AMERICAN HISTORY IN AMERICAN THOUGHT

CHRISTOPHER COLUMBUS TO
HENRY ADAMS

by BERT JAMES LOEWENBERG

Simon and Schuster / New York

First printing

SBN 671–20856–X
Library of Congress Catalog Card Number: 79–139641
Designed by Irving Perkins
Manufactured in the United States of America

ACKNOWLEDGMENTS

I wish to thank the Rockefeller Foundation for the award of two grants which facilitated the early stages of research. Thanks are also due to three successive United States Members of the Comisión de Historia; Arthur P. Whitaker, Professor of History at the University of Pennsylvania, Robert Burr, Professor of History at the University of California at Los Angeles and Dr. Howard F. Cline, Director of the Hispanic Foundation of the Library of Congress. The latter deserves particular mention for encouragement and help which exceed the duties of his office. Dr. Cline, in addition to other courtesies, read the manuscript in several of its stages. I am grateful to Dr. Ray Allen Billington, Senior Research Associate of the Huntington Library, who gave me the advantage of his comments on Chapters I to XV. Mrs. Anita Brooks Abramovitz, one of my former assistants, read the entire manuscript and made many helpful suggestions.

The Sarah Lawrence Journal *permitted me to reprint from "The Heroic Historians—Prescott, Motley, Parkman" (Fall 1968), 5–21, of which Chapter XV is a somewhat expanded version. The substance of Chapter XVIII, "John William Burgess, Scientific Method and the Hegelian Philosophy of History," is based on an essay with the same title published in* The Mississippi Valley Historical Review (*now* The Journal of American History) *XLII (December 1955), 490–509. The editors have kindly allowed me to reprint it in different form.*

The first fifteen chapters appeared as one of the volumes of a series on historiographical studies sponsored by the Instituto Panamericano de Geografía e Historia under the auspices of the Comisión de Historia and was published in Mexico in 1968.

To my son, Robert James Loewenberg, I owe an enormous debt. He interrupted his own historical studies to copy edit, to proofread and to type the bibliography. He also provided perceptive comments and helpful criticism. It is a pleasure to record it.

BERT JAMES LOEWENBERG

Sarah Lawrence College
Bronxville, New York

FOR MY CHILDREN

Robert James / Judith Anne / Sarah Miriam

Contents

10 / Contents

Introduction

American History in American Thought is a history of ideas. While it undertakes to accomplish what the title implies, more than an account of representative historical scholarship is contemplated. Scholarship, like the history that combines to create it, is an organic part of culture. The concept of culture is most helpful when specified. American culture, and to a slightly lesser extent western culture, is the primary emphasis. The context of professional communities, particularly the professional community of historians once organized, is likewise of importance. Other contexts pertinent to the continuing aspects of this study will require appropriate identification.

Convention has assigned the writing of history and the writing of historiography to separate categories. The distinction has tended to become more rigid in modern times; the difference appears to be less an indication of labor divided than of substance discriminated. A study of the influence of French civilization upon Frederick the Great, for example, is viewed as history; a study of the literature dealing with Frederick is classed as historiography.

The distinction is misleading. Not only is the historiographer a historian, but the historian is almost always a historiographer. The meaning of both words was once the same. Unless the historiographer regards himself simply as a chronicler or as a bibliographer, his methods, problems, and functions are identical. His purposes are also identical. These, however, require clearer description.

Learning is an endless succession of critiques. Scholarship, as Charles Darwin said of *The Origin of Species,* is one long argument. It is a continuing dispute concerning the incredible variety of living experience. An astute critic of the logic of scientific discovery avers that all method, if respectable, is subsumed under the caption "rational discussion." Whether in science or philosophy, the logic of discovery proceeds by "stating one's problem clearly and . . . examining its various proposed solutions *critically.*" [1] Few historians, though they might wish to express it differently, would be disposed to deny that such a formula is also their own. They would be even less disposed to object to the same scholar's version of historical method, the method of "trying to find out what other people have thought and said about the problem in hand: why they had to face it: how they formulated it: how they tried to solve it." Importance attaches to this formulation "because it is part of the general method of rational discussion. If we ignore what other people are thinking, or have thought in the past, then rational discussion must come to an end, though each one of us may go on happily talking to himself." [2] Karl Popper's interpretation of this particular point is unexceptionable. One might complain that "rational" is too restrictive to include all the varieties of intellectual experience, but that is another matter relating to the problems of knowledge and the history of ideas.

Criticism in its broadest application connotes a perennial examination of attitudes, values, and assumptions. It is a constant assessment of principles, standards, and methods, a series of reflections on the achievements of mind and the mutation of civilizations. Criticism, comments George Santayana, "arises out of the conflict of dogma." [3] Dogmas are not only theological. They are philosophical, scientific, and historical. Criticism arises in part out of contending views and the emergence of new generative ideas. In the contention among them the insistent problems of mankind are clarified. Criticism fashions novel contexts for thought.

Testing is the litmus of scientific method. After a hypothesis is formed, all the devices imagination can suggest are used to test it. The ultimate test is an attempt to refute it. Great history is a refutation of the implicit hypotheses of other histories that fail to withstand the corrosion of time and the acuity of later analysis. The writing of history involves the necessity of attempts to refute hypotheses. Overt assumptions must be attacked, the tissues of subhypotheses aggressively examined, and the cogency of explanation assailed. Neither the writers themselves nor the reviewers of their works can examine the ultimate assumptions upon which studies are grounded. The latter are reared upon silent cultural assumptions, the unexpressed paradigms of a civilization that are taken for granted. Alfred North Whitehead lucidly defines this concept, a fertile concept for adventures in ideas, crucial for historians and philosophers alike. "There will be some fundamental assumptions which adherents of all . . . variant systems within the epoch unconsciously presuppose. Such assumptions appear so obvious that people do not know what they are assuming because no other way of putting things has ever occurred to them." [4] These are discoverable only after the impact of germinative ideas have contributed to transform them.

The historian must first shape his problem. He must disentangle the issues, separate the lines of his own inquiry from the massive complexities of individual and social life. He must determine what in intellectual conscience he cannot omit and still present a coherent sequence and a logical explanation. While no research can be inclusive, the price of self-imposed limitation is often high. A histological slide gives a sharper focus, but explanations based upon it are likely to be dangerous if the tissue is interpreted without awareness of the total organism. The doctor of medicine, however rarefied a specialist, is not expected to forget the whole to which the part vitally belongs. In these days, he is charged with remembering there is more to the nature of disease and its cure than the physical body over which he once exclusively ministered. Nor are doctors of philosophy any less absolved from cultivating the requisite correlatives demanded of a reasonably complete scrutiny.

Historical scholarship is accordingly a venture in criticism. If the historian seeks to avoid this role, he succeeds by silence alone. Historians are enmeshed in the critical process from the beginning. The historian is prompted to engage in a research project for multiple reasons. But when he decides to inspect a segment of the past, no matter how recent, he is already in some state of disagreement with his precursors. The ineptitude, inaccuracy, or incompleteness of those who predated him instigates his activity. Occasionally, a newer relation hitherto unperceived or unelaborated, ignites his imagination or stirs his talents. A new insight does not always suggest a previous oversight; it usually heralds innovation in the state of culture and learning.

Historical research and historical writing parallel the historical process. Historians must know what others have said about their subject, for it is disenchantment with older research that sparks a student to search again. Whether disenchantment derives from a contemporary stance or personality factors is immaterial in this connection. To ignore one's intellectual forebears is a minor sin in the decalogue of historians. To retrace the steps of one's progenitors and to be judged as not having done it better is a professional calamity. The first transgression violates the historians' respect for the past. The second frustrates the aspiration for recurring critical judgment.

To demand of an author that he "define his boundaries" or place his work in perspective is to invoke an obligation. The obligation is to establish its locus not only in the literature of the subject, but also to establish a presumed significance in the sequence of thought. Unless demarcation is arbitrary, it requires an informed and critical exercise—one moreover which alters markedly as the analysis proceeds. All boundaries trace imaginary lines separating one fragment of time, space, or experience from others, and all perspectives, by providing a certain cluster of entities with sharper focus, blur or actually exclude other clusters from a larger field of vision. Significance is implicit and the assumption of significance denotes a criterion or a quality. At an earlier stage in the sequence of historical explanation, the awareness of later refinements of meaning were omitted or inadequately understood. But criticisms premise judgment. Assessment sets a value, appraisal establishes worth. Judgment presupposes standards; standards imply principles, criteria, values.

Criticism is the leaven of creative thought. The more diversity of viewpoint and disposition critical thought elicits, the more enriched and insightful life and learning become for mankind. But the irrepressibility of criticism and its latent premises erupt in the form of dissonances: in opinion, attitude, belief. These in turn fabricate diverse approaches to method, frame new questions, and fashion different moods. Historians themselves, particularly in the modern period, posed questions that plumbed the sources of historical faith. They tunneled under the canons of method, the nature and quality of historical explanation, the character and reliability of historical judgment. What did they ask? How did their interrogations influence their own professional lives and those of others? Why were they prompted to review the catechism their ancestors had bequeathed them? To these and to other similar questions, the record of the history of history makes partial response.

The historian is perforce a critic; the historian of history is a critic of critics. Although he participates with all historians in the persistent problems of the craft, his materials are of broader dimension. If he assumes the formidable responsibility of treating scholarship within the sweep of an entire culture, he has hewn out the widest conceivable national domain. The historical scholar who makes a given civilization his province, a great venture now largely out of fashion in American letters, alone rivals him in comparable scope. The goals of the historian of history, however, and the nature of its materials give a special cast to his objectives.

Concepts of meaning and concepts of function intermittently agitate the placidity of scholars. Historians, partly because of the antiquity of the discipline and partly because of an affinity for public affairs, sometimes appear to have been less ruffled. Despite appearances, individual historians and, after the midpoint of the nineteenth century the historical guilds, were stirred by the ferment of periodic debate.

Once theology was deprived of universal dominion over learning, history was allied with philosophy and affianced to literature. The alliance with philosophy was uneasy; the marriage with literature was disrupted by the impress of science. In consequence of the latter, history became "scientific history." "Scientific history," in spite of regal gifts, propagated a flock of problems. One was prolonged controversy. The conflict, remaining similar in substance, continues under the guise of the cleavage between science and humanism. Since the supposed issues between science and other forms of learning, dating from the seventeenth century, have always been about humanistic values, methods, and ends, it is probable that something resembling continuity obtains in this realm of ideas. Intellectual strife, especially active during the lifetime of the last three generations, has raised ancient issues newly formulated in aggravated form.

With disquieting frequency historians discovered that the problems they felt compelled to answer were frustratingly elusive. Reflective students, when not in torrid pursuit of a specific quarry in archive or manuscript collection, were besieged by misgiving. Some questions close to the surface of activity presented themselves with unwelcome persistence. Does written history mirror the culture, reflect its purposes, register its changes, and record its failures? Why do historians judge past events and ideas, not excluding the-printed remains of fellow historians of earlier vintage, in terms of assumed consequences in subsequent presents? Why do they not also evaluate them in terms of the whole body of ideas of the culture that sired them? To the present and the future, it might well be argued, belong the fruitage of antecedent ideas and developments. But is Plato, for example, to be accounted wrong because Platonism ceased to be the regnant philosophy in later ages? Is the evidence for the maturity of a field of study unity or diversity?

Neither archival fidelity nor monographic expertise quelled precipitating issues. If some historians remained undismayed, others did not share their equanimity. To what extent do historians in recreating parts of the past mortgage its future? How much do they condition a later framework, interpretation, and content? To what degree, to formulate the question somewhat differently, do historians influence their own culture? What does the process of isolating slivers of intellectual and social inheritance entail? What methods of inquiry do historians profess and with what consistency do they practice them? Are there unknown and subtle considerations that encumber selection of data, limit views, and meter judgment? Since the historian deals with singular events and particular individuals, these considerations impinge upon character and personality, the idiosyncratic thoughts, motives, and behavior of specific men and women. If individuals are in some sense to be considered the causative agents of ideas that foment change, other components require elucidation. Novel or generative ideas, sufficient to induce conceptual change, are individually engendered and internally evolved. They are nonetheless hammered out and tested in altering contexts. Creativity is a private affair, unique in origin and scarcely less so in evolution. In "imagination," Santayana reminds us, "not in perception, lies the substance of experience, while knowledge and reason are but its chastened and ultimate form." [5] If we record only the external manifestations of thought and behavior, he continues, only the external manifestations are in fact recorded.

Gathering the data, organizing the materials in spruce patterns, and designing persuasive interpretations provoked almost as many questions as answers. While prodigious research and a glittering record of production provided many historians with a sense of supreme contentment, all historians were not content. Neither did the record of accomplishment blunt the barbs of specialists in other areas who, if they read the historians, were prone to direct piercing questions about evidence, method, and meaning to whoever cared to listen.

Disunity among historians contrasted oddly with the surface unity of other disciplines. The older sciences appeared tightly bound together in singleminded resolve. Debates concerning method did not apparently ruffle physicists, and the individual triumphs of its practitioners, redounding to the prestige of the scientific community, dramatically impressed observers. Among historians, on the other hand, there were contending schools and different interpretations of the same materials. There were divergencies about method, multiple opinion concerning functions and the ways of fulfilling them. The professional expansion of history—measured by numbers of guilds-men, the multiplication of graduate schools, the training of teachers, the hooding of doctors of philosophy, and their impressive bibliographies—was undeniable. Was this enough?

Devotees of history conceived its purpose as more than understanding. The study and teaching of history was a public office and a public trust. It was a cultural imperative. History in one of its functions was the coadjutor of citizenship; in another, it was an instrument of self-fulfillment. An "historical sense" deepened the channels of self-knowledge and personal enrichment. Awareness of the past, and particularly of the national past, made for intelligent and effective citizenship. Yet even the faithful could hardly suppress reverent doubts. The aspirations were majestic aspirations, but how were they actually achieved?

Historians ceaselessly repeated that the major function of research and study was to capture and preserve the past. What was the past once reconstructed? Was it in truth the past as it actually was or was it a version of what historians thought it to be? What transmutations occurred in the process of reconstruction? While few rejected the primal need to knit past and present together, it was a proud maxim blemished by resistant qualifications.

Man to be sure could neither identify with the consecutive stages of his own growth nor could he comprehend the nature of society unless the past and the present were genetically linked. The past we may assume endures and surfaces in futures beyond the invocations of prophecy. What then of the present? The present, often called specious, is simultaneously devoured by relentless pressures at both ends of the spectrum of time. Each moment teeters on the brink of an engulfing past, and each moment, in Henri Bergson's piquant phrase, "gnaws into the future." [6] History is time objectified, and change, the mark of time, serves as its most meaningful symbol. Philosophers scarcely took time seriously before the seventeenth century; by the nineteenth change was posited as a universal condition of existence. What meanings do historians attach to change as concept, and how do such meanings impinge upon its continuing problems?

The mercurial present and the fragile past converged to dissolve absolute conviction about either. That the historian abstracts from a vast totality is a commonplace. There can be no "definitive" history in the ordinary sense. Segments of the past are omitted in any quest; some segments of the past have never been retrieved. How can assessments be rescued from the inherent limitations of the historian?

If such irremediable limitations curtail the historical venture, history, as one noted historian lamented, was never more than a noble dream.

Dilemmas enveloping objectivity are accented by relative standpoints. How can the past be grasped if scholars are at the mercy of their own pasts: of affiliations with class, religion, nationality, ethnic origin? The situation is not improved if unconscious factors subtly blend with attitude and belief. The situation is intensified if these were attitudes and beliefs of which scholars were but dimly aware. Everyman, in the language of another famed historian, was then his own historian.

The internal structure of history is philosophically charged. Historical issues incite historian and philosopher alike. Techniques devised for solving problems are problems themselves. To assess the interplay of knowledge, imagination, and feeling in the balance of historical accomplishment and the potentiality of historical achievement is a challenging exercise. As an inquiry, history exemplifies ways of knowing; as an inquiry of special character, it represents ways of knowing the past. It demands insightful ways of fashioning conceptual relationships among receding pasts and transitory presents. Such relationships imply the use of inventive metaphor and creative discovery.

Historical Writing in American Culture is divided into four parts. The present volume surveys historical writing to the beginning of the present century. The study continues in the second with developments during the first half of the twentieth. The third is allocated to special areas cultivated by American historians from 1865 to 1970. While traditional themes, properly the concern of native scholars, are treated here, emphasis is accorded to adventures in relationship that inspired new ones. Discussion of contemporary historical literature, 1960 to 1970, is reserved for this section. The whole study is based upon logical rather than thematic organization. Therefore, monographs dealing with the Colonial Period, the Revolution or the Civil War, for example, are sometimes referred to in the first section, but receive extended treatment in the third. The final volume is devoted to philosophical issues organized substantively rather than chronologically.

Almost two hundred years ago Dr. Oliver Goldsmith described the powers and the limitations of the historian. "Great abilities," he said, in a conversation with Dr. Samuel Johnson:

> are not requisite for an Historian; for in historical composition all the greatest powers of the human mind are quiescent. He has the facts ready

to his hand; so there is no exercise of invention. Imagination is not required in any high degree; only about as much as is used in the lower kinds of poetry. Some penetration, accuracy, and colouring will fit a man for the task, if he can give the application which is necessary.[7]

The sagacious Dr. Goldsmith belittles himself and his time. *American History in American Thought* offers a variant judgment.

I

The New World
Before Columbus

The purpose of the present work is to trace the development of historical scholarship in the United States from the European sources of its origin until yesterday. Certain basic assumptions regarding the history of the United States and the nature of the historical process have conditioned both its form and its substance. A number of questions must be raised at the outset. What is meant by historiography? Who are the historians? How is the history of the United States delimited? Unfortunately, these questions pose problems which are not simple, nor is there any reason to believe that they can be satisfactorily, much less conclusively, answered. Indeed, some would doubt the wisdom and the propriety of raising them at all. Yet it is difficult to discuss the development of historical writing in the United States without tracing its conceptual boundaries just as it is unwise to discuss history without first discussing what possible meanings attach to the term. And the word "historiography" demands some preliminary comment.

Historiography is the cumulative appraisal and reappraisal of historical knowledge. History and historians are themselves events; historical analysis and understandings are themselves parts of the historical process. Professor Frederick J. E. Woodbridge makes this point with particular clarity, and it is a point as valid for historiography as it is for history. They are both "genuinely progressive," both are "worked out in the course of time, and . . . the sequence of events progressively exposes or makes [them] clear." [1] After all, living men can alone ask questions of the past and living men alone can answer them.[2] Historical knowledge involves both the assessment of historical understandings and an investigation of the philosophical issues involved in their acquisition. Although the actual events of history are not the same as the historical accounts of them, both are nevertheless parts of a temporal sequence. They must not only be discovered and recorded; they must also be understood and reappraised.

Historiography, a word as vague as it is ponderous, has sometimes been used synonymously with history. It has been described as the history of history or the history of the study of history. Neither phrase is more felicitous than the word itself, nor is either more meaningful. In practice the history of history has frequently turned out to be a somewhat briefer version of a library card catalogue. And since the philosophy of history has long been one of the favorite aversions of historians, historiographical studies have rarely been devoted to patterns of human behavior, to theories of knowledge, or to explorations in meaning. Volumes concerned with method appear with a regularity measurable by philosophical indecision, but they have seldom been concerned with the nature of the historical quest or with the problems of historical knowledge. Such studies have usually centered analysis upon an evaluation of procedures of research and the canons of evidence, together with criticisms of those who employed them.

· Critics frequently imply that only prevailing assumptions are respectable. Even those celebrated for professional virtue have been unable to repress an irritation with scholars whose attitudes are alien to contemporary standards. Men can hardly be censured for what they could not conceivably have known any more than they can be expected to entertain viewpoints foreign to the culture that helped to fashion them.

Herodotus, ancient master of the historian's guild, wrote history for a purpose. He undertook his investigations "in order that the things men have done might not in time be forgotten." Like many who came after him, Herodotus was anxious that "great and wonderful deeds . . . might not become unheard of." Scholars in America, early and late, have been mindful of their debt to the past and their duty to posterity. Great events of a cherished past have been immortalized in the stirring pages of great historians. Great men, having been weighed and found worthy, still remain the companions of the present they helped to create. Conscious of man's forgetfulness of other and earlier men and events, generation after generation of historians have sought to insure an awareness of the future by preserving the record of the past.

The writing of history in America has another and deeper purpose. American historians undertook the study of the past not only to record "great and wonderful deeds." Whatever his avowed purpose, Herodotus helped the Greeks to see themselves. He provided a continuity between the living experience of the present and the re-lived experience of the past. Historians in America helped Americans to see themselves, for all historical scholarship "aims at solving the basic problem of knowing how some present situation has come to be as it is." [3] History is always written because history is always made. Historiography is always revised because history is constantly remade.

Yet the Greeks did not see themselves as others later saw them. George Grote in the nineteenth century perceived a particular unity in Greek history which was not apparent to Herodotus. Later scholars discovered other unities in the whole period of the classical age. To view the Mediterranean world from Aegean times to the "fall" of the Roman Empire as a cultural unit, for example, was a view that writers during the reign of Diocletian could scarcely have entertained.[4]

There is accordingly a cultural approach to historiography as well as to history. History *is* culture, and historiography—by whatever name called—is an intrinsic segment of it. The ideas men fashion of historical processes and events are basic elements of the cultural tradition, for the function of history and the function of historiography "is to bind present life to past life so that the social continuity which supports social order is maintained." [5]

Historians in an age of professionalism are easily recognized by their works. In earlier and less specialized days the hallmark of the guild was not so plainly stamped on the product. Columbus, for example, was certainly no historian. Yet it would be as fanciful to discuss the evolution of America without reference to his accomplishments as to discuss the evolution of the written record in America without reference to his writings. Governor John Winthrop of Massachusetts made little claim to historical craftsmanship but few have ever thought of denying the *Journal* a place in the development of the historiography of the North American colonies.

While systems of classification are usually precise, they are almost always arbitrary. Rigid principles of historiographical classification would include local chroniclers whose avowed purpose was to preserve the record of a given past. Such principles would exclude documents, even if of greater significance, because written by explorers, administrators, or clerics. Thus a Catholic friar of old California, compiler of monastery annals, has an assured niche in the hierarchy of historical accomplishment, an assurance not guaranteed to the letters of Hernando Cortés. A divine whose sermons delineate the philosophical framework of Puritan historiography might yield his place to the earliest historian of the Woburn settlement in colonial Massachusetts.

Spanish monks during the period of American beginnings are as often historians as priests. Explorers, like English ministers, fulfill multiple roles, among them the role of historian. Difficulties, however, increase rather than diminish with time. Are the works of Thomas Jefferson, John Adams, Thomas Paine appropriately classified as historiographical? Is Woodrow Wilson to be considered less of an historian because he was primarily a political scientist? Is Theodore Roosevelt to be considered less of a student of history because so much of his energy was devoted to the making of history rather than to the writing of it?

To make distinctions in terms of craft is ordinarily simpler than to make distinctions in terms of national association. What constitutes an American is a question many have raised and few have satisfactorily answered. Were the natives of the continent its first representatives? The Norsemen from the Scandinavian peninsula unquestionably came next. Were they on that account the first Americans? Spanish grandees, French fishermen, Dutch traders planted the roots of European civilization in the new world centuries before the emergence of the United States. Are they, therefore, to be excluded?

Were such arbitary principles of exclusion to be adopted as a basis of selection, the historian of historical literature in the United States need not be concerned with the Icelandic sagas. Nor should he accord any attention to the *Journal* of Columbus or the voyages of Cartier. Upon what theoretical grounds should the historian exclude Bartolomé de Las Casas and include John Eliot, omit Peter Martyr and reserve space for Captain John Smith? De Las Casas, to be sure, was a Spaniard and Richard Hakluyt an Englishman, yet it is hard to see what Hakluyt, whatever his interests, would have written about without Columbus, Las Casas, and Cartier. Aztecs and Incas cannot be denied membership in the American community on chronological grounds without denying it to English Puritans, French Huguenots, and German Pietists.

The history of the Americas coincides with a new era in the history of man. Patriotic fervor and racial pride have often combined to fix beginnings in specific historical events and to associate meanings with particular peoples. But history which deals solely with parts of humanity is culturally provincial; historiography which deals with national fragments alone is conceptually partial. There is more than a grain of justice in Gaetano Salvemini's rebuke that "the historian amputates reality." [6]

The forces which brought the Americas into existence were world forces; the forces which conditioned their later development were global in scope. The whole world was involved in the mighty changes transforming society at the end of the Middle Ages. "Everything that grows or changes," a noted philosopher of history observed, "manufactures a past by realizing a future." [7] "History," he insisted, "is . . . not only the conserving, the remembering, and the understanding of what has happened; it is also the completing of what has happened." [8] Of these changes at the end of the Middle Ages, one of the major consequences was the discovery of the western hemisphere. And the future realized by these changes was not only the history of the Americas, but the future scope of the modern world.

American history, therefore, is part of a much larger movement. We may, if we wish, "mark off sections of history." Yet whatever our method of measurement, historical periods or historical movements are themselves "in a medium which includes . . . the time . . . they distinguish." They are themselves parts of the continuum of time, themselves events or processes that "we must . . . recognize just as we must acknowledge that the processes of the circulation of the blood and the beating of the heart are going on while we are discussing the question." [9] While it is true that "the only universal history is the exposition of what history itself is," [10] it is also true that there is more to the process of history than "can be placed in accordance with a map or dated in accordance with a calendar." [11] If history were indeed a universal history, it would simply be "the time process stripped of all its variety and specific interests." [12] Nevertheless, processes and events do have "structures in time." They have, in other words, "genuine careers, each with its own particular character and its own possibility of a future." [13] They are, to put it differently, never what they may subsequently become. Yet whatever they do in fact become "is always continuous with what they are." [14]

Long before Spain was ready for imperial ventures, the discovery of the western hemisphere was in the making. Long before England was ready to build an empire beyond the seas, events which were to culminate in the history of the United States were in process. History, to use a well-worn metaphor, is less a broad highway over which mankind travels than a stream in which mankind is forever immersed. If the "stream of history" is a cliché, it is an image as valid as it is graphic. Humanity is always in the stream of history. The events, the periods, the movements that man has fashioned in order to understand himself, while retaining their form, merge into the currents of time and change. "An historical fact," Woodbridge wrote, "is not only spread out in space and exists equally with all its contemporaries at an assignable place in reference to them, it also persists in time; comes before and after other persisting facts, and persists along with others." [15]

When, then, may the history of the United States properly be said to begin? Chronology, although the earliest partner of the historian, is scarcely conclusive. The adoption of the Constitution in 1789 launched the United States of America upon its national career. If the United States may be said officially to begin in 1789, does it follow that it begins historically in that year? An equally good case can be made for 1787, the date of the Constitutional Convention, or 1783, the date when colonial victory over Britain was legally recognized. An even better logic supports the claim of 1776. The Declaration of Independence marks a stage in the controversy between Britain and the colonies as well as in the internal struggle within British North America. To begin with Plymouth in 1620 or Virginia in 1607 is conventional enough, but why not with Sir Humphrey Gilbert in 1583, Sir Francis Drake in 1572, or John Cabot in 1497? Why not, indeed, with Christopher Columbus in 1492?

Actually no specific date will satisfactorily answer the question of beginnings. If historical events do in fact possess careers in time, then it is their emergence which historians record and their subsequent implications which historians seek to understand. An exclusive reliance upon chronology without reference to concepts and hypotheses leads to an infinite regress of related or causally connected events. The completely unique event, moreover, cannot be said to exist. Even if it existed, it could not be described. Any singular happening touches our understanding only in terms of the classes, categories, and concepts that relate to it. The landing of Columbus on October 12, 1492, was a singular, historic event and as such can never be repeated.[16]

But Christopher Columbus belongs not only to a class of human beings but also to a category of men who among other things were Europeans, mariners, and discoverers. His life career was connected with other men and women, among them the monarchs of Spain. The latter supported his activities for multiple and complex reasons bearing upon certain concepts such as trade, nationalism, kingship, and power. They did so for a variety of other human motives which, though no longer operative upon Ferdinand, Isabella, and Columbus, are still operative in the lives of other men and women. Finally, the date October 12, 1492, and the event that it signifies is vital not only for itself, but also for what preceded and followed it. "The narrative may begin and end where we please; and might conceivably, within its scope, be adequate. But the beginning and the end of the action are so interwoven with the whole time process that adequacy . . . becomes progressive." [17]

THE NORSEMEN

The first historical documents relating to America stem from the early Norse voyages. Although many aspects of Scandinavian activity in North American waters have been questioned, there can be little doubt that the Scandinavians discovered Iceland and the Faroes in the ninth century. At the same time these mariners sighted the east Greenland coast. Credit for the actual discovery of that island, however, belongs to Eric the Red, who also established a permanent colony in 986. An outpost of European culture existed for five hundred years, but although the experience doubtless affected the individual lives of the settlers and their kin in the European North, it exerted little influence on the larger movement of events.[18]

What finally happened to the Greenland colony, Brattahlid by name, is still an unsolved problem, but during its existence the inhabitants were actively engaged in the prosaic occupation of cattle raising and the less prosaic production of walrus tusks and white falcons. The produce of Brattahlid made its way to Norway together with an occasional voyager who yearned for a sight of the homeland. One such voyage was made by Leif, son of Eric, who, driven off his course on the return trip, first touched the North American coast. This was in the year 1000, and five years later an exploring party, headed by Thorfinn Karlsefni, undertook to plant a colony in "Vinland," so called because of a luxuriant growth of wild grapes. Since the native Skraelings there and farther south were far from hospitable, the plan of settlement was abandoned although subsequent trips were made to the region for the purpose of cutting timber.

The two great sagas recounting the experiences of Norse explorers constitute the earliest records of history in America. Written reference to Vinland first appeared in *Descriptions of the Northerly Lands* by Adam of Bremen, sometime resident at the Danish court, where he acquired information of Scandinavian exploits. Nevertheless, the sagas are the primary sources, earlier in origin, and provide the main basis for our information of these events.[19] Both sagas, *The Vinland History* or *The Flat Island Book* (which derives its name from the residence of one of its owners on Flat Island off the coast of Iceland) and *The Saga of Eric the Red,* treat of the same series of incidents. But unfortunately they treat of them differently—a fact which has resulted in considerable confusion among the learned. The saga of Eric is generally accounted the better source, and diligent internal criticism and other corroborative evidence have tended to confirm this.[20]

The Norse episode is suggestive of certain historiographical trends. That it was simply an episode now seems beyond doubt. Whatever Eric the Red, Leif Ericson, or Thorfinn Karlsefni did or did not accomplish, it apparently had no appreciable effect on the development of Europe. Leif Ericson may with justice be hailed as the discoverer of America, but his discovery yielded no large-scale results. Geographical knowledge was doubtless accumulated in the course of the Norse explorations, but it was of scant help to later navigators. Nor did the Scandinavian voyagers have any notion that Greenland was but a stepping stone to a new world. Even their periodic excursions in search of wood to the Labrador and Newfoundland coasts apparently did not induce them to think so. Indeed, Greenland is pictured on certain pre-Columbian maps as north of Iceland, jutting out from the Russian-Asian land mass. Persistent efforts have been made to uncover physical testimony in the form of remains—efforts sometimes of a highly questionable order—but none has been found. Since wild grapes do not grow north of Passamaquoddy Bay on the New England coast, this is a serious deficiency in the chain of inference. Other data make it seem unlikely that the Norsemen penetrated this far south, and hence the Vinland reference may not be accurate. Yet, sailing in the right direction, one could hardly have been blown off the course to Greenland without touching the continent, so that wherever Leif may have landed, his right to priority as the discoverer of America seems incontestable.

A disproportionate amount of effort has been expended upon the Norsemen and their connection with the discovery of America. Their voyages have been painstakingly traced, their explorations charted, their documents analyzed and re-evaluated again and again. Fantastic claims, it is true, whether generated by patriotic zeal or other motivation, demand scholarly response. Thus the Kensington Rune Stone, allegedly proclaiming Scandinavian penetration into what is now Minnesota in 1363, required careful and expert research before it could be pronounced a forgery. Similarly, the "discovery" of pieces of Norse armor in Canada, unquestionably genuine specimens, were probably brought over much later for purposes that little ingenuity is needed to unravel.

Beyond fantastic allegation and scholarly retort, there is another item that calls for mention. Efforts to establish racial priorities in the discovery and settlement of America run through the whole course of historical writing and reflect a cultural chauvinism identical in kind. Ultimate meanings and pervasive influences, ascribed to particular nations, peoples, groups, or sections, have been equally persistent. The sources of such motivation are understandable; these tendencies have frequently contributed only to a distortion of perspective.

THE WESTERN WORLD: PARTNERS IN CULTURE AND RIVALS IN TRADE

The centuries between the Crusades and the settlement of the American continent are sometimes called the Age of Discovery and Colonization. The larger period, of which the Age of Discovery is a part, is frequently referred to as the period of the Expansion of Europe. But what William R. Shepherd [21] had in mind when he used the phrase "Expansion of Europe" was something different from what has in fact been written under this caption. Shepherd was thinking primarily of the expansion of a system of culture over those areas of the earth previously isolated from it. He was thinking of the influence of European culture upon the civilization of peoples hitherto untouched by it. Above all, he had in mind the interpenetration of different cultures and the emergence of a new and evolving social synthesis in consequence.

Europe was a generic concept in Shepherd's thought. The men who sailed to Africa and America not only sailed from the rim of the eastern Atlantic seaboard; they were the carriers of Western culture. Western culture was not merely Venetian, Genoan, or Florentine; it was not simply Portuguese, Spanish, English, or French. It was European, and because it was European it was the culture of the Ancient Near East, of Greece, and of Rome. Shepherd was using a concept based upon a postulate of scientific method, the existence of patterns which appear to depend upon wholes. They are patterns that depend upon "the totality of parts rather than upon their simple addition." [22]

Much more has been written concerning the development of the European powers than of the development of European culture. Historians have devoted far more attention to the creation of national states than to the creation of human patterns of behavior. They have stressed the struggles of empire rather than the struggles of mankind. [23]

When we contemplate the era of colonial beginnings, we are much more likely to think of Portugal, Spain, England, and France rather than the *process* of discovery. We have been accustomed to think in the image of conflict. The Crusades, with which we customarily begin, were a struggle between East and West. Italian cities and their princely merchants grew rich in the brisk competition for silk and spice. And it was precisely the advantage of Venice, Genoa, and Florence that stirred Portugal to contest the commercial monopoly to which the Italian cities fell heir. Prince Henry of Portugal was doubtless interested in finding Christian kingdoms in darkest Africa and in bringing lost souls to a Christian God. But his mariners, merchants, and cartographers, though unquestionably devout, were not less concerned with the interest rate in the profitable Levantine trade.

Spain was stimulated by Portugal, England by Spain. Portugal's spectacular success in finding an all-sea route to the Indies, coupled with Spanish achievements after Columbus, gave new directions to the thoughts of men. Richard Hakluyt become the most traveled man in Europe by mastering the records of discovery and trade, a mastery he was later to place at the service of his English queen. Before this event, however, the monarchies of the Iberian peninsula had divided the world between them. The division was made with papal blessing, but the conflict for empire had only begun.

The struggle between Spanish Hapsburgs and English Tudors was greater than the rivalry between Spain and Portugal. Royal marriages, royal divorces, diplomatic intrigues, and wars on land and sea crowd the pages of those who have traced the course of national conquest. If the defeat of the Armada in 1588 changed the nature of the conflict, it did not end it. England continued to compete with France as she had earlier competed with Spain.

Competition for empire is attested by thousands of records and erupts in countless documents. But the documents and the histories based upon them obscure as well as clarify. The conflict of empires was real enough, to none more so than to the participants. Yet the nations of Europe, though rivals for power, were partners in the building of culture.

Popular writers frequently permit themselves a certainty that scholars sedately abjure. Writing of the Norsemen, Hendrik Willem van Loon commented that exclusive reliance upon documentary evidence has caused historians to overlook "such small trifles as currents and winds." Now that we have accurate maps of the Atlantic which, of course, the Vikings lacked, there is little basis for questioning whether the Vikings did or did not reach the coast of America, for "a Viking on his way from Norway to the Arctic colonies ran every risk of being picked up by the Greenland current and unless he were very lucky he would find himself the guest of the Labrador current and after that there was no escape. He was bound to land somewhere on the east coast of the North American continent." Data of this kind rule out questions of whether it was possible for the Northmen to "discover" America. We should ask rather: "Why did it take them so long to get there?" [24]

Knowledge of the currents of the gulf stream and of Labrador makes it clear that the claims made for Leif Ericson and his Viking followers are not absurd. Now that navigation is a science and ocean travel a commonplace we can legitimately construct hypotheses that the sagas and other records of exploration by themselves do not warrant. Apart from Van Loon and this special instance, an exclusive reliance upon the written record frequently causes us to overlook the obvious. Except by inference and data derived from other sources, there is comparatively little in the formal record of exploration which tells of the partnership of the western world in the process of discovery.

Yet the discovery and exploration of the new world was a joint venture of mankind. It was no more the sole accomplishment of Spain and Portugal than of England or France. Our conventional use of language suggests another view. We habitually speak of the *new world,* of the *western world,* of the dawn of a *new era.* We rarely refer to the "Spanish world" or the "English world," unless we are using the word "world" in a metaphorical sense or as a synonym for empire, nation, or local culture.

Documentary sources invariably present great events masquerading as historical movements. Great events lack the ultimate historical dimension—the dimension of movement in time—for every historical occurrence, however great, is a part of the future as of the past.

While the documents tell us a great deal about the structure of society at any given point in time, they tell us little about social processes. This is peculiarly true of the whole series of dramatic events associated with the discovery of the new world. Many of the participants recognized their relationship to the past; they rarely perceived their relationship to the future. The *Journal* of Columbus, for example, records a great and dramatic event with feeling and intensity. The reader is swept into the conflicts of a personal life and shares in the epic of high adventure. But while Columbus conveys the trials of living on the verge of the future, he does not comprehend it. He conveys the thrill of discovery, though it was the wrong discovery. Columbus himself celebrates the rediscovery of the Indies, not the discovery of the new world. Later generations heralded Columbus because he became the symbol of a process, the events that stemmed from the fact that he had indeed discovered a new world.

Momentarily to forget Hapsburg and Valois in Europe and the sad night of Cortés in America's Mexico, might perhaps allow us to see other events in sharper perspective. Charles V, of course, could not have anticipated our world any more than the contemporaries of Columbus could have anticipated the Labrador current. But maps in modern projection reveal Europe as a diminutive peninsula of the Russian-African-Asian land mass, and the earth as a globe.

Columbus and some of his contemporaries, to be sure, regarded the earth as a sphere. They could not, however, envisage the planet in the focus of modern projections. If the import of Columbus derives from the fact that he discovered the new world, regardless of what he believed he had discovered, there is a vital connection between the Genoese mariner and the Wright brothers. Together they united the world and made the planet a physical unit.

Explorers, discoverers, and conquistadors, following Columbus, linked the Mediterranean with the Caribbean by way of the Atlantic. Balboa discovered the Pacific. Magellan circumnavigated the world. And the Wright brothers discovered another way of circumnavigating the world, which caused man to measure distance between continents in air hours instead of nautical miles.

Perspectives such as these do not slur individual events. On the contrary, they sharpen their meanings and they emphasize the cumulative series of which they are parts. They suggest the continuing series of changes that they contributed to initiate. Balboa claimed the Pacific in the name of the Spanish monarch Ferdinand the Catholic, but the crucial point is that he discovered it.

Rivalry for trade and empire was real, bitter, and unrelenting.

Charles V entertained no motive more genuine than belief in his Catholic God, although he sacked the holy city and held the Roman pontiff hostage. Philip II and England's virgin queen regarded themselves as agents of the Lord, whether it was by bringing the Dutch to their knees in the one case or by robbing Spanish treasure ships in the other. Yet those who explored and settled the Americas were engaged in a co-operative task. The monarchs of Spain and England played leading parts, but they were only parts in the scenes of a continuing epic. Spain, whether in the reign of Ferdinand, of Charles, or of Philip, was a spur to England's ambition. And England's effort to participate in the race for western mastery was the consequence of the earlier efforts of Portuguese geographers, Italian mariners, and Spanish adventurers. As Columbus studied Aristotle and Seneca, Hakluyt studied Columbus and Las Casas. Geography was put to Spanish, English, and Dutch service, but geography belonged to mankind. Frenchmen and Englishmen marked out claims in Canada and Virginia for national acquisition and personal enjoyment, but the Americas belonged to the world.

II

New Spain, 1492–1607

History in America begins with Spain, and the history of Spain in America begins with Columbus. While there were Irish monks in Iceland before the Scandinavians founded Brattahlid, Christopher Columbus under royal Spanish patent discovered the New World. Other Europeans, seeking passage to India, may have touched American coasts, but Columbus created the first real impact on the European mind. It was Columbus who initiated the process of colonization. In consequence he initiated the whole series of developments from which both North and South America derive. If the career of the Americas dates from the Admiral of the Ocean Sea, the historiography of America dates from Columbus.

La Empresa de las Indias—the great enterprise of the Indies—was the consuming passion of Columbus, and Columbian literature appropriately commences with the formal documents that launched it. Among these were the Capitulations or Articles of Agreement in which the terms governing the relations between the navigator and the Spanish sovereigns were set forth. Among other matters, mention is made of titles, offices, and privileges formally elaborated in a special document:

> Whereas you, *Cristóbal Colón,* are setting forth by our command . . . to discover and acquire certain islands and mainland in the ocean sea . . . it is just and reasonable that, since you are exposing yourself to this danger in our service, you be rewarded therefor, . . . it is our will and

34

pleasure that you the said *Cristóbal Colón* after you have discovered and acquired the said islands and mainland . . . or any of them, shall be our Admiral of the said islands and mainland which you may thus discover and acquire, and shall be our Admiral and Viceroy and Governor therein, and shall be empowered henceforward to call and entitle yourself *Don Cristóbal Colón,* and his heirs and successors forever may be so entitled, and enjoy the offices of Admiral of the Ocean Sea, Viceroy and Governor of the said islands and mainland.[1]

The *Journals* of Columbus, unquestionably one of the most important sources about Columbus himself and his epochal adventure, has never been available to modern scholars in the original. After the completion of the first voyage, Columbus apparently submitted his manuscript to his royal employers, then at Barcelona. But the Spanish rulers, frequently on the move, were less concerned with the preservation of records than with the expulsion of the Moors. In any case, the manuscript was never heard of more, but copies had fortunately been made before its disappearance. It is from these copies that we trace our knowledge of the initial voyage and much of our impressions of the man and of his dreams.

Other men's words were first to reach the eyes of Europeans, but Christopher Columbus was the first European to write them. And what words they were! They are not simply the logbooks of an explorer, the journals of a navigator, or the testament of a discoverer. One does not need to call up the stereotype of the Renaissance mind to appreciate with what excitement readers of the fifteenth century responded to them. They are still exciting. Even after centuries of achievement, of centuries of adjustment to successive discoveries, the words of Christopher Columbus have lost little of their appeal.

Historians have learned to use restraint in speaking of beginnings. But this is an instance for which "first" is the only appropriate word. The writings of Columbus are the first literary interchanges between America and western Europe. Columbus not only begins Spanish-American literature, but his sentences begin the long cultural process, still continuing, of communicating the meaning of America to other Europeans. Columbus is the direct progenitor of Hernán Cortés, of Bernal Díaz del Castillo, and of Germán Arciniegas. He is the indirect progenitor of Richard Hakluyt, of Sir Walter Raleigh, of Charles A. Beard, and of Denis Brogan. It was the first account of strange new lands and of a great uncharted sea. New peoples, new customs, new languages, new fauna and flora paraded before the imagination of Europeans. And new dreams, new hopes, and new ambitions stimulated the ancient faith in the powers of man.

Homeward bound, after the successful completion of the first voyage, Columbus set himself down to compose a letter. Not addressed to anyone in particular, it was meant for all. Peter Martyr's place as the first historian of America remains undisputed, but the *Letter of Columbus* was the earliest published report of the discovery, a report, moreover, written by the discoverer himself.

The *Santángel Letter*,[2] as it has come to be called, was sent to the King and Queen of Spain together with another specifically addressed to them. Preceding the arrival of Columbus, a number of copies were made for official purposes, one of which was sent to Luis de Santángel who had long been associated with the initial undertaking. It was Santángel who apparently caused the letter to be printed.[3] Another copy was sent by Columbus to Gabriel Sánchez, treasurer of Aragón, hence the document is sometimes referred to as the *Sánchez Letter*.[4] From this copy a Latin translation was made by Leander de Cosco.

Whatever the lines of transmission, the letter had a wide currency. From 1493 to 1497, it was printed twice in Spanish and nine times in Latin. The Latin version enabled the news to permeate outside the Spanish-speaking borders.[5] One of the most popular Tuscan poets of the day, Giuliano Dato, made an Italian paraphrase of it which appeared in Rome, June 1497, and was five times republished, thus widening the arc of awareness. A German edition came out at Strassburg in 1497.

The language of Columbus best indicates what his message must have meant to those who read it and what he must have had in his own mind as he put the tinkling Spanish words together:

> In this there is incalculable gold; and concerning these and the rest I bring Indians with me as witnesses. And in conclusion, to speak only of what has been done in this voyage, which has been so hastily performed, their Highnesses may see that I shall give them as much gold as they may need, with very little aid which their Highnesses will give me; spices and cotton at once, as much as their Highnesses will order to be shipped, and as much as they shall order to be shipped of mastic,—which till now has never been found except in Greece, in the island of Xio, and the Seignory sells it for what it likes; and aloe-wood as much as they shall order to be shipped; and slaves as many as they shall order to be shipped, —and these shall be from idolators. And I believe that I have discovered rhubarb and cinnamon, and I shall find that the men whom I am leaving there will have discovered a thousand other things of value; as I made no delay at any point, so long as the wind gave me an opportunity of sailing, except only in the town of Navidad till I had left things safely arranged and well established. And in truth I should have done much more if the ships had served me as well as might reasonably have been expected. This is enough; and (thanks to) Eternal God our Lord who gives to all those who walk His way, victory over things which seem

impossible; and this was signally one such, for although men have talked or written of those lands, it was all by conjecture, without confirmation from eyesight, amounting only to this much that the hearers for the most part listened and judged that there was more fable in it than anything actual, however trifling. Since thus our Redeemer has given to our most illustrious King and Queen, and to their famous kingdoms, this victory in so high a matter, Christendom should have rejoicing therein and make great festivals, and give solemn thanks to the Holy Trinity for the great exaltation they shall have by the conversion of so many peoples to our holy faith; and next for the temporal benefit which will bring hither refreshment and profit, not only to Spain, but to all Christians. This briefly, in accordance with the facts. Dated, on the caravel, off the Canary Islands, the 15 February of the year 1493.

At your command,

THE ADMIRAL[6]

Scholars have agonized over Columbus for the last century. The "Columbus question" has produced an abundant crop of monographs and a vast bibliography of controversial literature.[7] Yet without disparaging the concept of infinity—the almost endless series of possible combinations—it seems difficult to believe that any pertinent questions still remain to be asked.

The Columbus legend is now almost a part of international folklore. Cristoforo Colombo, born of a noble Genoese house which traced its lineage to ancient Rome, received the kind of education appropriate to his station.[8] At the University of Pavia, he studied geography and related subjects which prepared him for his role as a great mariner. As a young seaman, once in the employ of the king of Provence, he conquered the seas—sailing to England as well as to the Arctic. Lured by the maritime greatness of Portugal, he went to that country where he married a distinguished lady whose ancestry was as proud as his own. In the course of his residence at the center of geographical knowledge and speculation, he continued his study. He sailed to the colonies of his adopted country and visited the coast of Guiana.[9] He not only read books but entered into correspondence with the geographer Paolo Toscanelli of Florence.[10] As a result of this intellectual activity, he concluded that the Indies could be reached by sailing westward. The king of Portugal, presented with the plan, rejected Columbus but not the information, for he sent other navigators to see whatever they could see—and find. Columbus, therefore, withdrew from Portugal and offered himself to the Spanish queen. After many disappointments, he succeeded in securing her sponsorship. He set sail in 1492, discovered what he believed were the islands lying off the shores of the fabulous East, and returned to the triumph he had so richly earned. Filled with honors and weighted down with fame, he was ruined by jealous and self-seeking enemies. Others reaped the glory that was rightfully his. But he had given a new world to Spain.

The sources of the Columbus legend as well as the Columbus history stem mainly from his own writings, those of his son Ferdinand, from the account of Bartolomé de Las Casas, and other sources equally distinguished.[11] Since these works were penned, an almost unbelievable amount of historical ingenuity has been expended in the effort to unravel them. It is now apparent that many of the allegations of the Admiral, of his son and grandson, and of scores of apologists, propagandists, and nationalists more ardent in behalf of country than accuracy have embellished the narrative. Far from being a son of noble parents, Columbus came from a family of humble weavers. The son followed in the footsteps of the father. Columbus came no closer to the University of Pavia than a school, maintained by the weavers' trade, located on a street called the Vico di Pavia. If he attended this school at all, he acquired such learning as the son of a weaver could. According to his own story, he became a sailor at the age of fourteen and served the king of Provence, but all the extant records, combed with a fidelity out of all proportion to their significance, identify him as a weaver or a woolmaker until he reached nineteen. Nevertheless, the tales of travel and wonder characteristic of all seaport towns in the fifteenth century could hardly have escaped his notice. Without doubt Columbus was able to pick up considerable nautical lore and was fired by the careers of others. He unquestionably took part in a voyage in the year 1476 and is to be found in Portugal by 1479. There he married Felipa Perestrelloe Moniz, whose mother was kin to the noble house of Moniz. Since his father-in-law had been made hereditary captain of Porto Santo by Prince Henry, it was easy for Columbus to mingle in social circles, which would otherwise have been closed to him. More importantly, it made it possible for him to come in contact with merchants, cartographers, and navigators. The account of a voyage to Guiana is probably correct; but most of the statements concerning his African travels are probably colored. Whatever they actually were, Columbus' African experiences quickened what had by this time become a sense of mission.

While these issues are interesting, they are not vital. Columbus almost certainly forgot some things and remembered others. And it is probably reasonable to infer that he forgot those items which at the time were irksome to recall, remembering what it seemed appropriate not to forget. Christopher Columbus was no saint. He was not even a scholar, and he had an average proportion of virtues and vices. Issues such as the date of his birth or even so compelling an issue as the geographical concepts he entertained at specific periods of his life bear on important problems, but they are not themselves the important ones. The central problem revolves around his purposes and intentions. What did Columbus intend? Does the phrase *la empresa de las Indias* mean what it says? In other words, did or did not Columbus hope to find another route to the Indies, to China and to Japan? And, having reached Watling Island (or some other place in the vicinity) on October 12, 1492, did he think he had reached his goal or did he actually expect to find some other place when he bravely set sail from the harbor of Palos?

The testimony of Columbus himself seems conclusive on this point. But the student does not need to rely upon the words of Columbus, for his actions are even more expressive of his purposes than his words. Had his objective been some place other than Asia, he would not have had to formulate a plan. In that case, elaborate schemes, precise programs, and the intercession of important personages would have been unnecessary. No one required influence to get permission to sail to unknown shores. Monarchs were entirely willing to grant title to lands not yet discovered, but it was just because the routes to Cathay were so well known that Columbus needed argument and patronage. The King of Portugal would not have found it difficult to grant accurate title to vague domains, but the Portuguese already had a virtual monopoly of the markets of the Indies. The plan had to be novel. It had to propose a better, shorter, or different route. But if novelty finds favor with scholars assessing the importance of the event long after it happened, novelty was a barrier to the success of Columbus' plan.[12]

Moreover, Columbus states his ambitions often enough. He would not, of course, have been averse to finding undiscovered lands on the way, but the East was his goal. Actually it was more; it was the driving motivation of his mature life. Had Columbus been headed for other parts of the world, it is hard to know why he carried credentials from the monarchs of Spain to the Grand Khan.[13] That the Great Khan was dead and the country over which he had ruled had ceased to exist matters little. Columbus did not know it. Neither did the King and Queen of Spain. It was not until Columbus had made three voyages of discovery and exploration that he changed his mind. It was only then that Columbus was finally convinced that the new world was in fact new.[14]

While scholars have never ceased to call attention to the gaps in our information, we really know a great deal about the discoverer of America. His associates left an ample record of their joint undertakings, and his friends, not unmindful of the meaning of the events with which their names have ever since been associated, have written fully. A large part of the Admiral's own account has been preserved, and at least four other individuals have contributed significantly to the understanding of posterity. These were Ferdinand Columbus, loyal son and avid biographer; Bartolomé de Las Casas, a noble priest and scholar; Peter Martyr, first historian of the New World; and Gonzalo Fernández de Oviedo y Valdés, first historian of Spain in America. These four men were contemporaries of Columbus, and all knew him in varying degrees of intimacy. Excepting Peter Martyr, all made the voyage to America. A considerable number of the letters of Columbus and books marginally annotated still exist. If the original manuscript has been lost, Ferdinand made notes from it in the preparation of the biography, and Las Casas abstracted large parts for his own literary purposes. The Las Casas document is still to be viewed in the National Library at Madrid, the source of current versions of the *Journals*. Las Casas' work and Ferdinand's biography therefore are particularly valued. The biography makes up in part for the loss of the *Journals*. The first voyage is covered by Ferdinand's notes from the original manuscript, and he recounts firsthand the fourth voyage which he made together with his father.

Las Casas' importance is incomparable. When he finally sat down to write, he had an impressive library of Columbus' papers, manuscripts, and documents.[15] Christopher Columbus and Bartolomé de Las Casas share pioneer honors. One discovered America; the other contributed significantly to the rediscovery of the dignity of man. Columbus defied the assumptions of his day; Las Casas was one of a notable company who, with equal boldness, dissented from conventional views. By providing a source collection and a primary historical account of American beginnings, Las Casas performed an inestimable scholarly service for which he is justly remembered. But by protesting together with others[16] against the Spanish treatment of the native population in America, Las Casas deserves never to be forgotten.[17]

After studying at the University of Salamanca, Las Casas left old Spain in 1502 for Santo Domingo in the new. Preoccupation with the material resources of nature was interrupted by a concern for the spiritual resources of man. The condition of the Indians, enslaved by their Spanish overlords, arrested Las Casas' sympathy and energy. Compassion for the oppressed natives was doubtless quickened after

1510 when he became a priest—the first to be ordained in America —and thereafter his activities in behalf of justice became the driving goal of his existence. Five years later he was officially styled "General Protector of All the Indians." [18]

Las Casas' mighty efforts yielded greater dividends in the eighteenth century than in the sixteenth. He was not unsuccessful in converting Indians to the faith, particularly in two provinces of Guatemala.[19] But the *Nuevas Leyes de Indias* of 1542,[20] abolishing Indian slavery and looking toward a basic change in the encomienda system, splintered against the hard core of economic drives. His *Brevissima Relacion de la destruycion de las Indias*,[21] however, is a forthright exposure of cruelty, greed, and the efforts made to rationalize them. If the language is intense and the narrative colored, as is often alleged,[22] it can only be countered that injustice is a subject humanists find it difficult to treat dispassionately. And it might also be added that it was better to discuss it violently than not to discuss it at all. Yet Las Casas' notable feat entailed a considerable price. A special pleader, he overstated his case, for the Indians were far less perfect than his account suggests, the Spaniards far less cruel. One result was the legend of Spanish cruelty, still perpetuated in popular imagination.

The *Historia de las Indias* is undoubtedly significant, but it is obviously less significant than the life history of its author. Yet Samuel Eliot Morison rightly remarks that if all the early histories of America were threatened with destruction, it is the work of Las Casas most students would seek to preserve.[23] This is true for a number of reasons. In the first place, Las Casas was an eyewitness to many of the events he recounts and he was a contemporary of the civilization in which almost all of them took place. He had, in addition, a personal knowledge of Columbus and the use of manuscript materials unavailable to others and since unavailable elsewhere. The journal of the third Columbian voyage, for example, is in the second volume of the *Historia*.[24]

Las Casas' *Historia*, divided into eight parts, begins with Columbus and continues to 1554. Begun in Spanish America probably in 1527, it was largely written in the old country in the interval between 1550 and 1563. Las Casas was still engaged in historical work at the age of ninety, and he left instructions preventing publication until forty years after his death. Although some historians were able to use the Las Casas history in unpublished form, it remained unprinted until 1875—three hundred years after it was written.[25]

The literate world, which was to be deprived of the benefit of Las

Casas for three centuries, was able to participate in the knowledge of Peter Martyr almost at once. Peter Martyr—Pietro Martire d'Anghiera—was born in the duchy of Milan in 1457. To the great distress of his humanist friends in Italy, he removed to Spain thirty years later, but not before they had exacted his promise to keep them posted on the great events then taking place in the Iberian peninsula. They had reference, of course, to the dramatic crusade of Spanish Christians against the remaining Moorish strongholds, events in which they had an avid interest. Peter Martyr fulfilled his promise faithfully, and his letters, written from 1487 to 1526,[26] the year of his death, so well accomplished the wishes of his correspondents that one historian later described his reports as "perhaps the best contemporary source for the history of Spain in her greatest age." [27]

But it was not as the reporter of Moorish defeats or of Spanish grandeur that Peter Martyr made so deep an imprint on the future. Instead, he became the chronicler of America, the special purveyor of news about geographical discovery, of the glamorous Indies, or, to use his own striking phrase, of the New World. As a humanist scholar, he was intrigued by cosmography and captivated by the customs of faraway places. When the grand Admiral returned from his first voyage with the electrifying report that he had reached the Indies by sailing west, Peter Martyr was witness to the event. And one may be certain that neither Columbus himself nor anyone connected with the venture could escape his sharp, probing questions.

Peter Martyr first makes reference to the discoveries in a letter from Barcelona, dated May 14, 1493. "A few days ago," he wrote, "there returned from the *western antipodies* a certain Christoforus Colonus, a Ligurian, who, because they thought that what he said was fabulous, only got three ships from my Sovereigns and that with difficulty. But he brought back proofs of many precious things but especially of gold which those regions produce of their own special nature." [28] A number of other communications followed in rapid succession, each with additional details, until November 1, 1493, writing fully, he remarked: "Although the opinion of Columbus seems to be contrary to the theories of the ancients concerning the size of the globe and its circumnavigation, the birds and many other objects brought thence seem to indicate that these islands do belong, be it by proximity or by their products, to India. . . . Happy at having discovered this unknown land, and to have found indications of a hitherto unknown continent, Columbus resolved to take advantage of favouring winds and the approach of spring to return to Europe." [29]

Peter Martyr's influence on the dissemination of geographical knowledge was as great as the influence of the Columbian discoveries upon him. He hoped to write an account of the discovery and settlement of the land to the west himself. Although detained by diplomatic assignments and other affairs, he completed the first section of his history in 1511. Consequently, until 1571, when the Italian translation of Ferdinand's biography of his father appeared, these letters and Peter Martyr's *Decades* were the only public sources of information. The *Decades* turned out to be a work so absorbing to contemporary readers that one of them, Pope Leo X, is said to have sat up all night reading it.[30]

When in 1493 Christopher Columbus made his dramatic entry into Barcelona, Gonzalo Fernández de Oviedo y Valdés—subsequently renowned as a scholar and writer—was present with the court to receive him. Twenty years after this memorable experience, Fernández de Oviedo himself went to New Spain, then no longer a vision in the dreams of explorers but a thriving part of an expanding empire. He went, moreover, not as an explorer but as an official, a royal supervisor of gold smeltings.[31] He lived in America for thirty-four years and spent such time as he could spare acquiring information about life in his new surroundings. Home again in 1525, he submitted a summary of Spanish colonial activity dedicated to the Emperor Charles V. He described the work as "La general y natural historia de las Indias, que de mi mano tengo escrita."[32] Having met with royal favor, Fernández de Oviedo was made official chronicler of the Indies and given authority to ask Spanish officials to provide him with documentary and other material to aid him in his work.[33] The result of these literary efforts was *La historia general y natural de las Indias Occidentales,* the first parts of which appeared in 1535 and upon which the author was still engaged at the time of his death in 1557. His narrative, compiled before the biography of Ferdinand Columbus and Las Casas' *Historia,* contains suggestive data derived from personal contacts. For valuable comments on native customs and for a general understanding of how the land and its people appeared to an active contemporary mind, Fernández de Oviedo is indispensable.[34]

Antonio de Herrera was another official historian of the Indies. Although he borrowed generously from Las Casas, he did not share Las Casas' attitudes toward the Indians. Like most writers of the early period who lived close to the events they described, Herrera reveals the opinions current of his time and place. But it is for this reason that he possesses such value for those who followed him.

Herrera was, in addition, a writer of large experience and fathered many other historical works, besides *The General History of the Indies,* which, according to prevailing critical opinion, is the least biased and the most useful of all his writings.[35]

Columbus discovered America; others explored and colonized it. Spain became the commercial adversary of other mercantile powers —of Portugal, of France, of England—but all combined in the process of exploration and discovery. As contestants for economic monopoly and for national power, they employed all the techniques of rivals in peace as well as in war. But international conflict quickened the organization and dissemination of knowledge. The result, though unconscious, was a cultural revolution from which the meanings of national rivalries derive. The separate explorations, discoveries, and settlements of the major powers were all parts of a larger social texture. To the emerging pattern of a new civilization neither New Spain nor New France supplies the dominant thread, and New Britain is but a single strand in the total design. On this point Edward P. Cheyney's characterization of the end of the Middle Ages is pertinent:

> It is an experience, not so common perhaps as it should be, but not unknown to some of us, to watch the increasing glow of the early morning spread over the landscape. Few of the objects disclosed are new, but all appear in an altered and constantly changing light. It is the dawn of a new day. The scene is set for a series of new occurrences. So it was with the coming on of modern times.[36]

Yet "modern times" is a concept inadequate to convey the implications, for the end product was the transformation of the whole world. Columbus and his successors emerged from a society already in the process of disruption, and what they accomplished disrupted it still further.

Between the second and third voyages of Columbus, in May of 1497, John Cabot discovered the North American continent on his own. Sailing under the English flag, he set out from Bristol and landed on Cape Breton Island on June 24. Back in England early in August, he hastened to report to his royal sponsor that he had discovered the lands of the Great Khan. Since he brought back neither spices nor silks, he promised on his next trip to sail further south where, he was sure, the island of Cipangu was to be found. Once there, spices would flow into London as Cabot had seen them flow into the cities of the East. Henry VII, the first Tudor monarch, was properly impressed, and so too were several enterprising merchants of Bristol, for London might indeed become another Alexandria.

Probing southward in search of Cipangu brought Cabot and his son Sebastian, on a second voyage in May 1498, to the northeast coast of Greenland, to Labrador, to Nova Scotia, and to the New England shore. Cabot returned in 1499 without finding Cipangu, and as his holds were empty of spice, silks, or brazilwood, his financial backers were not enthusiastic. Neither was his majesty the king.

John Cabot's discovery put England's colonial claims on the American map. But it was an "English discovery" only in a legal sense. Giovanni Caboto was an Italian, and his role in discovery should remind us of the contributions made by others who hailed from Genoa and Florence. As Caboto was no Englishman, Columbus was no Spaniard. And Hieronimo da Verrazano was not born in France. Queen Isabella of Castile's patronage of Columbus induced men of means—some of them Spanish only in name—to invest in the Columbian scheme. The Medici and Juanoto Berardi, Italians both, provisioned many a vessel which set sail from Cádiz. It was, as German Arciniegas remarks, "the last great adventure of the mariners of the Mediterranean," [37] the link between the civilizations of the Atlantic and the civilizations of the inland sea.

The discovery of America was a European movement. Voyages of exploration occurred with a regularity that only a similar core of interests could have inspired. Duarte Pancho Pereira, for example, was sent by King John of Portugal in 1498 to see what Columbus had accomplished. The following year, Vicente Yáñez Pingori, in the employ of Spain, tried his own luck, and in January 1500 made a landing near Cape São Roque, while at about the same time Diego de Lepe explored the Brazilian coast from that point. Nor did the explorers confine their activities to the south, for a passage to the Indies was sought in both directions. As the fifteenth century slipped into the sixteenth, Gaspar Corte Real, retained by Portugal, navigated around the eastern shores of Greenland and Labrador. Another attempt in the same region in 1501 resulted only in the loss of a great mariner. Gaspar never returned, and his brother, Miguel Corte Real, seeking to find him, met a similar fate.

A mariner's immortality was the lot of the brothers Corte Real. The lot of Amerigo Vespucci was the immortality of history. Vespucci has been a center of scholarly controversy since the days of discovery, and the debate is likely to continue as long as there is interest in logical analysis and inference. Whatever Vespucci accomplished or failed to accomplish, two continents share his name.[38]

Amerigo Vespucci was a sailor, a banker, and a writer. In addition he has become a legend and a symbol. Had he lived out his crowded days in his native Florence, history still would not have forgotten him.[39] The Vespucci name was illustrious. The great and near great of Florence had intimate connections with the Vespucci clan. One of their number, Giorgio Antonio, executed a literary commission for Savonarola. Marco Vespucci married the enchanting Simonetta. And Simonetta Vespucci inspired Botticelli and became the lady of *The Birth of Venus*. When Simonetta died prematurely at the age of twenty-three, Leonardo da Vinci followed her coffin through the streets of Florence together with Amerigo Vespucci and his grieving kinsmen.

Whoever recalled the Medici would also have recalled Amerigo Vespucci. The son of Lorenzo the Magnificent, Piero de' Medici, was his childhood playmate, and Vespucci wrote to him from the New World. Another of his correspondents was Piero Soderini, also a companion of his youth, who had become the gonfalonier of Florence. These sparkling letters, full of interest and information, were designed to amuse a tired noble and to lighten the cares of an official weary of the burdens of office. But they also informed a generation about the discoveries others had made. While Columbus of Genoa was the first European to write of America, Vespucci of Florence was the writer whom Europeans first read.[40]

Vespucci, however, has long been a central problem in American historiography. He left Florence for Spain when the Medici fell on evil days, but he did not go to sea until middle life. How many voyages he made is not precisely known, and only one has been established to the complete satisfaction of experts. A voyage in 1497, described by Amerigo himself, has been accounted spurious by many. The expedition of 1499 in the company of Alonso de Ojeda and Juan de La Cosa is held by Amerigo's critics to be only plausible. The "Morizo Vespuche," attested to by Ojeda, may conceivably have been another explorer, especially since the date, if correct, would make him a seaman for a period longer than seems justifiable. However, during the last years of his life, from 1502 to 1512, he was *Piloto Mayor* in the Spanish service which indicates that he was, at least by that time, a highly trained sailor. On the other hand, there is no extant original record of the voyage, and such Latin and Italian versions as do exist have increased the critical perplexities instead of solving them. As a matter of fact there is no record of a Spanish voyage in the year 1497 at all. When Las Casas refers to Vespucci he does so only to deflate his claims, and the Portuguese historians who describe the later voyages in which Vespucci is said to have taken part, make no mention of him whatever.[41]

Vespucci's significance in the record of discovery does not stem from his exploits either real or fancied. Vespucci's significance derives from what he wrote. Even his unkindest critics concede that his literary craftsmanship was masterly. Edward G. Bourne, whose study of the evidence is a splendid example of historical analysis, commented: "His place in the history of the discoveries is the most remarkable illustration of eternal celebrity won through a happy combination of . . . literary gift and self-advertisement, with the co-operation of the printing press." [42] Two letters, ascribed to Vespucci, comprise in effect the total body of evidence. One, dated at Lisbon in 1503, was addressed to Lorenzo Piero Francesco de' Medici, and recounts the events of his third voyage of 1501. Another, dated September 1504 and likewise from Lisbon, was written to Piero Soderini. The latter is an account of the four voyages.

Coincidence may perhaps have played a larger role than conspiracy. Early in 1504 or late in 1503, the letter to the scion of the house of Medici appeared under the title of *Mundus Novus*. The *Soderini Letter* was published at Florence in 1505. Of both originals no trace has been found; it was a Latin translation of the *Soderini Letter,* translated in turn from one in French, which formed a part of Martin Waldseemüller's *Cosomographiae Introductio* in 1507. Peter Martyr's entrancing correspondence was still in manuscript, the *Decades* remained unprinted until 1511, and his first published letter did not reach the Latin reading public until 1508.

The *Medici Letter* not only reached Latin readers in Europe earlier than the news of the discovery of Columbus, but it had a remarkable publication record. Vespucci's voyages, true or not, were known all over Europe; Columbus' voyages, unquestionably authentic and known in Spain, were not known in Europe until after data concerning Vespucci's exploits were already widespread. The *Medici Letter* went through fifteen Latin editions, seven German editions, and one Flemish edition, and by 1550 there were no less than forty. Although editions of the *Soderini Letter* were fewer, it was often added as an appendix to geographies and other texts and was thus widely disseminated. Waldseemüller's geography, though the most famous, is but a single example of this common practice. "I do not see why," Martin Waldseemüller wrote in 1507, the new land should not "be named Amerige, that is Americ's Land, from Americus the discoverer, a man of sagacious mind, or America, since both Europe and Asia derived their names from women." [43]

Vespucci gave America a name, but Europeans still viewed their new world as the old world of the East. Even after Vasco Núñez de

Balboa discovered the Pacific in 1513, the Spanish continued to believe that the Oriental cities were almost within their commercial grasp. It was not until Magellan made his fabulous global voyage that discerning men began to comprehend the full significance of the discovery of Columbus.

But Balboa looked out upon the wide Pacific with the narrow vision of a fortune hunter. "I am told," he wrote to Ferdinand his king, "that the other sea is very good for canoe navigation, for that it is always smooth, and never rough like the sea on this side . . . I believe there are many islands in that sea. They say that there are many large pearls, and that the caciques have baskets of them." [44]

Already the governor of Darien, rich with gold, Balboa wished to enlist royal aid for an expedition to Peru of which he had recently heard. But he had greater need of men and provisions. "I have taken care," he writes, "that the Indians of this land are not ill-treated, permitting no men to injure them, and giving them many things from Castile, whereby they may be drawn into friendship with us. This honourable treatment of the Indians has been the cause of my learning great secrets from them, through the knowledge of which large quantities of gold may be obtained, and your Highness will thus be well served." [45]

Balboa's report is succinct and to the king's point:

In this province of Darien many very rich mines have been found, and there is gold in great quantities. Twenty rivers have been discovered, and thirty containing gold flow from a mountain about two leagues from this town, towards the south. This mountain is towards the west, and between the town and the mountain no gold bearing rivers have been seen, but I believe they exist. Following the course of the great river of San Juan for thirty leagues on the right hand side, one arrives at a province called Abanumaqué, which contains much gold. I have certain intelligence that there are very rich rivers of gold in this province, from a son of a *cacique,* and from other Indian men and women whom I have taken. Thirty leagues up this great river, on the left hand, a very large and beautiful stream flows into it, and two days' journey up this stream there is a *cacique* called Davaive. He is a very great lord with large and very populous land. He has great store of gold in his house, so much indeed that he who does not know the things of this land would be very hard of belief. I know this of a certainty. All the gold that goes forth from this gulf comes from the house of the cacique Davaive, as well as all that is owned by the *caciques* of those districts, and it is reported that they have many pieces of gold curiously worked, and very large. Many Indians who have seen them, tell me that this cacique Davaive has certain bags of gold, and that it takes the whole strength of a man to lift one of them on to his back.[46]

Balboa had really discovered the great secret of the new world. It was a new world, a new continent, and "the other sea" was its boundary.[47]

The conquistadors wrote much concerning the natural beauties of the new lands, but they were hardly content simply to contemplate its charms. Balboa's discoveries induced a search for more gold and for swifter ways of reaching it. One passage across the isthmus of Panama might lead to another, and the next might finally lead to bustling Far Eastern ports. Wherever there were pearls and gold more might still be found, for there were no limits to the desires of of those who pursued them. And the natives, never as artless as they have usually been described, always told of treasures piled high as the hills over which they directed their unwelcome visitors.

Actually there was treasure north of Panama as well as south of it, and the Spaniards were not long in finding it. And now they had the means as they had always possessed the will to push their conquests. Solitary adventurers and their companions still had their problems. They died by the scores in tropical heat, they perished at sea, and resistant natives made the most of their comparatively few opportunities. Diseases, wars, and gentlemanly brawls shortened the lives of countless others. But official expeditions between old Spain and new Spain and to and from the settled portions of the Hispanic dominions had ceased to be tentative affairs.

Even in the latter days of King Ferdinand, Balboa's promise of gold in Darien opened the royal coffers. After Columbus had returned from Hispaniola with solid evidence of his successes—gold, parrots, and Indians—he was never sumptuously provided for his later trips. Sheets, pillowcases, frying pans, and utensils were doled out with a parsimony unbecoming a grateful sovereign.

But by the time King Ferdinand sent Pedrarias Dávila to succeed Balboa—and incidentally to despoil him of his gains—nothing was really lacking. The new governor sailed with a fleet of twenty-two ships and a company of two thousand men. The holds were bulging with stores sufficient to care for the whole entourage as well as to impress the population of Darien. The company was augmented by experts—doctors, lawyers, and a specialist in rare and precious stones. And among the stores were two hundred troughs for the purpose of washing gold. The starving time was over. More importantly, the route from Spanish ports to Spanish possessions was a much-traveled one. Hazards, of course, there were but they did not come from lack of knowledge of geography, navigation, or the economics of supply.[48]

Discoveries, explorations, and expeditions of conquest produced literary records as well as historical results. Narratives, reports, letters, and chronicles were the inevitable counterparts of activity, whether official or unofficial. Despite the magnificent work of generations of historians, the original documents possess an incomparable quality. They frequently tell us less than later analysis, because subsequent scholars had perspectives of which the actors were naturally unaware. But no later secondary accounts have been able to convey so real a feeling of intimacy or to offer such opportunities for vicarious participation as do the original documents.

Both are provided by the literary records of the exploits of Hernando Cortés.[49] Young Charles of Hapsburg thrilled with pleasure when he fingered the gold ornaments and intricate fabrics made by the subjects of Moctezuma. But the gold that delighted Charles V is for the most part no more. The gold lined the pockets of Flemish courtiers and paid the wages of those soldiers still living after the capture of Rome. Other soldiers on other battlefields were paid by the emperor-king with the profits of new-world exploitation, but even the monuments that marked many of the sites of those bloody encounters have since disappeared. The battles themselves fill the pages of historical accounts and crowd the columns of chronologies. But the letters of Cortés are still as vibrant as when they first were written, the intent of his words still as sharp.

And the experience of Cortés was novel, for he was the first European to encounter a mature civilization in America. Mexico fulfilled the Spanish dream. Spaniards had uncovered new continents. They had reported on the existence of bizarre peoples in the Caribbean. They had even found gold. Yet, until the expedition from Cuba to Yucatan, they had met only primitive peoples living in what Europeans could only regard as a state of nature. Mexico was both startling and shocking. Europeans, like Cortés, found the greatness of Moctezuma and his court, heathen all, difficult to comprehend. It demanded a new rationalization.

Yet glories still to be won and gold still to be acquired constantly recharged the dynamic conquistadors. However, it was not simply military prowess alone that makes Cortés and his companions important for history. Rather it was the Aztecs, of whom Cortés wrote in such simple and vivid detail, who give his letters a lasting place in American literature. European readers, certain of their modernity, were unfailingly interested in the exotic.[50]

The *cartas-relaciones*,[51] as the Cortés letters are called, were written to Charles V in the years between 1519 and 1526. Frequently compared to the *Anabasis* of Xenophon and the *Commentaries*[52] of Caesar, they somewhat resemble them without possessing the craftsmanship of either. But the prose is forceful, and there is never any striving for effect; the understatement, apparently undesigned, doubtless contributed to their power. There are five letters in all. The first, written in 1519, has never been recovered, but another based upon or copied from what Cortés had written, is still in existence. It recounts the founding of Vera Cruz. The second tells of the advance into the strange Mexican lands, of encounters with local chieftains and of the meeting with Moctezuma. If the pages describing the fabulous city of Tenochtitlán still read like a chapter from *The Arabian Nights,* it is easy to imagine with what feelings readers in the Europe of the sixteenth century responded. The rebellion of the Aztecs stirred Cortés only to reconquest which, together with the extension of Spanish power over other parts of Mexico, is the subject of the third letter. A notable section contains the description of the capture of Tenochtitlán. The fourth letter describes the organization of the new conquest and the fifth, the Honduran expedition.[53] Soon after the second and third letters were received in Spain they were published in Seville. On November 8, 1522, the second appeared; on March 30, 1523, the third. Almost at once they were translated into Latin and Italian and read in Germany and Italy. The fourth was published in 1526 at Saragossa and Toledo.[54]

Other men made perilous journeys into unknown lands. Others had vanquished brave men made desperate by fear of conquest and enslavement. Others, too, had found treasure to gladden the hearts of their comrades and their kings. But none had found the cities of Cathay, the bazaars of the Orient, or the prospects of trade and empire promised by organized wealth. Cortés alone discovered a thriving society and thus fulfilled a European hope current since the time of the Crusades. Columbus detailed encounters with primitive peoples, with cultures still in varied stages of barbarism. Although he called petty tribal chieftains and territorial divisions by glamorous names, they remained for the most part what they had been— squalid and barbarous and pathetic. But always, most eloquent evidence of all, there were towns, principalities, countries, and empires around the corner of rumor. One need only compare the account Cortés gives of Tenochtitlán with the descriptive passages in the *Journals* of Columbus.

> The great city in Tenochtitlán is built in the midst of this salt lake, and it is two leagues from the heart of the city to any point on the mainland.

Four causeways lead to it, all made by hand and some twelve feet wide. The city itself is as large as Seville or Córdoba. The principal streets are very broad and straight, the majority of them being of beaten earth, but a few and at least half the smaller thoroughfares are waterways along which they pass in their canoes. Moreover, even the principal streets have openings at regular distances so that the water can freely pass from one to another, and these openings which are very broad are spanned by great bridges of huge beams, very stoutly put together, so firm indeed that over many of them ten horsemen can ride at once. Seeing that if the natives intended any treachery against us they would have every opportunity from the way in which the city is built, for by removing the bridges from the entrances and exits they could leave us to die of hunger with no possibility of getting to the mainland, I immediately set to work as soon as we entered the city on the building of four brigs, and in a short space of time had them finished, so that we could ship three hundred men and the horses to the mainland whenever we so desired.

The city has many open squares in which markets are continuously held and the general business of buying and selling proceeds. One square in particular is twice as big as that of Salamanca and completely surrounded by arcades where there are daily more than sixty thousand folk buying and selling. Every kind of merchandise such as may be met with in every land is for sale there, whether of food and victuals, or ornaments of gold and silver, or lead, brass, copper, tin, precious stones, bones, shells, snails and feathers; limestone for building is likewise sold there, stone both rough and polished, bricks burnt and unburnt, wood of all kinds and in all stages of preparation. There is a street of game where they sell all manner of birds that are to be found in their country, including hens, partridges, quails, wild duck, fly-catchers, widgeon, turtle doves, pigeons, little birds in round nests made of grass, parrots, owls, eagles, vulcans, sparrow-hawks and kestrels; and of some of these birds of prey they sell the skins complete with feathers, head, bill and claws. They also sell rabbits, hares, deer and small dogs which they breed especially for eating. There is a street of herb-sellers where there are all manner of roots and medicinal plants that are found in the land. There are houses as it were of apothecaries where they sell medicines made from these herbs, both for drinking and for use as ointments and salves. There are barbers' shops where you may have your hair washed and cut. There are other shops where you may obtain food and drink. There are street porters such as we have in Spain to carry packages. There is a great quantity of wood, charcoal, braziers made of clay and mats of all sorts, some for beds and others more finely woven for seats, still others for furnishing halls and private apartments. All kinds of vegetables may be found there, in particular onions, leeks, garlic, cresses, watercress, borage, sorrel, artichokes, and golden thistles. There are many different sorts of fruits including cherries and plums very similar to those found in Spain.[55]

The more Cortés and his followers saw, the more they marveled. Even before they had an opportunity to test the extent of the kingdom or to evaluate the wealth of the mighty emperor, they saw many evidences of both. The court of Moctezuma was magnificent, his retinue large and impressive, his power apparent. The pomp of imperial ceremony and the scale of living could not fail to impress the men who had just marched overland from Vera Cruz and who knew only the standards of Spain. Nobles of high degree waited on the emperor's pleasure. His diet consisted of innumerable dishes which, scarcely touched, were passed on to his retainers. Elaborate meals were daily served to throngs of courtiers and servitors. The service was rich and elaborate, the armor embellished with silver and gold; the gardens lush and exotic.[56] "And there was so much to see in these gardens as in everything else," wrote Bernal Díaz del Castillo, "that we could never feel surfeited to behold his great power." [57] The court of Moctezuma did not take the place of the court of the Grand Khan, but Cortés succeeded Marco Polo in the imagination of Western Europeans. Search for a passage to Cathay continued unabated but another Mexico might be found on the way.

To find a passage to the Spice Islands was the mission of Ferdinand Magellan who sailed out of Sanlúcar in 1519.[58] The voyage turned out to be one of the most memorable in the entire history of navigation, for Magellan first circumnavigated the earth. Although Magellan neither envisaged this result nor lived to witness its completion, he was in command of the armada that finally accomplished it.[59] Magellan actually did what Columbus attempted; he discovered a western route to the Far East—twenty-seven years after the maiden voyage of the great Admiral. Thereafter the world appeared to Europeans in something like its actual shape, for Magellan revealed the extent of the Pacific. And in discovering the Philippines, he introduced Europeans to another new world although it was in fact a part of the Asiatic region of which almost all mariners had dreamed.

Magellan's ships flew the Spanish flag, but his crew was by no means exclusively Spanish. In addition to Spaniards and Portuguese, there were Frenchmen, Italians, Flemings, Germans, Greeks, and Moorish sailors, together with a solitary Englishman. The Emperor Charles V, whose boundless ambitions for the house of Hapsburg required limitless funds, was interested in checkmating Portugal; Antwerp merchants were interested in profit; Magellan wanted fame as well as his due share. But the significance of Magellan's voyage is to be found in the expansion of human knowledge and the growing extension of human mastery.

Among the ship's company was Antonio Pigafetta.[60] A Lombard gentleman, he had come to Spain in the very year of the voyage and sailed aboard the *Trinidad* as servant to Magellan. He was vastly intrigued by "the great things of the Ocean," and his elaborate account of the perilous trip is one of the most celebrated in the literature of travel.

Bernal Díaz del Castillo was to Hernando Cortés what Antonio Pigafetta was to Ferdinand Magellan. Pigafetta accompanied Magellan's fleet from Spain to the Far East and back to Spain again. Díaz followed Cortés from the embarkation at Santa María to the end of the disastrous Honduran expedition. Both did far more than tabulate picturesque incidents of which there was certainly no lack. As historical narratives they are almost without parallel in their respective areas. Together with other data, they make historical reconstruction possible and bring us as close to the actuality as we are ever likely to come. But they are also social documents in themselves. Pigafetta's account reveals the mind of the sixteenth-century mariner; his response to danger and trial, his reaction to hunger, fear, and despair. Díaz's narrative reveals the mind of the sixteenth-century soldier and his response to victory and defeat, as well as the attitudes of Europeans to the natives of Mexico, of the Philippines and of the Moluccas. In doing so, they unconsciously recorded their concepts and ideals.

The history of Díaz has a particular relevance. When Cortés returned to Spain, a distinguished cleric and scholar, Francisco López de Gómara, entered his employ in the capacity of chaplain. He began to write a history of his own in which the triumphs of Cortés were second only to the triumph of Spain. Published in 1552, Gómara's story, already generally popularized, rapidly went into a second edition and was translated into French, English, and Italian. While gifted with an easy flowing style, there were certain difficulties that Gómara could not overcome. Among them Las Casas noted:

> About this first going of Cortés as captain on this expedition, the ecclesiastic Gómara tells many thing grossly untrue in his history, as might be expected from a man who neither saw nor heard anything about them, except what Fernando Cortés told him and gave him in writing: Gómara being his chaplain and servant, after he was made marquis and returned to Spain that time.[61]

The errors of Gómara prompted Díaz to write his version of the Conquest. But Díaz did not only correct Gómara, he corrected Cortés. While he had an old soldier's affection for his leader, he resented the way in which both Cortés and Gómara told the story. Whatever may be said in praise of the Cortés letters, they certainly suggest, whether tactfully or not, that their author performed his miracles largely unaided. Cortés is unmistakably the leader whose wisdom, courage, and foresight brought glory to Spain. He describes the victories in war and statecraft achieved by himself and his army. Díaz, on the other hand, recounts the achievements of the army Cortés led. He tells how the army overcame its difficulties and met its successes.[62] It matters little whether or not Díaz was moved by pique. It does matter that Díaz presents a picture of the conquest which nowhere else exists. Díaz speaks for the army, for the individual soldier. And he speaks with such intense sincerity and such a memory for detail that his history, together with the account of Cortés, gives us a sense of completeness. In addition, he loved Cortés so well that he was even able to censure him when he felt censure was due.[63]

Aided by Bernal Díaz and men of the Díaz stamp, Cortés conquered Mexico. And following the conquest of Mexico, the Spanish poured their energies into further expansion both north and south of the Aztec lands. Honduras, Guatemala, and Peru were added to the dominions of the Hapsburg crown, and territories that were to become parts of the United States also came within the orbit of Spanish expansionism.[64]

Exploration of the eastern region began with Florida and Luis Ponce de Léon in 1513. That he found neither gold nor the fountain of youth was no deterrent to others. Pánfilo de Narváez,[65] who would have liked to emulate Cortés or Pizarro, led an expedition up the Florida peninsula in 1528. When failure dried up what was left of hope, the survivors tried to reach home in Mexico by sea. But courage and ingenuity, adequate to improvise primitive sailing craft, were no match for the currents of the Mississippi's mouth. Out of the catastrophe of shipwreck only four men survived. But one of the survivors was Álvar Núñez Cabeza de Vaca whose record of the adventure has become a minor classic of early American historiography. With three companions he wandered over vast areas of Texas before returning to Mexico six years later.[66]

Cabeza de Vaca had found neither treasure nor civilization. Yet when he visited Spain a year after his miraculous escape from futility, he allowed his imagination to play tricks with his reason. To his credulous auditors who thought only of Aztec gold and Peruvian silver he gave a glowing account. Among his listeners was a gentleman of high quality who had recently acquired the rights of Narváez in North America. Hernando de Soto had a plan that he was ready to put into execution.[67]

When De Soto sailed from Spain in 1538, there were more applicants for passage than his ships could accommodate. Cuba was reached in safety, and in 1539 a great company of six hundred armed men with supplies and equipment to match landed at Tampa Bay. During four barren years De Soto and his ever-dwindling band wandered through the American wilderness. They covered an estimated 350,000 square miles, the first Europeans to march through Florida, Georgia, South Carolina, Alabama, Mississippi, Arkansas, Oklahoma, Louisiana, and Texas. They reached the site of Memphis, Tennessee, and roamed over a part of the Ozark country. De Soto discovered the Mississippi River, but there was no sign of precious metals, no trace of the fabled cities he had come to find.[68]

De Soto's failure was personal. Spain learned finally that the easy wealth of Mexico and Peru were not to be found in eastern North America. Spanish officials also learned that settlement was more rewarding than exploitation, and a new phase of imperial organization dates from De Soto's frustration.[69] In addition, the expedition added enormously to the store of knowledge, knowledge of the interior, of its waterways, and of its inhabitants. And this knowledge was first presented in an account of the venture written by one of the participants, Alvaro Fernández of Elvas.[70]

Alvaro Fernández, known as the gentleman of Elvás, was a Portuguese nobleman and a member of De Soto's party. His narrative, carefully edited by Theodore H. Lewis, was written after the events he describes, apparently without benefit of notes or other reference. Parts are almost certainly imaginative, other parts erroneous. But once these deficiencies are taken into consideration it remains, as Lewis avers, "the best full account that has been handed down to us." There is no other place where the discovery of the Mississippi is described, no other source that records the death of its discoverer. And there was thereafter no other man, wrote the spirited historian of the Spanish borderland, "in the Spanish islands who desired to tempt heaven in the barren land of Florida." [71]

If Florida eased to beckon the adventurous and the avaricious, California and the Pacific slope was still believed to hold the secret of the conquistador's dream. Francisco Vásquez de Coronado, governor of New Galicia, in glittering coat of golden mail, set out at the head of an army of three hundred to find the cities of Cíbola. The expedition which started so bravely in 1540 penetrated as far north as Kansas. Indian villages they found in abundance but no resplendent cities. They found poverty and simplicity but neither great lords nor great riches.[72]

Some twenty years thereafter Pedro de Castañeda, a private in Coronado's army, wrote the history of the expedition. Wisely he commented: "Granted that they did not find the riches of which they had been told, they found a place in which to search for them and the beginning of a good country to settle in, so as to go on farther from there . . . time has given them a chance to understand the direction and locality in which they were, and the borders of the good country they had in their hands, and their hearts weep for having lost so favorable an opportunity." [73]

Spaniards still continued to search for personal glory and personal wealth, but the government of Spain had an empire to administer. Expansion continued, but gradually requirements of organization and defense came to dominate official policy. St. Augustine was founded in 1565 to check French designs, and Florida, no longer viewed as the preserve of individual adventurers, was regarded as a part of the system of imperial defense. When Spanish galleons, homeward bound with cargoes of gold and silver, spread their sails to the Atlantic winds off the Florida coasts, no marauding privateer could be permitted to lurk along its shores. Conquistadors did not disappear, but they were finally succeeded by missionaries. Members of religious orders became the new pathfinders, the mission the outpost of the Spanish frontier. California became the land of missions, and by 1606 they stretched as far north as the Carolinas on the eastern coast.[74]

The Spaniards were first to grapple with the American continent. Their activity initially revealed the basic geographical contours of the new world lands. They first exploited its natural treasures and informed the old world of its riches and opportunities. But this was far from all, for they amassed knowledge as well as treasure. Letters of navigators, journals of explorers, and documents of conquistadors initiated the process by which data about America were acquired. These were the documents that created images of power and dreams of conquest just as they provided the elemental facts for trade and commerce. Balboa, Magellan, and Cortés were to the Europe of the sixteenth century what Marco Polo was to the Europe of the thirteenth.

Such prodigious feats and the men who accomplished them belong as much to historiography as to history. They were not only doers of great deeds, but the authors of great records which recounted them. And all have been the subjects of historians who strove to recapture their spirit and to ascribe meanings to their thought and action in the movement of time.

While the thrill of discoveries and tales of conquest excited Europeans, there were other factors no less consequential. The results of discovery and conquest became the links of history and the materials of historiography. Exploration was the basis of new knowledge; settlement the prologue to new experience. Spain first navigated the globe, and the exploits of her captains and pilots first defined the dual continental nature of the western hemisphere. Fortune hunters followed explorers into the unknown on land and sea. They discovered the great Amazon and the great Mississippi, they laid startled eyes on the peaceful South Sea, as the Pacific Ocean was first called. They reared up cities, built churches, set up printing presses, and established universities. As early as 1524 schools for the Indians were in existence, and in 1575 the Spanish were publishing books for the Indians in several native tongues.

It was Spanish exploration, Spanish achievement, Spanish wealth that spoke to the imagination of Europe. It was Spanish conquests, Spanish grandeur, Spanish struggles that inspired chroniclers, historians, dramatists, and poets then and since. They encouraged emulation, invited competition, previsioned rivalry. A full century before England entered the international race, Mexico and Peru were provinces of the Spanish empire. Hernando Cortés might well have boasted to his emperor that he had given more provinces and kingdoms to the Castilian crown than the forefathers of Charles V had themselves been able to conquer. Mexico was larger by far than England, and what Cortés accomplished, Pizarro bettered. Vasco Núñez de Balboa, after trudging across the wastes of Panama, beheld the South Sea, which quickened the explorers' urge to find speedier routes to the never-fading glamour of the Indies. Ponce de León reached St. Augustine and gave to the "island" he thought he had discovered the name of Florida. Álvar Núñez Cabeza de Vaca walked from Florida to the Gulf of California. When Jamestown, the first permanent English colony, was founded more than a hundred years after Columbus landed in the West Indies, the Spaniards were masters of a whole new world.[75]

III

New France, 1524–1607

The discovery of Christopher Columbus altered the history of the world by changing the history of Europe. European culture, already moving into Africa, crossed the western sea. Spanish pilots, French mariners, and English explorers transformed the Atlantic into a commonplace route of traffic. Together they charted the shape of continents, mapped the course of internal rivers, and catalogued the fauna and flora of the interior. The published accounts of navigation and discovery were tools of international trade as well as weapons of international rivalry. Reports of exploration and books of travel were instruments of economics and instruments of understanding. Rivalry, conflict, and the printing press gave knowledge to a growing world.

The records of French activity in the earlier centuries of discovery became the sources of French colonial history. Historians of the United States have been charmed by the rise and fall of the French empire in North America. French nobles and French *coureurs du bois* have fascinated scholars as much as armored Spanish knights. The forests of the Canadian North, the majestic St. Lawrence, and the Great Lakes waterways leading into the limitless West stirred the historical imagination no less than the jungles of Central America, the subtropical lands of Florida and Aztec cities. French successes in discovery and French failures in administration have received painstaking and continued attention. But the ultimate decline and fall of the French Canadian empire has tantalized scholarly ingenuity as much as the decline and fall of imperial Spain.[1] In the mid-nineteenth century, Francis Parkman, whose descriptions of the French pioneers and their successors have never been equaled, focused his supple intellect on the problem.

> The springs of American civilization, unlike those of the elder world, lie revealed in the clear light of History. In appearance they are feeble; in reality, copious and full of force. Acting as the sources of life, instruments otherwise weak become mighty for good and evil, and men, lost elsewhere in the crowd, stand forth as agents of Destiny. In their toils, their sufferings, their conflicts, momentous questions were at stake, and issues vital to the future of the world—the prevalence of races, the triumph of principles, health or disease, a blessing or a curse. On the obscure strife where men died by tens or by scores hung questions of as deep import for posterity as on those mighty contests of national adolescence where carnage is reckoned by thousands.[2]

The light of history, although dimmer than in Parkman's days, now partly reveals the role of France in the making of America. First came the hardy fisher folk from Brittany's coast. Like their English counterparts from Bristol, they lay in wait along the waters of the Grand Banks and adapted their existence to the unpredictable rigors of the northern climate and the predictable habits of marine life. Besides providing the bases for rival national claims and counterclaims, they quietly amassed nautical information and nautical skills. If the Atlantic remained perilous, it gradually ceased to be mysterious.

Parkman's writing underscored national stereotypes:

> When America was first made known to Europe, the part assumed by France on the borders of that new world was peculiar, and is little recognized. While the Spaniard roamed sea and land, burning for achievement, red-hot with bigotry and avarice, and while England with soberer steps and a less dazzling result, followed in the path of discovery and gold-hunting, it was from France that those barbarous shores first learned to serve the ends of peaceful commercial industry. That industry was fishing, and in this occupation the French took an early and prominent part. The Normans, offspring of an ancestry of conquerors, the Bretons, that stubborn, hardy, unchanging race, who, among Druid monuments changeless as themselves, still cling with Celtic obstinacy to the thoughts and habits of the past,—the Basques, that primeval people, older than history—, all frequented from an early date the cod-banks of Newfoundland.[3]

The exploratory activity of Giovanni Verrazano supplied the legal basis for French territorial claims. A Florentine in the employ of the French monarch, Verrazano nosed the prow of his ship into American waters in the vicinity of Cape Fear during the year 1524. Verrazano wrote little himself, but there is an extensive literature about him.[4] In fact, he wrote only a single letter of historical importance. The letter has never been found, and its very existence is part of the dispute concerning him. If it was actually written, it was composed July 8, 1524, at Dieppe, and addressed to King Francis I, and if authentic it would be the first known description of the coastline of what was to become the United States. Verrazano's exploits initiated a controversy as sharp as any in American historiography.[5] Francis Parkman, following his usual procedure of evaluating all the availble evidence, concluded that the probability in favor of the Verrazano voyage was greater than the doubts concerning it. Nevertheless, Verrazano has remained an argument. Although Verrazano disappeared from history, his part in the making of historiography continued. Partisans of the French crown instanced his accomplishments as proof of French priority. And scholars have intermittently revived and elaborated the evidence.

The undisputed accomplishments of Jacques Cartier rendered the assertions of Verrazano, true or false, largely irrelevant. The discoverer of the St. Lawrence, born in Brittany, sailed from St-Malo, April 20, 1534. Cartier's picture, still preserved, impressed Parkman with the character of its subject whose "bold, keen features" bespoke "a spirit not apt to quail before the wrath of man or of the elements." [6] Such characteristics were demanded of men in the sixteenth century who made the search for wealth and glory their life mission.

Wild wheat and the mild summer climate of the south Labrador coast pleased Cartier, and he returned to St-Malo to prepare for a second expedition. The following year, he entered the St. Lawrence River and approached the site of what later became Quebec. Parkman is at his greatest in describing what Cartier saw, for he had trained himself to feel what his heroes must have experienced and he knew what was to follow:

> As he drew near the opening of the channel, the Hochelaga again spread before him the broad expanse of its waters. A mighty promontory, rugged and bare, thrust its scarped front into the surging current. Here, clothed in the majesty of solitude, breathing the stern poetry of the wilderness, rose the cliffs now rich with historic memories, where the fiery Count Frontenac cast defiance at his foes, where Wolfe, Montcalm, and Montgomery fell. As yet all was a nameless barbarism, and a cluster of wigwams held the site of the rock-built city of Quebec. Its name was Stadacone, and it owned the sway of the royal Donnacona.[7]

The natives were as awed by the white men as they were curious of the natives. Told that they were in the kingdom of Canada—the Indian name for village—the French proceeded inland to Hochelaga, where Cartier gave the name Montréal to the nearby mountains. Thereafter privation, disappointment, and death, in typical pioneer rhythm followed: after two additional voyages, Cartier's work of exploration and colonization was finished.

But Cartier's work in the movement of exploration and colonization had only begun. The experiences of the first exploratory venture were set forth in *Relation originale du voyage de Jacques Cartier au Canada;* the second in the *Récit.* By 1600 the indefatigable Richard Hakluyt, compiler extraordinary, had provided a translation in English. Jacques Cartier had not found the Indies, but like Columbus he had made spectacular discoveries. And like Columbus he made history not for his contemporaries alone but for posterity. In 1843, just in time for Francis Parkman, the Literary and Historical Society of Quebec published *Voyages de découverte au Canada, 1534–42,* in which the Cartier writings appear.[8]

Notwithstanding the valiant effort of Jacques Cartier, Samuel de Champlain was true founder of New France. Son of a French naval captain, Champlain was born in a small town off the Bay of Biscay in 1567. The "Father of New France" had an apprenticeship to serve before he was ready to lay the foundations of a colonial empire. Not an adventurer himself, Champlain was enticed by the spirit of adventure and he longed to visit the West Indies. His yearning was compounded of fascination for the exotic and an irritation with Spanish exclusiveness. The Spanish, possessing geographical and economic secrets, were anxious to keep them. They were hardly eager to entertain curious foreigners within their domains. Foreigners were not only enemies but usually heretics, and Frenchmen were frequently both. Champlain, however, was a Catholic, and to lay such secrets before his king and at the same time to taste the excitement of travel was his ardent wish.[9]

Family influence in Spain secured Champlain the command of a ship in the fleet of Don Francisco Columbo. After landing at Vera Cruz, he remained in the Spanish colonies for over two years, visiting, among other places, Mexico City and Panama. On the occasion of his visit to the latter place the idea of a canal across the isthmus occurred to him. This idea, together with his impressions of life and labor in Spanish America, were recorded in his journal, *Bref Discours des Choses plus remarquables que Samuel Champlain de Brouage a recognues aux Indes Occidentalles au voiage qu'il en a*

faict en icelles en l'année 1599 et en l'année 1601, comme ensuits.[10]
Henry IV of France saw possibilities in Champlain's first literary product, and he saw possibilities in Champlain. Royal favor in the form of a small pension was Champlain's reward, and when in 1603 colonial plans were next proposed to Henry, he approved both the plans and the appointment of Champlain as geographer royal. Champlain returned to France in September 1603, with his head filled with geographical data about the Gulf of St. Lawrence and a ship filled with furs. Having promised Henry IV "a true report of what should befall," he began at once to prepare it. *Des Sauvages: ou Voyage de Samuel Champlain, de Brouage, faict en la France Nouvelle, l'an mil six cens trois,* was published in 1604.[11] As the title indicates, *Des Sauvages* presented abundant fresh material on the ways of the natives, a knowledge valued as much for commerce as for science. If furs were to make Frenchmen rich—at least until gold and a passage to the East made them richer—it behooved them to learn as much about the Indians as they could. For the rest, Champlain's report simply amplified what Cartier had already established.

Champlain took ship for America again in April 1604. At this point he began his journals, and the journals supply a continuous history of his life. But they provide much more than the history of the life of Champlain, for they constitute the first history of Quebec. As such, his writings became the first histories of the French colonial empire.

Although Champlain's life is intertwined with the history of Canada, it is also linked with the history of British America. The conflict between France and England was a conflict for the mastery of Europe and each phase of the struggle had an American colonial counterpart. But it was as an explorer rather than as an empire builder that Champlain exerted his greatest influence upon American history. Champlain first gave geographic clarity to the coastline of New England. In the course of his explorations, he sailed as far south as Boston Harbor, and his lucid descriptions, quickly translated and made available in Europe, provided merchants and cartographers with reliable information. His knowledge of the Maine coast was better than that of the early English navigators. Champlain's "three voyages," wrote a close student of Maine geography, "are the first thoroughly intelligible contributions to the cartography of Maine." Bartholomew Gosnold and Martin Pring, said another, "had touched the coast; but their brief stay and shadowy notes are to the historian tantalizing and only faintly instructive."[12] Inadequate credit has been accorded Champlain for these accomplishments. "While the trials of the settlements of Plymouth and Massachusetts Bay are known to every school-boy," comments W. L. Grant, the editor of the Champlain voyages, "the connection of Champlain with the history of the United States has often been disregarded, and he has been considered solely as the founder of Quebec. The exclusive attention paid to the English colonists has glorified Massachusetts at the expense of Maine, and one of the noblest names in the history of exploration has been passed over." [13]

Frequently the original narratives of exploration and discovery are no more than what they purport to be: reports to royal officials or merchant princes, impromptu journals or diaries. Usually they were conceived for immediate purposes with little or no concern for the future. Occasionally, however, they were written by men historically minded and intended as much for posterity as for those to whom they were directed. Las Casas, Cortés, Bernal Díaz del Castillo, for example, were writers who had history in mind. Samuel de Champlain was also conscious of history. The opening paragraph of the *Voyages* begins with these words:

> The inclinations of men differ according to their varied dispositions; and each one in his calling has his particular end in view. Some aim at gain, some at glory, some at the public weal. The greater number are engaged in trade, and especially that which is transacted on the sea. Hence arise the principal support of the people, the opulence and honor of states. This is what raised ancient Rome to the sovereignty and mastery over the entire world, and the Venetians to grandeur equal to that of powerful kings. It has in all times caused maritime towns to abound in riches, among which Alexandria and Tyre are distinguished, and numerous others, which fill up the regions of the interior with the objects of beauty and rarity obtained from foreign nations. For this reason, many princes have striven to find a northerly route to China, in order to facilitate commerce with the Orientals, in the belief that this route would be shorter and less dangerous.[14]

Champlain's historical view reflected his own disposition, for his inclination was to build a new French world in spacious Canada. When Englishmen with similar inclinations began their own efforts to facilitate commerce and to find a northerly route to Asia, Samuel de Champlain and his compatriots had already well begun.

French colonial attempts in the south were less successful. Admiral Gaspard de Coligny, Jean Ribault, and René de Laudonnière founded a southern colony only to lose it. An earlier effort made in Brazil in defiance both of Portugal and the pope ended in disaster.[15] Commanded by Nicolas Durand de Villegagnon,[16] as incredible a character as ever tempted Providence and the Portuguese, the colony crashed to disappearance as much because of physical trials as because of theological disputation. Portugal and Spain remained securely in possession of their domains, leaving France without an outpost of settlement and the Huguenots without a new world home. But the Florida Huguenots, despite their failure, represent a dramatic episode in American history,[17] an episode with an unusual literary record.[18]

Ribault, native of Dieppe, put out from the port of Le Havre on February 18, 1562 and reached the coast of Florida at the end of April. In *The Whole and True Discoveries of Terra Florida,* he described the scenic wonders and the habits of the natives; the trees, the plants, and the climate. The land, he wrote, was "the fairest, fruitfullest, and pleasantest of all the world." In addition to the beauties of nature and the inducements of climate, he believed he had discovered a rare treasure in silkworms, silver, gold, turquoises, and pearls. Despite such great expectations, the colony disintegrated after Ribault left for home. *The . . . Discoveries,* references to which adorn Parkman's chapter on this episode, was printed in London in 1652.[19] Although Ribault's original document, like the colony he left behind him, disappeared, a translation by Richard Hakluyt, the great English compiler of world travel accounts, was published only eleven years later.[20]

René Goulaire de Laudonnière, colleague and successor of Ribault, led the next French sally into Florida. On the twenty-fifth of June, 1564, he arrived off the Florida coast at the head of a fleet of French ships to achieve what Ribault had failed to accomplish. Huguenot fortunes had not improved in France, but the fortunes of the French monarch had declined. Laudonnière, a member of the house of Châtillon, of which Gaspard de Coligny was the head, owed his colonial chance to the devout admiral's influence at the court of Charles IX. Although Coligny's motives were as pure as French nationalism and high-principled piety could make them, Laudonnière's companions, like Ribault's, did not all share them. The membership of the company was ill fitted for colony planting. Gold, so essential an ingredient of impoverished nobility, accounted for many young lords who were willing to endure temporary discomfort in order never again to encounter it. Ignoble men who believed the alchemy of wealth would enoble them also made up a considerable part of the band. Swords and pikes were assuredly needed, but farmers, artisans, and home builders were needed even more. Laudonnière's colony failed; most of the conventional causes of colonial failure entered into the tragedy, but there were some unique causes as well.[21]

Laudonnière was his own historian. In a series of letters written on the spot during the period 1564–1565, he spelled out the ideals and the heartbreak of French Florida. *L'Historie notable de la Floride . . . mise en lumiere par M. Basamier,* published in Paris in 1583, shares with other primitive accounts the exuberance inspired by untamed nature. Florida's woods and semitropical jungles captured the French imagination. While waiting for an exploring party to return, Laudonnière climbed a hill. "I went right to the toppe thereof, where we found nothing else but Cedars, Palme, and Bay-trees of so sovereigne odour that Baulme smelleth nothing like in comparison." Added to the details of internal treachery and the trauma of misery and rebellion, these letters are filled with specific observations on the Indians and their intertribal relations.[22]

Other descriptive writings buttress and amplify Ribault and Laudonnière. Antoine Le Moyne, artist to Laudonnière, set down his impressions in drawings as well as words. As map maker to the expedition, he was to keep the physiographic record so that tentative exploration might be followed by permanent settlement. While his cartography leaves much geography to be desired, his drawings, in part because of their rarity, are invaluable. Vivid and realistic, they give us a clear notion of what a trained observer thought he observed. Accompanied by a "declaratio," explanatory of each drawing, plus his narrative, they indicate how the country, the natives, and their way of life impressed themselves upon an active European mind.[23]

The actual events in the history of these French colonial ventures follow a sequence all too familiar in the original records of discovery. Selfish ambition jostled with selfless zeal. Personal advancement combined with loyalty to God, country, or king were among the motives driving Europeans to America. The old-world pageantry in the virgin forest possessed a sublime majesty and a weird unreality. The inevitable ritual of medieval Europe, secular and divine, awed or amused the natives and heightened the disparity between the new environment and the symbols of European order. Drawn swords, the ponderous Latin phrases echoing in startled Indian ears, royal and ecclesiastical standards unfurled in breeze or gale were frequently as useless in the business of colony planting as feudal titles, royal investitures, and rival territorial claims.

The ritual over, there were the first exciting explorations. If the countryside was bleak and forbidding and the climate severe, ardor cooled, and only hope was left to moderate bitterness. If the sun shone and the landscape was rich in beauty, only reason was left to moderate enthusiasm. Always, regardless of climate and regardless of terrain, there was the expectation that around the bend of the river, at the next estuary, over the next mountain, or at a given distance leagues away, the goal was to be found. There, with but time, patience, and divine help, were the passage to the Orient, the gold, the silver, the rubies; there were the shimmering seven cities, the better fishing spot, the greater loot of furs. Almost always such dreams were shattered by the commonplace reality. For men unprepared, either physically or spiritually, who sought an easy road to wealth, the disappointments were almost too great to endure. Desperation sometimes brought out the best in man, but frequently it brought the worst attributes of human conduct to the surface.

Ultimately there was the splitting up of the adventuring group. A part returned home to report, to gather additional supplies and reinforcement. A part remained to protect the newly acquired corner of empire while awaiting the return of their compatriots. Usually the garrison met with such superhuman difficulties that its members were forced to revert to subhuman behavior. The literature of the French in Florida recounts the tragedy in picturesque and convincing detail and has enabled others to retell it. The volumes of the French explorers have become so much a part of the American tradition that, when not forgotten, they are taken for granted. Historians of the Huguenots begin their accounts with these occurrences, Floridians are as much beholden to them as to the sources provided by the chroniclers of Spain. And Parkman's superlative account owes much of its splendor to these primary documents.[24]

IV

New Britain, 1497–1607

Eager guides in Lisbon relate that the Americas began at the waterfronts of that picturesque Portuguese city. From there the Infante Don Henrique—later familiar as Henry the Navigator—and his bold sailors set out to master unknown seas. At the busy wharfs ancient mariners spun out yarns of the fabulous East. Sage cartographers checked the writings of Aristotle, Seneca, Ptolemy, and the glamorous Marco Polo against fresh geographical data that arrived with every cargo from the African coast. At the docks, merchants and traders mingled with ships' carpenters avid for news of spice and pearls. And nobles of church and state were ready to wager prestige and money against fortune's odds in behalf of personal gain and national glory. Men of high and low estate—saints and sailors alike —were devout servants of the one true faith, militant crusaders of the universal Church dedicated to bring comfort and salvation to those without the holy pale. Knowledge of geography, of ship making, and of nautical science; yearnings for fame, for riches, and for power were ingredients of colonial motivation; but they were not confined to the Portuguese.

Across the Portuguese border a different tradition exists. The Admiral of the Ocean Sea himself walked through Andalusia's winding streets. Granada, Cordova, and Seville are woven into the life pattern of Columbus, where, following the peregrinations of the Spanish court, he pled his cause and outlined his successive plans.

Spanish nobles and Spanish monks gave him aid and encouragement. And Spanish monarchs, granting him such powers as he later possessed, endowed him with the titles he so proudfully bore. The *Niña,* the *Pinta,* and the *Santa María* sailed out of Palos, near Cádiz, and the standard of Ferdinand and Isabella in the hands of Columbus laid claim to the new discoveries in the western world. Later, students from everywhere came to visit the shrines associated with American beginnings in Spanish cities and to study the precious documents stored in her archives.

The royal arms of Spain flew from the mastheads of ships sailing out of Palos, but French standards flew from the mastheads of other ships that put out of St-Malo. Early in the sixteenth century, fishermen from Norman and Breton coasts cast their nets off the shores of Newfoundland. French merchants quickly learned how to make fish yield coin of the realm, and French princes, lay and clerical, dreamed of empire too.

English fishermen were just as skillful with net and rigging, and English merchants later found the game of trade just as alluring. Backed by English capital, men of Bristol and other port towns made their way to Canadian waters. In time the wealth derived from fish came to seem less exciting than the savor of the spice trade and the luster of imperial power. But before Englishmen could think in terms of imperial power, England had to think in terms of imperial Spain. And Spanish power was formidable in the old world, in part because Spain had been so conspicuously successful in the new. While France had been active both in exploration and in settlement, she had signally failed to diminish the strength of her rival. The world seemed to be in the hands of the Spanish and the Portuguese. And notwithstanding the sturdy competitive drives of others, the bulk of world trade seemed also to lie in Iberian hands.

The prime English objective during the sixteenth century was to clip the wings of Spain. Trade was the double-edged instrument directed both toward badgering the enemy and building up the economic resources of Britain. Explorers, freebooters, and incipient merchants were not alone in serving these purposes. They were also served by the expansion of knowledge: knowledge of discoveries, of natural resources, and of commercial prospects. Expansion of knowledge was a work of publicity and promotion, of generating interest and awareness among men of affairs in business and statecraft. England needed her Sir Francis Drakes and her Sir Walter Raleighs, but she also needed her Richard Edens and her Richard Hakluyts.

Spain was the starkest reality of English national life. "The passions that stirred men's souls," Charles M. Andrews, an incisive modern student of colonial beginnings, suggested, "were not born of a desire for peaceful expansion, they were brewed in the crucible of hate for Spain . . . During the years from 1580 to 1596 these passions were at their height and until their intensity had been relieved by the breaking of Spanish power, men could not be persuaded to turn aside from pursuing the quarry." [1]

The connections between English reactions to Spanish power and the literary record of America are apparent. Exploits of discovery, settlement, and trade had to be analyzed, distilled, and propagated. Englishmen who performed this function supplied one of the most important links in the chain of the colonial process. Their literary labors mark the beginnings of English literature concerning America.[2]

England's history in the new world commences with John Cabot. In 1497, Henry VII gave John Cabot and his sons "full and free authority to sail over all parts," but the voyage netted little to the merchants of Bristol. Except for establishing England's claim to North America, Henry Tudor had every cause for disappointment. After a lapse of thirty years, Sebastian Cabot averred that nothing followed his father's discovery, because the nation, politically disturbed and intimidated by Spain, was not prepared to exploit the elder Cabot's achievement. This was no doubt true, but it was also true that since neither China nor spices figured in John Cabot's report, his commercial backers, not to mention the king, lost interest.[3]

Interest, however, gradually revived. Four years later, after John Cabot had approached Cape Breton Island, Henry VII issued another patent. The grantees, Richard Warde, Thomas Ashurst, John Thomas, and their associates, returned to England in 1502 with "three men brought out of an Iland forre beyond Ireland, the which were clothed in beestes' skynnes and ate rawe flesh and were rude in their demeanure as beastes." [4] While this discovery was exciting to some, it failed to stimulate the imagination of Henry Tudor; neither did it encourage English merchants to risk their capital. Little change occurred in England's position as a commercial and colonial power though patents continued to be granted and voyages continued to be made. In terms of English commercial longing, all roads led to Cathay. A northwest passage regularly appeared on European maps, although no one had as yet been able to find it.

Meanwhile, during this period the Spanish ambassador in London served as a geographical information center for his country. Whenever English mariners acquired data, he made gallant and usually successful efforts to acquire them too. Some of this information assisted Juan de La Cosa in drawing his celebrated map, made in 1500, which became the first American map to bear a date. Sebastian Cabot also made a map that reveals the extent of English geographical knowledge in 1544, a map that traces the North American coast from Labrador to Florida. Sebastian Cabot's map was lost soon after it was completed and was not discovered again for three hundred years.[5] England needed to absorb the knowledge she already possessed, to acquire still more knowledge, and to make it available to those who had the will and the wit to use it. Englishmen had already discovered the new world; it remained for England to discover America.[6]

Commercial and colonial failure induced some writers to conclude that geographical exploration was foolish and vain.[7] But the appearance of Sir Thomas More's *Utopia* in 1516 indicates that the significance of America had at least begun to register upon the English mind. Sir Sidney Lee considered the *Utopia* "a convincing testimony to the stirring effects on English genius of the discovery of an unknown, an untrodden world." [8] And just because the new world was untrodden, it challenged the imagination to build anew. It offered an opportunity, in More's case an intellectual one, to construct a new society free of the social and institutional inhibitions of the old. But the *Utopia* represented much more than the persistent nostalgia for the primitive, for, as a modern scholar has put it, Sir Thomas More was "the first Englishman to reveal in print an appreciation of the geographical revolution." [9] While he did not know the name of America, he knew and had read Vespucci, and it is of little moment in this connection how far Vespucci had wandered from the truth. The importance of Sir Thomas in the history of the Americas is that he "discovered the discoveries which were superseding Ptolemy." [10]

Utopia, of course, was nowhere, but More's ideal society was set in the new world. What had once been dreams had become realities. The world was spherical, the Atlantic could be navigated, and the lands on its farthest shore were filled with wonders. Other wonderful discoveries—physical, social, intellectual—might yet be made; it remained for the English to make them.

More's intellectual interest in America was closely seconded by John Rastell. Rastell, a man of letters, lawyer, and printer, was also brother-in-law to Sir Thomas More. The *Interlude of the Four Elements,* probably written in 1517, has been brilliantly analyzed by Richard Hakluyt's chief biographer who describes it as "a lecture, disguised as a play, on natural science." [11] Rastell, himself a promoter, had sponsored a voyage to the land of the Cabots which met with disaster. The disaster, however, was not of the ordinary kind. Rastell's ships did not founder; they were looted. And they were looted not by Spanish enemies but by the very sailors employed to make the voyage, who robbed "under the promoter's very eyes." [12] In writing the play, Rastell had a double motive. One was revenge, the other to encourage support for additional American undertakings.

Whatever the merits of this interpretation, the play is filled with sound geographical information. Indeed, it is the only writing, published before the accession of Queen Elizabeth, for which any such claim can be made. When, for example, Rastell comes to treat of America, it is not South America with which he deals. Rather it is North America, the territories so recently uncovered by English seamen. As if this were not sufficiently novel, he defines North America as a continent in defiance of the conventional practice of making it an appendage of Asia or a group of islands. The facts of geographic life, well known to mariners and pilots, were not yet current knowledge. Rastell, moreover, speaks in commercial accents, of economic value, and business prospects. He was interested in fish and timber, and he obviously knew whereof he spoke.[13]

Rastell was a distinguished man of considerable influence. Yet neither his distinction nor the brilliance of his brother-in-law, Sir Thomas More, were by themselves sufficient to acquaint Englishmen with America. If, at this period, Englishmen thought of America at all, "they must have thought of it as a fishing station near Iceland, or as an obstacle on the road to Cathay." [14] They certainly did not think of America as a home for hundreds of thousands of their countrymen and as a thriving part of some future British Empire. When peace came to England after the war with Spain in 1604, no English colony existed either in Asia, Africa, or America. Yet less than a hundred years later there were twenty colonies along the Atlantic seaboard and in the West Indies alone with a total population of almost two hundred and twenty-five thousand.[15]

So remarkable a transformation was obviously the result of many factors. George Louis Beer, an early and persistent student of colonial policies, suggests that the work of the "sea dogs" and the later activity of the colonizers were basic. Others contend that the role of the entrepreneurs was dominant. But in the intricate web of explanation, forces of a different kind also operated. No variety of analysis that excludes the organization and transmission of knowledge encompasses all the elements. Discoveries already made required exploitation. The exploitation of discovery awaited understanding of geographical information. Essential to entrepreneurial understanding was an appreciation of the economic possibilities in the newly discovered areas and their relation to the national economy. Kings and their ministers were ever attuned to rhythms of power, but they had to be informed how exploration and settlement could enlarge the scope of royal prestige. Prospective migrants to modern colonial utopias might be induced to leave the motherland, but the inducements could not be formulated before they were comprehended. Even when other social forces closely related to expansion, such as religious and economic change, altered the nature of English life, colonial movements had still to be organized in terms of geographical realities.

Disseminating knowledge was not simply the function of propagandists. Colonization could not have occurred without propaganda, but the early masters of the propagandist's art were needed at various levels and for different purposes at different times. Kings and queens were moved by one set of considerations; merchants and traders by another. Colonists responded to many forms of inspiration comprising elements of both. After Spain ceased to be the menace she had been before 1588, a specific kind of cultural situation existed. James I responded to an intellectual and social environment quite different from the one that moved Queen Elizabeth and her subjects.

Propagandists were aided by pilots. Geographers were assisted by translators, by compilers, by scholars. Normally they worked in unconscious union, occasionally in active collaboration. Regardless of the method by which they performed their tasks, the ultimate result was the movement of trade. English commerce was the parent of colonization; colonization and commerce initiated the movement of culture.[16]

In 1553 English commercial development entered a fresh phase. In that year Sebastian Cabot, recently summoned back to England, set out on a new expedition. The expedition, like so many which preceded and followed it, was destined for Cathay. But Cathay, resistant to newer ways of approach, remained so. Yet a discovery was made; it was the discovery of Russia. Cabot, in 1555, became the first governor of what later became the Russia Company, "the parent of England overseas." [17]

The expedition of Sebastian Cabot had hardly left the English coast when a literary event appeared to signalize it. While the subject matter of the book had little to do with the specific purposes of the expedition, it had much to do with its general purposes. The volume was devoted to expansion overseas. It was a translation of Sebastian Münster's *Universal Cosmography,* the first significant English publication on discovery and exploration to appear since Rastell's play. Richard Eden, the translator and compiler, featured particularly the voyages of Columbus, Vespucci, and Magellan, who were viewed as the distinguished predecessors of Sebastian Cabot, then engaged in renewing the search for the China passage. Eden's subtitle reads: *A treatyse of the new India with other new-founde landes and Islands, as well eastwarde as westwarde, as they are knowen and founde in these our dayes.*[18]

When the Russia Company was incorporated in 1555, Eden produced a second volume. Like the *Universal Cosmography,* it was a work of translation, but unlike the *Cosmography* its title did not fully suggest its contents. Eden entitled his translation *The Decades of the New World,* but only the first three of Peter Martyr's famous letters were included. These accounts detailed the conquests of Spain up to 1521, to which Eden added the record of Magellan, the papal bull of 1493, and additional material from Fernández de Oviedo and Gómara. He had in effect compiled a dossier of western explorations. To make the compendium complete, he inserted translations from the Italian of Cabot's expedition to Newfoundland as well as information on Russia.[19]

Richard Eden had performed a signal function. *The Decades of the New World* was the first English publication of so complete a nature. It was the first book published in English which brought the materials of exploration and discovery together. English readers were not only referred to Spanish sources and to the Spanish historians of America, they were introduced to the Ramusio collection— the first great source book of travel then being published in Italian.[20]

Deeper familiarity of America awaited an extension of knowledge of the kind amassed by Richard Eden. Settlement of America awaited its commercial use. Meanwhile, English literature of western lands, literature which was to become a part of the early American record, continued to appear. John Hawkins, gentleman buccaneer, successfully breached the Spanish commercial wall at Hispaniola in 1562. "A right worshippful and valiant knight," [21] he persuaded the reluctant Spanish to trade, albeit at the point of arms. With his holds filled with hides, ginger, sugar, "and a small quantitie of pearles," [22] he negotiated a respectable profit. The profits were the greater since he earned a goodly part by exchanging slaves kidnaped on the Guinea coast. They were ample enough in any case to warrant another expedition made in 1564–65. During this second expedition Hawkins, Puritan "sea dog" of England, landing at Fort Caroline, met Laudonnière, Huguenot captain of France, in the Florida wilderness. The encounter was as friendly as it was dramatic. Beleagured and weary, Laudonnière welcomed Hawkins, who, successful and confident, could afford to be kind. They had their reformism to bind them and a common hatred of Spain served as the basis of mutual trust.[23] Hawkins behaved magnanimously, but he secretly rejoiced at the apparent French failure. To Hawkins it seemed that Florida was much more suited to the English genius than to the French temperament. Hawkins brought home valued merchandise, but he also brought Englishmen the first authentic news of Florida and the South. On a third foray, this time to the West Indies in 1567–68, Hawkins was accompanied by his kinsman, Francis Drake. Later extolled as the "Indian Neptunian paire" they remained for Englishmen, at least, "these two Ocean peeres, Hawkins and Drake." [24]

Francis Drake followed in the footsteps of his famed relation, but he followed him in seven-league boots. Hawkins trifled with Spanish laws and tapped the seemingly limitless reserves of Spanish colonial wealth. Drake defied Spain and looted Spanish treasure on a scale of truly kingly proportions. Hawkins was a bold and intrepid mariner who made the routes from England to Guinea and from Guinea to America his own. But Drake, like Magellan, circumnavigated the globe to "the utmost island of Terra Incognita," where both the great oceans of the western world met "in a most large and free scope." [25]

Drake's reputation as the good queen's knight-errant of the sea dwarfs the real greatness of this admiral of England. Sallies off the coasts of Chile and Peru were romantic as well as hazardous, and adventures on the Spanish Main long continued to stir English nationalism. But Drake's voyage itself was remarkable. Drake sailed around the world, and he was the first Englishman to do it. When the Virgin Queen boarded the *Golden Hind* to make Drake Sir Francis, she may have rewarded him for the silver bars removed from Spanish galleons, but history has remembered him for setting his course through the Strait of Magellan and coming home with an epic to relate.

The geographical moral of Drake's magnificent seamanship was exemplified by Martin Frobisher's search for the illusive Northwest Passage. And in 1578 Captain George Best, Frobisher's friend, published an interesting account of it in *A true discourse of the late voyages for the finding of a passage to Cathaya by the north-west, under the conduct of Martin Frobisher, Generall.* Earlier, in 1576, Sir Humphrey Gilbert's *A Discourse of Discovery for a New Passage to Cataia* had appeared, although it had actually been written ten years before.[26]

Gilbert's deeds were as good as his words. He had long been identified with ideas of exploration, and it was to promote them that he wrote the tract on the passage. Queen Elizabeth finally agreed to grant permission, and in 1578 he received a patent to venture into American waters. This patent entitled Sir Humphrey to explore and to possess such land that might be discovered. He was enjoined from plundering "by sea or by land," a circuitous way of admitting that Drake had done so. While Sir Humphrey Gilbert was swallowed up by the waves of the Atlantic, his voyage had uncalculated results for both English and American history. His was the first English voyage "that carried people to erect an habitation and government in these Northerly countreys of America." Like Martin Frobisher, Gilbert was still seeking Cathay, but Gilbert, for whatever purposes, brought an English colony to America.[27]

Neither Frobisher's failure nor Gilbert's death abated English commercial interest in the Far East. The Northwest Passage retained its place on conventional maps, and geographers and merchants were as anxious to reach it as ever before. But more writing, research, and activity followed Frobisher's expedition. Translations in particular multiplied with the result that almost all significant writings, theretofore inaccessible, were rendered into English.

Foremost among translators was Richard Willis. *The History of Travayle in the West and East Indies* represented a considerable improvement over the previous work of Eden. Actually an expansion of Eden, its emphasis was on the East. At long last an adequate description of India, China, and Japan could be read in the buoyant English of the queen.[28] "In Willis' book Asia and the roads to Asia were for the first time made real to the English reader." [29]

Search for a "way towards the fruitfull and ryche Moluccaes" persisted as long as men believed that they were rich and exciting and as long as any hope of reaching them remained. The experience of Sir Humphrey Gilbert, however, registered a change.[30] America began to vie with the East, and colonial prospects as well as commercial prospects began to obtain financial consideration. Once this change took place, a question of immense practical importance emerged. What about North America? Who among Englishmen really knew about these regions? And how were they to find out?[31] Gilbert's exploration of 1584 had in part been planned to solve these problems. But Gilbert probed no farther south than Sable Island, and Gilbert himself had been lost. Willis had undertaken to supply similar information for the Far East; to supply it for North America was the work of Richard Hakluyt.

Walter Raleigh inherited the rights of his half brother, Sir Humphrey Gilbert, but he also inherited his difficulties. That Raleigh was confronted with the need for starting afresh underscored Elizabethan ignorance of the northern new world. Elizabeth, with a generosity induced as much by zeal for England as zeal for Raleigh, granted him a patent in 1584 which endowed him with Gilbert's rights, unrestricted as to time.[32] An expedition headed by Philip Amadas and Arthur Barlow[33] sailed in May, reached Pamlico Sound, and remained for two months. The account of this "most plentiful, sweet, fruitful, and wholesome" province written under the scrutiny of Raleigh by Amadas and Barlow so charmed the queen that she accepted the suggestion to call the land Virginia in her honor, and Raleigh was made a knight.

And Virginia it was. Three years later a colony under Sir Walter's auspices, made its way to the new land. Out of this venture stemmed the British colonies in North America, and two of the most noteworthy books concerning them. One was by Thomas Hariot, the other by John White. Thomas Hariot, Oxonian, mathematician, and expert in the Raleigh entourage, was the author of the first volume devoted to Virginia: *Brief and True Report of the new found land Virginia*. John White, governor of the second Roanoke colony and an English Le Moyne, drew the first pictures of the English new world. Together they gave Englishmen an initial picture of the virgin colony named in honor of Raleigh's queen.[34]

Hariot was an incisive observer, White an inspired one. Both deservedly rank with Gilbert, Raleigh, Eden, and Willis in the intellectual history of the discovery of America. But Hakluyt it was who assembled and edited the most comprehensive collection of travel literature and made it available in the English language just when it was most needed. Eden and Willis helped to lead England out of her insularity, but Hakluyt gave a scholarly unity to the written record of discovery and infused it with epic qualities. It was Richard Hakluyt who put Britain on the map of empire.

Yet praise for Hakluyt has frequently been faint.[35] Some contend that the forerunners of Hakluyt are entitled to greater approbation, since their books and pamphlets battered against English ignorance and indifference. Hakluyt's editorial craft, on the other hand, was christened on the full tide of English interest. Nevertheless, James A. Williamson, an especially competent judge, wrote: "The history of Elizabethan expansion is to a great extent the work of Richard Hakluyt, to a greater extent perhaps than the record of any other large movement can be ascribed to the labors of any one historian." Williamson's judgment, based on an intimate knowledge of the entire process of expansion, is supported by George B. Parks who has made a thorough and detailed analysis of Hakluyt himself. In the opinion of Parks, the "history of Hakluyt's career is in large part the intellectual history of the beginnings of the British empire." [36]

If the age of Hakluyt was an age of dashing personalities, Hakluyt, a cleric with a taste for secular learning, is not ordinarly accounted one of them. Sir John Hawkins who boldly defied the might of Spain and Sir Humphrey Gilbert who defied danger with equal boldness inevitably seem more arresting than the author of the *English Voyages*. Sir Francis Drake, after all, made one of the most spectacular of voyages; Hakluyt simply incorporated it in his encyclopedic volumes. And few scholars, even in Elizabeth's robust kingdom, could compete with Sir Walter Raleigh's grand exploits in adventure, whether in the art of politics or the science of love.

The glamour of Richard Hakluyt is not, however, without an appeal of its own. His was the romance of inquiry and the adventure of understanding. In one sense, he was himself an agent of the changes he catalogued, for he gave aid to all who looked to the sea. He was a scholar, a collector of books and documents, a master of language. He was also consultant to the rising lords of trade who fathered the lords of plantations. Ministers of state sought and followed his advice, and the queen herself lent ear to his suggestions. Hakluyt, moreover, did what others could not do. His connections with men of geographical learning abroad gave him access to information vital to his beloved England—information it would otherwise have been difficult to obtain. As Spanish secrets were tightly locked in official Seville, Hakluyt went to France instead. French seamen and disgruntled Spaniards resident in French commercial towns were in possession of such Spanish knowledge as there was. And material on ships and seas was plentiful in thriving ports such as St-Malo. Hawkins came home from new-world waters with a "quantitie of pearles"; Hakluyt came home from old-world France with quantities of priceless data. Raleigh dreamed of a colony to inflate his power and to gladden the heart of his queen. Hakluyt prepared a *Discourse on Western Planting* to further Raleigh's schemes. And it was the *Discourse* that outlined the colonial policy of a future empire.[37]

Hakluyt's adult life coincided with the great awakening of English commerce. He received his master's degree from Oxford the year after Frobisher made his initial voyage to America in 1578. By the year of Hakluyt's death in 1616, the Armada had been met and crushed, Jamestown founded, and the settlement of colonial Britain in America begun. He was still a lad in his twenties when he published Jacques Cartier's report of French explorations in Canada (Paris edition, 1586), followed the next year by a new edition of Peter Martyr's *Decades*.[38] Hakluyt had started his career with translations of inestimable value. Apart from the problem involved in simply getting books, Cartier was written in French, Peter Martyr in Latin. Peter Martyr had been translated only in part, Cartier had not been translated at all. Gilbert was then contemplating maneuvering in the mystic area defined as "north of Florida," Raleigh in Virginia. Verrazano's letter was reprinted in Eden; Cartier's narration, made available by Hakluyt, reduced the void of conjecture by just that much.

Hakluyt's objectives had already assumed precise direction. Other commitments, particularly the East, mortgaged his energies, but America soon became a competing goal. The East remained in Hakluyt's vision because he pursued every prospect of commerce, and his zeal for geography embraced the known world. Unlike those who had gone before him, Hakluyt did not document his works by references to the speculations of antiquity. Instead, he cited on-the-spot observations of contemporary explorers.

Divers Voyages touching the discovery of America, published in 1582, exemplified his method and presaged his future. Within its pages Hakluyt crammed all the materials on North America then available to him. Here his readers were to find the Cabot voyages, Verrazano, and his own translation of Cartier. In addition, Ribault's narrative on French Florida, a particularly scarce item, enriched the volume. The study, intended as tentative, was prelude to an intensive period of research. After seven years of investigation, including a five-year sojourn in France, he presented his countrymen with *The English Voyages.* Hakluyt gave his compilation a fuller and more suggestive title: *The Principal Navigations, Voyages, and Discoveries of the English nation, made by Sea or over Land to the most remote and farthest distant Quarters of the earth at any time within the compass of these 1500 years.* Patriotic pride prompted Hakluyt. "I both heard in speech, and read in books," he wrote in the familiar strains of nationalism, "other nations miraculously extolled for their discoveries and notable enterprises by sea, but the English of all others for their sluggish security, and continual neglect of the like attempts, especially in so long and happy a time of peace, either ignominiously reported or exceedingly condemned." [39] To the end that England might no longer be condemned by others, Hakluyt continued to spark British interest and imagination with additional navigations and voyages. The expansion of Britain became the creative purpose of his life; the expansion of *The Principal Navigations* one of the means of satisfying it.

The last volumes of *The Principal Navigations,* appearing at the end of the century, celebrated a reputation already firmly established. In the intervals Hakluyt became consultant extraordinary. He was retained by merchant capitalists and commercially-minded gentry now sufficiently well informed to plan colonial enterprise and sufficiently astute to seek expert counsel. His collaboration with Sir Walter Raleigh is historically the most significant of these associations. For Raleigh he wrote a memorandum which turned out to be as cogent a summary of British colonial purposes as ever was written. The *Particular Discourse on Western Planting* of 1584 served its immediate purpose and was then lost for nearly three hundred years. Beyond its influence upon Raleigh and the queen, it had few historical results. But its importance historiographically is far from lessened because of it. The *Discourse* is an affidavit of English colonial intention. That Englishmen during the three hundred years of its disappearance followed Hakluyt's prescription, without being able to read his words, suggests that Hakluyt's other labors had successfully made Hakluyt's point.

The *Discourse on Western Planting* is a nationalist manifesto. Hakluyt wrote out the mercantilist creed in the enticing language of self-interest that could hardly fail to win assent from a royal heart. The knightly mind of Walter Raleigh had long been won over, and Hakluyt had only to give geographical chapter and commercial verse in order to make the royal wish appear as father to resistless logic. And the logic was as tight as a master of publicity could make it. Since the shadow of the Spanish empire darkened English prospects, Hakluyt stressed the possibilities for naval bases in American colonies. The memorandum was not, after all, for publication, and its author had no reason for diplomatic reticence. A colony was an outpost by definition, but defense was not its only function. An American colony could also serve as a base of attack on Spanish strongholds and Spanish fleets. Inducements such as these were no less attractive than the exhaustive lists of products and occupations latent in the wealth of American natural resources. Nor were these lures of trade and industry the wishful dreams of a promoter's fancy. They were specific items culled from documentary references and the observations of experienced explorers. Cartier may well have been in error when he wrote of gold and silver, but he had in fact written about them. But French profits from fish and furs did not proceed from Hakluyt's imagination any more than the commercial inferences he rightly drew from the existence of forests, rich soil, cornfields, and fruit trees. And the consequents were implicit in the premises. If colonies could be established and settled, if the natural resources could be exploited, then the mother country would become less dependent upon her neighbors for the commodities she lacked and the colonies would become natural markets for the products of the homeland. To be free of dependence upon Europe was both economically profitable and strategically wise. No plan can be better than perfect, and Hakluyt's plan was perfect if the objectives were national supremacy and self-sufficiency.[40]

The *Discourse* is a masterful document. Hakluyt had perfected a technique and achieved a competence in his specialty which none in the sixteenth century could match. All geographical roads led to Richard Hakluyt. When the famed engraver Théodore de Bry of Liège, moved to Frankfort and became interested in discoveries, it was Hakluyt to whom he came. Since he contemplated an illustrated history, he journeyed to London to consult with the expert in England. And it was Hakluyt who put de Bry in touch with Jacques Le Moyne, who, in spite of the excellence of his drawings, was having trouble getting them into print. Governor John White of Roanoke apparently had no difficulty finding a publisher. But his drawings of Virginia, if more widely diffused, could do England's first American colony little harm. Hakluyt also made the White illustrations available to de Bry. The result must have pleased Hakluyt, as it certainly pleased other Virginia promoters. In 1590 de Bry published Hariot's *Virginia* in four languages—French, German, Latin, and English— embellished with pictures by White. In 1591 a second volume with Le Moyne's Florida illustrations initiated a series still esteemed for history as well as for the twin arts of engraving and bookmaking.[41]

No sixteenth-century literary work on the discoveries compared with Hakluyt's *Principal Navigations*. Highly valued during Hakluyt's lifetime, it retained its eminence throughout the years and is still an indispensable source—not only for the voyages, traffics, and discoveries of the English nation, but also for the mood, temper, and spirit of the Elizabethan age. When completed in 1600 and enormously expanded,[42] it canvassed sixteen hundred years of English maritime and commercial history from the time of King Arthur. And the whole magnificent collection represented Richard Hakluyt. The *Principal Navigations* was the spiritual autobiography of its creator. Here in its thorough and exhaustive coverage was Hakluyt the scholar, the editor, the collector. To the title of the new edition he had added the significant word—traffics—symbolic of his passion for trade, his career as consultant, his role as colonial promoter. Traffics, voyages, discoveries, and explorations were at once Hakluyt's tribute to England's past and Hakluyt's contribution to England's future. Criticisms of Hakluyt's literary results have been constant.[43] But no stricture on his scholarship, his accuracy, his powers of analysis has ever been able to impair either the essential greatness of the man or the essential greatness of his work. One may doubt the validity of his ultimate purposes, but none may doubt that his purposes were abundantly fulfilled.

V

History and Historians in the British Dominions Beyond the Seas, I, 1607–1763

The original narratives of English colonization during the seventeenth century closely resemble the original narratives of Spanish and French colonization. They depict the initial clash of man and nature in the new world. The literary expressions of the first Americans reveal the pioneer mind, and disclose the discordant human motives that created it. The quest for God and the quest for gold, the lust for power and the passion for tranquillity, the building of an empire and the search for a home, joined in subtle combination to stimulate colonial men to action.

Early contributions to historical writing in America were of two types. Native Hakluyts, like later promoters, spun shimmering webs of enticement to lure the dissatisfied from the old world to the new. Weaving the perennial yearning for fame, fortune, and future into a glowing prospect of opportunity, they whetted desire, encouraged hope, and stimulated ambition. Drab lives were filled with the glow of adventure; London merchants already counted the gold in bursting moneybags, and petty shopkeepers imagined themselves lords of broad Virginia acres. Such writers offered freedom of conscience to the oppressed as well as stellar imperial parts to restless patriots who had long awaited their cue. Mindful of their obligation to posterity, self-conscious autobiographers and chroniclers set forth the leading events in accounts of noble adventure. Pilgrim, Puritan, and Anglican, deeply impressed with their roles in furthering the kingdom of

Christ or Britain, recounted their trials with devil, native, and misguided papist in wresting His Majesty's dominions from their grasp. If American historiography does not actually begin with Captain John Smith, it is not because of any lack of effort on his part. Explorer, sailor, and gentleman adventurer, John Smith represents the literature of promotion and autobiography in the grand manner. He is the epitome of Jacobean grandiloquence, the swashbuckling hero as anxious to singe the beard of the king of Spain as to amass wealth and power. But clashes with Castilian cavaliers on the Spanish Main contributed less to the building of America in the first years of colony planting than the prosaic occupation of clearing the forest and the sowing of crops.[1]

Virginia was but a year old when Smith published the first of two books relating to the colony. Written during the first thirteen months of Virginia's existence, *A True Relation* was as symbolic of the future as it was suggestive of the past.[2] The account of the first permanent English settlement appeared in 1608, the year in which John Milton was born. And the name Smith, as the famed historian of American literature, Moses Coit Tyler, insisted, symbolizes the democracy to which Milton's ideas of freedom were later dedicated.[3]

A True Relation tells as much of Smith as of Virginia. In it Smith portrays the landing of the colonists, initial tilts with the Indians, and the groping struggles with an unfamiliar life. The bold assertiveness of his style, however, together with pointed verbal thrusts aimed at his enemies, has diluted the reverence that scholars usually accord primary documents.[4] Yet criticism can hardly destroy its value as a living record of seventeenth-century hopes. "In after times," he wrote in conclusion, we may expect "to see our Nation to enjoy a Country, not onely exceeding pleasant for habitation, but also a very profitable for commerce in generall; no doubt pleasing to almightie God, honourable to our gracious Soveraigne, and commodious generally to the whole Kingdome."[5]

The career of John Smith, fantastic even in terms of his own dashing age, is stirring enough to goad the envy of the sophisticated. The excitement which marked his Virginia days was simply a climax to a youth crowded with unbelievable escapades. Born less than a decade before the defeat of the Spanish Armada, he started his adult life conventionally enough by becoming a tutor in a noble household. Soon thereafter, however, circumstances drove him half over Europe and the Levant. He saw service in the armies fighting the Turks (in the course of which he is said to have overcome three Turkish nobles —one is almost compelled to say singlehanded), and was sent into slavery from which he escaped after a number of thrilling exploits. Yet when finally he arrived in England he was scarcely twenty-four. That he should have taken an interest in Virginia is hardly surprising if only because life in England must have seemed rather dull in comparison with Constantinople and Varna.[6]

Smith's second volume, *The Generall Historie of Virginia, New-England and the Summer Isles,* consists of reprints from his own writings and the works of others.[7] The *Generall Historie* bristles with partisanship, but the fourth part of the book preserves the Captain's lively comments on the opinions of his contemporaries, historically important regardless of their accuracy. Here, too, appeared the first full account of the Pocahontas incident, object of so much romantic embellishment and historical ingenuity.[8] While Smith was certainly intemperate and deeply devoted to himself, modern scholarship has vindicated many of his judgments. Comparison with other sources suggests that he was correct in his appraisal of colonial conditions as well as in his estimate of the Virginia Company. Throughout the narrative one finds nuggets of suggestiveness of which the following is typical.

> And this is as much as my memory can call to mind worthie of note; which I have purposely collected, to satisfie my friends of the true worth and qualitie of Virginia. Yet some bad natures will not sticke to slander the Countrey, that will slovenly spit at all things, especially in company where they can find none to contradict them. Who though they were scarse ever 10 miles from James Town, or at the most but at the falles; yet holding it a great disgrace that amongst so much action, their actions were nothing, exclaime of all things, though they were never adventured to knowe any thing; nor ever did any thing but devoure the fruits of other mens labours. Being for the most part of such tender educations and small experience in martiall accidents: because they found not English cities, nor such faire houses, nor at their owne wishes any of their accustomed dainties, with feather beds and downe pillowes, Tavernes and alehouses in every breathing place, neither such plenty of gold and silver and dissolute liberty as they expected, had little or no care of any thing, but to pamper their bellies, to fly away with our Pinnaces, or procure their means to ·returne for England. For the Countrey was to them a miserie, a ruine, a death, a hell, and their reports here, and their owne actions their according.[9]

Although the irrepressible "Coronell" is usually associated with Virginia, he also belongs to New England. Virginia entrepreneurs may have had their fill of John Smith, but his lust for adventure was far from sated. Only five years after his return to England, he undertook a voyage to New England in 1614, during which he prepared a map of the region between Cape Cod and the Penobscot River. On a second trip he was captured by the French and made prisoner at New Rochelle. After what for him was quite a conventional escape, he returned to England where he died in 1631 without again leaving the country. Smith was an exemplar of the newer motif in colonization. Like Richard Hakluyt he was impressed by the commercial prospects of New England. The "benefit of this salt and fish," he remarked with a realistic eye on the wealth of the English nation, "for breeding Mariners and building ships, will make so many fit men to raise a Common-wealth, if but managed, as my generall history will shew you; it might well by this have beene as profitable as the best Mine the King of *Spaine* hath in his West Indies." [10] Smith could be an incisive commentator when he chose.

> It is true, that Master *John Wynthrop,* their now Governour, a worthy Gentleman both in estate and esteeme, went so well provided (for six or seven hundred people went with him) as could be devised, . . . but all complaining, and all things so contrary to their expectation, that now every monstrous humor began to shew it selfe. . . .
> This small triall of their patience, caused among them no small confusion, and put the governour and his Councell to their utmost wits; some could not endure the name of a Bishop, others not the sight of a Crosse nor Surplesse, others by no means the bookes of common Prayer. This absolute crue, only of the Elect, holding all (but such as themselves) reprobates and cast-awaies, now make more haste to returne to *Babel,* as they tearmed *England,* than stay to enjoy the land they called Canaan." [11]

Many responded to the glittering prospects of the New Eldorado; others placed their faith in the prospects of a New Canaan. William Bradford, something of an American Herodotus, was leader of the Pilgrim band and easily a leader among early colonial literary craftsmen.[12] The simple, cadenced English prose of his *History of Plimouth Plantation* bespeaks Bradford's intimacy with the Bible, just as its unadorned forthrightness bespeaks his undeviating belief in the mission he had undertaken to fulfill.[13]

> It was answered, that all great, and honourable actions, are accompanied with great difficulties; and must be both enterprised, and overcome with answerable courages. It was granted the dangers were great, but not desperate; the difficulties were many, but not invincible. For though their were many of them likly, yet they were not cartaine; it might be sundrie of the things feared might never befale; others by providente care and the use of good means, might in a great measure be prevented; and all of them (through the help of God) by fortitude, and patience, might either be borne, or overcome. True it was, that such atempts were not to be made and undertaken without good ground, and reason; not rashly, or lightly as many have done for curiositie, or hope of gaine, etc. But their condition was not ordinarie; their ends were good and honour-

able; their calling lawfull, and urgente; and therfore they might expecte the blessing of God in their proceding. Yea, though they should loose their lives in this action, yet might they have comforte in the same, and their endeavors would be honourable.[14]

Bradford's history has immortalized the Pilgrims of Plymouth. His entrancing prose still invites his readers to share the Pilgrim's trials and to enter into the Pilgrim's hopes. He recalls the moment of arrival on the shore of Massachusetts Bay. ". . . for which way soever they turned their eys (save upward to the heavens) they could have little solace or content in respecte of any outward objects. For summer being done, all things stand upon them with a wetherbeaten face; and the whole contrie, full of woods and thickets, represented a wild and savage heiw. If they looked behind them, ther was the mighty ocean which they had passed, and was now as a maine barr and goulfe to separate them from all the civill parts of the world." [15] But Bradford, truest of Pilgrims, was never without hope, for Bradford's hope was faith. "That when they came a shore they would use their owne libertie; for none had power to command them, the patente they had being for Virginia, and not for New-england, which belonged to an other Government, with which the Virginia Company had nothing to doe. And partly that such an act by them done (this their condition considered) might be as firme as any patente, and in some respects more sure." [16]

Bradford's history tells us more of the Puritan character than of the Puritan mind, but the one cannot be understood save in terms of the other. His narrative charts the course of the Separatists from their initial persecutions abroad to the year 1648. It remains, as it was from the beginning, the best source for a study of the Plymouth group.[17]

Bradford's manuscript itself had a curious though not uncommon career. Bradford and his descendants did not undertake to publish the history of Plymouth, although it was considered vital for future historical reference. Used by scholars in manuscript for over two hundred years, it was not actually printed until 1856. The manuscript was believed to have been deposited in Boston's Old South Church, but during the occupation of that city at the time of the Revolution, the British converted the church into a riding school. Since the manuscript was never heard of again until it was discovered in London, it can only be inferred that the officers of George III had something to do with its disappearance. References to Bradford's *History* were made in other works published in the mid-nineteenth century. In any case, an unknown reader with a footnote eye found mention, while consulting a volume by Bishop Samuel Wilberforce, of a manuscript history of Plymouth which the Bishop averred he had read in the library of the Bishop of London. Finally, it was determined that the history there referred to was indeed the work of Governor Bradford, and following the intervention of members of the Massachusetts Historical Society, arrangements were made to publish it. It was not, however, until 1896 that the manuscript itself came back to America.[18]

Nathaniel Morton, neglected nephew of the famous Pilgrim, was one of the first to use the Bradford manuscript. When Morton's father died the year after arriving in Plymouth in 1623, he came under the guardianship of his uncle. As a result he was personally associated with colonial leaders and colonial events. In 1645, still in his early twenties, Morton was elected secretary of Plymouth, a post he occupied until he died forty years later. The first account of the colony comes from Morton's pages rather than Bradford's, for *New England's Memorial* (1669) is frankly based upon the unpublished *Plimouth Plantation*. Thus it was the secretary of Plymouth rather than the famous governor who first told of the Mayflower, the landing of the Pilgrims, and registered the leading events.[19] "It is very expedient," commented those who wrote the remarks "to the Reader," "that (while sundry of the Eldest Planters were yet living), *Records* and *Memorials of Remarkable Providences* be preserved and published . . . that New England, in all times to come, may remember the day of her smallest things." [20]

Virginia had its Smith, Plymouth its Bradford, and Massachusetts Bay its Winthrop. John Winthrop was a gentleman of consequence. His paternal grandfather, following the well-grooved path from profitable trade to country retirement, bought an estate in Suffolk. Here in 1588 John Winthrop was born, the son of Adam, a lawyer and country gentleman. As squire of Groton and member of the Inner Temple, Winthrop, already middle-aged, had attained success and inner peace when the Puritan revolution changed the course of his life.

Winthrop's motives for leaving England illumine the whole course of the Puritan migration. They likewise illumine the scope and purpose of Puritan historiography. Life was changing in the second decade of the seventeenth century. Men of high degree and low income, who lived sedately in the English countryside, found the pace of the wealthy aristocracy too swift. Social customs, extravagant and often lusty, were as distasteful to the devout as they were beyond the emulation of the provident. Such difficulties could have been managed, but threats to security came from other quarters. Charles I sat on the English throne, but Bishop Laud scurried over the land in search of nonconformists. Nonconformity was certainly heresy; it was also perilously close to treason. If His English Majesty was head of the Church, it was hard to see how he could be served faithfully as lord temporal while denied as lord spiritual. At least the king and his ministers could not see the distinction or, perhaps, they perceived it only too well. To divide the kingdom of God from the kingdom of the Stuarts was an exercise in logic that many dissenters performed with skill, but the demonstration failed to impress the king's ministers. Was it possible to divorce the policy of the government in domestic and international affairs from religion in an age when church and state were inseparably one? The Puritan revolution resulted from the fact that it was not. Archbishop Laud himself cautioned Parliament that if the attack upon the government of the Church succeeded, the next step would be "to have a pluck at the throne of David." Or, as another less famous Anglican had it, "Kings must bee subject to Puritan Presbyters. . . . Thus the oaths of Supremacie, and allegiance are broken. This Puritan is an Arch-traitor." [21]

Parliament was Puritan, and Charles I determined to govern without it. When Parliament resolved that all who supported the High Church and the royal prerogative were enemies to the kingdom, the issue was joined. Leaders of the Puritan party were taken to the Tower, Parliament was dissolved, and Charles began his eleven years of personal rule. While these events marked an era in the history of England and the history of democracy, they also marked a stage in the history of English colonization and the history of John Winthrop.

While Puritan and Pilgrim differed widely in temperament and outlook, they were more closely related to each other than to the rollicking captain of Jamestown. Winthrop exerted an abiding influence on the Massachusetts project and kept a faithful record of the events he helped to shape. His *Journal* has none of the conscious artistry of Bradford's style, but is a detailed exposition of life in the settlement from 1630 to 1649. Students have never ceased to be grateful for this record, as it not only discloses the erstwhile lord of Groton and the vicissitudes of the colony, but also is a revelation of the upper-class Puritan mind. [22]

Every diary or journal is as much a record of its writer as of the developments it seeks to describe. Other accounts testify to the events catalogued in Winthrop's *Journal,* but Winthrop's version of those events have added value. No one could supply a more cogent analysis of Winthrop's view of man and society than the governor himself. No one could relate more revealingly the course of the recurring conflicts that spelled out the disintegration of the Bible Commonwealth even before it occurred. Anne Hutchinson's heresy may be traced in many a source, yet what Winthrop chose to write and what he chose to omit have permitted later scholars to reconstruct the essential climate of Puritan opinion.

> The court also sent for Mrs. Hutchinson, and charged her with divers matters, as her keeping two public lectures every week in her house, whereto sixty or eighty persons did usually resort, and for reproaching most of the ministers (viz., all except Mr. Cotton) for not preaching a covenant of free grace, and that they had not the seal of the spirit, nor were able ministers of the New Testament; which were clearly proved against her, though she sought to shift it off. And, after many speeches to and fro, at last she was so full as she could not contain, but vented her revelations; amongst which this was one, that she had it revealed to her, that she should come into New England, and should here be persecuted, and that God would ruin us and our posterity, and the whole state, for the same. So the court proceeded and banished her; but, because it was winter, they committed her to a private house, where she was well provided, and her own friends and the elders permitted to go to her, but none else.[23]

And as with Mistress Hutchinson, so with Roger Williams whose sin was no less grave.

> The governor and assistants met at Boston, and took into consideration a treatise, which Mr. Williams (then of Salem) had sent to them, and which he had formerly written to the governor and council of Plymouth, wherein, among other things, he disputes their right to the lands they possessed here, and concluded that, claiming by the king's grant, they could have no title, nor otherwise, except they compounded with the natives. For this, taking advice with some of the most judicious ministers, (who much condemned Mr. Williams' error and presumption,) they gave order, that he should be convented at the next court, to be censured, etc. There were three passages chiefly whereat they were much offended: 1, for that he chargeth King James to have told a solemn public lie, because in his patent he blessed God that he was the first Christian prince that had discovered this land; 2, for that he chargeth him and others with blasphemy for calling Europe Christendom, or the Christian world; 3, for that he did personally apply to our present king, Charles, these three places in the Revelations. . . .[24]

The builders of Zion's kingdom cannot be understood without an understanding of the purposes that impelled them to create it. Pilgrims and Puritans crossed the ocean, fought the Indians, and wrote history with conscious purpose. Whatever assessments later generations have made concerning the Puritan way of life, much of the American intellectual tradition commences with it.

While the historical development of Puritanism is familiar enough, the historical interpretation of Puritanism has frequently altered. Puritans, dissatisfied with the Elizabethan settlement, wished to purify the Anglican Church; but this urge did not alter their character as seventeenth-century Englishmen. Nor did it alter their character as seventeenth-century Europeans. There was a larger amount of agreement between Anglicans and Puritans than some later historians have allowed. Great issues divided them, but the views they shared in common have all too often been obscured. Even when the differences sharpened—sufficient to inspire migration to America—the Puritan revolution was a movement within the English cultural situation, not outside of it. Puritans acted both as Englishmen and Europeans even while they acted as dissenters from the established ecclesiastical order of seventeenth-century England.

An understanding of Puritanism demands, of course, that the distinctions between Puritans and other Englishmen be made clear. But an evaluation of Puritan influence on American thought requires that the similarities between Puritans and other Englishmen and between Puritans and Europeans should not be obliterated. Puritans, for example, were no less the legatees of the Middle Ages than other seventeenth-century groups. They were Protestants both before and after they became Puritans. Although hostile to Catholicism, Puritans shared many assumptions with Catholic Spaniards, and Catholic Frenchmen. Although hostile to France and to Spain, they acted in response to attitudes identical with those of other Englishmen. Later critical of Anglicanism, they were more closely akin to the members of the Church of England than to Antinomians, Quakers, and Baptists.

As Englishmen they were patriots; they detested the enemies of the mother country as intensely as other Britons. As Protestants they regarded Catholicism as the supreme foe against which, like all other reformers, they were forever committed. But with the sons of Rome they believed religion to be central to life; the controlling purpose of thought, inquiry, and action. With other Christians they were never in doubt about the ultimate nature and destiny of man. Man had sinned, and salvation was possible only through Christ. The reign of God was supreme and unchallenged; his will everywhere manifest. Whatever differences separated Christians from one another—and they were crucial differences—these were assumptions unequivocally held.

For Puritans the will of God was revealed in his word. God not only revealed himself in the Bible but in "wonder-working providences." God spoke to man through these manifestations, not by special revelations to the inner spirit of individual men. Such revelations when asserted were spurious. They were "enthusiams," and Puritans and Anglicans alike would have none of them. Divine purposes were not discoverable by immediate inspiration; they were extracted from the record by reason and logic. Careless use of such terms as "supernaturalism" and "otherworldliness" have blurred the Puritan emphasis upon reason and learning. Nor is repetition of the word intolerance sufficient to explain the treatment Puritans accorded Anne Hutchinson and the Quakers. English Anglicans acted as harshly toward Quakerism and similar heresies, and for the same reason. Quakers responded to an "inner light"; they were in direct communion with God. Both were blasphemous.[25]

Doctrines such as these violated sanctified precepts. Mind and feeling were one and inseparable. It was an essential article of Puritan faith and therefore a conscious part of Puritan effort to preserve the unity of nature and supernature. And religion and science, intellect and emotion, were no less indivisible. There could be no "supernaturalism" if nature and supernature were actually indistinguishable, no "inner light" or a single guide to truth if emotion and intellect were complementary. Comprehension of Puritanism and Puritan historiography alike depend upon an awareness of these assumptions.

Puritanism was a religion for the learned. The intellectual level of the faithful was not up to the demands of the faith, but neither the Puritan leaders nor God himself regarded ignorance as an excuse. A certain degree of understanding and knowledge was essential to salvation. Puritans rarely failed to give close attention to the long sermons of their ministers. And poor New England farmers helped support Harvard, founded almost at once in order to insure a learned clergy. The leadership of the clergy was a social as well as an intellectual fact.[26]

In this respect, as Perry Miller points out, Puritans had taken a step revolutionary in its social implications. They built a theological and institutional system that eliminated the ecclesiastical middle man. By bringing religion directly to the people, Puritanism (with other types of Protestantism) broke with the conventional Christian tradition. If nothing need stand between man and God, what need of a learned ministry, of rational demonstrations of the existence of God, of books, and of logic? It is important to note, however, that this suggestion is clearer to us than to seventeenth-century Puritans. The logical development of this position, in other words, was the result of other and later factors within as well as outside of Puritanism.[27]

Men of high estate were rarely challenged by the lower orders in the sixteenth and seventeenth centuries. Puritanism constituted no exception to this general cultural rule. Whatever the spiritual reasons for Protestantism, it did not result in a social and political equalitarianism. The social and intellectual dominance of scholars and churchmen was as much a fact in sixteenth-century England as in seventeenth-century Massachusetts. "The New England theocracy," writes Miller, "was simply a Protestant version of the European social ideal, and except for its Protestantism was thoroughly medieval in character." [28]

Puritans were not only rationalists, they were also humanists. The preconceptions of humanism testify to a Puritan affinity with the Renaissance as well as with the Reformation. While classical scholarship by itself no more guaranteed admission to Heaven for Puritans than for Anglicans, both would have concurred with John Cotton's judgment that "knowledge is no knowledge without zeale" and "zeale is but wilde-fire without knowledge." [29] With this emphasis on knowledge or "natural reason," the Puritans as humanists took their stand in the intellectual revolution which initiated modern times. With all other Protestants they arrayed themselves against scholasticism which they identified with the Catholic Church. To this extent at least they broke with the Middle Age synthesis of knowledge and faith, symbolized by Saint Thomas Aquinas, and embraced what they believed was a new synthesis unsullied by Catholicism.

Although they abjured scholasticism, the Puritans did not abandon it. They could with impunity deny scholasticism to the degree that it was a part of Catholic apologetics, for they could put the Bible in its place. But they could not abandon scholastic notions in regions of thought where no substitutes existed. Puritan thought was governed by scholastic premises in physics, for example, until quantities rather than qualities—the mathematical concepts of Newton and Descartes—succeeded them. When this occurred, there was no problem of reconciling a new science with an older religion as later Protestants felt compelled to do, for between science and religion no cleavage existed. God's majesty was as apparent in one way as in another.[30]

While Puritans momentarily retained the syllogisms of physics, they were quick to separate themselves from scholastic logic. Whatever its origins in Greek philosophy, it was the child of Rome; it failed to satisfy the Puritan need for clear and rational exemplification. Puritans sought a new logic, and they found it in the work of a French Protestant, Petrus Ramus.

The connection between Ramus and Protestantism is explicit. A humanist, he defended his candidacy for the M.A. in 1536 with the thesis that Aristotle had been in error. This was to say in effect that scholasticism was in error, since the schoolmen had organized knowledge upon Aristotelian principles. Ramus embraced Calvinism in 1561, and his followers carried his doctrines to England where, especially at Cambridge, they were studied with enthusiasm. The Ramist logic came to Cambridge, Massachusetts, from Cambridge, England, and early secured the approbation of Harvard professors. If the new science—the mathematical science of Descartes and the inductive method of Bacon—penetrated Puritan thought with ease, it was because the logic of Ramus paved the way.

The Ramist logic was essentially Platonic. The Puritan theory of knowledge, the Puritan aesthetic, and Puritan morality have their sources in Plato. Human ideas mirror the ideas of the divine mind. Knowledge derived from nature and experience represent imperfect copies of anterior ideas perfect in the thought of God. Truth is therefore antecedent to experience because it existed in the mind of God before the world and man were created. Mortals grasp or apprehend truth, but once apprehended, it was no mere transitory insight; it was eternal, the reality lying behind the world of mutable experience. Although imperfect, such knowledge, once grasped by the natural reason, was certain and changeless.[31]

The function of history in Puritan thought is inseparably part of the Puritan view of the world. Puritan history and Puritan historiography are one and the same. Indeed history is philosophy registered in events just as philosophy is theology exemplified—the ways of God spelled out and explained. Ministers were historians and philosophers were ministers; all men were engaged in thinking God's thoughts after him. Ultimate meanings in history as in theology were transcendent meanings. Both referred to a reality existing prior to human experience, and human experiences were but intimations of the ultimately real.

While God moved in many ways to perform his wonders, all the wondrous ways were God's. Hence minor events were no less divine than major ones, calamitous events no less than beneficial ones. And great men as well as little men, the powerful and the humble, were alike the agents of providential design. Since all events shared a measure of divinity, all were to that extent of equal import. Some events, weighted with specific purpose, were more important than others. Accordingly, it was the function of the historian to record everything, for it would be impious of man to intrude standards of human value in seeking to unravel divine intent. But it was just as important a part of the historian's role to reveal the hierarchy of purpose whenever it was possible to fathom it.[32]

New England was the temporal and spiritual center of the universe because the purposes of God were most clearly demonstrated in New England experience. New England succeeded ancient Israel; the Puritans were the successors of the Jews. Following the life and times of Jesus, the years from the English Reformation to the building of Zion in Massachusetts were, in Puritan historical perspective, the most important years in the history of the world.

The history of New England was a history of special meanings. To make the divine intent as clear as mortals could make it was the supreme purpose of historiography, as it was the supreme end of all Puritan learning. Already familiar with the larger outlines of divine purpose, they had only to disclose, illustrate, and interpret it. Unity of Puritan thought and purpose transcends conventional divisions of intellectual function. Historians were preachers of the divine intent; preachers historians of the significance of life. William Bradford and John Winthrop rendered the past meaningful by recording illustrious providences; Puritan theologians related those meanings to the larger universe of spiritual discourse.

Puritan life was dominated by the Bible, and Massachusetts life was dominated by the men who interpreted it.[33] Of these the Reverend Thomas Hooker was one of the greatest. He was so famous a Puritan divine in the old country that Bishop Laud accorded him the special brand of attention devised for nonconformists. After being summoned before the High Commission in 1630, Hooker fled to Holland where he ministered to uprooted English Puritans like himself. During his residence in Rotterdam he met William Ames, a great and learned theologian, by whom he was both instructed and inspired. The *Survey of the Summe of Church Discipline,*[34] the foremost exposition of Congregational polity and Hooker's greatest work, was in part a result of this contact. Not long after his removal to New England, he took his congregation westward, to Hartford, where, until his death in 1647, he remained the undisputed leader of the Connecticut plantation. Despite certain brief passages in his writings, frequently misinterpreted,[35] Hooker was neither liberal nor democratic. On the contrary, he was as thoroughly conservative in his political and social views as he was orthodox in theology.[36]

Though scarcely the equal of the learned Hooker, Thomas Shep-

ard was among the powerful leaders of the first New England generation. Of lowly origin and of limited capacity, he had the stuff of
character and temperament which endeared him to his fellows. He
was a "soule-ravishing minister" [37] who devoted his life to his Cambridge flock. Long after the mighty of New England were forgotten,
Shepard was remembered, and a volume of his sermons, many times
reissued, was republished as late as the nineteenth century.[38] He perfectly reflects the Puritan historical mood:

> What shall we say of the singular Providence of God bringing so many
> Ship-loads of his people, through so many dangers, as upon Eagles wings,
> with so much safety from yeare to yeare? The fatherly cares of our God
> in feeding and cloathing so many in a Wildernesse, giving such health-
> fulnesse and great increase of posterity? What shall wee say of the
> Worke it selfe of the kingdome of Christ and the form of a Common-
> wealth erected in a wildernesse, and in so few yeares brought to that
> state, that scarce the like can bee seen in any of our English Colonies
> in the richest places of this *America,* after many more yeares standing? [39]

John Cotton closely approached Hooker in scholarship and probably surpassed him in prestige. As the "unmitred pope" [40] of the Bay
Commonwealth, it was often felt that God could scarcely have permitted Cotton to err. So great were his powers as a preacher that

> Rocks rent before him, blind received their sight,
> Souls levelled to the dunghill stood upright.[41]

A graduate of Trinity College, Cambridge, in 1603, he was a powerful personage for more than a quarter of a century before Laud was
able to silence him. When the Winthrop fleet set sail in 1630, Cotton
preached the farewell sermon and when, together with Shepard, he
arrived in New England, he became one of its leaders at once.[42]

Puritan writings are strange only if we are insensitive to their purpose. Bradford's *History,* like all its lesser counterparts, is not only
an historical record but a divine testament. Shepard's sermons are
historical accounts as well as spiritual exercises. God spoke through
his servants in Boston and Plymouth just as he had earlier mani-
fested his will at Sinai and in Jerusalem. The voice was that of
Moses or Jesus, of Bradford or Hooker; but the word was the word
of God.

Hooker, Shepard, and Cotton provide an index of the Puritan
conception of history. Intimately associated with Puritanism in Old
England, they were just as intimately connected with the new Puritan commonwealth. The truths for which they struggled in Europe as
nonconformists led them to stamp out nonconformity in America.
Cotton, seemingly on the side of Anne Hutchinson when Puritan rule

was first seriously threatened, soon joined forces with the elect. Hooker journeyed from Hartford to Boston to serve as one of the moderators at the synod that condemned Mistress Hutchinson's "blasphemous" opinions. Grounded in the logic of Ramus, Hooker wrote the classic exposition of Congregational polity. But it was not because of the theologian of Hartford that Congregational theory later blended with democracy, for he was fully committed to uniformity and the moral obligation of the ruled to obey. John Cotton, adversary of Roger Williams in the debate over toleration, was no less identified with the concepts of uniformity and obedience. Democrats, looking back upon this early controversy, are beholden to Williams rather than to Cotton for confirmation and inspiration.[43]

The fame of the great clerical trinity of New England—Hooker, Shepard, Cotton—has dwarfed the reputation of other divines who gave vivid expression to the objectives of seventeenth-century life. Despite the rigidity with which the scope of history has often been defined, the clerics remain the best exemplars of Puritan historiography because they were the best exemplars of Puritan values and ideals.

Edward Johnson, though not a cleric, was a loyal follower of the Winthrop way, admirably representing the combination of history and the divine in the Puritan world of life and letters. Inspector of arms, militia captain and deputy to the General Court, Johnson came to Massachusetts Bay with the Winthrop fleet, and in 1640 became one of the principal founders of the town of Woburn. *The Wonder-Working Providence of Zion Saviour in New England*[44] is more than a narrative of conventional events; it is the spiritual log of the divine process. Some unknown prefacer, in addressing the "Good Reader," correctly summed up its purpose:

> As large Gates to small Edifices, so are long Prefaces to little Bookes; therefore I will briefly informe thee, that here thou shalt find, the time when, the manner how, the cause why, and the great successe which it hath pleased the Lord to give, to this handfull of his praysing Saints in N. Engl.[45]

While *The Wonder-Working Providence* is an excellent source for the origins of town government and church polity, it is an even better source for the basic ideas of Puritanism. The Puritan venture in New England was guided by the divine hand: "The mighty Princes of the Earth never opened their coffers for them, and the generality of these men were meane and poore in the things of this life, but sure it is the work is done, let God have the glory, who hath now given them food to the full, and some to spare for other Churches."[46] Johnson's words accurately register the Puritan conception of the historian's calling and trace the broad outline of Puritan attitudes toward life, nature, and society.[47]

Edward Johnson was by no means alone in recording illustrious providences. Indeed special evidence of divine activity was consistently a part of Puritan thought. John Winthrop's record of early life in New England contains abundant reference to the occurrences which testified to God's superintendence over the colony.[48] There was a mouse that, passing over the New Testament, exercised its teeth on the Book of Common Prayer. And the child of a man who desecrated the Sabbath fell into a well. These and other instances caused Winthrop to believe that "the Lord hath owned this work, and preserved and prospered his people beyond ordinary ways of providence." [49]

Special providences in the time of Winthrop and Johnson were common rather than uncommon events. Unlike miracles, which are virtually absent from Puritan thought, special occurrences were natural occurrences. They did not indicate any gross deviation from natural processes; rather, in the words of one Puritan minister, they indicated a situation in which "Nature is turned off its course." [50] God in these cases did not alter his laws but worked with and through them. But in the later years of the century when the new science of Copernicus and Newton suggested the universal applicability of natural law, Puritan thinkers began to stress the unusual character of special providences rather than their conformity with the forces of nature. This change, writes one of the leading students of the subject, constitutes "almost the only respect in which they were compelled to reorientate their thinking or overhaul their doctrines in order to adjust themselves to the new era." [51]

Even before the process of time and change corroded Puritan intensity, some New Englanders regarded the experiment with something less than the full measure of approbation. Thomas Lechford,[52] migrating to Massachusetts Bay in 1638, was its first full-fledged lawyer. Not being in accord with Puritan theology, he was debarred from church membership and hence from the franchise. Later in 1641 he was deprived of the right to practice law because he had used his persuasive powers on a jury in a manner which the authorities did not approve. After he left the colony, he wrote *Plain Dealing: or Newes from New-England,*[53] a volume which, uncommitted to Puritan assumptions, provides an admirable aid to reflection on Puritan thought.

The thrusts of Lechford's jabbing pen pained the devout, and

Thomas Morton's conduct distressed Pilgrim and Puritan alike. Even the gentle Bradford was sufficiently provoked to use angry prose:

> And Morton became lord of misrule, and maintained (as it were) a schoole of Athisme. And after they had gott some good into their hands, and gott much by trading with the Indeans, they spent it as vainly, in quaffing and drinking both wine and strong waters in great exsess, and, as some reported, 10 *li.* worth in a morning. They allso set up a Maypole, drinking and dancing aboute it many days togeather, inviting the Indean women, for their consorts, dancing and frisking togither, (like so many fairies, or furies rather,) and worse practises. As if they had anew revived and celebrated the feasts of the Roman Goddes Flora, or the beasly practieses of the madd Bacchinalians. Morton likwise (to shew his poetrie) composed sundry rimes and verses, some tending to lasciviousness, and others to the detraction and scandall of some persons, which he affixed to this idle or idol May-polle. They chainged allso the name of their place, and in stead of calling it Mounte Wollaston, they call it Meriemounte, as if this joylity would have lasted ever.[54]

Traffic in arms and traffic with the devil made Morton a threat and a nuisance, but his book *New England Canaan* widens our comprehension of colonial life. If one cannot agree with Charles M. Andrews that the whole Puritan story is mirthless,[55] one cannot fail to agree that the *New England Canaan* is among the few spontaneously humorous accounts to come out of New England in the seventeenth century.[56]

The writing members of the New England community were more often within than without the fold. John Eliot who died in 1690 was minister of the church in Roxbury, Massachusetts, and devoted missionary to the Indians. He was, wrote Cotton Mather, "one who lived in heaven while he was on earth." [57] As the first missionary to the natives he translated the Bible into the Algonquin tongue. He well deserved Cotton Mather's comment: "our *Eliot* was in such ill Terms with the Devil." [58]

John Eliot was chief apostle to the Indians but he was only one of many who wrote with them in mind. Indians were more than interesting examples of men in a state of nature or hapless natives with souls to be saved. They were a threat to the citizens of the Bible Commonwealth, and Indian wars quickly produced chroniclers and historians. William Hubbard, graduate of Harvard's first class and minister of the First Church at Ipswich, was "almost a professional man of letters." [59] In 1677 he produced *Narrative of the Troubles with the Indians in New England*.[60] Although Hubbard's work was carelessly done, his history surveys English contact with the Indians from the beginning. It represents the "unmeasurable rage" [61] of the

European inhabitants and stands in marked contrast to the humane tolerance of John Eliot. Moses Coit Tyler held that "if, in the seventeenth century . . . any prose work which, for its almost universal diffusion among the people, deserves the name of an American classic, it is this work." [62]

Hubbard was also the author of *A General History of New England from the discovery to MDCLXXX* written as a tribute to God's providential interest in the Puritan Commonwealth.[63] When Hubbard died in 1704 at the age of eighty-three the *General History* was still in manuscript as it remained until 1815 when it was published by the Massachusetts Historical Society. Often mentioned together with Bradford and Winthrop, it really does not compare with either. While Hubbard was prized by such writers as Cotton Mather, it was largely because of his unimpeachable orthodox tone.[64] The narrative was hardly more than a transcript of Nathaniel Morton's *New England's Memorial* and John Winthrop's *History*. But it must be remembered that Bradford's manuscript was "lost," and Hubbard had the value of a primary source.

Hubbard's *Narrative of the Troubles with the Indians* was supplemented by the *A Brief History of the Pequot Wars,* written by Captain John Mason. Another participant, Colonel Benjamin Church, added his *Entertaining Passages Relating to Philip's War* in 1716. *History of the Wars of New England with the Eastern Indians . . . 1703–1725* was the work of Samuel Penhallow, chief justice of New Hampshire. A noted chronicler of New England-Indian relations was Daniel Gookin, who was superintendent of the Indians of Massachusetts. Unlike the Indian fighters, Mason and Church, Gookin sought to understand the Indians and to explain them to the whites. *Historical Collections of the Indians of New England* presented a minority viewpoint. Efforts to mollify popular antipathy stood little chance against the published recollections of captives who escaped from Indian imprisonment. Of these the most famous was Mrs. Mary Rowlandson, seized during King Philip's War, whose account of life with the Indians still makes exciting reading.[65]

Indians certainly constituted a serious menace to the external security of the Bible Commonwealth. But the internal security of the Bible Commonwealth was also menaced, no less seriously, by the slower and less dramatic process of social change. Although the seventeenth century had but reached its meridian when John Winthrop died in 1649, the forces which were to change America were already remolding colonial perspective. Before Winthrop left his native

Suffolk, Virginia acres were yielding half a million pounds of tobacco for annual export. If the economy of the southern region was not yet reared upon foundations of smoke, as one contemporary asserted, plantations manned by slave or servile labor were discernible through the haze. The distinguished governor of Massachusetts Bay was still alive when an iron foundry operated in New England, and mills appeared in the wilderness of Maine and New Hampshire. Only forty years after he had launched the good ship *Blessing of the Bay,* Massachusetts was producing over seven hundred vessels during a twelvemonth. What were once straggling outposts of empire, lonely fishing villages, and rude dwellings clustered on the fringe of the forest had become seventeenth-century towns. The starving time was over. Tobacco piled on southern wharves, and the white sails which put out from Salem and Newport symbolized the changing culture reflected in social organization and mental outlook. The dominance of the supernatural was challenged by the advance of the secular traceable in the Halfway Covenant of 1662 as well as in the counting rooms of Boston merchants. With the new royal charter of 1691, banning religious qualifications for the franchise, the Puritan theocracy felt a seventeenth-century gust of the winds of eighteenth century doctrine.[66]

Increase Mather, mightiest of theocrats and fearless spokesman of the orthodox, watched these events with deep foreboding. With regret he watched the work of the founders reforged by the profane hands of a secular generation. Prudence coerced him into adjustment, but he could never allow himself to forget, in the words of the Reverend John Norton, that Massachusetts was a *"Plantation Religious,* not a plantation of Trade." [67] The great clerics and magistrates were already "laid asleep in their beds of rest till the day of doom," [68] but whenever possible Mather held firm to the old truths from which he himself never wavered.

It was a difficult if not an impossible task. During the year 1681, for example, an Anabaptist congregation in neighboring Watertown likened itself to the founders of Massachusetts Bay. Using an argument long familiar, they insisted that their own theological cause was no less just, for they too had sought the liberty of nonconformists in the freedom of the new Massachusetts world. To this one of Boston's ministers, Samuel Willard, replied: "I perceive they are mistaken in the design of our first Planters, whose business was not Toleration; but were professed enemies of it, and could leave the World professing they *died no Libertines.* Their business was to settle and (as much as in them lay) secure Religion to Posterity, according to that way which they believed was of God." [69] Increase Mather endorsed these sentiments in an unhesitating preface. But in 1721 he joined with his son in the ordination of a Baptist preacher and himself delivered a sermon calling for harmony. The eighteenth century had indeed arrived, for the theology of Cotton, Hooker, and the Mathers had lost its hold over the minds of men. "Puritanism, in the true sense of the word, was dead." [70]

The Mathers represent the early history of New England. They also represent the rise and fall of Puritanism. Son of the Reverend Richard Mather, Increase Mather was born in Dorchester, Massachusetts, June 21, 1639. The Mathers were a family of clerics, for the distinguished father had four clerical sons. And Increase Mather was himself the father of Cotton who added the greatest luster to the family renown.[71] At the age of twelve Increase Mather matriculated at Harvard from which he was graduated at seventeen. His commencement oration—a critique of the Aristotelian philosophy—was not an unusual subject but was performed with unusual learning. When he was nineteen, in 1657, he delivered his first sermon in his father's church. He returned to Massachusetts in 1661 after having acquired an M.A. at Trinity College, Dublin. At twenty-six, he became minister of Boston's North Church, a position he held until his death when he was succeeded by his son Cotton.

A scholar in the best Puritan form, Increase Mather was the author of more than a hundred and fifty separate items, ranging from religion to history and science. Profoundly solicitous of the future of New England, he was also concerned with preserving its hallowed past. He attempted to insure the writing of New England history and himself made significant contributions to this end.

Increase Mather's historical venture was an account of King Philip's War, followed in 1677 by a second account dealing with the larger topic of Indian relations. Both were marked by a power of narrative selection and an appreciation for color and drama. But color and drama were permitted to crowd out significance. As later critics have indicated, the most important aspects of the struggle, certainly known to Mather, simply did not appear. *An Essay for the Recording of Illustrious Providences* was undoubtedly his most important work, for nothing better illustrates the Puritan view of history than the intimate record of providential design.[72] The completion of this task, however, was reserved for Cotton Mather, his son and successor, who inherited his father's position as leader of the conservative party and his standing as scholar extraordinary.

Cotton Mather, unquestionably the greatest of Puritan scholars, was doomed to a life of disappointment. He failed to become the leader of his age because he failed adequately to represent it. When his father left for England in the year of the Glorious Revolution, Cotton Mather was elevated to the pulpit of the North Church, but the issuance of the new charter three years later deprived the ministers of much of their prestige if not of their power. In the witchcraft frenzy of 1692, an episode intimately related to the decline of theocracy, Cotton Mather's reputation was pitted against the trends of change. While in theology he lagged behind his era, in science he was ahead of it. He espoused the cause of inoculation for smallpox only to meet with vociferous disapproval and general disdain. When the elder Mather lost the Harvard presidency, the younger Mather tried desperately to obtain it, and was twice refused. He was too conservative to have faith in the people and too orthodox fully to please the rising bourgeoisie who had become unsympathetic to the intensity of primitive Puritanism.

But if the ways of Cotton Mather were not the ways of the newer world in which he lived, he successfully built a world of his own. He was the "literary behemoth of New England" [73] and his reputation, particularly abroad, surpasses that of any American of the colonial era except Jonathan Edwards and Benjamin Franklin.[74] No one can think of Puritan New England without thinking of Cotton Mather. He may, in the forthright language of one critic, have become "a vast literary and religious coxcomb" [75] but his historical work is as indispensable as any work can be. Puritan priest and keeper of the Puritan conscience he undoubtedly was, but Barrett Wendall adjudged the *Magnalia* one of the most important English works of the seventeenth century. And Charles Francis Adams, never effusive about the patriarchs of Massachusetts, wrote:

> But it is a fact worthy of note that the *Magnalia* stands to-day the one single literary landmark in a century and a half of colonial and provincial life,—a geological relic of a glacial period,—a period which in pure letters produced, so far as Massachusetts was concerned, absolutely nothing else,—not a poem, nor an essay, nor a memoir, nor a work of fancy or fiction of which the world has cared to take note.[76]

Cotton Mather was more successful as trustee of his father's historical ambitions than as his spiritual and intellectual executor.[77] He quadrupled the literary output of his prolific parent, who would have been proud and thankful for the *Magnalia Christi Americana; or the Ecclesiastical History of New England* which, after much tribulation, appeared in 1702.[78]

The *Magnalia,* upon which Cotton Mather's reputation rests, was not simply a history of ecclesiastical affairs. In addition to a chronology of governors, magistrates, and distinguished clerical leaders, a record of "remarkable providences," and an analysis of the place of Harvard in the realm of learning, the book essayed to prove that the theocracy of the founding fathers was worthy of preservation. He ignored the economic interests of the past perhaps because economic interests were everywhere so apparent in his own day.

As preface to the final book of the *Magnalia,* Mather turned his attention to what he called "the Wars of the Lord." Here Mather dealt with the internal and external threats to the society of saints; the threats of religious dissension and of Indian attack. This important section offers a suggestive clue to the life history of Cotton Mather and the life history of Puritanism. Mather was neither tyrannical nor bigoted. He was a great man whose genius was squandered in the conflict of generations.

But it was not simply the conflict of generations that embittered Mather's life. The intensity of primitive Puritanism passed away with the passing of the first generation, because Puritanism was personal, intimate, and individual. The nature of the Puritan spirit altered because Puritanism was only part of the total process of individual life and only a part of the total process of history. Puritanism was imperiled from the very beginning of its existence. Removal from England to the rim of the wilderness was no permanent guarantee of isolation. Seventeenth century reformers could not build a Puritan wall around Zion's kingdom on the shores of Massachusetts any more than they could insulate the Bible Commonwealth against the mutations of the future. The same factors—intellectual, social, and individual—which produced Puritan views of Bible and commonwealth produced different views of both. The very ideas, attitudes, and institutions that Puritans sought to escape in Old England followed them to New England. The Atlantic was an obstacle, not a barrier. If the impact of difference was registered more slowly in New England than in Old England, it was registered nevertheless. The colonial impetus of Western Europe not only moved Pilgrim and Puritan; it also moved Catholics, Baptists, and Quakers. The nonconformist impulse was not confined to Puritans nor could the Puritans confine it.

Pressure in the direction of spiritual or intellectual conformity breeds dissent. The greater the degree of intensity with which ideas are held, the more deviations become crucial. What to an objective observer appears to be relatively minor is in reality of major import. Puritans were particularly vulnerable to the "dissidence of dissent" because theirs was a certainty based upon reason. And reason,[79] unlike revelation, as Catholic and Anglican disputants never wearied of pointing out, produced variation rather than uniformity. To achieve intellectual unity reason must be put in its proper and subsidiary place. Chaos and confusion, not the infallibility of universal agreement, was the reward of reason. Anne Hutchinson was followed by Roger Williams, Roger Williams by other Baptists, and the Quaker thrust was perennial. "Intolerance," wrote Samuel Eliot Morison, "was stamped on the very face of the Bay Colony by the conscious purpose of its founders to walk by the ordinances of God, as interpreted by themselves." [80] Morison was doubtless right, but it was one thing to claim the right to interpret the ordinances of God; quite another to interpret them to everyone's satisfaction. It was one thing, again, to assert the right; another to maintain it. Accordingly, the key to Puritan disintegration is to be sought in the sway of Puritan power. When the Bible Commonwealth simply became a commonwealth, it was apparent that the Puritans had lost their power.

These problems have provoked the most probing questions. Not the colonial period of American beginnings alone, but the total American experience has been involved. Actually, these analyses go to the very heart of the American matter, for they relate to the ultimate democratic issues.[81] Assessments of the Puritan conception of government as well as the entire Puritan heritage are implicated in the discussion: Puritan assumptions of toleration, of the nature of society and of man.

Cleavages stemming from these controversies have embraced virtually the whole scope of historical interpretation. There is, of course, no larger framework in American historiography than the meaning of American experience. And pivotal to any assessment of the American experience are the intellectual and institutional sources of democracy.[82] Various groups of New England writers have found the answers to America's greatness in Plymouth and Boston. "Despite the failure of the Puritan experiment," wrote Thomas J. Wertenbaker with some asperity, "it is a widely accepted belief that it was largely instrumental in moulding the character not only of modern New England, but of the entire United States. Plymouth is spoken of as the birthplace of the nation; the Puritans, it is claimed, came to America as the champions of religious freedom, they founded American democracy." [83] Exponents of this point of view have been devout and zealous, but they have often allowed themselves to forget that the world did not begin in Boston and end at the southern tip of Cape Cod. Connecticut, Rhode Island, Maine,

New Hampshire, and Vermont early enlarged the world by becoming parts of the New England triangle.

Superciliousness, however, recognizes no geographical boundaries. Providence and New Haven chroniclers have been just as piously self-contained as antiquaries from Boston, Cambridge, and Plymouth.[84] Other sections and other regions have also had their partisans. Each has produced its ancestors ready made to worship and there is practically no geographic place so unhallowed as to be without a shrine. But geography by itself is too narrow to contain an idea. Wider cultural perspectives—European and global—finally challenged the most devoted provincialisms. Puritan emphases have fared no better than New England emphases. Other religious traditions and the tradition of no religion entered the speculative field to counter the claims of unitary exclusiveness. As secular postulates demanded a hearing from later generations of scholars, new canons of interpretation—economic, institutional, psychological, cultural—demanded inclusion in the process of testing the multiple hypotheses of social causation.

Puritan attitudes toward the religious ways of others have been the subject of prolonged and acrimonious debate. In older and presumably less reverent days, it was assumed that the Puritans, having themselves suffered persecution, could scarcely suffer others to endure it. It is still regarded as the equivalent of patriotism in some quarters to believe that Puritans were the apostles of tolerance and the guardians of democratic virtues. Recent scholarship has dissolved these assumptions. Perry Miller, the accomplished modern interpreter of Puritanism, has indicated how alien such notions actually were.[85] Puritans did not consider themselves separatists. They did not separate from the church; others had in fact separated from it by perverting its doctrines. The Puritans were reformers. They were the "purifiers," for they alone possessed the truth. How, they often asked, could truth be tolerant of error? This conviction explains Richard Mather's answer to certain Presbyterians who sought liberty to worship in Massachusetts. If, he argued, the appointment "by Jesus Christ for his churches is not arbitrary," and if the Puritan church "which we here practice be (as we are perswaded of it) the same which Christ hath appointed, and therefore unalterable," [86] there was but one answer.[87]

Puritan theology was as uncongenial to democracy as it was incompatible with toleration. Puritan ideas of the nature of society and of man were as hostile to democracy as the metaphysics from which they derived. John Winthrop's famous speech on liberty in 1645 reflects Puritan thought in classic form. "There is," wrote Governor Winthrop in the sure prose of firm conviction,

> a twofold liberty natural (I mean as our nature is now corrupt) and civil or federal. The first is common to man with beasts and other creatures. By this, man, as he stands in relation to man simply, hath liberty to do what he lists; it is a liberty to evil as well as to good. This liberty is incompatible and inconsistent with authority, and cannot endure the least restraint of the most just authority. The exercise and maintaining of this liberty makes men grow more evil, and in time to be worse than brute beasts: . . . This is that great enemy of truth and peace, that wild beast, which all the ordinances of God are bent against, to restrain and subdue it. The other kind of liberty I call civil or federal, it may also be termed moral, in reference to the covenant between God and man, in the moral law, and the politic covenants and constitutions, amongst men themselves. This liberty is the proper object of authority, and cannot subsist without it; and it is a liberty to that only which is good, just, and honest. This liberty you are to stand for, with the hazard (not only of your goods, but) of your lives, if need be. Whatsoever crosseth this, is not authority, but a distemper thereof. This liberty is maintained and exercised in a way of subjection to authority; it is of the same kind of liberty wherewith Christ hath made us free. The woman's own choice makes such a man her husband; yet being so chosen, he is her lord, and she is to be subject to him, yet in a way of liberty, not of bondage; and a true wife accounts her subjection her honor and freedom, and would not think her condition safe and free, but in her subjection to her husband's authority. Such is the liberty of the church under the authority of Christ, her king and husband; his yoke is so easy and sweet to her as a bride's ornaments; and if through forwardness or wantonness, etc., she shake it off, at any time, she is at no rest in her spirit, until she take it up again; and whether her lord smiles upon her, and embraceth her in his arms, or whether he frowns, or rebukes, or smites her, she apprehends the sweetness of his love in all, and is refreshed, supported, and instructed by every such dispensation of his authority over her. On the other side, ye know who they are that complain of this yoke and say, let us break their bands, etc., we will not have this man to rule over us. Even so, brethren, it will be between you and your magistrates. If you stand for your natural corrupt liberties, and will do what is good in your own eyes, you will not endure the least weight of authority, but will murmur, and oppose, and be always striving to shake off that yoke; but if you will be satisfied to enjoy such civil and lawful liberties such as Christ allows you, then will you quietly and cheerfully submit unto that authority which is set over you, in all the administrations of it, for your good. Wherein, if we fail at any time, we hope we shall be willing (by God's assistance) to hearken to good advice from any of you, or in any other way of God; so shall your liberties be preserved, in upholding the honor and power of authority amongst you.[88]

John Cotton's letter to Lord Saye and Sele is equally famous and even more explicit:

Mr. Hooker doth often quote a saying out of Mr. Cartwright (though I have not read it in him) that noe man fashioneth his house to his hangings, but his hangings to his house. It is better that the commonwealth be fashioned to the setting forth of Gods house, which is his church: than to accommodate the church frame to the civill state. Democracy, I do not conceyve that ever God did ordeyne as a fitt government eyther for church or commonwealth. If the people be governors, who shall be governed? As for monarchy, and aristocracy, they are both of them clearly approoved, and directed in scripture, yet so as referreth the soveraigntie to himself, and setteth up Theocracy in both, as the best forme of government in the commonwealth, as well as in the church.[89]

In much the same language, the Reverend Henry Ainsworth declared more emphatically, "So then for *popular government* we hold it not, we approue it not, for if the multitude gouern, then who shall be gouerned?" [90]

Yet there was a democratic impulse latent in Puritanism. But it was a contribution that matured afterward. If Puritanism contributed to the growth of democracy, it was because of Puritanism, not because of the Puritans.[91] There is justice in Samuel Eliot Morison's conclusion "that the reward came two hundred years later." Then "the sturdy, sufficient tree of puritanism, well rooted in New England soil by the jealous gardeners of the first generation, burst into flower with such as Channing, Emerson, Hawthorne, and Thoreau." [92]

Long before the flowering of New England, however, changes in the locus of power took place in Puritan Massachusetts. Such changes in social and political relations, not specific Puritan intent, resulted in the merger of Puritanism and the developing process of democracy.[93] Disputes concerning the motives of early Massachusetts settlers have added zest to scholarship and suggestive monographs to historical literature.[94] The debate, of course, continues but on some points there is now general agreement. Most disputants— except the most partisan members of one school or another—endorse the view that the majority of the migrants to the Bible Commonwealth were never of the elect. Whether they came to the Bay with Winthrop or followed him, they were not equally identified with the spiritual ends of the founders. Some were not identified at all; others were more than merely indifferent. It scarcely follows that those who felt themselves safely within the community of saints were either insincere in their belief or indifferent to the affairs of the world.[95] Division still separates the experts. But little doubt remains that the control of the elect over colonial life, whatever the motivation, was successfully challenged by the majority without control, whatever their religious attitudes.

Absence of a majority never disturbed the governing group. Since majority rule concepts, except for purposes of refutation, were not parts of Puritan theory, the Puritan minority never thought in such terms.[96] Puritan social and political theory was exemplified in early Puritan practice,[97] and explicitly set forth in Governor Winthrop's discourse on liberty.[98] But long before Winthrop gave it such clear expression, an unbroken line of Puritan theologians, drawing upon post-Reformation political premises, had already established its logic.[99]

Regardless of the lineage of political theory, New England society was originally reared upon the social compact.[100] But the New England theory of social compact did not permit full community participation.[101] Only those who could unequivocally demonstrate regeneration were allowed to serve as lawmakers and magistrates. No real distinction existed between state affairs and church affairs, and the Congregational churches were governed by the same principles. Membership was confined to those who could prove their right to membership. And the right to membership depended exclusively upon the demonstration of grace determined by the ruling elders already in possession of it. Church members alone could vote and hold office. Residents of the Puritan Commonwealth—as distinguished from its citizens—had equal rights before the law. They were equally taxed, equally protected, and equally entitled to justice. But in any real political sense, they had no role, no rights, and no means of political redress.

The Puritan covenant was a covenant between man and God. It did not become a social compact in terms of modern usage until almost the eighteenth century. God, not man, ordained the laws and delimited the scope of man's governance on earth as well as in heaven. Unrestrained liberty, as Winthrop pointed out, was a liberty of beasts. Such "natural liberty" led to evil; only submission to the laws of Christ promised true liberty for mankind. Submission to the laws of God was like the loving submission of a wife to her husband; both were according to divine ordinance:

> It may be of some good use, to inform and rectify the judgments of some of the people, and may prevent such distempers as have arisen amongst us. The great questions that have troubled the country, are about the authority of the magistrates and the liberty of the people. It is yourselves who have called us to this office, and being called by you, we have

our authority from God, in way of an ordinance, such as hath the image of God eminently stamped upon it, the contempt and violation whereof hath been vindicated with examples of divine vengeance. I entreat you to consider, that when you choose magistrates, you take them from among yourselves, men subject to like passions as you are. Therefore when you see infirmities in us, you should reflect upon your own, and that would make you bear the more with us, and not be severe censurers of the failings of your magistrates, when you have continual experience of the like infirmities in yourselves and others. We account him a good servant, who breaks not his covenant. The covenant between you and us is the oath you have taken of us, which is to this purpose, that we shall govern you and judge your causes by the rules of God's laws and our own, according to our best skill. When you agree with a workman to build you a ship or house, etc., he undertakes as well for his skill as for his faithfulness, for it is his profession, and you pay him for both. But when you call one to be a magistrate, he doth not profess nor undertake to have sufficient skill for that office, nor can you furnish him with gifts, etc., therefore you must run the hazard of his skill and ability. But if he fail in faithfulness, which by his oath he is bound unto, that he must answer for. If it fall out that the case be clear to common apprehension, and the rule clear also, if he transgress here, the error is not in the skill, but in the evil of the will: it must be required of him. But if the case be doubtful, or the rule doubtful, to men of such understanding and parts as your magistrates are, if your magistrates should err here, yourselves must bear it.[102]

A system of this type could not function without the support of society. As it depended upon exclusiveness, those excluded had to accept the conditions of exclusion as well as the consequences stemming from it. Or, failing to accept the conditions, they had to be without the power requisite to alter them. The system did not evoke universal approbation; dissent paralleled the history of the colony from the moment of its planting. With the advance of secular interests and the decline of the original intensity of Puritanism, came a change in culture. Cultural alteration was followed by the alteration of attitudes, beliefs, and ideas. Among them was the secularization of institutions and the secularization of political theory. Something of the spirit of Puritanism remained, but the day of the Puritans had ended.

VI

History and Historians in the British Dominions Beyond the Seas, II

Settlement of the western continents was the work of Europeans; the building of European civilization in North America was the work of the western world. Greek philosophers and Roman geographers spurred Dutch navigators and English sea dogs alike, and innovations of a German printer influenced the life cycle of Cotton Mather and his Puritan culture as it had earlier conditioned the intellectual outlook of Spanish mission fathers. Gallic counterparts of the Reverend John Eliot also learned Indian languages and customs by means of which French Jesuits and French traders were able to penetrate the wilderness and build a chain of forts linked together by pelts of fur. Despite miles of distance and decades of time, Pilgrims and Puritans were not alone.

There were religions neither Puritan nor Protestant, regions in addition to New England and Massachusetts Bay. Virginians, Georgians, and Carolinians made history and wrote it. New York, New Jersey, and Pennsylvania also celebrated their trials in literature and fused their primitive struggles into classical historical traditions. Virginia, Maryland, and Georgia were South and New Hampshire, Vermont, and Connecticut were North, but all were frontier communities before their status altered in response to later settlement. The West in American history is a cultural concept, not simply a geographical location and is represented by different geographical areas at different periods of colonial and national growth. New York, New

Jersey, and Pennsylvania were in part "western" as well as "middle" colonies. Vermont remained western in character long after Massachusetts had become irrevocably New England even though a frontier psychology distinguished the inhabitants of the region west of Boston, Cambridge, and Concord. John Winthrop was scarcely accustomed to the taste of power when Thomas Hooker led his faithful followers westward to Connecticut. Jonathan Edwards later terrified Boston's Puritans from the wilds of western Massachusetts, first from Northampton and then from Stockbridge.

Puritan culture, however, touched the South but lightly. Writers of the South were often men of serious purpose and lofty character but they were seldom elevated to the heights of Puritan goals. More frequently their zeal was circumscribed by insular loyalties and private desires. An earthy self-interest permitted them to record the beauties of nature without metaphysical disquisitions and to detail their impressions with a minimum of theological parallel. Unquestionably the most important writer of early Virginia, if not of the South, was Captain John Smith. Whether we look for information or for piquancy of style, he is without real competition. His writings, to which preliminary reference has already been made, supply invaluable information. The historian, ever doubtful, reserved, and critical about Smith, has never been able to escape his influence. Yet it is not so much because of the specific data of his maps, books, and tracts that Smith is so incomparable an asset to historical reconstruction. It is rather because Smith himself recreates the atmosphere and defines the spirit of seventeenth-century adventure. That he fabricated and embellished has been established beyond critical peradventure. Prejudice rather than justice tinged his conclusions to a degree far greater than scholars are wont to allow their predecessors. And as his critics delight to recall, he certainly failed to consult the records of the Virginia Company.

All this is doubtless true. But Captain Smith had his virtues as well. He was not one whose virtues in practice became his vices; his very vices were his virtues. His conscious adornment of the facts permit us to measure the depth of his passions, and the intensity of his disapproval is in turn the measure of the goals he approved. And his goals are those of a Jacobean seeker after fortune in a land where fortune and honor were to be made. To Hakluyt's stirring *Discourse,* Smith wrote an equally stirring sequel:

> The mildnesse of the aire, the fertilitie of the soile, and the situation of the rivers are so propitious to the nature and use of man as no place is more convenient for pleasure, profit, and mans sustenance. Under that

latitude or climat, here will live any beasts, as horses, goats, sheep, asses, hens, &c. as appeared by them that were carried thither. The waters, Isles, and shoales, are full of safe harbours for ships of warre or marchandize, for boats of all sortes, for transportation or fishing, &c. The Bay and rivers have much marchandable fish and places fit for Salt coats, building of ships, making of iron, &c.

Muscovia and Polonia doe yearely receave many thousands, for pitch tarre, sope ashes, Rosen, Flax, Cordage, Sturgeon, masts, yards, wainscot, Firres, glasse, and such like; also Swethland [1] for iron and copper. France in like manner, for Wine, Canvas, and Salt, Spaine as much for Iron, Steele, Figges, Reasons, and Sackes. Italy with Silkes and Velvets, consumes our chiefe commodities. Holand maintaines it selfe by fishing and trading at our owne doores. All these temporize with other for necessities, but all as uncertaine as peace or warres: besides the charge, travell, and danger in transporting them, by seas, lands, stormes, and Pyrats. Then how much hath Virginia the pererogative of all those florishing kingdomes for the benefit of our land, whenas within one hundred miles all those are to bee had, either ready provided by nature, or else to bee prepared, were there but industrious men to labour. Only of Copper wee may doubt is wanting, but there is good probabilitie that both copper and better munerals are there to be had for their labour. Other countries have it. So then here is a place a nurse for souldiers, a practise for marriners, a trade for merchants, a reward for the good, and that which is most of all, a business (most acceptable to God) to bring such poore infidels to the true knowledge of God and his noly Gospell.[2]

Hakluyt was a great and astute compiler; Smith a close observer and active participant. Both were conscious propagandists. Smith's account evoked opposition among contemporary foes as he has engendered irritation among historians ever since. Nonetheless he stimulated interest in America and migration to Virginia. He certainly struck the right colonial note as true for Virginia as for any other colony:

> For in Virginia, a plaine Souldier that can use a Pick-axe and spade, is better than five Knights, although they were Knights that could breake a Lance: for men of great place, not inured to those incounters, when they finde things not sutable, grow many times so discontented, they forget themselves, and oft become so carelesse, that a discontented melancholy brings them to much sorrow, and to others much miserie.[3]

Other eyes bore witness to the judgments of Captain Smith. George Percy's *Observations* supplements the *True Relation,* for the *Observations* details the incidents of the first voyage to Virginia and the initial settlement up to about June, 1607, after which date Smith's narrative is full.[4] Percy was the son, albeit merely the eighth, of the earl of Northumberland. He was a member of the first expedition to Virginia which set sail from England in December

1606, and was president of the colony during its most trying period. Edward Maria Wingfield's, *A Discourse of Virginia* . . . belongs in the *Observations* class. One of the original colonists in 1607 and himself a patentee, Wingfield kept a diary upon which this record is based. Like Smith he was involved in disputes with fellow members of the council which unmistakably protrude from his pages.[5] Ralph Hamor's *A True Discourse of the Present State of Virginia* is a somewhat more dispassionate account.[6] Together Smith, Percy, Wingfield, and Hamor present an almost consecutive narrative of Virginia's first perilous days.

William Strachey arrived in Virginia with Sir Thomas Gates in May 1610. His *True Reportory of the Wrack and Redemption*[7] transmits in splendid prose the story of his voyage and the story of the colony under Lord De La Warr. Shakespeare himself is said to have found material in the storm which tossed Strachey and his companions "upon and from the islands of the Bermudas" for his own *Tempest,* which, though far less real, is far more famous. Elizabethans who influenced William Shakespeare were, of course, fewer than those who were influenced by him.[8] Yet the Englishmen who wrote from the first English settlement in America established their own claims to recognition. To have left Europe in the seventeenth century was to enlist in one of the great movements of history. While all men in some sense make history, some men make a greater impact on change and continuity than others. But the impact is not registered exclusively in speech or prose. Even in crucial times, activity is not the sole index of historical importance. Degrees of importance suggest that significance is qualified by relationships. Men and women whose lives were built into the founding of America, whether they remained in Europe or ventured abroad, performed creative acts in the process of change even when they were unaware of them. Numberless men who planted crops and mended sails and numberless women who helped gather in the crop and mended clothes, as truly made history as other men and women for whom the convergence of personality factors and the convergence of events gave opportunities for greatness. Literacy in colonial America was less common than literacy in the United States now and the urge to write under the press of difficulty and excitement was less frequent.

These considerations give a continuing worth to the writers of early America. Better histories of Massachusetts have been written since John Winthrop put his journal together. But the later histories of Massachusetts cannot be compared with the work of the governor of the Bay. Winthrop must be compared with other seventeenth cent-tury Puritans, not with such later New England historians as John Gorham Palfrey, Charles Francis Adams, or Perry Miller. By the same tokens of evaluation, the study of seventeenth-century institutions in Virginia by Philip Alexander Bruce are not to be weighed against the judgments of Captain John Smith. William Strachey of all the first inhabitants of Virginia furnished Shakespeare with material for a plot. Alexander Whitaker alone of all the clergymen of Virginia converted Pocahontas to Christianity. Strachey's experiences were parts of the process of the colonization of Virginia. Intellectual linkages with Shakespeare suggest the tightly knit fabric which is called western civilization. Shakespeare was more than a part of the Elizabethan renaissance. He built new ideas into an evolving language, a language which was to aid in carrying the ideas that were to create democracy in a growing world.

The Pocahontas incident has assuredly been overstressed in the folklore of America. Dramatic emphasis has conventionally been placed on the ephemeral aspects of this encounter between the vanguard of English civilization and the barbaric splendor of Indian power. The events were unquestionably events of dramatic force. But the importance of Pocahontas does not derive from the fact that John Smith married her or that she later became the wife of John Rolfe who, in turn, became associated with tobacco, at once the economic mainstay and the economic problem of early Virginia. Pocahontas is significant not only because the words of Smith created a legend, but also because the Smith legend created a movement of historical criticism. Historical criticism, provoked by the Pocahontas legend, tried the wit of generations of historians including the scarifying wit of Henry Adams. These critical excursions developed criteria of evidence and the canons of historical verity. These analyses, in addition, yielded hitherto unsuspected insights into Indian attitudes, the behavioral traits of Europeans and the relationship between the two. As an important intellectual by-product, much was learned about the values and standards of the seventeenth century, not to mention the intellectual insights into the attributes of the critics who investigated them.[9]

There is no dearth of dramatic and spirited narrative during the period of American beginnings. John Pory, who arrived in Virginia in April 1619 and departed in 1622, wrote so entertaining an account that John Smith was prompted to include it in the *General History*. During his brief sojourn in the colony, Pory made three visits to the Indians and on his homeward journey he paid a call upon the Pilgrims in Plymouth.[10] But much more distinguished both by birth and association was George Sandys. Sandys was the son of the archbishop of York and brother to Sir Edwin Sandys. Sir Edwin enjoyed a double distinction: he was the friend of Richard Hooker and the enemy of James I. George Sandys' fame, however, was made in a different province of human enterprise. He translated the sixteen books of Ovid's *Metamorphoses,* thus marking the seventeenth-century commencement of classical scholarship in America.[11] Another Latin contribution was made by Father Andrew White, a Jesuit. White wrote a history of the first Maryland colonists in Latin which classicists still regard as excellent.[12]

The Maryland associates of Father White were content to write in English. John Hammond's humorous piece, *Leah and Rachel,* was published in London in 1656. Hammond, like his literary offspring, was a blend of Virginia and Maryland. He came first to Virginia in 1635, where he resided for almost twenty years. Until 1656 Maryland was his second home. Two aspects of life in the colonies particularly impressed him. One was the condition of the poor; the other, the misconceptions about America then circulating in Europe.[13] A decade later George Alsop's sparkling account, *A Character of the Province of Maryland,* secured for that colony a commendable niche in letters as well as in bibliography.[14]

As the tranquillity of permanence settled over the British colonies, the writing of its citizens acquired a more mature outlook. Practitioners of promotional literature never slackened their activities, but purposes other than advertising became more common. The elegant Latin of Father White or Sandys' preoccupation with Ovid were unique in the seventeenth-century South, for the classics were largely incapable of satisfying the emotional needs of colonial pioneers. Pressures of need, physical and psychological, were too constant to permit a literary detachment that viewed the present in the perspective of the past alone. Life was too tentative, elemental demands too great. Men felt the need to justify themselves and their deeds, to air their hopes, and to explain their ways of life. By the middle of the century, time had already tested colonial institutions and colonial institutions sharpened internal distinctions. Differences in social structure and mental outlook between north, south, and west were already apparent.

With the eighteenth century there was enough of a past to command interest and enough native glory to command respect. An increasing division of social labor furnished leisure and skill for literary avocations that inspired private men of means and public men of power. Sensitive self-consciousness remained, but it was gradually overtaken by a critical self-awareness. Colonial Britons who were economically secure and socially established were resentful of misinformed and disdainful prejudice. They took pride in new world accomplishments. As writers of history men of affairs had by no means succeeded clerics, but secularly minded men more frequently devoted attention to the colonial past. And in eighteenth-century fashion they tended to emphasize the mundane rather than the spiritual and they increasingly sought explanations in the meaning of life rather than in the meaning of death.

Robert Beverley of Virginia typifies these trends. He belonged to the lesser gentry in England before he removed to Virginia in 1663, where he became a leader in the political and social life of the colony. Although he was educated in England and spent a good deal of his time there, he was engrossed in colonial affairs. He was clerk of the General Court, the Council, and the General Assembly. It was during one of the periods of his English residence that he read an account of the British in America. He was so exasperated by the section on Virginia that he decided he had a duty to write his own. *History and Present State of Virginia,* published in 1705,[15] was the product of Beverley's irritation. Whatever the justification for his dissatisfaction, the result was an enrichment of American history. The appearance of Beverley's small volume, still highly readable and highly useful, constitutes something of an event. Great books like Bradford's *History* and Winthrop's *Journal* had already graced the language in which they were written. The number of useful, interesting, and vibrant books produced in the seventeenth century alone is so great that none can question the significance of colonial writing. Yet Bradford's history, while majestic, is but rarely amusing. Winthrop's pages, filled with moral intensity, are seldom humorous. Mather is always learned but almost never urbane. All three, moreover, though they deal with universal issues, are frequently provincial. Beverley, on the other hand, is informative and witty, learned and humorous, and sufficiently cosmopolitan to be detached from petty affinities—qualities which scholars in all fields have ever striven to attain.

Beverley's *Virginia* is composed of four parts. The first deals with "The History of the First Settlement of Virginia, and the Government thereof, to the Year 1706." Natural conditions and "Conveniencies of the Country" comprise the second section, Indians are the subject of the third, and the final section contains a survey of conditions of the country particularly "as to the Polity of the Government, and of the Improvements of the Land." For his guidance as a magistrate Beverley compiled *The Abridgement of the Publick Laws of Virginia, in Force and Use, June 10, 1720.*

It was the volumes of John Oldmixon which roused Beverley into historical action. Oldmixon, an Englishman, was the author of *The British Empire in America, containing the History of the Discovery, Settlement, Progress and present State of the British Colonies, on the Continent and Islands of America.*[16] One volume was reserved for a review of the North American colonies; another for the settlements in the West Indies. Oldmixon's standpoint, traditional enough for the era, regarded the mother country as central to the national economic effort and the colonies in whatever part of the world as subsidiary. This view implied—as a whole generation of American colonial historians were to forget—that from the center of mercantilism, all colonies were theoretically one. Michael Kraus[17] rightly indicates that the historiographical tendency to regard the American colonies as peculiar was an attitude more largely confined to North America than to Whitehall. So warped an emphasis was not corrected until comparatively recent years and, for this reason alone, Oldmixon deserves credit for not sharing it.

Yet the effectiveness of John Oldmixon's services to historical scholarship were strictly limited. Centuries passed before it was recognized that he had earned the right to a corroborative footnote. The services of James Blair, on the other hand, produced almost immediate consequences. "Probably no other man in the colonial time," wrote Moses Coit Tyler, "did so much for the intellectual life of Virginia."[18] A native of Scotland and a graduate of the University of Edinburgh, Blair came to Virginia in 1685 and at once made the future of the College of William and Mary his own. For fifty years he served as its president, and he made it a powerful force not for the Church of England alone but for the life of the entire South. Together with others he wrote *The Present State of Virginia and the College,*[19] a title which indicates how closely he associated the life of learning with the life of society.

The Blairs and the Beverleys intimate that southern society was changing, the Byrds indicate that southern society had in fact changed. William Byrd of Westover, father and son, were among the first gentlemen of Virginia and easily among the founders of the historiographical tradition in America. The first William Byrd acquired the fertile acres that the second William Byrd managed enormously to increase. Ensconced as Virginia aristocrats, all the symbols of status were amassed at Westover. There was the invariable silver plate, the lace, and the gleaming mahogany furniture. But there were also books, for it was the habit of the gentlemen of Virginia to build up private libraries. In spite of the cares incident to tobacco growing or the demands imposed by the fox hunt and the ball, libraries were more often designed for reading than for conspicuous emulation. The library at Westover, consisting of four thousand volumes, was the largest colonial collection and William Byrd, second of the name, made full use of it. "If no other records had survived except those of the Byrd family," concludes one prominent historian of the South, "they alone would have made it possible for later generations to understand the social development of Virginia and to trace the evolution of an aristocracy that attained a mellow splendor." [20]

The writings of William Byrd II, however, are not simply records, crucial though records undoubtedly are. William Byrd II wrote history and his books are four in number: *A Progress to the Mines in the Year 1732, A Journey to the Land of Eden, Anno 1733,* and two histories of the Dividing Line. The histories of the dividing line grew out of the labors of a boundary commission appointed to adjudicate the joint frontiers between Virginia and North Carolina. Of this commission Byrd was a member, but it was many years before his account, written between 1728 and 1738, was published. Another century elapsed before the second history appeared.[21]

Byrd's book is more than a report of the work of the commission. *The History of the Dividing Line* is prefaced by an historical sketch and includes the general topics fancied by colonial essayists—descriptive natural history and the cultural state of the native inhabitants.[22] Byrd is as shrewd as he is cultivated, as witty as he is wise. His sharp humor is revealed in the comment concerning the original settlers of Jamestown. There were among them, he wrote, "about a Hundred men, most of them Reprobates of good Familys" who "like true Englishmen . . . built a Church that cost no more than Fifty Pounds, and a Tavern that cost Five Hundred." [23] The second version of the Dividing Line, called the *Secret History,* is appreciably briefer than the first, and adds considerably to our specific knowledge of the boundary. Both contribute to our knowledge of Virginia and of the frontier which stretched to the west of it.[24]

Knowledge of the American past constantly increased. The more men exerted themselves to understand the history that preceded them, the more those who followed were able to understand both. William Stith, Anglican minister, chaplain to the Virginia House of Burgesses, and president of the College of William and Mary composed a valuable history of the province from its discovery and first settlement until the year 1624.[25] The most favorable of circumstances combined to make his labors pleasurable and his results noteworthy. He wrote in the leisure of retirement, with a full awareness of colonial tradition and with relatively easy access to materials. To set the record straight was his objective, for time, he felt, was already scattering and destroying the irreplaceable data of history. Not unlike many other historians before and since, he regarded much of what had already been written as "learned Trumpery." On the other hand, Stith promised: "To give a plain and exact History of our Country, ever regarding Truth as the first requisite and principal Virtue in an Historian, and relating nothing without a sufficient Warrant and Authority." [26] In large measure, or at least in as large a measure as one could reasonably expect, he succeeded. While chronologically limited, the value of Stith's history lies in its elaborate detail. The value is enhanced by the use Stith made of the records of the London Company for the second part of the book. For these among other reasons Stith has sometimes been called the most modern of colonial historians.[27]

Virginia's greatness is in no way lessened by the recognition that geography is not a necessary correlate of intellectual interest and spiritual achievement. Maryland, the Carolinas, and Georgia had their founding fathers whose deeds generated as much devotion as the patriarchs of Jamestown and Williamsburg. They had intellectual as well as institutional beginnings, and the consequences of both are integral parts of the development of the United States.

North Carolina's historian, John Lawson, was a surveyor who came to America at the very commencement of the eighteenth century. Nine years after his arrival, he published a report which like other similar ventures discoursed upon the advantages of the region for colonization and the ever-fascinating appeal of the Indians.[28] Seventy years later Alexander Hewat wrote a much more significant work. The author, who was a Scotsman and minister of the Presbyterian Church, took South Carolina and Georgia as his historical preserve. The year 1728 served as a division between his two volumes. In that year South Carolina became a royal province, an event in accord with Hewat's basic ideas. As the first history of South Carolina, the study is of special historiographical moment, and considerable attention is accorded Georgia as well. The narrative extends to the verge of the revolution with which Hewat, a staunch royalist and later a Tory, was completely out of sympathy. Notwithstanding his political preferences, there is comparatively little of politics in Hewat's study. There is, however, much of the natural and social structure of the southland, for it was Hewat's purpose to tell other

Englishmen what awaited them in these untried lands should they be courageous enough to make them their own.[29]

In quality as well as quantity of production Virginia was undeniably first among the southern group. But in the middle colonies New York was no more than the equal of Pennsylvania. The first separate account of the province of New York written in English was from the pen of Daniel Denton. Denton moved to New York from Connecticut in 1644, and his small brochure consisting of twenty-four pages, *A Brief Description of New York; Formerly Called New Netherlands* . . . appeared in London in 1670.[30] Although Denton's pamphlet is hardly more than a promotional tract with immigrants very much in mind, it is an exceedingly good one.[31] It is so suggestively and pleasantly written that it has often been reprinted, latterly by the Scholars' Facsimile Text Society in 1937.[32] Denton's main theme was true of New York in the seventeenth century as it was subsequently true for all America. "If there be any terrestrial happiness to be had by people of all ranks, especially of an inferior rank, it must certainly be here." [33]

Quite as charming and just as instructive is a journal by two ecclesiastical visitors who came to New York and to Boston. Jasper Danckaerts and Peter Sluyter were emissaries of a sect of the Dutch Reformed Church—the Labadists—some of whose members had settled in Maryland and Delaware during the last twenty-five years of the seventeenth century. They journeyed from Holland to see their brethren and, having performed their duties, they took the opportunity of seeing something of the country. Before returning to Holland they visited New York and Boston. One can scarcely determine whether those visited were more amused by the two Dutch clerics or they by them. Fortunately they kept a journal which informs us at least how they felt about the things they saw and heard. They inform us, therefore, how Boston and New York appeared when viewed through Dutch clerical eyes.[34]

Both were disturbed by the state of religion, especially in New England. "We heard preaching in three churches," we read in the journal, "by persons who seemed to possess zeal, but no just knowledge of Christianity. The auditors were very worldly and inattentive. The best of the ministers whom we have yet heard is a very old man, named Mr. John Eliot, who has charge of the instruction of the Indians in the Christian religion." [35] Even zeal to them seemed to be declining.

> They are all Independents in matters of religion, if it can be called religion; many of them perhaps more for the purposes of enjoying the

benefit of its privileges than for any regard to truth and godliness. I observed that while the English flag or color has a red ground with a small white field in the uppermost corner, where there is a red cross, they have dispensed with this cross in their colors, and preserved the rest. . . . When we were there, four ministers' sons were learning the silversmith's trade.[36]

And of Harvard, the seat of godly learning and wisdom, Danckaerts wrote:

We went to it, expecting to see something unusual, as it is the only college, or would be academy of the Protestants in all America, but we found ourselves mistaken. In approaching the house we neither heard nor saw anything mentionable; but, going to the other side of the building, we heard noise enough in an upper room to lead my comrade to say, "I believe they are engaged in disputation." We entered and went up stairs, when a person met us, and requested us to walk in, which we did. We found there eight or ten young fellows, sitting around, smoking tobacco, with the smoke of which the room was so full, that you could hardly see; and the whole house smelt so strong of it that when I was going up stairs I said, "It certainly must be also a tavern." . . .

. . . They knew hardly a word of Latin, not one of them, so that my comrade could not converse with them. They took us to the library where there was nothing particular. We looked over it a little. They presented us with a glass of wine. This is all we ascertained there.[37]

As in other colonies, Massachusetts alone excepted, the most mature and well-rounded works appeared in the eighteenth century. The first great contribution of New York was written by Cadwallader Colden, one of the most celebrated citizens of the English community in North America. A doctor, statesman, and student, he was devoted to the expansion of empire. Many of his contemporaries in the colonies took a narrow provincial view, while those in Britain took an equally narrow administrative view. But Colden thought in broad imperial strokes. He worked with a controlling purpose: to present a case for the Iroquois nations. The Indians constituted part of a much larger problem. And the Indian issue was understandable only in terms of the internal situation in the American West and the external situation of European diplomacy. The latter furnished the basis for an understanding of the struggle between England and France; the former for an understanding of the Iroquois in the balance of world diplomatic power.

Dominance was the ultimate prize. The Indians, the fur trade, and the control of the American West were counters in an international struggle for mastery. These considerations made Colden an historian not alone of New York, but of the Indians and of the frontier as well. He bespoke civilized treatment for the red men lest the French profit from British inhumanity. Nevertheless, he was passionately interested in the evolution of the Indian past and the prospects of the Indian future. *The History of the Five Nations Depending on the Province of New York* came out in 1727. Such were the pressures of Colden's public life, that more than fifteen years passed before the second section of his work was published. The narrative progressed from 1689 to 1697 in the second section and is filled with ample discussions of Indian customs, government, and their relations with Europeans. A collection of Colden's remaining papers were published in 1935 by the New York Historical Society. These contain additional materials on his major theme plus a significant section dealing with Peter Zenger and his famous trial.[38]

William Smith, another noteworthy New York historian, was born in the year following the appearance of Colden's first volume.[39] After being graduated from Yale, he returned to his native colony to pursue the study of law. Then, even more than now, law was the gateway to public office, and he followed in the political footsteps of his father, who had held posts of importance. A conservative during the struggles preceding the Revolution, he became a loyalist when the war came and he left New York together with the redcoats. When he returned to America after the colonies had become the United States, it was as Chief Justice of Canada. Smith's history begins with the discovery and continues to the year 1732. Additional data, extending the account to the commencement of Colden's governorship in 1762, were printed after his death. In 1829 the New-York Historical Society produced a two-volume edition entitled *The History of the Late Province of New York from its discovery, to the appointment of Governor Colden, in 1762.*

Because of his Tory sentiments, Smith has often been rejected. But as a Tory he was intimately conversant with the shifting arguments of the loyalist case. For the same reason, he represented loyalist reaction to the course of colonial argumentation. As an aristocrat, Smith was sometimes resented, but because he was a member of governing social and political groups, he could, more or less accurately, report their opinions. As a practicing lawyer, he had direct experiences with judges, courts, and the operation of the law. For these reasons, Smith's history has the stature of meaning.[40]

The consequences of historical events are the measures of importance; ideas, not geography, the measures of distinction. Cadwallader Colden was the chief executive of the province of New York, but he is distinguished because he perceived a dynamic relation between England, France, and the Five Nations. William Smith resided in the

New York colony but he is important because he wrote a history reflecting events that merged into larger and continuing historical sequences. John Adams was jealous of the reputation of Massachusetts. George Washington, though not the father of Virginia as he was of his country, was nevertheless her loyal son. Local patriots of lesser stature have ever pressed the claims of Massachusetts, Virginia, and New York. Those with regional loyalties have clamored for the recognition of the middle group, of New England, or of the South. There are histories of individual colonies and of individual states. There are histories of physiographic regions and political sections, of cities, towns, counties, and villages. But the history of America is the history of colonies, states, regions, and sections in the process of becoming the United States.

Geography is a vital component of every historical equation, and localism is a recurring psychological response. Both have exerted profound influences on American development. The whole course of American history has often been interpreted in terms of one or the other. But geography has never been absent from any human situation, and identification with time and locale is as inescapable for human beings as the force of the physical environment. Particular combinations of physical influences and particular varieties of localism have ever combined to produce particular results. It is precisely the combination of such particulars that initiate change and difference, but the changes and the differences thus created are at once the consequences and the causes of other differences and other changes. American meanings are not to be found in the contours of geography or the human expressions that are partly conditioned by them.

The history of America is the history of an idea. But it is an idea of many plantings with a rich and varied yield. Geography, the diversity of peoples, special human motives, and human aspirations combined to give meaning to the American experience. The greatness of colonial Massachusetts and colonial New England, for example, was Puritanism; its achievement a tradition of earnestness, of moral intensity, and reverence for the uses of reason. But the achievement of Puritanism in the history of democracy is also its decline. Institutions altered, and ideas, attitudes, and aspirations were separated from one set of social impulses and attached to others. If a prime American characteristic is a preoccupation with man and society, it is partly the heritage of Puritanism and the legacy of the attitudes and institutions which took its place. The Mayflower Compact, to instance a single revered event, was no democratic document. No more so were the other great charters of Pilgrims,

Puritans, Anglican, and Catholics. But they had profound democratic results. Carl Sandburg later remarked that men must be careful how they use proud words as other men later put their own meanings to them. Virginians and Carolinians, Yankees and Yorkers all made use of the noble language of their time. Rights, privileges, and immunities are the great and recurrent words of grants and charters. The agreement drawn up on the Mayflower was drafted for the better ordering of society and bespoke an interest in the general welfare. The precise legal connotations "rights" and "privileges" once possessed came to mean different things to other generations of Americans. And they came to mean different things because America gave measurable reality to their newer meanings.

William Penn and his colony of Pennsylvania gave new meanings to liberty and equality. Bradford unmistakably impressed his personality and his purposes upon Plymouth, but it was more truly the Plymouth experience which impressed itself upon Bradford and his history. Winthrop was the product of Puritanism and its new world colony, notwithstanding the formative power of his influence upon Massachusetts Bay. But William Penn created the commonwealth of Pennsylvania. As the son of a distinguished admiral, William Penn had every social and individual advantage. His father's friendship with the Duke of York opened wide avenues of special favor and virtually guaranteed a brilliant career for his son. But the younger William had talents of mind and a largeness of spirit almost certain to achieve greatness without the favor of the powerful. An Oxford education was supplemented by further training at a Huguenot school in France and completed by legal studies at Lincoln's Inn, in London. Oxford, however, expelled him for joining dissidents in religious worship, a lapse from conformity which did little to gladden the admiral's heart. For this reason his father sent him to France in the hope that he would acquire wit enough to see that the richest English political plums grew on episcopal trees. On another trip, this time to Ireland to oversee the paternal estates, he met a Quaker preacher and was converted to the faith. Quakerism was a bitter pill for a seventeenth-century admiral of the King's navy to swallow. Although there were quarrels between father and son, each had too great a confidence in the integrity of the other to allow the breach to endure. William Penn went his Quaker way to the great advantage of his personal development and to the equally great advantage of the land that was to become the United States. Quakerism gave William Penn a faith as well as a mission, and it gave America the "Holy Experiment" which was Pennsylvania.[41]

William Penn was no scholar in any formal sense. He was nevertheless the first historian of Pennsylvania. To encourage immigration to his colonial province, he wrote a number of promotional tracts. While it is strictly accurate to describe them in this fashion, to do so is to ignore what they meant to him and what they still mean to us. They are, in the first place, unlike the conventional promotional tract of that time or of this. *Some Account of the Province of Pennsylvania,* written before he came to America, was Penn's first attempt in the literature of advertising. But he did not permit the pecuniary wish to become father to the purposive thought. Instead he submitted his copy "to Traders, Planters, and Shipmasters, that know these parts, and finally to the most eminent Friends." [42] He was trying to tell the truth as well as to encourage settlement. What he wished to establish was not simply a prosperous colony, but a prosperous free colony. Hence he directed his words to men and women who desired to build homes and cultivate farms, not to financial investors in lands and lives. He addressed Germans, Dutchmen, Frenchmen, and Englishmen too. He invited conformist and nonconformist, Gentile and Jew, Protestant and Catholic. And when he promised freedom of worship, he meant to grant it. Actually Jews and Catholics were granted something less than full liberty to worship in their own respective ways, but there was more liberty of conscience in Pennsylvania than anywhere else in the colonies except in the Rhode Island of Roger Williams. Limitations on revelry, on card playing, and dancing were imposed, but the Frame of Government was a humane and liberal system. [43]

An apparent immediacy does, of course, cling to Penn's words. Yet he did not write primarily to achieve immediate results. He had other objectives beside economic gain, for his pamphlets outline the biography of an idea just as they outline, somewhat more vaguely, the autobiography of a spiritual pioneer. They are historical documents of the first importance and unconscious history of the first order, for Penn was really writing an account of Pennsylvania in an advertisement to the likeminded. The accounts were addressed to those who like him wished to secure their future by helping to secure liberty.

The "Holy Experiment" was a democratic experiment. William Penn and his Pennsylvania represent many of the separate elements out of which democracy in America was finally built. William Penn himself represents Quakerism; Pennsylvania, both the left-wing religious sects and the variant eighteenth-century ethnic groups. Dissident nonconformists and diverse immigrant stocks symbolize the patterns of cultural difference, the free association for all social and individual purposes—the differences and the freedoms that make unities for other purposes democratically possible. Penn's "Holy Experiment" was the American experiment in miniature.[44]

Among the groups to whom William Penn appealed were the Pietists and the Mennonites of Germany.[45] Partly as a result of his visits to Frankfort in 1677, a contingent of these sects moved to Pennsylvania. Their agent was Francis Daniel Pastorius,[46] who arrived in Philadelphia in 1683 and founded Germantown. For the rest of his life Pastorius remained the guiding leader of his coreligionists who made their faith a guide to living and their living a warrant of faith. Pastorius brought learning to Philadelphia. Adept in a wide variety of skills, he was versed in agriculture and medicine, history and theology, science and business. A proficient writer, his letters, particularly those addressed to his father, still bear reading for their own intrinsic merit. These together with his autobiography contain much that is pertinent to the early history of Germantown, Philadelphia, and of Pietism in America. He was in complete accord with William Penn's devotion to religious liberty. In 1698, he wrote to his father: "As experience testifies that by the coercion of conscience nothing else than hypocrites and word-Christians are made, of whom almost the entire world is now full, we have therefore found it desirable to grant freedom of conscience." [47]

Whether it was William Penn's battle cry of freedom or the warming impulses of the eighteenth century, Pennsylvania attracted men whose love for ideas was second only to the urge to put them into practice. James Logan, secretary to Penn, classical student and scientist, was responsible for the first copy of Newton's *Principia* that came to America. His notable collection of books was fused into the Library Company of Philadelphia and became its initial core. Penn, Pastorius, and Logan in one sense belong to Pennsylvania, but in another and larger sense they belong to the world.[48] Benjamin Franklin is also properly a member of this illustrious company. Pennsylvania's claim to Franklin is attested by residence, documents, and learned footnotes. But even the cogent arguments advanced by eighteenth-century students are less persuasive than the irresistible case presented by the learned doctor himself. Franklin is a citizen of the world.[49]

Benjamin Franklin's intellectual history is a synopsis of world forces. That Franklin was "the child of the eighteenth century" has been repeated in almost every study of which he is a part. But it was not only as the child of the eighteenth century that Franklin serves as one of the chief transitional figures between the medieval and the modern age. Franklin is as much the offspring of the revolutions in religious thought and feeling as of the commercial revolutions. Together these revolutions were responsible for the founding of America. Taken together they were responsible for much of the later development of America. Religious and economic forces exerted a continuing influence from the period before the discovery of Columbus up to and including the present. But these influences were neither singular nor isolated. The economics of changing trade routes and changing class arrangements were not the only forces which brought the new world and modern society into being. Nor was it solely the altering ideas and institutions affecting organized religions.[50] None of these elements by themselves channeled the emerging culture of modern Western Europe.

Religious influences and economic influences are remarkably constant in the evolution of the current world. Yet the nature of the merger and the substance of the results are no less remarkably different. Economic and religious motives, attitudes, and institutions, united in diverse ways at different times and in different places. They had, therefore, quite different results. There could hardly be a more obvious generalization. But if the generalization is obvious for history, it is not obvious for historiography. Until examined, it appears as a startling anomaly. But where are the religious histories of America? Where are the histories of theological ideas? Customary linguistic usage is suggestive. We habitually speak of "sectarian" and "denominational" histories with which we are well supplied. But where is there a full analysis of religious ideas? Perry Miller has produced the *New England Mind* and with Thomas H. Johnson *The Puritans*. These are histories of a single group in a single time and place. Other studies of different groups at different periods of our history likewise exist.[51] While they compare with Miller's study in scope, they do not always compare in quality. H. K. Rowe's *Religious Forces* was an attempt in this direction that others, with varying degrees of success, have striven to emulate.[52]

There are few studies in the whole literature of America that essay what Thomas C. Hall's *Religious Background of American Culture* endeavors to accomplish. While Hall achieved far less than his title implied, he presented a revisionary thesis. However one may judge it, the intellectual effects were salutary. Hall called attention to the patent fact that there was a reformation in Europe before Luther and Calvin. He made it difficult for later scholars to ignore the earlier reformation and its English antecedents or the fact that the historical background provided by Wyclif had historical results. Yet this volume, though latterly cited with encouraging frequency, has still really to affect historical interpretation.[53] Two arresting monographs by foreign scholars have added to historical excitement in these regions of interest. Max Weber's *Protestantism and the Capitalistic Ethic* and R. H. Tawney's *Religion and the Rise of Capitalism* have succeeded in substituting acrimony for lethargy, and in general they have stimulated more debate than reflection. Ralph Barton Perry's *Puritanism and Democracy* has the advantage of being written by a philosopher and the disadvantage of dealing with a restricted topic.[54]

There is no synthesis of American experience based upon ideas to which social and institutional changes are related.[55] Scholars have combined to produce the *Cambridge History of American Literature* and its successor the *Literary History of the United States*.[56] Both are filled with references to ideas. There are, however, few integrated referents, bibliographical or conceptual. The *Dictionary of American Biography,* a triumph of systematized learning, is crammed with neat sketches of leaders of thought in all domains, the religious and philosophical included. The *Dictionary of American History* lists religious and philosophical leaders with bewildering brevity.[57] But none of these works clarifies interrelations and meanings. There is not a single volume of the *History of American Life,* the most consequential co-operative venture of the modern era, geared to the study of religious or philosophical ideas.[58]

Monographs on this level of analysis do in fact exist. Foster's *Genetic History of the New England Theology*[59] is in many ways an excellent performance, yet it is limited both in subject and in style. There are many biographies of leading figures in the intellectual history of American religious experience.[60] Some like Samuel Hugh Brockunier's *The Irrepressible Democrat: Roger Williams,* Ola E. Winslow's *Jonathan Edwards,* and Perry Miller's treatment of the same great philosopher have been outstandingly successful.[61] Special works by philosophers covering mainly philosophical ideas—Herbert W. Schnieder, Harvey G. Townsend, and W. H. Werkmeister—have also supplied helpful aids.[62] Vernon L. Parrington, Reinhold Niebuhr, Merle E. Curti, and Henry Steele Commager have recently accorded sustained attention to aspects of the religious influence in the making of the American mind.[63] But the whole area remains genetically unsurveyed. The indictment of William Warren Sweet, whose efforts to remedy this situation have been nothing less than valiant, is irrefutable, for religion has in fact "been the most neglected phase of American history." College students, he avers, "could pass a better examination in Greek mythology than on American Church history." They are "better informed on the Medieval popes than . . . on the religious leaders of America." [64] Whether the mastery of tests in Greek mythology and the medieval popes is an adequate measure of understanding has yet to be demonstrated, but the major point is fully revealed in the record of American scholarship.

The philosophical and institutional import of religion has impressed historians from the very beginning. Yet the overall results have been far from encouraging. Despite the brilliant researches of modern scholars, Puritanism is still confused. The role of Catholicism in the colonial period—as a body of living ideas rooted in living relationships—has never received understanding appraisal. The Jews have been accorded no more than antiquarian treatment. Protestant bodies are hardly more than names to those not affiliated with one of them. And the so-called left-wing sects, the Quakers alone excepted, are ordinarily confined to the index of volumes in which they are simply mentioned. Older studies—collections of documents and sources—together with newer works repose on the library shelves to which scholars, not specialists, have consigned them.[65]

These are intriguing problems basic to history as well as to historiography. The absence of a synthesis of American religious history, of an evaluative scholarly account of religious ideas and institutions, presents the issue in the sharpest terms. And this is but one of the quandaries in the historical development of scholarship. Unitary interpretations of the American past have not only blurred the significance of religious ideas and their consequences, of their philosophical affiliations with other controlling ideas; they have also obscured the formative role of cultural differences,[66] of ethnic varieties, of intellectual distinctions.[67] When other factors finally began to reshape the historian's view of history and the historical function, new forces conspired to narrow the scope of the historian's effort. But long before the machine and the city had created an age of specialism, the Revolution gave Americans a common experience. The political and social struggles resulting in American independence likewise resulted in American nationalism. The revolutionary struggle gave the American people a tradition; it also gave American historians a hypothesis of social meaning.

VII

The American Revolution in American History and American Historiography

The American Revolution shattered the complacency of western Europe. Ordeals of battle and the vicissitudes attending the emergence of statehood were watched with interest. But it was the sharp edge of difference that cut deeply into the European consciousness. The principles underlying the revolutionary struggle were common enough. There was hardly a revolutionary argument unfamiliar to educated Europeans. Locke, Rousseau, Harrington, and Montesquieu were as widely studied as the classics of Greece and Rome. But the doctrines of equality and natural rights had never before been employed as the foundations of a commonwealth.[1] A nation dedicated to the proposition that all men were created equal was a historical novelty. Americans and Europeans were conscious of the novelty, and succeeding generations in both parts of the world have been conscious of it since.[2]

Roots of loyalty lie deep within the consciousness of a people, and American loyalties were new. Not only were American loyalties young in years, they were also different in kind. While nationalism as a psychological development reveals similar characteristics everywhere, specific historical processes and events condition its content and direction. Nationalism in the United States was different from any variety that had preceded it. And it is more important to understand its meanings than to date its beginnings.[3]

The events of the American Revolution, dramatic though they

were, are less suggestive of basic meanings than the long-term processes of which the Revolution was a part. Patriotism, loyalty, and nationalism were variant expressions of American differences, differences which began before 1763 and continued long after 1789. When St. Jean de Crèvecoeur asked: "What then is this American, this new man?" he posed a basic question that Americans have always felt compelled to answer. They felt compelled to explain the nature and source of American difference to the rest of the world. They were also compelled to explain Americans to themselves. And Europeans, Asians, and Latin Americans have subsequently found it necessary for psychological as well as cultural reasons to understand the phenomenon that is America.

While differences between America and Europe predate the American Revolution, the Revolution marks the beginnings of a mature self-awareness. Between Americans and other peoples differences do exist, and the differences are fundamental. It is not that Americans are "practical" or that their outlook is "pragmatic." The most pragmatic of formal philosophies subsequently stimulated by the American environment is hardly less spiritual than any of the schools stemming from the Academy. If Americans are more inventive than others, it is not because they are natively more ingenious. Inventiveness is a cultural trait, not a cultural ideal; boastfulness is a pattern of behavior, not a spiritual end. And the meanings that can be attached to respect for work and wealth refer to historical developments which combined to make America different.[4] The American experiment was unique in the history of the world. The uniqueness of the American experiment is the source of American ideals and the origin of the distinctive aspects of American culture.

Belief in man is the essence of the American faith. The American faith belongs to all the peoples of all the world from the Hebrew prophets to the French *philosophes*. But the great American contribution was to translate the ideal goals of humanity into possible goals. America, in other words, gave concrete substance to the timeless aspirations of mankind. And the American experience gave man a renewed faith in himself. Faith in mankind is the American spirit. The creation of institutions for the further development of mankind is the American experiment. The ideal of America, to state it somewhat differently, is mankind; the contribution of America was to expand the possibilities of mankind. The succeeding problem of continuing generations of Americans has been to discover newer means for the attainment of this end.[5]

Subsequent historical developments were woven into the evolving pattern, but belief in man and belief in human progress remained the core of American nationalism. Differing loyalties conditioned the interpretation of later events, for tradition characteristically serves multiple purposes and acquires multiple meanings. Tempered by change and molded by time, the American tradition often hardened into a sacred myth piously repeated. For others again it remained simply folklore more interesting as tales of a long dead past than as the sustaining belief of living men. For democrats, however, in America as elsewhere, the American faith served as a guide for present action and as a basis for future hope. Whatever the meanings attached to the tradition, it has always been central to the writing of American history.[6]

John Adams regarded the American Revolution as the "history of mankind during that epoch." If he erred, it was only because he narrowed the scope of the concept and limited the sweep of the temporal span. The nationalism of the postrevolutionary period was a cosmopolitan nationalism, for American nationalism, paradoxically, was an internationalism. It was rooted in humanity not in geography; it looked to the future as well as the present. The Declaration of Independence made no reference to a particular race, to a special religion, or to a distinctive nationality; it refers only to man. France, for example, is the nation of the French, England of the Angles and Germany of the Germans. The United States of America derives its power from the people and is created in their name. Long years afterward Supreme Court Justice Oliver Wendell Holmes commented that the very existence of the United States government constituted a threat to authoritarianism everywhere.

Oliver Wendell Holmes was doubtless correct. Democratic theory views government as an instrument, designed to fulfill the changing needs of man. The Declaration of Independence therefore was a challenge, not directed to Great Britain alone, but to the rulers of mankind. To "enlightened men" of the eighteenth century, the Declaration was a vindication and a hope; to others, it was an affront. That all men are created equal was an assertion that skeptical eighteenth-century aristocrats could dismiss with scorn. But the existence of a government deriving its just powers from the consent of the governed was an ideological threat. Discussions in the pages of John Locke or Jean Jacques Rousseau were simply sketches of heavenly cities by philosophers, whether of the eighteenth century or any other. But the establishment of a government dedicated to such notions was clearly an event of a different order. Divine monarchs and their royal ministers may for a time have permitted themselves the luxury of a doubt. Yet kings, princes, and ministers could not permit themselves the luxury of a frontal assault. And Thomas Jefferson had declared quite emphatically that "whenever any form of government becomes destructive of these ends, it is the right of the people to alter or abolish it."

Those for whom the ideas of Voltaire, Diderot, and Condorcet became a living faith believed that a common humanity gave all men the right to life and liberty, the right to happiness and to freedom in its pursuit. But the tough residues of history obstructed the attainment of the Enlightenment's view of progress. Men of the Enlightenment were confronted by a culture of caste and class, by a society which institutionalized inequality, by the fact of slavery, and by poverty everywhere. Cosmopolitanism, to be sure, was the credo of the enlightened brotherhood, but nationalism, social inequalities, and national antipathies were the persistent facts. Church and state were still tied in political and social partnership, and the union, when spelled out in dynamic political terms, meant official uniformity and a monopoly of official truth. The eighteenth century, like earlier and later eras, was mortgaged to the processes of history, but the great Declaration awakened ancient yearnings and promised the dissipation of ancient fears.[7]

American men of the Enlightenment felt with Thomas Paine that they had it in their "power to begin the world over again." And men in America have in fact constantly started the world over again. They mastered a continent and bent it to their wills. They attacked nature and held it hostage to their goals. They built settlements, villages, towns, and cities. They created machines and countless other devices for the living of life. But they also contributed to the remaking of the world by the reshaping of ideas. They gave concrete dimensions to human wants. They "laid an ax," in Thomas Jefferson's words, "to the foot of pseudo-aristocracy." Primogeniture went the way of entail, and quit rents followed state-supported religions into social oblivion. Gradually the abolition of imprisonment for debt, of barriers to education, of demeaning punishments, of property qualifications for the franchise molded an environment for the democratic experiment and made the hope of democracy safe for the world.

"The concept of freedom," wrote the philosopher Alfred North Whitehead, "has been narrowed to the picture of contemplative people shocking their generation. When we think of freedom, we are apt to confine ourselves to freedom of thought, freedom of the press, freedom for religious opinions. Then the limitations to freedom are conceived as wholly arising from the antagonisms of our fellow-men.

This is a thorough mistake. The massive habits of physical nature, its iron laws, determine the scene for the sufferings of men. . . . The essence of freedom is the practicability of purpose. Mankind has chiefly suffered from the frustration of its prevalent purposes, even such as belong to the very definition of its species. The literary expression of freedom deals mainly with the frills." [8]

Once the Declaration of Independence was written, its ideals continued to sustain American democrats. The fight for democratic freedoms in America is rich and varied and constitutes in a large and very important sense the history of the United States. It is the struggle to achieve the promise of America, the struggle to overcome human obstacles, to overcome human opposition, and to overcome human despair.

American experience gave the substance of reality to human purposes long considered beyond human reach. It enlarged the scope of the possible. In consequence of the extension of the area of "practicability," the literary expression of freedom acquired a hard texture of solidity. History is a part of the literature of freedom, for history traces the shifting frontiers of human "practicability" and records the changing boundaries of human purpose. And the writing of history in America, continuing the record, destroyed a whole series of limitations that older experience had imposed upon the purposes of man.

Americans, obviously enough, were deeply inspired by the role of their country in the endless struggle for human freedom. Historians were moved to tell the glowing story and to attempt to measure its significance. Some, less analytical than patriotic, proclaimed their version of the American message with prideful certainty. Others sought to comprehend the merger of past and present, to give meaning to their heritage, and to project its future course. They collected the records of achievement with tender care, gathering together all that remained of their heroes and of their heroic events. Libraries, museums, collections, letters, and a seemingly endless succession of documents, pamphlets, and books bespeak their unflagging belief and devotion. And the history they wrote contributed to one of the undeviating trends of American nationalism.

Enthusiasm for the American Revolution was not confined to America. Many Europeans shared with Americans a conviction that Concord, Lexington, and the Declaration of Independence revealed a segment of the future. Liberals and revolutionaries all over Europe took courage from the American experiment and sought to emulate it. Americans, on the other hand, warmed by approbation from overseas, were bolstered in their faith. Nor was it simply the specific, resounding events from the beginnings of the imperial conflict to the emergence of the United States. Rather it was the impact of continuing processes which deepened eighteenth-century belief in progress and the perfectibility of man.

Dissident Europeans were inspired by American events. Such European interest in the American struggle for independence suggests the vitality of the western tradition of liberty as well as the hopes yet remaining to be fulfilled. The writings of Frenchmen, Germans, and Irishmen document the international scope of the American Revolution and disclose important connections, intellectual and political, between thinkers in the western world. Affluent praise together with critical comment are projections of European dissatisfaction with the structure of contemporary society. European adulation tightened American determination, and produced conviction of the singular nature of the American Revolution and its role in the history of civilization.

America and the American Revolution were unique. America, its first citizens believed, was to modern history what Greece was to Rome. Democracy was to America what philosophy was to Greece. What became basic to the development of American nationality became basic to the development of the American historical tradition. Without an understanding of the sources of nationalism in America, it is difficult to understand the ideology of American historical writing. The American Revolution became the central theme of American historiography, and the Revolution remained central to the writing of history until the Civil War. The development of democracy, the major consequence of the Revolution, has always been the underlying concept in the writing of American history. It was, as Carl L. Becker said of eighteenth-century thought, "related to something that came before and to something else that came after." [9]

The impact of the American Revolution upon Europe was almost as wide as Europe itself. Contacts between France and America, for example, are legendary—to such a degree that much of it still remains legend rather than fact. Famed were the works of the provocative Abbé Raynal, whose influence upon the revolution in his own country is said to have been even greater than the influence of Jean Jacques Rousseau. Whatever his part in the French Revolution, he was the author of a volatile book: *Philosophical and Political History of the Settlement and Trade of the Europeans in the East and West Indies.*[10] Like his greater compatriot Voltaire,[11] he was far more interested in society and culture than in the dynasties of kings and the wars of men. His was a study of economic factors and their ramifications in the life, the thought, and the destiny of peoples. Following the prevailing literary convention, he held up the mirror of new-world society in which the inequities of Europe were garishly reflected. But Raynal did not always rely upon oblique techniques. He could, in the words of Bernard Faÿ, "give God a piece of his mind for having permitted so much suffering. A priest himself, he could curse the priests." [12]

That Raynal's writing was a strange blend of fact, fiction, and prejudice did not detract from its popularity. Other students of America copied from it generously without either permission or recognition; for America was in the public domain. Parts of it were republished in American journals, and the whole, after its translation in London in 1776, was circulated in America. In addition to the *Philosophical and Political History,* Raynal was the author of *Sentiments of a Foreigner on the Disputes of Great Britain with America* as well as a study of the American Revolution. If Europe suffered from his sharp condemnations, America emerged as the hope of the world. Americans were a living refutation of the European theory that men could not order society without priests, nobles, or kings. The free citizens of North America had but to keep steadfast in order to bring peace and happiness to the rest of mankind.[13]

To the adulation of American courage was added praise for American works. The American constitutions were reprinted and circulated in the capital of the French Bourbons as widely as Dr. Benjamin Franklin and his Gallic friends could manage. Louis Alexandre de La Rochefoucauld d'Enville, the very model of a liberty-loving duke, was one of those who early published such translations. Particularly favored was the constitution of the state of Virginia with its ringing declaration on human rights and human liberties.[14]

The American and the French revolutions stand together in sharp chronological outline. Great names and great movements, moreover, at once suggested an intellectual affinity which investigation has richly confirmed. If Benjamin Franklin was the first civilized American, it was partly because the first minds in Paris called him friend. One remembers the anecdote of Voltaire who, rebuked by his niece for speaking in English that she did not understand, answered: "I am proud of being able to speak the language of a Franklin." Jefferson recalls Gallic contacts as does Thomas Paine and Joel Barlow. The Baron de Montesquieu is almost as much a father of the Constitution of the United States as James Madison. And Jean Jacques Rousseau is as clearly a patron of democracy as Thomas Jefferson is its American saint. Indeed, the intellectual reciprocity between American and French culture in the era of revolution and reaction has dwarfed the contacts between America and other European states. Whatever the specific contributions of America to the internal revolt in France, the French Revolution delayed reform elsewhere. But while social and constitutional changes were postponed, liberal thought and action were stimulated by the controversy dividing the British Empire. Particularly was this true of the influence of the American Revolution on Great Britain itself. The American Revolution was one of the prime factors in the collapse of the Georgian reaction, although the French Revolution delayed constitutional reform until the following century.

Awareness of the nature of the English response to American resistance added new meanings to the Revolution. As understandings of the American Revolution altered, the significance of opinion on the other side of the Atlantic came to be appreciated. Once the conflict was viewed as a conflict within the empire as well as between Great Britain and colonial North America, it could no longer be explained in unsophisticated, unitary terms. The "Great Event" could thereafter hardly be explained as a contest between the forces of evil resident in the British Isles and the forces of virtue resident in America. The myth-making process, to use Sydney G. Fisher's uncompromising phrase, was challenged by a rigorous process of scholarly analysis. In consequence, the American Revolution emerged as a world movement which began before Concord and Lexington and continued after the Treaty of Paris in 1783. Rigid categories such as Whig and Tory, Patriot and Loyalist, turned out upon examination to be similar to rules that frequently prove the exception. Even today, as one student of the subject of British opinion in the revolutionary era suggests, we rarely think of the American Revolution as a civil war. Instead we tend to think of it as "the War of the Revolution, and then forget the significance of the word 'revolution.' " [15]

Colonial agitation coincided with a movement for parliamentary reform. George III was no "royal brute," but his kingship was dedicated to the maintenance of things as they were. For many an Englishman living in thriving port towns or in growing factory cities the slogan "taxation without representation" had very specific connotations. It meant rotten boroughs, the sale of parliamentary seats, and corruption in the royal administration. The rights of Englishmen seemed to be threatened once again, and British reformers viewed the threat in broad political terms rather than in narrow geographical ones. The emergence of the American issue induced a reexamination of basic constitutional premises.[16]

Disgruntled Englishmen in Britain concurred with disgruntled Englishmen in America. John Wilkes, idol of constitutional reformers, was a heroic figure, despite subsequent doubt regarding his devotion to the principles with which he was identified. After attacking the King's speech in 1763, he was deprived of his place in the Commons and put under an outlaw's ban. He was thrice elected to Parliament and thrice denied his seat. Finally, the pressure of public outrage dissuaded the government from continuing this unwise policy. To Americans, as to Englishmen, Wilkes was a symbol, and Boston's Sons of Liberty sent him heartening messages and more tangible aid in the form of money.[17] A member of the Patriotic Society in London wrote to "Mr. Adams of the American Congress": "Your cause and ours is one and the same. The present parliament of England, not being duly elected, has no right to make any laws, and consequently the people are not obliged to obey such as may be made by them. Be assured in us you will find every support in our power to give."[18] And Dr. Richard Price, whose *Observations on Civil Liberty*[19] sold more than 60,000 copies in a year, warned his readers that "we are not maintaining but violating our own constitution in America."[20]

Such attitudes were confirmed by Lord Effingham, who dramatically resigned his commission in the British army rather than fight against the colonials.[21] Major John Cartwright, a leading proponent of constitutional revision, took an active part in the war of pamphlets. Among other items he wrote *American Independence, the Interest and Glory of Great Britain* and *The Legislative Rights of the Commonality Vindicated; or Take Your Choice.*[22] A copy of the Declaration of Independence adorned the walls of his dining room, and he declined the offer of a lieutenancy in Lord Howe's command. These men believed with Richard Price that America was "the hope, and likely soon to be the refuge of mankind."[23]

Whatever the feelings at various levels of English society, American affairs received full press coverage. Colonial happenings had always been a lively topic, and the mounting differences within the empire directed an increasing amount of public attention to the conflict. Periodicals all over Europe gave the American colonies added space.[24] In London, *The London Review of English and Foreign Literature,* initiated in 1775, reported the imperial issue thoroughly.[25]

If English liberals found echoes of their own struggle in American resistance, Irish patriots found a model. Britain had long stored grapes of wrath in the fertile Irish vineyard, and British policy in North America confirmed ancient Irish animosities. All sections of the empire were apprehensive lest coercion in one part threaten the whole.[26] Large immigration from Ireland to America supplied palpable evidence that all was not well. And Irish reformers were quick to urge the connection between an oppressed peasantry and the constitutional issue in Ireland, Great Britain, and North America. American events received frequent attention in the Irish press. American disquisitions on grievances, liberally reprinted, were augmented by generous native contributions. Actually the relation between Ireland and America was far from remote. Grenville's financial program encompassed Ireland as well as America, and troops, requisitioned in Ireland, were to be maintained with Irish money. That Irishmen and Irish gold were to be used "to crush the spirit of the colonies" was an argument too obvious for any controversialist to neglect.[27]

The American appeal to a candid world did not go unanswered. Europe replied to American words and American deeds in thought as well as in action. New world events after 1763 spelled out in realistic detail what old world exponents of social change had long believed. Colonial defiance confirmed European assumptions about America. It also confirmed the fact of difference between America and Europe and suggested the meaning of that difference to the future of world society. But above all else Europe's response confirmed the faith of Americans in themselves.

Revolutionists in America undoubtedly hoped for foreign encouragement, but they could not have anticipated such widespread acclaim. English liberals often thought of Americans as Englishmen fighting the good fight in the tradition of Pym, Hampden, and Burke. German constitutionalists viewed the rift in a similar manner. To follow certain lines of American propaganda was not hard for such Germans. Although of a German dynasty, George III (unlike his grandfather, whom he succeeded) was born in England, and was an English king. But he yearned to be every inch a royal personage and took no pleasure in tendencies that threatened to limit monarchical prerogatives.

Even among lovers of kingship, there was restrained approval of the American cause. But German liberals for the most part had little reason to love their rulers, whether kings, princes, or grand dukes. One would expect the author of *Nathan the Wise* to find inspiration in the American upsurge, and Lessing does not disappoint us. Neither do Goethe and Schiller.[28] And the mighty Kant in far-off Königsberg expressed the opinion that no form of government had so much to recommend it as democracy. One enthusiastic German author, J. C. Schmohl, who wrote *Ueber Nordamerika und Demokratie*, actually set out to join the American revolutionists, only to be drowned en route. He not only believed in America, but he believed further that the hope of Europe depended upon the maintenance and development of American democracy.[29]

Like the remainder of Europe, the people of the Low Countries had aspirations that outside domination and antiquated institutions continued to frustrate. And like people all over the Continent they saw, first in America and later in France, the outlines of a pattern of resistance. The Austrian Netherlands, under Hapsburg rule, were almost constantly discontented until they finally became Belgium. Their Dutch neighbors were equally restive. In both sections local patriots hailed the Americans with unreserved feeling. The Belgians called one of their generals *Washington Belgique;* one of their leaders *Franklin des Belges.* Fomenters of an abortive Flemish uprising flung the very words of the Declaration of Independence in the teeth of Vienna. And Dutchmen openly identified themselves with the American Revolution, although endorsement of revolutionary sentiments was little favored by the aristocratic rulers of Holland.[30]

Italians reacted to the American Revolution in a similar manner. Disunited and oppressed, they were prepared to follow—if only they could—in the course of the rising western star which was America. Benjamin Franklin's very name had a kind of political magic in Italy as elsewhere. The strange combination of democrat and savant is still a combination somewhat mystifying to many class-conscious Europeans. *Poor Richard,* made available in several Italian cities, offered a prescription to other lowly apprentices. If artificial barriers were once broken, ability and hard work could be made to tell in favor of what an outworn social structure labeled "ordinary" men.[31]

European liberals shared with Americans the belief that the United States was to play a stellar role in the history of freedom. "The genuine liberty on which America is founded is totally and intirely [sic] a New System of Things . . ." wrote Thomas Pownall in 1783. "This is a principle in act and deed, and not a mere speculative theorem." Americans, Joseph Priestley declared, had created *"a completely New Government* on principles of equal liberty and the rights of man without Nobles, without Bishops and without a king." [32]

Praise, although enthusiastic, was far from universal. Liberal reformers were heartened, conservatives were either scornful or depressed. Kings, princelings, and their ministers were no more willing to accept the revolution in America than they were willing to accept the revolution in France a few years later. The American Revolution was for them a reversal of divine command, violating the fundamental principles of religion, of elemental decency, and of sound political theory. To advocate philosophical views of popular government was heresy; to put them into practice was treason.[33]

The United States of America was an ideological menace. Conservatives thereafter were no longer able to dismiss democratic government as visionary and absurd. They were compelled to revert to ridicule and to prophetic warnings of the imminent dissolution of the American experiment. Fear was also an ingredient of conservative European malice. What had happened on one side of the Atlantic might just as well happen on the other. And the feelings of the opponents of democratic government turned out in fact to be correct. The inauguration of George Washington as first president of the Republic took place in March 1789; the storming of the Bastille in July of the same year. The French Revolution was followed by others. If the eighteenth century signaled the era of natural rights, the nineteenth century might be called the era of revolutions.

European reflections on the course of American events constantly recharged the vigor of American patriotism. As Europeans mockingly discounted the democratic future, Americans came more deeply to believe in themselves. Each succeeding European revolution was hailed as a vindication. Each succeeding outburst against dynastic and aristocratic government demonstrated the continuing influence of the "spirit of '76." Whether European reflections were favorable or unfavorable, it was Europe after all that provided Americans with a measure of comparison. Only by comparing existing institutions could Americans evaluate the quotient of social difference; only by comparing degrees of difference could Americans project the curve of probable change. The record of what men in America had in fact accomplished offered a solid basis for confidence. Although European awareness of America was constant from Christopher Columbus to Benjamin Franklin, the Revolution gave a new political dimension to the process of interaction. Old-world images of America were fashioned out of yearnings and frustrations. They were also fashioned out of the hardest social and economic realities: the realities of power and privilege.

VIII

The Makers of American History
and Their Historians, I

"When I look back on the processes of history," wrote Woodrow Wilson, himself an historian, "when I survey the genesis of America, I see this written on every page: that the nations are renewed from the bottom, not from the top; that the genius which springs up from the ranks of unknown men is the genius which renews the youth and energy of a people. Everything I know about history, every bit of experience and observation that has contributed to my thought, has confirmed me in the conviction that the real wisdom of human life is compounded out of the experiences of ordinary men. The utility, the vitality, the fruitage of life does not come from the top to the bottom; it comes, like the natural growth of a great tree, from the soil, up through the trunk into the branches to the foliage and the fruit. The great struggling unknown masses of the men who are at the base of everything are the dynamic force that is lifting the level of society. A nation is as great, and only as great, as her rank and file." [1]

History is in fact made by all men. But, to paraphrase Cicero's famous remark, all men do not do the same things nor do they perform them in the same way. Woodrow Wilson was too intimately aware of the function of creative leadership in a democracy to be heedless of such a critical distinction. He was a democratic leader, and he understood the role of leadership in the making and remaking of history.[2] He was deeply conscious of what he owed to the people, and others, if not Wilson himself, were conscious of what the people owed to him.

Wilson was probably right. A society is no better than its people, and the types of men thrust into positions of leadership provide a reliable index of cultural values. Stated differently, what it is possible for men to become expresses the social spirit. But Woodrow Wilson was far from suggesting an antithesis between society and the individual, for in Wilson's historical terms individual growth and social development were parts of an organic process. The logic of process makes every historical period a continuous part of the flow of change. Some periods, however, seem at given points of time to be more consequential than others. The American Revolution was such a period. For Americans it was *the* period, it became the "Great Event." The men and women who dramatically contributed to the making of independence, to the winning of the war, and to the establishment of the state and national governments became the makers of American history. Places associated with such events and the documents connected with them—meetings, battles, buildings, and official papers—became almost as meaningful for posterity as for those who were alive when the events were made. Mount Vernon is a national shrine; the Declaration of Independence a part of the American Scripture. The signers of the Declaration are the heroes of democracy; the "founding fathers" of the Constitution are the patriarchs of the Republic. The Constitution itself is the American Covenant.

Enthusiasm for the formative years of the nation has always been something more than undiluted patriotism. Undiscriminating loyalties helped to manufacture the more elegant legends, and the fertile crop of patriotic myth thrives as lustily as debunking critics. Myth and legend have both nurtured American nationalism. The national spirit, in fact, has received so much patriotic nutriment that it threatens periodically to burst its bonds.

Every variety of need and emotion entered into the American identification with the revolutionary epoch. There was no symbol of American unity in 1776 or in 1783: no royal house, no patron saint, no mythical beginnings. Unity of feeling and a sense of participation in shared purposes were blurred by thirteen political entities separated by geography, history, and tradition. New England was over a hundred and fifty years old at the time of the battle of Lexington, an age the United States was not to reach until Calvin Coolidge became president.

The thirteen commonwealths were inhabited by different ethnic groups; by people who came from different countries and who practiced different forms of religion. They were identified with different social classes, differing aspirations, and diverse ideals. Americans were under compulsion to create a unity and to create a tradition. Nor did they simply have to create unities out of national, sectional, and religious diversities. They also felt compelled to emancipate themselves from cultural dependence upon Britain. To bind Germans, Irishmen, and Englishmen together, to fashion a social fabric ample enough to contain Catholics, Congregationalists, and Methodists, to unite North, South, and West within a national framework —all these were difficult enough. But to create a new nation with the history, the language, and the values of the former English enemy was more difficult still. For Americans who had so recently been Englishmen resident in the colonial dominions of the British Empire, it was the dominating cultural drive. The American Revolution alone provided a body of common experience. The experience of the Revolution evoked a response that nothing else could quite supply. These experiences were confined neither to the North nor to the South. They were peculiar neither to Massachusetts nor to New Jersey, to Quakers nor to Baptists. They were, in fact, American.

Need for unity was negative as well as positive. Americans required social coherence to withstand divisive internal stress. They also required social coherence to withstand external intellectual assault. They were under the most desperate urge to justify themselves in a condescending monarchical world. "It was very doubtful whether the states would be able to come together and form a national government," Sydney G. Fisher wrote later. "Many thought that some of them might go back under British control. When a national constitution was at last adopted, it was regarded by the rest of the world and even by ourselves, as an experiment which very likely might not in the end succeed. In Europe, it was largely regarded as a ridiculous experiment. Our democratic ideas and manners were despised and our . . . crudeness contrasted with the settled comfort and refinement of the old nations. We felt all this keenly. . . . They [the revolutionary generation] strove to give dignity and respect to everything; to make no damaging admissions. . . . It was, therefore, perhaps too much to expect that they would describe the factions and turmoil of the Revolution. . . . So they described a Revolution that never happened and never could happen." [3] Americans had to justify independence less than they had to justify the theory of independence. Independence justified itself; Saratoga, Yorktown, and the Treaty of Paris had established it. The theory of independence was a matter on a different level of social need. Secession was rebellion from constituted authority, and rebellion in the name of human rights belonged to a different category of human experience. Successful rebellion presented Americans with embarrassing problems. The pale precedents of Greece, Rome, and the Italian city states supplied little guidance for a new republican society. Ideals of human equality were hardly more than literary affirmations unsullied by attempted human practice. Full-bodied words are the referents of individual deeds and social experiences. Democracy had to be experienced before democracy could be vindicated. Americans had to test out their attitudes and to experiment with their faith. They had to revise old institutions and to create new ones. They had even to formulate a language appropriate to the task. Pressures such as these account for the conscious striving and the unconscious myth-making among the first American patriots. They also account for much of the aggressive nationalism during the early decades of statehood. But the purposes ascribed to the lives of the revolutionary generation and the meanings derived from their activities gave Americans an enduring faith and an enduring tradition.[4]

The Revolution is one of the major themes in American historiography because the Revolution marks the beginning of the American democratic experiment. But while America had its enemies in Europe, it also had plenty of detractors at home. Democratic idealism was combated as ardently on the western side of the Atlantic as on the eastern side. Other ideals, equally powerful, disputed the claims of democracy as the primal American faith. Two levels of revolutionary tradition were immediately apparent. One phase of the Revolution represented a thrust against the oppression of a remote king whose emissaries seemed bent upon thwarting the legitimate yearnings of colonial men of affairs. This was the revolution against the tyranny of the metropolis versus the colony, a tyranny that sacrificed colonial interests to imperial interests. Whether the interests were concerned with commerce, industry, or expansion westward, it was a clash between national and local power and advantage. But there was another revolution genetically related to the first, yet separate from it. This was the revolt which, in the words of Tom Paine, centered in "the new method of thinking that hath arisen," the new thinking about the rights of man. American common sense stressed the contrast between the old Europe and the new America. Many concurred with the sagacious Dr. Benjamin Franklin that Europe, including England, was verging upon decay. Most Americans shared an already well-established conviction that the new world represented the hope of the future. At least it held what future there was for the underprivileged of the eighteenth century. In any case there was hope in America, for Europe to them meant an aristocratic class system and restricted social and economic opportunities. Unclear though many aspirations were, Britain suggested the past and the maintenance of privilege, while America promised an immediate future of opportunity compounded of land, a vote, and a broadening highway to social status. That Englishmen in Great Britain participated in this vision with Englishmen in North America gave substance and reality to these humanitarian dreams.

But all Americans were not in accord. They were in disagreement during the perilous years from 1763 to 1776, and the basic division of attitude continued throughout the course of national development. Early patriarchs of Massachusetts Bay and New Haven, for example, were strangers to democracy and could truthfully say that they regarded it as the worst of all possible social arrangements. Modern critics of democracy, no less truthful though less forthright, look to history to justify the assertion that democracy was never the intention of the colonial leaders or the founding fathers. Modern research seems to corroborate their history of events, but it does not confirm their interpretation of historical process. The theory of democracy developed in spite of efforts to stifle or to curtail it.[5]

The earliest advocates of human rights invited men to think of liberty; American experience invited men to struggle for it. Roger Williams wrote in 1644: "The sovereign, original, and foundation of civil power, lies in the people. . . . And if so, that a people may erect and establish what forms of government seem to them most meet. . . . It is evident that such governments . . . have no more power, nor for no longer time than . . . the people consenting and agreeing, shall betrust them with." Slightly more than a century later, Jonathan Mayhew, pastor of Boston's West Church, expressed the same doctrine in almost secular terms. "What unprejudiced man," he asked, "can think that God made *all* to be thus subservient to the lawless pleasure and frenzy of *one,* so that it shall always be a sin to resist him? . . . For a nation thus abused to rise unanimously and resist their prince, even to the dethroning of him, is not criminal, but a reasonable way of vindicating their liberties and just rights: it is making use of the means, which God has put in their power for mutual and self defence. And it would be highly criminal in them not to make use of this means." And Thomas Paine, propagandist extraordinary, allied himself with history: "Every spot of the old world is overrun with oppression. Freedom has been hunted round the globe. Asia and Africa have long expelled her. Europe regards her like a stranger, and England hath given her warning to depart. O! receive the fugitive, and prepare in time an asylum for mankind." [6]

Once the Declaration of Independence was written, its ideals served to sustain American democrats. But for Americans of 1776, the Declaration of Independence had at least two meanings. All who agreed upon separation from Britain were technically revolutionists. Yet all who agreed to independence or who acquiesced after independence was declared did not do so for identical reasons. Regardless of the differences prompting those who supported or later condoned secession, they all became Patriots. Although actions and attitudes suggested the varieties of motivation during the struggle itself, distinctions became less clear after the events. In fact the large, all-inclusive distinction between Patriots and Loyalists became standard. Crises are uncongenial to subtleties, and the emotional demands of patriotism make simplicity rather than honesty the best policy. Oversimplification obscured the nature of the revolutionary conflict, the period of Confederation, and the movement for the Constitution.

Whenever the Revolution was regarded as a clash between Patriots and Loyalists alone, it became a clash between colony and mother country. So single-minded a view warped fundamental meanings. Englishmen, Americans among them, were engaged in a movement for political, social, and economic change. If other Englishmen, wherever they chanced to live, opposed it, the contest was nonetheless more international than local. Only in the narrowest historical terms can the Revolution be regarded as a secessionist uprising followed by an effort to repress it. Since, as a matter of fact, the American nation appeared at the end of the war, the conflict has often been viewed as a war between nations instead of a war within an empire, a war, moreover, with global repercussions. The American Revolution was a civil war and an ideological revolt. The heritage of patriotic intensity positing a clear-cut division between virtue and justice on the one side and tyranny and oppression on the other made discrimination a virtual affront. Fixation by propagandists upon the king as the "royal brute of Britain" or upon the Parliament that deprived upright colonials of their traditional liberties deflected analytical attention from the underlying assumptions of both: power, its uses, and the responsibilities of governments for the common weal.

More than the Revolution was confounded by the testament of uncritical idolators. Reverence for the sacred years 1763 to 1776 or the years 1776 to 1783, a span no less sacred, has metamorphosed a chronological segment into an era of historical continuity. There was a revolutionary period, but there was also a revolutionary generation. And the generation who made the Revolution had historical antecedents and historical consequences. John and Samuel Adams, Thomas Jefferson, and James Madison were eighteenth-century gentlemen who lived on into the nineteenth. John Adams survived the movement for the Constitution and his own presidency and mellowed sufficiently to entertain an appreciation of Jefferson, if not of Jeffersonian principles. Jefferson, like Adams, lived long enough to see the Revolution, the Constitution, and his own tenure as chief executive become history. Sam Adams, very much on the scene when the proponents of the new frame of government were making their bid for popular approval, found it a cause to which he could not lend his enthusiastic support. And Madison was in the White House himself when Napoleon Bonaparte was tearing up the map of Europe and sowing new seeds of revolution from the Rhine to the Volga. The decades from the end of the Anglo-French War in 1763 to the advent of Jeffersonian Republicanism constitute a series of sequential developments, which began earlier than Britain's conquest of New France and which still continue.

The problems of 1783 to 1789 were of course different from those of 1763 to 1776. The underlying issues and the underlying motives of behavior were not, however, dissimilar. Problems of ordering society, of forming governments, of distributing and controlling power in terms of the perennial conflict of interests remained constant. Altered circumstances produced altering perspectives, but the nature of society and the nature of man remained in the background of motivation and in the foreground of debate. The conservatives of 1763 for the most part were the conservatives of 1776. The radicals of 1776 remained the radicals of 1789. Those who became "reluctant revolutionists" [7] at the time of independence remained so even if they took the title of Whig and were called Patriot. There were exceptions on both sides. Yet without hypotheses of multiple causation and the thesis that the Revolution was a continuing revolution, comprehension eludes us. When Yorktown and Saratoga ended the war, as Dr. Benjamin Rush of Philadelphia proclaimed, the Revolution had only just begun.

Among the men who helped to begin the war there were those who wished no part in revolution. They wished to achieve revolutionary ends without revolutionary means. The means they employed were far from decorous and often explosive, but war with

Britain and separation from the British crown were never parts of their plan. Pressure was legal, and agitation stemmed too smoothly from resistance. Reluctant revolutionists were saved from becoming loyalists by the movement of time, not by conviction. When decision had at last to be made, Tories found they had become Whigs by virtue of acts that neither an irate king nor a badgered government could easily condone. While they had always been extremely clear about the imperial threat to home rule, they had always been just as clear about who should rule at home. If this made them Whigs and Patriots, it did not make them social reformers. They helped to make the civil war with England, but any part they may have had in the revolution for social change was affected against their will and without their conscious assistance.

The American Revolution was also made by men even farther removed from the spirit of revolt than conservative colonials who resented commercial and administrative restraints. Philip Guedalla suggestively remarks that Louis XVI, George III, and the Right Honorable Lord North fathered the American Revolution.[8] Louis XVI never said that he was the state and rarely acted as if he believed it. The sixteenth Louis was not even the shadow of a proper autocrat, but his ministers whose urge to humble Britain had become a passion, made Louis the ally of the American Revolution.

George III was no Bourbon but he consistently confused the royal prerogative with the facts of British life. The royal prerogative should be confined to royal times, and however regal George III accounted himself, England, though far from democratic, was not royal either. England was on the verge of her career as a monarchy without monarchical principles. Though not obtuse, George was dull. He was too dull to permit his people to lead him and he was too regal to lead his people. Granted that from the royal park at Windsor the issues of American defiance appeared less volatile than from mercantile houses on Boston's King Street, the imperial mind could only see that "the colonies must either submit or triumph." The royal prerogative, well suited to subjects awaiting the sovereign's pleasure in the antechamber, was ill suited to colonials who cherished the symbols of kingship less than they cherished the traditions of 1688. George III gloried in the name of Britain, as his two Hanovarian predecessors did not, but he understood neither British history nor human passions. The equestrian statue in London's Cockspur Street might well adorn Broadway in New York, for, as Guedalla points out, George III himself sired revolution.

Others on the English side abetted the coming of separation. One was George Grenville, whose name attached to the tax acts has made him a minor figure in the schoolboy roster of tyranny. Alone of the men in the government, Grenville had made a study of America. But Grenville's study was the study of an administrator, solemn, competent, and unrelieved by imagination. He was able and conscientious, a reasonably competent lawyer and a faithful public servant. But he had the mind of an accountant, which, though valuable for the science of profit and loss, is something less than the wisdom demanded by the crises of history. Charles Townshend, chancellor of the exchequer, equally able and equally well informed on many matters save those immediately pertinent to the American issue, contributed to the making of the United States by well-intentioned ignorance. And Lord North, henchman to His Majesty George III, followed Grenville and Townshend in an attempt to prove a point that could be proved only by not making it. For students of the American Revolution Woodrow Wilson's conclusions are obvious. Grenville, Townshend, and North could not serve their king by defying him, and loyalty to George III put a premium upon slavish obedience. The king was England, and no party was great or powerful enough —nor indeed sufficiently a party—to destroy the figment that the crown magically canceled out differences. Even Pitt, Earl of Chatham, who rejoiced that the Americans had resisted, wished that all factions might be absorbed under the symbol of royalty. Chatham's wish was no more consistent with reality than the contention of unlimited parliamentary supremacy and the constitutional impropriety of American taxes. It almost seemed that he abjured consistency, a virtue sometimes less valuable than it appears, for as a consummate essayist has written, it "provides dull politicians with a convenient substitute for judgment." [9] The nature of British society during the reign of George III placed men of a certain type in public life. They were men who, regardless of their excellencies and qualities, were unable to grapple with history. Great Britain, on the eve of the Revolution, had no institutional resources to meet it. George I and George II flouted the authority of Parliament; George III, in spite of his professions of respect, circumvented Parliament by creating an oligarchy of aristocratic cliques. England had yet to develop a responsible system of party government, and only a responsible government or an autocratic government can successfully meet a crisis. The government of George III was neither.[10]

Dissent is a part of the logic of human association. Intellectual differences and differences of social and economic interest invariably exist. Dissent may be inarticulate but it is always latent, and there is never complete unanimity on any public issue. The margin of dissent may not be politically significant, but there is always a margin of difference. Whenever the channels for the expression of difference permit, differences emerge. The ineptitude of Britain's governing class provoked opposition on both sides of the Atlantic. And the opposition to the government's American policies aided not only in the making of the Revolution but in the making of democracy. Resistance provoked debate and debate in turn gave new life to the political principles of the English tradition, of Magna Carta, of Pym, of Hampden, and of the seventeenth-century Bill of Rights. American resentment, whatever Lord Chatham actually thought, was also historically important because it revived the British legacy of individual liberty and accelerated the Georgian collapse. The American reaction to the specific programs of Grenville, Townshend, and North stimulated resistance to other grievances objectionable on the same principles and the same theoretical grounds. George III and his ministers could not silence John Wilkes and Joseph Priestley, and James Otis, John Adams, and John Dickinson spoke and wrote with the impunity of freeborn Englishmen living three thousand miles away. Conservative Britons in the American colonies—Daniel Dulany, Joseph Galloway, and Samuel Seabury—argued with the even-tempered insistence of loyal subjects of the crown whose ministers threatened to destroy a common nation. Such conservatives, even if they had no intellectual connection with reformist desires, buttressed them simply by entering their protests. The history of democratic development is a history of protest, and in the eighteenth-century British context virtually every protest was a thrust at Georgian complacency.

American Loyalists eloquently supported the monarchical principle and the unity of Britain. If they left the colonies, leaving meant a painful uprooting; if they remained, remaining meant a painful adjustment.[11] Before leaving and while remaining, many had the courage to speak out their minds. Their feelings and their arguments became parts of the American design. Intelligent and articulate Loyalists anchored intemperate flights of patriot extremism in reason and supplied a hard core of history and logic against which democratic polemics had to make their way. The American Revolution was also an evolution. And in the evolution of ideas, the spirited conservative dialectic was indispensable. Conservatives, ardent Englishmen and ardent opponents of government programs, made expanding privileges for ordinary men possible, however much they objected to them. All kinds of men with all varieties of motivation united to make the American Revolution. Virginia orators and Massachusetts lawyers collaborated with periwigged gentlemen in Whitehall to shape the conditions leading to independence. Pennsylvania farmers and Westchester parsons, a well-known corsetmaker, and thousands of unknown militiamen channeled events into the flow of social change. Tories have but recently received the discrimination which is their due. A faint odor of treason still clings to their reputation and even when absolved of intellectual dishonesty they stand convicted of disloyalty. To the victors belong the plaudits as well as the spoils. Defeat is the road to oblivion, but victory and the historian's zeal cannot always recreate the hero remembered as a general or the founding father who was less of a patriarch than he was a man.

The Revolution was fought with words before it was fought with deeds. British tradition is to defend fundamental rights with musket in hand only after a constitutional brief has failed to secure them. Before Concord and Lexington, as well as afterwards, Englishmen objected to their government with the legal weapons of learning and the carefully balanced thrusts of argument. Debate produced a sparkling literature, and the literature of debate became the basis of national historiography.

The era of the Revolution is the era of the pamphlet.[12] Between the beginning of the controversy at the end of the French war in 1763 until the end of the American war in 1783, approximately nine thousand items came off the American press. Of these books, newspapers, and broadsides printed by the two hundred American presses,[13] some two thousand were pamphlets dealing with the divisive issues of society. Whether regarded as books or pamphlets is a convention, for it is their importance that really matters. Together with books, journals, diaries, letters, and state papers written in America and elsewhere, they constitute an evocative part of the literary record of the Revolution.

For the purpose of the communication of ideas, pamphlets were better than books. They were inexpensive to produce and could be circulated easily and cheaply. Time is the essence of crisis, and pamphlets took less time to write or to read than books. On the whole they were excellent, in part because the authors were trained in the eighteenth-century school of literary journalism and in part because they were versed in law, politics, and history. Those who wrote them believed what they wrote and were conscious of the personal and social consequences of the issues. Though the immediate issue has long since been settled, the ultimate issues—the governance of man and the nature of society—are still uppermost in the thoughts of large segments of humankind.

Among the early pamphleteers of the Revolution was James Otis whose writs of assistance have become parts of American folklore, and Otis himself is also something of a legend.[14] Born in Massachusetts and graduated from Harvard, he was kin to the indomitable Warrens and colleague of the Adams clan. He spoke "the prologue"[15] of revolution and after the year 1769, he held his melancholy peace. John Adams was present in court when the argument on the writs of assistance was made. Always happy with a pen in hand, Adams took full notes on the legal sources and afterward recalled that "his argument, speech, discourse, oration, harangue—call it by which name you will—was the most impressive upon his crowded audience of any I ever heard before or since, excepting only many speeches by himself in Faneuil Hall and in the House of Representatives. . . ."[16] George Bancroft, whose passionate search for liberty often caused him to find evidence when none existed, regarded this episode as "the opening scene of American resistance."[17] It was an important argument, even if not as weighty as Adams assumed. Yet it suggests the intensity with which Englishmen in America were attached to English liberties and the extent to which some Englishmen had forgotten them. "I argue this cause"—Otis declaimed—"as it is in favor of British liberty, at a time when we hear the greatest monarch upon earth declaring from his throne that he glories in the name of Briton, and that the privileges of his people are dearer to him than the most valuable prerogatives of his crown; and it is in opposition to a kind of power the exercise of which, in former periods of English history cost one king of England his head, and another his throne. . . . The writ prayed for in this petition, being general, is illegal. It is a power that placed the liberty of every man in the hands of every petty officer. . . . Every one, with this writ, may be a tyrant."[18]

This dramatic plea made James Otis a power within the Massachusetts radical group. His writing was as eloquent as his courtroom oratory, but he was too "disordered" intellectually and too "unsteady"[19] temperamentally always to be consistent. He wrote tellingly and with fervor, but his prose is distinguished by a controversial style rather than by grace or learning. His first essay, published in 1762, *A Vindication of the Conduct of the House of Representatives of the Province of Massachusetts Bay*,[20] indicates all his stylistic and mental characteristics. Without accepting Adams' extravagant enthusiasm,[21] it would be unwise to reject its virtues: humor, irony, strength. It had, in addition, ideas some of which Thomas Jefferson was to set forth in his own finished prose. "1. God made all men naturally equal. 2. The idea of earthly superiority, preeminence, and grandeur are educational;—at least acquired, not innate. 3. Kings were—and plantation governors should be—made for the good of the people, and not the people for them. 4. No government has a right to make hobby-horses, asses, and slaves of the subjects, nature having made sufficient of the two former, . . . but none of the last,—which infallibly proves they are unnecessary." [22]

It was in the *Vindication* that Otis presented his thesis of British constitutionalism. Here he offered the proposition that as colonists of Britain, Americans were entitled to all the rights of Englishmen. It followed that none could be taxed without consent. But *The Rights of the British Colonies Asserted and Proved,* 1764, advanced his more fully matured political doctrine. "We love, esteem, and reverence our mother-country, and adore our king. And should the choice of independence be offered the colonies, or subjection to Great Britain upon any terms above absolute slavery, I am convinced they would accept the latter." [23] At the same time he insisted that ultimate power rested with the people who in turn delegated such power for specific purposes. Among those purposes, he said in accents soon to have a familiar national ring, was "the good of mankind . . . to provide for the security, the quiet, and happy enjoyment of life, liberty, and property." [24] Again, in the following year, 1765, he answered a Briton's defense in *Considerations on Behalf of the Colonists*. Still professing allegiance to king and country, he provocatively called attention to the fact that revolutions could occur in the future as they had in the past. [25]

Considerations on Behalf of the Colonists was a great effort. Moses Coit Tyler, [26] whose opinions have rarely been injudicious, regarded this piece of Otis' as having become "for a time one of the legal text-books of the opponents of the ministry; it was a law arsenal, from which other combatants, on that side, drew some of their best weapons." [27] Otis himself had finished his work. Although he continued to write, he added little to what he had already accomplished.

Otis dominated the first stage of the literary debate; the second stage was dominated by John Dickinson. While the services of Otis cannot be dismissed, Dickinson was a thinker of far greater power, and his genius for subtle distinction quite surpassed the Otis analytical touch. [28] He was so subtle, so given to splitting the thinnest hair of logic into a principle of political difference, that his critics, who latterly outnumbered his steadfast friends, regarded this capacity as his greatest failing. Edward Rutledge of South Carolina, who had once stood by his side, felt that his besetting weakness was "refining too much." [29] Once the heat of debate was succeeded by the fury of combat, there was no place for Dickinson's verbal dexterity.

Dickinson hailed from the Chesapeake Bay area of Maryland, a region noted for the wealth of its great plantations and the gentility of its proprietors. He began the reading of law in Philadelphia and completed his legal studies in the years from 1753 to 1756 at the Middle Temple in London. They were happy years for Dickinson, but they acquainted him with the England suggested by the constitutional maxims of 1688. Such a vision of the old country did not conform to reality, especially after the colonial controversy had begun. His conciliatory attitude toward Britain was based in part upon expectations that the actual state of society made impossible.[30]

A master pamphleteer, Dickinson wrote swiftly, incisively, and well. He was a brilliant lawyer, a prosperous landed proprietor, and a successful man of affairs. Public life occupied the greater amount of his time and energy. From 1760 to 1776 he was almost constantly a member of the Pennsylvania Assembly. In 1765 he was in the Stamp Act Congress and from 1774 to 1776 he served in the Continental Congress. After another term in 1779, he became successively president of the supreme executive council—or governor—in Maryland (1781) and in Pennsylvania (1782).[31] His production was prodigious. Among the many state papers of which he was the author were the "Declaration of Rights" and the "Petition to the King," both promulgated by the Stamp Act Congress. He also prepared the Pennsylvania "Revision of the Bill of Rights" in 1776 and the first draft of the Articles of Confederation.[32]

John Dickinson spoke out for the inalienable rights of Englishmen, but he spoke with the voice of moderation. He yielded to none in his unreserved criticism of English acts that he regarded as acts of aggression, bordering on tyranny, but there was no more consistent advocate of conciliation. Dickinson never wavered in the belief that Great Britain alone could make America independent. Misguided ministers, for the moment in power, might commit acts of folly capable of precipitating it. But if Dickinson could prevent any similar rashness coming to the aid of the king's servants from the American side, he felt it his duty to do so. Opposed to independence, he later reconciled himself to its existence after the fact. Independence, however, came in spite of all he could do to prevent it.[33]

Following passage of the Townshend Acts, Dickinson wrote the

Letters from a Farmer in Pennsylvania to the Inhabitants of the British Colonies,[34] pronounced by Moses Coit Tyler "the most brilliant event in the literary history of the Revolution," [35] Dickinson acquired both a continental and an international reputation. The *Letters* were carried by almost every newspaper in America.[36] They were translated into French, and Benjamin Franklin wrote the introduction for an English edition. Altogether eight separate editions appeared in the colonies, one in Virginia prepared by Richard Henry Lee; another by James Otis in Massachusetts. Known thereafter as the Pennsylvania Farmer, he was welcomed by London, and the College of New Jersey (later Princeton) awarded him an honorary degree.[37]

Letters from a Farmer were worthy of every admiration, for Dickinson was not one to rely upon mealy words. Independence was at all costs to be shunned, but there was nothing of concession to fundamental principle in his plea. Patriotism there was, but the roots of loyalty were embedded in English culture and reflected in the majesty of the English crown. Liberty there was, but it was the ancient liberties of Englishmen to which Dickinson referred and the law owed to each class its privileges and its rights. "Let these truths be indelibly impressed on our minds: that we cannot be happy, without being free; that we cannot be free, without being secure in our property; that we cannot be secure in our property, if without our consent, others may, as by right, take it away; that taxes imposed on us by parliament, do thus take it away." [38] Dickinson the constitutional lawyer as well as Dickinson the controversialist was too astute to make a distinction between internal and external taxes. He admitted the sovereignty of Parliament, but denied its right to tax the American colonies at all. By virtue of its supremacy, Parliament could regulate the trade of the empire. If revenue derived from the power to regulate imperial trade, it was hardly the same as imposing a tax upon the colonies. Like the good lawyer he was, Dickinson maintained that it was the intent of a parliamentary act, not its consequences, that governed. Yet all constitutional schemes which aimed to set the imperial organization aright collided with events. And the Townshend Acts, far from ending the struggle, simply shifted the great controversy into another and far more acrimonious stage.[39]

There were arguments on all sides to meet every event. Another Philadelphia lawyer offered a solution which, if inappropriate for the needs of the British Empire in the eighteenth century, became the essence of the solution in the twentieth. James Wilson, addressing Englishmen and Americans alike, proposed in *Considerations on the*

Nature and Extent of the Legislative Authority of the British Parliament, that the colonies were actually beyond the legislative authority of Parliament.[40] Unlike most members of the fraternity of constitutional lawyers, Wilson was not under the spell of the doctrine of absolute sovereignty. The king was the sovereign thread that tied the dominions together. "Allegiance to the king and obedience to Parliament are founded on very different principles. The former is founded on protection; the latter, on representation. An inattention to this difference has produced, I apprehend, much uncertainty and confusion in our ideas concerning the connexion, which ought to subsist between Great Britain and the American colonies." [41]

Wilson holds a towering place in the history of American law. Authorship of *Considerations* at the age of thirty-two was hardly short of precocity and a brilliant performance at any age. As an eminent professor of law in the United States, he wielded a commanding influence upon developing legal ideas and institutions. But it was his public record in the period before the University of Pennsylvania professorship that gives James Wilson a special historical place. At the beginning of the revolutionary war, he was a member of the Second Continental Congress. Only six men were the signers of both the Declaration of Independence and the Constitution. Of these six, Wilson was one. And he alone of the whole large contingent representing Pennsylvania at the Convention of 1787 sat in the state constitutional convention that ratified the national document.

The heroes of the revolutionary era were men of ample talent. Tradition has perpetuated numerous character types. Washington has become the national hero, Thomas Paine the propagandist, Sam Adams the master of politics. Benjamin Franklin is the philosophical sage, Thomas Jefferson the philosopher of democracy. Franklin was too wise to be simply a patriarchal sage, Washington too human to be simply a national hero. And Thomas Jefferson was the philosopher of democracy because he was the first mature practitioner of it in the actual realm of politics. Patrick Henry, Richard Henry Lee, and John Dickinson were peerless orators, but Henry was at least nominally a general, Lee a statesman, and Dickinson a constitutional theorist. James Otis too was an orator as well as a trial lawyer and a political organizer. And these characteristics were as true of Patrick Henry as of James Wilson. Samuel Adams, the political genius, was no less of a genius in the writing of electrifying prose. His was a personality that brought out hidden strengths in others, making determination grow where only indecision had existed before.

Unlike biography, which has its own limitations, the literary sweep of historical narration frequently splits the human personality. Representatives of the revolutionary generation in many instances lived to complete independence, to frame the Constitution, and to preside over the fortunes of the new republic. While men altered their views, they did not alter their personalities. The age of the Revolution began before and continued after the events of revolution. "It is . . . [the] continuity of conflict that gives coherence to political history . . . ," writes one of the most cogent students of the Confederation years. "Many men and events must be ignored, or their significance distorted, if they are fitted into a pattern that assumes a sharp break in political history in 1776." [42] And what is true of the period after 1776 is also true in a more restricted sense of the period before 1776.

The conflict of ideas and the struggle for power continued only in part because the leading participants were often the same, or because men at various points of the political spectrum passed on their ideas to their intellectual heirs. The contest was continuous because the nature of the social task was similar—the task of organizing a government based upon popular sovereignty coupled with the task of controlling power. At this intellectual juncture the central historical and historiographical problems converge. These problems are among the most important in American historiography, for they have complicated American thought and American historical writing since the Revolution. Men who believed in the traditional liberties as then understood did not believe in democracy as now understood. Men who believed in democracy believed also in the historic principles of English liberty, but they had little experience and few institutions capable of operating popular sovereignty. The philosophy of democracy had begun to develop; the political theory of democracy had yet to mature. Popular sovereignty grew out of the principles of English liberty as well as the experiences of the American people. But in the era of the American Revolution they were not the same.

Patterns of ideas were changing, but all men did not alter their views of man and society at the same time or in the same degree. Liberty did not want for defenders, but liberty had many and diverse meanings. There were "crown men" in the colonies as well as partisans of the people's cause. These words and their conceptual referents have an honorable background of historical usage. Yet like Patriot and Loyalist, Whig and Tory, they have not always served as aids to understanding. Patriots were not always democrats and loyalists were not always monarchists. Followers of liberty were not always advocates of the people's cause at least in the sense in which democrats came later to understand it. And defenders of the people were not always intellectually one with their allies, however resolutely they defended the precious liberties of English law and custom.

English liberties had no more loyal or learned champion than honest John Adams.[43] As genuine a maker of history as any of his contemporaries, Adams worked in the people's cause without fully believing in the people. Always a sturdy opponent of the "crown men," he helped to further the growth of democracy although not himself a democrat. While historians have been appreciative of John Adams, history has treated him less generously. George Washington, Thomas Jefferson, and Benjamin Franklin had never to pursue recognition, but John Adams has to be recalled. When he is remembered it is all too often for the purpose of condemnation. Somewhat petulantly, Adams himself predicted that the strictures passing for criticism during his lifetime would continue to blacken his memory in after years. Statues and monuments, he wrote to the renowned Philadelphian, Dr. Benjamin Rush, "will never be erected to me." Statues and monuments were in time raised up to his memory, and it was forgotten that he had once been dubbed "His Rotundity" in derision. He was correct in predicting that his services would not be transmitted "to posterity in brilliant colors." [44]

Adams was brilliant without being colorful. And much of his difficulty proceeded from himself. He made enemies more easily than friends, but friends might have been more numerous, had he permitted himself to say in public what he confided in private to his diary. He admired Franklin's many capacities but envied him as he did George Washington. To Dr. Rush he revealed his fears that the history of the Revolution "will be one continued lie from one end to the other. The essence of the whole will be that Dr. Franklin's electrical rod smote the earth and out sprang General Washington. That Franklin electrified him with his rod—and thence forward these two conducted all the policy, negotiations, legislatures and war." [45]

Adams found fault with other men's weaknesses, but he was no more charitable of his own. The severe judgments of his compatriots attest the lack of popularity during his lifetime; it does not explain the lack of appreciation since. But of all the truly great men of the Revolution, John Adams is generally the least understood. Much of his distinction, ironically enough, derives from the greatness of his descendants. As the grandsire of the Adams clan, a strange twist of historical inversion has made their virtues his.[46] John Adams was a speculative thinker of rare insight and power. The depth of his erudition has been matched by others, but experience gave a range to his mind and a vital center to his intellectual drive. His lucid distinctions make it possible to trace the evolution of republican principles before the age of democracy.

The great bulk of Adams' voluminous writings, long accessible only to scholars in manuscript form, are now in the process of publication. A century ago, Charles Francis Adams edited a ten-volume edition of the second president's works, of which the first volume was a biography.[47] George Washington early came to light under the somewhat too careful guidance of Jared Sparks.[48] Jefferson's letters and papers, though not definitively edited until our own time, were scarcely unknown.[49] Since a large proportion of Adams' writings have been preserved, the black-bound Charles Francis Adams edition, described as possessing "the chill of an ornate mausoleum," [50] was hardly more than a fragment. But John Adams was always his own best spokesman, and the *Diary* made up, to some extent, for the decorous propriety of Charles Francis' account. An earlier compilation of Jefferson-Adams letters, published in 1823, was excluded by Charles Francis Adams, because it was originally published with the intention of injuring John Quincy Adams, then a candidate for the presidency. Failure to include them in the first collected edition of Adams' works was a greater reflection upon the editor than upon the subject, for Thomas Jefferson was probably the only man of the whole generation whom John Adams truly loved and respected. The letters unquestionably exposed Adams in a vain and petty mood. But since they concerned his relations with Jefferson, who forgave him, the general public, less intimately concerned, might also have done so.[51] Theodore Parker,[52] less squeamish, made use of them in an essay on Adams. He did so on the more manly and more reasonable hypothesis that if there is good in great men the evils can take care of themselves. The exchange of letters between Adams and Mercy Otis Warren,[53] in which Adams attempted to extricate himself from the charges made by the historian of the Revolution, appeared in 1878. And in 1892 a number of Adams letters written to Dr. Benjamin Rush were privately printed in a limited edition of fifty copies. These, of course, soon disappeared from general currency.[54] Excellent biographical studies of John Adams[55] have been made; the most recent by Catherine Drinker Bowen has done much to restore John Adams to his proper place in history.[56]

Yet the broad outlines of Adams' thought are almost as clear as his character. Publication of the extant Adams papers is a stellar event, but they are unlikely to alter the shape of his thought. While it is certainly easier to comprehend his public career from the written record of his principles, additional manuscript data can only add an appreciation of his speculative range. In 1815, full of the wisdom of his many years, he confided "the fundamental article" of his "political creed" to Thomas Jefferson. "Despotism, or unlimited sovereignty, or absolute power, is the same in a majority of a popular assembly, an aristocratical council, or oligarchical junto, and a single emperor. Equally arbitrary, cruel, bloody, and in every respect diabolical." [57]

How then was tyranny to be prevented? The tyranny of the one was to be avoided no less than the tyranny of the many. And the despotism of the few remained a despotism in any and every case. The science of government forever plagued the house of Adams, but it plagued other Americans throughout their lives. John Adams, in writing his creed, previewed subsequent American doubt and confusion. In these few sentences John Adams wrote the biography of a multiple series of ideas that were to have a long career in the developing history of democracy.[58] And they are still actively, if often unconsciously, behind many a current dilemma. Unchecked power in a single hand is absolutism. We no longer identify such power as monarchical; we call it dictatorial power. But it remains despotic, however called, even if exercised with benevolence. Among our political fears the tradition of a tyrannous majority ranks second only to a tyrannous minority. How to avoid tyranny and achieve liberty remains a basic democratic question. But in modern democratic terms this is simply another way of asking how the delegation of power, inescapable if government is to function, can be made responsible rather than irresponsible.

Like so many of his contemporaries, John Adams found the answer in the doctrine of the balance of powers. Only when the system of government was so ordered as to prevent the encroachment of one group upon the interests of another could tyranny be avoided. Men have a natural propensity to follow their interests, and interests have a natural propensity to clash. These were the facts of life, of the lives of individuals and the lives of societies. To create a structure capable of holding the natural drives of men and groups in check was the supreme purpose of government. But if it was simple to hold the impulses of men in check by arbitrary means, it was not so simple to provide a framework that would accomplish this purpose and yet assure men of their liberties. Such a structure and such a structure alone assured liberty. Liberty premised a government of laws and not of men, and the laws by which men were governed were ultimate principles.[59]

Balance-of-power doctrines are not to be confused with rigid theories of the separation of powers. Adams carefully explained that although the executive must be balanced against the legislative power, the former could not be deprived of a legislative role. The Adams thesis, elaborated in the three-volume *A Defence of the Constitutions of the Government of the United States of America . . . ,* announced in the preface that popular government derived from representation, not from collectivities of the people, and was based upon "a total separation of the executive from the legislative power, and of the judicial from both." [60]

Adams, who always wrote in haste, was sometimes confusing. But his purposes were seldom unclear. The executive power demanded a certain freedom from legislative interference, for the fundamental purpose motivating Adams was to assure a balance within the legislative process itself—among the senate, the house, and the chief magistrate. That supremacy gravitated to the legislative branch was apparent, and it was exactly for this reason that balances of power were demanded within the parliament. Therefore the executive must participate in the process of legislation, else the chief of state would be at the mercy of the legislature, which might at any time dispose of him. The executive in the Adams theory had a balancing function of its own. By operating in the legislative function a mediating influence could be exerted between the upper and lower houses.

To acclaim the virtues of a balanced system was to acclaim the virtues of the Baron de Montesquieu. And the greatness of the baron rested upon his brilliant description of the English Constitution, which to Adams, as to most American thinkers, did "honor to human understanding." All parties to the political controversy called upon Montesquieu, of whom it was said by James Madison that the British Constitution was to him "what Homer has been to the didactic writers on epic poetry." [61] But the most significant point to be made of the noted Frenchman in this connection is that he was wrong. The British Constitution was changing at the time he was describing it. And the view of the British system entertained by Americans in the eighteenth century, insofar as it was based upon Montesquieu, was incorrect. As Walter Bagehot was later to point out, the importance of the English Constitution was the fusion, not the separation of powers. "The Americans of 1787," wrote Bagehot, "thought they were copying the English Constitution, but they were contriving a contrast to it." And the English Constitution, unlike the American, was of "the type of *simple* constitutions, in which the ultimate power upon all questions is in the hands of the same persons. The ultimate authority in the English Constitution is a newly-elected House of Commons." [62] The political theory of John Adams was a political theory rooted in history; it was conceived without benefit of experience with popular party government. But it created a tradition which was to confuse the meaning of political parties. With the advent of parties came a new period in the development of democracy. But the intellectual history of democratic party government remains to be written.

IX

The Makers of American History
and Their Historians, II

Honest John Adams was an honest revolutionist. He believed in the principles of English justice and in a government structure as perfectly balanced as the wisdom of man could make it. His aim, the same in 1789 as in 1776, was a government "well ordered, mixed, and counterpoised." [1] There were elements of Puritanism in Adams' spirit, there were also elements of Aristotelianism in his thought. If, as the philosopher Charles M. Bakewell urged, western philosophy was hardly more than a footnote to Plato, western political philosophy has often been a succession of commentaries on the *Politics*.[2] It was characteristic of John Adams that he should defend an unpopular cause and wager his political future by defending a group of frightened British soldiers charged with murder. The heritage of impartial justice and the inalienable right to a fair trial had to be upheld. Having taken his side with men already convicted of murder in the public mind, Adams marched in a solemn procession to the graves of their victims. Adams could honestly do both without violence to his conscience, for the legal process alone, impervious to momentary passion, insured the constitutionalist's faith in free government, a government of principles modulating events. It was no less a matter of principle to honor the memory of those who, having transgressed the constitutionalist's code of virtue, had died in the name of liberty.

John Adams was no revolutionary firebrand. Samuel Adams, a

firebrand, was still no revolutionary incendiary.[3] John and Samuel Adams were cousins, friends, and coworkers, but they differed as much in political convictions as in psychological temperament. Long historical usage suggests the extent of difference. John Adams has been called many things—honest, doughty, vain, erratic—but no one has ever called him anything but John. Samuel Adams, "The Publican," "The Maltster," has always been and remains invariably "Sam." Politically they differed even more widely than this popular convention would indicate. If Sam Adams in Tom Jefferson's brimming tribute was "truly the *Man of the Revolution*," [4] it was because he had a faith in mankind that John Adams was never able to share unreservedly. Both believed in checks and balances. John Adams espoused them to balance popular whimsy against seasoned reflection and to check man's innate lust for personal power which forever threatened the general welfare. Sam Adams espoused checks and balances to prevent aristocratic power from limiting the popular will.[5] Before the Revolution John Adams perceived an unprincipled oligarchy within the British government, whose behavior resulted in the perversion of liberty. For him the Revolution offered an opportunity of creating a model framework to prevent tyranny of the one, the few, or the many. Sam Adams, whose faith in mankind and in education was less qualified, hoped to breach contemporary barriers to human advancement. "From my youth," wrote Sam Adams in later life, "my mind has been strongly impressed with the Love of Mankind; and tho' I am old, the lamp still burns." [6] John Adams and Sam Adams experimented with party organization during the revolutionary years. These experiences furnished data for the hypothesis later developed that in a free society parties may provide a natural system of checks and balances.

Historians have found it possible to neglect a president, a general, or a man of large public affairs. They have not been able to ignore Sam Adams, for he is indispensable to the understanding of the transition from colony to commonwealth. Even had Sam Adams never lived in Boston's Winter Street or wandered along the town wharfs and North End alleys, the American Revolution would doubtless have taken place. Given Adams, however, no history of the Revolution can be complete without taking him into precise account. Considering the movement for American independence without Adams would be like viewing the history of modern Europe without Napoleon or without Bismarck. Jefferson acclaimed him the Man of the Revolution because he was the master propagandist, the master organizer, and the master politician.

Yet as a man of letters, Adams has been insufficiently considered. His power as a writer made him the master propagandist; his skill in the use of words for political purposes made him the master organizer. That "of literary art for art's sake, he was entirely regardless" [7] is probably true, but his letters, state papers, speeches, and pamphlets were creative parts of the movement for independence. None of John Adams' adversaries ever paid him so glowing a tribute as Governor Thomas Hutchinson paid Sam Adams. He acquired, lamented the harried chief executive of His Majesty's Bay Colony, "a talent of artfully and fallaciously insinuating into the minds of his readers a prejudice against all whom he attacked beyond any other man I ever knew." Another royal governor, equally harried, was even more eloquent: "Damn that Adams," cursed Sir Francis Bernard, "every dip of his pen stings like a horned snake." [8]

Sam Adams cultivated the arts of democratic politics. He revived the idea of committees of correspondence[9] and crisscrossed the Massachusetts Bay province with a network uniting the rural communities with Boston. In doing so, Adams effected a bold, extralegal stroke the importance of which has been overlooked. The committees of correspondence, a political increment of free association dating from the John Peter Zenger trial of 1734, institutionalized political organization. When the committees assumed a broader intercolonial basis, they began to resemble modern national party organizations. As such, colonial leaders employed them as techniques for self-government on a popular basis. The committees of correspondence, under the guidance of Sam Adams, defeated the more conservative elements in the struggle for power. Under the guidance of the radical leaders, the First Continental Congress precipitated the final break with England. The First Continental Congress presaged the accelerating growth of intercolonial union. In the revolutionary struggle, it also intimated the growth of the popular element that was largely responsible for bringing the Congress into existence and for selecting its more important members, among them Sam Adams. The Continental Congress of 1774 was something else. In the institutional terms of subsequent democratic development, the Continental Congress of 1774 may be considered the first national convention of the first national party in American history.

The pen of Sam Adams and his adroit maneuvers made him the Man of the Revolution. Passion caused him to write in behalf of the immediate issue, and expedience induced him to write behind the shield of fictitious names. Articles signed "A Son of Liberty" or "An Elector of 1771," as easily identifiable as his famous red cloak, mark the rise and fall of radical argument. They outline the purposes of Sam Adams, and the purposes of Sam Adams finally became national goals. Sam Adams' aims demanded true self-effacement. "It was not Samuel Adams," Tyler wrote, "that Samuel Adams cared to put and keep before the public,—it was the ideas of Samuel Adams." [10] And these ideas, if taken together as written, would make a "fair-sized library." [11] Among Adams' works are the controversial tracts that drew his loyalist adversaries into debate plus his endless replies to their provocative retorts. They also include his state papers, which provide a continuous record of the spirit and substance of colonial revolt.[12]

Sam Adams fought the propagandist battle for independence, Tom Paine the propagandist battle of the war. Adams was a political genius, Paine an incomparable journalist. Thomas Paine's electrifying words helped to win the Revolution, and it was the Revolution that secured for Paine his position both in history and historiography. Before his arrival in America, Paine had known only mediocrity. After January 1776, when *Common Sense* appeared, all those identified with the patriot cause borrowed courage from his words. American independence owes much to Thomas Paine, more, in fact, than has been credited to the account of his memory.

When Tom Paine arrived in Philadelphia late in 1774, he had little money and less of a reputation. Armed with a letter of introduction from Benjamin Franklin, he soon made his way among the leaders of revolutionary thought and action. Nothing in his past suggested that he would figure in the making of the American nation. The training of law, the experience of mercantile affairs, or the benefits of general education provided equipment for most of the intellectual founders of the Republic. Paine had none of these advantages. He had only energy, passion, and a genius for putting English words together.

Paine was born in the Norfolk village of Thetford in 1737. His father, a maker of stays, passed on his technical skill to his son, whose education was cut short at the age of thirteen. Staymaking and Thetford held few charms for Paine, who ran off to fight at sea during the Seven Years' War. He returned to staymaking and later shifted to the excise department as a government employee. Twice dismissed from the government service and with nothing left but desperation and courage, he ventured on a new life in America. Such was Paine's life history to the year 1774, a history rich in failure and in poverty.[13]

Franklin's patronage gave Paine access to the patriot leaders in and out of Congress. He met Benjamin Rush, David Rittenhouse, and John Adams and like them he immersed himself in the flow of events then combining to produce the Revolution, the Declaration of Independence, and the United States. One of these events was the publication in January 1776 of *Common Sense.* It was appropriately titled, for it shifted the level of argument from legal and political theory to immediate practical considerations within the comprehension of all. *Common Sense,* a pamphlet of forty-four pages, "written by an Englishman," was "addressed to the inhabitants of America." [14]

Common Sense, remarkable neither for its learning nor logic, is remarkable for its evocative language. Tom Paine said what many Americans were thinking and he said it with a lusty conviction and a flair for the unforgettable phrase. Society, argued Paine, "in every state is a blessing, but Government, even in its best state, is but a necessary evil," [15] an argument faintly reminiscent of the philosopher of Geneva, who contended that man, though born free, was everywhere in chains. But Paine and Rousseau were thinking of governments of unlimited monarchs who had all too frequently made statecraft a sadistic art.

"In the following pages," Paine promised, "I offer nothing more than simple facts, plain arguments, and common sense." [16] What the argument lacked in sophistication, is more than made up in linguistic color. And the logic of Paine's language left little room for rebuttal. His was not an argument for reconciliation; it was an argument for independence. He asked Americans to think of the future of mankind before they thought of themselves. Only by thinking in terms of the future could they really be worthy of the present and of themselves. "The sun never shined on a cause of greater worth. 'Tis not the affair of a city, a county, a province, or a kingdom, but of a continent—of at least one-eighth part of the habitable globe. 'Tis not the concern of a day, a year, an age; posterity are virtually involved in the contest, and will be more or less affected even to the end of time by the proceedings now. Now is the seedtime of continental union, faith, and honor. The least fracture now will be like a name engraved with the point of a pin on the tender rind of a young oak; the wound would enlarge with the tree, and posterity read it in full grown characters." [17]

Paine made short shrift of the case for reconciliation. To assert that because the colonies once flourished as dependencies of Britain the same desirable state would necessarily continue defied common sense. "We may as well assert . . . that the first twenty years of our lives is to become a precedent for the next twenty." [18] That the mother country had protected the colonies did not impress him either, for "she would have defended Turkey for the same motive." [19] Paine had a ready answer for the claim that America was the child of England: "Europe, and not England, is the parent country of America. This new world hath been the asylum for the persecuted lovers of civil and religious liberty from *every part* of Europe. Hither have they fled, not from the tender embraces of the mother, but from the cruelty of the monster; and it is so far true of England, that the same tyranny which drove the first emigrants from home pursues their descendants still." [20]

Thomas Paine, a citizen of America, has been properly regarded as a citizen of the world. More than an eighteenth-century cosmopolite, he was an internationalist; he advocated internationalism out of a genuine aversion for provincialism. But as Paine well knew, there was no sharper point with which to puncture his adversaries' case. "Not one third of the inhabitants, even of this province, are of English descent. Wherefore, I reprobate the phrase parent or mother country applied to England only, as being false, selfish, narrow, and ungenerous." [21] The example of Pennsylvania was certainly a good illustration, but Paine's argument was really tighter. "The first king of England, of the present line (William the Conqueror) was a Frenchman, and half the peers of England are descendants of the same country; wherefore, by the same method of reasoning, England should be governed by France." [22]

A finished propagandist, Paine was unwilling to rely upon a finely spun web of reason. There were other ways of pinning down the issue. "I challenge the warmest advocate for reconciliation to show a single advantage that this continent can reap, by being connected with Great Britain. I repeat the challenge, not a single advantage is derived." [23] He made a direct appeal to special interests. No other markets were open to America except those of Europe, and hence there should be no organic connection with it. " 'Tis the true interest of America," said Paine in words that were to be repeated for centuries, "to steer clear of European contentions, which she never can do while by her dependence on Britain she is made the makeweight in the scale of British politics." [24] Europe was "too thickly planted with kingdoms to be long at peace, and whenever a war breaks out between England and any foreign power, the trade of America goes to ruin, *because of her connection with Britain.*" [25]

The first series of the *Crisis* papers followed *Common Sense* on December 19, 1776. All who were connected with the war in any way were aware that crisis had overtaken the patriot cause. The battle of Long Island, on August 27, 1776, had resulted in a complete defeat for General George Washington. It was the first real test of strength, and the Americans seemed to be decisively beaten. A few weeks later, on September 15, New York had to be abandoned, a disaster followed by the unsuccessful engagement at White Plains in October. Misfortunes pursued the Continental armies as Washington marched over New Jersey and crossed the Delaware. These were times "that try men's souls," and it was Paine's function to rally the flagging spirits of weary men. How well he succeeded is a part of the national legend, for he not only wrote courage into the hearts of soldiers made desperate by weariness and defeat, but he wrote deathless words into popular American speech. "The summer soldier and the sunshine patriot will, in this crisis, shrink from the service of his country; but he that stands it *now,* deserves the love and thanks of man and woman." [26] He did not seek to minimize the gravity of the dangers. He capitalized them, for "tyranny, like hell, is not easily conquered." [27] Thomas Paine had just begun to fight. He fought not only with the pen but with the sword and he would not have been impressed with Edward Bulwer-Lytton's aphorism as to which was the mightier. He was concerned only with winning the battles of the Revolution, since that, he believed, was the way man could win the war for human independence. He fought the battles with Washington at Valley Forge and as aide-de-camp to Nathaniel Greene, and he fought them with the sixteen *Crisis* papers.[28]

The Continental Congress made Paine secretary of the committee on foreign affairs in 1777. In connection with these duties, he became involved in a controversy with Silas Deane, the Congressional agent in France, as a result of which he resigned in 1779.[29] And in December 1780 he published a pamphlet, *Public Good,*[30] to further those who believed that the western lands, claimed by the states, should be ceded to the national government. The line of argument employed in this essay, interesting in the light of the disposal of the public domain, suggests Paine's large-minded statesmanship.

> A question may arise whether a new state should immediately possess an equal right with the present ones in all cases which may come before the congress.
> This experience will best determine; but at first view of the matter it appears thus: that it ought to be immediately incorporated into the union on the ground of a family right, such a state standing in the line of a younger child of the same stock; but as new emigrants will have something to learn when they first come to America, and a new state requiring aid rather than capable of giving it, it might be the most convenient to admit its most immediate representation into con-

gress, there to sit, hear, and debate on all questions and matters, but not to vote on any till after the expiration of seven years.[31]

Paine's point of view was also that of certain land speculators, notably the Morris group, but the motives of real estate operators scarcely destroyed its validity.

The American revolutionary movement molded the earlier phase of Thomas Paine's thought, the French revolutionary movement molded the later phase. Private affairs sent Paine to France in 1787. Public affairs quickly involved him in French politics. Thomas Jefferson, then United States minister to France, was in frequent touch with Paine, and both were observers of the early stages of the French Revolution. The key to the Bastille, to be given to General Washington, was entrusted to Paine by the ever-present Lafayette. And in February 1791, having denounced monarchy in *A Republican Manifesto* which, as befits manifestos, was nailed to the door of the Assembly, Paine published the first part of *The Rights of Man*.[32]

The Rights of Man, Thomas Paine's reflections on the French Revolution, was partly an answer to Edmund Burke. There is much in this first installment directed to the English statesman; there is also a great deal of Paine on revolutions, constitutions, and the nature of humankind.

> Sovereignty, as a matter of right, appertains to the nation only and not to any individual; and a nation has at all times an inherent, indefeasible right to abolish any form of government it finds inconvenient, and establish such as accords with its interest, disposition, and happiness. The romantic and barbarous distinctions of men into kings and subjects, though it may suit the condition of courtiers cannot that of citizens; and is exploded by the principle upon which governments are now founded. Every citizen is a member of the sovereignty, and as such can acknowledge no personal subjection; and his obedience can be only to the laws.[33]

This, we may be sure, did not convince Mr. Burke, but it certainly irritated him. Paine was now moving along the road to the political left. But before long his French colleagues were to regard him as a moderate, if not as a conservative. Those who have misinterpreted him could not have understood his own analysis of the history he witnessed. "The Independence of America, considered merely as a separation from England, would have been a matter of little importance had it not been accompanied by a revolution in the principles and practice of government. She made a stand, not for herself only, but for the world, and looked beyond the advantages which *she* could receive. Even the Hessian, though hired to fight against her, may live to bless his own defeat; and England, condemning the viciousness of its government, rejoice in its miscarriage." [34] It was the revolution in ideas, not the revolution itself. The revolution in ideas gave independence and the founding of America world significance. America indeed was the one place on the whole planet where these "principles of universal reformation" [35] could have begun. Here the vastness and grandeur of the continent possessed "something in it which generates and enlarges great ideas." [36] Here Europeans with differing personal and cultural backgrounds gathered as allies rather than as enemies. They had to leave their older national affinities behind them and embrace a new and larger allegiance, an allegiance rooted not only in geography but in a unifying set of ideas. And Paine concluded in the patois of the Enlightenment later absorbed by Frederick Jackson Turner in the early stages of his development: "The wants which necessarily accompany the cultivation of a wilderness produced among them a state of society which countries long harassed by the quarrels and intrigues of governments have neglected to cherish. In such a situation man becomes what he ought to be. He sees his species not with the inhuman idea of a natural enemy but as kindred; and the example shows to an artificial world that man must go back to nature for information." [37]

America created unities out of diversities demonstrating that reason rather than force provided the basis for civil society. To establish the rights of man Paine pursued the hereditary principle and Mr. Edmund Burke over every crag of argumentation.[38] He routed his adversaries who had persistently branded him a leveler with the neatest of turns:

> We have heard the *rights of man* called a *leveling* system; but the only system to which the word leveling is truly applicable is the hereditary monarchical system. It is a system of mental *leveling*. It indiscriminately admits every species of character to the same authority. Vice and virtue, ignorance and wisdom, in short every quality, good or bad, is put on the same level. Kings succeed each other, not as rationals, but as animals. Can we then be surprised at the abject state of the human mind in monarchical countries, when the government itself is formed on such an abject leveling system? It has no fixed character. Today it is one thing; tomorrow it is something else.[39]

The history of the United States provided Paine with the primary source materials of democracy. After the outbreak of hostilities and the proclamation of independence the colonies formed independent governments of their own. The process of constitution-making exemplified by the several states, by the Confederation, and by the Constitution represented democratic methods in action. In Paine's estimation, as many now concur, this was one of the greatest contributions of America to the rest of the world.[40] Referring to Pennsylvania, with the constitution of which Paine was personally identified, he said: "It was the political bible of the state. Scarcely a family was without it. Every member of the government had a copy." [41] The constitutions of the other states and of the country were "the property of the nation, and not of those who exercise the government. All the constitutions of America are declared to be established on the authority of the people." [42]

The United States of America was a representative government. It was a government dedicated to the general welfare, a *res publica*.[43] By this Paine meant that it was "representation ingrafted upon democracy. It has settled the form by a scale parallel in all cases to the extent of the principle. What Athens was in miniature, America will be in magnitude. The one was the wonder of the ancient world—the other is becoming the admiration and model of the present." [44]

The Rights of Man promptly involved Paine in a conflict with English law. Charged with sedition, he had to make a quick removal across the English Channel, urged on by discretion and duty. Although the date of his trial in England had already been set, he had also been named to the Convention of the French Revolution. From the comparative safety of Paris, he wrote an address to the English people urging them to follow in the footsteps of the French. For this last outburst of what English conservatives regarded as incitement to revolt, he was formally outlawed.[45]

Paine left his English brethren to their own political devices and offered his revolutionary devotion to his French colleagues. He served on a committee to draft a constitution for the new French Republic, a constitution which never went into effect. When the Convention decided to send Louis XVI to the guillotine, Paine had the temerity to oppose the decision.[46] The price of opposition to the dictates of the Convention ran high, and Paine soon was imprisoned in Luxembourg. He remained a prisoner for ten months until James Monroe, American minister to the French Republic, intervened to secure his release.

Paine's term in prison sapped his health and embittered his mind. When Washington and the government of the United States failed to take active steps in his behalf, he changed his opinion of the first president, whom he had once revered. The famous letter to Washington, written from Paris on July 30, 1796, is one of the most caustic he ever wrote. Washington's friends, who were countless, were so enraged that they believed Paine in the pay of radical French elements who desired to divide American opinion. After citing what he believed to be the defections from true republican principles, Paine wrote: "Could I have known to what degree of corruption and perfidy the administrative part of the government of America had descended, I could have been at no loss to have understood the reservedness of Mr. Washington toward me, during my imprisonment in the Luxembourg. There are cases in which silence is a loud language."[47]

Just before taking up residence in the Luxembourg,[48] Paine entrusted an unfinished tract, *The Age of Reason,* to an American friend, probably Joel Barlow, who was then in France.[49] Neither learned philosophy nor learned theology, the book was profoundly suggestive of Thomas Paine and the century in which he lived. Paine's reputation as a democrat rests upon *Common Sense,* the *Crisis* papers, and *The Rights of Man;* his reputation for godlessness rests upon *The Age of Reason.* But Paine was no more an atheist than he was a leveler. He simply considered hereditary government a vestige and conventional religion an anachronism. Each stood in the way of human enlightenment. Paine's attitude toward the social institutions of his day reveal him as a primitivist. To be free, mankind had first to secure release from the inhibitions of outworn cultural modes. Such social doctrines were too radical for English Tories or American Federalists. Such theological doctrines were too unconventional to satisfy the orthodox anywhere. Yet they were far too conservative for revolutionary French radicals, who were by this time ready to embrace Robespierre and the goddess of Reason.

Clergymen in New England and elsewhere were vigorous in their denunciation of Paine's heresies. For them *The Age of Reason* represented a vicious and unprincipled attack upon religious truth. Such clerical reactions distorted Paine's ideas and created a perverted image in the public mind. Far from being an atheist, Paine was a thoroughly conventional eighteenth-century deist. To Sam Adams he wrote in 1803: "The people of France were running headlong into atheism, and I had the work translated and published in their own language to stop them in that career, and fix them to the first article . . . of every man's Creed who has any Creed at all, *I believe in God."* [50] Undeterred by the evidence of Paine's faith Theodore Roosevelt, more than a century later, called Paine "a filthy little atheist," a remark which damaged two reputations.

Tories were likewise able to forge weapons out of fine English words. As such they too were the makers of history, for it was in response to Tory logic that patriots like Paine felt impelled to make answer. It was in response to Tory efforts to manipulate events that

Sam Adams made his well-thought-out political moves. Until the Declaration of Independence made the debate academic, the Tory rebuttal to colonial agitation was powerful and constant.[51] Tory debaters cut the heart out of the American remonstrance by admitting the principle that taxation implied representation. They simply denied that the principle had been transgressed. They made virtue an active partner of polemics. Law was on the side of the Loyalists; order was violated by their opponents. Sentiment and affection were also their emotional allies, for the defenders of the empire sought to preserve an historical attachment, not to sever it. The friends of Britain possessed an almost insuperable advantage. It was the radical group who had to implement the existing situation and to create conditions favorable to unprecedented change. The true measure of a Paine or an Adams can be taken only against the Tory background; their accomplishment is apparent only in relation to the magnitude of the task.

But the men who were loyal to Britain, irrespective of politics, were enrolled in a lost cause. The American colonies did not have to be independent in 1776, but they had to be acknowledged. When the compulsion of consistency led to an awareness that change was reasonable, dogged resistance and administrative ineptitude obstructed it. Nor was it simply an unregenerate conservatism or a blind stupidity, for the conflict itself dissolved attitudes and loyalties more swiftly than the understanding of those in power could mature. The British government had a part in making America independent, and the loyalist argument was as often directed to noble lords in London as to politicians and lawyers in Boston and Philadelphia.[52]

Among Tories there were men of every stripe. From his pulpit at St. Mary's Church in Caroline County, Virginia, the Reverend Jonathan Boucher thundered denunciations in the name of God, who had appointed rulers for society and ordained a proper government. Precepts of obedience to constituted authority were repeated with pedantic monotony. Not all were content to repeat scriptural maxims masquerading as political theory. Samuel Seabury of Westchester County, New York; Myles Cooper, president of King's College (later Columbia); and Joseph Galloway of Pennsylvania looked forward as well as backward and tried to temper their convictions with new understanding.[53]

Samuel Seabury, Anglican divine, wrote under the name of A. W. Farmer.[54] After the Continental Congress had determined on nonimportation as a method of pressure, Seabury condemned extralegal conventions and congresses. He maintained with eloquence that the path of constitutional virtue was the narrow one of appeal through the regular channels of the colonial assemblies. With rustic directness and a prose uncluttered by legal citations, he suggested that farmers would bear the brunt of such economic pressure following the "non-importation, non-exportation, and non-consumption agreements." [55] Such measures would immediately and disastrously affect manufacturers and producers in Britain, in Ireland, and the West Indies. "They have been no ways instrumental in bringing our distress upon us. Shall we then revenge ourselves upon them?" [56] This was simple justice, and it was also simple economics. If Americans by their conduct precipitated the unoffending inhabitants of these regions into difficulties, why should they continue to purchase American produce? Specifically, it would be miraculous if the Irish, despoiled by American embargoes, should respond by buying American flaxseed. "The sale of your seed," warned the Anglican parson disguised as a Westchester farmer, "not only pays your taxes, but furnishes you with many of the little conveniences and comforts of life. The loss of it for one year would be more damage to you, than paying the three-penny duty on tea for twenty." [57] The Westchester farmer could pivot an argument as well as the Thetford staymaker. "Will you be instrumental in bringing the most abject slavery on yourselves? Will you choose such committees? Will you submit to them, should they be chosen by the weak, foolish, turbulent part of the country people? Do as you please; but, by Him that made me, I will not! No, if I must be enslaved, let it be by a KING at least, and not by a parcel of upstart, lawless committeemen. If I must be devoured, let me be devoured by the jaws of a lion, and not gnawed to death by rats and vermin!" [58]

Had the Westchester farmer been what he purported to be rather than a learned Episcopalian clergyman, he might not have been capable of such subtle, though unembellished, argumentation. He ridiculed the claim that the representatives of the colonies in congress assembled were truly representative since the congress had no legal validity and the delegates no legal right to office. This was a lethal thrust, for without the argument for representation there was scarcely a colonial case, and two representative wrongs did not make a congress right. Just as lethal was his thrust at the proposition that the colonial governments owed allegiance to the crown rather than to Parliament.

> It is a distinction made by the American republicans to serve their own rebellious purposes,—a gilding with which they have enclosed the pill of sedition, to entice the unwary colonists to swallow it the more readily

down. The king of Great Britain was placed on the throne by virtue of an act of parliament; and he is king of America by virtue of being king of Great Britain. He is, therefore, king of America by act of parliament. And if we disclaim that authority of parliament which made him our king, we, in fact, reject him from being our king—for we disclaim that authority by which he is king at all.[59]

Myles Cooper, signing himself "A North American," asked a number of pertinent and sharply worded questions.[60] In *The American Querist*, the president of King's filed a list of a hundred interrogations which, though unanswered, left no doubt how men of principle and education would answer them. Another pamphlet—*A Friendly Address to all Reasonable Americans*[61]—made the point that grievances must be settled in a reasonable manner, and the only reasonable method for the solution of imperial problems was the constitutional method.

> The great object in view should be a general American constitution on a free and generous plan, worthy of Great Britain to give and of the colonies to receive. This is now become necessary to the mutual interest and honor both of the parent kingdom and of its American offspring. Such an establishment is only to be obtained by decent, candid, and respectful application, and not by compulsion or threatening. To think of succeeding by force of arms, or by starving the nation into compliance, is a proof of shameful ignorance, pride, and stupidity.[62]

The most famous plan for salvaging the empire was presented by Joseph Galloway. Galloway was a native of Maryland, well known as a practitioner at the bar and as a member of the colonial assembly of Pennsylvania. Critical of the policies of the British ministries, he felt misunderstandings were inherent in the clumsy governmental system. As a conservative member of the Continental Congress he offered his "Plan of a Proposed Union between Britain and the Colonies" on September 28, 1774. Under this scheme, the colonies would have attained virtual home rule, and Britain might have saved an empire. "As the colonies from their local circumstances," ran the wording of the resolution, "cannot be represented in the Parliament of Great Britain, they will humbly propose to His Majesty, and his two Houses of Parliament, the following plan, under which the strength of the whole Empire may be drawn together on any emergency; the interests of both countries advanced; and the rights and liberties of America secured." [63]

Galloway's plan appeared more reasonable in after years, but it remained a museum piece until the Statute of Westminster reorganized the British colonial system and reconstituted the British Empire. The radical elements of the revolutionary party were unimpressed by Galloway's proposals just as they were irritated by Myles Cooper's questions. They rejected Galloway and harried Myles Cooper out of the land. Critics of the victorious in war and of the successful in peace continue silent and vanquished. Advocates of conciliation in times of crisis are celebrated only if conciliation has been successful in averting it. Crusaders for lost causes attain immortality only as a consequence of change, which is then said to have vindicated them. Critics of successful causes attain immortality only from historians.

The winning of independence gave America her heroes. The creation of the republic gave America her founding fathers. Epochal events acquired heroic proportions as Americans wove their early traditions into integrated patterns of thought and feeling. To the first generation of American citizens no events were more momentous than the struggles of the war, and no hero was more revered than the general under whose command those struggles were won. General George Washington reflected the image of America at home and abroad. No other figure symbolized American virtue and American unity so admirably. At home he was so devoutly worshiped that he sometimes seemed more god than man. Abroad he was the model of republican rectitude, the victorious general who could never accept a crown. To European republicans, Washington was the reality of the American dream. To his countrymen, he was the incarnation of the American spirit.

Second only to Washington was Benjamin Franklin. If the Virginian was the model of selfless devotion, the Pennsylvanian was the model of unmatched wisdom. Washington was the soldier-statesman, Franklin the philosopher-sage. Franklin's fame as a man of science was established in Europe long before he went abroad to plead his country's case. Europe honored him not only for what he had accomplished, but also for what he was. And he was a living proof of a major eighteenth-century premise: that equal opportunity gave ordinary men the chance to become extraordinary. General Washington symbolized the American dream; Dr. Franklin vindicated it. Franklin was the representative American. He represented American democracy, the emergence of individual talent, and the application of that talent to the practical issues of a changing society.[64]

Secure among the makers of American history, Benjamin Franklin and George Washington have inspired historians at every stage of scholarly development. Their towering achievements have "drugged historical enquiry with a whiff of hero-worship," [65] for great men have a beguiling way of making history seem much simpler than in fact is the case. It may be more accurate to say that historians are beguiled into making their heroes greater than any individual man can be. The age of the Revolution, precisely because it was a creative age, has provided posterity with heroes as well as with an abundant crop of representative men. But representative men are *representative of something;* they represent the forces which make them and they represent the ideas, aspirations, and personalities by which the forces are shaped.[66]

The age of the American Revolution possesses a unity, but every unity is composed of parts. Certain aspects are unquestionably best represented by George Washington; others by Benjamin Franklin. An incorruptible devotion to duty and the responsibility for welding American effort are the virtues that belong to Washington's character and reputation. The essence of democratic opportunity and its fruition are revealed in the career of Benjamin Franklin. But the chief architect of the American Republic was Thomas Jefferson.

Thomas Jefferson was the architect of the American Republic because he was its leading thinker. Among the philosopher-statesmen of the early Republic Jefferson was pre-eminent for a variety of reasons. His prime interest was the philosophy of society; his major objective the study of government. Yet it was more than a passion for scholarship which motivated his efforts. He was engaged in creating a society and in building a democratic government. Alexander Hamilton, John Adams, James Madison, and Thomas Jefferson were the pioneers of American self-government. It was no mere intellectual adventure; it was an adventure in learning by doing. They were engaged in the practice of knowledge. Realization that they were innovators gave a zest to their thought and a passion to their activity.

But Thomas Jefferson, more than any of his collaborators, was the representative man of democracy. More than Alexander Hamilton, James Madison, or John Adams, he stamped his convictions upon the American character. America came to resemble Jefferson's dream. To be sure, America is urban not rural. Hamiltonian principles still operate in the marketplace and the paradoxes of Adams still pursue those striving to give modern form to a more perfect union. But the Declaration of Independence, though its ideas, as John Adams insisted, were common intellectual property, was set to Jefferson's words. And the Declaration of Independence remains the core of democratic philosophy. Democratic government in America is government by party, and Thomas Jefferson gave to the concepts of majority rule, minority rights, and the principle of continuing majorities their classic formulation. Explication of democratic precepts in crystal prose is the least of his accomplishment. Jefferson explicated democratic precepts in political action. He organized majorities, he formulated dissent, he belonged to minorities.[67]

The quality of his mind and the quality of his temper combined to make him first among the builders of the nation. He was the ideal scholar, one of a long line of successful scholars in American politics. There was little that eluded him, nothing that escaped his active interest. His was a quest for understanding, a search for newer and deeper meanings. He was impatient of certainties and was constantly prepared to examine his premises and to revise his methods. James Madison was also great, but Jefferson was his master. John Adams was, in the view of Harold Laski, the most original of American political thinkers,[68] and he left an abiding imprint on American patterns of thought. But John Adams, whatever else he was, was not a democrat. Alexander Hamilton, brilliant, colorful, impetuous, was ideologically closer to Adams, his archenemy, than to Jefferson, his political opponent. If democracy is the name for America, Thomas Jefferson is first.

The Declaration of Independence was written by Thomas Jefferson, but fifty-six men endorsed its principles with their names. John Hancock's florid signature led all the rest, and the signers by this very act alone furthered the history of democracy in America. The "signers of the declaration," whose autographs are avidly sought by collectors, are less well known than they deserve to be. The two Adamses of Massachusetts, the two Lees of Virginia, Pennsylvania's Robert Morris, Benjamin Rush, and James Wilson were famed throughout the land.[69] But who remembers William Paca of Maryland or Thomas Heyward, Jr., of South Carolina?

While the "signers" made their mark in the halls of Congress, other revolutionary heroes walked with history on the battlefields of the war. American generals besides George Washington—Nathaniel Greene, Horatio Gates, Charles Lee, Henry Knox, George Rogers Clark—fought, intrigued, and struggled. Others were later induced to write about their influence upon the course of the war that brought about the emergence of the American people. In addition to native American military leaders, there was the legion of foreign aides—Lafayette, Steuben, Kalb, and Pulaski—each of whom evoked biographers, essayists, critics, and adulators. There were border captains as well as generals, traitors as well as heroes, whose plans, motives, and campaigns were endlessly rehearsed and reexamined. There were allies and enemies both commanded by men whose deeds required appraisal and who received it.[70] But it was the nameless soldier on both sides who made the history of the Revolution. "Where, looking closer," asked Philip Guedalla, "is the man to take the credit of the French, the American, the Russian Revolution. There were so many of him. He stood about the streets; he stoned the soldiers; he put the leaders up and pulled them down; he died at Valmy, at Saratoga, behind Archangel. He is an elusive hero with far too many names. How much easier to select one figure, cast him in bronze. . . . Yet even Governments . . . must have their moments of uncertainty, when they elbow aside the eager claimant for Valhalla and bury an Unknown Soldier. The wise historian will search history for its Unknown Soldiers. For though there is never, perhaps, a great man, there is sometimes a great age." [71]

Because it was a great age, it was an age crowded with important events. And the events and those who participated in them have been celebrated in legend and in history. The diplomats of the war years and the peacemakers who negotiated with Britain, Spain, and France have earned the careful consideration they have received. Historians have dissected tarnished warriors who grasped at transient satisfactions, and they have evaluated the statesmen whose qualities of mind and heart go by the name of devotion. But once the war was won and the peace declared, historians, following the strict chronology of events, described the steps leading to the formation of the national government. The years from 1783 to 1789 became "the critical period of American history." [72] The critical period provided a dramatic background of political chaos and economic confusion from which the American experiment was rescued by the Constitution. The movement for the Constitution, the Convention, the process of ratification, and the establishment of the United States in 1789 supplied conceptual boundaries for description and analysis. The historical convention of separating development before and after 1776, perverted the meaning of men and movements. The struggles of 1763 were the struggles of 1783. "It is this continuity of conflict that gives coherence to the political history of the age of the American Revolution. Otherwise many men and events must be ignored, or their significance distorted. . . . And the issues of the struggle were the same. The issues were those of democracy. The debate was white-hot and was carried on with utter frankness. It was white-hot because for a moment in history self-government by majorities within particular political boundaries was possible. Those majorities could do what they wanted, and some of them knew what they wanted. Democracy was no vague ideal but a concrete program: it meant definite things in politics, economics, and religion." [73]

X

Historians of the Revolution

American affirmation altered in response to colonial victory as loyalist dissent shifted in response to British defeat. The surrender of Lord Cornwallis marked both the triumph of colonial arms and the triumph of the colonial cause. If Jefferson's declaration was a manifesto addressed to a monarchical culture, the formation of the union was an unprecedented venture in government on trial in a skeptical world. The Declaration was based upon a philosophy of human rights; the American union was based upon a faith in man. Historians of the early republic set out to expound the one and to vindicate the other.

The Revolution is central to American historical writing, as it is central to American development. Colonial separation from imperial Britain is the ultimate point of reference in the political history of the United States. The Revolution marks the beginning of separate statehood, of a heightened feeling of national self-consciousness, of a newer integration of culture. But if the Revolution points to beginnings, it also marks developments. The Revolution was not only the culmination of an historical process, but the process itself was a continuing one. The American Revolution, in other words, was a continuing revolution. History remains intensely absorbing to Americans, because the history of the United States and the history of the modern world is history of a special kind.

Many related trends came into focus with the events of 1776 and the years thereafter. The Revolution was, in fact, a revolution because it was based on a philosophy, a complex of ideas of nature, of man, and of society. While these philosophical notions had older roots and were reformulated by the great systematic thinkers of the eighteenth century, they were given a new emphasis and direction in the world of Thomas Jefferson and of Benjamin Franklin. They developed, moreover, into an ideological framework of American thought. When J. Franklin Jameson in 1925 reassessed the American Revolution considered as a social movement, he was simply saying in the chaste words of modern scholarship what the writers of American history in the eighteenth and nineteenth centuries had said in a more fervid literary prose. The phrase "rise of the common man"—a phrase as inept as it is inaccurate—is no more than what Richard Hildreth, one of the most remarkable of American historians, meant by the term "The Age of the People." [1]

The eighteenth century was not yet the age of the people. But the age of the people seemed nearer to realization than ever before. It was an era noteworthy for a reawakening interest in the process of history. The two are not unconnected, for historical interest was not simply confined to a rediscovery of the past. On the contrary, effort was centered on the understanding of the present and in projecting such understandings into the future.

An early historian of the American Revolution was the Reverend William Gordon. More frequently remembered for his vices than for his virtues, Gordon was born in Hertfordshire, England, in 1728. Trained as a dissenting minister, he later became a warm defender of the colonial position. The purposes of the colonial leaders, with whom he was in correspondence, so far became his own that he decided to leave England the better to serve them. He resigned his post in 1770 and removed to Massachusetts. Two years later he became minister to the third Congregational Church of Roxbury and in 1775 he became chaplain to the Provincial Congress sitting in Watertown.[2]

The stirring scenes preliminary to the outbreak of the war and the creation of republican governments transformed the patriot into an historian. Gordon regarded these events as crucial to the future of mankind, which he, as an alert contemporary, was under obligation to record. He undertook an extensive correspondence with Americans everywhere and enticed many leading military and civilian figures into revealing interviews. After collecting and investigating what source collections he could find, he was ready to write his history of the rise, progress, and establishment of the independence of the United States.[3]

Whatever the subsequent judgments of his work, Gordon was keenly aware of the historian's problem. "I shall endeavor," he wrote General Horatio Gates, "that what I write shall be not only the truth truly represented; for you may tell the truth so as to make a lie of it in the apprehensions of who reads or hears the tale." [4] He determined to publish in England to avoid the turmoil of partisanship, for, as he put it, "The credit of the country and of individuals who now occupy eminences will be most horribly affected by impartial history." [5] Impartial history, however, was no less offensive to those who occupied eminences in Britain. Nor was "the truth truly represented" more kindly to the motives and actions of the English. All this he confessed to John Adams, who again met him in England, and wrote that Gordon altered his original manuscript in terms of British preferences.[6]

Despite such literary indelicacies, Gordon achieved a long and important influence. His volumes, widely used for over a century, were among the most frequently cited secondary works in England as well as in America.[7] A later American critic, undeterred by the sanctity of reputations, reported in elaborate detail that Gordon had borrowed copiously from the famed *Annual Register* without benefit of quotation marks.[8] While this devastating exposure damaged the reputation of a highly prized study, it was less of a discovery than an analysis, for Gordon acknowledged his great indebtedness to the *Register*[9] and quotation marks were not so essential a part of scholarly decorum in the eighteenth century as they have since become. Regardless of such uninhibited borrowings, Gordon's account remains an invaluable reference of firsthand impression and opinion. Sydney G. Fisher, whose comments on the historians of the Revolution are usually more devastating than laudatory, judged Gordon somewhat kindly. Admitting his copying from the *Register* and his pro-American sympathies, he was, says Fisher "unquestionably very painstaking and accurate." [10]

Historical production, from the War of Independence to the early decades of the nineteenth century, was undistinguished only by comparison with present-day critical standards. It is true that America was culturally impoverished by the exodus of the Tories, the natural patrons of the arts and sciences. But it is also true that a new culture was emerging, and that the writers of the early republic represented it. While scholarly techniques of investigation had yet to mature, it is well to remember that those who began the historical tradition in the United States were without the physical and social accoutrements of learning. Leisure, always at a premium in undeveloped countries, awaited the coming of the industrial revolution as did the progress of education, the growth of libraries, and a more broadly cultivated intellectual awareness.

If the output of the United States before the literary reawakening of New England fails to satisfy the rigor of scientific standards, it was neither unimpressive nor insignificant. In fact, it was both impressive and continues to be significant. It is impressive because it represents a philosophical mood, and it is significant because the mood it represents is essential to an understanding of the evolution of democracy. In addition, it is this literature which has enabled subsequent historians to recreate the atmosphere of crisis. Some of these writers were unquestionably impassioned, but their volumes provide relatively accurate barometers for gauging the attitudes of men. Others were certainly biased, but they furnish a key to the riddle of prejudice. The very reasons that detract from their historical worth, in the narrower sense, are precisely the reasons that make them invaluable to the student of ideas.[11]

The writings of David Ramsay deftly illustrate this contention. Investigators, seeking to check their own version of the American Revolution against the opinions of the times, could scarcely have wished for a more enticing observer. Born in Lancaster County, Pennsylvania, in 1749, Ramsay was graduated from Princeton in 1765. He then matriculated at the University of Pennsylvania Medical School and after finishing his studies settled in Charleston, South Carolina, to practice. He became a surgeon in the army of the Revolution, took part in the siege of Savannah, was captured at Charleston, and spent eleven months in prison at St. Augustine. These were qualifications enough. A childhood spent in the western backcountry of a colony whose history was crucial to the revolutionary movement and education at a college famed for the study of moral and political ideas provided a background sufficient for the making of any mind. Yet this was only the beginning of Ramsay's career. He served in the state legislature of South Carolina from the time of the Declaration of Independence until a year before the treaty of peace and again from 1784 to 1790. To this must be added membership in the Continental Congress and several terms in the state senate of South Carolina.[12]

Activities such as these furnished the motives and the materials for the writing of history. In 1785 the *History of the Revolution in*

South Carolina appeared, followed soon thereafter by the *History of the American Revolution.* Like many patriots who handled a pen, he paid his personal tributes to the father of the country in a *Life of George Washington,* all of which were preludes to *The History of the United States* from the settlement at Jamestown to the year 1808. He also wrote a volume on the development of South Carolina, and after his death his last contribution, revealingly entitled *Universal History Americanized,* was published.[13]

Like Gordon, Ramsay's study of the Revolution laid the materials published in *The Annual Register* under contribution in an all too literal sense.[14] Critics of his style have noted that he was "obscure and tedious" to such a degree that "he could never have much effect." Yet his turgid style neither dampened the zeal with which he wrote nor detracted from the enthusiasm that he accorded his subject.[15]

Vivacity of style may insure fame but does not guarantee historical significance. Mercy Otis Warren wrote with verve and charm[16] but her place in the American record rests upon other grounds.[17] As a woman of letters she was one of a rare company in eighteenth-century America, and historians among females of the species were even rarer. Prophecy may be dangerous, but it is scarcely prophetic to suggest that interest in the American Revolution is likely to endure as long as there is interest in the development of democracy. And as long as the Revolution continues to stir the imagination, Mercy Otis Warren will continue to have a place in the chronicle.[18]

Had Mercy Otis Warren escaped the impact of the Revolution, it would have been remarkable. That she was immersed in it was unavoidable. James Otis was her father, James Otis of Writs of Assistance fame her brother, James Warren, leading opponent of British measures, her husband. She knew both the great and the near great. John Adams was her lifelong friend; George Washington and Thomas Jefferson thought well of her, and Thomas Hutchinson, Sam Adams, and John Hancock paraded their strengths and their weaknesses before her searching eyes.

Mercy Warren was born in Barnstable, Massachusetts, in 1728. When she was eleven, her brother James went off to Harvard; Mercy remained at home reading Sir Walter Raleigh's history. But Mercy Warren not only read history, she lived and recorded it. A woman of her temperament and ability would doubtless have found ways to participate in the great events of life. Mrs. Warren had other reasons. Her husband, her brother, and all her male acquaintances were playing exciting and meaningful roles, and Mercy Warren was not one to hide behind her femininity.[19] "At a period when every manly arm was occupied," she wrote in the preface of her history, "and every trait of talent or activity engaged . . . I have been induced to improve the leisure Providence has lent, to record as they passed . . . new and unexperienced events. . . ."

The History of the Rise, Progress, and Termination of the American Revolution was Mercy Warren's contribution to liberty. But the subtitle of this historical work—*Interspersed with Biographical, Political, and Moral Reflections*—actually defines its range and lasting import.[20] The value of Mercy Warren's history lies in the revealing estimates of her associates. While she was hostile to the leaders of the "malignant party," which included all those who leaned in the "aristocratical direction," she was no less sharp and penetrating about those who shared her democratic preferences. Here, for example, is her characterization of John Hancock, which more than 175 years of research and study has done little to change:

> Mr. Hancock was a young gentleman of fortune, of more external accomplishments than real abilities. He was polite in manners, easy in address, affable, civil, and liberal. With these accomplishments, he was capricious, sanguine, and implacable: naturally generous, he was profuse in expense; he scattered largesses without discretion, and purchased favors by the waste of wealth, until he reached the ultimatum of his wishes, which centred in the focus of popular applause. He enlisted early in the cause of his country, at the instigation of some gentlemen of penetration, who thought his ample fortune might give consideration, while his fickleness could not injure, so long as he was under the influence of men of superior judgment. They complimented him by nominations to committees of importance, till he plunged too far to recede; and flattered by ideas of his own consequence, he had taken a decided part before the battle of Lexington, and was president of the provincial congress, when that event took place.[21]

It was this incisive gift of character analysis which prompted Moses Coit Tyler to remark that "Mercy Warren was unable to exhibit that twice-blest quality somewhat ironically announced in her baptismal name." [22] She reached an acrimonious height in her evaluation of Thomas Hutchinson.[23] He was, she writes, "dark, intriguing, insinuating, haughty and ambitious, while the extreme of avarice marked each feature of his character." At this point she might well have stopped, for hardly more could be said by way of damnation. But, she continued, "His abilities were little elevated above the line of mediocrity; yet by dint of industry, exact temperance, and indefatigable labor, he became master of the accomplishments necessary to acquire popular fame." [24]

None would seek to absolve Mercy Warren of partisan devotion to the democratic cause. Yet John Adams' stricture, "Your History has been written to the taste of the nineteenth century, and accommodated to gratify the passions . . . of the party . . . now predominant," [25] actually tells more of John Adams than of Mercy Warren. At the height of their growing friendship, Adams had instructed Mrs. Warren on the duties of the historian. "The faithfull Historian delineates Characters truly, let the Censure fall where it will.—The public is so interested in public Characters, that they have a Right to know them, and it becomes the Duty of every good Citizen who happens to be acquainted with them to Communicate his Knowledge. There is no other way of preventing the Mischief which may be done by ill Men; no other Method of administering the Antidote to the Poison—." [26] But when Mercy Warren followed John Adams' prescription with reference to John Adams, the second president of the United States was not so pleased. "It was viewed as a kind of political phenomenon," wrote Mrs. Warren, "when discovered that Mr. Adams' former opinions were beclouded by a partiality for monarchy." The patriarch of Quincy, then seventy-two, took up his pen once more, but whether his irritation stemmed from the above-quoted remark or the following it is difficult to be sure. "Pride of talents and much ambition were undoubtedly combined in the character of the president who immediately succeeded General Washington." In any case, a long and delicately barbed correspondence ensued, and an old friendship was momentarly imperilled. That it ended in victory for Mrs. Warren is attested by Adams' ultimate refuge: "History is not the Province of the Ladies." [27]

Mercy Warren was unusual but not unique. She unquestionably earned the title later accorded her—"penwoman of the Revolution" —but the first professional American penwoman was Hannah Adams.[28] Hannah Adams, born in Medfield, Massachusetts, in 1755, stemmed from the Adamses of Braintree. Hence she was distantly related to President John Adams and belonged to the famed Adams clan. Her father, as his nickname "Book" suggests, was more interested in cultivating his mind than his farm, so that the former improved as the latter deteriorated. "Book" Adams soon found it necessary to invite paying guests to the farmstead. Both these factors influenced the life of his daughter. She acquired her father's taste for learning and the boarders, mostly students of theology, greatly aided her education. They not only helped her to learn the classical languages, but introduced her to geography and the elements of logic. One of them placed a compendium of religious knowledge in her hands, and she read it with her usual enthusiasm for the printed word. This particular volume so irritated her because of what she considered its inadequacies that she decided to write a better one herself.[29]

The result of this irritation was an *Alphabetical Compendium of the Various Sects* . . . , which had an immediate and lasting success. A more significant consequence was Hannah Adams' resolution to make writing her career. In 1799 she published a *Summary History of New England* later abridged for school use. A goodly portion of this study deals with the Revolution, of increasing interest to students, since the whole revolutionary period was coincident with her life.[30]

An avid public interest in the history of the Revolution met with prolific literary response. Lavish approbation was matched by crochety dissent, but occasionally there were solemn and calm appraisals. Whatever the tenor or temper, there was a lively sense of participation and an identification with history at a majestic moment of change. And the color of personality glowed as brightly as the color of events. Ramsay and Gordon outraged the scholarly convention that historians later developed, but they lived exciting lives. Subsequent standards of historical deportment and literary excellence caused their volumes to suffer by comparison, but the remarkable point is not that they wrote histories tinctured with feeling, but that they found time and energy to write them at all. Literary ladies like Mercy Otis Warren and Hannah Adams were as dashing as Massachusetts females in the waning years of the eighteenth century could be. Braintree, Milton, and Medfield resembled neither Paris nor London. And even dullness, of which Mercy Warren and Hannah Adams could scarcely be charged, is not without interest, for the wonder is how one could succeed in making an account of the Revolution dull.

Colorful personalities and significant historical writing were not infrequently united. Few, however, had more entrancing careers than John Daly Burk of Ireland, Boston, New York, and Petersburg, Virginia.[31] An Irish emigré, he first settled in Boston, where he started a newspaper, *The Polar Star and Boston Daily Advertiser,* in 1796. Failing to make journalism pay in Boston, he tried again in New York with the *Time-Piece.* Burk had more luck with the drama and is remembered as one of the first to use battle scenes in an actual stage presentation. Two literary works preceded his *History of Virginia: A History of the Late War in Ireland* and "An Historical Essay on the Character and Antiquity of Irish Songs." [32]

Burk's *History of Virginia*,[33] left unfinished because of his un-
timely death in a duel, is noteworthy on two counts. While centered
on Virginia, it is in fact a history of the region told in terms of all
British settlement. The *History of Virginia* also enjoyed the sponsorship of Thomas Jefferson. Divided into four volumes, the third, *A
History of Virginia from its first Settlement to the Present Day,* carries developments up to the critical year of 1776. The final volume,
completed after his death, deals with the war years. Jefferson's patronage, acknowledged in the dedication, gave Burk the use of his
library, including certain manuscript sources. When Jared Sparks,
the first great compiler of national records, used these volumes, he
found the last volume meager. But he believed it was "doubtless
authentic, as it was written under the eye of Mr. Jefferson." [34]

Charles Botta was one of several Europeans sufficiently impressed
by the American Revolution to write a history of it.[35] Botta, a Pied-
montese, studied medicine at the University of Turin, became an
army surgeon, and later a member of the provisional government of
Piedmont in the seventh year of the French Republic. Like other
Europeans who were drawn to a study of America, Botta perceived
in American experience a genetic kinship with his own. He followed
the progress of the American Revolution in the pages of *The Annual
Register* and in current pamphlets, and a translation of his work was
published in Philadelphia (1820–21).[36] His success was enormous.
Fourteen editions of his work were sold in the United States in a
single year.[37] Later students have had some difficulty in explaining
the generous reception accorded his volumes,[38] but a suggestion may
perhaps be found in the observations of Thomas Jefferson. Jefferson
applauded Botta because his pages glowed with a "holy enthusiasm
for the liberty and independence of nations. Neutral, as an historian
should be, in the relation of facts, he is never neutral in his feelings,
nor in the warm expression of them . . . and of the honest sympathies with . . . the better cause." [39]

Unlike Charles Botta and Mercy Otis Warren, there were others
who, though chronologically a part of the revolutionary period, were
immersed in historical problems only incidentally connected with
imperial issues. Jeremy Belknap, the great historian of New Hampshire, was such a figure.[40] Critical, rational, tolerant, he exhibited the
best scholarly traits of his age. A product of Boston and Harvard, he
was called to a church in Dover, New Hampshire, where he offici-
ated until 1786, after which Boston again became his home. In 1787
he accepted another pulpit in his native city which he held for the
rest of his life. This position gave him leisure, and easy access to

materials made it possible for him to indulge his historical interests.[41] The first volume of Belknap's *History of New Hampshire* appeared in 1784, the second in 1791, and the third in 1792.[42] Long a model of its class in composition and suggestiveness, it evoked Tocqueville's elaborate praise[43] and in truth, though equaled, it has never really been outclassed. Belknap also served the historical craft by helping to found the Massachusetts Historical Society and became one of its most loyal members. He communicated his enthusiasm for research to his associates and was largely responsible for the publication of the Society's *Collections* in 1792, a landmark in cooperative historical effort.[44] But the historians of America were then engaged in a more immediate work of collaboration.

While Belknap was restrained and judicious, his liberalism and nationalism were faultless. Criticisms of the American viewpoint during the years of the imperial clash, however, served only to strengthen patriotic conviction. Blemishes in the record of the recent past there might well have been, but the incidents of conflict were scarcely regarded as important as the meaning of the conflict itself. The record of the progress of mankind had yet to be written. And it had to be written, moreover, in great and living deeds as well as by chroniclers whose office was to recount them. To blur the past by criticism was understandable but to doubt the future stamped critics with an unmistakable brand. It was possible to comprehend the conservative temper; it was impossible to condone it. While few expected the vanquished to be generous, some expected them to be wise. The truth, after all, was clear and indisputable.

Democrats were judged by the beliefs they held, just as they were soon to be judged by their actions. Democrats not only believed in liberty and freedom; they believed in liberty and freedom for man. They rested their faith in mankind, and their faith in popular government was proportionate to their belief in humanity. Accordingly, the historic function of the American Revolution and the historic role of the newly created republic was clearly etched in the perspective of progress. Denial of the logic, whether in its premises or in its correlates, convicted critics by the very fact of denial. To limit the potentialities of man was to limit the case for popular government. To question the qualifications of the people to govern themselves was to sanction the principle of aristocracy. Aristocracy led to monarchy, monarchy to despotism. The myopic alone could fail to see the mission of the American Revolution and the destiny of the United States.

Yet it was not primarily the strictures of the unreconstructed loyalists that motivated the historians of the Revolution. Although they were quick to resent what they conceived to be a misconception and just as quick to correct it, they were too engrossed in other matters to pause overlong for critical combat. The heroic deeds of their countrymen had to be set down quickly lest younger generations, robbed of the actual experience, should forget them. Even more important than the deeds themselves were their meaning, and none could tell them as well as those who had lived close to the events.

While ardent Americans were convinced that they had served the cause of justice well, their critics of the 1770's still remained to dispute them. Jubilant writers, complacent in victory, were confident that their fellow countrymen had but to reap the rewards of the future, but vigorous critics constantly rose up to say them nay. Among them was Thomas Hutchinson, historian of Massachusetts and the last royal governor of the colony of the Bay.

Among the adversaries of colonial independence many were of greater astuteness than Governor Thomas Hutchinson. Others lived and wrote during those swiftly moving times of confusing change. Others, too, sat in the seats of power, which gave special significance to their official deeds and words. Nevertheless Hutchinson's position was a singular one. If some of his loyalist colleagues were of a more subtle turn of mind, he alone was the king's chief emissary in Massachusetts in this period of crisis and decision. If many of his Tory associates wrote with sharper understanding and with ampler cogency, he alone held a post that, in the hands of a different personality with different qualities of mind, might for a time have veered the course of events. It was not that Thomas Hutchinson was more of a Tory than Daniel Leonard or Jonathan Boucher;[45] he was not. But he expressed the conservative doctrine in official terms. For this reason the third volume of his *History* is an incomparable document; it represents the Tory mind in crucial action.[46]

Many men wrote of the revolutionary years, but Hutchinson is one of the few remembered. *The History of the Colony of Massachusetts Bay*[47] continued to be cited in almost every account of these troubled decades. The first two volumes, dealing with the years from 1628 to 1750, have acquired a kind of primary authority, and even his most caustic critics refer to the documents he so carefully collected. The third volume is equally authoritative, although for different reasons. Beginning where the second volume ends, the concluding section carries the story down to 1774, the year in which the governor relinquished his stately office. Although sixty-one years intervened between the publication of the second volume in 1767 and the appearance of the final one, the latter documents a cultural attitude with unique effectiveness and illustrates a typical frame of mind. Later generations have not found it easy to fix Hutchinson's place in American letters. Tories acclaimed him; patriots reviled him. To the latter he appeared as a stiff-necked aristocrat; to the former he seemed a loyal and conscientious servant of constitutional principle. Mercy Otis Warren, a fervent republican historian, thus assessed his leading characteristics:

> He was dark, intriguing, insinuating, haughty and ambitious; while the extreme of avarice marked every feature of his character. His abilities were little above the line of mediocrity; yet by dint of industry, exact temperance, and indefatigable labor, he became master of the accomplishments necessary to acquire popular fame. Though bred a merchant, he had looked into the origins and principles of the British Constitution, and made himself acquainted with the several forms of government established in the colonies; he had acquired some knowledge of the common law of England, diligently studied the intricacies of Machiavelian [sic] policy, and never failed to recommend the Italian master as a model to his adherents.[48]

Modern students differ no less widely. The learned Tyler, full of praise for Hutchinson's greatness as a scholar, accounted him "the ablest historical writer produced in America prior to the nineteenth century." [49] James Truslow Adams, a more recent student of the revolutionary ferment, regarded Hutchinson's three volumes as "the best historical work done in America during the colonial period." [50] But Vernon Louis Parrington in his provocative study of the colonial mind characterized Hutchinson as "marked for a reactionary." [51] He lacked, believed Parrington, "the creative imagination to reconstruct the past" and could scarcely ever "rid himself of narrow partisanship." [52] Parrington's estimate represents the minority view. James Savage, editor of Winthrop's *Journal,* had even more robust praise for Hutchinson than Tyler. Before 1765, wrote Savage, Hutchinson "was incomparably the most popular and most influential statesman in New England." Savage, moreover, felt that "from the year of the Stamp Act until that of his own death in London fifteen years afterward, [he] was the most powerful American statesman in the ranks of the Loyalist party." [53]

As Thomas Hutchinson has always been a central figure in the historiography of the Revolution, these conflicting judgments demand appraisal. In addition, it is vital to examine the critical standards upon which such evaluations are based. While the verdict of Tyler and Adams has frequently been confirmed by the weight of scholarly reputation, it is difficult to see the grounds upon which it rests. Hutchinson was not alone in searching out documents. He was hardly more diligent than Prince or Stith;[54] no more "modern" than scores of his contemporaries. Virtually all are in agreement on the limitations of his style, the meagerness of his insights and the narrowness of his conceptions. His historical research was the by-product of a busy life, and he was no more a "professional" historian than other writers. Hence his results may properly be compared with the achievements of others who wrote with different purposes. William Bradford and John Winthrop, for example, are easily his superiors in literary craftsmanship, in conceptual scope, and in imaginative qualities.[55] Jeremy Belknap, more strictly an historian, was also more consequential as the creator of an intellectual legacy. One cannot fail to agree with Parrington that Hutchinson's knowledge of political theory was severely limited, a limitation fatal to his scholarship and statesmanship alike. His reaction to Samuel Adams' use of the natural rights theory indicates, as one of Adams' biographers has stressed, a complete and thorough unfamiliarity with Locke. Indeed, there is little to suggest that he ever read Locke, a suggestion which, if true, was remarkable among eighteenth-century American men of letters.[56]

Parrington's estimate is as limited as Tyler's is generous. It will hardly do to say that Hutchinson was "marked for a reactionary" simply because he successfully manipulated his father's mercantile business. Nor will it suffice to allege that he was "avaricious for power." [57] Merchants' sons and merchants there were aplenty on the patriot side, and the lust for power was no special attribute of royalists. If as Parrington insists—and correctly—that Hutchinson never examined the basis of his political faith, it can only be answered that the process of critical self-examination is very rare indeed—even in a period when many men are seemingly forced by circumstances to undertake it.

Yet in historical terms few can compare with the great royalist governor of Massachusetts Bay. Loyalist writers following him, while sharing his preconceptions, wrote under a different dispensation. The significant literature of loyalist dissent appeared between 1774 and 1776, between Hutchinson's retirement from office and the Declaration of Independence. During these years Joseph Galloway, Samuel Seabury, Jonathan Odell, Daniel Leonard, and Jonathan Boucher[58]—loyalists all—presented a forthright demurrer against the trend of colonial action. After 1776 it was still possible to write, but it was no longer possible to hope that writing alone could stay the direction of change. If, after the issuance of the great Declaration, the movement for independence was no longer debatable, after 1783 and British defeat, the United States of America was no longer vulnerable to the logic of words.

The organization of learning, often deflected by war, nevertheless continues. Certain scholars manage to insulate themselves from the implications of violence;[59] participants can rarely evade the impact of issues. Following independence, dissenters from the patriot cause within the colonies acquired a different set of purposes; following expulsion, most Tories acquired a different set of mind. Such writers were less dispassionate than passionate, but they called attention to attitudes that an accelerating avalanche of opinion threatened to extinguish. However partisan, these attitudes possessed a cogency later generations on both sides of the Atlantic were to appreciate. Tory writings provide an important measure of self-criticism. Americans, aware of their existence, tended for obvious reasons to dismiss them. The British, for different reasons only slightly less obvious, tended to ignore the loyalist point of view.

But the loyalist point of view and its later development outlined the forthcoming revision in the historiography of the American Revolution. The more loyalists acclaimed the virtues of the British Constitution and the validity of their special brand of political theory, the more it was evident that error in the application of both had been committed. By loyalist definition at least, legal power indisputably lay on the British side of the ocean, and it was hard to escape the conclusion that the British wielders of power had erred. An early British history of the Revolution appeared simultaneously with the event. *The Annual Register,* a year-by-year account, later became a convenient source for students frequently consulted and not infrequently copied. Largely written by Edmund Burke until his death in 1797, it was in the main factually accurate. But it was unequivocally Whig in its interpretation. The leading assumption running through the narrative was that the Americans had never wanted independence. Since, argued the English Whigs, separation was never the colonial aim, it followed that a different—and more intelligent—handling of the issues of controversy would have resulted in peace rather than war, in preserving the empire rather than in dismembering it. The intellectual genesis of this mode of analysis is easy to comprehend, but its sequel follows less smoothly from the premises. Tories, who so often accused colonials of wanting nothing short of independence, ended by agreeing with the Whigs. According to Sydney G. Fisher, it was this unpredictable merger of Whig and Tory historiography which resulted in the legendary and mythmaking process by which the American Revolution was long misconceived. If no one wanted independence, why did it come about? [60]

Whatever the validity of Fisher's special argument, it establishes the import of Tory polemics. Tory writers will always remain basic in any attempt to reassess the intellectual course of the Revolution. But they are just as basic in any attempt to reassess the social and intellectual course of democracy. There is no material more significant for the history of democracy than the written remains of its opponents. They reveal with the sharpest clarity the social and intellectual circumstances of democratic evolution. Such writings are more than anachronisms preserved for the delectation of antiquaries and the use of historians. They were themselves spurs to action. None knew better than colonial patriots and the early American historians who succeeded them that they were disputed by powerful opinion both learned and devout. Advocates of the philosophy of the Declaration were conscious that its precepts were as frequently condemned as endorsed. While this was more generally true outside the boundaries of the United States, there was nothing like unanimity within the nation. The United States appeared in a world neither friendly nor sympathetic, a fact that defined the objectives and edged the fervor of its proponents. Opposition, overt and latent, demanded the best that analysis could provide and the highest patriotism devotion could inspire. Loyalist criticisms and conservative reservations were integral parts of the dialectics of democracy.[61]

"A history of the histories of the American Revolution," wrote Professor Arthur M. Schlesinger, Sr., "should go far toward realizing the ideals and purposes which have governed historical writing in this country in the various periods of the past." [62] Altering viewpoints concerning the Revolution actually reflect altering perspectives in scholarship. These mutations in scholarly perspective provide a cross-section of historiography because they are in themselves aspects of a changing culture. Complexity succeeded simplicity in history as well as society. Single causes no longer sufficed for social understanding. Multiplicity took the place of uniformity in social structure and in social analysis. Unsophisticated theories of historical causation or of social organization appeared as inadequate to later generations, as they had seemed adequate to former ones. Black was evil, and white was good, and if the twain sometimes appeared to meet, they rarely ever intermingled. For subsequent scholarship, the fact of intermingling was given. It remained to factor out combinations and to evaluate them in the process of historical reconstruction. Transcendental assurance gave way to the method of experimentation by hypothesis. Accordingly, it became possible to pose the most outrageous theorems for historical exploration. Ideas that had become conclusions by default were reexamined; reputations based upon hearsay were reappraised. Forces, endowed by myth with causal powers, evaporated with exposure to fresh concepts and fresh data. Hallowed reputations were made and remade as scholars with newer intellectual formulations were led to forgotten treasure troves of materials and to the re-examination of older concepts fertilized by newer ones.

The writing of the history of the Revolution altered as passing centuries added experience to time. Historical scholars before 1800 enjoyed certain advantages denied to those who followed them. Eighteenth-century writers, present on the spot, believed they saw history as it actually happened. Many were privileged to go straight to the general rather than to the general's memoirs. They could interrogate the makers of the Revolution and the builders of governments, instead of asking themselves the questions that forgotten papers in family attics and official archives suggested. They moved among the men who were themselves made by revolutionary events. These were the men who in one critical period after another were the *dramatis personae* of history and who were regarded—or who regarded themselves—as the heroes of a great social tradition. Later historians had the great social tradition, the archives, and the concepts of social science.

XI

Historiography and Nationalism

The American Republic in 1783 was an alliance of states rather than a union of peoples, a legal rather than a social fact. Independence was not only political separation from Britain; it was also a separation from British imperial power. Power was not focused in the national congress; it was divided among the several states. The process of transition from colony to commonwealth, from states to nation, governed political as well as intellectual history in the decades following Yorktown and Saratoga. The idea of nationalism was central to both.

Americans were confronted by the dilemma of the unprecedented. If the spirit of '76 was strong, the Republic was weak. Although Americans often knew what they wanted, ways of effecting their desires were limited by history. The first citizens of the Republic wished to establish republican government in a world uncongenial to republican principles. And the tasks of America's philosopher-statesmen were intensified by the irremediable facts of existence.

America was enormous. American territory, according to one contemporary estimate, stretched over an area of a million square miles. There were 589,000,000 acres of land and 51,000,000 acres of water and in the West the public domain amounted to 220,000,000 additional acres.[1] To administer so vast an area required resources the nation did not possess. Europeans predicted the new venture would dissolve into anarchy before it could fairly be tested. America, moreover, had achieved independence from Britain, not isolation from Europe. England remained an American continental power. Spain, through mastery of the Mississippi's mouth, retained a hold on the straggling western settlements. Behind the fine Iberian diplomatic hand, were the designs of Bourbon France. More than a third of the total acreage of the United States was unoccupied except for the Indians, whose efforts to survive provided schemers on both sides of the Atlantic with a pawn in the ancient game of balance of power.

History was weighted against the republican experiment. Administrative techniques for the ordering of large territories were inventions of kings and their ministers. Loyalty was a response to the monarchical principle, the dynastic house, the royal person. It was a loyalty supported, moreover, by force. Behind the royal person and the royal bureaucracy was the royal army. Power had always been associated with force; it remained to be demonstrated that power, voluntarily delegated, could be exercised without use of force. Administration depended upon transportation and communication; America was not only large but undeveloped. Transportation in Britain, for example, was infinitely superior, while the distance between Land's End and the Orkneys hardly compared with the distance from Maine to the Georgia frontier. According to the blueprints of historical experience, republics were small. And the record of the small republics of history, if republics they were, was bleak and depressing.

America was rural. American historians, while aware of the rural nature of America, have written its history with scant regard to its rural character. Ninety per cent of the population lived on farms; most studies have been written from urban sources and from urban points of view. Historians studied their Jefferson with care, but some Jeffersonian maxims were stressed to the neglect of others. There was little attempt until recently to align the precepts of Jeffersonian philosophy with political, economic, and psychological realities. Republican leaders thought of small units of government loosely federated in a decentralized system. Local power alone was believed to be controllable. All central power, remote from the sources of origin, was dangerous. These propositions seemed the more apparent because based upon historical experience. Political assumptions were the social and psychological counterparts of rural and agricultural assumptions, the political and economic expressions of rural attitudes and agricultural behavior patterns. Americans were individualistic because they were themselves relatively self-sufficient. They were distrustful of power in strange hands because they placed their trust in the face-to-face contacts of a folk society. They believed less government was better than more government, because the task of controlling big government strained their imagination. Big governments were despotic governments. They believed in doing things themselves, because many things were and could be accomplished without apparent aid. The Articles of Confederation, the state constitutions, and the legislative record in many states between 1776 and 1789 expressed these experiences in political terms.

The results for historiography were consequential. Merchants and business groups during the Confederation era and the period of the formation of the Constitution were the articulate elements in society. "They exported the produce of farm and forest," concludes a competent modern student, "and in turn imported the necessaries and luxuries which were paid for by that produce. They were the middlemen who made fortunes and had influence in the American states out of all proportion to their numbers. Their power was born of place, position, and fortune. They were located in or near the seats of government and they were in direct contact with legislatures and government officers. They influenced and often dominated the local newspapers which voiced the ideas and interests of commerce and identified them with the good of the whole people, the state, and the nation. The published writings of the leaders of the period are almost without exception those of merchants, their lawyers, or of politicians sympathetic with them. Thus it is that subsequent thinking about the period has been guided in one direction." [2]

The founding of the American Republic was first interpreted by men who shared such experiences and such views. Men with different experiences and different views, though far more numerous, were scattered, unorganized, and for the most part unlettered. The farmers—the small, inarticulate, relatively self-sufficient farmers—were silent, and their hopes and desires were not preserved in literary form. And it was from the documents that historians later wrote the story of American beginnings. The small farmers, however, did "influence elections and the policies of legislatures. So powerfully did they make themselves felt during the Confederation that by 1786 seven of the thirteen states had once more adopted some form of paper money as a means of agrarian relief. It is significant that later historians have usually discussed such measures in terms of unsound finance, or even of morality, but almost never in terms of an attempt to solve the pressing problems of an agrarian society." [3]

"The pressing problems of an agrarian society," however solved, were solved neither by its agrarian elements nor by agrarian conceptions. The concept of centralized power, the opposite of decentralization, was employed to order the affairs of the early Republic. American historical writing, interpreting the documents that recorded these occurrences, created an American tradition of national power.

An expansion of national power, warranted or not, was neither an agrarian device nor a majority view. Scholars who transmitted the notion of a self-defeating localism under the Confederation also transmitted the notion of a revivifying nationalism under the Constitution. American nationalism became a synonym for national power. If, as in some accounts, chaos ruled society after the Revolution, order governed the nation after the Constitution was adopted. The "new roof," the arresting metaphor invented to describe the constitutional framework, fails to evoke an image of the architectural underpinnings the Constitution had crowned. When the historians had established the Constitution in their reconstruction of events, they began at once to stress the difficulties inherent in the federal system. They emphasized the division of power between the individual states, sovereign for some purposes, and the federal government, sovereign for other purposes. States' rights and sectionalism, forces operative from the beginning in the shape of localism and regional differences, reappeared as explanations of internal conflict and the continuing crisis leading to civil war. The divisive threats of the so-called critical period persisted during the national period.

The hypothesis of centralized power and the dominating role of national government conflicted with the facts of eighteenth-century American life. They failed to square with the living realities of existence, realities reflected in agrarian political concepts. Fear of centralized power was the psychological and intellectual response of the small American farmer in postrevolutionary America. It was a response rooted in history and conditioned by a rural way of life. Decentralization and the limitation of power were countervailing traditions to centralized national power. If the former were not always explicit in the sources, they were implicit in the historical reconstruction of them. State governments, not the federal government, exercised the greatest influence over their citizens, a condition true before the adoption of the Constitution and which continued, as one historian asserts, to the brink of the twentieth century. Most of "the normal governmental contacts of the citizen were with his state," writes Thomas C. Cochran, but "historians . . . persisted in writing a national history revolving around presidential administrations and constitutional law." [4]

There was no disparity between the flowering of early national loyalties and diverse theories of political power. American loyalty was loyalty to an idea.[5] Americans were identified with Massachusetts, Virginia, or Maryland, but before the Revolution, as after it, they accounted themselves the champions "of rights which were confined by no boundary line." [6] The rights of man were not confined by state boundaries or barricaded within the national frontier. American nationalism, comprising a number of elements simultaneously, was a confession of faith and a mechanism of defense. It was blatantly aggressive and confidently optimistic, a quiet hope and a confession of disquieting inferiority. It was parochial and global, universal and local. Despite its diversities, it was uncompromisingly humanitarian. Humanitarianism provided the compelling drive that countered its diversities. America's hopes for mankind were woven into its literature, its art, and its architecture. America's hopes for mankind were written into American history.

Patriotism colored all American activity in the decades following the Revolution. A philologist, for example, conducted a campaign to purge American English of aristocratic vestiges latent in British speech. Republicanism required a language suitable to its principles and a coinage suitable to its institutions.[7] Erasmus Root, author of *An Introduction to Arithmetic* (1796), exhorted: "Let us, I beg of you, Fellow-Citizens, no longer meanly follow the British intricate mode of reckoning. Let them have their way, and us, ours. . . . Their mode is suited to the genius of their government, for it seems to be the policy of tyrants, to keep their accounts in as intricate and perplexing a method as possible. . . . But Republican money ought to be simple and adapted to the meanest capacity." [8] Even the literature of the nursery did not escape the patriotic zeal of custodians of national virtue. The fathers of democratic education attempted to purify children's rhymes, folk tales, and fairy stories. One such patriotic editing altered *Mother Goose* so that "Four and Twenty Blackbirds" was made to read:

> *When the pie was opened*
> *The Birds they were songless*
> *Was not that a pretty dish*
> *To set before the Congress?* [9]

Desire to match intellectual independence with political independence moved all classes of society. Philip Freneau, a leading poet of the young republic, spoke out sharply:

> *Can we never be thought to have learning or grace*
> *Unless it be brought from that horrible place*
> *Where tyranny reigns with her impudent face?* [10]

Noah Webster, foremost advocate of American cultural individuality, corroborated Freneau's sentiments. "Europe is grown old in folly, corruption, and tyranny—in that country laws are perverted, manners are licentious, literature is declining, and human nature is debased. For America in her infancy to adopt the present maxims of the old world would be to stamp the wrinkle of decrepit age upon the bloom of youth, and to plant the seed of decay in a vigorous constitution." [11] Other commentators, though less effusive, repeated the same theme. When the American Academy of Arts and Sciences was established in Boston in 1780, the founders proclaimed among their objects the cultivation of "every art and science which may tend to advance the interest, honor, dignity, and happiness of a free, independent, and virtuous people." [12] Prideful writers of textbooks for the unsuspecting young took it upon themselves to see that spelling, geography, and arithmetic carried no subtle monarchical implications. The English language itself, one affrighted writer suggested, was alien to the purposes of a free culture. He proposed that Hebrew or German should be the language of the schools and used as the official tongue for public documents. More temperate was the comment of President John Witherspoon of the College of New Jersey (later Princeton) that the peculiarities of American speech already differentiated it from the English spoken in the Old World.[13]

Organized religion no less than popular literature responded to the nationalistic impulse. Quickening the movement of separation between church and state, a process already begun, the Revolution deprived formal ecclesiastical establishments of their privileged place in society. Churches in America declared their independence from European administrative controls.[14] A Philadelphia printer, Robert Aitken, published in 1777 an American version of the New Testament and later printed a complete English Bible both of which represented the first American ventures of their kind.[15] America was to be free of dependence upon Europe even to the extent of the importation of Bibles, and Congress passed a resolution endorsing Aitken's labor of patriotic love. Isaiah Thomas, famed printer of Boston and Worcester, felt a similar urge. By 1800 there were twenty complete editions of the Bible in its Roman Catholic as well as in its Protestant forms.[16]

Americans were concerned with both present and future. It was in the present that the future was to be made. Two possibilities suggested themselves to contemporary minds: one was the reform of education, the other the teaching of history. The former would insure the gains to liberty that the revolutionary heroes had won; the latter would preserve the glorious record they had made. Reticence was no part of the loyal design for national salvation. Most of the intellectual architects of the new nation doubtless felt with George Washington, who wrote in 1783: "It appears to me that there is still an option left to the United States of America—that it is in their choice, and depends upon their conduct, whether they will be respectable and prosperous, or contemptible and miserable as a Nation. This is the time of their political probation." Benjamin Rush, scholar, patriot, educator, set out his thoughts on these matters in 1786. The new government had "created a new class of duties to every American." These duties were specific and they carried instructions for historians, artists, and writers of textbooks for future citizens. The young "must be taught that there can be no durable liberty but in a republic, and that government, like all other sciences, is of a progressive nature." Let Americans be taught "the history of the ancient republics, and the progress of liberty and tyranny in the different states of Europe." [17] Rush's ideas served as models for many. A detailed prescription was hardly needed, for all who shared the general assumptions emerged with similar injunctions.

Jedidiah Morse, minister at Charlestown, Massachusetts, was an unqualified devotee of the principles of Benjamin Rush. Doubly famed as "the father of American geography" and the father of Samuel F. B. Morse, he set himself to revise the teaching of geography in the United States.[18] As a cultural patriot he was exceedingly irked that Americans should be forced to rely upon foreign accounts of the contours and resources of their own land. He disliked the manual then in use as much because it was the work of an Englishman as because it was inadequate. *Geography Made Easy* was Morse's contribution to accuracy and Americanism, and the result of his resolve to do better than anyone had yet done. The text, the first work of its kind to appear in the New America, became in effect the outline for later expansions and additions. *The American Geography,* an expanded version of *Geography Made Easy,* appeared in 1789, and was followed by *The American Universal Geography,* a two-volume work, approximately half of which was devoted to the United States.

Morse found something of a correlation between American independence and accuracy.[19] Before nationhood, the Europeans, who alone had written on the subject, purveyed incorrect information to the world. "But since the United States have become a separate nation," he wrote in the preface of *The American Geography,* "the rest of the world have a right now to expect authentic information." [20] Morse soon traveled from geography to history. *The American Gazetteer,* a work consisting of seven thousand separate pieces, was published in 1797.[21] Like his geographies, the *Gazetteer* was conceived as a means of introducing America to the world. His most interesting and memorable historical effort is the *Annals of the American Revolution* (1824).[22] Interest attaches to this compendium—for it can hardly be said to be more—because the sixth part of it contains a section on the causes of the civil conflict. The chapter entitled "Causes of the Revolution, assigned by Dr. Franklin, and the late President Adams," contains a number of letters from John Adams written to Morse in response to queries.

Jedidiah Morse was as impassioned a Federalist as Thomas Jefferson was an uncompromising democrat, but neither yielded to the other in love of country. Independence was an American need. Whether for geography, arithmetic, or the importation of Bibles, the demand for independence was both patriotic and ideological. Hugh Henry Brackenridge's *United States Magazine* insisted with gentle but unmistakable conviction that "we are able to cultivate the *belles lettres,* even disconnected with Great-Britain; and that liberty is of so noble and energetic a quality, as even from the bosom of a war to call forth the powers of human genius, in every course of literary fame and improvement." [23] Royall Tyler, pioneer American dramatist, expressed the same yearnings in *The Contrast* (1787):

> *Whilst all, which aims at splendour and parade,*
> *Must come from Europe, and be ready made.*[24]

America's citizens believed in America. Belief was compounded of pride in the way things were and confidence in what they might yet become. The recent revolutionary past supplied them with the confidence; they had only to put reason and wisdom to work for mankind to avoid the agonies that had afflicted less fortunate generations. With Jefferson, they gazed at the rising western star and read their future in it. That "we are to look backwards," wrote the American philosopher of democracy to his friend Joseph Priestley, "instead of forwards for the improvement of the human mind, and to recur to the annals of our ancestors for what is most perfect in government, in religion and in learning, is worthy of those bigots in religion and government, by whom it has been recommended, and whose purposes it would answer. But it is not an idea which this country will endure." [25] When Jefferson wrote to John Adams, "I like the dreams of the future better than the history of the past," [26] he gave expression to what was already a dominant democratic characteristic and was to become one of the most pervasive of national traits.

Thomas Jefferson and Benjamin Rush had their dreams, but they also had concrete plans and specific proposals. Their trust in the future was not misplaced, for they helped to make it. Great though Thomas Jefferson was, he did not work alone. Jefferson gave expression to democratic yearnings in his own characteristic prose; Noah Webster virtually fashioned a democratic prose for Americans. Few individuals have ever wielded so great an influence in the making of the popular mind. America, wrote Webster in 1783, then an unknown pedagogue, "must be as independent in *literature* as she is in politics." She must, he further proclaimed, become "as famous for *arts* as for *arms*." [27] If Webster did not himself succeed in making the United States famous for the arts, he created an audience capable of responding to the literary artistry of others. But he did make Americans conscious of their language, of their idiom, and of the creative instrumentality of words. His *Spelling-Book* sold some fifteen million copies before 1840; sixty million by 1900.[28] "No other secular book," concluded his principal biographer, "has reached so many minds in America . . . and none has played so shaping a part in our destiny."

> Webster became our greatest schoolmaster. He passed successively from the desk of a Connecticut log schoolhouse to the lecture platform, to the editorial chair, and finally to the home library table as the arbiter of every English-speaking reader's and writer's diction. His schoolbooks were carried from the hills of New England across the Alleghenies; his were among the first books printed in every new settlement. Across the prairies and over the Rocky Mountains his carefully marshalled columns of words marched like warriors against the ignorance that tended to disrupt the primitive society of thinly spread and localized culture of America. Dialect variation disappeared from our writing and spelling, and to his blue-backed Speller . . . America owes its remarkable uniformity of language. No other book, the Bible excepted, has strained so many heads, or done so much good. It taught millions to read, and not one to sin. And today the monolithic "Webster" . . . bears silent testimony to Noah Webster's enduring labors and superb genius.[29]

Noah Webster was unsuccessful as a lawyer, indifferent as a singing master, and he made no fortune out of teaching. But as a grammarian and a lexicographer he is unsurpassed. He invigorated the American language and himself became a part of it. Webster is the word for dictionary, and wherever English is spoken Webster is known even though many who speak his name are unaware that it is Noah to whom they refer.[30] He was schoolmaster to America, and he taught Americans the uses of their language. He also taught them to recognize its distinctive qualities. He did not instruct historians how to write, but he instructed the readers for whom the historians wrote. To Webster grammar was a passion. But he was no dry-as-dust grammarian who viewed himself as the guardian of the sacred principles of syntax and pronunciation. Words were tools, and he would have his people use them for the living of individual and national life. Webster practiced the grammar he preached, and wrote and lectured to exemplify it.

To free the American language from dependence upon England was more than a chauvinistic loyalty. It was for the purposes of making American English a vehicle for American objectives. He lectured on American issues and pamphleteered to win acceptance for his particular brand of them. By doing so he was teaching by example and demonstrating the social function of words and the internal logic of their arrangement. When he first presented the outline of his program to Ezra Stiles for approval, he followed the advice of the president of Yale and entitled his work *A Grammatical Institute of the English Language*. Webster was no Calvin, he was not an oracle of immutable precepts, and besides he had an American end in view. He had first thought of "the American Instructor" as a proper title which was much more to Webster's point, and in 1778 the *Speller* became *The American Spelling Book*.[31] The dictionary, *An American Dictionary of the English Language,* in two volumes, appeared in 1828.[32] Webster was still fighting the war for cultural independence. It was the *American* dictionary, and he spelled out his challenge in the preface: "I may . . . affirm with truth that our country has produced some of the best models of composition. The style of . . . many . . . writings; in purity, in elegance, and in technical precision, is equalled only by that of the best British authors, and surpassed by that of no English composition." In 1890 Webster's commercial successors brought out a new edition of the dictionary, *Webster's International Dictionary.* Gone was the adjective "American" from the title page, but gone too were the needs that Webster served. By 1890 internationalism was no longer a fighting word, and even Noah Webster himself might have given his approval.[33]

Webster never wavered in his fidelity to American cultural nationalism, but he changed his mind about democracy. Webster wrote a piece on "The Theory of Government" in 1785 in which he extolled representative democracy as "the most perfect system that is practicable on earth." This dictum he later repudiated as a "chimerical" notion that he "had imbibed from the writings of Dr. Price and Rousseau." [34] Even when his approval for popular government ran most strongly, he favored more extensive powers for the central government of the Confederation. A lecture tour in Massachusetts coincided with the outbreak of Shays' Rebellion, from which he recoiled. Law and order, he affirmed, were the prerequisites of reasonable societies. Paper-money panaceas were lawless deprivations of property. The great educator of the people finally concluded that the people were too uninformed to be entrusted with the management of their own affairs.[35] When the Federal Constitution was promulgated, Webster became one of its most articulate champions, and he always believed he had anticipated the founding fathers in projecting its most characteristic features.[36] Just before he died in May 1843, an honored and respected patriarch, he said: "I have struggled with many difficulties. Some I have been able to overcome, and by some I have been overcome. I have made many mistakes, but I love my country, and have labored for the youth of my country." [37] Noah Webster was right.

Another Yankee from Connecticut, Webster's friend and college classmate, was Joel Barlow. While Webster embraced democracy only to abandon it, Barlow abandoned an aristocratic superciliousness for democracy.[38] His was a democracy that came out of long European experience and provided insights into the meaning America held for him and for the world. As a member of the famous Hartford coterie of wits, he put words together with an easy grace in the manner of his conservative associates and indulged in the fashionable criticism of popular foibles.[39] But the company he kept and the pose he cultivated were no measure of his feeling for America. His epic poem, *The Vision of Columbus,* nine books and almost five thousand words long, was contrived to portray what the new world had come to mean, not only to Barlow and his countrymen, but to all mankind. First published in 1787, Barlow reworked it in the course of the next twenty-five years, and a new and final version, *The Columbiad,* appeared in 1807.[40] The first version was dedicated to Louis XVI, the gracious sovereign of America's ally, France. Significantly, Barlow had something to do with the loss of this particular king's head, for he was later immersed in the currents of liberal European politics. The second edition, dedicated not to Napoleon, was inscribed to the inventor of steam navigation. But it was not until Barlow had been long enough in Europe that he really learned what he himself had written:

> Think not, my friends, the patriot's task is done,
> Or Freedom safe, because the battle's won.[41]

Barlow took up the patriot's task. Fourteen years after graduation from Yale,[42] he went to Europe on a mission for the Ohio Land Company.[43] He had a pleasant but financially unrewarding career as an army chaplain, a lawyer, and a writer.[44] Barlow was not quite Virgil, with whom patriotic reviewers sometimes compared him,[45] but *The Vision of Columbus* was the best of its kind America had to offer, and its readers were charmed to have their own ideas so well expressed in metrical verse. Even if he had little money, Barlow had a reputation. Since he had taken Ruth Baldwin[46]—whose brother, Abraham, represented Georgia in the national legislature—as his wife, he required more than he could earn at the writer's trade in a literary world unprotected by copyright. When the offer from the Ohio Company presented itself, together with the chance to improve his material prospects, he was too much the Yankee to refuse.

When Barlow, then just thirty-four years old, set sail for France in 1788, he began a new and adventurous life. He arrived in Europe when France was on the brink of revolt and with Jefferson, Paine, and Gouverneur Morris he was among the fortunate company of Americans in Paris who were witnesses to it. As American minister to the Bourbon court, Jefferson maintained a decorous neutrality. With the knowledge of some of the ministry, his house was used as a meeting place during the initial stages of respectable political plotting.[47] But Barlow, like Tom Paine, had no official position and was unrestricted by protocol. Paine wrote *The Rights of Man;* Joel Barlow wrote *Advice to the Privileged Orders.*[48] As in *The Columbiad,* Barlow interpreted the history of the United States. In the United States, he told all who would listen, "the science of liberty is universally understood, felt and practised, as much by the simple as the wise, the weak as the strong. Their deep-rooted and inveterate habit of thinking is, that all men are equal in their rights, that it is impossible to make them otherwise; and this being their undisturbed belief, they have no conception how any man in his senses can entertain any other. This point once settled, everything is settled. Many operations, which in Europe have been considered as incredible tales or dangerous experiments, are but the infallible consequences of this great principle." [49]

Barlow's *Advice* had nothing like the vogue of *The Rights of Man*. Both writings plunged their authors into difficulty with British officialdom and into favor with French radicals. Barlow also became a citizen of the French Republic to which he gave good democratic counsel. In "A Letter to the National Convention of France," he laid down the rules for framing a constitution and instanced the theoretical principles supporting them. He expressed confidence that "any people . . . are the best judges of their own wants relative to the restraint of laws, and would always supply those wants better than they could be supplied by others." Once the doctrine of equality was accepted and incorporated in the fundamental law, "It ought to be the invariable object of the social compact to insure the exercise of that equality, by rendering [the population] . . . as equal in all forms of enjoyments as can possibly be consistent with good order, industry and the reward of merit. Every individual ought to be rendered as independent of every other individual as possible; and at the same time as dependent as possible on the whole community." Barlow was now no longer a novice in the philosophy of democracy: "Those who are selected to be the organs of the people, in making and executing the laws, should feel this dependence in the strongest degree. The easiest and most natural method of effecting this purpose, is to oblige them to recur frequently to the authors of their official existence, to deposit their powers, mingle with their fellows, and await the decision of the same sovereign will which created them at first, to know whether they are again to be trusted." [50]

Robespierre and the Terror cured him of French politics, for totalitarian certainties made no sense to a democratic Yankee. He had reason to congratulate himself that he had not like Paine been elected to the Assembly. Paine went to prison, and Barlow was free to go about his business. Home began to look good to him, and he was making plans for his return when the American government sent him to Algiers in 1795. On the Barbary Coast in the eighteenth century, foreigners either died or accomplished the miraculous. Barlow did not die. Instead, he established himself with the dey, which helped to smooth out the tangled relations between the Barbary states and the United States government.[51] Connecticut and America continued to fill the Barlows with longing, but years were to pass before they could go home again. Finally in 1805 Barlow came back and settled down in Washington to finish his *Columbiad,* to write a history of the American Revolution,[52] and to accomplish all the ambitious things busy men outline in their dreams. James Madison, then president, sent him off to Napoleon's France to try his luck at securing a commercial treaty with the unpredictable Corsican. These were to be his last travels. After negotiating the details of a treaty with the French foreign office—a job wilier diplomats had failed to accomplish—Barlow and other ambassadors were invited to meet Napoleon at Vilna. The march to Moscow had begun, and Napoleon anticipated a triumphant return. Vilna was to be an object lesson in power. Joel Barlow never met Napoleon in that Polish town. Napoleon managed to get back to Paris, but Barlow, at the age of fifty-eight, died of pneumonia and was hurriedly buried, far from the Connecticut hills, in the little village of Zarnowiec, near Cracow.[53]

To George Washington's countrymen the commander in chief of the revolutionary armies was first in their hearts. And first he remained in peace and in war. Other leaders in American life have enticed more biographical talent and study—notably Abraham Lincoln—but at least until the Lincoln legend had achieved its full maturity, George Washington was the unchallenged folk hero of American history. The patriotism of the Revolution and the early national period reached astronomical heights in the adulation of George Washington. Magazine and newspaper writers together with local versifiers strained their ingenuity in search of ample adjectives.[54] Washington was the:

> *Illustrious patriot, hero, sage,*
> *Ordained to save a future age*
> *Before Columbia's birth, . . .*
> *Grand base of freedom's fed'rate dome,*
> *More glorious far than Greece or Rome,*
> *The noblest man on earth.*[55]

The first gentleman of Virginia and of the Republic, he had a career that was one long record of devotion to the nation that so richly rewarded him. As the victorious commander of the army of independence, presiding officer of the Constitutional Convention, and chief executive of the United States, he appeared as the physical embodiment of American genius and American virtue. Later students have found it difficult to see the living man through the blur of myth; those closer to the events experienced no such difficulties. For them he was the symbol of statehood. He was an American David who had freed his people from the menace of a sinister modern Goliath. An American Cincinnatus, he was twice called from his Virginia acres to perform public duties. Twice he returned to his ancestral fields to resume the rural life after having first surrendered the tokens of power. His was a career out of which heroes were made, and Americans were eager to worship.[56]

The first and most notorious item of Washingtoniana was the work of Mason Locke Weems. Familiarly known as Parson Weems, he started life as a medical student, switched to the Anglican ministry, and ended as an itinerant vendor of books.[57] When he published his life of the first president, he tapped a field up to that time unexploited and made money for himself and the publishing firm he represented. Sydney G. Fisher, for whom the exposure of historical myths was a specialty, regarded Weems as "a writer of the highest order of popularity." As a popular writer he had a fabulous influence, and "in that sense" he was "the ablest historian we have produced." Weems, he wrote, "will live forever. He captured the American people. He was the first to catch their ear. He said exactly what they wanted to hear. He has been read a hundred times more than all the other historians and biographers of the revolution put together." One may well differ with Fisher's final assessment.[58]

The Life and Memorable Actions of Washington,[59] published in 1800, was written for the edification of the young, but absorbed the youthful of all ages. Weems had a superlative talent for storytelling. Whether he just talked to people in the rural lanes of the South or put the same tale on paper by the light of his campfire at the end of the day's journey, he made the most obdurate indifference quicken into interest. The peerless character who materialized by Weems' deft use of words was already the national idol. All the shining attributes with which he endowed his subject were the commonplace attributes, honored by everyone and capable of universal emulation. There but for the grace of a devil's luck any could go, for hard work, perseverance, and temperate living were the opportunities of all men. Weems was one of the earliest exemplars of a sturdy American literary genre, the biography of success. And the cult of success, even though hardened into a sentimental axiom by unimaginative dullards, is deep in the American grain. He was the pioneer Horatio Alger of American literary culture, the author of the most popular biography of American letters. *The Life . . . of George Washington,* in Alger's patois, was the story of a successful career from colonial surveyor to first president of the United States.

Parson Weems' flamboyant success is easily measured. That his *Washington* went through innumerable editions—variously estimated as between thirty and seventy[60]—is not so conclusive as other evidence. Then as now people bought books they never found time or inclination to read, and mere statistics of volumes printed and sold is only a partial index of the penetration of ideas. But the popular image of George Washington painted in the lush colors mixed by the good parson's own hand is evidence almost indisputable. The story of Washington and the cherry tree, a creation of the author's pure imaginative genius, became part of the national mythology, as indestructible as Plymouth Rock and the pioneer log cabin. George Washington had been presented with a hatchet useless to a young boy unless put into action. In this particular instance, it was employed to demolish a cherry tree in the Washington garden, an act of childish vandalism all too easily discovered. Questioned by a remarkably self-controlled father, George Washington confessed to the deed in the now famous words: "I can't tell a lie, Pa, you know I can't tell a lie. I did cut it with my hatchet." There is hardly an American now alive who did not learn as a schoolboy that among the many virtues distinguishing the first president honesty was paramount. Contemporaries of Weems probably also remembered the substance of the response to the brave confession by George Washington's proud parent. "Such an act of heroism in my son is more worth than a thousand trees, though blossomed with silver, and their fruits of the purest gold." [61] Weems made George Washington and Parson Weems parts of American folklore.

A famous life of Washington, now more noted because of its author than because of its subject, was written by John Marshall, chief justice of the Supreme Court of the United States.[62] The project was suggested to Marshall by Bushrod Washington, the general's nephew, whose financial resources needed as much bolstering as those of the chief justice. Pecuniary motivation does not guarantee a bad book, and no two men in America were in a better position to sponsor this particular one. Bushrod Washington had the materials. Marshall, able to observe Washington closely at Valley Forge (1777–78), knew his subject as well personally as Washington ever permitted himself to be known. As a leading Virginian and a leading Federalist, Marshall participated in much the same intellectual experience and could be expected to understand certain complexities incomprehensible to others. But Marshall had even greater disadvantages for this undertaking. Learned is an adjective ascribed to lawyers and jurists by courtesy. Marshall was able and versatile, but his wide reading in literature was no substitute for his deficiencies in history. There was hardly a busier man than the chief justice of the Supreme Court, and the writing of a superlative brief is not the best preparation for writing biography. To what extent Marshall was the sole author of the Marshall decisions is not so important as the fact that he had no experience and little real interest in writing itself.[63] The five discursive volumes that finally appeared, though appropriately labeled, were quite inappropriately balanced. The first, more or less justified by its subtitle, *A Compendious View of the Colonies Planted by the English in the Continent of North America,* covers the colonial period from John Cabot to the close of the war in 1763. The whole series, like the first volume, is much less an assessment of Washington than a study of the times. As Jared Sparks, the editor of the Washington papers, was later to discover, Marshall's contacts with the Washington kin were of inestimable help. These intimate and rich materials Marshall himself could have exploited, had he been so disposed. This was reserved for others to accomplish. Marshall's study remains a museum piece, helpful for grasping the nationalistic mood but otherwise without profound historical meaning. But there are vital segments of Marshall's discussion which by their nature and authorship can never be duplicated. This is especially true of the analysis of political parties in the last volume, which, in lieu of a face-to-face conversation with a living Federalist in the new day of the Federal Constitution, is second to none. The chief justice stamped his pages with the Federalist party seal so unmistakably that many regarded *The Life of George Washington* as a Federalist polemic. To Thomas Jefferson it was "that five volumed libel," [64] and he felt that something ought to be done about it by way of refutation. The fat of party conflict had long been burning in the fire of political difference, and there were already two traditions of the national heritage, as there had always been differing traditions of the nature of man and the nature of the social order.[65]

If time conspired with experience to weight the differences between rival philosophies of man, nature, and society, they were kinder to the Washington legend. The world of George Washington passed away and with it passed many of the standards of value and judgment by which he and his associates had been accustomed to measure it. Historians and editors collected papers and documents, contemporaries wrote their memoirs, and even Mount Vernon, preserved with rugged devotion, continued to reflect its image in the quiet Potomac. But the essence, though not the substance, of the eighteenth century died with the men who had once given it life. Thereafter only the dexterity of human thought made it possible for others to relive its experiences and to reconstruct its aspirations. The past is recaptured through the instrumentality of concepts, and it is the function of historians, among others, to invent, refine, and employ them. The eighteenth and early nineteenth centuries glorified George Washington. In the process George Washington was all but stultified, for a truly real hero must be truly unreal. Washington was elevated to Olympus, but unlike the heroes created by the Greeks, Washington was forced to leave his humanity behind him. Historians later recovered something of his personality, which, though increasing his stature and enriching his character, discomfited the growing horde of idolators who have always confused purity with greatness.

Francis Glass, a revering pedagogue, wrote a life history[66] of George Washington in the stateliest Latin prose, since Latin alone was sufficiently dignified and elegant for a paragon of Washington's caliber. No elaborate psychological hypothesis is needed to realize that in an era when only educated gentlemen could read it, a Latin biography restricted the Washington legend to the learned elect. Less elevated was Aaron Bancroft's attempt to make a true biography out of Marshall's history. The father of the eminent George Bancroft, himself a worthy and erudite Unitarian minister, regretted that so few were likely to read five ponderous volumes, even when written by a Supreme Court Chief Justice. Washington was too important for Americans to neglect, and if the Reverend Aaron Bancroft could save his compatriots from the deprivation involved in neglecting him, a rewriting of Marshall was all too small a price. Aaron Bancroft was so faithful to his purpose that he successfully achieved it. But he achieved no more.[67] Dr. David Ramsay, the South Carolinian author of a history of the Revolution, added to the literature of Washington, centering his narrative on the public life of the Virginian, which he treated more interestingly and with greater clarity than either Marshall or Bancroft.[68] Jared Sparks gave George Washington's letters to a receptive public in one decorous volume after another. When the twelve chaste tomes were completed they crowned Washington with added dignity. Whatever the reasons Sparks or others later assigned, he was so solicitous of the reputation of Washington that he edited away every suspicion that might blemish the sanctity of the national hero, who was also his own.[69]

American historiography has a Washington theme. The theme is not simply George Washington, but what George Washington represents. For two centuries the finest literary and historical talents have accorded the first chief executive major attention. To find the appropriate niche for Washington in the American hall of fame has been far from simple. The ablest critics had first to unravel a legend in order to discover the man who lay buried in its shrouds. No less a literary personage than Washington Irving tried his practiced hand at a life of the national hero. Following *A History of New York,* published in 1809, he subsequently turned to Washington. To a patriotic citizen and a literary artist, Washington had a great appeal. A Spanish interlude deflected him from Washington to Columbus, and *A History of the Life and Voyages of Christopher Columbus* still holds a respected place in the literature. Irving did far less well with the *Washington*. But even after all the critical weaknesses are noted, Irving's *Washington* cannot be completely disregarded. The usual Irving touch is assuredly lacking, for the *Washington* does not have the irresistible fascination of either *A History of New York* or the *Columbus*. Irving was already an old and sick man when this biography was actually written, and it was published in 1859, the year of his death. While it lacks the charm of other Irving writings, it attempts what none of the biographies of Washington preceding undertook to accomplish. Irving tells about Washington. After the volumes have been read, something like an impression of the man and his work emerges. The five volumes of the first edition have a logic and a sequence. They suggest that Irving worked out a plan, and having adopted a method of presentation, he made some effort to follow it.[70] The pen portraits of the leaders of thought and action whose lives touched Washington and his history are often splendidly executed. Irving's *Life* had little constructive effect upon the writers who elected to publish on Washington. He was rarely referred to during the years before 1895, and one examination of Washington biographies indicated that his study was hardly used.[71] Legends die hard. Revisionary estimates of the life of Washington only began to appear toward the end of the century. Woodrow Wilson and Henry Cabot Lodge presented reasonable portraits of an understandable man, which, together with Worthington Chauncey Ford's edition of *The Writings of George Washington,* published in the nineties, opened the modern phase of Washington scholarship.[72]

Democracies must offer a choice of heroes. For those who found Washington in some respects deficient, there was Benjamin Franklin. Franklin is the patron of Pennsylvania and the saint of Philadelphia. But Benjamin Franklin is everybody's hero. *Poor Richard's Almanac* made Franklin a popular figure; his scientific achievements made him a world celebrity. As a poor boy without sponsorship who more than made the grade, he suggested to Americans and Europeans alike the validity of democratic faith in equality. Franklin's career was too many-sided to create a single, unified tradition. Diversity, however, for obvious reasons is a considerable advantage to heroes and their worshipers. "Almost everybody claims Franklin. He is 'The father of all Yankees' . . . He is invoked by printers, merchants, Masons, Sons of the Revolution, publicists, diplomats, postmen, efficiency experts, scientists, advertisers, newspapermen, purveyors of correspondence courses in success, inspirational preachers, Christians, deists, and atheists. The manufacturer of a popular safety razor once built an advertising campaign upon Franklin's observation in the *Autobiography* that 'if you teach a poor young man to shave himself, and keep his razor in order, you may contribute more to the happiness of his life than in giving him a thousand guineas.' " [73]

The best account of Franklin was written by Franklin himself. Published for the first time in 1791, the *Autobiography* provided a rich source of quotable maxims and aphorisms which in turn provided a prolific crop of multiple interpretations.[74] But there is no better life of Franklin. Even Bernard Faÿ, Carl Van Doren, and Carl L. Becker could do little more than build on the foundations that the learned doctor supplied. Scores of worthy men tried, for until the avalanche of Lincoln studies overwhelmed him, Franklin was the most popular American biographical topic. And again Mason Locke Weems led all the rest. Weems, always anxious to turn an honest penny even at the cost of a deviously turned phrase, commenced the development of one aspect of the Franklin tradition. *The Immortal Mentor; or, Man's unerring guide to a healthy, wealthy, and happy life*[75] showed how health could make wealth and how wealth could make joyous contentment. Already in possession of a formula, Weems was able to turn out a smooth performance. By 1845 Weems' *Franklin* had piled up eleven editions, not a very good record for the manufacturer of the cherry-tree fable. The parson may have been disappointed, but he was never dismayed. "When we think of what we have done with his illustrious compat. Washington," he wrote to his publisher, "we must keep up our hopes." [76] Jared Sparks, who had venerated Franklin since boyhood, placed ten volumes of the Franklin papers within reach of the public. As was his editorial custom, he added a biographical piece. He expanded the *Autobiography* by treating Franklin's later years. The Franklin of Sparks is the kindly sage, upright and public-spirited, the Franklin which in truth he was.

All have observed that the first heroes of America were heroes of a special kind. One was a soldier; strong, reserved, dedicated to duty. The other was almost too human to qualify for idolatry, but brilliant, warm, and generous enough to qualify for greatness. Franklin was a genius, but he was a convivial genius. Franklin was a philosopher, but he was a philosopher who formulated his philosophy from the experience of living, and he lived most of the time by the precepts he formulated. He was a scientist and a great one, but his science, though fully enjoyed, was cultivated in order to serve mankind. In Franklin, doing and thinking were as nicely blended as theory and practice were logically combined in the instrumentalism of John Dewey. Thomas Jefferson, the third American hero, was the true scholar whose greatness was thrust upon him by history. Had he been able to make his choice, which ultimately no man can, he would probably have elected to read, to think, and to write in the peaceful quiet of Monticello. It may be said of Washington—as it has in fact been said—that he was made to be a hero. Franklin had the makings of a successful diplomat and man of affairs. But Jefferson had too subtle a mind to pursue an overweaning goal and too warm a heart to be content had he achieved it. Jefferson was as many-sided as Franklin because both were incurably restive and curious. Jefferson was as dedicated to duty as George Washington, but Jefferson responded to the call of public duty at the cost of personal development. Music, architecture, letters, and political philosophy lost whenever democracy gained by Jefferson's service. But such loss is the inescapable price of democratic living and Jefferson cheerfully paid it.

George Washington, Benjamin Franklin, and Thomas Jefferson had an arresting characteristic in common. Jefferson was a speculative thinker, Washington a man of resolute action, Franklin an active doer. Washington wrote moving state papers, but he never made a moving oral appeal. And it was no part of Franklin's many-sidedness to sway audiences by forensic skills. Jefferson admired great oratory but was skeptical of its virtues. Patrick Henry enraptured all who heard him, and Jefferson recorded that he "appeared to me to speak as Homer wrote." But Jefferson was prone to look for logic and was never sufficiently swayed by rhetoric not to sense its absence. Jefferson himself had a weak throat and was always more at ease in small conversational groups, over after-dinner wine, than with large audiences. America's first heroes were not orators, they were relatively silent men. Their great deeds spoke for themselves.

XII

Jared Sparks and the Records of the Republic

Views of the Revolution and the founding of the American nation have frequently been revised, but older writers, rarely studied thereafter, achieve little more than a doubtful immortality in critical bibliographies. To quarrel with such judgments is not only warranted but imperative, for the result of neglect is confusion. While the accumulation of time compels us to contract the writing of the past, judgments must constantly be reviewed in order to validate the standards by which contractions and omissions are made. Students who jar us into fresh perspectives earn the reward of being read, but students who once created perspectives now no longer fresh deserve a better fate than polite citation. A footnote, long repeated, inevitably shrivels a personality or stereotypes an idea. It is impossible to compress a lifetime or an intellectual history into the small lines reserved for documentation.

Jared Sparks, of course, is not unknown to scholars. But the place in the record of scholarship to which he is usually assigned robs him of justice and distorts his significance. Follower of a long line of collectors and editors,[1] he outdistanced them all. Indeed, Jared Sparks is the first great editor of American history. He was, in the judgment of a deservedly well-known historian who was also his biographer, "the first great discoverer of the original sources of American history by means of travel and research. In him the spirit of the independent explorer can never be separated from that of the editor, the biographer, and the historian. His tours of historical inquiry throughout the United States and Canada; his repeated visits to European archives; his constant collection of fresh material for American history, materials which, through his own and others' labor, have now entered into the very substance of American historical literature,—all this is better understood when Jared Sparks is viewed in the light of an original discoverer, an investigator, and a pioneer." [2] Others who came later unquestionably surpassed him. But comparisons with Jared Sparks must be tempered with appropriate qualifications. Later collectors had the inestimable advantages of the library and the card catalogue; they were able to travel by rail with source-material inventories and portable typewriters as parts of their essential luggage. Contrasts with Sparks must be weighted by the mechanisms of duplication and other aids to learning as well as the general organization of scholarship.[3] And they must also be weighted by Jared Sparks himself, for every subsequent editor in American history was indebted to Sparks for his courage, imagination, and industry.

As an editor Sparks is all too frequently remembered for tampering with historical documents in the interest of national piety. The editorial controversy surged about him during his own lifetime and still eddies in our own.[4] By some he is still regarded simply as a more learned Parson Weems who carefully fashioned unstained heroes for his compatriots to worship. His association with the Unitarian pulpit, *The North American Review,* and his Harvard connections have identified him with a New England provincialism, thus blurring the catholicity of his interests. The incredible list of his editorial achievements has eclipsed his achievement as a writer. The popularity of his biographical studies has obscured the lasting character of his research. But the conventional image of Sparks as an editorial drone has distorted the real personality, of a life filled with rich human contacts and exciting adventures. It was a life, moreover, which converged with other lives to the enhancement of his own development and that of his friends.

Befitting one whose public career was largely identified with America, the epochs of Sparks' life coincide with the epochs of American history. Born together with the Republic in 1789, he was graduated from Harvard when the United States concluded its second war with England; he died in the crucial year 1866, a date signalized by the Congressional victory of the radical reconstructionists, which placed them at the wheels of political control. The financial substance of Sparks' parents was no larger than the town of his birth—Willington, Connecticut—and both facts account for the irregularity of his early education. Until he was sixteen, his formal schooling averaged scarcely two months a year. Circumstances such as these were not of a kind to deter young Sparks. As a youth he read and was greatly impressed by Benjamin Franklin's *Autobiography,* of which he later wrote: "It taught me that circumstances have not a sovereign control over the mind." [5] The life of Sparks exemplifies Franklin's maxim and his own indomitable conviction.

When Sparks seriously set out to study, he quickly excelled his master, who, unlike ordinary teachers, was as quick to recognize it. Accordingly, he was sent to a larger school in the small nearby town of Tolland. There he also excelled, and when he returned to his home he was apprenticed to the local carpenter. Although he was an apt and faithful apprentice, it was clear that books interested him more than building tools, and his master graciously released him from the bonds. At this point his scholarly career began, for the selectmen of Tolland, acquainted with his school work, offered him a teaching post for four months at four dollars a month. His success as a teacher so pleased and gratified him that he decided to make it his profession. Having made up his mind, he took a trip through eastern New York in search of a more rewarding position. He covered three hundred miles, supporting himself at the carpenter's trade, but he found no satisfactory post.

In Arlington, Vermont, Sparks undertook to teach the young. There he helped to organize the Arlington Philosophical Society, for which he kept the records. The important points about this phase of Sparks' life are that he brought along his books, that he had a lively interest in ideas, and that he was always eager to learn by expounding them to others. His fleeting membership in the Arlington Philosophical Society is indicative of a concern for natural history that he never abandoned.

When he returned to Tolland to teach, he again took up his studies with the local minister. He concentrated particularly on Latin and algebra, and when examined he surpassed even the exacting standards of the learned clergy. Fortunately for Sparks, he was examined by the Reverend Abiel Abbot whose cousin, the Reverend Benjamin Abbot, was master of Phillips Exeter Academy. It was arranged that Sparks was to go to Exeter; financial help was provided, and the Reverend Abiel Abbot agreed to transport his trunk. Jared Sparks himself walked to Exeter, and as a young man of twenty-one began his program of studies in September, 1809.[6] At Phillips Exeter Sparks met John Gorham Palfrey, a classmate and lifelong friend, who became a well-known New England historian. Here, two years later, one of the most famous of American historians, George Bancroft, was to matriculate. Despite his proven ability to work hard, Sparks learned at Exeter to drive himself even harder. In addition to his regular studies, he tried to make up deficiencies in his background although he still needed his vacation time to make up deficiencies in his purse.[7] How well he succeeded is attested by the fact that after two years he was ready to enter Harvard.

While at Exeter he wrote articles for a New Hampshire newspaper on astronomical subjects, an area of science that had always intrigued him. He was also concerned with education, and contributed an argument to the *New Hampshire Patriot,* published in Concord, in behalf of higher education for women.[8] Sparks was twenty-three when he entered Harvard, an age at which students normally were graduated. He was the outstanding student of his class in mathematics and he had begun to take an active interest in theology. To supplement his income, he accepted a tutorial position with a family living at Havre de Grace, Maryland.[9] While there, he witnessed an engagement of the War of 1812 with his own sharply focused eyes. In 1813 a British naval contingent under the command of Admiral Cockburn descended upon the community. Sparks watched the burning and the pillaging and later served briefly as a private in the Maryland militia, summoned to watch over the area. *The North American Review* in 1817 carried an account of this episode by Jared Sparks, his first venture in historical writing.[10]

American history, however, was not yet his goal. Still an active reader of science, he carefully studied Newton's *Principia* in his junior year, which resulted in a prize essay entitled "The Character of Newton, and the Influence and Importance of his Discoveries." Theology still had a large place in his plans, and he began to study seriously with the Reverend Nathaniel Thayer of Lancaster, Massachusetts. But his mind was still unfettered by a specific decision. While reading Priestley's *Lectures on History* his imagination was stirred by Africa, and he weighed the possibilities of going to Africa to trace the career of John Ledyard, "the American Marco Polo," who continued always to fascinate him. After graduation from Harvard in 1815, he served as tutor in geometry, astronomy, and natural history for a two-year period. Parallel with his Harvard teaching, he was editor of *The North American Review* from May 1817 to March 1818 as successor to William Tudor. At the same time he finished his theological studies at Harvard. Baltimore was selected over a church in Boston; the Unitarian ministry over the offer of a Harvard teaching position. Answering a request for information on the motivations of his choice, he is said to have replied: "The world has done much for me, and I must do something to repay it. There are hundreds of students who can fill that chair as well as I can, but they can't go out in the world and do what I can."[11]

This was a statement of faith and courage, for to preach the doctrines of Unitarianism in the South in 1819 required both. The ministry had a profound influence upon his development. He was forced to defend his creed against hostile critics, which helped him to clarify his own philosophical position and provided an opportunity for him to improve his literary and forensic skills. The editorial tasks undertaken during the Baltimore period prepared him for his post on *The North American Review* and for his later historical work. Some of the projects of these years provided the models for the larger work of the historian. During the Baltimore days he first began his biographical investigation, probably as a direct result of his southern experiences. Formal preaching plus theological debate aided him in his dual role of public lecturer and college teacher.[12] Residence in the South gave Sparks his first real contact with slavery. Sparks did not approve of it. "Slavery, in the abstract," he told the Honorable Thomas W. Cobb of Georgia, "I consider a great calamity, and a reproach to free government, and one which every true patriot should desire to see removed." But he hastened to qualify "in the present state of things we can have little to do with the question in the abstract. Slavery exists by the Constitution and the laws; rights have grown out of this institution. . . . I hold it to be wrong . . . for any person, except those immediately concerned, to interfere with those rights."[13]

Regardless of his views on slavery, direct contact with its existence turned Sparks' thoughts to Africa, never far below the surface of his interests.[14] He now firmly resolved to undertake the biography of Ledyard and he began to collect materials by correspondence. In 1822 he made a visit to Stonington, Connecticut, where Ledyard was born. "If I had six months," he wrote in 1822, "I do believe the 'Life of Ledyard' would come out a book that might be read. But I am overwhelmed with theology."[15] The Ledyard was deferred because Sparks bore the major editorial responsibility for *The Unitarian Miscellany* and the *Collection of Essays and Tracts in Theology, with Bibliographical and Critical Notices.*[16] His prominence in local religious circles and his writing in the field resulted in his election as chaplain of Congress in 1821. If his new position was a gesture to liberal religion, it did not please the orthodox. One of his clerical colleagues, though regarding Sparks as personally able and honest, felt that to appoint a Unitarian to so high a post was like appointing Thomas Paine.[17]

The intellectual climate of Baltimore and Washington was not sufficiently invigorating for Jared Sparks. This, rather than provincialism, induced him to say: "There is nowhere so much refinement and general intelligence in society as in Boston." [18] Sparks would doubtless have continued the good Unitarian fight in Baltimore, despite nostalgia for Boston, but hard work impaired his health. Accordingly, he resigned his pastorate in 1823 and returned to his idyllic Boston. *The North American Review* was offered for sale, and Sparks, partly with borrowed money, purchased it. For seven years, from 1823 to 1830, he remained its editor and he was instrumental in making the *Review* the leading literary journal in America.[19]

Theological polemics on the brink of philosophy were unquestionably rewarding, but Sparks' full intellectual maturity dates from the end of his Baltimore sojourn. Boston, Cambridge, and the *Review* afforded creative stimulation and richer contacts that Sparks had missed, and he was quick to take advantage of them. As editor of the leading literary journal in the United States, he found the "refinement and general intelligence" that he, together with Boston, so greatly prized. Daniel Webster, Henry Clay, Lewis Cass, Joseph Story, and Caleb Cushing were public figures of such eminence that they were certain to be associated with *The North American*. Sparks also enjoyed association with the Everett brothers, Alexander and Edward, William H. Prescott, Henry Wadsworth Longfellow, George Ticknor, John Gorham Palfrey, and George Bancroft. It was an invigorating circle, and however exacting the editorial duties, Sparks could well have felt that they were worth it.

The function of *The North American Review* in American intellectual history has often been set forth, but Sparks' relation to it has not usually been recalled. Largely through his activity, the *Review* became a medium for the diffusion of knowledge about Latin America. Americans were conscious of the existence of their southern neighbors, and many Americans were actively interested in the revolutionary upheavals then disrupting the Spanish empire. Accurate information about the Latin American communities was almost completely lacking. Sparks broadened the scope of the *Review* by becoming an ardent exponent of inter-American understanding and accord. For Boston, New England, and *The North American Review,* at least, sympathy with Latin America was a novel attitude.[20]

Only two years before Sparks assumed the editorship, his good friend Edward Everett, himself a former editor of the *Review,* had written:

> We have no concern with South America; we have no sympathy with them. We are sprung from different stocks, we speak different languages, we have been brought up in different social and moral schools, we have been governed by different codes of law, we profess radically different codes of religion. But they would not act in our spirit, they would not follow our advice, they could not imitate our example. Not all the treaties we could make, nor the commissioners we could send out, nor the money we could lend them, would transform their Pueyuendons and their Artigoses, into Adamses or Franklins, or their Bolivars into Washingtons.[21]

Sparks took a completely opposite view, which implied a shift in the policy of the *Review* from a provincial to a national position. It was a shift not only from a New England outlook but also to a North American outlook. Sparks took a continental stand, and a stand with democratic implications. Two years after President James Monroe's famous pronouncement, Sparks wrote to a high Mexican official: "I wish to do all in my power through the channel of the 'North American Review,' to disseminate the knowledge so much desired, and to draw more clearly the bonds of union and interests between the free governments of the Western World." [22] Perhaps for this reason Alexander H. Everett, brother of Edward, wrote from Madrid that there were few positions charged with such responsibility as the editorship of the *Review.*[23]

Sparks was by no means unaware of his responsibility. And when Sparks committed himself, it was a full commitment. In typical Sparks fashion he bought himself a map of South America in 1823 and set about collecting documents and sources. John Quincy Adams, secretary of state, was asked for assistance and urged to contact the United States minister's residence in South America for aid. Never one to do things by halves, Sparks set himself to learning Spanish, for when he thought of "bonds of union" he really meant it.[24] Sparks not only carried on an extensive correspondence with Latin American readers, but he also wrote a number of informative articles for the *Review* and encouraged others to do so. The Latin American articles were characteristic. No light journalistic response to popular interest, they were painstaking efforts to master a fresh subject. First he learned all he could himself; then he undertook to convey his information to others. Genuinely intrigued, he believed the readers of the *Review*—as well as the general public—should be apprised of the state of affairs south of the border.[25] Other sentiments also fed his industry. Like so many of his countrymen, he looked upon the "decrepit" monarchies of Europe with republican disdain. The rebellion of almost all the states of South America from Spain seemed but another step in the progress of political freedom. It was the American Revolution all over again, and Jared Sparks could not fail to be on the side of George Washington and Benjamin Franklin. James Monroe and John Quincy Adams were Washington's heirs. So, indeed, was Jared Sparks.

The plan of collecting and publishing the Washington papers was formed while Sparks was editor of the *Review*. The formation and execution of the plan is the central fact in the life of Sparks the historian. Once the plan took shape and the work had begun, all his ambitions as scholar, editor, writer, and teacher revolved about the Washington project. Because of it American history became his passion and the collection of materials one of his consuming goals.

The evolution of the Washington program has a significance of its own. Shortly after graduation from Harvard, Sparks requested one of his friends about to make a pilgrimage to Mount Vernon, to bring him a "scrap" of George Washington's handwriting.[26] Sparks' devotion to the father of his country was shared by most nineteenth-century Americans, but it was not until 1824 that the idea of a collection of the Washington papers was presented to him. As Sparks had lived in the South, he was considered something of a specialist in Cambridge on southern life. Charles Folsom, then associated with a Cambridge printing firm and who contemplated "a handsome and correct edition of Washington's writings complete," [27] asked Sparks who in the South should be approached. Sparks, whose pen was always at hand, wrote Associate Justice Bushrod Washington,[28] who had acquired the papers of his uncle. The judge was not particularly disposed to help, and Folsom seems to have been disposed to let his project drop. Sparks, however, continued to press the matter, curious to discover the whereabouts of Washington's sacred scripts. And those with whom he corresponded shared his anxiety that the longer the nation waited for a collection of Washington's letters and papers, the more difficult and inconclusive the result would be.

So stimulated did Sparks become that he planned a tour of the southern and middle states in search of materials. After making the tour he wrote Alexander H. Everett in September 1826: "I have got a passion for Revolutionary history, and the more I look into it the more I am convinced that no complete history of the American Revolution has been written." [29] Jared Sparks had determined to do the job himself, and as the first step in gathering the necessary materials he contemplated the editing of the Washington papers. Hence in September 1826 he took up his case with Bushrod Washington again and enlisted the aid of Chief Justice Marshall to further his cause. Together they were able to persuade President Washington's nephew, and an agreement was finally reached on January 17, 1827.[30] A few weeks later Sparks wrote to the president of the United States, suggesting the publication of the diplomatic correspondence relating to the Revolution.[31] Congress had already authorized its publication in 1818, and Sparks' request indicates the nature of his research plan. Jared Sparks was to write the history of the American states during the Revolution. All his strivings were directed to this end; that he did not accomplish it was due to the fullness with which he performed his other labors.

With his literary ambitions rapidly taking precise form, Sparks was admitted to Mount Vernon and for a full and exciting month he was alone with the spirit of George Washington. From the fourteenth of March to the sixteenth of April, 1827, he made a quick survey of the manuscript treasures[32] to discover what he possessed and what was missing. Having made arrangements with Edward Everett to operate the *Review,* Sparks planned a trip to Europe to collect materials in European archives relating to American history. He arrived in Liverpool in April 1828, almost exactly a year after he had completed his preliminary survey of Washingtoniana at Mount Vernon. Although most of his time was devoted to the discovery of sources, reading in the archives, and making arrangements for the copying of documents, he managed to see many interesting people and many interesting things.[33] Like all Americans in England, he visited the Commons, and like most then if not since, he came away convinced that the quality of debate was no higher than in the American Congress. He was moved to find himself "on the spot where Franklin sustained . . . his examination at the bar of the House of Commons," and was stimulated by the mighty Wordsworth with whom he had tea.[34]

From England Sparks went to Belgium and from Belgium to Germany. At Göttingen, where he talked with the great and the near great, he found "the best and most extensive collection of books relating to America that is anywhere to be found, except at Harvard College." [35] Lafayette came to his assistance in Paris with introductions that thawed out official indifference to American research and opened up drawing rooms for delightful interviews. One such interview was arranged with the Marquis de Barbé-Marbois, then eighty-four, formerly French minister to the United States and French representative during the negotiations for the Louisiana Purchase.[36] Sparks' main goal was never out of his mind and in a conversation with Guizot he made tentative arrangements for a French translation of the life of Washington. Washington's influence, he later wrote Guizot, "on the destinies of the Western world has been incalculable," and he congratulated himself that "his fame, in regard to that portion of mankind who read the French language, will be in your hands." [37]

Sparks' initial European trip coincided with the publication of his first historical biography, the *Life of John Ledyard*.[38] Ledyard, Sparks' early biographical love, gave him justifiable pleasure, a pleasure that William H. Prescott's praise did much to heighten. In a letter written soon after Sparks had left for Europe, Prescott wrote: "It is one of your best letters of introduction. You have written nothing, in my judgment, and not mine alone, in a better manner." [39] The full title of the *Ledyard* carried the words "comprising selections from his journals and correspondence," which became a Sparks technique. First the documents, the letters, and the sources; then the life and usually a part of the original materials was published together with the biographical study. The *Ledyard,* containing a journal of a four-year cruise with Captain Cook, was republished in England at once and translated into German in 1829. Sparks was working at full literary steam. After his return from Europe he was engaged in editing the diplomatic correspondence and was also at work on the *Washington.*

The magnitude of Sparks' labor can best be judged by an appreciation of its extent. *The Diplomatic Correspondence of the American Revolution* appeared in twelve volumes between 1829 and 1830. In 1832, in one sense a by-product, *The Life of Gouverneur Morris* was published in three volumes. And between 1834 and 1837 *The Life and Writings of George Washington* finally came off the press in twelve additional volumes, a total of twenty-seven volumes in a six-year period.[40] Nor was this all, for Sparks was still at the helm of the *Review,* and in 1829 he projected *The American Almanac,*[41] designed as a periodical dealing with the statistics of the United States. Sparks himself did most of the *Almanac* for 1830, but was later forced to sell out his interest because of other pressures. *The American Almanac,* the first of a series of periodicals cataloguing the economic and institutional development of the country, continued to be published for thirty-three years until it was succeeded by the *National Almanac.* At about the same time Sparks became involved with *The Library of American Biography.* J. G. Flügel, the lexicographer, asked Sparks in 1830 if a biographical dictionary of famous Americans had ever been compiled.[42] Sparks was forced to reply that no such biographical dictionary, save one on the signers of the Declaration of Independence, existed. In 1832 there is an entry in Sparks' journal making mention of a plan for an historical and biographical series.[43] The first volumes of this new venture appeared in 1834, and the first series of ten volumes was completed between 1834 and 1838. William H. Prescott contributed a life of Charles Brockden Brown, Edward T. Channing wrote on William Ellery Channing, and the philosopher Francis Bowen wrote the biographies of Baron Steuben and Sir William Phipps. Sparks planned and edited the entire series and supplied it with studies of Ethan Allen, Benedict Arnold, and Père Marquette.[44]

Laurels were not made for Sparks to rest on. Even during the final stages of the diplomatic correspondence, the Washington and the Morris, he turned over other editorial possibilities in his active mind. Hamilton suggested itself to him, but was quickly rejected because of difficulties in securing access to the manuscripts. An attempt was made to get at the Jay papers with no more success. Permission to edit the letters of Lafayette was graciously accorded. As the most noted biographer in the country, he was wooed by the families of General Nathaniel Greene and George Clinton.[45] But it was Benjamin Franklin who next captured his talent. Franklin had been one of his boyhood inspirations, and many had urged him to give the noted Philadelphian his historical due. George Bancroft, already favorably known but not yet famous, wrote Sparks in 1832 on the occasion of the life of Morris: "I should have made a public call on you to write the life of Franklin. Gain the glory of being the vindicator of his fame to all posterity. . . . Defend in a permanent form the honor which has been wantonly assailed by the invidious. John Adams sowed the seeds of calumny respecting Franklin; it will be an act of some merit to root out all the crop of slanderous imputations."[46]

Sparks had already taken a position on Franklin. In a critical notice of Timothy Pitkin's *History of the United States,* written for *The North American Review* in 1828, he had dissented from current notions about Franklin.[47] In a preliminary one-volume study of Franklin, published in 1833 and limited to an edition of a thousand copies, he indicated how much further in dissent he was willing to go.[48] Franklin was often portrayed as more crafty than wise and more careful than honest.[49] Sparks objected to Pitkin's version with spirited candor,[50] and George Bancroft sent him fine words of encouragement. "Your defense of Franklin was excellent; to every unprejudiced mind highly satisfactory." [51] When Sparks forwarded the last of the ten-volume edition of *The Works of Benjamin Franklin; with Notes and a Life of the Author*[52] to the printer in February 1840, he commented: "The work has been more than four years in the press; a very laborious undertaking, of which I had not formed a proper estimate when I began it." [53]

The high price Sparks paid in terms of his own ambition was always a price of his own making. He already had a neat shelf of volumes to his credit, but the history of the American Revolution remained unwritten. There were compensations. To so relentless a collector of materials the thrill of discovery was exhilarating, and the Washington papers at Mount Vernon were but one such collector's delight. While working on Benjamin Franklin he unearthed an historical treasure trove. As he told John Quincy Adams: "I have been very successful in procuring materials for this edition. In a garret seven miles from Philadelphia I found two large trunks of Dr. Franklin's papers, which have lain there undisturbed for forty years." [54] There were other rewards, although Sparks did not live to experience them. Justin Winsor, one of the most noted American bibliographers, considered that the Sparks edition of Franklin remained standard for half a century, a lapse of time, it seems safe to say, no history of the American Revolution could have endured. Paul Leicester Ford, one of the most celebrated of Franklin's editors, credited Sparks with adding six hundred and fifty items to the Franklin documents never printed up to that time. Ford's judgment that Sparks' critical notes were still of value can hardly fail to impress all but Franklin specialists. [55]

Citizen as well as scholar, Sparks had from the first been concerned with educational problems. His career had begun with teaching, and his Baltimore ministry, no less than his *North American Review* editorship, were primarily ventures in communication. From 1838 to 1841 he sat on the Massachusetts Board of Education, a body forever memorable because Horace Mann, an indefatigable leader of the public-school movement, was its secretary. [56] Possibilities for political office were twice offered to him. When Edward Everett, Harvard scholar and Massachusetts politician, was governor of the Bay State, he tried to induce Sparks to stand for Congress. [57] Earlier, when Everett became governor, Sparks was frequently mentioned as his successor in Washington. [58] Sparks gave these flattering inducements the attention they deserved, and after serious consideration, he politely declined. If, as once was said, the Harvard professorship of Greek was valued more highly than a seat in the United

States Senate, it seemed more important to Sparks to write the history of the Revolution than to represent Massachusetts in the national capital.

While public service in the political life of the nation did not tempt him, public service in the educational life of the nation did. Devotion to his special subject and a desire to discuss it led him to accept an invitation from the Society for the Diffusion of Useful Knowledge to give a public course of lectures. These lectures, first delivered at the Masonic Temple in Boston, were favorably received. Covering the period 1763 to 1783, the topical outline indicates how far we have departed from the old scheme of presentation although it also indicates how much of it we still retain.[59] Sparks repeated the lectures in New York and other places to groups often as large as two thousand. During the same year, 1838, Sparks became professor of history at Harvard. Herbert Baxter Adams regarded his appointment as the McLean professor of ancient and modern history as marking "the dawn of a new era in American scholarship." There were two cogent reasons for his opinion. Sparks' appointment was the "first recognition of historical science by an American college as worthy of a distinct professorial chair." This was reason enough, but there was also another. Because of Sparks' interests and accomplishments, this choice was "the first academic encouragement of American history, and of original historical research in the American field." [60]

Sparks was no great teacher. Dedicated and conscientious, he wrote out his weekly lectures, which were based upon original sources and the products of his own unending research. He was saddled by an educational process he could alone do nothing to alter, and he never wished to halt his own investigations. To discuss the Revolution with anyone who would listen was a pleasure, but he was much more anxious to write about it. At the first opportunity, he went off on his second trip to Europe.[61] The contest between teaching and research was an unequal one. Sparks could never resist a manuscript collection, and he sailed abroad filled with new enthusiasm for his much postponed opus. Success in discovery again made him hopeful, and in October he confided to a Baltimore friend: "I am preparing to write a formidable history of the American Revolution." [62]

Sparks already knew more about the sources of American revolutionary history than anyone then living, and this research tour yielded startling documentary finds. Notwithstanding official apprehension that he might unearth something on the Maine "boundary question," [63] then agitating diplomats on both sides of the water, he really found no difficulty in gaining admission to the depositories. In the State Paper Office he uncovered the correspondence of the colonial governors, who, regarding the government papers as their own, brought them back to England when they were forced to leave America. Among these documents were the letters of British ministers containing instructions, directives, and observations of all kinds. "They are all original," wrote Sparks with the collector's respect for the initial source, "and none of these papers are in America." [64] He was granted permission[65] to examine the eleven volumes of military correspondence of General Gage and others, which he found "ample and important beyond my expectation." [66] Through personal contacts, constantly accumulating, he was introduced to Sir Thomas Phillipps of Middle Hill, Worcestershire,[67] the owner of the manuscript of Arthur Homer's *Bibliotheca Americana.*[68] Of the existence of Homer, Sparks already knew from a printed prospectus in the Washington collection, but he knew nothing of the contents of Homer's *Bibliotheca* nor could he discover anything about the bibliography. Sir Thomas permitted him to take the five volumes of sixteen hundred pages to London in order to copy them. It was a rare example of uninhibited co-operation. Homer listed books in all languages relating to America, and Sir Thomas, himself a great collector, put his own incomparable library of books and manuscripts at Sparks' disposal.

One document almost invariably leads to another, even though it may not be the particular document sought. But Sparks was the most fortunate of seekers. Quite "by accident," while examining Sir Thomas Phillipps' catalogue, he found a reference to fifty-six volumes of manuscript dealing with the American war in the library of the Royal Institute. As soon as he returned to London from Worcestershire, he went to investigate and found to his happy surprise that they were the papers of Lord Dorchester, famous in the Revolutionary War as Sir Guy Carleton.[69] This collection turned out to be an almost complete record of military correspondence. When the originals themselves were missing, there were duplicates, apparently placed in Sir Guy's keeping by those who preceded him in command.[70] Though pressed for time and drained by excitement, Sparks was not too busy to execute a mission for his good friend William H. Prescott. While examining Spanish manuscripts, particularly a letter from Cortés to his avaricious king, he came upon an old document of the early period of Mexican history. This document, recounting Mexican habits of existence, contained almost half a hundred illustrations, among them a portrait of Moctezuma. Sparks made careful notes for Prescott's use and secured the aid of Sir Thomas Phillipps' daughter, Henrietta, who copied the Moctezuma picture for him.[71]

For the next nine years editorial work and literary output continued. The history of the American Revolution remained in progress and was preceded by other writings. The ten-volume Franklin was completed in 1840, a few months prior to the second European exploration. A year before, a German edition of the *Washington* had been published. Fifteen volumes of the second series of *The Library of American Biography* appeared under his editorship between 1844 and 1848.[72] When, in 1849, Sparks accepted the presidency of Harvard, he allowed himself to be distracted from his main purposes.[73] With "the history" still unfinished and many scholarly assignments remaining to be done, further involvement, especially in administration, was certainly a mistake. Actually, he soon wearied of the details of office,[74] and as his health deteriorated after 1851,[75] he longed to be relieved. On October 30, 1852, he tendered his resignation to the board of overseers.[76] But Sparks could never leave documents alone. During his Harvard presidency, he rearranged and reclassified the records of the college, a chore that badly needed to be done.[77] Sparks was not a gifted administrator, and his tenure of leadership at Harvard was undistinguished.[78] Herbert Baxter Adams has summed up this phase of his life neatly: "He did not owe his scientific distinctions to his presidential office; he distinguished it by his own published works of history and biography, which were the occasion of all his honors." [79]

Sparks lived quietly in Cambridge for the remaining thirteen years of his life.[80] He made another trip to Europe with his family,[81] but for the most part he retired to the house on Kirkland Street, honored for his prodigious editorial work and his great historical knowledge. The same old passion for accomplishment still smoldered, but his dwindling vigor could no longer obey its command.[82] A neuralgic ailment almost deprived him of the use of his right arm, and he never accommodated himself to dictation. The "unfinished history" pursued him mercilessly. An intimate friend accounted his failure to write it the great frustration of his life.[83] Increasingly, he gave his energies to others who sought his aid and advice. He gave without measure, and men like Edward Everett, George Bancroft, Robert Winthrop, George Ticknor, and William H. Prescott always felt free to call upon him. Help frequently went far beyond counsel.[84] Henry D. Gilpin had recourse to Sparks while preparing his edition of the Madison papers and asked him to supply material for the first volume. Henry

Randall required and received data on Thomas Jefferson's relations with Washington for his large-scale biographical study of the third president. What he cordially did for Randall and Gilpin, he did for many others.[85]

The Correspondence of the American Revolution, four additional volumes of preparation for the diplomatic history, appeared during these years. George Bancroft's full measure of praise gave him pleasure not unmixed with regret, for Bancroft said exactly what Sparks must have felt. "I pray that you may live long, alike to write the history of the period with which you are so familiar, and to make further publication from the vast stores." [86] Just when Sparks was about to retire from Harvard in 1852, William H. Trescot, a young Charlestonian, published on the subject. Sparks applauded and urged him to go on. Trescot did so, and six years later a diplomatic history of the Washington and Adams administrations was completed.[87] Trescot did not steal Jared Sparks' literary thunder; Jared Sparks stole his own.

Sparks never formulated a philosophy of history, but he did have a theory of historiography. Within this intellectual framework there was a philosophical position, had Sparks ever felt prompted to develop it. George E. Ellis, historian of the Puritans, in a memoir published for the Massachusetts Historical Society,[88] remarked that Sparks was "neither poet nor enthusiast." Rarely, he went on to say, "are his pages kindled with any glow or fervor. . . . He was not a man of theories." Ellis was only partly right. There is much, in the letters and journals, not to mention his formal writings, that glow abundantly. An enthusiast for America, for American history, for the revolutionary era, for documents, Sparks most certainly was. Particularly in view of the controversy relative to the proprieties of editing, his own attitude, early formed, is suggestive. During his New England tour of 1826, Sparks engaged in a long discussion with an author who proposed to write a constitutional history of the United States from 1787 to the administration of John Quincy Adams. The work was planned in advance to "illustrate, defend, and vindicate the views of the Federal party." Sparks regarded this position "highly objectionable in a writer of history." "He said he thought it proper," Sparks confided to his journal, "not to bring out the defects of the great actors in our historical drama, but only to set forth such of their virtues and good acts as are worthy of the admiration and imitation of posterity. This principle I hold to be pernicious. The character and turn of events more frequently take their coloring from the foibles and waywardness of the actors than from their merits or elevated qualities. The causes of evils must rest on somebody, and justice requires that they should fall on the right head. History which keeps men's defects out of sight tells but half the tale, and that half but imperfectly." [89] These accusations were almost exactly those later directed at Jared Sparks.[90]

If Sparks had no clearly worked-out philosophy of history, he did have a precise theory of biography. Although he followed the principles he set forth in his own biographical compositions, they contained only implied speculative aspects. There were in his view three types of biographical writing. Historical biography "admits of copious selections from letters and other original papers." A second classification, described as memoirs and related to historical biography, was "more rambling, and related more to affairs of a private nature." "Personal narrative" comprised the third category "in which the individual is always kept before the reader, and the incidents are made to follow each other in consecutive order. This last is the most difficult to execute, because it requires a clear and spirited style, discrimination in the selection of facts, and judgment in arranging them so as to preserve just proportions." [91] Sparks apparently was never intellectually aware that there was a logical gap between his theory of historical propriety and his prescriptions for biography.

But Sparks performed gigantic services for history in America. The diplomatic history of the Revolution, now after almost a hundred years, is somewhat differently conceived from what Sparks envisaged. Sparks' contribution to the thinking of Americans is not a monument to an individual scholar, it is a monument to a generation of scholarship. The character of George Washington, etched by Sparks, has been many times revised. Edition after edition of the Washington papers have crowded Sparks from the minds of students and from the shelves of libraries. What is true of the *Washington* is true of the *Franklin*. The *Library of American Biography* has served its purpose of reference and stimulation and has had to make room, together with most of its successors, for the *Dictionary of American Biography* which, in turn, will one day be relegated to the storage rooms to be handed out only for purposes of research. Yet this is no adequate measure of Jared Sparks. Greater men are enshrined in the obituary columns written by the editors of rare booksellers' catalogues. The rare bookseller's catalogue is telling evidence that, whatever treatment contemporaries accord a writer, scholars in the main have not abandoned him. Every reprint of a rare book, apart from commercial impulses, suggests that something of continuing value has been neglected that modern methods of duplication allow us to preserve and revive. Sparks, to be sure, is in the booksellers' catalogues and the library indexes, but he has not yet been reprinted. We do not reprint him because his contributions still continue to serve scholarship in every collection of Washingtoniana and in every biography of Franklin. He still lives in the pages of *The Library of American Biography* because the *Library* was a pioneering editorial idea which has many times served as a model for other co-operative programs.

Admirable progress in the collection of sources had been made before Sparks, but to him belongs the editorial crown. No one did more. He rekindled enthusiasm for the period of national beginnings and transmitted a heritage. Collecting, preserving, and editing the papers of the revolutionary age was critical, for each item identified and salvaged by Sparks was almost literally salvaged. Indifference and ignorance of the past still threaten understandings of the future, but scientific means of preservation and the microfilm insures the safety at least of what we know we possess. Scarcely less than a century ago, there was no adequate treatment of American development in print. Sparks attempted to cure this deficiency by *The Library of American Biography*. Students of colonial evolution often turned to the work of a Scotsman; for the Revolution, to the work of an Italian. That there was no satisfactory account from an American pen is suggested by the popularity of Carlo Botta's *History of the War of Independence* and the favorable comment that greeted James Grahame's survey of colonial history from the era of discovery to the Revolution.[92] Together Jared Sparks and George Bancroft gave American historiography its first modern scope and direction.

XIII

George Bancroft: The Making of a Tradition

The career of Jared Sparks echoes the resounding changes taking place during his lifetime. America had not yet fully matured when Sparks died at the close of the Civil War, but it was growing intellectually at a pace much faster than a comparison with material development indicated. Time and the gradual acquisition of the social elements, upon which the cultivation of the arts and sciences depend, mellowed the American mind and broadened the democratic spirit. While Americans in the Belgian city of Ghent were signing a treaty of peace,[1] other Americans in Göttingen, Heidelberg, and Berlin entered into spiritual covenants with scholarship. Beginning what was to become a migration to German universities, young scholars like Joseph Green Cogswell, George Ticknor, and Edward Everett carried the inspiration of learning and the passion for inquiry back to their beloved New England. And among these early migrants was George Bancroft. Not long thereafter, James Marsh of the University of Vermont initiated a new period in American thought by introducing German philosophy to receptive minds.[2]

In the northeastern section of the United States, the earlier industrial development and its urban counterpart quickened scholarly traditions. New England, ready to yield its second fruits, flowered in a resplendent renaissance—not, however, confined to letters.[3] Emancipation from European imperialisms was celebrated by the War of 1812, but another kind of emancipation was indicated when, in

1818, *The American Journal of Science and Arts* was founded by Benjamin Silliman, a pioneer scientist at Yale.[4] It was also an emancipation from provincialism, a recognition that scientific thought in America required circulation not only within the confines of the United States but everywhere. The converse point did not have to be made, for the *Journal* was filled, as was every other learned periodical, with references to discoveries, reports, and results from one end of the scholarly globe to the other. American scientists who wrote for the *Journal* were proud of their achievements, but they did not have to be told that individual and national advancement rested on universal foundations. Thought was science, and science was thought, and the two met wherever there were scholars. Less than twenty years after the founding of the *Journal,* Charles Darwin was studying the whole *Journal* series, as he studied everything else, seeking additional data on the hypothesis of evolution. Everett and Ticknor—and Bancroft—sojourning at continental universities, suggest a similar emancipation from provincialism. The aggressive self-sufficiency of early American nationalism had been tempered by critical self-awareness. Bancroft and his fellow Americans in Europe looked for fresh data and fresh inspiration in the old world in order to better the new. It was not so much that they were sentimentally in love with the past as that they were incorrigibly devoted to the future.

In the Puritan acropolis, William Ellery Channing, a scholarly Boston clergyman, submitted ancient Christianity to a searching critique and contrasted its claims with those of Unitarianism. Channing's declaration of human independence signalized the breach between Augustinianism and mid-nineteenth-century Americanism and opened the New England dykes to the oncoming Transcendentalist surge. Soon after John Lothrop Motley was graduated from Harvard,[5] Ralph Waldo Emerson's *Essay on Nature*[6] furnished supercilious European critics with a yardstick for the measurement of American breadth, and Henry Wadsworth Longfellow, freshly ensconced in a Harvard professorship, was about to furnish them with others.[7] Washington Irving's *Sketch Book* was already a classic model when Bancroft returned from Germany,[8] while James Fenimore Cooper and William Cullen Bryant had earned a place for American letters in the firmament of recognition.[9] Horace Mann, a sagacious Boston lawyer, was remodelling American education,[10] the Lowell Institute had opened its doors,[11] and Nathaniel Hawthorne published *Twice-Told Tales* a year before William H. Prescott's *Ferdinand and Isabella* appeared.[12] Edgar Allan Poe and James Russell

Lowell were names enshrined in the halo of print previous to the advent of the great Francis Parkman,[13] and George Bancroft had stores of energy still unspent after Herman Melville and Walt Whitman had freed themselves from the literary inhibitions of the past. If American historiography came of age with George Bancroft, it was because America itself had come of age.

Bancroft was born in Worcester, Massachusetts, in 1800. His early boyhood, not untouched by poverty, was blessed by domestic peace and stirred by parental learning. The qualities that marked his adult personality were acquired from his ministerial father and his understanding mother. Together they created a home where the virtues were practiced as well as preached. Here, before leaving for Exeter at the age of eleven, George Bancroft was fortified by a philosophy of tolerance and a sympathy for ideas not his own. Scholarship and a reverence for it were as much a part of Aaron and Lucretia Bancroft's temperament as an unflinching Unitarianism was the core of their faith. It was characteristic that George Bancroft should have done with Caesar before he was ten. But even for the Bancrofts it was unusual that a boy of six should decide a moot point in Roman history which arose between his father and a truly learned judge.[14] Though one of the youngest of students, he was the leading classical scholar at Exeter; at thirty-four he was the leading historian of the United States.[15]

Bancroft's years were the years of America. His lifetime links the generations of American history together.[16] Born in the year of Thomas Jefferson's election to the presidency—a twelvemonth after the death of George Washington—he died in the last decade of the nineteenth century, two years after Benjamin Harrison had succeeded Grover Cleveland.[17] The American Revolution had only begun when Bancroft's father was a Harvard undergraduate and Bancroft himself matriculated during the second war with England. James Monroe issued his memorable proclamation when Bancroft was still a student in Europe, and he was, of course, in Cambridge when President Monroe made his triumphal visit to New England in 1817. During the national struggle over slavery, Bancroft was alive to the meaning of public affairs. The makers of America's future in those perilous days, who gave their names to the events historians were later to describe, were subjects of daily conversation in the Bancroft circle. He was witness to the war with Mexico and the war of secession. Jared Sparks and Edward Everett were his friends; Ralph Waldo Emerson, George Ticknor, and James Russell Lowell were within the orbit of his intimate contacts. Francis Parkman, William H. Prescott, and John Lothrop Motley moved in the path of his life, and virtually every historian, great or small, touched either the center or the periphery of his existence. When New England had its flowering, Bancroft shared in it.[18] When Unitarianism altered the intellectual vision of its leaders, Bancroft experienced it. And after Transcendentalism gave philosophy and nationalism a new impulse, Bancroft represented it. He was political advisor to Martin Van Buren, official counselor to James K. Polk, and, on one important occasion, ghost writer to Andrew Johnson. He was ambassador to Prussia when Otto von Bismarck changed the face of Germany and the balance of power in the western world. Long-lived men inescapably parallel the great changes of history, and many men exercise an influence in the making of it. But on the roster of American historians, George Bancroft is unique.

Had Bancroft never written a solitary line of historical prose, he could not have avoided historical scrutiny. He wrote varieties of prose. He wrote letters, notes, and dispatches as American representative at the British court just prior to the European revolutions of 1848 and from the Prussian court during the crises of Metz, Sedan, and Versailles. He had ideas about the classics, literature, education, and political theory. Pieces in *The North American Review* and the *American Quarterly Review,* translations, and reviews constitute a considerable body of written materials telling about educational methods, aesthetic standards, German culture, and Greek scholarship.[19] Hardly a Democratic politician in Whig Massachusetts before the Civil War, not to mention an articulate one like George Bancroft, has eluded the biographer's scalpel. Bancroft's speeches, good enough to elicit a response from such national figures as Martin Van Buren and William L. Marcy, were certain, if only on that account, to be caught in the net of historians constantly fishing in troubled political waters. Public officials in high places have rarely been able to insulate themselves from family pride. Even when the charity of forgetfulness seemed clearly indicated, chaste memoirs invariably appeared to be followed by lusty biographies not usually so eulogistic. But Bancroft displayed the same qualities in public office that he did everywhere else. He was too able and too restive not to improve a situation when he was in a position to do so. He was too active, too verbal, too aggressive not to leave his mark whether on politics, literature, or education.[20]

Bancroft's record of achievement bears no reasonable comparison. An early worshiper at the German shrine, he was influential in breaking down academic provincialism in the United States.[21] He brought the invigorating historical ideals of his German tutors to this country directly as well as by application.[22] Failing to make an appreciable impression at Harvard,[23] except with the students, he joined with his friend Joseph Green Cogswell to establish the Round Hill School at Northampton, Massachusetts, an innovation in teaching and in learning which commanded respect and attention.[24] He had found Harvard on his return "a sickening and wearisome place," [25] but the eleven years from 1823 to 1834 he devoted to Round Hill were not without despair and discouragement. "I like the sound of the word schoolmaster," [26] he wrote, but he wanted to teach a larger and more consequential audience than the somewhat inappreciative lads who came to him and Cogswell at Northampton. Jared Sparks was only one of those who commended what was being done at Round Hill. Bancroft was duly appreciative, for he and his associate could not have wished for a better advertisement than the article written in *The North American Review* by the widely acclaimed historian and biographer. "The praise we covet . . . ," he replied to Sparks' comments, "is of contributing in our sphere to the promotion of letters in our country, and patriotism is the most inspiring of the motives by which we are influenced." [27]

Bancroft amply contributed to letters while serving as schoolmaster, but history offered fairer fields for Bancroft to conquer. Sparks aided Bancroft by editorial assistance that Bancroft did not always appreciate, and by encouragement that Bancroft always did.[28] The pages of *The North American Review* were receptive to his literary offerings, and Sparks urged him to try his hand at historical topics. Bancroft, however, had carved out a large assignment for himself. He confessed to Sparks that "there is nothing half so delightful to me in the moment of exertion as the hope of thus being a useful citizen; of contributing in my humble sphere to disseminate the principles of justice, liberty, and learning. There is no man who may not find a fit sphere for exertion; and if there are any who can produce no results, it is because they err in judgment, or devote their powers in the wrong service. There is no faculty I would more desire to possess in an eminent degree than cool, practical judgment." [29] Bancroft offered up his considerable talents to the promotion of justice, liberty, and learning, and he took intelligent care to see that he should not devote his "powers to the wrong service."

Scholarship and politics were the spheres Bancroft chose for the exertion of his powers. Industry and the city had not yet succeeded in arbitrarily dividing human functions, and the lines which came to separate men of thought from men of action were not yet rigidly drawn. Thomas Jefferson, James Madison, and John Quincy Adams were scholars whose response to the call of public duty made them greater and more effective ones. Had they cultivated a single line of specialist activity, they might have made larger gains within a restricted area, but the restriction of the area of cultivation might have limited their gains. Scores of public figures, not from Boston and Cambridge alone, were convinced that a true and flourishing republic of letters was possible only in a true and flourishing republic. Bancroft chose his spheres well. Certainly, one sphere interfered with the other, and his most prolific literary years were those in which he was free of civic cares.[30] Yet he reached heights in both, far greater than many of his contemporaries undistracted by a division of occupational loyalties. For Bancroft there was no deep psychological conflict either of loyalty or interest. For him scholarship and politics were separable parts of a unitary purpose; they were neither inseparable nor irreconcilable.

Bancroft had chosen to promote liberty and justice. He hoped to inculcate their values and to explain, to learned skeptics and unlettered believers alike, how liberty and justice were developed, expanded, and preserved. The means by which they were promoted mattered less than the accomplishment. Politics in a democracy places responsibility upon those with knowledge and sensitivity. They have an obligation to serve, if only the people choose them. Bancroft liked the office of schoolmaster; he would help to educate the people. He would exchange the Greek verbs and the little boys of Round Hill for the harder lessons of democracy and the larger classroom of America. The political forum offered the opportunity for clarifying ideas and sharpening the issues dividing society. The forum of scholarship offered the opportunity of examining and expounding ideas. One could consecrate one's life to the common weal: a public life of party debate and service in office and a private intellectual life of study and writing. Bancroft attempted in both areas to expound the evolution of the concept of commonwealth and to explain the politics of liberty and its institutions.[31]

Bancroft plunged into politics early.[32] On the fourth of July, 1826, Bancroft appeared in Northampton, Massachusetts, as the orator of the day. One of numerous orations delivered to commemorate the half century of independence, it could easily have been a conventional and fulsome performance. Few had any reason to expect that anything other than a flurry of local approbation would follow. Actually, all his affiliations of background and association suggested a mildly conservative approach, filled with references to the wisdom of the founders and patriotic injunctions to the populace. These were not the themes for Bancroft, and he boldly took his stand with Jeffersonian rather than with Federalist doctrine. He sketched the development of popular government against a background of universal history and assigned a fundamental and continuing influence to the United States. "There is no safe criterion of opinion but the careful exercise of public judgment;" declaimed Bancroft, "and in the science of government, as elsewhere, the deliberate convictions of mankind, reasoning on the causes of their own happiness, their own wants and interests, are the surest revelations of political truth." [33] These dicta were as clear as any Fourth of July orator could make them. "We give," continued Bancroft, "the power to the many in the hope and to the end, that they may use it for their own benefit; that they may always so legislate, as to open the fairest career to industry, and promote an equality founded on the safe and equitable influence of the laws." [34]

To some of Bancroft's friends this was apostasy; to most of his family it was embarrassing heresy.[35] Far from recanting, he contributed a piece on the Bank of the United States question to *The North American Review*. He took a strong Jacksonian position, advocating that the charter of the Second Bank of the United States should not be renewed.[36] This line of argument represented neither the view of *The North American* nor of the wielders of political power in New England. There was sufficient disquiet in the editorial rooms of *The North American* to require an advance announcement that a forthcoming article would take the other side. An article representing the Whig case, supporting recharter, did appear, and Bancroft was ready and eager to answer its contentions, but the editors of the *Review* had had enough.[37] In a letter, appearing in the *Boston Courier,* Bancroft had his unequivocating say. "Of all political heresies the most baleful is that which would base political power on wealth. It is too late to invent theories on the subject; history has solved the question. Where the people possess no authority, their rights obtain no respect." Bancroft allowed himself to use fighting words, but the ideas were those with which Andrew Jackson was fighting the party battle. "Show me one instance where popular institutions have violated the rights of property, and I will show you a hundred, nay a thousand instances, where the people have been pillaged by the greedy cupidity of a privileged class. There is more danger from monopolies than from combinations of workmen. There is more danger that capital will swallow up the profits of labor than that labor will confiscate capital." [38] Had Bancroft desired to call public attention to himself, he could have chosen no more effective way. Jacksonian leaders on both national and local levels were forced to recognize his existence.[39]

Democratic strategists soon began to think of Bancroft as a Congressional candidate. Bancroft took himself out of the running by choosing to stand for the lower house of the Massachusetts legislature as a candidate of the Workingmen's party. He lost the election but won a place in the thick of Democratic party politics.[40] In the presidential campaign of 1836, Bancroft publicly supported Van Buren and after the Democratic victory he was appointed collector of the port of Boston. This position, a modest party plum, placed him in the party councils, provided a moderate income, and gave him sufficient leisure to write.[41] Meanwhile in 1834, Volume I of *A History of the United States, from the Discovery of the American Continent,* appeared, and George Bancroft had become a figure of national prominence.

The first volume of Bancroft's monumental history was almost unreservedly applauded. Edward Everett could hardly bear to put it down except to nourish his spirit at church and his body at table. When he finished after twenty-four hours of almost constant reading he wrote: "It will last while the memory of America lasts, and . . . will take its place instantly among the classics of our language." [42] William Hickling Prescott, whose approval for neophytes was success itself, was equally generous. "I have read your book with great pleasure, interest, and instruction. . . . In your first volume you have given us a pledge of an enduring, impartial, readable history— such as we greatly need." [43] European scholars added their approbation for the new historian of America, and after the passage of a year one out of every three New England homes possessed a copy.[44] But responses were not all laudatory. John Davis, Whig governor of Massachusetts and husband to Bancroft's sister, chided the author for permitting his political sentiments to color his historical judgments. George Ticknor, whose scholarship carefully followed the best Germanic forms, struck an identical critical note. "You are not made," he warned Bancroft, who had followed him in the sacred halls of German universities, "by your talents or your affectations, by your temperament or your pursuits, to be either the leader or the tool of demagogues." [45] There was more to the comments of Davis and Ticknor than their own political bias. Jackson men took the *History of the United States* to their hearts. If Bancroft's volume could not have been said to have voted for Jacksonian principles, it was certainly taken as an endorsement of them.[46]

Succeeding volumes followed quickly. The second appeared in 1837, and the third three years later. The next two volumes, delayed by politics and research, were not published until 1852. Three volumes were issued at periodic intervals: the sixth in 1854, the seventh in 1858, and the eighth in 1860. The final volumes, nine and ten, came off the press in 1866 and 1874 respectively. Not many works have enjoyed so long and so steadfast a popularity. They were so popular that writers of manuals and textbooks have relied upon them extensively, too extensively in the opinion of some.[47] Methodological foibles, since detected, must be balanced against the fact that few, up to that time, had laid so many sources of information under contribution. Scholars have matched the extent of his output, if not the number of years expended in preparation, but none has matched his activity. Even to Bancroft's bounding energies, there were limits. His history, originally projected as *A History of the United States from the Discovery of the American Continent* did not extend beyond the close of the Revolution. He later enlarged his narrative to include the years to 1789 with a two-volume study of the *History of the Formation of the Constitution of the United States of America* (1882). The whole work is divided into three units: the period of discovery and colonial beginnings, the era of the American Revolution, and the formation of the Constitution. Of these the Revolution is accorded the largest space and emphasis.

Bancroft made his intentions clear in the preface, and the introduction carries an explicit statement of his purpose. "I have formed the design," he wrote in the former place, "of writing a History of the United States from the Discovery of the American Continent to the present time. . . . I have dwelt at considerable length on this first period, because it contains the germ of our institutions. The maturity of a nation is but the continuation of its youth. The spirit of the colonies demanded freedom from the beginning." [48] If Bancroft had a special interest, none at least could accuse him of concealing it. And Bancroft's special interest was the relation of American history to the development of the concept of democracy. The United States of America "have the precedence in the practice and the defence of the equal rights of man. The sovereignty of the people is here a conceded axiom." Nor was this all. "Our government, by its organization, is necessarily identified with the interests of the people, and relies exclusively on their attachment for its durability and support. Even the enemies of the state, if there are any among us, have liberty to express their opinions undisturbed; and are safely tolerated, where reason is left free to combat their errors. Nor is the constitution a dead letter, unalterably fixed: it has the capacity for improvement; adopting whatever changes time and the public will may require, and safe from decay, so long as that will retains its energy." [49] The mission of the United States of America was democracy, and George Bancroft was its historian.

The nature of history and the function of the historian were as clear to Bancroft as the goal of his effort. A year after the publication of the first volume of his *History,* Bancroft delivered an address presenting his philosophy as a historian and his creed as a citizen. "The Office of the People in Art, Government, and Religion" was Bancroft's confession of faith in humanity and in progress. Belief in man stemmed from the eighteenth-century enlightenment, belief in progress from nineteenth-century German idealism. Bancroft's dedication to scholarship and his dedication to the betterment of society were based upon the philosophical principles outlined in this lecture. No "passive destiny" attached "to the inhabitants of the earth. For them the expectations of social improvement are no delusion; the hopes of philanthropy are more than a dream." The inhabitants of the earth for Bancroft meant all the people everywhere. "There is a *spirit in man:* not in the privileged few; not in those of us only who by the favor of Providence have been nursed in the public schools: IT IS IN MAN: it is the attribute of the race. The spirit, which is the guide to truth, is the gracious gift to each member of the human family." [50]

To all but genuine democrats this was heady doctrine. But it was rooted in a theory of knowledge soon to find distinguished votaries in the United States. George Bancroft was a transcendentalist before there was a transcendentalist movement in America.[51] "The five senses do not constitute the whole inventory of our sources of knowledge. They are the organs by which thought connects itself with the external universe." There was more to the universe, however, than its external aspects and relations. "We have functions which connect us with heaven, as well as organs which set us in relation with the earth. We have not merely the senses opening to us the external world, but an internal sense, which places us in connexion with the world of intelligence and the decrees of God." This was the world of the ultimate, the world of reason, the source of all knowledge and insight which provided the criteria for judgment and certainty. There could be no mistaking of Bancroft's meaning. "I mean not that faculty which deduces inferences from the experience of the senses, but that higher faculty, which from the infinite treasures of its own consciousness, originates truth, and assents to it by the force of intuitive evidence; that faculty which raises us beyond the control of time and space, and gives us faith in things eternal and invisible." [52] Let us disagree with Bancroft if we will—as who among historians has not—but let us disagree with his philosophy, not with the intellectual consequents of his logic, once the philosophy was accepted.

Reason was not the special endowment of special men. "The intellectual functions, by which relations are perceived, are the common endowments of the race." Common men were potentially uncommon men, and progress was a law of the universe. "If it be true, that the gifts of mind and heart are universally diffused, if the sentiment of truth, justice, love and beauty exist in every one, then it follows, as a necessary consequence, that the common judgment in taste, politics, and religion, is the highest authority on earth, and the nearest possible approach to an infallible decision." Democracy and progress were thus grounded in the universal reason, and "government rests on the people and not on the few, on persons and not on property, on the free development of public opinion and not on authority; because the munificent Author of our being has conferred the gifts of mind upon every member of the human race without distinction of outward circumstances." [53]

Bancroft's democracy rests upon his theory of knowledge; his *History* is an exemplification of his philosophy. The original ten volumes of the first edition were later reduced to six, the result of vigorous cutting, pruning, and change.[54] The first three volumes cover the colonial years to 1763; the remaining three to 1782. Volume I begins with the beginnings in 1492 and reaches the period of the English Restoration and its repercussions in the colonial world. Bancroft's approach frequently resembles what later came to be known as the "new history." Although he seldom 'failed to celebrate "the heroes who had won laurels in scenes of carnage," he urged consideration "for the founders of states"; and for "the wise legislators, who struck the rock in the wilderness, so that the waters of liberty gushed forth." [55] The second volume carries the account through the exciting happenings of the Glorious Revolution and continues colonial evolution to the mid-eighteenth century. While pages are appropriately devoted to events on the English side of the waters, Bancroft's eye is fixed on the American Revolution. Nevertheless, Bancroft allowed himself the space and the time, unlike later historians, to discuss the progress of France in America at length and to detail the linguistic patterns of the aborigines east of the Mississippi. Following the discussion of Indian languages, several chapters describe

Indian manners, polity, and religion as well as their nature and origin.[56] He had a genuine flair for synthesis, and his summary "Twenty-Six Years of Colonial Administration Under the House of Hanover" is a brief but cogent statement of contemporary historical knowledge.[57]

Bancroft was unquestionably fond of the grandiloquent phrase,[58] but he frequently employed such phrases with telling effect. If the following sentences are florid, they also make the point. "Tyranny and injustice peopled America with men nurtured in suffering and adversity. The history of our colonization is the history of the crimes of Europe." When he chose he could also write with epigrammatic brevity. Of the early days of Virginia he commented: "If America had no English town; it soon had English graves." Of Sebastian Cabot he wrote: "He gave England a continent, and no one knows his burial place." [59] So much has been made of Bancroft's qualities of style that his qualities of greatness have often been overlooked. It was not his style but his ideas that make his history notable, not his grandiloquence but his scholarship. The magnificent periods of Gibbon fascinated him, but he seems not to have sensed that a style appropriate for the decline and fall of an empire was inappropriate for the rise and growth of a democracy.[60]

The fall of the European colonial system from 1748 to 1763 is the grand theme of Bancroft's third volume. And the overthrow of the European colonial system meant the overthrow of the European political system. Bancroft was approaching the core of his subject; the first epoch of the American Revolution. "The hour of revolution was at hand, promising freedom to conscience and dominion to intelligence. History, escaping from the dictates of authority and the jars of insulated interests, enters upon new and unthought of domains of culture and equality." [61] In a typical Bancroft paragraph, flamboyant but suggestive, he outlined the direction his history was to follow:

> For Europe, the crisis foreboded the struggles of generations. The strong bonds of faith and affection, which once united the separate classes of its civil hierarchy, had lost their vigor. In the impending chaos of states, the ancient forms of society, after convulsive agonies, were doomed to be broken in pieces, and the fragments to become distinct, and seemingly lifeless, like the dust; ready to be whirled in a deadly sand-storm by the tempest of public rage. The voice of reform, as it passed over the desolation, would inspire animation afresh; but in the classes whose power was crushed, as well as in the oppressed who knew not that they were redeemed, it might also awaken wild desires, which the ruins of a former world could not satiate. In America, the influences of time were moulded

by the creative force of reason, sentiment, and nature; its political edifice rose in lovely proportions, as if to the melodies of the lyre. Peacefully and without crime, humanity was to make for itself a new existence.[62]

When Bancroft returned to America in 1849 after three years as United States minister to Great Britain,[63] he set about the task of historian in earnest. He abandoned Boston for New York, and with his boxes of manuscripts collected abroad and his large and ever growing library, he made the completion of the *History* the mainspring of his life. Bancroft remained the great historian of America, but he was no longer in undisputed possession of the historical domain. William Hickling Prescott's books on imperial Spain, Francis Parkman's studies of colonial France, and John Lothrop Motley's accounts of his liberty-loving Dutch vied with Bancroft for popular attention and offered other historical accomplishment for comparison.[64] While two of the three heroic historians dealt largely with European phases of history, there were historians who made American themes their own. Jared Sparks, hardly ever inactive, still dreamed of a history of the American Revolution, but was too busy collecting, editing, and publishing documents and biographies to write it.[65] Local historians carved out sections and regions for their own research, which they cultivated with varying degrees of interest and competence. Bancroft's fellow alumnus from Exeter, John Gorham Palfrey, made the history of New England a monument to his noble ancestors,[66] while others chose Virginia, New York, or Louisiana as their special fields.[67] Richard Hildreth, whose father had been Bancroft's master in the old Exeter days,[68] and George Tucker, a versatile southern scholar who graced the faculty of the University of Virginia,[69] alone attempted to write of America from its beginnings. Yet Bancroft's reputation insulated him from serious rivalry. The unchallenged master for almost a quarter of a century, he eclipsed his predecessors and outranked his contemporaries. The volumes of *A History of the United States* already written continued to sell; those he was yet to write would no doubt do as well. Bancroft was the leading historian of America, and for most Americans Bancroft's version of their country's past was American history. In the opinion of the most recent student of George Bancroft: "his position in the field was as unshaken as that of Herodotus among the Greeks." [70]

Although politics had not lost its allure for George Bancroft, finishing the *History* was now his career. But politics in one form or another cut deeply into Bancroft's life plans. The decade of the fifties were peaceful and productive years, of which five volumes were the fruit. The Civil War and his diplomatic duties in Berlin from 1867 to 1873 interrupted the rhythm of his creative activity. To Bancroft, for whom the history of democracy was an integral part of life, it was almost impossible to remain aloof from the events that threatened to disrupt it. He came to the public support of Abraham Lincoln[71]—for whom he had failed to vote in 1860 [72]—because he agreed that the only way to preserve democracy was to preserve the Union. The materials for the final volumes of the *History* gathered dust in his Washington study, while Bancroft wrote letter after letter to William H. Seward and to Salmon P. Chase with the encouragement they always needed and the sage advice they could never do without.[73] Requests for historical data became routine,[74] and President Lincoln himself tapped the historian's knowledge on the subject of the suspension of *habeas corpus,* once he had suspended it.[75] After Lincoln's assassination, Andrew Johnson acquired Bancroft's support and counsel, for Bancroft and Johnson had Jefferson, Jackson, and a love of the Union in common. Charles Sumner, the brilliant but erratic senator from Massachusetts, was Bancroft's old friend, but Bancroft had little sympathy with Radical Republican plans for the reorganization of the South and the nation.[76] Johnson not only acquired Bancroft's support, he acquired his active collaboration. Bancroft composed Johnson's presidential message to Congress of December 1865, which, in the view of both, would either make or break the new administration.[77] Shortly thereafter, Bancroft appeared before both houses of Congress to deliver the Lincoln eulogy, which he performed in the best Bancroft oratorical manner.[78] And the Bancroft manner was graceful, rhetorical, and impressive. It was a courageous performance, in addition, for he could not do Lincoln justice without offending Johnson's Congressional opponents nor could he give Lincoln his due as the preserver of the Union without offending those nations whose leaders had placed every obstacle in Lincoln's way. He offended them both, but he spoke his convictions with unabashed candor and rugged consistency.[79]

Even during these upsettingly crowded years, Bancroft managed periodically to turn to the *History,* and in 1866 the ninth volume was finished. Following the dictates of chronological development, he related the military history of the first stages of the Revolution from the outbreak of battle to the treaty with France in 1778. But other matters also required extended treatment. He commenced building the federal union by discussing the state constitutions, and he was careful to emphasize that, while the colonists had broken the bonds of political allegiance, they had not severed the linkages of political thought. When he reached the Articles of Confederation, it was plain that localism was the enemy of union, whether in 1783 or in 1861. The destiny of America was democracy, and for Bancroft union was the historical instrument of democracy in 1783, as reunion was the historical instrument in 1866. Bancroft's judgment on the issue of union was as clear before the Civil War as after it, and the events from Fort Sumter to Appomattox were hardly needed to confirm it.[80]

Bancroft's analysis of the Confederation was perverted by his preconceptions of American historical meanings, but the volume on the outbreak of the Revolution remains masterly both in conception and execution. He conceived of the American Revolution in large historical terms. Like some of his predecessors who were contemporary to the events he placed the great conflict in global perspective—a movement that directly or indirectly influenced the subsequent course of historical change. His presentation of the impact of the Declaration of Independence set a standard of balance, though not necessarily of comprehension, rarely equaled even by his more "objective followers." [81] "The conflict between England and her colonies," he affirmed, "sprang necessarily out of the development of British institutions," [82] a point that immediately made ludicrous the view of the struggle as a split between English oppressors and colonial guardians of English liberties. Bancroft did for the diplomacy of the war what Sparks had hoped to do, and nothing approaching a challenge to such inclusiveness appeared for many a year. Never guilty of suggesting by omission that the struggle within the British Empire occurred in a European void, he wrote chapters on American contacts with Spain and with France and he traced European reactions from Russia to the kingdom of Naples.[83] Critics have always resented his lengthy discussion of Germany from the dawn of Christianity to the emergence of the United States.[84] It was not simply that things German were close to Bancroft's heart. Rather it was that German thought had provided him with a philosophy of history, that the House of Hanover was a German house, that Hessian troops fought American colonials, and that German immigrants in colonial Pennsylvania and in the New York of Bancroft's own day tied Germany and America together. Regardless of its faults, Bancroft's section, "The Independence of America Is Acknowledged," was incomparably the best that had yet been written. The dean of historians, already past his middle sixties, had reached his full intellectual stride, and the end of the *History* was now in sight. At this point President Johnson, anxious to honor the man who had given so much without official reward, appointed Bancroft American minister to Berlin.[85] And the Senate, unaware that Bancroft had been Johnson's ghost,[86] confirmed the appointment without delay.

Bancroft, always sentimental about Germany, accepted with alacrity, for Europe was fascinating, and Berlin was an important diplomatic post. Once again the *History* played second to politics. Bancroft liked good company, good talk, and good food, and there was plenty of aristocratic *Gemütlichkeit* in Berlin court circles.[87] In addition there was Bismarck, whose genius for *Machtpolitik* rarely interfered with his capacity for the lively give-and-take of companionship.[88] Even with the pleasant distraction of society and the demands of diplomatic business, the *History* was not completely neglected. Whenever he could, Bancroft searched for fresh data in the royal library and the state archives. And diplomatic colleagues in European cities, together with his own personal research staff, were always on the alert.[89] Yet it was not easy for Bancroft to write notes for the next volume while Bismarck and Moltke talked uninhibitedly of plans for the unification of Germany and the war with France.[90] Not until he was re-established in America and ensconced in his Washington home was Bancroft really able to resume historical work. In 1874 the final volume of the *History* was ready.[91]

The last part of Bancroft's work was a fitting climax to the impressive whole. The American Revolution was brought to a resounding close. Again, events were framed in a wide international setting. Again, the widely ramifying maneuvers of diplomacy were recounted in rich detail but with sharply defined perspective.[92] Bancroft, now seventy-four, with a record of accomplishment few had ever equaled, had more than earned the right to indulge in the pleasures afforded by his friends, his roses, and his fame. All these pleasures were his, but there were also continuing pleasures of work. The *History* was to be twice revised, a biography of Van Buren was to be written, and two fresh volumes on the formation of the Constitution were yet to come.[93]

The first volume of the revised edition came out the year after the last volume of the *History*.[94] America lacked but a year to make a century, and Bancroft was not far behind. Revision was a lethal process and a swift one. "Slaughtered adjectives" [95] helped to cut the ten volumes to six, and much of the exuberant rhetoric disappeared with vicious strokes of the author's own editorial pen. Mindful of the objections raised over the years by all manner of critics, he appended an index to each one of the volumes and toned down provocative references particularly when unsupported by satisfactory evidence. When the "Centenary Edition" was completed in 1879, Bancroft was free to surrender himself to the Constitution. The surrender was virtually complete, and Bancroft, the old pioneer, was again engaged in breaking new ground.[96] He studied his single predecessor, George T. Curtis,[97] with care, but he had resources at his command possessed by no one else. He had talked with Madison in 1836, and as was then and always thereafter his practice, he made notes of the interview. His distinction as a scholar gave him easy access to manuscript collections in private hands and in public trust, and his personal means permitted his research assistants to comb repositories all over the world for pertinent data.[98] The two volumes of the *History of the Formation of the Constitution of the United States,* ready in 1882, crowned Bancroft's works.[99] He never quite relinquished the idea of bringing his *History* down to "the present," [100] but he had "been able to trace step by step the march of the people of the United States toward a union." [101]

It was indeed a march, and a dramatic one. His philosophy of history, the same as it had been fifty years ago, guided the American people to the fulfillment of their divinely sponsored mission. The old Bancroft hand had lost none of its democratic touch. But there was also the old Bancroft skill in narrative art, in the marshaling of new and unused primary sources, and the keen perception of interactive forces. The two volumes at once became the best available reference on the origin of the Constitution. Not until the "scientific school" devised new tools of research and analysis was Bancroft superseded.

But Bancroft was not yet ready to call it a scholar's day. "The Last Revision" appeared in 1886,[102] shorter, sharper, and in every way improved. He was weary, but his mind churned with projects: lives of Van Buren, Polk, Shakespeare.[103] He still spent long hours among his books, still enjoyed his friends although toward the end he mistook them. He still took his walks and loved his roses. Despite a cold, he took a usual walk in January 1891 which turned out to be his last. He died on January 17, 1891, full of honors and full of years.

Bancroft deserved the rich reward of approbation and the richer reward of encouragement. The praise accorded him was neither casual nor perfunctory, and came from men whose opinions none could fail to value. Their opinions indicate how truly Bancroft stirred his generation and how accurately he echoed men's own private thoughts. Ralph Waldo Emerson was almost lyrical in his own Emersonian way. "The history is richer not only in anecdotes of great names, but of the great heart of towns and provinces than I

dared believe; and—what surprised and charmed me—it starts
tears, and almost makes them overflow on many and many a page.
. . . It is noble matter, and I am heartily glad to have it nobly
treated." [104] Theodore Parker, whose learning matched his generous
nature, could not make up his mind which characteristic of Bancroft
most excited him: "the mighty diligence which collects all the facts
and words—even the minutest particles of characteristic matter—or
the subtle art which frames them into so nice a mosaic picture of the
progress of the People and the Race. I think you are likely to make,
what I long since told you I looked for from *you,* the most noble and
splendid piece of historical composition, not only in English, but in
any tongue." [105]

Everyone, obviously, was not so complimentary as Emerson and
Parker. But criticism was grist to Bancroft's second thought, and he
was forever struggling for accuracy of judgment and precision of
detail. Henry Hallam, a well-known English historian with whom
Bancroft had had many a delightful encounter when at the court of
St. James, reproved him for gross one-sidedness and reminded him
that "an historian has the high office of carrying the scales." This
latter reminder could have disturbed Bancroft but little, for carrying
the scales was exactly what he thought he was doing. But Hallam
had other objections with which to reproach him. "I must fairly tell
you, that I do not go along with all your strictures on English statesmen and on England, either in substance, or still more, in tone. You
write as an historian, but you must expect that we shall read as Englishmen. Faults there were, but I do not think that all were on one
side. At all events, a more moderate tone would carry more
weight." [106] Bancroft tried valiantly to remedy these two defects over
the years, and to his credit it must be said that he succeeded.

The balances of the historian weighed all things, but what was
placed in the scales made a vast difference. "You give us," wrote
Edward Everett, who certainly did not endorse Bancroft's political
philosophy, "not wretched pasteboard men, not a sort of chronological table, with the dates written out at length, after the manner of
most historians:—but you give us real, individual living men and
women with their passions, interests and peculiarities." [107] The
critics, however, did grasp Bancroft's essential weakness. "All things
have light *and* shadow" said Carlyle,[108] and even the stoutest of Bancroft's defenders would have to concede that, in the grand theme of
the *History* at least, there was little of shading. The philosophy of
history that Bancroft espoused made progress certain and purpose
clear, but in the mundane history of living experience no scholar has

ever found such unshakable assurance. Guizot confided to Jared Sparks that the *History* was "très démocratique," [109] which was undoubtedly true, but this for Bancroft was far more of a compliment than a criticism.

If Bancroft's *History* was too philosophical in the sense in which modern historians have come to abhor the term, it was nevertheless a speculative synthesis. If it was "too democratic," it was rooted in the logic of a respected theory of knowledge. Bancroft was not alone among historians who believed that the world was in "a constant state of advancement" and historians still believe "it is the office of history to write the changes in humanity." During ancient times, Bancroft wrote, historical writers had "sought the causes of events in the personal genius and purposes of individuals." Scholars who came after the classical historians "considered events in connection with one another, yet without observing the general principle by which that succession was controlled." There was, in other words, a causal connection beyond the simple relation that explained the sequence of a series of successive events. The "true historians" applied the inductive method that led "to the perception of general principles in the cause of events." [110] The inductive method was the instrument of reason, but for Bancroft it was reason as expounded by Hegel and Coleridge; not by Darwin and Thomas H. Huxley.

The words Bancroft used are still the words used by historians, but the philosophy has altered. Scholars have complained of Bancroft's "unphilosophical tone" and his uncritical spirit. They object to his style and his unabashed assurance. His "exuberant confidence" and his "uncritical self-laudation" [111] has irked many an exponent of the scientific method in historical study. Yet Bancroft's critics have seldom attacked his fundamental assumptions. While modern scholars have abandoned Bancroft's world view without having refuted it, they have not abandoned the substance of Bancroft's social view. Historians still share his ultimate faith in the future of democratic man. They are not, however, so confident or so complacent. Modern scholars could not abandon the Bancroft faith without at the same time abandoning America. Bancroft placed his trust in man and man's potential. Modern historians have simply exchanged metaphysics for science, transcendental imperatives for the concepts of biology and physics. They have substituted working hypotheses for ultimate certainties.[112]

XIV

Richard Hildreth and the
Philosophy of History

George Bancroft, though he hailed from Worcester, added Boston to his conquests in spite of his politics. Many a dowager on Beacon Hill refused to accept him, but Boston, Cambridge, Harvard, and all New England claimed him as their own.[1] Boston and Massachusetts also produced Richard Hildreth.[2] Hildreth was born in 1805 in Deerfield,[3] and he had eminently respectable Massachusetts associations. He went to Phillips Exeter and to Harvard, he taught at Concord, studied law in Newburyport, and practiced in Boston. His fame, however, rests on grounds more substantial than geographical fortuities. *The Theory of Morals, The Theory of Politics,* and *The History of the United States* are solid contributions to American scholarship.[4]

Honors and wealth were Bancroft's lot; distinctions and successes came to William H. Prescott and to Francis Parkman. Hildreth struggled vainly to achieve recognition.[5] Bancroft worked prodigiously and reached almost all of his goals. Hildreth worked no less hard—for none could work harder than Bancroft—and reached but few of his objectives. In politics Bancroft lost elections but won important political office and important political results. Hildreth, on the other hand, scarcely less able and on the side of the majority party in Massachusetts politics, made no deep political dent. His *History,* different from Bancroft's but by no reasonable standards inferior, was dwarfed by Bancroft's ever-growing prominence. Ban-

258

croft's historical writing yielded what Hildreth would have regarded as a fortune. Hildreth earned less than five thousand dollars after more than seven years; Bancroft's early volumes brought him fifty thousand dollars after twenty.[6] Bancroft spent his last years in Washington. They were years as full of happy living as they were full of pleasurable satisfactions. Presidents, statesmen, and scholars enjoyed the sparkle of his company and the sheen of his mind. The Senate of the United States voted him the privilege of the floor—a signal gesture of honor—and his visits to that body resembled occasions of state. The American Historical Association, august even in infancy, elected him its president and invited him to speak. National events and celebrations found George Bancroft at the speakers' table, in the reviewing stand, or in the special places reserved for the chief executive, the justices of the Supreme Court, and the diplomatic corps. Bancroft, the historian of the forces of American history, became the hero of American historiography.

Hildreth's declining years were even more frustrating than the middle years of robust ambition.[7] By contrast with Bancroft's they were pitiful years. His last days were spent in Trieste where as American consul—a post secured for him by friends—he hoped to recapture health of body and vigor of mind. "Do you not think," wrote a desperate but courageously loyal wife to Governor John Andrew of Massachusetts, "that his country should award him something of honor?"[8] Never had it been necessary to write such a letter for Bancroft; it was Bancroft who wrote President Polk that he preferred a diplomatic post but would consider membership in the cabinet.

Caroline Hildreth succeeded. Abraham Lincoln, moved by John Andrew and Charles Sumner, gave Richard Hildreth the appointment. But Hildreth was already a dying man. William Dean Howells, American consul at Venice, recalled him: "He had worn himself out on a newspaper when he got his appointment at Trieste, and I saw him in the shadow of the cloud that was wholly to darken him before he died. He was a tall, thin man, absent, silent: already a phantom of himself, but with a scholarly serenity and dignity amidst the ruin, when the worst came."[9] He died in 1865 and was buried not far from Theodore Parker in the Protestant cemetery at Florence.

Even death did not secure Hildreth the anonymity of fame. The *History* has offered scholars ideas,[10] and those who have traveled over the same ground have been wise enough not to refuse its guidance. But Richard Hildreth was a problem from the beginning. His philosophical excursions and the ideas which prompted them have been largely neglected.[11] His career as critic, lawyer, journalist, reformer—the urges of his life that fashioned the texture of his growth —has eluded those who have studied him as historian alone.[12] Hildreth's dedication to a broader understanding of democracy still deserves attentive scrutiny.

Hildreth was a student of philosophy before he became a student of history. *The History of the United States* exemplifies his philosophy; his philosophy was an attempt to construct a science of man. Hildreth's historical researches followed his philosophical explorations projected more than a decade before the *History* was composed. *The Theory of Morals* appeared in 1844, five years before the completion of the first volume of the *History,* and *The Theory of Politics,* drafted earlier, was published a year after the last three volumes of the *History* in 1852.[13]

By training a lawyer and by profession a journalist, Hildreth was not simply a research scholar. He was a reformer who investigated philosophy to discover the limits of the possible in human improvement. He explored American history to discover what in fact had been done and what lessons for men were latent in the record. The reformist spirit gives purpose to Hildreth's life. Like Jeremy Bentham, a thinker who inspired him, learning was hostage to the fortunes of mankind. Eighteenth-century French *philosophes* and representatives of the British radical movement of the early nineteenth century were the intellectual company he elected to keep. Like Bentham, he was interested in law as an instrument of social change and social control. Discussion and education were served by journalism and pamphleteering. They were also techniques of pressure, in short of politics; and politics, the means of the democratic process, resulted in the ends of reform. Bentham looked to Parliament; Hildreth, reflecting a basic difference between America and Britain in the nineteenth century, looked to democratic party structure and the social forces that stimulated it.

Hildreth's philosophy and Hildreth's *History* frequently appear to be in conflict. And Richard Hildreth often seems to be at odds with both. The first three volumes of the *History* are supposedly at variance with the concluding volumes of the series. The pamphlets are at war with the *History* and sometimes with the philosophical treatises as well. Hildreth's works and Hildreth himself present a series of problems.

The problems, however, are less real than apparent. Hildreth was not a technical philosopher. He never developed a logically coherent system, although he strove to achieve consistency and to apply his precepts concretely. He was far too occupied, far too immersed in responding to life. John Stuart Mill's memorable description of Jeremy Bentham, an early idol of his own, tells a great deal about them both. Bentham, he wrote,

> had neither internal experience nor external. . . . He never knew prosperity and adversity, passion nor satiety; he never had even the experience which sickness gives. . . . He knew no dejection, no heaviness of heart. He never felt life a sore and weary burthen. He was a boy to the last.[14]

Inaccurate as a description of Bentham, the inventory, if reversed in every particular, fits Richard Hildreth exactly. Hildreth suffered from indifferent health. He suffered from disappointment and unrequited ambition. He struggled to make the straggling ends of existence meet. He was dissatisfied, frustrated, and occasionally embittered. Moreover, he was captive of his own trying formula: "I pay no attention to what I have been taught, except so far as my own examinations confirm it." [15] That he deviated from Bentham and Mill and followed Adam Smith, Locke, and Hume only in spirit is as natural as his own fluctuations of mood and concept. He was consistent in devotion to his own maxim and his own compulsive urge. His inconsistencies are less the results of logical lapses than of additional probings, less the results of rigidity of mind than intensity of feeling. If there is a single clue to the Hildreth paradox it may reside in comparison with his English Utilitarian mentor. Jeremy Bentham, no less hostile to the French Revolution than to Edmund Burke's reflections on it, looked to Parliament for an affirmative response to his reforms. When Parliament failed to respond, Bentham turned to the people. His ends were the most important elements of his life, and his reforms turned out to be almost as radical as those advocated by groups he despised. The reforms of Richard Hildreth were likewise the all important ends of his life. If he did not break with his Federalist heritage completely, he gradually found himself out of harmony with its spirit. Like Bentham, he moved closer to the side of his former antagonists. He came closer in some respects to the Jeffersonians than he probably wished and shared a larger affinity with the Jacksonians than he would probably have relished.

Persistent repetition of stereotyped opinion has made Richard Hildreth and George Bancroft the classic models of antithesis. Bancroft belonged to the old school of historians, Hildreth, who predeceased him, heralded the advent of the new. Recalled as the passionless exemplar of scientific techniques, Hildreth is just as frequently remembered as a pleader for a partisan cause. Bancroft has been so completely identified with a philosophy that one critic suggested the propriety of retitling his history, "The Psychological Autobiography of George Bancroft, as Illustrated by Incidents and Characters in the Annals of the United States." [16] Hildreth is asserted to have written without embellishment, while Bancroft's meanings were shrouded in the orotund phrase. Bancroft was a transcendentalist, Hildreth an empiricist; Hildreth a realistic nationalist, Bancroft a romantic one. Hildreth's reputation rests on fidelity to the sources and a resolve to recount the past as it actually occurred. Bancroft, on the contrary, recorded the meanings of God's providences in America as revealed by the Democratic party. Hildreth later emerged as a philosopher whose history only seemingly bore the scientific hallmark. Both wrote the history of the United States, but neither could escape the coincidence of their New England origin, which in each case slanted its emphasis out of national proportion. Bancroft's volumes allegedly marched with Jefferson's Jacksonian successors to the polls; Hildreth's volumes voted solidly against the heirs of Martin Van Buren. The historiographical record, when not patently inconsistent, is assuredly confused.[17]

The words of the "Advertisement" in Hildreth's opening volume have frequently been quoted. "Of centennial sermons and Fourth-of-July orations, whether professedly such or in the guise of history, there are more than enough. It is due to our fathers and ourselves, it is due to truth and philosophy, to present for once, on the historic stage, the founders of our American nation unbedaubed with patriotic rouge, wrapped up in no fine-spun cloaks of excuses and apology, without stilts, buskins, tinsel, or bedizenment, in their own proper persons, often rude, hard, narrow, superstitious, and mistaken but always earnest, downright, manly, and sincere. The result of their labors is eulogy enough; their best apology is to tell the story exactly as it was." To identify these words as a direct and personal indictment of Bancroft tells us less of what Hildreth actually thought than what some have thought of Bancroft. That the two men and their histories were basically different is not the same as asserting that Hildreth wrote in direct philosophical reply.

Each studied the other with competitive interest, but the speed of Hildreth's treatment left Bancroft far behind.[18] Hildreth had already reached the year 1821 when Bancroft momentarily paused at 1748. Actually less than two Hildreth volumes meet Bancroft on the same historical ground. As Donald E. Emerson in his penetrating study suggests, Bancroft may just as reasonably be considered as replying to Hildreth. Bancroft's *History* and Bancroft's vogue were probably no more than a stimulus to Hildreth. His real stimulation, Emerson concluded, "came from his own interest in history, from his definite opinions concerning American history, and especially from very deep convictions about the way in which that history should be written." [19]

Bancroft and Hildreth were separated by differing philosophical assumptions. They proceeded from different intellectual premises and were distinguished by different qualities of mind and temper. Yet there is much that is similar in their lives Both were sons of ministers, a coincidence that partly explains their passion for learning and their determination to cultivate and disseminate it. [20] Bancroft preceded Hildreth at Exeter; Hildreth followed Bancroft at Harvard. [21] Each experimented before deciding upon a career. Bancroft experimented with theology, teaching, criticism; Hildreth with teaching, criticism, law. History was the final choice of both, but the choice in each case was sparked by an urge for reform. [22] Hildreth and Bancroft were reformers, and both recognized politics as an instrument of reform and regarded history in part as a guide. For Hildreth the law was once a means of social change and he served a legal apprenticeship before becoming a political journalist. [23] For Bancroft it was teaching, and he served an apprenticeship at Round Hill before becoming a politician and a writer. Both historians were descended from the sturdiest of Federal stock. Bancroft deserted the political faith of his fathers early. Hildreth's deviation, which came later, was more hesitant and confused.

When Hildreth set himself up in Boston as a lawyer, he simply changed the scene of his activities and gave new directions to his career. As a law student in Newburyport, he had found his studies fascinating enough, but it was writing that intrigued him. In Boston law was his profession, but writing with a social end in view his occupation. Soon he became affiliated with the Boston *Daily Atlas,* a political sheet dedicated to the embarrassment of Andrew Jackson and the advancement of Whig principles. Ill health forced him to abandon journalism and politics alike, and he tried to recover his strength in Florida. Here he first came into direct contact with slavery, and his novel *Archy Moore* (1836) [24] and his antislavery tract, *Despotism in America* (1840), [25] were the literary results. There were other results as well. Hildreth widened his experience, improved his powers of observation, and acquired a new focus for his reformist urge.

Hildreth's physical constitution was not made to stand the strains he constantly placed upon it. Once again he retired from active work and sought a more congenial climate. He went to British Guiana in 1840, where he successively edited two local papers[26] and so arranged his schedule that he had ample leisure for a full program of study and writing. He had long and earnestly desired both, and he made full use of his opportunity. The South American interlude, though far from free of editorial strife and controversial encounters, was intellectually rich. He projected a program of writing—including a history of the United States—which was quite impossible of fulfillment. He read a prodigious amount, put in long thoughtful hours, and wrote, among other things, his *Theory of Morals* and his *Theory of Politics*. Studies of Jeremy Bentham, earlier begun, were continued, and he emerged with a philosophical outlook.[27]

Richard Hildreth's effort was more spectacular than its outcome. To achieve "a total revolution in the whole system of philosophy relative to man considered as an intellectual and active being" [28] was a task of Kantian proportions, and Hildreth did not achieve it. The important point, however, is not that he failed but that he undertook it. The undertaking was the more important historically because his philosophical position was uncommon in the America of a hundred years ago. To the orthodox his ideas were heretical; to the unorthodox they were unphilosophical. Christian philosophers found them blasphemous;[29] Transcendentalists saw only the glittering arguments of the Enlightenment, which for them had long since lost their gleam.[30]

Hildreth's interest in science and philosophy was an interest of long standing. Originally stimulated by his learned father, the old Exeter teacher, his own intellectual yearnings made thought and study a lifelong aim. It was not his journalistic career alone which accounts for his participation in the controversies of the day. Every movement in thought and society evoked an immediate response, for Hildreth was creating a synthesis of understanding built out of the joint experience of living and thinking. When orthodox Unitarians clashed with Transcendentalists, Hildreth took a position antagonistic to both. He denied the orthodox Unitarian contention that ultimate authority of faith and conduct resided in scriptural texts.[31] Transcendentalist reliance upon intuition hardly pleased him more. Hildreth championed the cause of science and the philosophies inspired by the scientific advance. "I am a rational man," he announced, "not in the German, but in the English sense." [32] The South American interlude provided Hildreth with his intellectual opportunity. Here he made the system of Bentham his own and here he began to write *The Rudiments of the Inductive Philosophy of Man*.

My system of the philosophy of human nature is to be included in eight treatises. 1. Theory of Morals, 2. Theory of Politics, 3. Theory of Taste and Criticism, 4. Theory of Political Economy, 5. Theory of Human Nature, or a statement of the Laws of Human Thought and Action including a refutation of the mystical or spiritual philosophy. . . . These treatises are of the nature of theorems, or demonstrations of certain scientific facts. The three following treatises, namely, 6. Theory of Education, 7. Theory of the Administration of Justice, 8. Theory of Law are of the nature of problems, containing the practical application of the preceding theorems.[33]

Hildreth took a speculative stand that the future was partly to vindicate. "My principle," he explained to a correspondent, "is to apply to the principles of man's nature the same inductive method which has proved so successful in advancing what is called natural philosophy." Hildreth's language is reminiscent of the language of the post-Darwinian world. "Man is a part of nature; the philosophy of nature is a part of natural philosophy; and it ought to be investigated by the same methods." Yet the science to which Hildreth appealed was physical rather than biological, post-Newtonian rather than pre-Darwinian. Nevertheless, his appeal was prophetic. Science and its methods, he explained, "for powerful but temporary reasons" had "been very partially employed." The scientific study of man accordingly had made substantially little progress. "The . . . increasing interest with which that science is regarded, and the great social problems which depend upon it for solution, seem to demand for its several branches a more patient, thorough, comprehensive, experimental investigation, than they have yet received. Such will be the aim of these Treatises. However short of that aim I may fall, I shall at least claim the merit of an earnest, honest, thoughtful, laborious endeavour." [34] Historians who strove to construct a philosophy of man and society were as rare then as they have since remained. Hildreth is entitled to credit for honest and laborious endeavor.

Ethical bases for action and judgment were Hildreth's quest in *The Theory of Morals.* Intellectual curiosity alone did not spur him; he sought explanations of human behavior in order to emancipate mankind. Ethical relativity served as his starting point, and he reduced the standards of competing schools to logical chaos. Universals—Platonic, Christian or Transcendental—failed to satisfy him since human sources, not absolutes, were the primary data of conduct. Hildreth placed no more faith in classical ethics than in traditional Christian systems. He dismissed the Christian code of conduct as a "mystical theory of morals," rooting righteous action in the approval or the disapproval of deity. Rules of conduct based upon individual fear of retribution or upon individual hope of reward did not impress Hildreth as either safe or intelligent. Individual motives and individual needs he observed were frequently identified with divine will.

Conduct and morals were grounded in human behavior. This was Richard Hildreth's great contribution, for if not new it was a prediction of a future trend of philosophical development. Axiomatic was the postulate that actions have consequences not only for those directly involved but for others within the boundaries of their effects. A microscopic probing of human action illumined by the record of history, was central to his investigation. Man pursued pleasure and avoided pain, but man was capable of feeling either or both as a result of what happened to others or of what happened to him. Standards of morality were not abstract. Morality, "instead of being an abstract thing, independent of human nature, something external to it, whether originating in the abstract nature of things, in the decrees of God, or in the arts of man, grows, in fact, out of man's very constitution." [35]

Benevolence, a virtue as much prized in the eighteenth century as later by Benthamites, equipped man with sensitivity to impersonate the feelings of his fellows. In Hildreth's logic human benevolence varied in direct proportion to the prevalence of pain.[36] Existence of pain and the conditions inducing it were the constant threats to human happiness. The greater the knowledge of the causes of pain-producing conditions and the greater degree of control exercised over their operation, the greater the degree of happiness and progress.[37]

The Theory of Morals is to be honored more for its search than for its solutions. As Hildreth became more deeply involved, he became more certain of his own precepts and less cogent in expounding them. The "sentiment of benevolence," upon which distinction between choices rested, was no less an assumption in Hildreth than in Bentham and as vulnerable as those they rejected.[38] Hildreth cut through the fabric of other men's logic, but the same logic might have been employed to cut the fabric of his own. Much more consequential than success or failure to establish an ethical system was his critical, historical examination of the systems of others. Still more important was his credo:

> I am a mere experimental inquirer. I pay no attention to what I have been taught, except so far as my own examinations confirm it. I do not suffer my wishes to run away with my judgment. It is my object to investigate human nature as it is, not as I or others might desire it to be.[39]

The reception accorded *The Theory of Morals* was devastatingly hostile. Polite reviewers used gentle language that effectively made their point. Hildreth was praised for industry and high purpose, yet neither motive nor labor could transmute mistaken principles into acceptable doctrine. Orestes A. Brownson, a passionate pilgrim who meandered from Unitarianism to Catholicism, was neither gentle nor restrained. He branded the volume as containing "blasphemous sneers at the existence of God," and warned that the faithful would find nothing but delusion within its covers.[40] Hildreth himself was so identified with his crusade to free the human mind that he replied with similar abandon. He assailed Orestes Brownson as a "walking *variorum* edition of all sorts of opinions." He attacked another reviewer who published in *The North American,* indicting both the writer and the journal for maintaining silence on slavery, which, he concluded, was "the conduct of a skulk, a coward, a sycophant, a hypocrite, a liar." Hildreth postponed the publication of *The Theory of Politics* for almost a decade.[41]

The Theory of Politics is even less clear than *The Theory of Morals.*[42] In the second treatise as in the first, Hildreth employed the fundamental categories of pleasure and pain. Governments have varied enormously in historical development, but men who seek to govern are always motivated by the pleasure of superiority. In pragmatic political activity this motive, akin to if not identical with ambition, may also be stimulated by desire for wealth. Any or all of these attributes on the part of the governors might incite revolt, but the vital cause of social upheaval was found in the pain of inferiority felt by the governed. That the authority of the rulers had to be recognized by the ruled was clearly enunciated. Government without power was impossible, but although governors had to be granted power in order to function, they were denied the right to govern arbitrarily. How they were restrained is answered by a Benthamite formula. ". . . with the growing force of the sentiment of benevolence, which acts always with the most energy among those in comfortable circumstances, a disposition springs up to contribute, by all feasible and promising means." [43] While tyrannical government was beyond the pale of right, Hildreth did not establish the criteria of justice or the nature of political obligation. Of the role of personality and power in any modern sense, he had little more than a glimmer.

More pertinent to his history was his treatment of the origin of states. He followed the conventional practice made common by writers influenced by the idea of progress of dividing history into eras and stages. After sketching the evolution of man through the ancient, middle, and modern periods of history, he raised a significant question:

> Is there never to be an Age of the People—of the working classes? Is the suggestion too extravagant, that the new period commencing with the middle of this current century is destined to be that age? Certain it is, that, with the last three quarters of a century, advocates have appeared for the mass of the people, the mere workers, and that movements, even during this age of the deification of money, and of reaction against the theory of human equality, have been made in their behalf such as were never known before.[44]

Statements such as these had nineteenth-century socialistic implications, and readers of *The Theory of Politics* were not slow in calling attention to them. Hildreth was no Marxian, though he gave large weight to economic factors and to simple economic motivation. Karl Marx published his great work after Hildreth had written, and it is doubtful on other grounds whether socialistic principles can be ascribed to him. If he had any socialistic sympathies at all, they were of an evolutionary rather than a revolutionary sort.

> This socialist question of the distribution of wealth once raised is not to be blinked out of sight. The claims set up by the socialists, based as they are upon philosophic theories of long standing . . . cannot be settled by declamations and denunciations, and mutual recriminations, any more than by bayonets and artillery. It is a question for philosophers; . . . what the party of progress needs is not action . . . but deliberation and discussion.[45]

The philosophy of *The Theory of Politics* is the philosophy of the Enlightenment, its ideology the theory of progress. "To raise the mass of the people to a more equal participation in the goods of life is essential to the further progress of civilization." It was equally essential if the devastations caused by pain were to be checked in the interests of social and personal happiness. The barriers which barred the progress of civilization in America were the barriers Hildreth wished to destroy. Sentiments of this type find no place in the orthodox Federalist-Whig[46] canon.

The History of the United States was published after *The Theory of Morals* and before *The Theory of Politics*. When Hildreth returned from South America in 1843 at the age of thirty-six he married Caroline Negus. His marriage was probably the most important event of his adult life. Caroline Negus was beautiful, talented, and stable. Her temperament complemented Hildreth's and gave him a balance and direction. She also gave him more of peace, tranquility, and happiness than he had ever known. Richard Hildreth wrote

The History of the United States, but Caroline Negus made it possible. For the next ten years, from 1843 to 1853, although many other activities absorbed him, the *History* became his chief literary occupation.

Hildreth's *History* consists of two series of three volumes each. The first three volumes were published in 1849; the second group of three volumes from 1851 to 1852.[47] Historiographical judgment has severed the Hildreth *History* in two. The first three volumes have been described as scientific, temperate, and objective, those following as intemperate, partial, and colored by a political and social predisposition. Hildreth himself regarded them as a unit, different neither in intent nor execution. "It has been my earnest endeavor," he wrote in October 1850, as preface to the second series:

> now, as formerly, guarding as far as might be, against these current illusions, to present, through a pure medium of impartial truth and justice, the events and characters of the times of which I write, undistorted by prejudice, uncolored by sentiment, neither tricked out in the gaudy tinsel of a meretricious rhetoric, nor stretched nor shortened to suit the purposes of any political party.
>
> Yet the nature of the subject and the extended method of treatment—the chief of the narrative being now mainly concentrated upon a few leading and conspicuous characters, whose personal qualities and particular views come to exercise a not inconsiderable influence over the progress of affairs, and whose opinions and actions are dwelt upon at length must naturally give to some portions of the present work somewhat more of an emotional character than was consistent with the multiplicity and rapid succession of events in the former volumes, and the reduced scale upon which almost every thing had in consequence to be exhibited. Very likely the charge of partisanship may now be urged by some of those same critics who thought those volumes too apathetic and coldly impartial. For, though both works have been written in the same spirit, and, with allowances for the variations above pointed out, on the same plan, a few figures, large as life, and kept for a length of time before the eye, though the general style of art be in no respect different, will naturally produce a different effect from numerous groups, mostly in miniature, succeeding each other with panoramic rapidity.[48]

Hildreth, one may be sure, composed his preface with care. When he wrote that the shift in the nature of his data "must naturally give the present work somewhat more of an emotional character," he obviously meant that his readers might be expected to react with greater emotion. Although now dealing with personalities in historical depth, he would continue to be critical and unprejudiced. He had chosen to deal with men as typical of change, but he felt as free to evaluate their personalities, ideals, and actions as in the earlier volumes he had evaluated forces, movements, and events.

Between the volumes of the two series there is less difference than has commonly been taken for granted. Hildreth was an honest man and an honest scholar. He followed the rules of procedure as scrupulously as his understanding of them permitted and as faithfully as the limitations of his humanity allowed. The quality of Hildreth's scholarship depends upon the quality of his philosophical premises and the logical rigor with which he employed them. The process of induction was as natural in history as in science, and Hildreth was scarcely less objective at the end of his historical series than he was at the beginning. If a real question exists, it was probably the result of his shift in focus rather than conscious intent. If the question is legitimate, it concerns the sufficiency of his data and the validity of his inferences. Like Bancroft, Hildreth had a philosophical point of departure and return. Bancroft, the kind of "speculatist" Hildreth deplored, made his premises explicit in advance and consistently underscored them throughout his work. Hildreth, the kind of empiricist Bancroft never understood, strove to eliminate his speculative preconceptions while accumulating his facts, but did not repress his judgments after the accumulation of facts permitted him to induce an appraisal. "Fictions" that dissolved after logical analysis remained "fictions," whether philosophical, theological, or political. They were as undemonstrable in ancient Greece as in nineteenth-century America. To ask whether Hildreth failed is valid enough, but it is an inquiry of a different kind. But inquiries of this kind must take into account that his postulates are no longer accepted in the way in which he understood them. Nor are the hypotheses of science, conceptions of scientific methods, and notions of objectivity identical with those then current. And theories of history used by Hildreth's critics early and late were not those of Hildreth.

Reviewers of the first series were restrained in their praise. In general, the *History* was lauded for its comprehensiveness, the scope of its research, its clarity, and its value. Concerning its tone and style there was almost universal agreement: it was cold, precise, unadorned. If it was useful and accurate, it was none the less without spirit and barren of philosophy. Theodore Parker, a scholar to whom even his critics listened with respect, wrote the most comprehensive appraisal.

> Everywhere we see marks of the same intellectual vigor which distinguishes the former writings of Mr. Hildreth. There is strength and freshness in his style. He writes in the interests of mankind. He allows no local attachment, or reverence for man or classes of men, to keep him from telling the truth as he finds it. He exhibits the good and evil qualities

of the settlers of the United States, with the same coolness and impartiality. His work is almost wholly objective, giving the facts, and not his opinion of the facts.[49]

Theodore Parker's elaborate review of 1850 might well have nourished Hildreth's famished ego. He pronounced the work well executed "without a single idle word," and he applauded its sustained devotion to the "interests of mankind." While Parker's approbation was not unqualified, his complaints were not distressing. The *History* was, to be sure, much less philosophical than Parker wished, but for Parker it required a democrat fully to understand the American past and properly to write it. Hildreth had no doubt that his history was philosophical and he had no reservations about his democratic faith. He could have been neither surprised nor alarmed to discover that others held dissimilar views of philosophy and history. Parker conceded that Hildreth had "written in the American spirit," even though he had done so "in spite" of himself. If the *History* did not at once bring Richard Hildreth wide acclaim, it bolstered two of his persistent objectives. He had succeeded, in the opinion of Theodore Parker, in writing American history in the interests of mankind, and he had written it scientifically.

The first three volumes are indeed without a scheme of interpretation explicitly stated or a philosophy of history explicitly announced. Hildreth did, however, remark in the preface, dated January 1, 1849, that no extant history "comprehends the same circuit of inquiry, or has anything like the same plan and object." [50] Hildreth's attitudes did not elude immediate detection. Intolerance he disliked with the same intensity as Bentham or Mill. Hildreth had a particular aversion for "mystical or spiritual philosophy," which he had vowed in his speculative studies to refute. The Puritan he found had the same "horror of tolerance" that was "an inherent characteristic of every theocracy." [51] Francis Bowen, a Harvard professor of history to whose position Hildreth had once aspired, objected to the manner in which these topics were treated. "Mr. Hildreth cannot write history without making it one uniform record of the pernicious consequences of allowing the state even to recognize the existence of Christianity." Bowen perceived a purpose in the *History* that gave it a unified point of view, even though the viewpoint rendered it partial. "The evils of a theocratic form of government, and the folly and hypocrisy of rulers who profess to act upon religious principles, are the only topics of so frequent recurrence in his work to give it an air of unity and a distinctive character." [52]

Mystical philosophies collided with Hildreth's empiricism. They were the "fictions" of Bentham, deductions from *a priori* postulates which confused and obstructed thought. The Quakers, whom Bancroft had so lavishly praised, put Hildreth, the apostle of scientific method, on his intellectual guard.

> But this "inner light," on which the Quakers relied, and to which, when it prompted them to speak or act, they gave the name of "the Spirit," was not, in their idea of it, man's natural reason, which they held in as great contempt as religious enthusiasts commonly do. They described it rather as a sort of inspiration, a divine illumination superior to reason, and often apparently in contradiction to it. It was, in fact, but a whimsical, superstitious, ill-informed, passionate, narrow, ill-regulated reason, right, no doubt, upon many important points, but often exaggerated; unable or unwilling to justify itself by argument or fact, and hastening to cut short all objections and to make a deep impression on the imagination by claiming for itself somewhat of intuition and divinity.[53]

Hildreth had unloosed the most lethal shaft in his quiver. Without fact or argument there was no position to defend or attack. There was really nothing to add, but Hildreth used six redolent adjectives to blunt his sharp empirical point. No elaborate exegesis was demanded of Francis Bowen to demonstrate that the author of *The History of the United States* was hostile to certain types of philosophy. If Parker did not find enough philosophy in Hildreth, Bowen found too much of the wrong kind. If most critics noted the absence of a structural theme, other critics had no difficulty in discovering one.[54] George Bancroft subsequently found little favor among the scientifically wise, and Richard Hildreth later received little credit from the philosophically mature.

Hildreth desired to court posterity less than he desired to influence the measurable future. He cared less about the strictures of speculative opponents than for continuous analysis of the speculation that hovered over issues. Slavery was his personal crusade and nothing save lawful abolition would satisfy his insatiable indignation. Already abolished by Great Britain in 1832, slavery provided a model instance of the complex of Hildreth's thought—although he did not explicitly recognize the merger of evangelical benevolence and liberal politics in the British victory.[55] Under any system of involuntary servitude, the slave earned only pain, for slavery deprived him of liberty and robbed him of choice. Nor was there a compensatory happiness for slave owners in the calculable balance of good and evil. Like the slave, the slave owner was debased in a system that stunted and perverted personality growth. Vicious traits of character and behavior erupted in both master and slave, infecting the whole culture from center to periphery. Even were one to stretch the utilitarian point beyond the endurance of meaning, the master-slave relationship offered no increment of recompense. When the six volumes were done, Hildreth planned to continue the narrative:

> My history is now finished to 1821. The account at the close of it of the Missouri Compromise contains some good Antislavery matter particularly in the speeches of the New York members. It is my desire and intention . . . to write two more volumes closing with Fillmore's administration, and continuing the history of the Antislavery struggle thus far.[56]

Differences between the first and second series of the *History* account for Hildreth's reputation among historians. He became in consequence a New England historian, an apologist for the Federal-Whig view, and a partisan of conservative political theory. During the remainder of his life as well as later, his standing as a dispassionate scholar was impaired. Such judgments have resisted correction. "His first series is impartial enough," concluded one student, "but in the second the temptation to write history for an ulterior purpose proved too much for him." In the second series Hildreth was described as a "shrewd and powerful advocate but a poor historian." [57] Some critics have not found this explanation entirely satisfactory, particularly those familiar with other Hildreth writings. The reputed apologist for New England Federalism advocated doctrines unacceptable to the Whig trustees of Federalist ideas. A chaste presentation of brittle facts, marking the *History*, contrasted sharply with the fervid prose Hildreth employed elsewhere. *Archy Moore*, his antislavery novel and the first of its kind, was as torrid as the *History* was cold. His *Despotism in America or, an Inquiry into the Nature and Results of the Slave-Holding System in the United States,* bristled, and every sentence was later described as "a declaration of war." [58] Richard Hildreth, the crusader, contrasted sharply with Richard Hildreth, the historian. If Hildreth supported the Federalist conception of society, how could he propound a social creed in conflict with it at so many vital points? Hildreth's social philosophy was in fact neither strictly Federalist nor strictly Whig. His antislavery attitudes, vigorous, consistent, and outspoken, were clearly out of harmony with the party stand. There was scarcely any resemblance between Hildreth and the national party leaders, Clay, Webster, and Calhoun.[59] Out of sympathy with the makers of national party policy, he was not in full accord with the leaders of abolitionist extremism. With the extraconstitutional measures of coping with slavery advocated by William Lloyd Garrison, Wendell Phillips, and others, he would have nothing to do. Reform of slavery was to be affected, not by violence or nonlegal means, but by party politics and party organization.[60] Had Hildreth's reformism been confined to the antislavery crusade, it might have been easier to resolve the paradox, for many men, stirred by antislavery impulses, abjured their faith in analysis. But Richard Hildreth was not a man to abdicate the sovereignty of reason.

Hildreth participated in the controversy on rechartering the Bank of the United States. In 1837 he wrote a diminutive *History of Banks,* which carried the subtitle *A Demonstration of the Advantages and Necessity of Free Competition in the Business of Banking.* While banks themselves were not necessarily bad, monopolies were evil. Hildreth presented a vigorous case for free enterprise, a doctrine he espoused with as much conviction as Adam Smith or Jeremy Bentham. But for good Whigs of the mid-thirties rechartering the Bank of the United States was as sacred a principle as vilification of Andrew Jackson was a public duty. Bancroft's pronouncements on banks and banking may have been more volatile and Democratic, but Hildreth had certainly veered from the Clay-Webster-Biddle political line. When in 1840 he refurbished the booklet, now *Banks, Banking, and Paper Currency,* he still remained unchastened.[61] Whigs tirelessly repeated the accusation that the Jackson-Van Buren policies, the Bank among them, had caused the depression, but Hildreth argued that banks as such had nothing to do with the panic.[62] He supported William Henry Harrison for the presidency in 1840 and wrote a campaign biography of "good, old Tip," but his support could have had no connection with the currency program of Harrison and the party. "The People's Candidate," as Harrison was called by Hildreth and the Whig high command, was the candidate of the people only in the sense of the party's new tactics.[63] The new Whig tactic was designed to win elections by filching Democratic slogans and Democratic objectives,[64] by which Hildreth could not have been completely deceived.

The politics of democracy are geared to allow for changes of mind. Hildreth could disagree with the party leadership on slavery and the Bank question. He could remain a loyal supporter of a party holding mutually exclusive propositions if only for the reason that he preferred his own. But the "Age of the People," while not socialism, was as remote from Federalist-Whig assumptions as the ideas of Karl Marx. Whig leaders were content to advocate equality of condition as long as political controls remained safely in Whig Congressional hands.

Recognition of economic considerations constituted no deviation from Federalist attitudes. Federalist-Whig theory was itself an economic interpretation of society and of politics. The inferences Hildreth derived from current controversies, however, flouted the specifics of the Federalist creed. His vision of equality which the "Age of the People" suggested was the antithesis of conservatism whether Whig or Federalist. And Hildreth's call for full discussion of the socialist indictment was completely ignored by America's Clays and Websters. John Adams, despite Hildreth's copious praise, would have spurned doctrines that destroyed "equipoise" in the structure of society. Jefferson, despite Hildreth's sullen barbs, would have responded to reformist programs in the democratic idiom of alternating majorities.

Hildreth's activity strained the ties of allegiance to Whig conformity. He excoriated orthodox religionists in polemic and monograph. Their faith was "mystical," their piety often a pretense, and their power frequently marshaled behind the opponents of reform. He attacked sabbatarianism on the plea that everyone had the privilege of deciding how to spend Sunday without legal restraint.[65] Together with Ralph Waldo Emerson, Theodore Parker, and George Ripley he took up the fight to permit Abner Kneeland to say what he believed about God in Boston. He wrote a pamphlet in Kneeland's support with the revealing title: *Appeal to common sense and the constitution on behalf of unlimited freedom of discussion.*[66] He crossed swords with Andrews Norton, the "Unitarian pope," on the authority of the Bible and boldly entered the lists against those Transcendentalists who offered intuitionalism in its place.[67] When traditionalists branded him an atheist, he took up the issue, and, after venting his anger in thoroughly unobjective fashion, sought to prove his accusers the true unbelievers.[68] He scouted the assumption that morals depended upon divine will and held his intellectual own against all theological comers. Hildreth certainly agreed with John Stuart Mill that "no one can be a great thinker who does not recognize that as a thinker it is his first duty to follow his intellect to whatever conclusions it may lead." He would also have concurred with Mill's historical induction:

> Truth gains more even by the errors of one who, with due study and preparation, thinks for himself, than by the true opinions of those who only hold them because they do not suffer themselves to think. Not that it is solely, or chiefly, to form great thinkers, that freedom of thinking is required. On the contrary, it is as much and even more indispensable to enable average human beings to attain the mental stature which they are capable of. There have been, and may again be, great individual thinkers in a general atmosphere of mental slavery. But there never has been, nor

ever will be, in that atmosphere an intellectually active people. . . .
Never when controversy avoided the subjects which are large and important enough to kindle enthusiasm, was the mind of a people stirred
up from its foundations, and the impulse given which raised even persons
of the most ordinary intellect to something of the dignity of thinking
beings.[69]

Neither position nor wealth deterred him. He denuded the pretensions of Boston's rich in an anonymous pamphlet, which left them
nothing but their moneybags for comfort.[70] He unmasked the arguments of native Americans, and exposed anti-Catholicism in a sear-
ing democratic rebuke.[71] He appeared on almost every sector of the
social battle, the foe of monopolies of any kind, whether they were
monopolies of truth, opportunity, piety, or wealth. The area of temperance reform alone was relatively safe, but even in this twilight
zone of respectability he ran into difficulties with the party organization.[72] If Richard Hildreth was an apologist for Federalist conservatism, he did not unquestioningly accept its principles.

While commitment to diverse reforms charts the course of Hildreth's Federalist defection, it confounds the problem of Hildreth's
biased scholarship. If he wrote the *History* with partisan political
intentions, his parallel activities become even more paradoxical.
While completing his final volume, he was reading Rousseau and
preparing a second edition of the antislavery novel. The second edition of *Archy Moore* appeared in the year of the third volume of the
second series, and *The Theory of Politics* immediately thereafter in
1853. The next year a new edition of *Despotism in America* came
off the press. During the whole decade of the fifties he was on the
staff of Horace Greeley's *Tribune,* as much involved in reform as
ever.[73]

His prefaces, though brief, make charges of willful prejudgment
unbelievable. Either he did not mean what he wrote or he did not
know what he was writing. Neither is credible. He believed he was
performing in the same way, with the same purposes, and employing
the same principles. He was persuaded that he could understand and
discuss the past, even the more or less immediate past, with equanimity. He was under the impression that he was doing precisely
what he has been accused of not having done.[74] There is no evidence
that he faltered in his philosophical faith during these years. On the
contrary, all the evidence points in the other direction. Hildreth may
have failed, but that is not the same as saying that he did not attempt
to succeed.

The difference between the first and second series of the *History,*
if a real difference in fact exists, is quantitative rather than qualita-

tive.[75] Hildreth reached conclusions in the former as well as in the latter, for induction was the rule of science and the purpose of history. Mystical philosophies were among the barriers to rational progress in modern as in ancient times and alterations of the variety did not affect the specific type. Theocracies were always social combinations in restraint of free discussion, regardless of the historical time and the geographical place. Puritans and Quakers and those who took a similar philosophical stance could not avoid censure from a rationalist historian. Cotton Mather, for instance, was no Hildreth hero. Mather was branded a "dupe" for his part in the witchcraft hysteria. Of him Hildreth said he was "fully conscious of all his gifts, and not a little vain of them. . . ." and "he believed himself to be often . . . in direct . . . personal communication with the Deity." [76] Yet Hildreth absolved Mather of all complicity in the witchcraft trials. "The suggestion," he insisted, "that Cotton Mather . . . deliberately got up the witchcraft delusion, and forced it upon a doubtful and hesitating people, is utterly absurd." [77]

Criticism of Thomas Jefferson placed Hildreth on the minority side of modern historiographical opinion. He rarely lost an opportunity to belittle Jefferson's contributions or to demean Jefferson's character. Jefferson "was ever ready to allow his most cherished theoretical principles to drop into silence the moment he found them in conflict with popular currents." [78] He praised Jefferson for his tolerance and liberality in matters religious, but in political matters he accounted him "a complete bigot." [79] Jefferson in this sphere was repeatedly deluded by an "ardent temperament." [80]

> Though himself separated from the masses of the people by elegance of manners, refined tastes, and especially by philosophical opinions on the subject of religion, in political affairs Jefferson was disposed to allow a controlling, indeed absolute authority to the popular judgment. The many he thought to be always more honest and disinterested, and in questions where the public interests were concerned, more wise than the few, who might always be suspected of having private purposes of their own to serve. . . . To sympathize with popular passions seemed to be his test of patriotism; to sail before the wind as a popular favorite, the great object of his ambition; and it was under the character of a condescending friend of the people that he rose first to be head of a party, and then chief magistrate of the nation.[81]

For him Hildreth reserved his sharpest critical thrusts:

> In quitting the cabinet, Jefferson had the satisfaction to carry with him Washington's testimonial of continued belief in his integrity, almost extorted by a somewhat bold assertion, in Jefferson's leave-taking letter, of a "thorough disdain of all means which were not as open and honorable

as their object was pure." He retired to his patrimonial estate of Monticello, as he said, to withdraw from politics after twenty-four years of public service, and to devote himself to the pleasures of rural life; but in fact, like a spider, drawn into a corner, yet still sensitively feeling every thread of his wide-extended net, to play, no less assiduously at Monticello than he had done at Philadelphia, the part of a watchful, zealous, untiring party leader. According to Jefferson's theory of politics, to aspire to office was a breach of that equality without which liberty could not exist. What right had any man to desire to be elevated over the heads of his countrymen? Ambition was the political sin which he charged upon Adams and upon Hamilton. Could the idea be tolerated that the same evil disposition lurked even in his pure soul?[82]

Jefferson's opponents were more sympathetically drawn. John Adams, for example, though driven by "an unextinguishable thirst for eminence" was yet virtuous and public-spirited. He was, Hildreth thought, always "a leader rather than a follower," and unlike Jefferson he did not "sail before" public opinion.[83] Hildreth was never able conceptually to resolve the conflicts in democratic leadership. He was seldom able to distinguish between the gift of social vision and the equally great gift of social timing. The courage to advocate policies tinged with future insights was no greater than the wisdom required to defer advocacy of a program if the barriers were too great or the cost too high. Part of the difficulty, he correctly perceived, was imbedded in the character and temperament of personality, although he was not invariably just in assaying them.

Hamilton was the ideal statesman. Hildreth admired Hamilton for many reasons. Particularly noteworthy was the cast of his mind: "he possessed talents of the highest practical order." Hamilton, Hildreth appropriately concluded, was "much less of a . . . speculatist than either Jefferson or Adams" and Hildreth prized those of whom this could be said. Hamilton, not Adams or Jefferson, was one of makers of history whose "theory of government seems to have been almost entirely founded on what had passed under his own observation during the war of the Revolution and subsequently."[84] Hildreth and Hamilton were in pragmatic accord. No tribute was too high a recognition of his service. But Hildreth's adulation was tempered by his democratic commitment and his skepticism of unqualified Federalist faith in conservative influence.

. . . he had become very strongly impressed with the impossibility of duly providing for the public good, especially in times of war and danger, except by a government invested with ample powers, and possessing means for putting those powers into vigorous exercise. To give due strength to a government, it was necessary, in his opinion, not only to invest it on paper with sufficient legal authority, but to attach the most wealthy and

influential part of the community to it by the ties of personal and pecuniary advantage; for, though himself remarkably disinterested, acting under
an exalted sense of personal honor and patriotic duty, Hamilton was
inclined, like many other men of the world, to ascribe to motives of
pecuniary and personal interest a somewhat greater influence over the
course of events *than they actually possess.* Having but little confidence
either in the virtue or judgment of the mass of mankind, he thought the
administration of affairs most safe in the hands of a select few; nor in
private conversation did he disguise his opinion that, to save her liberties
from foreign attack or intestine commotions, America might yet be
driven into serious alterations of her Constitution, giving to it more of a
monarchical and aristocratical cast. He had the sagacity to perceive, what
subsequent experience has abundantly confirmed, that the Union had
rather to dread resistance of the states to federal power than executive
usurpation; but he was certainly mistaken in supposing that a president
and senate for life or good behavior, such as he suggested in the Federal
Conventions, could have given any additional strength to the government. *That strength, under all elective systems, must depend on public
confidence, and public confidence is best tested and secured by frequent
appeals to the popular vote.*[85]

Hildreth has occasionally been quoted out of context. The much-
cited remark on the revolution of Daniel Shays of Massachusetts has
been held to establish his Federalist loyalties. Hildreth commented:

Nor were there wanting artful, restless, discontented individuals, de-
ceivers rather than deceived, such as always step forth on such occasions
for the gratification of their own uncomfortable feelings, or for the
sake of a little notoriety, to inflame public discontent, and to flatter popular delusions. The example of the Revolution so lately accomplished
naturally enough suggested an appeal to arms and the overthrow of the
existing state government as an appropriate means for the remedy of
social evils. To that point matters in Massachusetts seemed to be fast
tending.[86]

But, on the page preceding, there is a succinct account of the
grievances of the residents in the southern and western counties of
Massachusetts. "The real difficulty," he wrote, "was the poverty and
exhaustion of the country consequent upon the war; the want of a
certain and remunerative market for the produce of the farmer, and
the depression of domestic manufacturers by competition from
abroad. But, as often happens in such cases, the popular mind
glanced only at the surface. The fundamental difficulties were overlooked." [87] Hildreth disliked extralegal methods as much in the
eighteenth century as in the nineteenth. The plight of the slaves and
of the nation in consequence was not less grievous than the plight of
the dispossessed in postrevolutionary America. But Hildreth could
endorse violence neither in the one case nor the other. In both instances redress could be secured only by "appeals to the popular

vote." The role of democratic government and democratic leadership was to cure difficulties, or at least to assuage them before violence came to seem the sole and last resort.[88]

Hildreth approved of the Constitution of the United States and of the men who made it. In his judgment it was an excellent solution of existing problems to which the major portion of the nation assented. Even the opposition did not dispute the larger intentions of the farmers. Opponents of the Constitution were in agreement with its supporters regarding the ultimate purposes of government; they differed on methods and details. Debates were real enough, but Hildreth would not have them obscure so fundamental a unity. While he applauded the Constitution he did not, as later fashion was to dictate, scoff at the Confederation. The Confederation inspired him with respect for his fellows, for "the really difficult, the truly admirable thing is to accomplish great objects by merely human means." His tribute to the Continental Congress, closing the third volume of the *History,* was written with a warmth his prose is customarily said not to possess.

> The dying embers of the Continental Congress, barely kept alive for some months by the occasional attendance of one or two delegates, as the day approached for the new system to be organized, quietly went out without note or observation. History knows few bodies so remarkable. The Long Parliament of Charles I, the French National Assembly, are alone to be compared with it. Coming together, in the first instance, a mere collection of consulting delegates, the Continental Congress had boldly seized the reins of power, assumed the leadership of the insurgent states, issued bills of credit, raised armies, declared independence, negotiated foreign treaties, carried the nation through an eight years' war; finally, had extorted from the proud and powerful mother country an acknowledgment of the sovereign authority so daringly assumed and so indomitably maintained. But this brilliant career had been as short as it was glorious. The decline had commenced even in the midst of the war. Exhausted by such extraordinary efforts—smitten with the curse of poverty, their paper money first depreciating and then repudiated, overwhelmed with debts which they could not pay, pensioners on the bounty of France, insulted by mutineers, scouted at by the public creditors, unable to fulfill the treaties they had made, bearded and encroached upon by the state authorities, issuing fruitless requisitions which they had no power to enforce, vainly begging for additional authority which the states refused to grant, thrown more and more into the shade by the very contrast of former power— The Continental Congress sunk fast into decrepitude and contempt. Feeble is the sentiment of political gratitude! Debts of that sort are commonly left for posterity to pay. While all eyes were turned—some with doubt and some with apprehension, but the greater part with hope and confidence—toward the ample authority vested in the new govern-

ment about to be organized, not one respectful word seems to have been uttered, not a single reverential regret to have been dropped over the fallen greatness of the exhausted and expiring Continental Congress.[89]

The crisis of 1792, precipitated by European chaos following the French Revolution, and the domestic political struggle offered Hildreth an opportunity to dissect American democratic theory. In one of the most penetrating sections of the entire series, Hildreth discussed the nature of late eighteenth-century American politics with reflective comments on the course of democratic growth. His analysis, derived from his own intellectual pilgrimage and his own political experience, enlivens the Hildreth narrative. Thomas Jefferson fared no better than elsewhere in the *History,* but he is condemned on conceptual as well as personal grounds.

The antagonistic modifications of political sentiment prevailing in the United States were very far indeed from being monarchical and republican. Whatever fancies some individuals might indulge in, monarchy, as a practical matter, was just as little thought of then as now. The only real controversy was as to the amount of democracy which safely could be and ought to be infused into the republican system adopted as well by the Union as by the separate states; for all admitted the distinction taken by Madison in the Federalist, that the American governments were not proper democracies, but representative republics, the difference being this, that in democracies the main conduct of affairs is directly in the hands of the people, whereas, in representative republics, instead of acting directly themselves, the people intrust the conduct of affairs to certain agents selected for that purpose.

Though the American governments gave great weight to the voice of the people, acknowledged to be the source and origin of all society—a weight which has gradually and generally increased with the increased diffusion of political intelligence—they were very far from being such purely democratic republics as Paine advocated in his "Rights of Man," and as Jefferson, by his approbation bestowed upon that work, seemed theoretically to approve. This was especially the case with that Federal Constitution of which Jefferson now claimed to be the true friend and supporter against its unnatural fathers, accused of seeking to distort it into a monarchy; and the case also especially with that particular construction of the Constitution upon which he insisted as the only one consistent with republican liberty. How was it possible to reconcile with the democratic theory of the sovereign power of numerical majorities that doctrine of state rights of which, as leader of the late anti-Federal, now Republican party, Jefferson was the special champion? The very fundamental compromises upon which the federal constitution rested, the equal vote of the states in the Senate, the extra weight given to the South by allowing a representation of slave property, were remarkable departures from the democratic idea.[90]

If a special point of view permeated the *History,* it was not the Federalist theory of a statically balanced society. It was rather an incipient theory of power, the power of special interests and states' rights—symbolized for Hildreth by the slavery struggle—pitted against the sovereign power of the people.

Hildreth acknowledged himself a rational man in the English tradition, by which he meant to claim kinship with post-Newtonian empiricism. Hume, Locke, and the French *philosophes* had a place on the roster of his inspiration, but the nineteenth-century Utilitarians and their antecedents influenced him directly. Hildreth was one of the first Americans who studied Bentham's work seriously, and he translated a part of it from the French in 1836.[91] Although Bentham retained a special place in the spectrum of his thought, his conceptual ties with Adam Smith and John Stuart Mill were firm and vital. Bentham wished to reform "the state the human mind was in," a desire Hildreth passionately shared. But Hildreth was no mere disciple. Bentham in fact derived the doctrine of utility from Hume, and Hildreth derived it from both. What Hildreth and all Utilitarians owed to Bentham was a skepticism of "fictions," a semantic approach to language and an irresistible urge to probe.[92]

Like Hildreth, Bentham represented the faith in reason and the eighteenth-century science on which it was based. Reason supplied the key to knowledge. Reason was ever and always the final test of beliefs, institutions, or social programs. The credibility of a belief had little to do with its historical antecedents, its conformity to nature, or its establishment by God. An institution was justifiable only if it was reasonable, and it was reasonable only if its utility could be satisfactorily demonstrated. The test of reasonableness was a social test and depended upon functioning relationships of human artifacts in the economy of pleasure and pain. Maximum utility, and therefore reasonableness, existed whenever ideas or institutions were negatively related to pain, and positively related to pleasure; criteria of proof were social criteria discernible in individual and community results. Since individual results obviously varied, the impact of consequences likewise varied. If one man's pain was another man's pleasure, a wide latitude of difference was always theoretically possible. And within the inevitability of such a sliding scale of individual reactions, the community goal became the greatest good of the greatest number. For all the emphasis of the Utilitarians on individuals, Bentham created a social morality and Mill in explaining him approached an organic view of society. Hildreth was a social reformer committed to the party process. For Bentham in the beginning the reform of Parliament was nothing more than a practical means to a reformist end. For Hildreth democratic politics was always the preface "to the highest kind of moral action." [93]

Bentham made the science of human behavior the major object of inquiry. Such knowledge was prerequisite to happiness, and happiness—or the avoidance of pain—was the persistent drive of man. Only by knowing the mainsprings of human behavior, by an awareness of the social and individual consequences of human action was it possible to legislate wisely, to secure justice, to promote progress. Hildreth's *Rudiments of the Inductive Science of Man* was a contribution to this end. While Bentham hoped to improve the quality of thought, Hildreth determined to participate "in the assault upon tyranny and error." [94]

Bentham's assumptions were unsophisticated by modern standards of human complexity and later social science has discovered qualifications and subtleties demanding refinements of his concepts and conclusions. Hildreth never completed his projected analysis and what was completed failed to elicit prolonged attention. But Bentham and Hildreth both insisted upon the cultivation of rational method. Relentlessly they urged the need for investigation, for deliberation, for sustained analysis. And by explicit pleas and the implications of their thought they stressed the never-ending import of consequences in the understanding and the living of life. Bentham, the father of Utilitarianism, profoundly influenced modern philosophy and modern democracy. Hildreth was an early protagonist of the scientific viewpoint in the United States.

Hildreth's dismissal of "mythical" systems was proportionate to his reliance upon science. He was not antireligious; he was antiauthoritarian. His defiance of orthodoxies of whatever kind stemmed from his abhorrence of monopolies of truth.[95] Any "truth," rigidly held, was a barrier to thought. Nothing was sacred enough to avoid examination. Even after it had once been examined, it had to be examined again. Science was the only method, because human reason was the only guide. Whatever blocked the way of investigation, however reasonable and useful in itself, impeded a higher utility. Orthodox religionists and transcendentalist philosophers offered man absolutes based upon authority, which he was therefore disposed to question. Absolutes were barred by definition, but no proposition was admissible until after its scientific credentials had been demonstrated. The proposition that freedom of speech was necessary to the well-being of society was not admissible until proved. Hildreth was a stalwart defender of the principle not because nature ordained it or because divine commands enjoined it. Freedom of speech was vital because it was demonstrably useful to society. Without such freedom there could be no investigation, no discussion, no science. There could also be no politics, and without politics there could be no legislation, no change, no progress. And if there were no politics, no legislation, and no change, there existed no way of translating the increments of scientific knowledge into the growth of human happiness. Reformism was an injunction of reason, a solemn mandate imposed by the discipline of thought. "I am impelled by an irresistible impulse to act,—or rather to write—, for the sharpest point of a goose quill is the most potent instrument in my power to employ. . . ." [96] Hildreth did both. In Hildreth's conception—as in Jeremy Bentham's and John Stuart Mill's—the discovery and presentation of fact constituted the principal office of science. Generalization came after the presentation of fact. And if the search for the data was sufficiently objective, sufficiently persistent, and sufficiently ample, the facts themselves supplied the generalization. The task of the historian was to be aware of his prejudices, to struggle to control them, and to allow the facts to speak for themselves. Uninvestigated assumption distorted history; the importation of extraneous authorities in the form of mythical postulates destroyed it. [97]

Hildreth's view of the function of history and the method of writing it reflected these intellectual mandates. The characteristics of the *History* result from convictions regarding method, not stylistic preference. Hildreth shared Bentham's concern for the values of scientific method. He did not share his indifference to historical evidence and historical studies. The historian of society did not differ from the historian of nature. Once the data in either area were presented in original form, induction followed. Galileo and Newton were masters of the inductive process in natural science. David Hume and George Grote were masters of the inductive process in historical science. Richard Hildreth strove manfully to emulate them. [98]

Richard Hildreth raised a basic problem and presaged a deep speculative conflict later to divide historians. Francis Bowen, one of Hildreth's penetrating critics, anticipated the lines of future controversy.

> . . . it is impossible to write history without seeking, either avowedly or stealthily, or unawares, to verify some hypothesis, or establish some theory, which furnishes a reason and a guide for the selection and arrangement of materials. It is not necesary to draw the inference, or set forth the doctrine, which the course of the narrative is calculated to

illustrate or defend. What is skillfully left to implication generally strikes the reader's mind with more force than that which is boldly and earnestly inculcated. The facts have no connection with each other, and the story has no unity, unless some doctrine lies at the bottom to which they are all more or less related. Without giving one false assertion or positive misstatement, a writer may give any tone to a narrative that he pleases, simply by an artful choice of events to which predominance is given, and a studied collocation of the circumstances. And he may do this unconsciously, or while sincerely striving to elucidate the truth.[99]

Neither Carl L. Becker, for whom every man became his own historian, nor Charles Beard, for whom reliable historical knowledge became a noble dream, ever stated the issue more clearly.

XV

The Heroic Historians:
Prescott, Motley, Parkman

Richard Hildreth, George Bancroft, and Jared Sparks were notable men and notable scholars. Devoted to the American past and the American future, they contributed to the growth of democracy and to the growth of an historical tradition. Each made his vital mark in the world of learning, for Hildreth, Bancroft, and Sparks were men of stalwart minds. Regardless of criticism, which is the earned increment of scholarship, their accomplishments were formidable. Yet neither Sparks nor Hildreth became America's great historians and although George Bancroft was the leading historian of the United States, he was rivaled by William Hickling Prescott, John Lothrop Motley, and particularly Francis Parkman.

Prescott, Motley, and Parkman stemmed from the same social roots—from Harvard, Massachusetts Bay, and New England. While they had no interest in formal philosophy, the nature of their work involved them in philosophical issues. They were historians of cultures. The drama of peoples, the clash of civilizations, the role of great men, stimulated their imagination. They were literary historians only because they wrote with the practiced skill of craftsmen. They were romantic only because they identified with a point of view which later scholars, identified with other viewpoints, have labeled with a name. Qualities of style and powers of imagination caused them to be read; the subjects they chose to treat made them heroic. For Prescott it was the idyll of Spain, for Motley the epic of the

Netherlands, for Parkman the struggle between Europeans and natives in the North American wilderness. Prescott traced the shadow of the Catholic cross as it gathered darkly over the Moorish crescent, Motley charted the deepening Protestant threat to Catholic supremacy, and Parkman narrated a later stage of the conflict between Catholic and Protestant forces.

The heroic historians are linked together by a series of genetic connections. All were of Boston's impeccable elect, and all were reared in the bracing climate of New England's second awakening. Another intellectual thread binds them even more closely. Each pursued themes related to the genesis of America. Motley was drawn to the study of the Dutch because in the Dutch striving for independence from Spanish absolutism he perceived an earlier phase of the historical process that later took place in America. The rise of the Dutch Republic was akin to the rise of the American Republic, the United Netherlands to the United States. Motley's hero had a Dutch name, and he is indisputably a part of Holland's national annals. But for Motley, William the Silent was a George Washington.[1] Prescott made the beginnings of America his personal intellectual domain, and America did not begin in Plymouth, in Jamestown, or even in the islands of the Caribbean. It began in Europe, and for William H. Prescott it began with Moors and Spaniards whose struggles for the control of a peninsula separating the Mediterranean from the Atlantic had a determining effect on the cast of modern civilization. He weighed the lives of the Catholic sovereigns of Spain, who succeeded in uniting a country and in conquering new world empires.

Parkman and Prescott divided their intellectual spheres at the Pyrenees, and partitioned the western continent. Canada and the French northern domain became Parkman's historical territory; Spanish America belonged to Prescott. Parkman made history speak through the lives of Jesuit missionaries and colonial administrators. La Salle and Frontenac served him as Cortés and Moctezuma served Prescott. And the natives, whether of Peru, Canada, or the Illinois country, could not be kept from their volumes any more than European kings and their ministers, whose fortunes were frequently made or broken by the movement of events in the far off Americas.

Comparisons yield contrasts as well as similarities, and the differences among Prescott, Motley, and Parkman are important. All were men of means, which made the pursuit of history possible in a period before mechanics simplified the labor of scholarship. But Prescott and Parkman were afflicted with physical infirmities of such magnitude that only independent financial resources rendered their work feasible. One of Parkman's greatest literary virtues was his capacity for the reconstruction of scenes and events, a technique perfected by on-the-spot experiences. Motley's vividness of description derived not merely from close examination of sources in European archives, but from living contact with the places where his history was once made. Prescott alone was forced to rely upon words and concepts— in books and documents usually read to him—for the transmission of feeling and idea. Prescott's experience, of course, was not necessary to prove that great history is made up of more than words alone,[2] but it demands the kind of imaginative genius that Prescott possessed. Parkman and Prescott disciplined their imagination by a rigorous analysis of evidence. Motley had no wish to do so and took pleasure in the warmth of his passion. He was not averse to calling "fancy to the aid of history"[3] in order to make it more lively, a practice of which neither Prescott nor Parkman would ever have approved. Prescott, periodically incapacitated by ill health and partial blindness, found salvation in a career of writing. Once he charted the bounds of his subject, he followed his quarry with a fidelity bordering upon compulsion. Parkman made up his mind while still a sophomore that the "war that ended in the conquest of Canada"[4] was to occupy his mental life. The war that ended with the expulsion of the French in 1763 virtually consumed it, for it was not long before he "enlarged the plan to include the whole course of the American conflict between France and England."[5] Almost at once he began to prepare himself for this central project. He began to keep notebooks on all manner of topics that bore on the subject. He spent his holidays in the areas where the happenings he intended to write about had taken place. He tracked down stories, anecdotes, reminiscences, and the people who treasured them. "My theme fascinated me," he later wrote with restrained understatement, "and I was haunted by wilderness images day and night." He was more than fascinated, he was possessed. And it was more than a boyhood enthusiasm for Indians; it was a dedication. When Parkman promised to write "the history of the American forest," he had undertaken a history of civilization.[6]

Prescott likewise undertook the writing of a history of civilization, although such was not his initial intent. The call of duty was in his bones, and he tried to suppress a natural inclination toward self-indulgence. The New England conscience easily blended with ambition. The pleasurable life of the Boston *literati* made up of talking clubs and carefully polished reviews for *The North American* was not enough for William Prescott.[7] He set out to find a subject large enough to match the needs of his mind and rewarding enough to match the needs of his spirit. When George Ticknor, brimful of knowledge and impressions, returned from his European wanderings, Prescott received his first real introduction to the glamour of Spain. Ticknor brought back a Spanish library to Cambridge and entranced Harvard audiences with his lectures. In 1824 Prescott wrote Bancroft that he was "battling with the Spaniards" and by 1826 the *Ferdinand and Isabella* had grown into a plan.[8] Ferdinand and Isabella led Prescott to Mexico, to Peru, and finally to Philip the Second.

Prescott's volumes are notable for the labor involved in their preparation and the care with which they were executed. Perhaps to compensate for his infirmity and his pleasure-loving tastes, he made it a point of duty to get at everything he could.[9] Scholars have criticized Prescott's sources, but scarcely a word has ever been directed in criticism of his industry or the precision with which he drew his conclusions from the data at his disposal. His data sometimes led him astray, his fidelity almost never. John Fiske, a cosmic historian with a cosmic philosophy, found an "unsound element" in Prescott: Prescott's sources betrayed him.

> In reading Prescott's account of the conquest of Mexico, one feels one's self in the world of the "Arabian Nights"; indeed, the author himself, in occasional comments, lets us see that he is unable to get rid of just such a feeling. His story moves on in a region that is unreal to him, and therefore tantalizing to the reader; his Moctezuma is a personality like none that ever existed beneath the moon. This is because Prescott simply followed his Spanish authorities not only in their statements of physical fact, but in their inevitable misconceptions of the strange Aztec society which they encountered; the Aztecs in his story are unreal, and this false note vitiates it all. In his Peruvian story Prescott followed safer leaders . . . ; but he lacked the ethnological knowledge needful for coming into touch with that ancient society, and one often feels this as the weak spot in a narrative of marvellous power and beauty.[10]

Prescott's errors were not made because of any want in preparation. In fact, his perseverance would have taxed a man in full possession of his physical faculties. Eight years of preliminary reading were required before the *Ferdinand and Isabella* was begun in 1829. Prescott had to absorb his materials by listening to another read,— and manuscript reading was strictly forbidden. The first time he ever read his own results was from a printer's proof set in special type. Against this background of obstacles his production record is striking. *A History of the Reign of Ferdinand and Isabella* appeared in 1837, *A History of the Conquest of Mexico* in 1843, *A History of the Conquest of Peru* in 1847, and *A History of the Reign of Philip the Second* between 1855 and 1858, not yet finished when Prescott died.[11] Collateral as well as direct lines of preparation were carefully marked out before Prescott considered himself ready to write. He worked at language, the principles of style, and the theory of history. He studied Voltaire, Montesquieu, and the Abbé de Mably with the same care he accorded everything else. Prescott felt the Abbé's *De l'étude de l'histoire* so important for his purposes that he read it ten times. He developed a theory of style and a prescription for the writing of narrative history which by implication constituted a philosophy of history.[12]

The problem of the nineteenth-century historian remained the problem of the twentieth-century historian. How does the historian discover a thematic unity within the diversity of multiple events? Prescott's dramatic sensitivity was heightened by what he learned from Mably. With most nineteenth-century historians, Mably was of the opinion that history should be presented in an interesting fashion. One of the ways of accomplishing this purpose was to give dramatic elements full narrative play. No one denied that the sources in the archives were absorbing to some and frequently to many. Yet someone had to give order and meaning to the documents, to select the materials on the basis of some set of criteria, and to evolve a scheme of narration. This was exactly what Prescott planned, and he planned to do it in such a way that the heroes in the center of the stage where history had placed them would carry the narrative by their action.

Prescott thought out his plots with infinite creative care. He followed the Continental devotees of Sir Walter Scott and the laird of Abbotsford himself. In *Ferdinand and Isabella* he displayed a mastery of the eighteenth-century mode of literary craftsmanship; the metaphor, the sharp contrast, and the counterpoint of the balanced sentence. He mastered this technique so well that his early prose seemed contrived rather than a natural vehicle for the flow of his thought. The lucidity of his expression and the clarity of his logic accounted for the charm of the *Ferdinand and Isabella* volumes.[13] American comments were largely favorable, for few save George Ticknor had any real familiarity with the sources. European critics were laudatory, except for a few high Tory reviewers for whom scholarship in America was a contradiction in terms. The historians Hallam, Milman, Guizot, and Sismondi granted Prescott the honors he craved.[14] With energy renewed, he turned to his next and greatest project, *A History of the Conquest of Mexico.*

Prescott first applied himself to a study of the lives of great men and their exploits. He read Voltaire's *Charles XII,* Livy's account of Hannibal, and Washington Irving's *George Washington.*[15] Prescott was in his element. Cortés was the unquestioned hero, and his dashing exploits and crushing reverses supplied enough dramatic intensity to keep even the most jaded at a high point of excitement. While reading Washington Irving's *Columbus,* he jotted down some notes revealing his method and intent. He agreed with the general opinion that the *Columbus* was a "beautiful composition," but found it "fatiguing as a whole to the reader." The subject of the great discovery, admittedly "full of sublimity," was a model topic for historical investigation, and Irving had performed with enviable skill. But "all after that event is made up of little details,—the sailing from one petty island to another, all inhabited by savages, and having the same general character. Nothing can be more monotonous, and, of course, more likely to involve the author in barren repetition." The subject of the conquest of Mexico, on the other hand, "though very inferior in the leading idea which forms its basis . . . ," was much more suited to Prescott's conceptions and devices. "The event is sufficiently grand, and, as the catastrophe is deferred, the interest is kept up through the whole. Indeed, the perilous venture and crises with which the enterprise was attended, the desperate chances and unexpected vicissitudes, all serve to keep the interest alive." [16]

The *Mexico* brilliantly exemplifies Prescott's method and Prescott's genius. It established his reputation and still remains in print, a genuine tribute after more than a century of minute study. Prescott followed his own literary formula precisely. Cortés is the central figure around whose victories and defeats the story revolves. After Hernando Cortés completed the Conquest, William Prescott completed his history. The remainder of the *Mexico,* the results of the conquest and the rest of Cortés' life, are compressed into the smallest compass. There were to be no repetitious details in Prescott, no barren monotony. He took care not to violate dramatic requirements. "I must . . . not . . . make this tailpiece too long." Prescott had thought out a method and elaborated it in practice.[17]

Prescott's *Peru,* well known though it is, does not compare with the *Mexico.*[18] If the *Mexico* is infinitely superior to the *Peru,* it is in large part because Pizarro was not Cortés and the Incas were not the Aztecs. Pizarro was simply not in the same class with Cortés as a hero, and the Incas were not so novel or intriguing as the Aztecs. A creative artist can construct an epic out of the fertility of his imagination, but even a great creative artist, relying on the facts of history, cannot transform a relatively minor encounter into a major epoch. Prescott recognized this difficulty himself. The Peruvian adventure suffered from a "want of unity." While it was "a connected series of adventures," it did not possess "the especial interest that belongs to the *Iliad* and to the *Conquest of Mexico.*" It is this, of course, which is the inherent weakness of history of the Prescott kind. Epochal events, however intense and spectacular may actually obscure the long-term historical processes of which the events are merely parts. The dramatic intensity, necessary to Prescott's technique, did not exist in the Peruvian episode of Spanish conquest to the same degree that it existed in Mexico. Once Pizarro had his way with the Incas early in the story, there was little Prescott could do to sustain the narrative pitch. The whole story in his own words was "second rate,—quarrels of banditti over their spoils." [19] But even in the *Mexico* a larger logic is sacrificed to dramatic consistency. The Spanish conquerors destroyed a civilization. Even if, as in Prescott's estimation, Cortés and his followers were the agents of history, there was a cultural clash accompanied by cultural borrowings and cultural results. Prescott is forced to assume, especially in the *Peru,* that the Spanish conquest is a "tendency of history" and the establishment of Spanish control in the new world "the great result." He is also forced to assume in consequence that Spanish culture was somehow better than Aztec or Inca culture, for the Spanish had become the carriers of civilization. Prescott is on the weakest ground when, in response to the demands of dramatic climax, he brings his story to a close. A story must have a conclusion. But historical processes end only with the limits of the historian's vision and understanding. And these insights, inevitably limited by the historian's position in the span of time, are not limited by the historian's own chronology.

After the *Peru* and the *Mexico,* however, Prescott was securely ensconced among the literary great. He took a four-month trip to England, where, among other marks of esteem, Oxford awarded him an honorary degree. Prescott was enormously pleased with this tribute. In spite of academic honors elsewhere received, the Oxford degree was a special prize. "I am a *real* Doctor," he wrote to George Ticknor.[20] The French Institute and the Royal Society of Berlin elected him to membership in 1845.[21] When he began his final work, *Philip the Second,* which he never lived to complete, he was universally recognized and acclaimed. *Philip the Second* did not lend itself to the Prescott method. No one could make Philip a hero, and no one could build up the events of his reign to a dramatic climax, unless it was the climax of degradation. The drama of Philip and the drama of Spain were in the realm of historical consequences. But in his narrative style Prescott had rarely if ever done better.[22] John Lothrop Motley, who covered the same period with equal thoroughness, paid *Philip the Second* its highest compliment. "I am astonished at your omniscience," he wrote to the author. "Nothing seems to escape you. Many a little trait of character, scrap of intelligence, or dab of scene-painting which I had kept in my most private pocket, thinking I had fished it out of the unsunned depths, I find already in your possession." [23]

Motley generally shared Prescott's social views but did not share all his qualities as an historian. Motley and Prescott were separated by almost a generation—Prescott died in 1859, Motley was born in 1814, when Prescott was graduated from Harvard.[24] They were even farther apart in temperament. Prescott, the wealthy Bostonian, every Brahmin inch the gentleman, was restrained and calm in his historical judgments. Motley, no less the Brahmin and equally the gentleman, lacked judicial balance. Prescott, for whom the dramatic was an authentic sense, never consciously permitted the pressures of form to mold his understanding of history. Motley was usually more responsive to drama than to history. Prescott's historical conclusions were seldom distorted by warped judgments or by lack of perception. When his judgments were in fact warped, it was the result of fidelity to the sources and fidelity to the dramatic instinct that so often confounded history with arresting parts of it. Motley, indoctrinated with Carlyle's version of great men and history, frequently wrote as if the players were more important than the play, when there could not have been the one without the other. "I am always in a passion," [25] Motley wrote Prescott, but his passion for liberty was initially confined to the sixteenth and seventeenth centuries. Identification with the liberalism of the remote past and a disdain for the liberalism of the immediate present was a characteristic by no means peculiar to Motley. Motley was actually somewhat less remote from the mid-nineteenth century than either Prescott or Parkman. Social ambivalence was a phenomenon not uncommon in Brahmin Boston. Both Prescott and Motley found Spanish absolutism distasteful to their prejudices, and Parkman's comments on French Catholicism still draw angry fire from the exponents of certain schools of history. Yet Prescott remained all but impervious to the disruptive social clashes of his day. Parkman was an outspoken critic of "the rule of the mob," and even the Whiggism of the forties seems to have been rather too democratic for John Lothrop Motley.

Motley's early career was not unusual for the wealthy Boston set to which he belonged. He was a pupil at the Round Hill School where George Bancroft was one of his teachers, and he entered Harvard at the age of thirteen. Thirteen was a fairly youthful age for Harvard freshmen, just as seventeen was a fairly youthful age for graduation. But graduated he was, and with membership in Phi Beta Kappa. He was not an assiduous scholar, and his formal academic record did not warrant this final honor. Yet he was so charmingly precocious and so unpretentiously learned that, as one commentator had it, "he could not be passed over." [26] European travel after Harvard was almost a convention of the leisure class, and Motley spent two exhilarating years abroad. Due to Bancroft's enthusiasm for German, Motley had begun to study it at Round Hill, which made his stay at Berlin and at Göttingen immediately rewarding. He had a romantic time tramping over beautiful German mountains and tarrying in picturesque German villages. Motley made friends easily and among others he learned to know Otto von Bismarck, with whom he later kept up a correspondence.[27]

Law was on the agenda when Motley returned to Boston, but he was never actually very serious about it. He wanted above all else to write, and since there was nothing to prevent him, he wrote two novels. *Morton's Hope,* published anonymously in 1839, demonstrated Motley's unusual flair for words but had no shadow of a plot. Kindly Dr. Oliver Wendell Holmes spoke of it harshly as a "series of incidents which are flung together with no more regard for the unities than a pack of cards." Ten years later *Merry Mount,* a romance dealing with Massachusetts in 1628, established Motley's difficulties with plot construction as an undeniable fact.[28] Motley did more than write two bad novels during this period of his life. In 1841 he went to Russia as secretary of the American legation. He found the post so uninteresting and St. Petersburg so dull that he resigned after a few months' stay. As a Clay Whig, he was elected to the Massachusetts state legislature in 1849, but politics was no more to his liking than the lower rungs of the diplomatic ladder.[29] Neither was congenial to his talents.

While a member of the legislature, he served as chairman of the committee on education. His legislative record consists of the sponsorship of a bill for the endowment of institutions of higher learning at the expense of the secondary public school system. One of his colleagues, George S. Boutwell, who knew his political way about, remarked that the bill could not have been passed even had it been championed by Daniel Webster. Motley could never understand why.[30] Motley's experience in public life did not enhance his opinion of the democratic process, but Motley made little effort until the outbreak of the Civil War either to explore or to improve it. The competition of the market place repelled him no less than its reverberations on Beacon Hill. With other proper Bostonians who cherished Anglo-Saxon notions of an ordered society in which social groups were neatly checked and balanced, he wondered how gentlemen could take any part in the struggle for wealth and power. Bancroft was a Brahmin rebel. Edward Everett, Rufus Choate, and Daniel Webster, if not considered quite Brahmin enough, were not at least on the wrong side.

For Motley's personal development the years from 1839 to 1849 were not fruitless years. Like Prescott and Parkman, he wrote for *The North American*. The success of his historical pieces helped him to make up his mind about a career. History was to be his *métier*.[31] As an historian, he would have to do no more than borrow the plots that history had already made, and he could put his gift for resplendent prose to best advantage.[32] The Dutch crusade for independence provided such an opportunity. He was ecstatic. The subject, he wrote, has "taken me up, drawn me on, and absorbed me into itself." [33] But a seemingly insuperable obstacle marred his pleasure. The renowned Prescott was engaged in a study of Philip the Second, a study already begun and already announced. Motley approached his older friend and was assured that no real obstacle existed. Prescott gave Motley his encouragement and his blessing in much the same way as he had received both from Washington Irving with whose work he feared the *Mexico* would collide.[34] Reassured, Motley pressed ahead. *The Rise of the Dutch Republic* appeared in 1856, *The History of the United Netherlands, from the Death of William the Silent, To the Twelve Years' Truce* in the years from 1860 to 1867, and *The Life and Death of John of Barneveld, Advocate of Holland* in 1874.[35]

Motley did not emulate Prescott's mode of preparation by vast reading along direct and related lines. Instead, he did what Prescott could not do. He spent years in the archives of Brussels, The Hague, Dresden, and Berlin, and he seeped up local color wherever he could find it. The three volumes of *The Rise of the Dutch Republic* were crammed with ten years of single-minded effort. Publishers were as cautious about the commercial risk of the *Dutch Republic* as they had been about Prescott's *Ferdinand and Isabella*. Motley published at his own expense.[36] The first reviews were restrained and cool; few thought the subject or the style would attract many readers. In April 1856, James Anthony Froude, an historian whose reputation commanded authority, wrote in *The Westminster Review:* "the result of many years of silent labor, . . . the book will take its place among the finest histories in this or in any language." This was stunning praise from a Froude, and Dutch scholars, captivated by American interest in their national past, were generous and cordial. Bakhuysen van der Brink, a learned Hollander, gave Motley approbation where he thought approbation was deserved. "Motley shines in narrative," he admitted together with almost everybody else. But he continued, again reflecting a general view: "He is less fortunate in his explanations of cause and effect. What the witnesses whom he summons testify, he narrates better than they could tell, but he fails to weigh their personality and trustworthiness with sufficient accuracy." [37] Bakhuysen was more than accurate in his appraisal. So too was Froude, for *The Rise of the Dutch Republic* made Motley's reputation and kept it. Fifteen thousand copies were sold in two years, probably because the work was so brilliantly and captivatingly written. No subsequent writer on these topics has surpassed Motley in narrative power and in the vividness of his pen portraits, particularly of William of Orange. But later scholarship has rendered Motley's attempted explanations all but obsolete.

Motley was a lesser Prescott. Both attempted to capture historical meanings through vivid portrayal of the epochal. Motley was temperamentally unable to achieve Prescott's sense of balance, but he followed him in positing an elemental cleavage of forces resulting in dramatic fulfillment. Evil was challenged by good, the "great result" by opposing historical tendencies. Motley's heroes like William of Orange were great men, exemplars of the virtues he admired. His devils like Philip the Second personified the vices he most deplored. If altered standards of scholarship have changed some of Motley's strengths into weaknesses, they have not impaired his literary reputation. His descriptions of the defeat of the Spanish Armada, of the execution of Egmont, of the flight of Grotius are stories as fascinatingly told as anything in Parkman's superlative pages. But *The Rise of the Dutch Republic* and *John of Barneveld* are no longer the standard references for the subject of which they treat. While they have been superseded forever, they will always remain prime sources for the study of nineteenth-century values and for the study of John Lothrop Motley.[38]

Motley was surpassed by Prescott, and Francis Parkman surpassed them both. Parkman possessed all their strengths, and he possessed them in greater and in richer proportion. Except for detail, Parkman's history still stands as great and unimpaired as when he wrote it. Of Parkman's genius there has been little difference of opinion among historians. He was the greatest historian of America. Bancroft doubtless had a much wider general influence and was unquestionably the foremost historical writer in popular estimation, but Parkman had virtues Bancroft did not possess. In matters of style, there is simply no basis for comparison. Parkman was a prose artist; Bancroft wrote well on occasion. Bancroft was a man of action, and his insights were fed by the experiences of a rich and varied life. Life forced Parkman to become a man of thought, to immerse himself in the past of his chosen period. Parkman's logic is tighter and tougher; his organization smoother and more consistent. No writer of history in America, save Henry Adams alone, can reasonably be compared with Francis Parkman. Social conditions and professional goals have changed since the Civil War, but no one has matched his achievement or really equaled him in literary skill.

The history of Francis Parkman is as intriguing as the history he wrote.[39] Descent from a long line of reverential Puritans was a commonplace in Parkman's Boston. That he numbered John Cotton among his ancestors made him only more or less distinguished than some of his friends. Many were sons of ministers, and by 1823 it was socially fairly safe to be the son of a Unitarian one. Parkman's father, minister of the Unitarian North Church, had inherited a comfortable fortune which he bequeathed to his children. Parkman was able to write the series *France and England in America* because his grandfather's wealth secured his independence. His Harvard interlude, 1840 to 1844, turned out to be crucial. As he tells us in an autobiographical fragment, it was during his sophomore year that he made up his mind to write the history, and he was indifferent to whatever failed to bear on his plans.[40] It was also during his undergraduate days in 1843 that the infirmity which was to shape his existence began. He went abroad for a year and was able to return to graduate with the class of 1844. Parental pressure induced him to defer his historical project for another three years spent, without much enthusiasm, at the Harvard Law School. Almost immediately after he received his law degree, he set out on a trip along the Oregon Trail. During the later stages of this trip, he was afflicted with the malady which made him a partial invalid and finally deprived him, for normal reading purposes at least, of the use of his sight. Blindness for Parkman was not only a tragedy; it was a catastrophe.

He had a lust for the robust life and had evolved an elaborate theory on the relationship between an active mind and a virile body. "I held the creed," he later wrote,

> that the more hard knocks a man gets, whether in mind or body, the better for him, provided always that he takes them without flinching; and as the means of forcing myself up to the required standard, I put my faith in persistent violence which I thought energy. I held that the true aim of life was not happiness but achievement; had profound respect for physical strength and hardihood when joined with corresponding qualities of character; took pleasure in any moderate hardship, scorned invalidism of all kinds, and was full of the notion, common enough with boys of a certain sort, that the body will always harden and toughen with exercise and exposure.[41]

That like Prescott he was able to overcome his infirmities was heroic, but for Parkman physical incapacity involved a deprivation. Physical infirmity made Parkman a fragmentary man. He confided to his friend Ephraim George Squier, a noted ethnologist who became editor of *Leslie's Weekly,* that reports of activity "kindled in me a burning desire . . . a restless fit which is apt to seize me at intervals and which you have unmercifully aggravated." [42]

While Parkman's critics and biographers have stressed the connections between his blindness and his work, they have probably overstressed it.[43] His condition was certainly distressing, more distressing perhaps to his friends than to Parkman himself. The struggle to master the effects of his various maladies was doubtless the controlling factor in the development of Parkman's personality, but it was a struggle that Parkman won. To Squier he wrote with brave candor:

> I can bear witness that no amount of physical pain is so intolerable as the position of being stranded and doomed to be rotting for year after year. However, I have not abandoned any plan, which I have ever formed and I have no intention of abandoning any until I am made cold meat of. At present I am much better in health than when you last saw me, and I do not suffer from that constant sense of oppression which then at times annoyed me beyond endurance. I find myself able to work a little although my eyes are in a totally useless state, and excessively sensitive. The eyes are nothing to the other infernal thing which now seems inclined to leave me alone . . . ; so I contrive to dig slowly along by the aid of other people's eyes, doing the work more thoroughly no doubt, and digesting my materials better than if I used my own." [44]

Parkman did not permit his physical limitations to stand in the way of his purpose. To overcome them, however, demanded unusual determination and character. The eleven volumes of the series *France and England in America* are monuments not only to the scholarship of Francis Parkman but to his indomitable will.

Parkman truly made history the work of his life. The eight divisions that comprise the series *France and England in America* represent a full half century of devotion. Prescott's preparatory efforts were comprehensive; Parkman's were incomparable. His reverence for the primary source, no whit less than Leopold von Ranke's, made no effort too difficult. Neither distance nor expense ever stood in the way of Parkman and the documents. Almost two hundred folio volumes now in the possession of the Massachusetts Historical Society supply incontrovertible proof of his diligence. They contain the copies of hundreds of documents made at Parkman's direction and expense, documents he carefully studied and mastered.[45] When he was at work on *The Discovery of the Great West,* for instance, a large body of materials of "extraordinary richness" was known to be in existence in France. Pierre Margry, director of marine and colonies in Paris, had been engaged in collecting materials pertinent to the history of early French exploration. Margry had no intention of publishing a book on the subject, but he did intend to publish the documents. Until they were in print, he was unwilling to permit Parkman to use them. Since Margry had difficulty in finding a publisher, Parkman was forced to finish his volume without consulting these sources. He was later instrumental in arranging for the publication of Margry's valuable collection, and after it appeared he revised the book wherever the newer materials required correction.[46] After 1879, it was entitled *La Salle and the Discovery of the Great West.*

The prefaces of Parkman's books likewise demonstrate his respect for primary materials and his constant reliance upon such evidence. He once conducted a fifteen-year search for a batch of Montcalm letters and in the judgment of one Parkman scholar, he examined every relevant source either known or available in his day.[47] Nor was it only the written record upon which Parkman depended. His accurate and vivid description were products of direct and personal knowledge. Whenever possible he went over every inch of a battlefield, an approach, a town, or a village. These trips of observation supplemented the written accounts. The description of the siege of Louisburg is a masterpiece of accuracy as well as of prose. When he came to write this chapter in *Montcalm and Wolfe,* his notes tell us there were six primary sources before him. Among them were French diaries of the siege, an English officer's diary, and the actual plans of the siege operations. Parkman had been on the site, and when Parkman visited the scenes about which he was to write nothing missed his damaged eyes.[48]

Parkman's concept of history is implicit in his finished products;

his conception of historical writing is suggested by the method he employed. He was determined first to discover what actually happened, but he was not attuned to the issues involved in the use of the raw data of experience. It was enough to evaluate the evidence of documents and the actualities of time and place by ordinary rules of logic and common sense. He subscribed to the lawyer's faith that truth could be sifted out of conflicting evidence by assiduous and impartial analysis. Once in possession of the facts of the siege of Louisburg, as seen through the eyes of participants and checked against the actualities of the site—a rough measure of the possible—, the next step was to tell the story in clear and dramatic prose. His reviews in *The North American* and elsewhere distributed unqualified awards to writers whose knowledge had been amassed from primary materials. Those who really knew their subject matter and drew valid inferences with balance and proportion received his approbation. Those who wrote without the knowledge requisite to sustain their conclusions, he dismissed with impatience.[49]

Parkman admired colorful and dramatic writing. A vivid style enhanced rather than distorted truth. Cooper's prose pleased him, although he thought it suffered somewhat from want of "glow." It was marked by a "manly directness," and he admired Cooper particularly because his work was free "from those prettinesses, studied turns of expression, and petty tricks of rhetoric, which are the pride of less masculine writers." [50] But style for Francis Parkman was no end in itself; it was cultivated for a deliberate historical purpose. If history was to be real, it had to be alive. The dead past could live again only if the historian recreated it. To do so the historian had to enliven his material by imagination, an imagination trained to recreate without distortion, to add a creative dimension to the solidity of incorruptible fact. Parkman disciplined his imaginative faculties by documentary research and the logic of evidence, and his journeys, expeditions, and travels to the scenes of his histories were integral parts of his technique. Proof of the Parkman method is in the reading:

The main body of troops waited in their boats by the edge of the strand. The heights near by were cleft by a great ravine choked with forest trees; and in its depths ran a little brook called Ruisseau St.-Denis, which, swollen by the late rains, fell plashing in the stillness over a rock. Other than this no sound could reach the strained ear of Wolfe but the gurgle of the tide and the cautious climbing of his advance-parties as they mounted the steeps at some little distance from where he sat listening. At length from the top came a sound of musket-shots, followed by loud huzzas, and he knew that his men were masters of the position. The word was given; the troops leaped from the boats and scaled the heights, some here, some there, clutching at trees and bushes, their muskets slung at their backs.[51]

The past lived in Parkman, and he lived in the past. To write the history he desired he was willing to pay a high price.[52] And Parkman paid it. The difficulties under which his body forced his mind to work were not without compensations. He was aware that his trials and their specific tolls made him more acute, more sensitive, and more painstaking. They trained his memory, made discrimination a subtle sense, and transformed his mind into a practiced instrument of human measure. But illness and preoccupation took him out of his culture. He became a stranger to his times. But if he knew the America of his own day less, he knew the America of pre-Revolutionary days more.

The journey along the Oregon trail was one of Parkman's great fieldwork expeditions. The account, first published serially in the *Knickerbocker's Magazine,* appeared as a volume in 1849.[53] Still an exciting story, it was a trip of seventeen hundred miles on horseback, a feat of rugged masculinity sufficient to satisfy even Parkman's standards of the strenuous life. Here Parkman recorded his love of nature and his love of adventure:

> We had passed the more tedious part of the journey; but four hundred miles still intervened between us and Fort Laramie; and to reach that point cost us the travel of three more weeks. During the whole of this time we were passing up the middle of a long, narrow, sandy plain, reaching like an outstretched belt nearly to the Rocky Mountains. Two lines of sand-hills, broken often into the wildest and most fantastic forms, flanked the valley at the distance of a mile or two on the right and left; while beyond them lay a barren, trackless waste, extending for hundreds of miles to the Arkansas on the one side, and the Missouri on the other. Before and behind us, the level monotony of the plain was unbroken as far as the eye could reach. Sometimes it glared in the sun, an expanse of hot, bare sand; sometimes it was veiled by long coarse grass. Skulls and whitening bones of buffalo were scattered everywhere; the ground was tracked by myriads of them. . . . The naked landscape is, of itself, dreary and monotonous enough; and yet the wild beasts and wild men that frequent the valley of the Platte make it a scene of interest and excitement to the traveller. Of those who have journeyed there, scarcely one, perhaps, fails to look back with fond regret to his horse and his rifle.[54]

Parkman had already learned much about writing; he had also learned a great deal about history. But the history he learned was the history of the particular.[55] His powers of observation, already keen, allowed him to photograph the multitudinous details of the western sweep in his memory, but the significance of the westward sweep itself eluded him. That the Indian and Indian culture were mortgaged to the future, he saw clearly. The Indian, he wrote, "will not learn the arts of civilization, and he and his forest must perish together." But that the future, already taking industrial shape in Brahmin Boston and Yankee New England, was to destroy "the arts of civilization" as he understood them, he never quite fully grasped. Partly because he was young, but more because he was a Boston Parkman and wise in the manner of a recent Harvard graduate, he failed to understand the West. The reasons for his own western pilgrimage were clear, clearer perhaps in retrospect than earlier, but he had almost no inkling of the reasons inducing thousands of men to rip up their roots and move into an unknown future. He had less insight into the process by which the West, even while still the frontier, was to be molded into a mechanized appendage of urban America.

As soon as Parkman returned from his western excursion, he began the *History of the Conspiracy of Pontiac*. He laid down the plan he was to follow and presented the reasons for its importance. The conquest of Canada "was an event of momentous consequence in American history. It changed the political aspect of the continent, prepared a way for the independence of the British colonies, rescued the vast tracts of the interior from the rule of military despotism, and gave them, eventually, to the keeping of an ordered democracy. Yet to the red natives of the soil its results were wholly disastrous." [56] By any standard the *Pontiac* is a great book. As Parkman himself would have wished, the volume was to be judged on its merits without reference to the limitations under which it was written. Justly celebrated in historical literature, no other study of the subject compares with it. This would be immortality enough, yet few single volumes in all American historical writing can truly be said to rival its lucid and comprehensive scope.

Pontiac presents a double synthesis. It is a synthesis of the total struggle between France and England, a preview of what Parkman aimed to accomplish in detail, and a summary in advance of his life effort. It was also a synthesis of the historical setting as a preparation for the conspiracy of Pontiac, itself the background for the motif of "the American forest and the American Indian at the period when both received their final doom." [57] The entire volume, indeed the whole series, is an epitaph to Indian culture. But Parkman wrote the most eloquent of epitaphs to Pontiac himself, which was the epitaph of a race. It was also a memorial to a white civilization that passed from the cultural scene not long after the red men:

> Neither mound nor tablet marked the burial place of Pontiac. For a mausoleum, a city has risen above the forest hero; and the race whom he hated with such burning rancor trampled with unceasing footsteps over his forgotten grave.[58]

The unique character of the *Pontiac* is stamped on every page. With genuine modesty, the preface presents the historian's credentials: his residence among the primitive tribes of the Rocky Mountains and in a village of the western Dakotas, for he explained, "it is evident that other study than that of the closet is indispensable to such an attempt." Study of the closet, nevertheless, was not overlooked, and the "collection of the necessary documents" when completed numbered "about three thousand four hundred manuscript pages." General Lewis Cass, onetime American minister in Paris, made a collection of papers about the Indian siege of Detroit available and European and American state archives were searched with a lust usually ascribed to the so-called "scientific" historians alone. The list of acknowledgements for specific documentary services reads like a roster of contemporary scholarship: collectors, bibliographers, and specialists in early colonial history and Indian affairs. Among them are the names of Henry Stevens, Henry R. Schoolcraft, William Leete Stone, E. B. O'Callaghan, and Lyman C. Draper.[59] And with all this array of manuscript treasures, the *Pontiac* is not so celebrated for its reliance upon primary sources as it is for oral evidence culled from personal contacts with frontiersmen and the associates of pioneers.[60] The volume opens with an introductory chapter on the Indian tribes east of the Mississippi. A chapter on the French and English in America from 1663 to 1763 follows the digest of knowledge on the Indians and their way of life. Material on the French and the English, including a chapter on the French, the English, and the Indians, is the best brief account to be found anywhere in the language. Here is the sketch he was later to fill out with rich, varied, and elaborate detail.[61] The contrast between the two rival powers, a premise of his analysis and final conclusion, is set forth in bold and graphic lines:

> In the valley of the St. Lawrence, and along the coasts of the Atlantic, adverse principles contended for the mastery. Feudalism stood arrayed against Democracy; Popery against Protestantism; the sword against the ploughshare. The priest, the soldier, and the noble, ruled in Canada. The ignorant, light-hearted Canadian peasant knew nothing and cared

nothing about popular rights and civil liberties. Born to obey, he lived in contented submission, without the wish or the capacity for self-rule. Power, centered in the heart of the system, left the masses inert.

If we search the world for the sharpest contrast to the spiritual and temporal vassalage of Canada, we shall find it among her immediate neighbors, the Puritans of New England, where the spirit of nonconformity was sublimed to a fiery essence, and where the love of liberty and the hatred of power burned with sevenfold heat. The English colonist, with thoughtful brow and limbs hardened with toil; calling no man master, yet bowing reverently to the law which he himself had made . . .—such a man might well be deemed the very pith and marrow of a commonwealth.[62]

The great history had been long in the making, but *Pioneers of France in the New World* did not appear until 1865. The years between *Pontiac* and the *Pioneers* were dark years for Francis Parkman. His only son died in 1857, followed soon after by the death of his wife in 1858, and "the Enemy"—as he called his sickness—pursued him relentlessly. For large segments of time work on the history was out of the question.[63] In 1858 he went to Paris to seek a specialist's care and advice, while his friends in Boston feared that if he returned at all, he would not return whole. But return he did, and when he found he could not grind away on the English and French struggling in the primitive forest, he took to the cultivation of flowers in his domestic garden. With George Bancroft, Parkman shared a love of roses. For Bancroft the cultivation of roses was a means of relaxation; for Parkman it was a method of survival. When Parkman took up horticulture, he became an expert.[64] Between 1859 and 1884, the Massachusetts Horticultural Society granted him three hundred and twenty-six awards. He became active in the affairs of the society and once served as its president. Numerous botanical papers indicate how close his avocation came to be another profession, and his monograph, *The Book of Roses,*[65] became standard in its field. Harvard appointed him to a horticultural professorship at the Bussey Institution in 1871 and five years later he developed the *Lilium parkmanii.*[66] Likewise in the interval between the publication of his histories, he wrote *Vassal Morton,* a novel less distinguished as fiction than as an autobiographical record of Parkman's thought.[67]

Neither tragedy nor indisposition ever completely banished the history from Parkman's mind. Finally he was able to give it the sort of undivided attention that helped to bring him peace. *Pioneers of France in the New World,* the first volume of the grand series, was ready in 1865. The *Pioneers* had a Spanish as well as a French phase, and the ill-fated Huguenot venture in Florida preceded a discussion of Champlain's founding the French empire in Canada.

Parkman may have been content to let the facts speak for themselves, but his judgments of their meaning were as clear and full-
throated as the interpretations of Prescott or Motley. He made his
choice between the influence of great men and the role of historical
tendencies, and ranged himself on the side of human personalities
rather than on the side of impersonal forces. Yet he wrote that the
contest was one between "Liberty and Absolutism," between New
England and New France.[68]

The later volumes of the series appeared with greater frequency.
The Jesuits in North America in the Seventeenth Century was published in 1867; *The Discovery of the Great West* in 1869; *The Old
Regime in Canada* in 1874; *Count Frontenac and New France under
Louis XIV* in 1877; and *Montcalm and Wolfe* in 1884. *A Half Century of Conflict* which precedes *Montcalm and Wolfe* chronologically, was postponed by Parkman in order that the former and more
important volume could be completed. *A Half Century of Conflict*
appeared in 1892, a year before Parkman's death. *The Jesuits,* the
chronicle of French efforts during the seventeenth century, also portrays the heroic work of the Jesuit Order among the Indians. *La
Salle,* an eloquent tribute to a great figure whom Parkman could not
fail to admire, continues the narrative and centers in the discovery
and exploration of the interior valley and the region of the Great
Lakes. Colonial administration, royal policy, and missionary work
are the subjects of *The Old Regime.* The era of greatest French success as a colonial power in America is recounted in *Count Frontenac.* The last two volumes are devoted to the fall of New France. *A
Half Century of Conflict* covers the forty-eight years from 1700 to
1748, years filled with terror of Indian raids and a growing emnity of
the rival colonial powers. The struggle ends on the Plains of Abraham in *Montcalm and Wolfe* with the expulsion of France from the
American continent.[69]

Francis Parkman's praise has been as magnificent as his achievement. Henry James and James Russell Lowell, both acknowledged
masters of the writer's craft, admitted Parkman to their own company. George Bancroft, Jared Sparks, and Justin Winsor, fellow historians, expressed pride and satisfaction in their colleague's production.[70] And Henry Adams, whose opinions of the historical guild
were not always high, wrote him apropos of the *Montcalm and
Wolfe:*

> The book puts you in the front rank of living English historians. . . .
> Your book is a model of thorough and impartial study and clear state-
> ment. Of its style and narrative the highest praise is that they are on a

level with its thoroughness of study. Taken as a whole, your works are now dignified by proportions and completeness which can hardly be paralleled by the literary baggage of any other historical writer in the language known to me today. George Bancroft has the proportions but not the completeness; for, as I often tell him, he has written the History of the United States in a dozen volumes without reaching his subject.[71]

Historians of a later generation, while respectful, have been more qualified. Even the critical have allowed Parkman his reputation for greatness, but only after establishing their own limitations. The majestic quality of his style is admitted, but it has often been thought necessary to categorize Parkman as a "narrative," "dramatic," "romantic," or "literary" historian.[72]

Among the more serious criticisms are those relating to Parkman's attitude toward Catholicism. Professor Wilbur Schramm argues persuasively that the charge of anti-Catholicism was inevitable. Parkman was not only a rationalist, but also an antisupernaturalist. He was not hostile to individual Catholics—many of them were his heroes—but he was a confirmed exponent of rational causation. Catholic doctrine and Catholic philosophy were for him unacceptable. Parkman did not scoff, he simply did not believe. He evaluated religious beliefs and the consequences of ecclesiastical acts in terms of his own understandings and convictions. What provoked Catholic critics is not difficult to perceive. But it is difficult to perceive how Parkman, or anyone else for that matter, could have satisfied such critics without subscribing to Catholic doctrine and the philosophy of the supernatural. He would have been less entitled to his place in historiography, if, having concluded that the rule of France was despotic and that one of the factors in French despotism was the Catholic Church, he had suppressed such conclusions. Prescott and Motley were just as unsympathetic, and only in part because they were Protestants of Puritan descent.[73]

Other charges have somewhat more substance. Parkman, it is said, could not have been truly impartial because he was identified with Anglo-Saxon institutions of the New England variety. On that account he was unable sympathetically to understand the West. Parkman, it is true, was a Bostonian, but he had as much love for nature and for the West as the most zealous follower of Frederick Jackson Turner. Theodore Roosevelt and Turner himself were inspired by Parkman's feeling for the West, and Reuben Gold Thwaites modeled much of his historical scheme on Parkman's volumes. Few apostles of the history of the frontier covered the Oregon Trail as did Parkman, however much more fully they may later have written about it. To argue that Parkman knew little about the West of which he wrote refutes itself; that others learned more and different things about the West needs scarcely to be maintained.[74]

French despotism was not the sole cause of French failure or of English success. There were many other elements that combined to bring about the expulsion of France from North America. Parkman failed to recognize some elements because of lack of knowledge; he failed to recognize others because of lack of understanding. Parkman gave full weight to geography, but he gave practically no weight to geography as a factor in multiple causation. The size of Canada and access from the sea only twice a year had something to do with the inequality of the conflict between the two colonial powers.[75] One has merely to read the final chapters of *The Old Regime* to see that Parkman had a grasp of economic forces and their political implications. If he failed to give them adequate stress, it was probably less because of his emotional ties then because of his conception of history.[76]

There are other facets to the argument of sectional bias. Parkman unquestionably preferred the New England way. At least he preferred the ways of New England in the days of his father's prime. But if a cultural identification precludes reasoned judgment of alien cultural forms, historical knowledge is unattainable. Parkman's natural affinity for his own cultural background did not necessarily induce him to prejudge the struggle between France and England. Parkman was almost as critical of Puritanism as he was of Catholicism.[77] During his adult life he was even more unsympathetic to the changing social patterns in New England.[78] An uncompromising critic of democracy, he was no more friendly to majority-rule principles than to the principles of absolutism.[79] His New England Anglo-Saxonism created biases of a different order. They were the prejudices favoring a certain set of social and political values, certain ideas of liberty and of social organization. But these attitudes and values were less sectional and national than universal.[80]

It is sometimes reasonable to censure a scholar for failing to do what he should. The limits he sets to his labors must be defensible, not arbitrary. Surely no one can be censured for failure to include what is not within the scope of knowledge as then organized and understood. Prescott could not have availed himself of developmental psychology in weighing the character of Philip II. Economic interpretations were not so clear and compelling to Sparks and Parkman as to Clarence W. Alvord and Charles A. Beard. Contemporary students cannot fairly castigate Parkman for sins of which they are themselves guilty. The very scholars who have exposed economic, political, constitutional, and political gaps in Parkman's writing reveal social, intellectual, and psychological gaps in their own.[81]

Theodore Parker discovered the nucleus of Parkman's weakness. "The historian," he wrote to Francis Parkman, "cannot tell all; he must choose such as, to him, most clearly sets forth the Idea of the nation—or man—he describes." Parkman sacrificed the internal logic of history to its drama. He identified the processes of history with the men and events who exemplified them:

> The title indicates that the *Conspiracy of Pontiac* is the chief theme. But in the book itself it seems to me this is not exactly so, that other things are not quite enough subordinated to the main theme, so as to give unity to the whole book. The *Barn* is a little too near the house. . . . This appears as you look over the table of contents, when Pontiac & his schemes are not the central object about which the rest is grouped. You do not tell the effect which his death had on Indian affairs. A special study like this requires at the end a general summary with the philosophical reflections which have grown out of the historical treatment of the theme.[82]

Theodore Parker was right. But Mason Wade, a careful and appreciative student of Parkman, is also right, for "there is no other explanation but sheer genius for his ability to reduce the conclusions of years of study of dusty documents and garbled accounts to a narrative of remarkable clarity and vigor." [83]

XVI

The Civil War in
American Historiography

The deepest meanings of American experience have been associated
with the dramatic episodes preceding and following the struggle between the States. Appomattox is not only a place name and 1865 an
unforgettable date; they have both become American symbols.
Abraham Lincoln's presidency marks a turning point in the history
of the United States and in the history of democracy. "The people of
the United States," a leading historian asserted, "did not compose a
nation until after the Civil War." Another scholar concluded that
"the conflict marks a bloody dividing line across American history
indicating a crucial stage in the transition from an agricultural, rural,
religious, and personalized America to an industrial, urban, secular,
and institutionalized America. This pivotal significance has made it a
basic factor in practically every attempt since 1865 to develop a
meaningful interpretation of American history." [1] Division is the
historiographical theme of America from 1820 to 1861; reunion the
dominant note from 1865 to 1900. The clash of "social and economic interests between these sharply differentiated sections" [2] not
only brought about the war; it was also followed for whatever reasons by the triumph of the industrial North. Pragmatic need and the
sentiment of shared tradition held North and South together during
the forty years of controversial bitterness. Before Appomattox the
United States was less a nation than a "confederation of sections;" [3]
it was the war which gave birth to the modern nation. The Civil War

therefore marked a stage between national adolescence and national maturity. Except for the Revolution, no single series of events seemed so climactic, so final, so devastatingly complete. None was so shattering to human life, even for those who survived the physical and emotional devastations of actual battle.

The cessation of hostilities, though failing to bring peace either to North or South, preserved the Union. But the cost had yet to be counted. A heavy price had to be paid for the corrosion of ideals and the debasement of values. For the moment there was relief, and most Americans rejoiced with James Russell Lowell that America was "ours once more." Democracy, though disrupted, had not been destroyed. Weakened by institutional collapse before the war and constitutional strains during it, democracy had survived. Democracy remained a noble dream, but why, men were compelled to ask, had secession been permitted to shatter it? The fact of secession and the experience of civil war reopened the debate concerning the nature of the Union and the nature of democracy. During the revolutionary era men had earnestly asked whether a people could break the bands of union and under what conditions they could be broken. Some searched for reasons to justify the events of 1776; others found reasons to condemn them. The Civil War raised similar questions. Students were led to examine the concepts of American government and the operation of American social institutions with a seriousness proportionate to their gravity.

The preservation of the Union was as dramatic as its original creation. William Archibald Dunning, a leading student of the Civil War and its consequences, regarded the salvation of the Union "a still greater miracle" than independence. After the peace American historians were irresistibly "forced to deal with the conflict of sections." [4] Southerners and northerners alike pursued justification for individual and sectional behavior, and many found a facile satisfaction in the pallid abstractions of irresistible forces. The evil of treason was pitted against the virtue of loyalty, the tyranny of majorities against the democracy of minority rights. Guilt was attached to northern aggression or to southern conspiracy, and retribution was discovered in southern defeat as well as in the chaos of northern victory.

Historical scholarship dealing with the Civil War covers the widest conceivable range. Broad not only in scope of subject matter, the Civil War has become one of the most productive areas of research. As the twentieth century approached its midpoint, the centennial impulse recharged the enthusiasm of scholars filling the learned journals, the publishers' lists, and the bibliographies, both general and special. The latter are crammed with titles of monographs devoted to every aspect of life North and South before, during, and after the war.[5] Publication has been so vast that a "problem of sheer quantity" [6] has overwhelmed the special student and general historian alike.

Civil War literature is enormous. There is hardly a phase which has not enticed its chronicler.[7] Diaries and letters have been endlessly discovered and gently edited.[8] Random jottings of soldiers and civilians, together with the studied recollections of generals and statesmen, struggle to find space in special library collections.[9] There are scores of biographies of the great, the near great, and the insignificant,[10] assessments of campaigns, battles, and overall strategies.[11] There are attacks upon reputations coupled with inevitable rebuttals, and eulogies fulsome and sincere.[12]

There are two main stages of Civil War historiography. Neither is chronologically nor conceptually precise, but both are clearly discernible. The first, beginning in 1861, continued until the twentieth century, when the second commenced. Both have an individual character, but the essential distinction between them lies in logic rather than in data. Materials have increased in quantity, perspectives have shifted, but the substance of argument has remained relatively constant.

From the outbreak of the war to the final nineteenth-century decades, there were two leading formulations. During these years, roughly parallel with the life of the war generation, conspiracy theories alternated with constitutional theories as explanations of national disruption. Meanwhile, the second generation, exponents of scientific method in historical scholarship, reviewed the conflict in an altered spirit. The passionate language of participants was abandoned for the temperate words of scholarship, and efforts were made to understand the conflict rather than to justify or to condemn it. The ethics of slavery, suppressed in Southern apologetics, again became a crucial factor, and the prewar assumption of an "irrepressible conflict" was revived. Slavery in this stage was viewed as a moral evil inconsistent with democratic principles. Individual and sectional attempts to justify slavery could be explained; they could not be condoned. Certain varieties of abolitionists, now rehabilitated, appeared as the upholders of moral virtue and their proslavery adversaries as mistaken extremists.

The twentieth century registered a change in emphasis. For at least the first thirty years thereafter economic interpretations became

paramount. Slavery, still a moral problem, appeared as a single, identifiable component within a complex of factors. Responsibility for
slavery and its social consequences was assessed impersonally. The
economic argument, constantly elaborated, was finally absorbed
within a larger framework of analysis. Historians, in response to
outer pressures and inner needs, adopted the anthropological culture
concept. The older theory of an "irrepressible conflict" of antagonistic societies continued in the anthropological terms of culture clash.

The cultural thesis gave the facts of sectional discord and the hypotheses designed to clarify them a more finely tooled comparative
stress. Economic interpretations, already questioned as fragmental,
appeared less convincing. The problems molded by economic explanations were sharpened by a fusion with culture-clash assumptions.
The data, now more comprehensively focused, merged venerable
questions improperly separated and introduced novel combinations.
The logic of comparative culture elevated the correlative query to
equal status: were the cleavages resolvable short of war? Was the
war needless, unnecessary, avoidable? Debate was thereafter once
again locked in a polar antithesis: the repressible *versus* the "irrepressible conflict."

Historians were subsequently as much concerned with what prevented peaceful solutions as with what brought about military action. The concept of a "blundering generation" was one immediate
response, a concept that posited human frailty, inept, blind, and fa-
natical leadership. While this transition in emphasis disparaged economic elements, it was also a frontal assault on impersonal cultural
forces. Yet fanaticism, especially if given psychological names, was
no less blind a force than the impersonality of culture or the immutable drift of economics. Scholars who regarded the war as prevent-
able were impelled to wonder where men had failed. The investigation of institutions, particularly political institutions, was an
emotional as well as a logical result. Since all men were not blind,
fanatic, or indifferent, what was the role of politics in a democratic
society? The problem of democratic politics emerged once again, and
with it the moral issues of slavery. While it was possible to keep
the ethics of slavery out of economics, it was as impossible to keep
ethics out of the politics of history as to keep it out of the politics of
life. Revisionists argued, as some Americans had always argued, that
slavery and democracy were incompatible. They likewise maintained
that democratic theory was designed to meet basic conflicts dividing
society. The discussion returned to the point where it had begun, not
with the controversy between North and South, but with the axioms

of the Declaration of Independence. The debate amplified far beyond its nominal limits. Were democratic methods sufficient to cope with social upheavals? Was democracy a system successful only when divisive issues were simply secular and unrelated to moral values? Was majority rule a device that worked only when defeats at the polls were relatively inconsequential, but not when such defeats frustrated the most sacred interests and the most sustaining beliefs? If these questions lie at the heart of democracy, they likewise lie at the heart of the dialectics of "irrepressible conflict" and of Civil War historiography.

Threats of conspiracy, real or fancied, were no less the extensions of "irrepressible conflict" theories and hence of democratic dilemmas. The charge of conspiracy, long an acrid part of mutual recrimination, was as comforting to its proponents after as before the war. Before the war such charges were held to have demonstrated the existence of an unholy intent; after the war began, the unholy purposes were demonstrated. The response to conspiracy was to frustrate it; failure to block it demanded resistance. The plotters of conspiracy alone were guilty and must bear full responsibility for their acts. The Northern view, based on an opposite reading of the same facts, was the obverse of the Southern view. And the facts marshaled in defense of both consisted virtually of the entire range of contact between the sections from the beginning. Southerners affected to have unmasked a plot to strip the South of power and to destroy its institutions. Northerners believed they had uncovered a scheme to control the federal government and to subvert the national purpose.

The North was called upon not only to free the Negro, but to save the basic American freedoms threatened by a "Slave Power Conspiracy." [13] This conspiracy, it was argued, designed to make the South safe for slavery, was also designed to spread slavery as a system of power over the nation. Amply documented in abolitionist literature, the arguments had considerable influence in attracting support from those who were repelled by abolition itself. Henry Wilson's *History of the Rise and Fall of the Slave Power in America* was one of the most effective postwar presentations,[14] but it was in the periodicals of abolition that the arguments were most extravagantly presented earlier. William Lloyd Garrison suggested in *The Liberator* that the conspiracy was in reality an alliance between the plantation owner and the northern industrialist. Such a conspiracy, nestled in the interest of class rather than in the interest of sections, transformed the simple and unqualified North-South cleavage into coincidence. Wendell Phillips, without benefit of Karl Marx, warned of an evil liaison between "the Lords of the Lash and the Lords of the Loom." In unrestrained and unambiguous language, he told the American Anti-slavery Society that organized wealth had conspired to destroy American freedom. The power of the cotton kingdom and the wealth of the industrial empire, warned another writer, "are combined to crush the liberal, free, progressive spirit of the age." This was the language of class struggle, not of sectional struggle.[15]

Living tissues of older antagonisms stretched across the years of battle and were projected into the atmosphere of an uneasy peace. Only the active verb differentiated earlier argumentation from the later dispute. Aggressive antislavery elements were responsible for the southern need for self-protection, and conspiratorial slavocrats remained a northern rationalization for violent self-defense. "Devil" theories, largely abandoned by historians in the closing decades of the nineteenth century, have not entirely disappeared. Eighty years after Fort Sumter, a respected southern university professor, Frank L. Owsley, wrote in the *Journal of Southern History:*

> . . . the Civil War had one basic cause: sectionalism: . . . Our national state was built, not upon foundations of a homogeneous land and people, but upon geographical sections inhabited severally by provincial, self-conscious, self-righteous, aggressive, and ambitious populations of varying origins and diverse social and economic systems; and the passage of time and the cumulative effect of history have accentuated these sectional patterns. . . .
>
> It was the egocentric, the destructive, the evil, the malignant type of sectionalism that destroyed the Union in 1861. . . . One has to seek in the unrestrained and furious invective of the present . . . to find a near parallel . . . neither Dr. Goebbels nor Virginio Gayda nor Stalin's propaganda agents have as yet been able to plumb the depths of vulgarity and obscenity reached and maintained by . . . Stephen Foster, Wendell Phillips, Charles Sumner, and other abolitionists of note.[16]

Another historian, writing in 1949, reviewed the evidence for the Southern conspiracy threat neither from the point of view of the North nor of the South:

> In the sense of the term as used . . . a secret and highly organized group with conscious aims of imposing restrictions upon traditional liberties . . . the "Slave Power conspiracy" had no real existence. The South was never so completely unified as to reveal evidence of a definite conspiracy . . . yet there evidently was agreement among certain Southern leaders that slavery was a good system, probably the best, and that it should be retained and possibly extended. Certainly the events of the period 1830 to 1860 showed that in preserving and extending it the South was willing to infringe upon basic civil and personal rights.

. . . While the "conspiracy" of which the abolitionists warned was no doubt simply an alliance of common economic and political interests, its inherent threat seemed to the times more than idle. The alliance itself was motivated by and founded upon the cardinal principle of slavery—the master principle—and the abolitionists were perhaps not so far wrong in believing that its existence jeopardized the American tradition.[17]

Constitutional arguments during the antebellum controversy persisted long after it.[18] Disquisitions on the nature of the Union continued to be written after Northern victory. For Southern apologists they provided a rationale; for Northern apologists they provided a vindication. Jefferson Davis, president of the Confederacy, and Alexander H. Stephens, its vice-president, pled the Southern case, which in the deepest personal sense was also their own. They insisted that expansion of federal powers had no constitutional warrant. Davis presented his plea in 1881 in *The Rise and Fall of the Confederate Government* and again in 1890 in the posthumously published *A Short History of the Confederate States of America*.[19] Regardless of the protocol of language, the inference was unavoidable. If the verdict of the battlefield went against the South, a proper reading of the Constitution nevertheless proved the Southerners to have been constitutionally right. Yet Northern exponents of the inviolability of the Union who crossed legal swords with former Confederate leaders found themselves in a weak forensic position. And the arguments of Stephens and Davis were likewise weakened by their successors in positions of Southern influence. In fact, the Northern victors in the period of Reconstruction changed constitutional sides with their recent adversaries. The Northern view in 1861 was premised upon the perpetuity of the Union and the illegality of secession. The American republic was not a compact among individually sovereign states; it was an indestructible union. Consistency demanded that the Southern states resume their normal relations within the federal structure. As secession was invalid, the Confederate States had never been out of the Union. States could not withdraw from the United States; they could only rebel against it. But it was Southerners who maintained after the war that the members of the Confederacy had never been out of the Union. It was Northerners who based theories of radical reconstruction on the premise that secession had dissolved the fabric of union.

But Southerners were constrained to show that slavery had little or nothing to do with either sectional conflict or secession. Slavery was collateral, an incident of economics and cultural growth. The

Union, as Southerners presented the matter, was breached following unlawful intrusions of a government committed to centralization. Misguided Northern groups and perverted anti-Southern agitators acted on mistaken premises. If the conflict was irrepressible, it was not because of slavery; it was an "irrepressible conflict" between opposing principles of constitutional government. Alexander H. Stephens compiled his own history of the war, *A Constitutional View of the Late War Between the States,* in which he expounded these notions as fervidly as he had in the period before the South was defeated.

> It is a postulate, with many writers of this day, that the late War was the result of two opposing ideas, or principles, upon the subject of African Slavery. Between these, according to their theory, sprung the "irrepressible conflict" in principle, which ended in the terrible conflict of arms. Those who assume this postulate, and so theorize upon it, are but superficial observers.
>
> That the War had its origin in *opposing principles,* which in their action upon the *conduct of men,* produced the ultimate collision of arms, may be assumed as an unquestionable fact. But the opposing principles which produced these results in physical action were of a very different character from those assumed in the postulate. They lay in the organic Structure of the Government of the States. The conflict in principle arose from different and opposing ideas as to the nature of what is known as the General Government. The conflict was between those who held it to be strictly Federal in its character, and those who maintained that it was thoroughly National. It was a strife between the principles of Federation, on the one side, and Centralism, or Consolidation on the other.
>
> Slavery, so called, was but *the question* on which these antagonistic principles, which had been in conflict, from the beginning, on diverse *other questions,* were finally brought into actual and active collision. . . .
>
> Some of the strongest Anti-slavery men who ever lived were on the side of those who opposed the Centralizing principles, which led to the War.
>
> The contest . . . which ended in War, was, indeed, a contest between opposing principles; but not such as bore upon the policy or impolicy of African Subordination. They were principles deeply underlying all considerations of that sort. They involved the very nature and organic Structure of the Government itself.[20]

As a responsible constitutional opinion, Stephens' case might have carried more conviction had he not himself earlier negated it. Speaking at Savannah, Georgia, March 21, 1861, to celebrate the new Constitution of the Confederate States of America, he took the other side:

> The new constitution has put at rest, *forever,* all the agitating questions relating to our peculiar institution—African slavery as it exists amongst

us—the proper *status* of the negro in our form of civilization. This was the immediate cause of the late rupture and present revolution.

The conceptions of Thomas Jefferson, he continued,

> and most of the leading statesmen at the time of the formation of the old constitution, were that the enslavement of the African was . . . wrong in *principle,* socially, morally, and politically. . . . This was an error. . . .
> Our new government is founded upon exactly the opposite idea; its foundations are laid, its cornerstone rests upon the great truth, that the negro is not equal to the white man; that slavery—subordination to the superior race—is his natural and normal condition.
> This, our new government, is the first, in the history of the world, based upon this great physical, philosophical, and, moral truth.[21]

John William Burgess, dean of the graduate faculty of Columbia and one of the deans of the new scientific school of historians, forcefully took up the rebuttal. In *The Middle Period 1817–1858,* published in 1897, and *The Civil War and the Constitution 1859–1865,* published in 1901, Stephens and Davis were controverted on their own legal grounds.

> The theory upon which the claimed right of secession was based was that the United States were a confederation of sovereignties, connected with each other by an agreement, from which each might secede at its own pleasure, without any legal power on the part of the others to prevent it. . . .
> It would be strange indeed if the fathers of the Union did intentionally legalize disunion and anarchy. . . . It is . . . entirely evident to any impartial mind that the Congress [which proposed the tenth amendment] never intended to reserve by it the power of disunion or secession to anybody.[22]

During the final decades of the nineteenth century, the scientific school of historians began to reshape professional standards and objectives. The scientific historians gave a new formulation to old problems and devised new techniques for solving them. Analysis succeeded narration, a search for "underlying causes" succeeded the search for guilt and retribution. The historians of the late nineteenth century, a generation removed from the age of hate, labored to snuff out prejudice. They schooled themselves to look at both sides, discarded pejorative symbols, and gave up simplistic theories of causation. The famed historians, James Ford Rhodes, James Schouler, and John Bach McMaster, presented a meticulous recital of events with noticeable restraint and candor. There were no Prescotts or Parkmans to recount the trauma of division and the epic of fratricidal war. But the scientific historians searched for the sources of human motivation and for the mainsprings of action; they traced the reverberations of events in human thought and emotion. Often they searched for them without explicit awareness, for values were implicit in the attempt. The ethics of slavery, the moral obligation involved in constitutional principles, fidelity to historic compromise were recurrent themes and were accorded full weight as decisive explanations.

Slavery remained in the foreground, for these historians found it difficult to comprehend the severence of the Union unless some place were found for one of the factors which helped to tear it apart. They freely granted that some abolitionists were fanatics; yet abolitionists, otherwise reasonable, seemingly were not unmoved by moral considerations. The South, as all shades of opinion admitted without argument, had erected a social and economic system in which slavery had a role. Patterns of Southern society, however various, possessed a strand of slavery, whether dominant or subdued in the motif. Land, transportation, and capital were segments of the economic whole, but the labor force was likewise a vital element. And the repeated references to the "peculiar institution" in the literature of Southern propaganda, not to stress the secession debate, offered confirmation to those who required it. In any case, the roster of historians and their imposing volumes testify to their earnestness. Slavery and politics were integral parts of the controversy for which adequate explanations had to be found if any satisfying meanings could be attached to the war. Beginning with John W. Draper's three-volume *History of the American Civil War* (1867–70) until well into the following century, this approach was persuasively and consistently argued.[23]

The war ended the rebellion and discredited armed revolt as a technique of American dissent. The war, however, did not end the states'-rights argument, although jurists and constitutional theorists have established the illegality of secession and the limitations of states' rights in a democratic federal system. Arthur M. Schlesinger, Sr., convincingly established that states' rights was more often a fetish than a viable method of balance of power. "The states rights doctrine," he wrote in 1922, "has never had any real vitality independent of underlying conditions of vast social, economic or political significance." States' rights remain in practice what they always have been, a shield of protection for special or local interests in defiance of majority will. The Southern states had no monopoly on the doctrine nor were they historically unique among sections or groups seeking particular advantages. "The group advocating states rights at any period have sought its shelter in much the same spirit that a

western pioneer seeks his storm-cellar when a tornado is raging." [24]
Constitutional arguments gave the late nineteenth-century dispute
a special legal character. Debate almost inevitably became an exegesis. Constitutional texts and other authorities were matched against
other constitutional texts and other authorities. An analysis of
American federalism turned out to be an analysis of what the
framers were thought to have intended rather than an assessment of
living changes and realities. [25] To make disruption a purely legal
problem distorted its essential nature. A conflict, primarily constitutional and involving a distribution of government power, circumscribed the range of thought. There were theoretical issues demanding elaboration, but they required cultivation beyond a narrow legal
focus. Charles A. and Mary R. Beard were convinced in 1927 that
legal and constitutional arguments were simply verbalizations.

> When the modern student examines all the verbal disputes over the
> nature of the Union . . . he can hardly do otherwise than conclude that
> the linguistic devices used first on one side and then on the other were
> not derived from inherently necessary concepts concerning the intimate
> essence of the federal system. The roots of controversy lay elsewhere. [26]

Many historians have since concurred. Some would probably cau-
tion that legal and constitutional issues powerfully moved the men of
the Civil War era just as the larger meanings have concerned their
compatriots ever since. Among the roots of the controversy was a
problem related to the constitutional phase, a problem unsolved except legally. In the democratic process of agreement and decision
real differences of interest and belief actually divide society.

The specific purposes of 1787, together with the correlates of
older constitutional premises, acquired a validity unqualified by seventy-four years of social change. But federal systems, as former Supreme Court Justice Felix Frankfurter observed, "are not the offspring of political science; they are the product of economic and
social pressures." [27] Social and economic pressures of the eighteenth
century, however, were not those of the nineteenth. While few historians failed to recognize some cogency in this contention, constitutional disputants often referred nineteenth-century changes to eighteenth-century standards of value and eighteenth-century institutional
arrangements. Twentieth-century standards and values, sometimes
read into nineteenth-century conditions, have confused historical
understandings. Arthur E. Bestor has carefully meditated this particular confusion.

> One simple fact is often forgotten. Secession was the *alternative* to, not
> the purported *outcome* of, the constitutional program that proslavery

forces advocated, in the name of state sovereignty, during the controversy over slavery in the territories. This alternative—dissolution of the Union —doubtless lay in the back of the minds of increasing numbers of pro-slavery leaders as the year 1860 approached. Nevertheless, the actual proposals they were offering from 1846 to 1860 presupposed the continued existence of the federal system. The defenders of slavery wished the constitutional machinery to function in such a way as to give maximum protection to slavery. This meant, of necessity, that they were still committed to the view that the Constitution was a machine that could and should be made to work. Only after they had opted for secession did they look upon the old Constitution as a wreck to be dismantled.[28]

The import of this distinction for historiography is far-reaching. If Southern exegetes presupposed the existence of the Constitution and the federal system, the "underlying causes" are not to be sought in the document alone, but in the methods fashioned to operate it. Secession, as a constitutional argument, was a final stand taken only after an institutional impasse had been reached.

For some historians, constitutional dialectic was often no more than a logical exercise. Efforts to diagnose the breach in a living culture by constitutional analyses alone was to view government and society in static terms. Hypotheses formulated in a social vacuum resulted in the paradox of stressing the written constitution to the neglect of the unwritten constitution. John W. Burgess, for example, highlighted this distinction in a brief portrait of Jefferson Davis.

> He saw very clearly, but not deeply. He was logical rather than intui-
> tive, and possessed little real imagination. From given premises he rea-
> soned with great exactness, but had neither the inductive power nor the
> power of insight necessary to the discovery of principles or axioms upon
> which he based his syllogisms. The letter of the Constitution, as the fa-
> thers made it, was his political bible, and he manifested nowhere the
> slightest appreciation of the consideration that the fathers might have
> failed to give exact expression, in the instrument, to the political and so-
> cial conditions, or of the consideration that those conditions might have
> so changed through the natural course of human development as to re-
> quire either a revision of the instrument, or the employment of methods
> of liberal interpretation, such as would enable the political forces and
> ideas, existing at any given moment, to find some expression through it.[29]

State laws, federal statutes, court decisions, tradition, custom, usage, and institutions appearing in response to innovation not only furthered social change, but also altered the Constitution. Political parties—themselves extraconstitutional devices—changed the Constitution and society as well. Constitutional historians gave these factors comparatively little argumentative weight. They rarely embraced the dynamic view represented by William B. Munro, a political scientist as well as a historian:

The makers of the American Constitution neither began nor finished their work in the summer of 1787. Their ancestors began it at Runnymede and continued it at Westminster. Their descendants have kept bravely at the work since the Great Convention adjourned. It is often said that the last framer of the Constitution passed off the scene with Madison's death in 1836; but Marshall and Jackson were giving new significance to the supreme law of the land when Madison died. Nor were they the last of the line. In a wider sense of the term the makers of the American Constitution form a great and still growing company. The list will not be closed until the end of time.[30]

Constitutional arguments, recast in the language of economic and political power, converged to produce the modern historical discussion. Slavery became an appendage to larger considerations as economics acquired increasing prominence. That slavery was a moral problem was, of course, granted, but its connections with land valuation and territorial expansion seemed to promise more fertile exploratory yields. Studies investigating markets, trade, sectionalism, population, and the westward movement amassed evidence of economic behavior and interactivity. The economic interpretation of the Civil War, advanced in countless articles and books, was fully developed between the two world wars. Based upon a staggering amount of original research excavated by a generation of scholarship, the economic interpretation wielded a pervasive influence and was not seriously challenged until the period of the second global war.[31]

Economic argument was modern rather than new. Strong undertones of economics were implicit in the thesis of conspiracy and in constitutional and moral interpretations. The great sectional divide, a cultural split dating from colonial days, separated South from North by differences in soil, climate, and economic activity. Slavery, a sin to Northern abolitionists and a virtue to Southern propagandists, was none the less a labor system. And the attitudes of sectionalism were expressed as violently in respose to tariff, land, internal improvements, subsidies to business, and immigration policy. Calhoun, Clay, Webster, and Jefferson Davis spoke in the accents of economic sectionalism, accents their descendants in Richmond and Washington rarely outgrew. If it was difficult to divorce one set of drives from another, it was easier to perceive a struggle for economic advantage and control. It was easy to infer that professions of moral indignation regarding slavery or of strict constitutional virtue relating to minority rights had something to do with economic and political power.

Historians did not always find it necessary to resort to inference. Senator Robert Toombs of Georgia informed the legislature of his state in 1860 that "the instant the Government was organized, at the very first Congress, the Northern States evinced a general desire and purpose to use it for their own benefit, and to pervert its powers for sectional advantage, and they have steadily pursued that policy to this day." [32] Identical forensics by statesmen, propagandists, and scholars informed the historians who devised the subtler interpretation of economic motivations and of revolutions in the power structure.

Elements of economic sectionalism were integrated in 1903 by Algie M. Simons. In an essay entitled "Class Struggles in America," followed in 1911 by *Social Forces in American History,* Simons presented the Civil War as a power struggle in Marxian terms. "Political struggles are based upon economic interests," Simons announced in the preface to the latter, and the Civil War became inevitable after the Republican Party, representing Northern capitalism, captured sectional dominance. "When that party obtained control of the national government, the chattel slave interests, realizing that no social system can hope to prosper within a government which it does not control, felt that secession was necessary." He also anticipated the interpretation of the power revolution subsequently allied with the economic view of Civil War causation:

> Out of the Civil War was born the elements of present society. It created the great capitalist and the great industry and the mechanical foundation upon which these rest. It placed these in control of the national government, and for the next generation capitalism was to find its greatest development in the nation the war had maintained as a unit.[33]

But *The Rise of American Civilization* by Charles A. and Mary R. Beard in 1927, a synthesis of scholarship, presented the economic interpretation with the luxuriant sweep of gifted minds. The roots of controversy, wrote the Beards, did not lie in contests over slavery or in differing views of the Constitution.

> The roots of controversy lay . . . in social groupings founded on differences in climate, soil, industries, and labor systems, in divergent social forces, rather than varying degrees of righteousness and wisdom, or what romantic historians call "the magnetism of great personalities." [34]

The clash between the agrarian South and the industrial North was irrepressible. If the leaders of competing sections were determined to capture the federal government in order to protect and expand their respective interests, a real adjustment was illusory. A conspiracy was on foot, though not a species of conspiracy outlined by Wendell Phillips. Adjustment was conceivable only if change was stabilized. But no artful compromise seemed capable of arresting events, events which not only altered the two hostile sections but altered the relations existing between them. The final breach could be deferred; it could not be prevented. The balance of change, now tipped in favor of the North, now in favor of the South, would ultimately outweigh the interests of one or the other. Either the South would be prompted to secede or the North would be induced to limit and subvert Southern institutions.

The historical reconstruction of economic sectionalism presupposed that each section had become a self-conscious unit, aggressive, militant, and confident. The two sections became so differentiated that they more closely resembled separate nations than different national regions. The outcome of the struggle for power, according to this scheme of analysis, was determined, once it became clear to the leaders of the minority section that economic forces, reflected in the census, in immigration, and the statistics of industrial potential, were leagued against the prospects of a workable adjustment. Equally determinable was the outcome, once it became clear to the leaders of the majority section that the "destiny" of the North was incompatible with the "destiny" of the South. The corollary of this insight suggested that the South obstructed Northern objectives through an unwarranted influence of power in the various branches of the government. Louis M. Hacker, economic historian at Columbia, gave particular attention to this theme of Civil War reinterpretation in 1935:

> War was nothing less than a conflict between two different systems of economic production; and with the victory at the Presidential polls in 1860 of the higher order, the young industrial capitalism of the North and Middle West, a counter-revolutionary movement was launched by the defenders of the lower order, the slave lords of the South.
>
> The politics of compromise of the two decades preceding the opening of hostilities have completely obscured the economics and class basis of the maneuvers: that the slave masters, in the interest of the maintenance of their peculiar institution, were using every agency at their command —legislative, executive, and judicial—to prevent the growth to power and maturity of rising industrial capitalism. . . . With its control over the instrumentalities of government in the decades before the war the South was able to frustrate every hope of the industrial capitalists of the North and block up their every possible avenue of expansion.[35]

Civilization in America was either to be industrial or agrarian. Either it was to be based on tariffs, banks, sound finance, immigration, and free domestic markets in the West or on slavery, one-crop systems, decentralized banking, revenue tariffs, and a closely stratified and technically homogeneous society.[36] This interpretation made constitutional arguments subservient to economics and moral arguments subservient to power. This interpretation seemed also to make man the victim of impersonal forces beyond his control. Sectional hostility making for "irrepressible conflict" evoked an image of Southern nationalism. The image of nationalism appealed to some Civil War scholars for its own sake, since nationalism, as its learned historian Hans Kohn remarked, "is first and foremost a state of mind, and act of consciousness." [37] In addition, another dimension of inquiry promised the discovery of neglected or unknown elements in the hidden equation of meanings. The concept of Southern nationalism was enticing because to unravel the mind of the South was a token of scholarship to which students had given their pledge. Irrepressible conflict was a clash of tragic proportions that left man with nothing but the power to retort. If man was gripped by inscrutable forces, he could at least respond with dignity. Economic interpretations stripped him of proud motives and tied him to the values of the slave auction and the ethics of double-entry account books. The thesis of sectionalism left each area starkly different without the blessed relief of similarity. Historians, like most other men, are too human to remain content with the irremediable cash nexus. Dominance of given factors there might well have been, but sheer unanimity and unqualified singularity were beyond credence. Fuller study of Southern culture might conceivably adjust the ledger of responsibility. Those unforgiving about slavery might find more in the South than slaves, overseers, and plantation owners. The concept of Southern nationalism also promised a calm exploration of the continuing sources of Southern life. Insistence on agrarian virtue as contrasted with industrial evil invited reassessment in historical depth. For centuries Southerners had taken their resolute stand with Jefferson's rural ways. If Southern nationalism actually represented an integrated agrarian culture that humanized man, there was more to Southern society than jasmine, gentility, and racial inequality.

Consciousness of nationalism developed in the South in the ten-year period before secession. At the Nashville Convention, November 14, 1850, Langdon Cheves, an esteemed South Carolinian, gave these sentiments fervent expression:

> Our Constitution has been completely and forever subverted. . . . What is the remedy? I answer: secession—united secession of the slave-holding States. Nothing else will be wise—nothing else will be practicable. . . . Unite, and you shall form one of the most splendid empires on which the sun ever shone, of the most homogeneous population, all of the same blood and lineage, a soil the most fruitful, and a climate the most

lovely. . . . O, Great God, unite us, and a tale of submission shall never be told.[38]

A nationalistic urge paralleled the growing acuteness of sectionalism which historians could hardly fail to note. Edward Channing entitled the sixth volume of his famed series *The War for Southern Independence,* but the most painstaking study of Southern nationalism was made in 1949 by Rollin G. Osterweis. Osterweis selected South Carolina as the most striking instance and the nationalism he described was a nationalism of a special kind.

> Southern nationalism . . . stressed the peculiarities of its particular traditions and institutions. In common with the romantic nationalisms of central Europe in the nineteenth century, the frontiers of the existing state and the rising nationality did not coincide. The movement expanded in protest against, and in conflict with, the de facto government. The effort was not to alter the existing political organization, as in the case of the thirteen colonies, but to redraw boundaries that would conform to mythical but credited ethnographic needs. That the realities behind the myth were the institution of Negro slavery and the plantation system do not affect the situation. They merely provide the identifying features.[39]

In the American environment of sectional struggle during the prewar years, Southern nationalism was the preface to secession. Although stressing factors other than economic, the hypothesis of Southern nationalism is a part of the irrepressible-conflict approach.

Irrepressible-conflict theories appealed to the "lost generation" of the years after World War I and to those for whom the great depression was an object lesson in economics. While economic interpretations continued to multiply, competing hypotheses organized the multifarious data in other ways. Scholars became involved in a review of their own methods and were led to query whether the questions they asked of the facts were calculated to supply the type of answers sought. World events between the wars impressed a growing number of students with the need to face values squarely. The centrality of the slavery issue as a "cause" of the Civil War reappeared as many investigators, stirred by the prologue to World War II, concluded that moral issues were ignored at a price too high to pay. World War II itself, and later Korea, also turned minds toward speculation about irresistible forces beyond the immediate control of men, and Freud and his successors induced others to think of irrational behavior as a potent factor in the affairs of men and of society. In Civil War historiography, these trends assumed two contrasting intellectual forms: one the "irrepressible conflict"; the other, "the blundering generation." Sophisticated notions of method effected changes in emphasis if not technique. On the one hand, efforts were made to frame more manageable hypotheses. On the other hand, there was a search for more inclusive ones.

Civil War scholarship informs American historiography. It provides a profile of the problems, confusions, and triumphs of historical reconstruction. Any previous major issue supplies a cross-section of the historian's dilemmas and achievements. But the Civil War has a particular significance in American historical writing because the Civil War has a particular significance in American history. Not merely because it was a war, although the largest and most destructive up to that point, were historians and other scholars unable to resist it. Not only because it was a civil war have American scholars felt charged to decipher it. Every historical reconstruction is involved in what Henry Seidel Canby, describing the war itself, called "the heavy payment of innocent men for the will of their ancestors." [40] The past exacts a price of every future, and historians, simply by writing, mortgage the outlook of their successors. The war itself shaped the milieu for the life of two generations; historians drew the frontiers of interpretation.

The battles of the war were fought over again in books and articles. Northerners armed with a thesis were arrayed against Southerners armed with a heritage. Southerners took a Northern stance, and Northerners acquired an affection for Dixie. Some with attachments to both or with allegiance to none took no stand at all, but they were nevertheless fighting the war of causes all over again. Regardless of avowed purpose or unconscious intent, all asked the same fundamental question: where did responsibility lie?

Whatever the variety of question, it was in some way linked to responsibility. Even if individual men were absolved, historians could not avoid weighing social responsibility. Were society and individuals held to be free of complicity, then factors beyond human power had still to be assessed. American historians following the Civil War had wide experience with war as a category of social occurrence. They were familiar with religious, dynastic, national, and defensive wars. They had an intimate knowledge of wars of revolution and wars of liberation. They were likewise familiar with civil wars. But the American Civil War was a war fought in the modern era, a war that disrupted a society conceived and dedicated to the propositions of democracy. It was their war. Until World War I bared the illusions of western society and World War II irretrievably shifted western perspectives, the Civil War appeared as the most shocking and incomprehensible series of events in American experience. But the meaning of the war—the processes fomenting its eruption and the consequences stemming from its occurrence—eluded unremitting labor and the subtlest ingenuity. After more than a hundred years there is no general agreement and no single explanation sufficient to satisfy the community of specialists. A century of search and research establishes each view and each interpretation as one previously expressed either before or shortly after the war. Scholars are unanimous only in concluding that the problem of the Civil War is a complicated one, far more complicated than any of their predecessors realized. It is also conceded with fair unanimity that no single explanation will suffice, a methodological principle to which Civil War historiography has simply added confirmation.

XVII

New Techniques and
New Perspectives

Long after time had transformed the great American conflict into the great lost cause, partisans continued to fight its battles and to debate its issues with belligerent words. But the continuing issues confronting historians in the years after the Civil War were older than Gettysburg and more crucial than the election of the critical year. Historical scholars had to explain their world to themselves. Challenged by events, they were forced to ask themselves, to use Henry Adams' phrase, if the standard formulas had failed. Division and reunion did not alter the nature of the historical quest, which remained, as always, the quest for understanding. There were, of course, few scholars like Henry Adams who had sufficient knowledge to make a frontal assault on confusion. But there were scores of men who, in varying ways and with varying results, strove to bring intellectual order out of the chaos presented by the unrelated flow of experience.

The Civil War demanded a re-evaluation of American historical experience. It was not only the war itself that required explanation but the meaning of the American experiment. Answers fashioned by the revolutionary generation and their successors in thought were no longer adequate. The splintering of the Union and its preservation added new data; the consequences of war and peace added new cultural dimensions. Patriotism and nationalism stimulated interest and inquiry, but patriotism and nationalism were surface manifestations of a profounder need for emotional justification and intellectual direction. Change influenced history and historians alike. War and reconstruction, industrial development, and urban growth altered historical emphases at the same time that they altered the conditions of life. The movements of events in time continued to mold the reconstruction of the American past after the Civil War as before it. The constant reappraisal of experience is central to human existence. Each generation must come to intellectual terms with its past, and the process can only take place in the present. Man is forced to face new events and to find place for them in "the scheme of things." Cotton Mather knew with certainty when he encountered a "remarkable providence." He knew with equal certainty where it belonged in the scale of Puritan meanings. George Bancroft was no less certain. He too embraced a metaphysics of value which enabled him to assign significance and direction to the movement of events in time. Between the underlying assumptions of George Bancroft and those of Cotton Mather there is less difference than has commonly been supposed. Historians after the Civil War were led to make other and different assumptions.

A task of synthesis became increasingly difficult. The organization and transmission of learning remained the social function of scholarship, but the conditions under which learning was organized and transmitted were transformed. Changing methods of organization, in scholarship as elsewhere, altered the content and direction of human urges and human drives. New processes changed both the life of everyday living and the life of the mind. The impact of technology and the growth of cities on learning was, in one controlling respect, the same as the urban impact on other forms of human activity. Roles and functions were divided, and then divided again. Scholarship became institutionalized as industry was mechanized.

The revolutions in economics created a new America, and Americans took pride in national accomplishment. They looked backward to the emergence of the federal republic and forward to the progress of American democracy. If discord and difference existed everywhere, there was always hope in the future. Yet those who found cause for apprehension were few compared to the many who identified with the symbols of national wealth and national power. Sectional bitterness continued to mar the memories of living men and women who lived out their lives in defiance of reality. But new issues and new problems absorbed the energies of succeeding generations. The Philadelphia Centennial of 1876 was a double celebration. It marked the hundredth anniversary of American independence, and it also marked a hundred years of American progress. Americans divided their pride between the greatness of history in the making and the great history that had already been made.[1] Patriotic enthusiasms expressed themselves in specific historical directions. The dramatic episodes of war and social turmoil provided an atmosphere favorable to historical pursuits. Attention was again directed to records and documents and to the ever-present need to preserve them. Those who struggled to understand and explain events were acutely conscious of the written record always imperiled by the callousness of time and the heedless pressures of immediacy. Patriotism lent motivation to historical effort in other ways. The nation had experienced its greatest trial, and the factors that had produced civil strife demanded explication. For loser and victor alike, causes and consequences had to be formulated into patterns of explanation.

Historiography involves more than the writing of books. Like all activity, historical craftsmanship became increasingly interdependent. The reliance of scholars upon other men's books is as old as the written word, but there were other forms of silent collaboration. It was still necessary, as in the time of Jared Sparks, to journey to distant places to consult materials. More and more, however, materials were collected in depositories under the care of experts. Such experts spent as much time, effort, and zeal in assembling, housing, and making their treasures available to the learned public as was expended by the writers of books and articles themselves. Multiplication of aids to historical learning facilitated scholarly production. They also foreshadowed the wider development of aids to scholarship characteristic of our own day.

Chief among the aids to learning was the growth of libraries and historical societies devoted to the gathering and preservation of materials. College and university libraries, and the establishment of special collections, followed the advent of graduate instruction and innovations in collegiate education. Public libraries furthered scholarship simply by housing books and records in central depositories and by serving as disbursing points for study. The free public library, supported by taxation, began in New Hampshire, Massachusetts, and Maine in the mid-nineteenth century. Their numbers increased after 1865, and by 1875 there were two thousand. In 1900 five thousand four hundred free libraries with collections numbering more than a thousand volumes apiece already existed.[2] The phrase "aids to scholarship" has become a part of the vocabulary of learning. The idiom of specialization has gradually crept into conventional speech, a clear indication of an expanding division of labor and function. Collecting of books, documents, and manuscripts was once the avocation of the wealthy, but librarians, editors, and archivists soon came to have a recognized status in the guild of scholars. Transformations such as these provided the basis for John Spencer Bassett's later observation that "although the United States contains at present [1921] several times as many educated people as in 1876, there exists among them no historian who has the recognition enjoyed fifty years ago by Bancroft, Parkman, and some others." [3]

Historians following the Civil War were not as well known to the general public as Parkman and Bancroft, but specialists were better known to each other. New techniques of scholarship, like the devices of technology, formed an institutional web of interrelated parts. Societies, libraries, universities, and their auxiliaries—manuals, textbooks, guides, and card catalogues—formed an environment for the practice of history similar to the environment formed for the practice of all other disciplines. The very proliferation of disciplines was the hallmark of a new culture. History divorced itself from philosophy as it had earlier divorced itself from theology. Bancroft became "too philosophical" in the estimation of modern scholars. Prescott, Motley, and Parkman were lavishly praised by historians who were quick to add that the heroic triumvirate were practitioners of literature, not of "scientific" history.[4] Historians began to proclaim their complete independence from literature as well as philosophy, an independence some were later to think was maintained with far too literal a devotion. The historical critics of Francis Parkman were assiduously studied by other historians; but many Americans, ignoring the critics, continued to read Parkman's epic.

History was devoted to the study of society, but scholarship divided as society became more diversified. Political science, economics, and sociology pursued learning in their own separate ways, and reunion of thought and activity was difficult to obtain. The work of scholarship was intensified; it was also narrowed. "We have partially lost sight of the relation of history to other universes of thought," complained a student of historiography fresh from a study of the eighteenth century, "and in particular to the ethical universe." [5] History, having become scientific, has lost its contact with values. Lord Morley's strictures in his study of Diderot were even more emphatic.

> The conception of history has, on the whole, gone back rather than advanced within the last hundred years. There have been signs in our own day of its becoming narrow, pedantic, and trivial. It threatens to disintegrate from a broad survey of great periods and movements of

human societies into vast and countless accumulations of insignificant facts, sterile knowedge, and frivolous antiquarianism, in which the spirit of epochs is lost, and the direction, meaning, and summary of the various courses of human history all disappear.[6]

These results were, of course, clearer in the future. Men engaged in following the urges which prompt them are unlikely to calculate the remoter cultural consequences of their actions. Patriotic enthusiasm and genuine historical interest were motives sufficient in themselves. The sustained vandalism of war had demolished libraries, scattered records, and destroyed manuscripts. For those who loved the past the sacrilegious destruction of irreplaceable materials was but a single element in the composition of drives. They were also conscious of the grandeur of events to which they had been witness. And the sensitive were aware, even though dimly, of the historical implications of the large events with which they were associated. The almost unbelievable qualities of the human spirit precipitated by the cruel demands of wartime existence moved others to gather the records that told as much as words could tell. Official memoirs, statistics, and communiqués were part of the tangled experience; journals, diaries, letters were another. Posterity, forever barred from direct participation in past experience by its uniqueness, is forced to accept the vicarious ghost of reconstruction for the red badge of courageous living. Only the creative imagination of scholarship and the creative power of insight—really aspects of the same thing—make it possible for historians to preserve the past.

And strive to preserve it they certainly did. But it was not alone the war which laid claim to their energies. Some fixed their attention on the settlements of the western frontier where, as Frederick Jackson Turner said, men and women were beginning life over again. Those who looked westward were determined that the press of survival and the lust for material accomplishment should not blot out stages by which survival was threatened and performance achieved. Others again looked further backward in time and place to rediscover the older historic links which had made the nation one before a "blundering generation" almost succeeded in permanently sundering it. To preserve these historical traditions was one of the functions of historical societies.

Historical societies had been in operation since 1791, when the Massachusetts Historical Society began its pioneer existence. Citizens in other states, initially stirred as much by local self-consciousness as by a consciousness of history, followed the example of the Bay State. The Massachusetts group was seconded in 1804 by the

New-York Historical Society and eight years later by the American Antiquarian Society, which, as such things were then reckoned, was a gain for the city of Worcester and the state of Massachusetts. Between 1822 and 1831 the Rhode Island, Maine, New Hampshire, Pennsylvania, Connecticut, and Virginia societies were established.[7] Members of these societies were often absorbed in family records, usually the records of great families, and devoted to historical affairs as local and minute as only a pious antiquarianism could make them. The first period of their history matched the first period of the history of the Republic: concerns were local, and the local concerns of the state were paramount. Yet they published reports, collections, and proceedings which, particularly for the states that made an early start, contained research materials of the highest relevance for the nation at large. J. Franklin Jameson, a most reliable authority on records and research, was severely critical of the positive contributions made by eastern historical societies. He conceded that they possessed materials "great and rich," but he knew of no "instance in which the publishing authorities of any eastern historical society" had "set on foot any serious researches. . . . Seldom indeed do they touch the period since 1783." [8] Jameson's condemnation is certainly too sweeping. The kind of research projects envisaged in 1910 when this comment was written were not ordinarily conceived during the forty years after the Civil War. And interest in American development before 1783 was, of course, a perfectly legitimate interest, provided only it was historical and not antiquarian. One cannot think of historical societies without thinking at the same time of the raw materials of understanding available in their proceedings and reports. Nor can one fairly ignore the ripe scholarship in the pages of the publications of the Massachusetts Historical Society and the Pennsylvania Historical Society, to name but two among many other claimants for inclusion. After the Civil War better organizations, better-trained personnel, and a clearer judgment of historical purpose produced both an improvement and an increase of activity. *The Pennsylvania Magazine of History and Biography* commenced publication in 1877, the *Virginia Magazine of History and Biography* in 1893.[9]

Western historical societies closely resembled their eastern counterparts. At first autonomous bodies dependent upon private support, they finally became state historical societies. As such they were in contact with the historians of the state universities, who in turn were in touch with historical activities locally and nationally. Wisconsin and Minnesota became the first state historical societies, to be followed, among others, by Illinois, Michigan, and Indiana. With the appearance of industrious and imaginative collectors, editors, and scholars these groups became centers of research and publishing easily the equals of the eastern historical associations.[10]

Continuing the formidable work begun by Jeremy Belknap and furthered by Jared Sparks, the compiling and editing of historical materials made remarkable advances. One of the most memorable editors and collectors was Lyman Copeland Draper, who probably did as much for the development of frontier history as anyone who came before him.[11] Immersed in frontier legends and tales of Indian struggles, he read whatever books dealing with American history that came his way. His reading did nothing to lessen his boyhood passion, although the quality of the reading matter persuaded him to think that he could do better. This resolve was induced less by the books he read—which were not of a high order—than by the conviction, shared by many men, that given the opportunity one could improve on what had already been done. He set himself to write the biographies of his frontier heroes and to insure accuracy and vividness, he tried to put himself in contact with their living descendants. Correspondence was the obvious method, and he used it wherever it would bring results. But he desired to get even closer to the sources. He stalked the survivors of the makers of early frontier history southward from western New York to Alabama and Mississippi.[12] The proceeds of these journeys were masses of anecdotes and recollections taken down from the lips of the aged who had witnessed the events and had known the participants. He also amassed a respectable collection of manuscripts in the course of his peregrinations along the Allegheny frontier. When in 1854, the State Historical Society of Wisconsin was reorganized, Draper was invited to become its secretary. He accepted, remaining in the post until 1886, when he retired after having built up the Society's library from virtually nothing to 118,000 volumes.[13] During part of his tenure he also served as state superintendent of public instruction, and it was in this office that he secured the enactment of a bill creating township libraries.[14] Funds had previously been allocated for this purpose but had been diverted to other uses during the Civil War. The first ten volumes of the *Collections*[15] of the Wisconsin Historical Society published under Draper's editorship, and with his notes, are a permanent tribute to his industry and scholarship.

Draper was followed in 1887 by Reuben G. Thwaites, who retained his connection with the Wisconsin Historical Society until 1913.[16] Not an outstanding critic or a writer of the first grade, he was pre-eminently an organizer and collector. As such he ranks with the highest. Under his direction the Library of the Society became "one of America's greatest historical workshops" [17] in the opinion of Frederick Jackson Turner, whose measured praise is a guarantee of accuracy. As a young instructor at the University of Wisconsin, Turner was in almost daily contact with Thwaites, and the image of Turner and his disciples working in the Library of the Historical Society is one of the traditions of American historiography.[18]

In sheer quantity of production Thwaites has few competitors. He wrote fifteen books himself, and more than a hundred and sixty additional volumes stand to his editorial credit. An eight-volume edition of the *Original Journals of Lewis and Clark*[19] provided a documentary record of the primitive west to which it is still difficult to find a comparable parallel. *The Jesuit Relations and Allied Documents,*[20] a triumph of skill and salvation, would by itself have secured any editorial reputation. Published between 1896 and 1901, these seventy-three volumes made it possible to comprehend the task and to assess the contributions of the Jesuit missionaries. Coming soon after Parkman's well-earned vogue, *Jesuit Relations* again revealed the European venture in colonization and settlement as a joint cultural enterprise. And for the students who were beginning to attach special national significance to the colonization and settlement of the West, the knowledge of French-Catholic activity during earlier times should have proved helpful. The unadorned records of the *Jesuit Relations* exposed in its fullness a magnificence of courage and selfless devotion that Parkman's Protestant bias occasionally obscured.[21] From the documents of the Jesuits a crystal conclusion emerged on virtually every page; if the French missionaries failed, it was neither because they were French nor because they were Catholic. A garnet of hypotheses stemmed from this generalization which few historians of the early American West chose to elaborate. *Jesuit Relations* comprised works previously printed but so rare as to be almost unattainable—to which Thwaites added manuscript sources. Of particular value were the annual reports filed in France that broadened information already supplied by the published accounts of such explorers as Champlain.

Thwaites buttressed the record of frontier evolution with a collection of western travels.[22] In thirty-two invaluable volumes, scarce and out-of-print books covering the years from 1748 to 1846, were finally incorporated into the public domain of scholarship. The *Early Western Travels*, wrote Turner, "present a picture of the irresistible tide of American settlement flowing into the wilderness, of societies forming in the forests, of cities evolving almost under our gaze as we see them through the eyes of these travelers in successive years." [23] Turner, of course, was right, and the achievement of collecting was not salvage alone but accessibility. Editors could hardly fail to operate on the assumption that historical documents are public documents and constitute a public trust.

That Reuben G. Thwaites was a master of organization is demonstrated by his collections, but he also demonstrated his capacity in administration. It was he who tightened the relationship between State University and State Historical Society, a relationship rewarding to both. Thwaites laid the groundwork for Wisconsin and supplied a model for others to emulate. Clarence W. Alvord, a student of British politics in the Mississippi Valley, who aided Illinois in building a distinguished State Historical Society, was clearly in Thwaites' intellectual debt. And when Thwaites was succeeded by Milo M. Quaife in 1917 and followed in 1920 by Joseph Schafer— both devoted investigators of western significance—they found a splendid basis from which to continue the admirable work.[24]

With the threat of national dissolution happily over and with the frightful war at last ended, the tranquillity of the remote past again exerted an irresistible appeal. The centennial year, centering attention on 1776, suggested the ultimate beginnings of American history. Whatever the reasons, the era of discovery and exploration excited new and sustained interest. John Carter Brown, wealthy member of a noted Rhode Island family and an assiduous collector of materials relating to early America, became the center of a like-minded group. Brown was seconded in what he called "the great subject" by James Lenox of New York,[25] and as a result of a tireless search for books they built up libraries that only great private wealth could afford. Both collections finally became the property of the public: the first as part of the John Carter Brown Library of Providence, Rhode Island; the second as part of the New York Public Library. The life and meaning of Columbus became almost an obsession, and Verrazano could never be ignored by those investigating the career of Spain's daring admiral. Samuel L. M. Barlow, also of New York, was thoroughly captivated by Columbian studies, which, together with other topics relating to exploration, were his passion. "Next to Christianity," he wrote, "the discovery of the New World was the greatest event of our era." [26]

"The great subject" prompted immediate research. A study of Verrazano by James C. Brevoort, a New York businessman for whom history was an avocation, appeared in 1874. Another New

York bibliophile, Henry Cruse Murphy, made Verrazano the subject of his investigations. One book on Verrazano usually provoked another, and Murphy's *The Voyage of Verrazano,* while not specifically in answer to Brevoort, took a decidedly different position.

One of the greatest exponents of the "great subject" was Justin Winsor, born in Boston in 1831, who early decided to make literature his career. Having made this decision, he forsook Harvard for an education planned by himself. He was soon forced to concede that he was not likely to make his mark in creative literature, although he wrote a good deal and projected a great deal more that was never written. His creative life really began when he was appointed librarian of the Boston Public Library in 1868. Winsor was a scholar's librarian, and in 1877 Harvard invited him to a similar post. There he remained until his death in 1897, serving scholars and scholarship alike.[27]

Justin Winsor's enthusiasm for the period of colonization was partly the result of his enthusiasm for cartography. On the subject of the cartography of colonization he was an early American master. His study of Columbus, *Christopher Columbus and How He Received and Imparted the Spirit of Discovery,* was primarily notable for its presentation of the evolution of geographical knowledge. In fact his maps and the text covering this portion of the topic represented the fullest and most reliable account available before the present century. Winsor continued his studies of discovery and exploration in *From Cartier to Frontenac, The Mississippi Basin,* and *The Westward Movement* with much the same emphasis and achievement. As these volumes demonstrate, Winsor was probably wise in substituting a career of research for a career of literary craftsmanship. His works are crammed with the evidence of copious learning and conscientious research. For his maps, his bibliographies, and his insights, those who have traversed the same ground have had ample reason to be grateful. But his capacities for organization and expression were distinctly limited. He confessed that he conceived history "a thing of shreds and patches."

> I have only to say that the life of the world is a thing of shreds and patches, and it is only when we consider the well rounded life of the individual that we find permeating the record a reasonable constancy of purpose. This is the province of biography, and we must not confound biography with history.[28]

Previous to the publication of his volumes on exploration Winsor had served as editor of a co-operative history of Boston. The *Memorial History of Boston* and Winsor's part in it were thought by the publishers to have been so successful that they asked him to plan and edit a comprehensive American history. The completion, between 1884 and 1889, of the *Narrative and Critical History of America* in eight volumes was a landmark in American historiography. Five of the eight volumes comprised a history of both hemispheres up to the eighteenth century, two volumes dealt with the United States from 1763 to 1850, and the final volume continued with a narrative of the colonial powers—Spain, Portugal, and Great Britain—in the new world. Although thirty-nine writers collaborated to produce the *Narrative and Critical History,* it was largely the work of Winsor. Almost half was his own writing, he planned and edited the whole, and the finished product bears the stamp of his scholarship. The emphasis of the *History* is among the factors making it distinguished, for two world wars and two generations of scholarship were necessary before American historians began to study history in global perspective. Winsor's rare competence in cartography and bibliography is apparent in virtually every volume. The most important service rendered by the *History* was to bring scattered materials together within a single compass. Winsor's unequaled bibliographical knowledge paid rich dividends to students and the notes and critical evaluation of sources have not yet lost their value. *Aboriginal America,* the first volume, attests Winsor's veneration for the remote past, but the terminal date, 1850, suggests an aversion for the immediate present.

More striking than Justin Winsor was the dramatic Henry Harrise. Brought to America while still a boy, Harrise was born in Paris and was graduated from the University of South Carolina. After his admission to the bar he moved to New York and became acquainted with Samuel L. M. Barlow. Barlow gave him friendship and support and imbued him with his abiding love for the history of colonial discovery. Harrise, a willing convert, formulated a grand plan for a history of Spain in America. To begin this project he compiled an extensive bibliography of the Columbian era based upon Barlow's collection and other materials available in New York. The *Notes on Columbus,* published in 1866, delighted the collectors no less than it pleased Harrise. His *Bibliotheca Americana Vetustissima—A Description of Works Relating to America*—came out the same year. The *Bibliotheca* was a magnificent compilation containing more than three hundred listings from 1492 to 1551. Specialists immediately applauded Harrise for his massive erudition and his equally massive industry, but the bibliography was nevertheless a commercial failure. It was such a colossal failure, even for a bibliography, that the publisher grasped the chance to unload a portion of the edition at a low price. Harrise was wounded, felt his work unappreciated, and set sail for France. The move turned out to be fortunate for Harrise and for scholarship. French scholars gave him an unrestrained Gallic welcome, acclaimed his work in French superlatives, and offered him assistance and encouragement. He took up the practice of law, specializing in international matters, and made an astonishing financial success which enabled him to devote as much time as he wished to the study of history.[29]

Harrise spent his time to excellent advantage. Thirty books and a large number of articles and pamphlets made him the most informed scholar in the world on the subject of his specialty. He explored the explorers and recharted the discoveries, and he did both with a lawyer's emphasis on detail and discrepancy. After an examination of European libraries in 1872, he published additions to his bibliography of 1866, which proved how thoroughly American collectors had ransacked the book marts of the European world. There simply were no European collections so adequate as those in America. Harrise now projected three critical biographical studies—on Columbus, Cabot, and Vespuccius—planned as a comprehensive analysis of the colonization movement. Actually, they proved to be a series of extended arguments between Henry Harrise and those who had preceded him. They also began a prolonged debate between Harrise and those who followed him, than which there can be no greater historical service. *Jean et Sebastien Cabot* (*1882*) took a very dim view of Sebastien, who, on Harrise's reading of the evidence, was a master dissembler "disguising the truth, whenever it was to his interests to do so." [30] *Christophe Columbe,* an affair in two volumes published between 1884 and 1885, contained new documentary material and was written in Harrise's provocatively argumentative style. The *Vespuccius,* posthumously published in 1910, was a work with which Harrise had struggled prodigiously. When Harrise was engaged in preparing a brief he let no scrap of evidence evade him and once he had the testimony, he presented it with superb conviction. His assertiveness encouraged dissension, and other specialists disagreed with him with a heartiness much like his own. But, as one historian had it, "No man has opposed him without acknowledging that Harrise made possible the investigations of his critics," [31] and when, in 1892, his *Discovery of North America,* an overall summary of the whole field appeared, Edward G. Bourne, himself an authority and no exponent of the Harrise interpretation on many an important count, judged him deserving of generous praise. "Unless we allow ourselves to become identified with some of Harrise's conclusions as partisans, we cannot fail to acknowledge him as a fine critical mind." [32] In spite of his long residence in the land of his birth, Harrise always considered himself an American. When he died he left many of his maps and manuscripts to the Library of Congress, where other scholars used them to destroy his conclusions without destroying their recognition of his service to history.

Henry Harrise and Justin Winsor were collectors and bibliographers as well as historical writers. Lyman Draper and Reuben G. Thwaites were editors, archivists, and librarians. Lines of expertness were to be still more tightly drawn, but the lines of development were already vaguely apparent. Books were published to be read; editing and collecting were undertaken for use. Volumes of learning were hardly more than mere possessions unless students knew of their existence and could reach them more or less at will. The former need called for catalogues, the latter for librarians and librarianship. Collections and bibliographies appeared before the Civil War, and the greatest strides were made after the end of the nineteenth century. Guides and bibliographies inescapably followed the increase in collections and publication of sources, documents, and the studies that were issued in response. Yet advances made from the time of Appomattox to 1900 suggest the marked shift in the direction of historical professionalization.

In the skilled craft of bibliography, Joseph Sabin is a name that only the educated public has forgotten. Bibliographers are the makers of one of the most important scholarly instruments, even though they play but a subdued role in the literary finale. Sabin, an Englishman who migrated to America in 1848, was a lover of the rare books he collected and sold. His plan for a listing of American books was announced in 1866, and parts of it began to be issued two years later. The monumental *Bibliotheca Americana. A Dictionary of Books Relating to America from Its Discovery to the Present Time* continued periodically under his guidance until 1881.[33] The *Bibliotheca Americana* was at once a record of achievement and an invitation to further historical exertion. More than anything else, it heralded the existence of a profession. Sabin was a technician of books, and the practitioners of bibliography owed their special existence to the librarians, editors, and writers who used them. Death interrupted the work of Joseph Sabin, but Sabin's *Dictionary of Books* was ultimately completed. After a lapse of forty-six years, Wilberforce Eames, a bibliographer of even greater competence, supervised the bibliography from 1885 to 1892. Eames also served as librarian of the Lenox Library and became the "bibliographer" of the New York Public Library when the Lenox and Astor Libraries and the Tilden Trust were amalgamated to create it. Robert W. G. Vail, a worthy successor to Sabin and Eames, brought the *Dictionary of Books Relating to America* to its majestic close with the publication of the twenty-ninth volume in 1936.[34]

Augmentation of materials was paralleled by newer methods in the organization of knowledge. Bibliography, "the science of books," was the scholar's response to publication, and research and writing responded to the activities of collectors, editors, and librarians. The Boston and New York public libraries, the Winsors, the Thwaites, and the Sabins were not only the precursors of a future which was to change the scholar's world, they had already begun to change it. The Massachusetts Historical Society and the Boston Atheneum no longer stood alone. Historical societies became the workshops of professionals, at the same time retaining their function as symbols of the cultural past. Collectors, being graduated from antiquarianism, became scholars, and fathered histories and historians alike. If scholarship became a profession as a result of the university graduate school and the rise of great teachers[35] with a zest for the organization of research, editors, bibliographers, and librarians were also members of learning's specialized guilds.

Guides to books multiplied with the additions to knowledge, although they hardly kept pace with them. Sabin was preceded by Orville A. Roorbach and followed by James Kelly.[36] The British Museum issued its first *Catalogue of Printed Books* in 1881, which, with supplements, extended to 105 volumes by 1905. In 1883 the Peabody Institute of Salem, Massachusetts, listed its literary assets in the first of five volumes, a practice the Boston Atheneum had already begun in 1874.[37] The *American Catalogue of Books,* beginning in 1876, appeared in 1881 and the *United States Catalog: Books in Print* emerged in 1889.[38] And the vast body of periodical literature surrendered to orderly classification with *Poole's Index* beginning in 1802.[39]

Publication of state and federal documents continued its endless course.[40] A pioneer effort to prepare a full listing of all government publications at the federal level—executive, legislative, judicial—was undertaken by Benjamin Perley Poore.[41] Poore, trained as a printer, became a journalist with an historical flair. He wrote biographies of Generals Zachary Taylor, Ambrose E. Burnside, and U. S. Grant, but he is best recalled for his chatty recollections of Washington life and for his editorial work. In addition to his bibliography of federal publications, he prepared a *Congressional Directory* and an index to the *Congressional Record*. Nevertheless, his index to government publications is undependable, and his listings are incomplete.[42] But as the first and only attempt to cover this enormous bibliographical area, his compilation has a definite historical interest. John G. Ames, chief of the documents division of the Department of the Interior, in 1893 prepared a two-volume index to government publications that is superior in almost every way.[43]

State publication of records seemed much more impressive in formal bibliographies than was actually the case. The Civil War dispersed and despoiled records, and postwar exigencies delayed the execution of plans to house and print official state proceedings. In the West, where county seats and state capitals often changed, developments were retarded. Only within the last half century has anything like a co-ordinated program of preservation and publication begun. Under the direction of William L. Saunders, North Carolina secretary of state, ten volumes of colonial records and sixteen volumes of state records from colonial beginnings to the adoption of the Constitution, were projected and completed.[44] While other states more or less matched this accomplishment, special mention must be made of Connecticut, which reprinted its seventeenth-century compilation in 1865,[45] and of the publications of Massachusetts, New Hampshire, New Jersey, New York, Ohio, Pennsylvania, Rhode Island, Vermont, and Virginia.[46]

Additional materials from official sources supplemented the documentary record. John R. Brodhead, earlier commissioned by the state of New York to transcribe documents relating to its history in Europe, completed his own two-volume *History of New York,* covering the years 1609–91, which derived much from the experience. William S. Perry assembled materials relating to the colonial church, and Henry M. Dexter, a minister and historian, compiled an exhaustive bibliography of Congregationalism. William B. Sprague completed his *Annals of the American Pulpit* in 1868 with the appearance of the tenth volume. Edmund Bailey O'Callaghan, a refugee of the Irish uprising in Canada in 1837, found his new home in Albany conducive to research. The *History of New Netherland* and *The Documentary History of New York* introduced him as a compiler and editor, and he improved his reputation among historians by bringing out, with Berthold Fernow, Brodhead's ten volumes of transcripts. John Dawson Gilmary Shea, the first significant Catholic historian in America, edited Pierre de Charlevoix's *History of New France* and the *Jesuit Relations* before he became generally known as the author of the *History of the Catholic Church in the United States.* Henry Martyn Baird did for the Huguenots what Shea did for the Catholics. His *History of the Rise of the Huguenots* followed by *The Huguenots and Henry of Navarre* and *The Huguenots and the Revocation of the Edict of Nantes,* usually favorable to the protesting French, gave the subject its first adequate coverage by an American student.[47] Personal records complemented official government papers and special source collections. Charles Francis Adams edited his father's memoirs in a dozen decorous volumes. Ulysses Simpson Grant wrote his own, as did Horace Greeley, Thomas Wentworth Higginson, George B. McClellan, Hugh McCulloch, Samuel J. May, and Josiah Quincy. Statesmen, generals, detectives, scholars, bequeathed their impressions to posterity, which, save for historians, has rarely expressed its gratitude.[48]

The memoirs of public figures like Grant and Sherman provided historians with a fresh point of departure, while the collection of primary material enormously lightened the initial burden of research.[49] Other devotees of the original source helped to make the evidence of the American past more readily available. Charles Deane, a successful Boston merchant who made American history the life of his retirement, edited William Bradford's *History of Plimouth Plantation,* John Smith's *True Relation,* and Edward Wingfield's *Discourse of Virginia.* Paul Leicester Ford and his brother Worthington Chauncey Ford contributed to make American editorial scholarship scientific in fidelity and artistic in execution. Paul Leicester Ford, born in Brooklyn, New York, in 1865, grew up with his father's remarkable collection of Americana with which he began his editorial career. He compiled a genealogy of his famous great-grandfather, Noah Webster, and with a boy's adoration of his family's past, tenderly printed it himself. Celebration of the centennial turned his attention to Alexander Hamilton and the makers of the Republic. When he was twenty-one he was ready with the *Bibliotheca Hamiltoniana* followed later by a list of Hamilton's treasury reports and a bibliography of editions of the *Federalist* papers. A checklist of American magazines printed in the eighteenth century literally blazed a trail which historians were later able to widen. The Pennsylvania Historical Society requested him to prepare the papers of John Dickinson for publication, which he accomplished with customary thoroughness. But *The Writings of Thomas Jefferson* was his finest editorial achievement. While slightly anti-Jeffersonian in tone, it is exceptionally well documented, and Ford's critical notes have undeniable insights and suggestiveness. His accuracy in reproducing the exact text of Jefferson's manuscripts made his collection the most authoritative until Julian P. Boyd of Princeton and his associates began to produce the definitive edition of Thomas Jefferson's works. Paul Leicester Ford was a tireless historian, and he also applied his capable hand to historical fiction. *Janice Meredith,* a romance of the Revolution, and *The Honorable Peter Stirling,* a novel of New York politics in the eighteen-seventies, despite their weaknesses in construction, remain of interest as sound historical dramatizations.

Worthington Chauncey Ford did more than continue the family devotion to his country's history. As editor of the Massachusetts Historical Society he elevated the publications of the society to an even higher standard of excellence, and his affiliation with the manuscript division of the Library of Congress enriched history and added luster to his name. His individual works, the papers of John Quincy Adams and those of George Washington, together with his biography of the first president, established his reputation. Ford's historical colleagues recognized their indebtedness by electing him to the presidency of the American Historical Association in 1917.[50]

Deepening specialization did not alter the substance of historical objective; it altered the nature of the historical enterprise. Two characteristics had already begun to dominate historical activity long before Bancroft died. One was the rapid growth of specialization in all branches of inquiry; the other was the need for larger and more encompassing meanings. Recent American historiography is the record of the development of these two tendencies. The division of learning, inevitable though it was, narrowed the scope of individual accomplishment. But division of labor was hardly more than a pragmatic acquiescence to mounting technicality and the growth of the total body of knowledge. Yet the price of efficiency in countless special areas was staggeringly high. Special competence, as Thorstein Veblen early indicated, resulted in the incapacity of the specialist in fields other than his own. In fact the more competent the expert became—the more, in other words, he mastered his particularized discipline—the more he was untrained by his capacity.

When in 1884 the American Historical Association was founded, the practice of history in the United States had become a professionalized activity. Libraries and librarians, editors and historical societies, graduate schools, bibliographers, collectors, and university professors were the evidences of a new and growing guild. New historians were fashioning the modern world of historical scholarship in the image of the modern world of science. George Bancroft, very much alive when the American Historical Association announced its existence, was its second president. But George Bancroft already belonged to a different era, as did Jared Sparks and the heroic Francis Parkman. The age of history as philosophy and of philosophy as history was followed by the age of the doctor of philosophy in history. A broad scope and a sharp perspective was followed by the narrower objectives of specialist inquiry. The age of the monograph succeeded the multivolumed panorama. And in the transition the university and the masters of the seminar exercised a commanding and lasting influence.

XVIII

John William Burgess:
The Scientific Method
and the Hegelian
Philosophy of History

Less than a hundred years ago America had no great universities. At least, in the opinion of William R. Shepherd, historian and political scientist of Columbia University, none was "properly entitled to the name." [1] Colleges there were in great number, some as distinguished for their historic past as for the reputations of their famous professors. But the development of the profession of history in America was the work of a group of men, who, employing the techniques of a new civilization, molded the university for the training of teachers and scholars. Under their guidance ancient colleges became modern universities; research became a calling and teaching a craft. The pioneers of modern history in America trained a generation of teachers and imbued them with their own enthusiasm and ideals. They elaborated a method, formulated a philosophy, and created a guild.

John William Burgess was one of the masters of social science in America. He was among the founding fathers of graduate education, a pioneer political scientist, and an early practitioner of "scientific" history. As an administrator he helped to remodel Columbia University and in 1880 he became dean of the faculty of political science. As a teacher he contributed to the education of a generation of scholars. He was not only the maker of historians and political scientists, but also of lawyers, judges, educators, and statesmen. Herbert Levi Osgood, first at Amherst and later at Columbia, was his pupil, and it was at his instance that Osgood undertook his massive study of colonial institutions. Nicholas Murray Butler acknowledged Burgess as his mentor, and Burgess acknowledged Butler as "the most brilliant student" he ever taught.[2] Theodore Roosevelt, briefly a member of Burgess' classes in 1881, was likewise marked by him for greatness. The German-trained professor taught many young historians and political scientists their first lessons in methodology. Scores of future lawyers and men of affairs learned the Burgess version of constitutional law and the Burgess concept of the state in the impressive Burgess manner. As historian Burgess fulfilled his planned purpose. History was the background for political science and the law. Through history, in his words, "we seek to find the origin, follow the growth and learn the meaning of our legal, political, and economic principles and institutions. We class it therefore no longer with fiction or rhetoric or belles-lettres, but with logic, philosophy, ethics. We value it, therefore, not by its brilliancy, but by its productiveness." [3]

Equally familiar are Burgess' intellectual kinships and affinities. He was an Aristotelian in political theory and a German idealist in philosophy. John Austin's notions of law and sovereignty gave substance to his concepts of the state and the sovereign power.[4] Theories of evolution inspired his thought, as they inspired the thought of other scholars in all branches of learning.[5] Like many of his colleagues in history and political science, he adopted the so-called "Teutonic hypothesis" to explain the origin and transmission of the institutions of ordered society. The principle of continuity and identification of Anglo-Saxons with the discovery of liberty merged with ideas of racial supremacy.[6] Devoted to Germany, he assigned Germans a special function as state builders and accorded them a unique part in the creation of free institutions.[7] A conservative by intellectual conviction, he was partial to constitutional checks and balances and suspicious of uninhibited popular rule. He is remembered as one of an active group of historians who, after the Civil War, created a school of "scientific" history and established a critical method of historical interpretation.[8]

But the history of ideas is more than mere classification. To understand Burgess requires an understanding of a broad field of thought. The central problem in Burgess is his interpretation of scientific method. The meanings that he attached to science explain his intellectual system, and his intellectual system had significant consequences for American life and thought. In the first place, Burgess differed from the historians with whom he is conventionally associated; if there was a school of "scientific" history, it was a school in which there were important distinctions. In the second place, Burgess differed from the scientists whose methods he is believed to have expounded. While he violated the presumptive canons of "scientific" history in his use of concepts, he differed from scientists in his use of hypotheses. Historians professed an allegiance to the Baconian method; but the Baconian method as historians conceived it was not the code of scientific procedure. If the Baconian method, or John Stuart Mill's version of it, had ever in fact been the method of science, the analysis of scientific method and practice was being changed just when the "scientific" historians were supposed to have adopted it. Burgess followed his historical colleagues in professing Baconian techniques, but he did not employ them. If he seemed to be following the principles that scientists were then enunciating, the appearance was illusory. Scientists and historians used the same words, but they used them with different meanings. Burgess used the current language, but the "scientific" historians would have been forced to reject his meanings, and the scientists could not have accepted his procedures.

That the "scientific" school of history was not as scientific as once supposed is no longer shocking. While the theoretical confusions in "scientific" historiography are vital, they are not so important as the historical consequences. Faulty notions of scientific method, stemming from the assumptions of the "scientific" school, have prejudged later attitudes regarding historical analysis. Priority being accorded to "facts" resembling the particulars of the material world, an induction or synthesis became the recognized mode of historical reconstruction. Concepts—Bacon's anticipations of nature—were thus theoretically avoided, and the perils of personality presumably escaped. Later assessments of historical practice resulted in a more sophisticated understanding of the problems of historical knowledge. Nevertheless, the historical enterprise, as many historians are still fond of saying, continued with excellent results, regardless of philosophical critiques. Historians who insist that thinking, for example, goes on perfectly well without knowledge of psychophysical processes are quite right. They are also right who insist that any human activity is more fully enjoyed and understood with deeper knowledge. A scientific bias, moreover, has induced the belief that meanings are likely to be clearer and more useful in the discovery of other meanings if assumptions are made explicit. Implicit assumptions may be difficult to discover, but their existence mortgages the accuracy of judgment. The historical enterprise, moreover, proceeded with mounting aversion to the use of hypotheses.[9] The conceptual techniques represented by Burgess did little to encourage historians to develop them. Burgess tended to confirm the historian's prejudice against the use of hypotheses. As a result, and irrespective of specific historical performance, historians still profess belief in but one part of scientific method.[10]

While confusions in scientific method were serious, there were other aspects of the Burgess legacy no less consequential. Under the guise of science, he propagated a body of social and political ideas that have lastingly conditioned American attitudes. The concept of the state as distinguished from the government and the unlimited supremacy of the sovereign power represented in the law and the Constitution were two of primary importance. No less important was his insistence upon extreme individualism and his advocacy of Teutonic racial supremacy. If these ideas and their correlates still operate in life, however, it is not solely owing to Burgess. Others read Herbert Spencer's *Social Statics* into the American Constitution. Others gave property protection in the name of liberty and resisted governmental activity in the name of political science. Burgess was not the only professed evolutionist who upheld immutable principles sanctified by nature's laws. Nordics had many champions upon whose shields "were emblazoned the Anglo-Saxon militant, the Teuton rampant, and the Aryan eternally triumphant." [11] Burgess had no monopoly on the theory of government by the elite, and lawyers were made guardians of the Republic long before the Columbia professor expressed an enthusiasm for an aristocracy of jurists. Others, too, had propounded doctrines as axioms of science derived from a strict observance of scientific rules.

Yet the influence of Burgess is unique. He was the leading figure in the establishment of graduate work in social studies at Columbia, where he served for nearly half a century. At the law school literally thousands of students were tutored in the principles of his constitutional faith. Some of them became professors of law, others became judges, most became practitioners at the bar. As a pioneer political scientist he had a part in training most of the scholars who filled the professorial chairs in the colleges and universities of the nation. Butler, when awarding Burgess an honorary Columbia doctorate in 1912, rightly hailed him as the "most potent organizer and inspirer of the study of the political sciences in America." [12]

John William Burgess was born into a slaveholding family in Giles County, Tennessee.[13] Ownership of slaves did not necessarily make Southerners secessionists, and Burgess' parents were as op-

posed to withdrawal from the Union as they were opposed to aboli-
tionism. The one was as violent a solution as the other, and what the
parents endorsed the son came to approve. War put Burgess' loyalty
to the Union to the severest test, for as Tennessee was overrun by
Northern troops in 1862, he felt he either had to don the blue or the
gray. He had little choice except to fight, and he chose to wear the
uniform of the Federal Army. Once mustered out, he matriculated at
Amherst, where the good teaching of Julius H. Seelye, a philosopher
who was later to become president of Amherst, helped Burgess to
develop his first-class mind. Amherst gave him all it had to give aca-
demically and shaped his maturing resolve into a course of action.
As a reflective volunteer, he could not fail to see that shot and shell
were inadequate substitutes for thought and feeling. Burgess wished
to discover ways in which reason could be made the arbiter of human problems. Law seemed to offer the natural course, and he
elected to follow the lawyer's way. No sooner had he finished his
legal training, an appointment to teach offered itself. Burgess accepted the appointment and changed the direction of his life. The
better to equip himself for teaching he went abroad to continue his
study. He went to Germany; to Berlin, Leipzig, and Göttingen; to
Theodor Mommsen, Leopold von Ranke, Johann Gustav Dorysen,
and Heinrich von Treitschke. When he returned in 1873 his old
alma mater summoned him to teach history, government, and political economy. In 1876, after three years at Amherst, he began his
association with Columbia which was to continue for the remainder
of his life.[14]

At Columbia, from 1876 to his retirement in 1912, he was at the
center of institutional change. In 1906 he became the first Roosevelt
professor at the University of Berlin where—as at Bonn and Leipzig
—he lectured on American institutions. Columbia, largely under his
direction and influence, was reorganized on the German faculty plan.
The faculty of political science was the first of its kind in the United
States, and Burgess was also responsible for the initiation of the *Political Science Quarterly,* the first learned journal devoted to the
study of government. None of these interests and activities interfered, apparently, with his teaching or his literary output in history,
in law, and in government.[15]

The constitutional and political crises of the Civil War were the
subjects of Burgess' four historical studies. *The Middle Period,
1817–1858,* concentrates on the sectional clash between North and
South.[16] *The Civil War and the Constitution, 1859–1865,* while
according military events a high priority, discusses the constitutional

status of southern secession and the constitutional validity of the use of the war power in the North. Extremists in both sections were treated to impartial condemnation, for neither northern nor southern extremists respected the Constitution and the limits it imposed.[17] In *Reconstruction and the Constitution, 1866–1876,* Burgess accepts the constitutional theory of Congressional reconstruction while denying the validity of Congressional measures. He agreed with Senator Charles Sumner of Massachusetts and with Congressman Thaddeus Stevens of Pennsylvania that secession deprived the Southern members of the Union of statehood. For the purposes of reconstruction they became territories, but he was certain that many of the measures of Radical Congressional policy departed from "sound political science and correct constitutional law." [18] *The Administration of President Hayes,* the final volume of this historical unit, resulted from a course of lectures Burgess had been invited to give at Kenyon College. Hardly a heroic figure, Rutherford B. Hayes has always taxed the ingenuity of biographers. Burgess could scarcely make him heroic, but he granted him his full historical due. He contended—for the conclusion demands contention—that it was President Hayes, who, by presiding over the statutory end of Reconstruction, deserved major credit for restoring the nation to "constitutional normalcy." [19]

The processes of thought and method that Burgess imparted to his students reached back to first principles. Few scholars were as eloquent in defining the methodological goals of historical investigation as applied to documentary research. "As to the internal principles . . . of our method of historical instruction . . . ," wrote Burgess, "we seek to teach the student, first, how to get hold of a historic fact, how to distinguish fact from fiction, how to divest it as far as possible of coloring or exaggeration. We send him, therefore, to the most original sources attainable." Principles of internal criticism, well known to historians, were carefully expounded. "If there be more than one original source upon the same fact," he continued, "we teach him to set these in comparison and contrast, to observe their agreements and discrepancies." Discovery and authentication of fact were the prerequisites of synthesis. "We undertake, in the second place, to set the facts which he has thus attained in their chronological order, to the further end of setting them in their order as cause and effect." Synthesis was but another name for induction, for this "process is the most delicate and critical which the historical student is called upon to undertake, in that he is continually tempted to account that which is mere antecedent and consequent as being cause and effect." [20]

Burgess was as emphatic in pointing out that the facts alone were without meaning. Even a series of facts in chronological sequence, fully authenticated, was not to be confused with cause and effect relationships. The historian, Burgess insisted, "must *construct* history out of the chaos of original historic atoms." [21] He must, in other words, construct a conceptual framework in which the "original historic atoms" would acquire meaning. On this crucial point Burgess was somewhat less adequate. "It is just in this process that genius is most necessary to accomplish anything valuable. It is therefore most difficult to formulate rules." Yet he averred that "a critical comparison of the sequence of facts in the history of different . . . peoples at a like period in . . . their civilizations," if pursued "with patience, care, and judgment" and "a moderate degree of true logic" would yield a meaningful synthesis of history.[22]

Precisely at this juncture, Burgess and the "scientific" historians were at intellectual odds. How is the "causal *nexus*" inferred and how is it established? If it was induced from the sequence of facts, compared, contrasted, and analyzed, it followed prescribed historical canons. Actually, however, Burgess organized his own thinking and derived his own conclusions by the use of previously defined concepts. This was the method historians of the "scientific" school had determined to avoid.

In using previously defined concepts, Burgess appeared to be following the methodological prescriptions of contemporary scientists. Charles Darwin, for many the very model of scientific exactitude, commented: "About thirty years ago there was much talk that geologists ought only to observe and not theorise; and I well remember some one saying that at this rate a man might as well go into a gravel-pit and count the pebbles and describe the colours. How odd it is that anyone should not see that all observation must be for or against some view if it is to be of any service!" [23] Thomas H. Huxley, Darwin's friend and co-worker, used even more forceful language. "It is a favourite popular delusion that the scientific inquirer is under a sort of moral obligation to abstain from going beyond that generalization of observed facts which is absurdly called 'Baconian' induction. But anyone who is practically acquainted with scientific work is aware that those who refuse to go beyond fact, rarely get as far as fact; and any one who has studied the history of science knows that almost every great step therein has been made by the 'anticipation of Nature,' that is, by the invention of hypotheses, which, though verifiable, often had very little foundation to start with; and, not infrequently, in spite of a long career of usefulness, turned out to be wholly erroneous in the long run." [24] Whether his American colleagues in social science approved or disapproved, the concepts of Burgess were not hypotheses designed to explore the social universe. Burgess' concepts of political science were based upon his concepts of the state, and his philosophy of the state was based in turn upon his philosophy of history. Both were rooted in the assumptions of post-Kantian idealism.

Burgess presented a scientific method derived from Hegelian philosophy; it was not a scientific method derived from experimental science. Confusion often arises from the fact that in Hegel as in Burgess empirical approaches are not only valid but inescapable. Hegel stated that in history, "Thought must be subordinate to what is given, to the realities of fact." He was particularly anxious to demonstrate at the outset of the *Philosophy of History* that history is not necessarily *a priori,* that "we have to take [history] as it is. We must," he stressed, "proceed historically—empirically." [25] Without the data of the phenomenal world, thought would have nothing to act upon. On the other hand, without the operation of thought, no meanings could be attached to the data of experience. Concepts, fashioned by thought, must be applied to the raw data of commonsense experience. This is fundamental in scientific analysis and merely exemplifies the principle that discrete particulars are beyond comprehension unless classified. And the categories of analysis, although developed later in time, are logically prior in terms of our understanding. But Hegel and Burgess both maintained that ultimate categories of thought, demonstrable by reason, existed. These ultimate categories were certain and changeless and gave meaning to the fragmentary character of experience. For Hegel as well as Burgess the sovereignty of Reason was the ultimate or final category. History yields general laws or principles, deducible from the facts, but, unless prompted by thought, laws or principles themselves cannot be established. Just as any particular aspect of the brute world would be meaningless unless conceptually related to other aspects, no particular event in historical experience is meaningful unless conceptually related. The philosophy of history, Hegel wrote, "means nothing but the *thoughtful consideration of it.*" [26]

While all historical experience is meaningful only in terms of concepts, Hegelian insistence upon the absolute sovereignty of Reason did not perpetuate the dualism between reason and the raw data of sense. On the contrary, Hegel's great philosophical effort was to close the gap between the two.[27] The objective world of fact and the subjective world of reason were not only connected; they were interconnected. Truth progressively developed was the consequence of the analysis of experience. But truth, although progressively discovered, was knowable and logically demonstrable in advance of progressively developed experience and discovery. The ultimate Reality, related to everything, gave a basic character and fundamental meaning to everything.

Burgess defined history as "spirit." [28] Spirit, by which he meant the ultimate Mind or Reason, alone possessed "the creative power of making the consequent contain more than the antecedent." The causal explanation, in other words, does not lie in the empirical relation between temporal progressions; it lies rather in the purposive intent of the creative power. History was thus "the progressive realization of the ideals of the human spirit in all of the objective forms of their manifestation, in language, tradition, and literature, in customs, manners, laws and institutions, and in opinion and belief. And history, in the writing, is the true and faithful record of these progressive revelations of the human reason, as they mark the line and stages of advance made by the human race towards its ultimate perfection." [29] The words of Burgess were substantially those of Hegel: "Universal History . . . is the exhibition of Spirit in the process of working out the knowledge of that which it is potentially. And as the germ bears in itself the whole nature of the tree, and the taste and form of its fruits, so do the first traces of Spirit virtually contain the whole of that History." [30]

Burgess gave these principles concrete form in the interpretation of American history. In *The Civil War and the Constitution,* he expressed his conviction: "A sound philosophy will undoubtedly hold that there is a plan of world civilization." [31] While the largest scope of the plan was not disclosed in this volume, Burgess was unreservedly precise about certain aspects of it. "We know now," he confided in his discussion of southern secession, "that the spirit of civilization was working for much more advanced results than the Republicans themselves consciously intended."

> Immediate abolition of slavery in the Commonwealths, and through nationalization of our political system, were consummations far beyond their hopes. Their hearts had to be fired to these results by the madness of the secessionists, who, upon the basis of their "State sovereignty" theory, sought to destroy the Union for the sake of perpetuating and extending the institution of African slavery. Not until then did the Republicans see that both slavery and "State sovereignty" must go, and in their places universal freedom and national sovereignty must be enthroned.
>
> This then was, in the plan of universal history, the meaning of se-

cession: The hastening of emancipation and nationalization. The United States were lagging in the march of modern civilization. Slavery and "State sovereignty" were the fetters which held them back, and these fetters had to be screwed down tight in order to provoke the Nation to strike them off at one fell bow, and free itself, and assert its supremacy, forevermore.[32]

The plan of civilization was so clear and certain that men "cannot thwart its ultimate realization." But, as Burgess pointed out in his comment on John Brown's raid, a sound philosophy will "also hold that man can and does, in large degrees at least, determine the nature of the means employed in the attainment of the predestined results." [33] Yet it is not only the results which are predestined, for the certainty of the results determines the proper means to be used in achieving them. John Brown was wrong because he consulted the oracle of his heart and not the guide of reflective reason. He did not reason about the proper means:

Whether they shall be destructive or constructive, or more or less destructive, whether they shall be vicious or virtuous, honorable or degrading, these are things which are within the power and control of man. Here lies his responsibility. Here is his realm of duty. It is from this point of view that the event at Harper's Ferry must be judged. And from this point of view it was crime, and nothing but crime, common crime and public crime, crime that made violent and destructive means possible and actual, and seemingly necessary for the attainment in the United States of that principle of the world's civilization which has decreed the personal freedom of all men.

While the logic of Burgess became more obscure as his intensity mounted, his philosophical intent was transparent:

Unless we are fatalists or Jesuits in philosophy, we are bound to condemn this crime to the end of time, and execrate the committers of it, even though we should ascribe to it the emancipation of the bondmen. It is an affront to Divinity itself to assert that the world's civilization cannot be realized except through violence and destruction, blood, crime, and sin. It is the cardinal fallacy of orientalism to hold that what has happened must have been inevitable, not only as to the end secured, but also as to the means by which the end was secured. It is the passionate haste of sinful man which dares to hurry the plans of Providence by the employment of means which rob the plans of their glory and their divinity.[34]

The predetermined course of world history is as patent in the historiography of Burgess as in the historiography of divine providence. But there is nevertheless an important difference. In the latter, history is predetermined in every respect, for an omniscient God foresees every event which manifests his will. The philosophy of history, as developed by Hegel and followed by Burgess, explains the nature of total reality, not the details of every historical experience. The explanation of the constitution of the universe in turn explains how things are what they are and why they must fulfill their potentiality; it does not undertake to explain each and every step in the process. Hegel, for example, as a leading commentator puts it, may have held "that the perfection of the Prussian constitution was philosophically demonstrable, but he made no endeavour to explain, from the nature of the Idea, the exact number of civil servants in the employment of the Crown."[35]

The precepts of Hegel were the precepts of Burgess. They alone render his definitions, axioms, and conclusions understandable. Political science, he wrote with unmistakable explicitness, "consists of something more than facts and logical conclusions from facts." Of what then does it consist? Political science, Burgess explained:

> contains an element of philosophical speculation which, when true and correct, is the forerunner of history. When political facts and conclusions come into contact with political reason they awaken in that reason a consciousness of political ideals not yet realized. Thrown into the form of propositions these ideals become principles of political science, then articles of political creeds, and, at last, laws and institutions. Now while this speculative element in political science must be kept in constant, truthful, and vital connection with the historical component, and must be, in a certain very important sense, regulated by the historical component, it is, nevertheless, the most important element in political science, because it lights the way of progress, and directs human experience towards its ultimate purpose.[36]

The ultimate purpose of human experience as defined by Burgess provides an exact measure of his social and intellectual values. The ultimate purpose of existence was the "perfection of humanity," and the perfection of humanity was the purpose of the state. When fully realized, the state represented "the civilization of the world; the perfect development of human reason; and its attainment to universal command over individualism." The true state, in short, represented "the apotheosis of man." Yet his conception was neither a perfectionist's dream nor the vision of a moralist. It was a logical postulate. The "political reason," having "come into contact with political facts and conclusions," had awakened "a consciousness of political ideas not yet realized." So conceived, the state was not only the final end of history, it was the final end of man. "This end is wholly spiritual; and in it mankind, as spirit, triumphs over all fleshly weakness, error and sin." Once the state was completely and finally formed, man, to use Hegelian language, would no longer be alienated from himself.[37] He would achieve the perfect freedom which was potentially his from the beginning. This, said Burgess, is "what Hegel meant by his doctrine that morality (*Sittlichkeit*) is the end of the state; and the criticism that this doctrine confounds the domain of the individual with that of the state so freely indulged in by most publicists, is a crude view, a narrow conception of the meaning of the term 'morality.' " [38] Man was fulfilled in and by human relations of which the state, like the Greek polis, was the highest expression. If, according to Burgess, Hegel erred, it was in thinking that man could reach his final goal more swiftly than in fact was possible. There were preliminary steps that had first to be taken. The national state must precede the world state. "The national state is the most perfect organ which has as yet been attained in the civilization of the world for the interpretation of the human consciousness of right. It furnishes the best vantage ground as yet reached for the contemplation of the purpose of the sojourn of mankind upon earth." [39]

To achieve nationality—the genius and spirit of a people—government and liberty had to be culturally instituted. Government and liberty were "proximate ends" by means of which "national civilization, and then the civilization of the world" were finally to be attained. The role of government was primarily to create and secondarily to preserve internal order and external peace. But peace and order, though a precondition to the "development of the national genius," do not by themselves create it. Law and obedience to its injunctions provide mankind with liberty, which it is the function of the state to prescribe, to maintain, and to cherish. "In the modern age, the state works . . . through government and liberty, and accomplishes many of its fairest and most important results for civilization through the latter." [40]

Burgess' philosophy of society therefore rests on three pivotal concepts. These are the concepts of the state, of sovereignty, and of government, concepts which reveal the design of his thought and the texture of his views. His definition of the state suggests his theory of knowledge. "There are two ways of reaching the definition. The one is the process of pure philosophy, the other that of inductive logic." And "the process of pure philosophy" turns out upon examination to be ultimate Reason. "The idea of the state," he continued in the idiom of Hegel, "is the state perfect and complete. The concept of the state is the state developing and approaching perfection." [41] To make the distinction in different words, the state, when perfect and complete, was the Hegelian "Idea," but the concrete manifestation of the state in historical experience was the state conceived as concept. Conceived as idea, the state was the product of reflective reason. Conceived as concept, the state was the actualization of the idea in the process of history. The former was an induction of logic; the latter an induction from the scientific analysis of empirical historical fact. The logic of the idea gave meaning to the empirical facts of historical change, while the empirical facts of historical change provided the data for the logic of induction. But it was the idea of the state, not the concept, which made the meaning and purpose of history understandable. For Burgess the theory of the state was rooted in history, and the development of the state was rooted in social change.

The idea of the state is the product of what Hegel called the creative power of reason. The concept of the state emerges as a consequence of the Hegelian reflective reason. Hegel's distinction between the creative power of reason and the reflective reason—the differences between the idea and the concept in Burgess—resembles Carlyle's familiar distinction between reason and understanding. Understanding, in the words of Carlyle, is "the mere mechanical and uncreative deduction and inference of given premises." Reason is the "direct spiritual perception, the ability to penetrate behind the shadows of formal logic and *see* the fundamental realities which lie beneath." [42] For Hegel the "knowing Reason" was Truth "because Truth consists in the harmony, or rather *unity,* of certitude and Being, or of certitude and objectivity." [43]

The distinction between the idea of the state and the concept of the state is for Burgess a controlling distinction. The idea of the state, an idea logically antecedent to experience, furnishes the key to the description of both. With the emergence of the state the "universal in man" was for the first time realized. With the evolution of the state, the "modern political era" first began. Society in the Hegelian sense could not exist before the idea of the state was actualized in experience, for the state alone, in the words of Burgess, marks "the sovereign organization over the particular." Before the process of civilization could properly commence, the state—"the product of the progressive revelation of the human reason through history"—had to become the form of human organization. Burgess was no less clear than Hegel. Hegel described the state in his *Philosophy of Law* as "the march of God through the world" in which "the individual . . . has his substantial freedom . . . the essence, purpose, and product of his activity." [44] Burgess described the state as *"the* product of history."* The state was "all comprehensive" because it represented the total culture. It was "exclusive" because it was the final social end. It was "permanent" because it was the ultimate realization of human development. It was "sovereign" because it was unlimited by its nature.[45] The Hegelian formula sharpens the Burgess definition. The state, as Hegel elaborated in the *Philosophy of Law,* "is nothing but the organization of the concept of freedom. The determinations of the individual will are given by the State objectivity, and it is through the State alone that they attain truth and realization." There is no qualification: "The State is the sole condition for the attainment of the particular end and good." [46]

Sovereignty is, therefore, "original, absolute, unlimited, universal power over the individual subject." [47] But though the state is unlimited the government is not. Government is the "limited agent for accomplishing certain of the state's purposes." [48] The two must never be confounded; the complete separation of state and government in theory as well as in practice is actually the guarantee of individual liberty. The conceptual separation is the logical ground of liberty, the practical separation is the social ground for its preservation. The state prescribed the nature of liberty, the function of government was to preserve it.

"The whole idea" of liberty, Burgess believed, "is that of a domain in which the individual is referred to his own will and upon which government shall neither encroach itself, nor permit encroachments from any other quarter. Let the latter part of the definition be carefully remarked. I said it is a domain into which *government* shall not penetrate. It is not, however, shielded from the power of the *state*." [49] Indeed the "deepest problem of political science," if not in fact of history, has been the reconciliation of government with individual liberty. This was the ultimate purpose of the political science of Burgess and the ultimate intellectual drive of his life. Yet once the abstract individual is separated from the abstract state, we are inescapably involved in the cleavage between the individual and society. Nor is the cleavage bridged by distinguishing between the government and the state. "The moment we utter the words 'The State,'" John Dewey observed, "a score of intellectual ghosts rise to obscure our vision. Without our intention and without our notice, the notion of 'The State' draws us imperceptibly into a consideration of the logical relationship of various ideas to one another, and away from the facts of human activity." [50]

The difference between Dewey and Burgess is not only the difference between an ideal and an instrumental view of politics. It is the difference between the science of ideal philosophy and the philosophy of experimental science. The facts of human experience are as essential for Hegel and Burgess as for Dewey and the practitioners of science. Concepts for scientists and for philosophers of science make it possible to classify, compare, and understand the facts of experience. But concepts are made and remade in an endless temporal process in response to the continuing impact of the facts of human experience on newer concepts and newer facts. Concepts are not immutable. Concepts control the growth of knowledge only by reason of their instrumental character and the growth of knowledge itself. The logical relationships of various ideas to one another in experimental science are parts of the method of inquiry. They are not, as in Hegel or Burgess, invariant truths intimating final reality and purpose.

Burgess wrote numerous volumes and essays on various phases of political philosophy, all more or less devoted to exploration of the subject he had described as the "deepest problem of political science," the reconciliation of government and liberty. But by separating state and government, he had emasculated government. If he assured liberty for the theoretical individual by the separation, he denied government the power to prevent encroachment upon the liberties of actual individuals in the world of practical life. Burgess made the state the anchor of social stability. He made sovereignty an effective barrier to social change. And he made government the ineffective creature of the state. Sovereignty, the state, and government were thus parts of a great chain of being, a hierarchy of predetermined ends and fixed purposes. Obviously, if the state was the end of man, government could be no more than a transitory human contrivance. And political parties, as creative instruments of social change, found little place in Burgess' speculative scheme.

Political parties were of scant theoretical significance because Burgess did not endorse majority rule democracy. He applauded Lincoln in extravagant terms,[51] but he was much more sympathetic to the notion of government *for* the people than government *by* the people.[52] He was apprehensive about popular government and did not think it necessary for the welfare of mankind. The unlimited power of sovereignty lodged in the ubiquitous state intentionally restricted the functions of government and, by definition, limited the role of parties. Most men had not attained their full capacities; all men had assuredly not. In a world governed by Reason there was a prescribed sequence. "Take these ends in their historical order, and pursue them with the natural means, and mankind will attain them all, each in its proper time. But this order cannot be successfully reversed, either in part or whole. The state which attempts to realize liberty before government, or the world-order before the national order, will find itself immediately threatened with dissolution and anarchy. It will be compelled to begin *de novo,* and to do things in the manner and sequence which both nature and history proscribe." [53]

Burgess frequently discriminated between those who governed for the people and those who were governed. In a proper and reasonable society, the former were educated and competent and possessed a high sense of public consciousness. They were mindful of the constitution and of the relations of state and government, and were careful to see that government never entered the sacred vestries of the state. People in general, regardless of caste or class, were likely to press for the attainment of their special interests. They were unlikely to preserve the general welfare. With this theory of interests, modern proponents of party government are probably in accord. But they would probably doubt that the general welfare could be created and maintained by a wise race of philosopher kings. Did such a society exist in fact, democrats would be inclined to call it benevolent despotism.[54]

Hegel, of course, was intellectually hostile to democracy. "The prevalent idea," he wrote in a mood which was the outcome of his whole philosophical approach, that "the people itself, best understand what would promote the common weal, and that they have indubitably the good will to promote it," was fallacious. "The people . . . stands precisely for the part that does not know what it wills. To know what one wills, and, what is more difficult, to know what the absolute will, viz., reason, wills, is the fruit of deep knowledge and insight; and that is obviously not a possession of the people." [55] The people were represented virtually, not actually represented. "To view the delegates as representatives has . . . an organic and rational meaning only if they are not representatives of mere individuals, of the mere multitude, but of one of the essential spheres of society and of its larger interests." [56] Burgess, for his part, subscribed to "natural and moral representation" as, for example, when a father represented a child, or a husband a wife.[57] Where, Burgess felt, "government is really *for* the people, it will almost surely be *of* the people, and *by* the people's faithful representatives. This might be true even though the suffrage should not be broadly extended and election should not be the sole method of designating the holders of governmental power." [58]

As Burgess distinguished between people, he also distinguished between ethnic groups.[59] His philosophy of the state required general identification of its citizens with a given culture, and their active participation in the dominant cultural values. Accordingly, he sharply separated a people from a population. The first suggested the culture; the second the statistical fact.[60] Next to the United States, Germany claimed his respect and affection. Teutons, he believed, were the great state builders, the creators and carriers of liberty. Aryans, Anglo-Saxons, Teutons possessed a greater share of the civilizing virtues and were destined to help other less fortunately endowed peoples to attain civilization.[61] Burgess accordingly called upon the American state to protect itself from immigrant cultural invasion. Immigration of the "right" kind was welcomed, but he was resolutely opposed to the so-called "new" immigration from southern and eastern Europe. Although racism is an ugly word, Burgess unhesitatingly classified ethnic groups into desirable and undesirable elements.[62] Some peoples possessed great political sagacity, others none at all. Some were prone to anarchy and violence; others were summarily classified as antidemocratic.

When the United States emerged as a world power after the war with Spain, the philosophy of Burgess neatly blended with zeal for the acquisition of colonies. The civilizing powers had a moral obligation to bring light and progress to the less fortunate peoples of the earth. While the theoretical position of Burgess did not differ essentially from that of Alfred T. Mahan and Josiah Strong, Burgess later qualified his enthusiasm for American expansion, lest expansion affect domestic government adversely.[63]

Burgess' conclusions stemmed logically from his premises. But his ultimate premises were philosophical rather than scientific ones. His contribution to the study of history, while considerable, was not as a forerunner of science and the scientific method. His words were often those of science, but his ideas were those of post-Kantian philosophy. He was an exemplar of the critical examination of documents, but meanings deducible from documents, or from any other variety of empirical fact, were definable only in larger philosophical terms, terms known logically in advance of human experience and development. Of him his colleague, William R. Shepherd, revealingly remarked: "The definiteness with which he forms his conclusions is equalled only by the tenacity with which he holds them. In the profound study and mature reflection upon which they are based he finds justification for their statement and maintenance. Doubt befits the man who does not know; certainty, the man who does." [64] The true scientist is always in doubt. He is certain only that what he thinks he knows should be doubted.

XIX

Herbert Baxter Adams
and American
Historical Craftsmanship

Herbert Baxter Adams achieved for the Johns Hopkins University what John William Burgess achieved for Columbia. With their colleagues at Harvard, Pennsylvania, Michigan, and elsewhere they made the teaching and writing of history a specialized technique. They impressed German methods of instruction upon the American university and gave graduate training its characteristic form. Themselves German-trained, they brought the seminar and the dissertation to the graduate schools and with them Continental ideals and objectives. Scholarship already had its acolytes, but Adams and Burgess tutored the makers of American historiography. They were specialists in the science of learning, masters in the art of teaching. Their major institutional role was the organization of knowledge; their major creative role was the training of scholars and teachers.

If great teachers are made rather than born, Adams and Burgess were made by their opportunities. They were the pioneers. Pioneers also have their difficulties, but the difficulties that blocked Adams and Burgess were easily overcome. Their struggles were within the universities they were seeking to reform, not within the culture that supported them. They required funds, status within the university hierarchy, teachers, and books. Public attitudes were favorable to specialized training and to the study of the history of the United States. Students asked only for the opportunity to be taught, and patriots were proud when Hopkins, Harvard, and Columbia were able to provide the facilities Americans had previously journeyed to Berlin, Leipzig, and Freiburg to procure.

The pioneers of modern history in America had the field virtually to themselves. The anonymity of numbers had not yet overtaken them. Teachers of American history and government with doctorates in philosophy were still uncommon enough to be rare. Moreover, they were engaged in the exciting work of beginnings. They were building new centers of education and shaping new traditions of the power of knowledge. Both Adams and Burgess—and other contemporary pioneers—were completely identified with their work. Theirs was no conventional daily round; it was a full-time life career. To the career of a pioneering teacher, Herbert Baxter Adams brought superlative qualities. An indefatigable worker, fondness for people, and a sharp mind made him a successful mentor and a successful administrator. Woodrow Wilson later called him "a great Captain of Industry, a captain in the field of systematic and organized scholarship," and another recalled that in Adams "the man overshadowed the professor." Always available to his pupils during and after student days, Adams influenced the continuing course of historical development in his contacts with former Hopkins men long after they had left the University to take up posts of their own.[1]

Adams was born in the small Massachusetts town of Shutesbury, near Amherst. Phillips Exeter, the training ground of historians, was his secondary school, from which he was graduated with honors in 1868. Amherst was his college, as it had been the college of Burgess, and after a year of teaching he made the academic pilgrimage to Germany. Amherst's Julius Seelye fired young Adams as he had fired young Burgess, and both recorded their indebtedness to him. "I remember," Adams wrote, "in the philosophical course by the President of the College one remarkable lecture on the Philosophy of History. After rapidly reviewing the course of civilization, Dr. Seelye said that history was the grandest study in the world. That sentence decided my fate. I determined to devote myself to that grand subject."[2]

Adams' fate was less easily decided than his words suggest, for he still had a future to conquer. Seelye had shown him many kindnesses and granted him many favors, none more lasting than the enthusiasm he was able to communicate and the splendid feeling for scholarship he was able to impart. At Heidelberg in 1874 he listened to Heinrich von Treitschke, whose sparkling eloquence enraptured his students. When Treitschke left for Berlin, his students followed him. Adams went with them, but in 1876, having returned to Heidelberg, he was awarded the coveted doctorate by the university. Johann Kasper Bluntschli, his chief professor, continued to influence his development even after he became a Hopkins teacher. Bluntschli, described by his student as "a trump," probably had something to do with his appointment as a fellow at Hopkins and almost certainly had a great deal to do with the formation of his ideas.[3]

The career of Johns Hopkins and the career of Herbert Baxter Adams began together. When Johns Hopkins became the first purely graduate school in the country in 1876, an active partnership in creativity was offered to the men associated with it. Adams was one of a notable company. Among the fellows of the University was Walter Hines Page, a young student from the South, and Josiah Royce, a young student from California. Page matured in the shadow of greatness; Royce himself became great. During the anxious days when Woodrow Wilson, another Hopkins man, was trying to keep the United States out of World War I, Page was American ambassador in London. Royce, one of America's outstanding philosophers, graced the Harvard faculty in the Augustan age of George Santayana, William James, and Hugo Munsterberg.[4]

Hopkins offered an intellectual environment almost unequaled in American experience. J. Franklin Jameson never forgot the brilliant and intellectually convivial atmosphere of 1876. "It was," he recalled later, "like the opening of the Pacific before the eyes of Balboa and his men. Here were no dated classes, no campus, no sports, no dormitories, no gulf between teacher and student where all were students, no compulsion toward work where all were eager." [5] Jameson's judgment is confirmed by the character of the student body, doubtless attracted to Hopkins by the conditions he described. Even had such an enticing situation not already existed, the men who came to Hopkins would have created it. Gatherings of bright young men have not infrequently occurred at American universities. But rarely has there been such a company of first-rate minds, all of whom were to achieve immortality in the history of ideas. At various colleges and universities a single class or a college generation contained a quota of men who made a deep impress in different areas of life. Many an educational institution cherishes such a record as part of its history. Seldom, however, has a group of men trained in the same place and within so short a time become a dominating force in so many branches of scholarship. Only at Clark University, more than a decade after Hopkins began, did such a phenomenon take place. There, in the second purely graduate school in the country, G. Stanley Hall began his work in psychology and education.[6] Hall's colleagues and students virtually staffed the faculties, laboratories, and journals in these disciplines. Not until the advent of John Dewey was any single man or group to wield so decisive an influence in education, psychology, and philosophy. After the Hopkins interlude, and with the exception of Frederick Jackson Turner, no single individual and no specific school exerted an influence comparable to the Johns Hopkins of the Adams era.

Between the years 1878 and 1889 there were three students at Baltimore whose capacities may well be matched but hardly outdistanced. Josiah Royce, Thorstein Veblen, and John Dewey comprise an intellectual trinity hard to equal. Royce became the most learned exponent of modern philosophical idealism. As a Harvard teacher and as a writer of books which guided men's minds, he solidified the tradition of western idealism in an era progressively unsympathetic to its outlook. John Dewey represented an opposite philosophical tendency. He initiated what one of his idealistic critics has called a "Copernican revolution" in philosophy and his teaching and writing caused two generations to reconstruct philosophy, a reconstruction in which students are still engaged. Dewey induced scholars to think in a new key and every division of specialized thought reflects the pervasiveness of his influence. Thorstein Veblen shocked his generation into self-criticism and forced students of history, economics, and sociology to expand the frontiers of their thought.[7]

Veblen, Dewey, and Royce were but three among many. Frederick Jackson Turner was also a student at Johns Hopkins, and it was then that he first began to look westward rather than eastward for the clue to America's significance. He remembered Adams not so much for the originality of his thinking as for the appeal of his teaching. Adams gave young scholars an "enthusiasm for serious historical work," and stimulated "the best that was in them." [8] He did not appreciate Adams any the less because he departed from the direction Adams gave to history at Hopkins. Writing in 1889, Turner, by implication hardly obscure, criticized the school of Herbert Baxter Adams. "America's historians have for the most part, like the wise men of old, come from the East; and as a result our history has been written from the point of view of the Atlantic coast. . . . General United States history should be built upon the fact that the center of gravity has passed across the mountains." [9] With these words, Frederick Jackson Turner opened a new phase in American historiography. Turner became the John Dewey of American history, for his reinterpretation of the American past forced historians to reconstruct the philosophy of American meanings. Subsequent reconstruction, stemming from Turner's synthesis, initiated still newer viewpoints in American historical thought. And Woodrow Wilson, also a student of Herbert Baxter Adams, not only wrote history and political science but also profoundly influenced the society about which historians and political scientists are still thinking and writing.

Adams' students and the University he did so much to make have acquired fame sufficient for Herbert Baxter Adams as well. But Adams has a fame of his own. He owes his fame among American historians to his talent as a teacher and his genius as an organizer. As an organizer of the so-called scientific study of history he has no peer. His was the most notable, if not the first, truly Germanic seminar in the United States, and he took infinite care of the smallest details concerning it.[10] He supervised the physical arrangements which gave him inordinate satisfaction and made a diagram illustrating how the furniture and the materials of study had been arranged.[11] "The Baltimore seminaries," he wrote, "are laboratories where books are treated like mineralogical specimens, passed from hand to hand, examined and tested." [12] The seminar was a means and not an end. It was designed to equip students with a respect for ordered knowledge and a reverence for the critical temper.

Adams was a crusader, and the object of his crusade was to establish historical study as a respected and flourishing discipline. In his Hopkins office was a map of the United States and whenever a student, freshly hooded with a Hopkins doctorate, took up a teaching post, a new pin appeared on the Adams map.[13] If this practice was not unique, it was certainly unusual. Each new position represented a Hopkins "colony," a new conquest in the educational wastelands. It represented a triple conquest: for history, for Hopkins, and for Adams. Adams kept in constant and close touch with the teaching situation. Ever on the alert for possible opportunities, he recommended his students for positions as they occurred. They in turn wrote to "the Chief" in Baltimore from every section of the academic frontier telling of vacancies, needs, and the possibilities for Hopkins men.[14]

Yet it was not so much Hopkins as history which moved Adams and his students. The loyalty of Hopkins graduates to "J. H. U." and the "fraternity" [15] of Baltimore scholars was deep and enduring. But scholarship was always first. John Spencer Bassett, teaching at Trinity College in Durham, North Carolina, wrote Adams about libraries, prejudice, and the need for expanded educational facilities.[16] William P. Trent, considering the prospect of moving from one academic post to another, confided to Adams: "As I have often told you my ambition is to do good historical work and to make whatever mark I can in that way without thinking too much of money or position. I would rather get a subordinate place in a large university with a *library* and the chance to make a scholar of myself than to be a *full professor* in a very *unfledged university* (so called! God save the mark!)." [17] Hopkins men studying abroad took pleasure in the scholarly attainment of America, with which their own University was so largely associated. David Kinley, writing from Berlin in 1901, asked "why American students come here to study?" The United States had developed first-rate men and institutions, and it was no longer necessary for aspiring scholars to covet a German degree. "I think far less of Germans, German education and German educational institutions than I did six months ago! I cannot help feeling that they (especially the *Prussians*) are a narrow people. . . . It seems to me that in all technical education, and in university subjects like economics, chemistry, all history *except* German, mathematics, literature & cc., Germany has nothing to offer that our students cannot get better in our own country." [18] Kinley's judgment was far from singular. John M. Vincent, who later became a Hopkins professor himself, told Adams he found nothing in Paris "that equals the *possibilities* of our American educational life. There are many advantages here, but methods are often petrified and fossilized beyond belief. I did not have the worship for Germany that I had when I went there as a student ten years ago, and in France things seem to be up to the hubs in ruts." [19] Kinley and Vincent may have overstressed European failings, but they insisted correctly that American graduate instruction in history was more than adequate.[20]

The high level of graduate instruction owed much to Herbert Baxter Adams, but Adams made additional contributions to professionalization. He was instrumental in the formation of the American Historical Association in 1884.[21] As its secretary from its inception to 1900, he was in an excellent position to make his influence felt. When the need for a journal was considered by historical scholars, the suggestion was made to Adams, who took a lively interest in the proposal. He could hardly have failed to do otherwise, for his passion for history was exceeded only by his passion for Hopkins.[22] George W. Kirchwey, of the office of the Regents of the State of New York, had written him: "Of course, if we once get it under way we shall lean heavily on the group of able men who have been trained by you at the Johns Hopkins, and we count not a little on your sympathy and cooperation." [23] Two years later, in 1890, he was able to tell former president Andrew Dickson White of Cornell: "We are now in position to begin the development of an *American Historical Review,* as *The Nation,* after the appearance of our last annual report, recommended us to do. What do you think of the idea? If you like it please send on your paper and I will put it into the first part of our proceedings." [24]

Honors for the initiation of the *American Historical Review* are divided, but Adams was primarily responsible for the *Johns Hopkins Studies in History and Political Science.*[25] The first issue, appearing in 1882, introduced a new scholarly genre, and succeeding issues demonstrated what kind of work was being accomplished by American historians centered in Baltimore. Edward A. Freeman, the noted English historian and the leading proponent of the idea of the continuity of Anglo-Saxon influences, contributed a preface to the series: "An Introduction to American Institutional History." [26] Adams was completely committed to institutional history, and it was an institutional history of a special kind. "I send you a letter from Mr. Bryce," Adams reported to President Daniel Coit Gilman of Hopkins,

> which I received this morning and which suggests a feasible plan of cooperation between the friends of History in the Old Country and the New. To my mind there is peculiar propriety in *united* English effort in the direction of historical science; for the history of the two countries is one. The whole tenor of our researches at the J.H.U. is to show the continuity of English institutions in America. Mr. Freeman has struck for me that key-note in his Introduction. Now my idea is this: supposing you write to Mr. Bryce slightly encouraging the main idea of an English journal of history, in a broad sense, including American contributions, which shall be subject to an American subeditorship. Taxation without representation is a bad principle. *Generous cooperation* must be the principle of the magazine. It should be English, *with American assistance.* It should be published through Macmillan in England and America, and through the cooperation of Johns Hopkins University. The thing would be a scientific tentacle reaching over England and drawing life to our little Baltimore centre from the best intellectual resources of the old world.[27]

To show the connection between English and American institutions was one of Adams' first objectives. If Adams had any speculative interest at all, it was the comparative study of institutions.[28] "I have no ambition to be known as a Professor of American History," he confessed to President Gilman. And his reasons, conceptual rather than national, made hypothetical sense. "At least five-sixths of my three years' course of lectures to graduates and *all* of my undergraduate classes are in the European field." Adams was not a European historian either, but if he taught Russian history it was because he was seeking historical meanings by comparing and contrasting institutions. "I do not object to the phrase 'Institutional History,' for that describes very happily the nature of my university-work in class and seminary. As Professor of Institutional History I could have a fair field for comparative studies in Church and State and in the Institutes of Education without being regarded as an American provincial." [29]

The Germanic hypothesis of institutional origins was initially elaborated by Adams and his seminary students at Johns Hopkins.[30] Originally a generalized form of the "great chain of being," a controlling idea of romanticism,[31] it was feelingly expressed by Bancroft's faith in the progressive development of democracy.[32] What Bancroft had absorbed during his Göttingen years, his German teachers of history had absorbed from their colleagues in linguistics. German savants, expert in philology, discovered a method in the comparisons of words. Resemblances among words induced concepts of their origin and meaning. Similarities implied cultural contact; cultural contact implied kinship. But the concepts of Adams rested on other and somewhat less tenuous assumptions. The Adams version of institutional history was also derived from the doctrine of biological evolution. Continuity of institutions and ideas were genetically related, and exponents of the comparative method acquired new insights from Darwinian emphases. The intellectual orientation of Adams, Burgess, and their associates reflected the triumphs of speculative science and applied science, which in the nineteenth century were symbolized by Darwinian evolution and the marvels of the machine. Scientific history which Adams and Burgess represented was partly an effort to emulate the methods and to achieve the results of physical science.[33]

Adams' formulation of the genetic relation of institutions, sometimes called the "germ theory" of politics, was not as Germanic as has sometimes been supposed. American institutions, according to the Teutonic interpretation, followed a precise geographical sequence. They first emerged in the primitive German forests, whence they were transplanted to the primitive English forests. Finally they were carried across the Atlantic by pioneering Englishmen, who planted them in the wilderness of the new world. Despite the Teutonic origin of the Anglo-Saxon interpretation, Adams relied less upon his early German masters than upon his later English friends. That his interest in "municipal history" was "first awakened in the Seminary of Prof. Erdmannsdoerffer at the University of Heidelberg in 1875" he himself stated, but it was an interest quickened at the time "by the reading of Carl Hegel, Arnold Von Maurer, Fustel de

Coulanges" and "was ultimately directed toward England and New England by a suggestion upon the last page of Sir Henry Maine's *Village Communities*." Adams could scarcely have been more explicit. The seminary at Heidelberg had been studying Otto of Freising. The reading of the *Gesta Friderici imperatoris* raised a question concerning the inception of city government in Italy. These discussions provoked young Adams to probe further, and in the course of his probing he came upon an arresting reference. Maine had quoted John Gorham Palfrey's *History of New England* and called "attention to the survival of Village Communities in America." These fertile suggestions for Adams resulted in research "verified in all essential details with reference to Nantucket, Plymouth Plantations, Cape Ann, Salem, and the oldest towns in New England, has been extended gradually to a co-operative study of American local institutions in all the older States and throughout the Northwest." [34] Adams himself contributed studies on the Germanic origins of New England towns and on Saxon tithingmen in America.[35]

But Adams was much more impressed by English scholars such as Edward A. Freeman than by German university professors. He may never have opened his German notebooks after his return from Heidelberg, as another Hopkinsonian Albion W. Small, a founder of American sociology, intimates.[36] W. Stull Holt, who edited a revealing selection of Adams' letters, was startled to find so few communications between Adams and his former German teachers. "I have long cherished the notion," Adams wrote to Frederic Bancroft, then in Paris, "that our American students devote too exclusive attention to Germany in their foreign study," [37] a comment which implies that his enthusiasm for German scholarship was not unreserved. Letters to English students and references to English works of historical learning are so numerous as to suggest, as it does to Professor Holt, "the possibility that the orthodox account of the dominant influence of German scholarship during this period may need revision." [38]

Germanic influences on American historians are less important than the consequences of Anglo-Saxonism on American historical writing. The study of comparative political institutions under the aegis of the "germ theory" gave colonial history a special appeal. And it was in the area of colonial institutions that some of the major scholars of the post-Civil War period did their noblest work. Absorption in colonial issues and colonial problems tended to localize the study of American history, to confine it to regions of colonial settlement in New England and the South. Since theoretical assumptions factored out certain institutions to the exclusion of others, only one institutional variety was assiduously studied. Freeman's well-known epigram: "History is past politics; politics is present history" was inscribed in an honored place in the library of Herbert Baxter Adams' Historical Seminary at Hopkins. Political institutions, and then only selected political institutions, became the objects of historical inquiry.[39]

Every principle of the Adams interpretation was ultimately challenged. Most of his theoretical precepts were finally abandoned or rigorously qualified. Classical evolutionism, positing a linear series of institutional descent, was searchingly examined by anthropologists in the latter decades of the century and rejected at its end. The comparative method of analysis as employed by Adams and Burgess was reviewed by colonial historians themselves and found conceptually wanting. Herbert Levi Osgood, student of Burgess, and Charles McLean Andrews, student of Adams, were by no means ready to reject comparative techniques. They required a more subtle evaluation and a more careful handling of such methods. Andrews and Osgood reported the "germ theory" too general, too unrefined to qualify as an instrument of synthesis. "All people will not develop wholly alike," objected Andrews as early as 1893. While similarities between peoples had customarily been obscured, differences were none the less crucial. "Inherent ethnological traits, climate, geographical location, adjacency to certain forms of animal life, completeness of commercial relations, attrition of nations and many other influences, will bring out marked social and political peculiarities, out of which has sprung that people's peculiar contribution to the civilization of the world." [40] And the critique of Andrews and Osgood was not made on speculative grounds alone. Both had learned from their study of colonial institutions that, however great the resemblance between English forms and American varieties, they developed different functions and produced different social results. Actually, the essence of the study of American colonial history was an effort to explain how English ideas and institutions became American.

The "germ theory" was exposed to a relentless examination by the younger students of its most famous proponents. Restriction of the study of American institutions to the Atlantic seaboard led to the intellectual rebellion of Frederick Jackson Turner. Turner had listened to the expositions of Herbert Baxter Adams and the institutional hypotheses of the classicist William F. Allen (1830–89) of the University of Wisconsin,[41] but he had been trained in critical analysis by both. The "germ theory" of politics did not demand endorsement of the heredity of acquired characteristics. Nor did it require a rigidly determined pattern of institutional continuities. But it did place an emphasis on the survival of cultural forms rather than upon social innovation. By stressing universal kinship, it narrowed the scope of cultural invention. The rebellion of Frederick Jackson Turner led to a search for the American origins of American institutions in the American West. "All peoples show development," Turner noted at the beginning of the most celebrated essay in American historiography, and

> the germ theory of politics has been sufficiently emphasized. In the case of most nations, however, the development has occurred in a limited area; and if the nation has expanded, it has met other growing peoples whom it has conquered. But in the case of the United States we have a different phenomenon. Limiting our attention to the Atlantic coast, we have the familiar phenomenon of the evolution of institutions in a limited area, such as the rise of representative government; the differentiation of simple colonial governments into complex organs; the progress from primitive industrial society, without division of labor, up to manufacturing civilization. But we have in addition to this a recurrence of the process of expansion. Thus American development has exhibited not merely advance along a single line, but return to primitive conditions on a continually advancing frontier line, and a new development for that area.[42]

Turner's language was mild, but the intellectual assault was devastating. "American social development has been continually beginning over again on the frontier." [43] Men did not, of course, shed their cultural equipment as they approached the frontier line. But unprecedented conditions coerced the colonizers of the West to readapt their heritage in order to meet the demands of a new, strange, and primitive environment. "The wilderness masters the colonist," and pressures of adaptation instigated novel formulations. Men from everywhere, with varied cultural backgrounds, made the West. The combinations of traits, attitudes, and institutions produced by the new environment together with the blending of cultures resulted in the evolution of characteristically American forms. "This perennial rebirth, this fluidity of American life, this expansion westward with its new opportunities, its continuous touch with the simplicity of primitive society, furnish the forces dominating the American character. The true point of view in the history of this nation is not the Atlantic coast, it is the Great West." [44] To concentrate on the East and its European background was to miss the crucial American point. Scholars, fascinated by the quest for survivals, who looked nostalgically beyond the Atlantic, neglected the most American part of America. The search for American origins soon succeeded the search for European origins. Among some of the disciples of Turner the search became so intensely absorbing that European origins and European influences all but vanished.

Historians captivated by Anglo-Saxonism neglected contemporary America as well as the American West. Turner's students, entranced by their master's early nationalism, likewise neglected the changing America in which they lived and thought and wrote. Historians under the spell of Anglo-Saxon interpretations equated cultural traditions with race; historians under the spell of the frontier interpretation equated cultural development with the forces of the environment. The Anglo-Saxon historians dealt with English immigrants who colonized America and transplanted old world institutions to the New England, whether in the South or in the North. The western historians dealt with immigrants from older America and certain portions of Europe, who colonized the great interior plains and valleys and created American institutions in the process. Together they managed to ignore urban industrial America, the growing American cities, and their immigrant populations. The former were largely interested in cultural forces outside the "Aryan" orbit; the latter were seeking the roots of American growth. The one discovered the American genius in the wilderness of ancient Germany; the other found the American spirit in the wilderness of the modern American West.[45] When immigration finally came to be studied seriously, it was studied against a background of Anglo-Saxon biases. Purporting to be free of bias, the scientific historians themselves became the carriers of racial prejudice. Anglo-Saxon cultural superiority was the result of racial superiority. Burgess extolled Aryan virtues and proclaimed the Germans, together with their English and American cousins, the great civilization builders.[46] Pervasive ethnocentricism and the pressures of nationalism combined to give the greatest movement of peoples in modern times American meanings alone. Emphases on Americanization, whether in public debate or in historical reconstruction, represented but a fragment of the cultural and psychological whole. As the trustees of the Anglo-Saxon tradition, students of immigration distinguished the older movement of colonial and early American settlement from the later movement after the Civil War. The first were the colonists; the latter were the immigrants. Lecturing to a glittering audience in the imperial palace in Berlin, John William Burgess said:

> On the other hand, the danger which arises from the powerful immigration of distinctly foreign race elements is . . . serious. So long as

> this immigration was confined to comers of the Teutonic races—Germans, Swedes, Norwegians, Danes, Dutch, and English—everything went well. They are people with a conscience, with a basis of self-control and, therefore, prepared for the enjoyment of civil and political liberty. But now we are getting people of a very different sort—Slavs, Czechs, Hungarians, South Italians. They do not know our language and do not learn it. They are inclined to anarchy and crime. They are, in everything which goes to make up folk character, the exact opposite of genuine Americans.[47]

Historians engaged in the study of the West unwittingly reenforced attitudes such as these. They were immersed in evaluating American rural culture, American rural attitudes, and an American rural way of life. They had little concern and less understanding of the Russian, Polish, or Hungarian workers who crowded the slums of America's great cities. Bent upon the discovery of what was truly American, they were as unlikely to think the essence of America was to be found in urban immigrant culture as they were unlikely to believe its sources were to be found in Teutonic or Anglo-Saxon contributions to eastern civilization. To endow one section of the world with a monopoly of cultural virtue warped human perspectives. To endow one section of the nation with the superlative virtues of civilization distorted national perspectives. The revolt against overstressing seaboard influences eliminated consideration of European influences. An uncritical emphasis upon the European heritage of Anglo-Saxonism robbed America of the heritage of other cultures and an appreciation of its own. Not until a leading historian of immigration reminded his colleagues that the Atlantic migration was a cultural movement in Western history did anything like a revision take place.[48] Historians had still to be reminded that immigration was not an American problem alone; it was a global process. While scholars were learning the implications of global processes, the history of immigration in America was provided with something called a European background. The "European background" was a contradiction in terms because it was a contradiction in thought. Immigration to the United States or elsewhere was a world movement. It had no European background; it had only European manifestations.

The Anglo-Saxon viewpoint exacted still another intellectual price. Freemanesque politics was the politics of law and constitutions. Adams and Freeman traced the development of shires, constables, and tithingmen from the old England to the new England in America. The moots and councils of unnamed Teutons in the language of Adams provided "the seeds of self-government, of commons and congresses." These ancient institutions were "the germs of our state and national life"; they were "the primordial cells of the body politic." [49] Freeman and Adams were immersed in the politics of the Middle Ages, in medieval concepts of representation and notions of social estates that emerged in response to struggles between king, nobles, and burghers. They were expert in the sources that detailed the political theory of mixed governments. In mixed governments conflicting groups were checked and struggling classes balanced to achieve social stability and to insulate change. Nineteenth-century exponents of Anglo-Saxon liberty upheld a static political theory, a political theory compounded of mechanical checks on the power of both absolute rulers and popular majorities, which, if adequate, yielded peace and freedom. Doctrines of virtual representation followed only if the classes thus virtually represented remained stationary. Social mobility and economic fluidity made estates and virtual representation logically untenable. And artificial checks and balances were incompatible with majority rule. Freeman, like Burgess, was an eloquent apostle of liberty, but the doctrines of liberty were not those of majority rule-process effected through institutionalized party systems.[50] For Freeman it was the self-government of the Witan, not the Commons of his own day. For Burgess it was Germanic origins, not the political innovations of American historical experience.[51] G. P. Gooch correctly suggests that Freeman, while a believer in continuities, was not an evolutionist.[52] Adams believed in both and understood Darwin better, but he frequently did not weigh the consequences of his own premises. When in the process of evolution the "primordial cells" vary significantly, the result is a new variety.

Herbert Baxter Adams studied Norman constables rather than the actual operation of politics. Lord Bryce, friend of Adams and friend of Hopkins, wrote *The American Commonwealth,* which called the principles of predetermined institutional evolution into question at a hundred points. Empirically descriptive and comparative within self-imposed bounds, it dealt with the realities of American politics, with the presidency, the congress, the courts, and the parties. Bryce enlarged the panorama of politics and liberty by examining novel institutions, different modes of adaptation, and different methods of social organization.[53] But it remained for Woodrow Wilson, a respected member of the Hopkins fraternity, to reveal the politics of democracy as dynamic rather than static, demanding evaluation of organic relationships between functioning institutional parts.[54]

Emphasis on politics as construed by Freeman, Burgess, and Adams was rejected together with the Teutonic hypothesis and gross comparative methods.[55] "With us," Burgess had written of the purposes of graduate teaching at Columbia, "history is the chief preparation for the study of the legal and political sciences. Through it we seek to find the origin, follow the growth and learn the meaning of our legal, political, and economic principles and institutions." [56] And once found, the meaning became a conceptual formula for the understanding of social and political change. History as past politics and politics as present history was also rejected. When John Richard Green, an early exemplar of social history and a protégé of Freeman's, reviewed Freeman's *Norman Conquest* he wrote harshly. "He passes silently by religion, intellect, society. He admires the people gathered in its Witan, but he never takes us to the Thegn's hall or to the peasant's hut. Of the actual life, manners, tastes of our forefathers the book tells us nothing. It is essentially a work of historic reaction." [57] The political-institutional interpretation was narrow in its outlook and limited in its vision. John Bach McMaster, Edward Eggleston, James Harvey Robinson, and Arthur M. Schlesinger, Sr.,[58] recoiling from the image of man as an institutional animal, devised a new history more in keeping with the humanistic tradition. Abandoning the Freemanesque model of political history did not mean the abandonment of politics in historical interpretation. But while rejecting the Adams concept of institutional origins, they did not substitute any other concepts. The serious study of politics became the special preserve of political scientists. Political history became for the most part the record of party battles and party organization written without benefit of hypotheses.

The interest of Herbert Baxter Adams in Saxon and Norman origins waned after 1883. After that date at least he no longer published monographs on these subjects. Instead, he directed his concentrated energy to education, and Hopkins and the seminary continued to remain the center of his life. To build the university and the history department was simply another way of furthering the careers of his students, who augmented the prestige of history and Hopkins alike. The American Historical Association and its *Review* received his undiminished support, a support beneficial both to history and to education.[59] University extension attracted his concern and he helped to set up courses on the British model for the general population of Baltimore.[60] The Chautauqua idea captivated him, and on several occasions he lectured under its auspices.[61] His educational activity extended from boys' schools to the development of libraries, which he aided by lectures, articles, and organizational work.[62]

The history of education was as meaningful to Adams as the reform of education. For one associated with the makings of a great university and with the organization of a learned discipline, the history of education was scarcely peripheral. Under an arrangement with the United States Bureau of Education in 1887, Adams became the editor of a series of monographs entitled, "Contributions to American Educational History." Twenty-nine items, of which a number dealt with higher education in specific states, were completed during his life. Hopkins men were well represented in the roster of authorship, and Adams himself was inscribed on the roll. *Thomas Jefferson and the University of Virginia,* because of its subject as well as its author, has remained one of the more important titles in the group.[63] Yet it was education for history rather than the history of education with which Adams had always been identified. *The Study of History in American Colleges and Universities,* a labor less of love than commitment, was published in 1887. By demonstrating all that had already been done to make history a respected and respectable academic subject, Adams showed what remained to be accomplished. Adams never wearied of the role of propagandist for more and better historical research and instruction. He supplemented his compendium on history in America's colleges and universities with special reports on educational developments at Harvard, Yale, Columbia, and William and Mary.[64] His article, "Special Methods of Historical Study," which appeared in G. Stanley Hall's *Methods of Teaching and Studying History* was a thoughtful recasting of two earlier pieces. Here he offered teachers and students chapter-and-verse advice based on his experiences with courses at Smith and Johns Hopkins.[65]

Adams' longest and most elaborate work was also devoted to history in America. In 1886 Adams agreed to prepare a biography of Jared Sparks, the great editor and collector of his country's documents. The two volumes stipulated in the contract duly appeared in 1893, a tribute to the memory of Jared Sparks and to the faithfulness of Herbert Baxter Adams.[66] While filled with interesting data about their subject still not readily accessible elsewhere, the volumes were lacking in proportion and balance. Sparks and the editorial controversies with which his reputation has been stained, placed Adams, as one of the foremost exemplars of scientific accuracy, in a somewhat difficult position. But he handled the sharp points at issue with delicacy and tact, for which the Sparks family and the judicious must always be grateful.[67] Historians, like other men, all too frequently err; their errors live after them, and their services are too likely to be obscured. Errors, of course, must be corrected, sometimes often, but the necessity of correction need not obliterate services rendered in spite of them. Adams too committed errors, but none can exaggerate them without distorting his fidelity to scholarship. History was his life, and Herbert Baxter Adams deserves well of it.

XX

The Impact of Science and
the Science of History

The achievements of the scientific historians are central to the growth of historiography. While they filled the great professional chairs and stimulated a widespread general interest, their vices have been more frequently celebrated than their virtues. They wrote weighty monographs and inspired scores of students who more than matched them in output and acumen. Public support came in response to their efforts and resulted in the creation of lasting institutions for the preservation and analysis of the human heritage. They also broke with the historiographical past. They set up new standards, established new criteria, and developed new aims for scholarship. Exactitude became a measure of perfection, factual detail a perpetual quest. Whatever assumptions hovered over their mental operations, accuracy became a value worthy of almost any intellectual effort. However much they failed to achieve the objectivity in which so many took pride, verifiable truth became the supreme value of scholarship. If they sometimes failed to practice in the monograph what they preached in the manual, they endlessly attested their faith in the power of intelligence to arrive at understanding of man and the world.

The rise of science was one of the most pervasive aspects of cultural change in the years following the Civil War. Beginning with the publication of Charles Darwin's *Origin of Species* in 1859, the most compelling influence upon thought and learning was the scientific renaissance initiated by the theory of evolution.[1] The impact of scientific developments spurred historians to render the study of history an accurate and ordered discipline. While historians honored the work of their predecessors, they were sometimes inclined to view it as a prescientific expression of the primitive urge to record and to understand the past. Theirs was the task of creating a science of history in the spirit of experimental method. Critical evaluation was a virtue in itself.

> The student of chemistry does not expect to gain from his own early and awkward experiments any new or startling results. He only aims to comprehend, as one can only do by personal experiment, those laws of chemical action already laid down by previous investigation. So the student of history may not expect to arrive at new results during the time of his apprenticeship, but he will certainly learn how other men have arrived at their results, and will thus know how to measure these at their true value.[2]

The meaning and implications of scientific method absorbed the historian. Method supplied the clue to historical practice and indicated the differences between earlier efforts and modern analytical triumphs. Ephraim Emerton, German-educated Harvard historian, proclaimed that there was "a science of history, with its apparatus, its schools, its devotees, and its great results already reached. . . ." [3] In answer to a chemist who did not grasp the meaning of scientific method as applied to history, Emerton explained: "Original work in history consists in an inquiry into the sources of authority for a given period or for a given statement or series of statements. Every conscientious historian of today goes through such a process in preparing his narrative." [4]

Emerton voiced the late-nineteenth-century historian's aspiration. The raw material of historical science was the original document just as the concrete particulars of the phenomenal world were the raw materials of physical science. For historians and scientists alike the particular, the discrete, and the primary were the ultimate elements of experience. "All science which is true science," declared an eminent historian in defense of the primal faith, "must rest upon the proved and correlated fact. . . . At the very beginning of all conquests of the unknown lies the fact, established and classified, to the fullest extent possible at the moment." [5]

Such facts were the sources of knowledge, the materials from which an intellectual synthesis was constructed. The first duty of the historian was to discover the facts. "What are the facts?" was the perennial historical question. "What is the truth?" was a phrase substantially equivalent. When the historical scholar sought answers to the query: "What actually happened?" he turned to the evidence, and the evidence was in the record.[6] The historical record, the primary source, contained the facts. Facts were real, tangible, irreducible. They alone were free from "anticipations" of nature, from speculative inference, from *a priori* assumptions. Facts, and the eternal search for them, permitted the historian to control if not to escape his prejudices, to seek if not to attain, the ideal of objectivity. Truth was elusive, the whole truth beyond human grasp. But truth was definable in terms of actuality revealed by the facts, not what someone wished or thought the actuality to be. The actuality revealed by the facts was the truth, and it was the historian's responsibility to discover it. This attitude toward fact, this striving for accuracy, for critical standards of documentary analysis made history a science for scholars during the latter decades of the nineteenth century and defined their concept of scientific method. George Burton Adams, an outstanding historian of the English constitution, writing in defense of scientific history, restated the faith of his predecessors:

> Can methods of investigation which are strictly scientific be applied to the study of the past action of the race in such a way as to give our knowledge of what happened greater certainty? The school of Ranke has never endeavored to go beyond this . . . question, but their answer to it has been a clear and, I believe, an indisputable affirmative. The actual result has been a science of investigation, and a method of training . . . . At any rate it is true that all technically trained historians . . . have been trained according to these ideas and they have all found . . . that the first duty of the historian is to ascertain as nearly as possible and to record exactly what happened.[7]

The historian's elemental function was to discover the sources.[8] Any source, however, was not enough. He was obligated to find the best sources—those contemporary with the events he wished to describe. Original sources were more reliable by definition, for the closer they were to the events the less likely they were to be tainted by later attitudes, values, and ideas. Such primary sources did contain attitudes, values, and ideas, but these inhered in the times and were parts of the factual whole. "History has at its disposal a limited stock of documents," concluded two of the most noted historical methodologists who would have riveted the historian to the written record,[9] and

> this very circumstance limits the possible progress of historical science. When all the documents are known, and have gone through the operations which fit them for use, the work of critical scholarship will be

finished. In the case of some ancient periods, for which documents are rare, we can now see that in a generation or two it will be time to stop. Historians will then be obliged to take refuge more and more in modern periods. Thus history will not fulfill the dream which, in the nineteenth century, inspired the romantic school with so much enthusiasm for the study of history; it will not penetrate the mystery of the origin of societies; and, for want of documents, the beginnings of the evolution of humanity will always remain obscure.[10]

The historian was to take the sources logically apart in the same way the chemist took any segment of the physical world logically apart. Both put their data together again according to rigorous rules of logic in order to discover their true nature. History could be as scientific in its methods as physics. As organized, verifiable knowledge it could also be classed as a science even if it could not be equated with the physical sciences. "In history knowledge is not obtained as in the other sciences, by direct methods; it is indirect. History is not . . . a science of observation, but a science of reasoning." [11]

Documents, from which the facts of history were quarried, possessed a logical priority. The documents came first in time, preceded only by the event itself. Since the event could not be made to recur, the primary account was necessarily the beginning of knowledge concerning it. Hence the absorption of the scientific historian with the documentary facts; hence his preoccupation with method, the means by which the primary record was discovered, preserved, organized, and understood. But once the documents were discovered by scientific techniques, once they were validated by scientific principles of internal criticism, how did the induction or synthesis—the "science of reasoning"—operate? Given the priority of facts, the facts preceded the induction on which it was inevitably based. Emphasis upon discovery of data and the inductive process made it possible for the historian to perform his scientific function with a minimum of bias or preconception. He did not ask any questions until he had the data of the document; he asked them only thereafter and then only in accordance with the rules of scientific procedure. He did not deduce conclusions from concepts or axioms accepted in advance of proof. Rather, he induced a conclusion from the facts themselves after they were discovered and ordered.[12] Having amassed the facts and as many facts as possible, the "facts spoke for themselves." [13] How the human mind operated in relation to the facts presented for analysis and how reason played its role in the process of synthesis, the nineteenth-century historians in America did not generally inquire. It was enough that this procedure was equated with the procedure of science. The nineteenth-century historian was simply following the method he believed the physical scientist had adopted and which had produced such grand results. Scientists, no less than historians, for the most part agreed that metaphysical issues were unprofitable. There was ample cause for both to be skeptical of undisciplined abstraction, but the validity of knowledge could not be accepted as given simply because some philosophical efforts had previously obstructed empirical research.[14]

American historians drew their major inspiration from German sources. German scholars, particularly Johann Gottfried von Herder, Barthold Georg Niebuhr, and Leopold von Ranke, initiated the modern movement in historiography.[15] Herder formulated the mission of history, and Niebuhr strikingly exemplified the principles of critical method. Ranke, Niebuhr's most celebrated pupil, illustrated and developed them.[16] American historians, whoever their teachers, universally regarded Ranke as the patron of scientific history and the unparalleled master of their craft. Nor was Ranke's reputation unjustified, for "in him," as a well-known scholar later affirmed, "historical consciousness reached a new height of maturity, and . . . in the enormous range of his works and teaching no modern scholar has equalled him." [17]

A new era of historical scholarship began with Ranke's famous seminar at the University of Berlin in 1833. When in 1876 Herbert Baxter Adams began his career at the Johns Hopkins University, Ranke was over eighty, and there was scarcely an historian in the western world who did not account himself an intellectual disciple or an intellectual adversary. When Ranke died [18] in 1886, the critical principles associated with his name—the method of Ranke—were the methods of history. History was everywhere defined in Ranke's words, an account of the past "wie es eigentlich gewesen." [19] Historians began their work where Niebuhr and Ranke had begun theirs: with the documents, the documents contemporary with the events. Scholars in America and elsewhere strove to borrow something of his critical genius, to capture something of his passion for truth.

Although Ranke is the Thucydides[20] of modern history, he has frequently been misinterpreted.[21] He redefined the scope of history as well as the nature of historical method. But he revised historical techniques in order to realize his conception of the purpose of history. Accordingly, if his understandings of the nature of history were misapprehended, his concepts of historical method were almost certain to be misunderstood. Disciples wrote countless monographs in what they believed to be the Rankean tradition, but Ranke himself always insisted that "there are other things than mere texts to examine." Excavation of the materials and a faithful summary of their contents were far from enough. No multiplication of evidence could result in history because[22] without the historian the facts remained forever silent. The historian himself—his life, his training, his artistry—was an indispensable party to the historical transaction. He whose methods did so much to create a guild of experts had only scorn for those merely learned in their specialty and nothing more. Ranke could afford to insist on the need for depth in historical training; he was trained in sufficient depth to appreciate his own inadequacies. He began his career in classical philology. He studied theology and learned to read the Old Testament in Hebrew. Thucydides intrigued him and he became something of a specialist on the early Greek historians. Prolonged study of Kant and Fichte prepared him for philosophy, an interest he finally exchanged for a professional career in history. He had little respect for the untutored specialist.[23]

Such considerations suggest a problem. Ranke, acclaimed as the greatest of scientific historians, was a great philosophical historian. He was a philosophical historian in exactly the sense that American scientific historians disparaged. Except for his devotion to documentary sources and the methods he refined for their use, he was scientific in precisely the sense they denied. While he disparaged philosophy, his thrusts were aimed at particular philosophies: certain rationalisms of the Enlightenment and a type of a priorism he associated with Hegel and his followers.[24] Ranke was to be sure supremely concerned with the discovery of what had actually happened; but he was concerned with what had actually happened because he wished to discover meanings in history. In fact, what actually happened could be discovered, if it could be discovered at all, only after an hypothesis relative to its meaning had been devised. What actually happened referred not to the uncoordinated elements of a situation but to a theory of its total significance. "Nothing," he wrote, "but universal history can be written. All our efforts tend to illuminate this. Detail never seems better than when it is seen in its relation with the whole."[25]

Ranke frequently stated that he wished to eliminate the self from historical analysis.[26] To eliminate the self would insure against the intrusion of the historian's personality and prevent distortion of observation. This was a methodological problem, not a methodological axiom. None knew better than Ranke that elimination of the self would eliminate the richness of background and the diversity of viewpoint that the investigator brings to historical study. Literally to eliminate the self would transform the scholar into an automatic collector of documents. Were this transformation conceivable, historical effort would yield only raw data devoid of meaning. Ranke knowingly involved himself in the observation and narration of history. He took "an active part in the events," he said with reference to the *History of Prussia,* otherwise "such a history would not be possible." [27] His *German History in the Age of the Reformation* was likewise written "with the deepest feeling for the events and of an unequivocal attitude concerning them." [28]

The greatest confusion concerning the Rankean method arises at this point. But it was here that Ranke made his superlative contribution to history as a discipline and as a form of thought. He succeeded "in determining and delimiting the part played by the 'personal.'" [29] In effect, Ranke made the personal a creative part of the "will to knowledge," [30] or, in a less enigmatic phrase, he made the personal an instrument of knowing. "That was what permeated, vitalized, inspired his research; but he would not allow it to prescribe in advance the conclusion which his research should reach." [31] He collected documents with a methodical passion and based his historical reconstructions upon the largest body of primary sources available. But he used the documents imaginatively. A psychologist of human motivation, he subjected the written remains to total and complete analysis. He cross-examined the witnesses of the past by every known device; he explored every avenue of insight before he established their internal logic and wrung them dry of the meanings they acquired for him. Even this was not enough. He entered into them psychologically; he identified with the men he tried to understand and impersonated the motives of the subjects whose lives he tried to recreate. "The historian's task," Ranke once said, "is to explain history by human motives." No other kind of history was possible for him. "It has not been doctrines that have overthrown the world . . . ," for doctrines move in living men, but "the powerful personalities who are the incarnation of these doctrines." [32] Far from the Ranke of popular imagination, his outstanding characteristic was "as a subtle analyst of human passions . . . in moral portraiture. . . ." [33] Normally he did not take sides. He resembled the gifted theatrical performer who lives a role rather than the partisan who pleads a cause.

Ranke ignored those who objected to his approach as failing to serve immediate practical needs. History, of course, offered wisdom to mankind, but Ranke believed wisdom was the end product of the historical scholar's total understanding. Wisdom did not result from the historian's *ex parte* judgments; it emerged after the past was fully understood. Only then did the historian know what really happened, *wie es eigentlich gewesen*. This was one of the profounder meanings of Ranke's much-quoted phrase, for no true judgment was conceivable until such understanding was attained. The historian, Ranke believed, did not judge in the usual sense of the word. By achieving an empathic relation with persons and events, he simply re-enacted in words what individuals had actually thought and felt and what movements and events had actually occurred in relation to them. The historian, to select an instance, did not pass judgment on Frederick the Great; history evaluated him and his role. The historian, by a successful effort to feel and think as Frederick did and by a successful merger of himself with Frederick's era, learned to sympathize with the motives and forces that impelled the king to think, to feel, and to act.[34]

The evolution of Ranke's own research and writing suggests his method and purpose. The history of the papacy was essential to the history of the Reformation, German history to French history, Spain to Venice, Venice to Turkey. Each was essential to the other, and all were necessary if the history of Europe were to be comprehended.[35] Leopold von Ranke was a universal historian. He was a universal historian, not in the sense of an historian of civilization, which he was not, but in the sense of one who sought universal meanings in the welter of particulars. In terms of the universal history of Europe, England was a particular that defied comprehension apart from a larger unity. The concept of the universal in Ranke was the concept of an idea, and it was by means of the idea that he hoped to discipline the particular. Ranke's "idea" was not Plato's: he did not seek ultimate meanings in a transcendental world beyond earthly experience. For him the particular facts of historical life were not mere appearances which were the imperfect copies of the immutable original. The historian's prime function was to deal with the particulars of past human experience, and he could hardly solve his problem by leaving the world of experience to find a solution. Hence he rejected the Hegelian expedient, which he regarded as another variety of Platonic dualism—a separation between the world of ultimate reality and the world of phenomenal experience. Ranke's universal or "idea" "cannot be known through any separate faculty of knowledge but only through the events themselves." The facts themselves are not enough for the historian who "like the draughtsman, produces only caricatures if he sketches detailed circumstances and events merely as they seem to present themselves and as they follow upon each other. The apprehension of events must be guided continually by ideas; yet on the other hand these ideas must not be added on to history as an unrelated appendage. . . . The 'idea' can appear only in the natural connection of things and can never be separated from them as something independent and existing for itself alone." [36]

Accordingly, Ranke did not separate life from meaning and truth; he did not separate truth from the irresistible urge to search for it. Yet, in the most important sense, the historian did not put life into the past, he reported the life he found throbbing in the past. Meaning was implicit in the data, but it could only be reported "in its relation with the whole." [37] Subject and object were merged in every experiment; they were living parts of every venture in creativity. Niebuhr, inverting Plato's image, spoke of the historian working in the darkness of a cave who could see what others, unaccustomed to darkness, could scarcely perceive even with assistance. Because he had himself become one with the life of ancient Rome, he was able to illumine the blur of flux with the light of meaning. He was able imaginatively to unite changing particulars by the creation of universal ideas. All history is in one sense histrionic—the power of finely trained and sensitive minds to live the lives of those who have lived them before. The historian immersed in the past impersonates the actors in a vital segment of the human drama and becomes sensitized to the spirit of an era. Henry Adams invited men to live in the Middle Ages as he did, and Ranke invited men to participate in his judgments.

Ranke made the implications of his historical theory explicit in his historical writings. He did not consider himself a reporter, stripped of personality, who, having discovered the so-called facts, transmitted them unsullied by meaning to posterity. On the contrary, he consciously sought to make himself one with the materials. The materials spoke to him, as to every great historian, through the medium of symbolic forms. This was his greatest contribution and his greatest virtue. When he expressed a preference for what actually happened rather than any fictionalized account, as in Sir Walter Scott's *Quentin Durward*,[38] it was not because he belittled Scott's imaginative creation but because the true sources offered the possibility of a more credible account. Only after one had grasped *wie es eigentlich gewesen,* could one capture the facts. Facts, after all, are captive only after they are endowed with meaning. Ranke's formula stated rather than solved the problems of historical knowledge. While there is an apparent mystical aspect in Ranke's formulation of the universal, it relates neither to the primacy of the concept nor to the validity of the symbolic form.

If Ranke's classic aphorism, *wie es eigentlich gewesen,* became the scientific historian's motto, it was a precept all too literally taken. It was Ranke's skill as an analyst of sources and as a historical craftsman, not as a philosopher, that scholars sought to emulate. Ranke's reputation as a teacher and the luster of his writing, not his elucidation of symbolic forms, account for his prestige. The cumulative influence of scientific innovation shaped attitudes of mind and objectives, for the scientific atmosphere encircled the practitioners of history. More often it was a general mood rather than the consequence of a sustained analysis of the problems of knowledge.

American historians, like other scholars, understandably wished to participate in the prestige of science and to escape from the fetters of uncertainty. They wished to be as objective about the past as they believed the physicist was neutral about the universe. History, they longed to believe, was as rational and scientific as mathematics. If mathematics also possessed form and beauty, neither form nor beauty alone distinguished it. If history also instructed and entertained, both these characteristics were secondary. History, they permitted themselves to hope, was neither solely art nor literature. History was also science.

Science became a cult, and empirical criteria prefaced credibility. While Darwin and the revival of evolutionary theories initiated a great age of biology, other sciences were also enriched by spectacular discoveries. The observations of Willard Gibbs in theoretical physics, beginning in the 1870's, were temporarily unappreciated, but Albert Michelson's measurement of light during the same period was a startling instance of understanding the ways in which the universe performed. Michelson's discovery was likewise evidence of the method of science, for it was the use of experimental devices that enabled Darwin, Gibbs, and Michelson to extract meanings from nature. They exemplified the injunction of Sir Ray Lankester, an insightful zoologist and a younger member of Darwin's coterie. "Nature," said Lankester, "gives no reply to general inquiry." Lankester's comment hardly accorded with stereotyped notions of scientific methods. Nature, he cautioned, "must be interrogated by questions which already contain the answer she is to give; in other words, the observer can only observe that which he is led by hypothesis to look for." [39] Contemporaries of Charles Darwin who applauded the results of physics, chemistry, and biology only half understood the methods by which they were obtained.

The scientific vogue did not require a tutored understanding. Fascination with electricity, locomotion or steel flourished without an exact comprehension of the theory of light waves, of diesel engines, or the process of oxidation. Reading of laboratory reports and research results in the scientific journals was no more necessary than familiarity with press accounts of paleontological findings and the wonders of applied chemistry. To be impressed with the application of science, Americans had only to be alive.

Historical scholars were as impressed by theoretical science as they were by applied science. Mental attitudes created by science made it almost mandatory for scholars to review their status if not their postulates. The credentials of history could not be less rigorously appraised than the credentials of biology. The method by which historical data was gathered and reconstructed had to be made to conform as far as possible to the method employed by science with such conspicuous success. As late as 1883 Professor Emerton asked somewhat petulantly:

> How does it stand now with history? Perhaps more than any other study, history has suffered, and is suffering, from that misconception . . . that it means only a dreary mass of facts, dates, and events, strung along like so many beads on a chain, and with no more distinction in value or meaning. It is the rarest thing to find a man who has any idea whatever about the materials of historical writing, or of the methods used in dealing with these materials. Even educated men are inclined to regard history as a collection of stories merely, more or less entertaining to read, but not having any really serious bearing upon the present active life of men.[40]

Only those disciplines which could satisfy the criteria supposedly established by science were worthy of respect. If the materials of history were different from the materials of the physical sciences, it could at least be asked that historical method conform to the methods of science as closely as the differences permitted. Historians were persuaded that the only way to discover the truth about the past was by refining the method of historical inquiry. By this was meant adapting the method of science to the search for historical verity. Every man would indeed become the arbiter of his own scholarly rectitude unless there were valid criteria to which all could assent, general principles to which all could agree, cumulative knowledge upon which all could rely.

The scientific historian's conception of scientific method provides an accurate self-image. The philosophy of science espoused by the scientific historians was based less upon scientific practice than upon descriptions of scientific procedures and criteria. Historians and others were indebted to the discussions of method presented by Francis Bacon and John Stuart Mill. Neither Mill nor Bacon was an experimental scientist, and each relied on secondhand experience of scientific research. For Bacon and Mill the idea of hypothesis was a limiting idea which pressed the facts into service, not a creative instrument consciously devised to order the facts and to explore the initial problems and those subsequently raised by the exploration. To avoid controlling ideas and to permit the facts freely to testify, Mill stressed the untrammeled search for undiluted facts. Only after as many facts relevant to the problem were collected and arranged in proper chronological and schematic sequences was generalization possible.[41]

This version of scientific method was based on a cluster of assumptions. Facts were envisioned as real in an ultimate sense, which, once discovered, fitted with other facts and permitted the historian to trace out meanings and relations. The nature and constitution of "fact" were seldom examined. Half a century later, Carl L. Becker, excavating beneath the crumbled temple of his own historical precepts, described what a historical fact had once meant to him and what it continued to mean to others.

> Historians feel safe when dealing with facts. We talk much about the "hard facts" and the "cold facts," about "not being able to get around the facts," and about the necessity of basing our narrative on a "solid foundation of fact." By virtue of talking this way, the facts of history come in the end to seem something solid, something substantial like physical matter . . . something possessing definite shape, and clear persistent outline—like bricks or scantlings . . . .

Becker gave fact a new character:

> Thus the simple historical fact turns out to be not a hard, cold something with clear outline, and measurable pressure, like a brick. It is so far as we can know it, only a *symbol,* a simple statement which is a generalization of a thousand and one simpler facts which we do not for the moment care to use, and this generalization itself we cannot use apart from wider facts and generalizations which it symbolizes. And generally speaking, the more simple an historical fact is, the more clear and definite and provable it is, the less use it is to us in and for itself.[42]

Like Becker, those who have analyzed the nature of fact, have endlessly reported that a fact is "simply the part of the picture on which we fix our attention." [43] To insist on a rigid demarcation between facts and concepts, between things and meanings, violates common-sense experience as well as logical analysis. Scholars did not have to be Hegelians, as Morris R. Cohen was not, to conclude that "meanings do not exist apart from the facts" and that there is no fact which does not "depend upon relations to other facts for its existence as well as for our knowledge of it." [44] Mill's version of scientific method assumed that facts can be known apart from hypotheses or concepts. Whether history is or is not a science in the ordinary sense is largely an honorific debate, but neither science nor history could exist without concepts. Mill's philosophy of scientific method was neither the method of science nor the method of history. Bacon indeed misstated the scientific method nor did he follow his own version of it. [45]

The actual practice of the late-nineteenth-century historians was frequently at variance with their methodological faith. John William Burgess, partial to original investigation and an exponent of the scientific virtues of textual criticism, did not operate without the use of concepts. Describing the method in use at Columbia, he affirmed: "After the facts have been determined and the causal nexus established we endeavor to teach the student to look for the *institutions and ideas* which have been developed through the sequence of events in the civilization of an age or people." [46] The state, for example, was not the "mere consequence of the sequence of events," but an ultimate idea which was the end of man. [47] President Andrew Dickson White of Cornell remarked that historical instruction in that university proceeded from "the empirical to the rational by encouraging the students to draw philosophical principles out of events before any connected discussion of philosophy of history is given as a whole," for he favored encouraging "the student to find in the progress of the world's affairs philosophical principles and underlying laws." [48]

Bacon's maxim—"man should bid themselves for a while renounce conceptions and begin to make acquaintance with things themselves"—was more frequently expounded than followed. Herbert Baxter Adams, pioneer extraordinary, wrote: "every pebble, every form of organic life, from the lowest mollusk to the highest phase of human society (might be regarded) as a perfect microcosm. . . . Natural history is of no significance if viewed apart from Man. Human history is without foundation if separated from Nature." [49] Many shared the purposes of Moses Coit Tyler, although few expressed them so frankly:

I confess that I adopt for American history the principle which Professor Seeley, of Cambridge, is fond of applying to English history, namely, that while history should be thoroughly scientific in its method, its object should be practical. To this extent, I believe in history with a tendency. My interest in our own past is chiefly derived from my interest in our present and future; and I teach American history, not so much to make historians as to make citizens and good leaders for the State and the Nation. From this point of view, I decide upon the selection of historical topics for special study.[50]

And in one of the most respected manuals of the day, two noted French scholars collaborated in saying:

In order to use the facts which have been observed under known conditions, it is necessary to apply criticism to them, and criticism consists in a series of reasonings by analogy. The facts as furnished by criticism are isolated and scattered; in order to organize them into a structure it is necessary to imagine and group them in accordance with their resemblances to facts of the present day, an operation which also depends on the use of analogies. This necessity compels history to use an exceptional method. In order to frame its arguments from analogy, it must always combine the knowledge of the particular conditions under which the facts of the past occurred with an understanding of the general condition under which the facts of humanity occur. Its method is to draw up special *tables* of the facts of an epoch in the past, and to apply to them sets of *questions* founded on the study of the present.[51]

Science nevertheless provided newer understandings for scholars in almost all branches of learning. Darwin, in Alfred Russel Wallace's abundant phrase, was the Newton of the nineteenth century. Darwinism presented a series of special hypotheses as well as a general one. Evolutionary biology suggested new concepts of the unity of time. Since evolutionary doctrines premised development without fixed beginnings and without precisely determinable ends, historians acquired a different series of temporal perspectives. Together with geological findings, evolutionary doctrines altered conventional historical categories. The course of terrestrial and human development, and hence of history, appeared to be infinitely longer than had previously been supposed. In consequence, many of the standard formulas—ancient, medieval, modern—had to be understood with tempered qualifications. From an evolutionary standpoint, Francis Bacon had been right in asserting that contemporaries are always the ancients. "Modern History," said Lord Acton in his inaugural lecture at the University of Cambridge in 1895,

is a subject to which neither beginning nor end can be assigned. No beginning because the dense web of the fortunes of man is woven without

> a void; because, in society as in nature, the structure is continuous, and
> we can trace things back uninterruptedly, until we dimly descry the
> Declaration of Independence in the forests of Germany. No end, because,
> on the same principle, history made and history making are scientifically
> inseparable and separately unmeaning.[52]

E. A. Freeman objected strenuously and repeatedly to the separation between ancient and modern history. History was "a brotherhood of all periods and all subjects, of all nations and languages."
Of this unity Freeman had no doubt "at least within the pale of
Aryan Europe." [53] Viscount Morley elaborated this point of view
before an audience at the University of Manchester. Continuity of
human societies was "orthodox doctrine, though accepted, as orthodox doctrines sometimes are, in various senses." [54] The noted French
scholar of medieval institutions, Marc Bloch, sensitively made the
same point much later:

> There is, then, just one science of men in time. It requires us to join
> the study of the dead and of the living . . . historical research will toler-
> ate no autarchy. Isolated, each will understand only by halves . . . ; for
> the only true history . . . is universal history.[55]

Questions of origins—of ideas, institutions, aspirations—assumed
commanding importance. American historians, no less than their
European counterparts, acquired a different set of inspirations. Continuities as well as origins instigated fresh researches and thought-
provoking comment. Herbert Baxter Adams, whose respect for the
present was deeper than some of his associates, observed:

> There is hardly a subject of contemporary interest, which, if properly
> studied, will not carry the mind back to a remote antiquity, to historic
> relations as wide as the world itself. A study of the community in which
> the student dwells will serve to connect that community not only with
> the origin and growth of the State and Nation, but with the mother-
> country, with the German fatherland, with the village communities
> throughout the Aryan world—from Germany and Russia to old Greece
> and Rome; from these classic lands to Persia and India. Such modern
> connections with the distant Orient are more refreshing than the gene-
> alogy of Darius the son of Hystaspes.[56]

The past, Adams discovered, resided in the present which, as Marc
Bloch remarked, contained an important historical prescript.

> In the last analysis, whether consciously or no, it is always by borrow-
> ing from our daily experiences and by shading them . . . with new tints
> that we derive the elements which help us to restore the past.[57]

While the past had often been conceived as "parent of the present,"
the doctrine of evolution supplied a living connection between spe-

cific aspects of specific pasts and their present manifestations. Professor William F. Allen, teacher and colleague of Frederick Jackson Turner at the University of Wisconsin, was moved by the study of institutions and "their organic relation to one another in constitutions of government." He became progressively immersed in "the political conflicts that have grown out of them" [58]—an area of analysis of which his foremost student was to become one of the foremost exponents.

Continuities based upon similarities implied comparisons. The doctrine of evolution restored the comparative method to historical study. More directly indebted to the sociologist Herbert Spencer and the anthropologist Edward B. Tylor than to Charles Darwin, comparative assumptions exhilarated the scientific historians. Herbert B. Adams wrote: "The world of human thought and research were expanding into new realms." American students were urged to compare

> the phases of historic truth here discovered with similar phases of discovery elsewhere; for example, the colonial beginnings of North America should be compared with Aryan migrations westward into Greece and Italy, or again with the colonial systems of Greece and of the Roman Empire, or of the English Empire to-day, which is continuing in South Africa and Australia and in Manitoba, the same old enterprise which colonized the Atlantic seaboard of North America. It would interest young minds to have parallels drawn between English colonies, Grecian commonwealths, Roman provinces, the United Cantons of Switzerland, and the United States of Holland.[59]

Adams drew the implications with clarity:

> The science of Biology no longer favors the theory of spontaneous generation. Wherever organic life occurs, there must have been some seed for that life. History should not be content with describing effects when it can explain causes. It is just as improbable that free local institutions should spring up without a germ along American shores as that English wheat should have grown here without planting. Town institutions were propagated in New England by old English and Germanic ideas brought by Pilgrims and Puritans.[60]

Scholars were later to correct such fanciful evolutionary correlations. One of the most glaring errors was speedily exposed by the colonial historian, Charles M. Andrews, who gently rebuked his former Hopkins mentors.

> As the study of anthropology continues, it becomes apparent that the people of this earth are not to each other as though they were inhabitants of different planets; that following the general lines of historical advancement, these people have developed from tribal life to political life

in much the same manner: that the stages of their growth have had, from the necessities of the case, certain points of familiarity, in consequence of which certain principles of development can be established; which, it is inherently probable, will apply to all peoples when they have reached a similar stage in social and political growth. We must, therefore, compare not anything and everything, but only that evidence which, as far as it can be determined, belongs to corresponding periods in the life of a people, and which alone we have an historical right to compare.[61]

The comparative method was an obvious historical device long before the advent of Darwinian evolution, as old in the study of man as in the study of natural science. George Bancroft, Francis Parkman, and John Lothrop Motley noted progressive differences in human culture, which they referred to differences in stages of civilization. Henry Adams began his Harvard survey of the Middle Ages with primitive man, although he later looked for general principles in physics instead of in biology. Distorted Darwinian analogies and oversimplified evolutionary interpretations were common enough nor were they confined to advocates of the "Teutonic hypothesis." [62]

Darwinian evolution exerted an influence far more revisionary than the "Teutonic hypothesis" and far more astringent than the comparative method. The nineteenth century was an age of science; it was also an age of history. Evolutionary biology conditioned historical theory and historical practice, but history and historical theory conditioned the development of evolutionary ideas and the development of science. The notion that science saturated the nineteenth-century mind has become a historical platitude; the correlative notion that history saturated nineteenth-century science remains relatively unexplored.

The concept of evolution, to anticipate later discussion, stimulated a creative merger between history and science. Ernst Cassirer, a German-American philosopher with wide historical interests, redirected attention to this fertile joinder in western thought. The nineteenth century, he wrote, "presents the first encounter and the first reckoning between two great ideals of knowledge. The ideal of the mathematical sciences, which had engrossed and dominated the seventeenth century, was paramount no longer." Developmental shifts in the nature of the understanding of knowledge resulted in "the *primacy of history* . . . proclaimed by both philosophy and science." [63] Restoration of history as a reliable form of knowledge was the other side of the decline of the mathematical view of nature. Reliance upon the ultimate truths of reason, seriously threatened in the so-called Age of Reason itself, was first effectively challenged in the mathematical sciences. The intellectual status of rationalist certainties reached a crisis in German romanticism of the early decades of the nineteenth century. But it was in the zoological sciences that fixed truths were questioned last, for the final truths of reason remained unassailed in biology until Darwin. Darwin and Darwinism performed a vital catalytic role. Darwinism, in the language of Cassirer, "opened to natural science a new *dimension* of thought . . . by showing that scientific and historical concepts are far from opposed but mutually supplement and need one another." [64]

Like every great historian, Darwin made the lifeless past a vital part of the living present. He coupled the scientific method of observation with the scientific method of ideal synthesis. He united the scientific method of physical experiment with the scientific method of logical analysis. Varieties of species were his particular data. The writings of travelers, explorers, breeders, and scientists were among his basic sources. Darwin discovered the theory of natural selection; he substantiated the theory of evolution. He created an hypothesis to explain the transmutation of species; he documented the history of the descent of living forms. Darwin enlivened a moribund segment of the whole past. But Darwin and the theory of evolution accomplished even more. Darwin and the theory of evolution succeeded in putting the whole of past life into every aspect of every form of present life. While the full meaning of the fusion of science and history was not immediately apparent either to historians or to scientists, the nature of the debate concerning the status of history altered in substance and direction.

Darwinian evolution was itself a history. History and biology both contributed to its hypothetical validity. The record of speculation from Aristotle to Darwin constituted a historical series no less than the record of geology and paleontology. But every experimental proof, each adaptation, variation, or mutation, was also an historical demonstration. Without historical examination "even the problems of pure classification and physiology" were not completely soluble. Ernst Rádl, historian of biological theories and an uncompromising Darwinian critic, summed up this novel intellectual phase explicitly.

> One could not possibly conceive of the true nature of an animal by any analysis, be it ever so profound, or by any comparison with other forms, however comprehensive, because there lies hidden in the organism traces of the past that only historical research is able to reveal.[65]

Darwinians, documenting the intellectual blockages in the history of evolutionary theories, declared that the evidence furnished by the material world was adequate to explain the history of life. "We no longer need indulge in airy speculations, for we are not in search of a general definition of the nature or essence of man. Our problem is simply to collect the empirical evidence which the general theory of evolution has put at our disposal in a rich and abundant measure." [66]

Confirmation of the general theory of evolution changed the framework of analysis for history as well as biology. Earlier biological theories of development were formal and metaphysical; post-Darwinian theories were nonmetaphysical and material. Aristotle, for example, explained biological development in the metaphysical language of appearance and reality. Changes in species were the appearances; the formal cause of variation was the final end toward which each species strove. "Accidental" causes could not explain material phenomena; explanations were satisfactory in terms of final causes alone. All material changes were particulars and were intimations of the ultimately real.

After Darwin, biological science gradually deserted this theory of knowledge. Physical rather than metaphysical explanations were fashioned to describe the nature and development of species and of man. The historical facts of organic life were no longer regarded as secondary and partial. After Darwin, evolutionary doctrines were premised on transmutation, not a genetically unconnected series in a great progressive chain of being. The concept of a gradual unfolding in which each form was referable to a transcendental category was exchanged for an evolution conceived as a great unbroken chain of life. Genetic transmutation was also a problem of history, the life history of the individual, of the species, and of the race. If evolutionary forms were rooted in the history of genetics, genetic changes were rooted in the history of life. From this point of view the biological sciences were historical. Darwin had not only put mind back into nature, he had put nature back into history.[67] The "idea of the historically evolved" [68] had become a vital category of the life sciences.

J. B. Bury, English historian of the idea of progress, noted some of the meanings of biological evolution applied to history.

> The present condition of the human race is simply and strictly the result of causal series (or a set of causal series)— a continuous succession of changes, where each state arises causally out of the preceding; and the business of historians is to trace this genetic process, to explain each change, and ultimately to grasp the complete development of humanity.[69]

Whether historians could in fact "ultimately . . . grasp the complete development of humanity" was a challenge scholars were infrequently disposed to accept. But the function of the historian was to explain change in terms of past connections and alterations precisely as the biologist delineated changes in living forms. Genetic transmutation revised the meanings attached to the historical concept of continuity. Differences in materials might demand differences in method, but all knowledge, including history, converged in the sciences of man. Science had provided the historian with a scientific faith. And history had provided scientists with a faith in science.

The scientific historians of the nineteenth century had perfected a method and elaborated a system of values. Yet the problems of historical knowledge were neither fully examined nor deeply explored.[70] Historians possessed a scientific method for the critical evaluation of documentary and other materials. They had still to develop theories of history based on the logic of symbols and the intricate textures of knowledge.

XXI

History at Hopkins:

J. Franklin Jameson, John Spencer Bassett,

William P. Trent, Woodrow Wilson

With the establishment of graduate departments in the leading American universities, the practice of history acquired identifiable cultural forms. Doctors of philosophy in history like Herbert Baxter Adams succeeded writers of philosophical history like Francis Parkman. History became a discipline taught by men who were university-trained and written by men tutored in the seminars of scholars. And the seminars were presided over by teachers who themselves had studied the principles of method and style from acknowledged masters. Historians became professionals as well as professors. Resembling their counterparts in physics and chemistry, they acquired the appropriate credentials entitling them to teach. They qualified as experts before venturing to add to the store of knowledge in the form of articles and monographic volumes on the history of the United States. Universities multiplied, and graduate instruction was both the cause and the effect of changes in teaching and research. Organizations—local, regional, national—indicated the spread of historical interest and the standardization of historical modes.

The course of specialization was swift and decisive. A dozen years after the formation of the American Historical Association in 1884, the transformation was complete. Jared Sparks in 1838 became McLean professor of ancient and modern history at Harvard.[1] In 1857 Andrew Dickson White began his historical career at the University of Michigan. In 1880 it was estimated that there were but eleven full-fledged professors of American history in the country.[2] Seven years later Herbert Baxter Adams, with admirable modesty, expressed confidence that Harvard could match foreign opportunities in graduate study and that it was no longer necessary to pursue the doctorate overseas.[3] Although France, England, and Germany continued to attract graduate students in considerable numbers,[4] America was ready to undertake the training of its own scholars.

Thereafter one notable event succeeded another with rapidity. Moses Coit Tyler moved from Michigan in 1881 to become professor of American history in Andrew Dickson White's Cornell. In 1883 the first volumes of *The Johns Hopkins University Studies* appeared under the guidance of Herbert Baxter Adams. The *Manual of Historical Literature,* prepared by Charles Kendall Adams, who in 1869 was offering his own seminar at the University of Michigan, indicated the growing awareness and accomplishment of American scholarship. The formation of the American Historical Association institutionalized the professional fact, and when the *Political Science Quarterly* appeared in 1886, evidence of the transformation of learning was no longer arresting. The first owed much to Adams of Hopkins; the second owed no less to Burgess of Columbia. Herbert Baxter Adams, who died in 1901, witnessed the alteration. With the death of Burgess in 1931 a new literature of American history had already appeared. Albert Bushnell Hart began to teach at Harvard in 1883, when the first volume of John Bach McMaster's *History of the People of the United States* was published. The *American Historical Review* emerged in 1895, and by 1900 James Harvey Robinson at Columbia was teaching his famous course on the "Intellectual Development of Modern Europe." [5] The "new history" had already reshaped Robinson's mind, and new historians were in the making.

Between 1884 and 1889, the eight massive volumes of the *Narrative and Critical History of America,* edited by Harvard's librarian Justin Winsor, came off the press. Thirty-four authors combined to produce this well-known and still usable compilation. Of these contributors but ten held academic appointments, of which two were in the field of history. Only one of these historians had received academic training in the subject.[6] When the *American Nation* series appeared under the editorial direction of Albert Bushnell Hart between 1904 and 1907, the statistics were weighted in the opposite direction. Twenty-one of the twenty-four authors were professors, all but two of whom had received graduate instruction in history.[7] A metamorphosis had occurred within the lifetime of a single generation.

The higher learning in America produced a phenomenally large number of students. They staffed the colleges and universities, filled the offices of the association, and wrote the books which became the manuals of the next generation. The intellectual relations between living historians and the founding fathers of modern historiography demonstrates their continuing influence. They stamped history with their hallmark, the hallmark of "scientific history." In their drive to make history "scientific," they provided points of return and departure for contemporary scholarship.[8]

As teachers the scientific historians entertained similar pedagogical notions. Recitations with emphasis on memory were to be substituted for independent investigations with emphasis on thought. "In every new school of learning," wrote a Harvard historian, who gave serious consideration to the goals of teaching, "a well-equipped laboratory is as necessary as a well-trained teacher. It remains to apply the same method to other branches of education." [9] The presentation of history "to be effective must not confine itself to lectures, but must supplement these by the method of original work." [10] Lectures, sometimes considered a necessary evil,[11] were variously regarded. Herbert Baxter Adams felt that any device "of teaching history which converts bright young pupils into note-taking machines" was a bad one. The general practice reminded Adams of Goethe's quip that students, admonished to pay close attention to their notes, were only able to be sure that the professor had not said anything outside of the lecture, a fate to which too many students had been consigned.[12] Ephraim Emerton's advice is still as sage as when he offered it:

> The justification of academic lectures on history, is that they shall contain *suggestion,* which shall enable students to do their own reading intelligently, and, therefore, profitably. They should contain the result of varied reading and research, summarizing the outcome of long controversies, showing how events of one period explain and are explained by those of another. It would take the inexperienced student weeks of reading to grasp the meaning of men and events which his instructor may present to him in a paragraph.[13]

Burgess approved of recitations on historical work at the lower levels of instruction. Textbooks, the drill of question and answer "for the purpose of fixing and classifying . . . the elements of historical geography, the chronology and outward frame of historic events, the biographies of historic characters, and the definitions of historical terms. . . ." he found admirable. But at the university level he endorsed the "original lecture" as the method of independent study. The original lecture was valid for both the professor and

the student. "The University professor must be a worker among original materials. He must present to his student *his own view* derived
from the most original sources attainable. He must *construct* history
out of the chaos of original historic atoms. If he does not do this, but
contents himself simply with repeating the views of others, it is probably because he is not capable of it; in which case he is no University
professor at all, but at best only a drill master of the Gymnasium." [14]

Original sources were an unqualified prerequisite for the graduate
student. Historians were to be *"trained"* and not merely *"learned."* [15]
Indeed Herbert Baxter Adams was convinced that it was almost as
important for the student to know *"how* to study history" as to know
history itself.[16] Textbooks, even when they could be said to exist,
were anything but popular. A broad familiarity with the literature
was essential, and libraries were the laboratories for scientific historical study. "What the laboratory is to physical science, that the library must be to moral science. The library must become, not a store-
house of books, but a place for work." [17] Accordingly the pioneer
historians were builders of collections, general and special, for ready
access to books was indispensable.[18] The seminar room was the
graduate student's private library and work room. Equipped with
reference books, monographs, and study alcoves, it was the scientific
historian's special pride. At least it was the special pride of Herbert
Baxter Adams, who with customary thoroughness drew a diagram of
the Hopkins seminar room. The Hopkins seminar, in addition to the
standard equipment, possessed a newspaper bureau, a map bureau, a
historical museum, and a portrait of Johann Kaspar Bluntschli.[19]

While the physical construction of the seminar was important,
what took place around the seminary table was much more so.
Ephraim Emerton gave an ecstatic description of his own experience
as master of the seminar:

> I can recall only with gratitude the inspiration which came from the
> generous enthusiasm of those young men who have sat . . . about the
> green table in the Harvard College library, working over, with a pure
> scholarly spirit, the dusty record of the middle ages. What a sense of
> discovery when they found themselves touching the very thought of the
> men who lived through the events they describe! What a triumph when
> they proved this book, bearing the imposing name of some famous
> scholar of our day, to be a tissue of gaps and errors! Nor could a
> scholar ask for any ampler reward than the repeated assurance of these
> young men that this power of independent thought was the best fruit of
> their student lives.

And the results for students were as salutary for scholarship as they
were gratifying for the participants.

The charm which has heretofore surrounded the names of great historians vanishes. He learns to accept nothing on their word. He demands the proof of every assertion, or if, as is often the case, proof be impossible, he demands at least evidence as to the degree of probability. And this he does not blindly, not in the spirit of mere carping criticism, but intelligently, under the guidance of men who are themselves makers of books, and who are on the watch at every step to detect a flaw in his argument, an error in his judgment, or a gap in his powers of perception.[20]

The proof of the seminar was in the learning. The students who grew to scholarly maturity in the seminars of Hopkins, Columbia, Wisconsin, and other rising universities were the best witnesses of the intellectual powers of their teachers who could not have done so well for historians had they not done so well for history.

The Hopkins seminar deserves its reputation in American intellectual history. Whether Michigan, Harvard, or Hopkins was first is not important, but the results of the work at Hopkins were of great moment. History at Hopkins was the work of Herbert Baxter Adams and the wise statesmanship of President Daniel Coit Gilman, who gathered a brilliant faculty at Baltimore and managed to keep them there.[21] The roll of Hopkins doctorates in history is practically a synopsis of modern American historiography. John Franklin Jameson, John Spencer Bassett, William Peterfield Trent, Woodrow Wilson, Charles Homer Haskins, Frederick Jackson Turner, and Charles McLean Andrews suggest the development of major themes in historical writing and research. Jameson is associated with archives, records, the Revolution, and the Constitution, Bassett with Jackson, the South, and historiography. Woodrow Wilson connotes division, reunion, and the theory and practice of democracy. The West, the frontier, and the section are the special domains of Turner, while Andrews recorded the foundation of the American colonies on a new level of thought. William Peterfield Trent is identified with the revival of Southern scholarship, and Charles Homer Haskins gave to the history of the Middle Ages and to the history of ideas a modern emphasis and a modern dimension.

Other associates added luster to Hopkins and to history. Johann Kaspar Bluntschli, teacher of Adams at Heidelberg, amassed a notable historical library, which came to Hopkins after his death. Presented to the University in 1882 by Baltimore citizens of German origin, the collection contained pamphlets and manuscripts as well as books. Among the manuscripts were Bluntschli's notes of his work with the historian Barthold Georg Niebuhr and the legal scholar Friedrich Karl von Savigny. Adams regarded the acquisition of the library and the library itself as an instance of "the internationality of modern science."[22] The manuscripts of Francis Lieber, German-born political scientist who served on the Columbia Law School faculty from 1857 to 1872, also became a part of the seminary library and were duly recorded on the Adams diagram. Another Heidelberg product, Hermann Eduard von Holst, who made America his special subject at Freiburg, lectured at Hopkins in his inimitable Continental manner.[23] Gilman made it a Hopkins practice to borrow talent from everywhere by instituting the visiting lectureship. Between 1877 and 1881 James Russell Lowell in literature, Francis A. Walker in political economy, William James in psychology, James Bryce in political science, and Charles S. Pierce in logic gave the Hopkins students an opportunity some of them never forgot.[24]

Associations with England were closer than those with Germany.[25] The incomparable Thomas H. Huxley came to celebrate the opening of Hopkins and charmed that part of the nation not hostile to Darwinian science.[26] Lord Bryce lectured at the University and was much interested in the work of the history department. Even before *The American Commonwealth,* Bryce wrote a monograph for the *Johns Hopkins Studies.* Edward A. Freeman, who fathered a school of interpretation in this country as well as his own, wrote "An Introduction to American Institutional History," which opened the *Studies.* Freeman provided Adams with one of his controlling assumptions and wielded a marked influence upon American historical interpretation.[27] The continuity of English institutions in America was a leading idea of the Hopkins seminar and remained an organizing principle among historians until challenged by Charles McLean Andrews, a Hopkins product.[28]

But American students made the Hopkins seminar great. John Franklin Jameson, first historian to receive his doctorate under Adams in 1882, became a member of the Hopkins faculty. He later taught at Brown and the University of Chicago where he succeeded Hermann von Holst in 1901. Like his mentor's, Jameson's contributions were largely in organizational and editorial spheres. He was active in the affairs of the American Historical Association and editor of the *American Historical Review* from its beginnings in 1895 to 1901 and again from 1905 to 1927.[29] In 1905 he became director of the department of research of the Carnegie Institution at Washington and was one of the editors of the guides which inventoried American materials in foreign archives.[30] Jameson earned his critical spurs as a scientific historian by the identification and location of the Pinckney Plan of 1787. The document containing the

Plan, sent to John Quincy Adams by Charles Pinckney in 1818 when the former was engaged on the *Journal* of the Constitutional Convention, was obviously different from the original. By diligent search and comparison of the sources, Jameson concluded that the "so-called Pinckney Plan" was really the report of the Committee of Detail with certain additions and deletions. That Jameson's inference was correct was confirmed by the appearance of the Pinckney document found among the James Wilson papers.[31] Jameson's historiographical writings, among the earliest statements made after history had become a self-conscious discipline, are marked by judicious balance and discrimination. Some of his later pieces on historiographical themes composed in moods of reminiscence have the value of primary documents.[32] *The American Revolution Considered as a Social Movement* sharply summarized the conclusions of a generation of thought and scholarship, in which there is a good deal of his own.[33] Items in a bibliography hardly begin to suggest the influence of a personality. Men of the intellectual and moral stature of Jameson invigorated their colleagues, their students, and the profession they did so much to serve.

John Spencer Bassett was another early Hopkins graduate, and Trinity College, North Carolina, secured his talents soon after he received his doctorate.[34] Young and dedicated, he reported to Adams that "it has been put on me to do God's work in the field of history." [35] God's work in teaching American history at Trinity was an uphill fight, as Bassett soon discovered. Just how strenuous is suggested by Bassett's request to Adams that a picture of Lincoln be presented to Trinity, so that the presentation might provide an excuse for a lecture on the Civil War president.[36] Yet, Bassett had some cause to be gratified, for the youth at least were receptive. To Adams he confided:

> I had an excellent meeting of our historical society. The students are interested and I hope for good results. I am trying to put a new spirit into the historical work of the South—so far as my influence extends. Last night I made a talk on our historical ideal. I spoke of the freedom of thought in the history department of this college. . . . I appealed to the boys to let it be so that our society would be at least one place in all the South in which a man could present his own opinions of our history and get a respectful hearing. At this point they cheered. I think we are making progress.[37]

Progress, however, was distinctly limited, and discouragement frequently imprisoned his hopes. The Negro problem in North Carolina politics distressed him, and he tried his single hand in an effort to

establish his conception of democratic justice. Of this venture in
1898 Adams read:

> Since the election . . . there is some reaction of opinion against the
> violence and passion of the last few days; but the great majority of
> people are in support of all that has been done. I have tried down in my
> portion of the vineyard to cause men to think. I have spoken as clearly
> as a teacher ought to speak on a partisan question; but I have had but
> little effect. I am going on in my way. But there is not much hope that I
> shall be able to reform the State. What would you do to meet the disease
> if you were the physician? [38]

Bassett made more headway in reconstructing the Southern past
than in reconstructing the Southern future. With Adams he felt that
Southern institutions had been too long neglected and he set himself
to explore them at least with reference to the state of North Carolina. Between 1886 and 1890 he busied himself with the colonial
records, the treasure trove of his earlier researches. His *Constitutional Beginnings of North Carolina* (1894), "The Regulators of
North Carolina" (1895), and *Slavery and Servitude in the Colony
of North Carolina* (1896)[39] owe much to the thoroughness with
which he used the primary archival materials. When *Slavery and
Servitude* was completed, he offered two courses in North Carolina
history, one for seniors and another for graduates.[40] In both the use
of source materials was required. Bassett was as much concerned
with the topics as the sources, and these monographs were followed
by his *Anti-Slavery Leaders in North Carolina* (1898) and *Slavery
in the State of North Carolina* (1899). The slavery system and the
public documents continued to crowd his research hours. A report
on the public archives of North Carolina was published by the American Historical Association in 1900, followed the next year by a
study of the Virginia planter and the London merchant. *The Federalist System* (1906), a volume in Albert Bushnell Hart's *American
Nation* series, gave him national standing. When he left Trinity for
Smith during the same year he simply exchanged the scene of his
operations.[41]

Bassett's study of the Regulator movement, a monographic gem,
called attention to the sectional conflict in the era of the Revolution.
The clash between the coastal settlements and the frontier communi-
ties offered a new focus of interpretation and helped historians to a
more mature understanding of the whole revolutionary movement.
Together with Jameson, Bassett edited a seven-volume edition of the
Jackson papers, which were enriched by his knowledge of the South.
On his editorial own, he produced an elaborately collated edition of

the writings of William Byrd of Westover and various letters relating to historiography which appeared in the *Smith College Studies in History*.[42] In this sector of effort his *Middle Group of American Historians* and his articles in the *Cambridge History of American Literature* are standard references.

Bassett's scholarship was characteristic of the scientific school. It was monographic in form and documentary in approach. Evidence, painstakingly collected, was presented without special pleading although Bassett's sympathies with Regulators, slaves, and free Negroes are by no means difficult to discover. And his emphasis, true to the early Hopkins format, was legal and institutional.

The Hopkins stress on institutions and the Southern past was further exemplified in the work of William Peterfield Trent. Trent was as Southern as Dixie. His ancestry was impeccably colonial, and his father and grandfather were both medical men. His father, a graduate of the University of Georgia, had been a Confederate surgeon, and found, as had so many others after the Civil War, that the family fortune was no more. Trent was graduated from the University of Virginia in 1883 and earned a master's degree the year after. During his student days at Virginia two future leaders of the Democratic party were also enrolled: Woodrow Wilson and Oscar W. Underwood.[43] Trent read law and taught in the Richmond schools until 1887, when he matriculated at Hopkins. At Hopkins he studied economics with Richard T. Ely, administration with Woodrow Wilson, Russian history with Herbert Baxter Adams, and American history with J. Franklin Jameson.[44] The graduate school in Baltimore had more than a decade to its growing credit, and its early pupils had already become its teachers. Trent, a member of Adams' seminar, earned the great man's coveted praise for his report on the influence of the University of Virginia on Southern life and thought. His data on nine thousand Virginia students between 1825 and 1874 were incorporated in Adams' *Thomas Jefferson and the University of Virginia,* a tribute from Adams and a boon for Trent. Trent's study of the University of Virginia led him to investigate Francis Walker Gilmer, whose letters were made available to him. Gilmer, charged with discovering appropriate talent in England to staff the University of Virginia faculty, intrigued Trent, who edited his correspondence in a volume called *English Culture in Virginia* (1889). Trent did not remain at Hopkins to take his doctorate, and in 1888 he was appointed professor of English and acting professor of history at Sewanee.[45]

Conditions at Sewanee, Tennessee, were no more exhilarating for

Trent than they were for Bassett at Trinity, in North Carolina. To Adams, always a friend as well as teacher, Trent unburdened his mind: "people around me consider me a traitor," [46] a feeling which might well have occasioned his apprehension. Loyalty to caste and class was almost a prerequisite for social acceptance in Southern academic towns, and Trent's theological views were also locally suspect. The South, he concluded, "will only be regenerated by *time. . . .*" [47] Although Trent was ready to make any reasonable sacrifice to hasten the process of regeneration, he felt there was little he could personally accomplish. Work gave him some satisfaction, and he plowed through the records to discover the colonial origins of bills of attainder[48] in state constitutions. In 1892 he completed his first full-length study, a life of William Gilmore Simms. Within the next seven years he published two additional biographical works, *Southern Statesmen of the Old Regime* (1897) and *Robert E. Lee* (1899).[49] The biography of Simms justified the feelings of his Sewanee contemporaries; he was not loyal to the old regime. He could not deal intelligently with the growth of ideas while ignoring the culture that conditioned them. He met slavery in the life of Simms and, far from evading its implications, he welcomed the opportunity of assaying them. He found that Simms and all other men were stunted by the existence of slavery, for it "dwarfed" the imagination and cramped the mind. These were among the consequences of slavery to which whites reacted even more grievously than blacks.[50] The book did not please the South, but north of the perilous line Brander Matthews and Theodore Roosevelt found much to praise.[51]

Southern Statesmen grew out of a course of lectures delivered at the University of Wisconsin. Two Hopkins men in Madison, Turner and Ely, had arranged the invitation, and Trent was on familiar ground.[52] George Washington was characterized as "a Sophocles in his perfect balance and mobility"; Jefferson as "the Shelley of our politics." [53] Trent was now a well-known scholar with a maturing style and a maturing interpretation. He presented a different and unconventional interpretation of the Southern past which, as Wendell H. Stephenson remarked, "was courageous for a Southerner of fifty or sixty years ago." [54] When he moved to Columbia to become a professor of American Literature in 1900, he already had a national reputation. As an historian of American letters he became an historian of American thought. As a teacher of graduate students and as an editor of the *Cambridge History of American Literature,* he made an enduring place for himself in the history of ideas.

While Trent was still at Virginia, Thomas Woodrow Wilson[55] left

Augusta, Georgia, for Baltimore.[56] Dissatisfied with the law for which Jefferson's university had helped to prepare him, he yearned to explore the world of ideas. Hopkins, he was convinced, was the best place to study, but study was a dedication to "profound and public-spirited statesmanship." The law might well lead to the state house or to Washington; a university might lead to a career of public service through "literary and non-partisan agencies." [57] Wilson was as earnest in scholarship as he was in everything else. Learning like life was real, and erudition alone was not his purpose.

Hopkins at first repelled him. He had dreamed of a community of scholars free of requirements, courses, and examinations. Princeton and Virginia had taught him how to handle the drudgery of examinations and the ways of making the grade. He did not wish to find himself "intellectually strait-jacketed";[58] he wanted learning, inspiration, and guidance. Hopkins presented him with a schedule from Monday through Friday, with fixed appointments for lectures and seminars, and with prescribed reading. Wilson's profound disturbance emerged in letters to his fiancee. He was "somewhat downcast." The mighty Adams also disappointed him. He was, thought Wilson, "too smooth," and offered his students "a very meagre diet of ill-served lectures." Finally he reached so low a state that he went to Adams, told him of his disappointments, and asked for the chance to give free rein to his bounding interests. Adams' response made Wilson a new man. Adams "received my confidences with sympathy, readily freed me from his 'institutional' work, and bade me go on with my 'constitutional' studies, promising me all the aid and encouragement he could give me, and saying that the work I proposed was just such as he wanted to see done! Do you wonder that I feel elated?" [59]

Enthusiasm succeeded dejection, and Wilson was on the high road to accomplishment. With Richard T. Ely and Davis R. Dewey he commenced a history of American economic thought for which he read with an avidity that only absorption could sustain.[60] Yet it was political thought, not economic thought, that provided the intellectual compulsion of his life. From the very beginning, government, constitutional history, and politics commanded the direction of his growth. With the full academic blessing of Adams, he returned to consider the problems involved in "Cabinet Government in the United States," an essay he had written as a Princeton senior and published in 1879. The climax was a small volume called *Congressional Government: A Study in Politics*. Done at Hopkins, first published in 1885, it was the greatest book Wilson ever wrote and one

of the truly significant books in the literature of American democracy.[61]

Congressional Government was remarkable by any reasonable
standard. When the book was written, Wilson was only twenty-eight,
and it displayed a critical talent and an intellectual grasp rare in one
so young. Wilson had steeped himself in the materials of government
ever since his undergraduate days, and to diagnose the weaknesses
of the American system had always been a compelling motive. But
the speed at which he managed to write the volume is almost unbelievable and demonstrated his command of the materials, his mastery of style, and the compulsion of his spirit, which in future was so
often to conquer him. The actual writing was begun in January
1884, and in early April he was ready to send the preliminary chapters to Houghton Mifflin to discover if they were interested in publication. Graduate study at Hopkins carried responsibilities that broke
into the steady pace required for concentrated writing. The summer
months gave him uninterrupted time, and when he returned to Baltimore, the manuscript was almost done. Completed soon thereafter,
it was dispatched to Houghton Mifflin, who informed him in late
November that they had accepted it.[62]

Wilson was fully aware that his dominating ideas were by no
means original. "I have simply grouped facts which have not before
stood together." He frankly disclaimed having "brought out any
hitherto unseen facts" and he was just as mindful of his indebtedness
to Walter Bagehot. Bagehot's treatment of the English Constitution
"has inspired my whole study of our government." Wilson aspired to
do for the American system what Bagehot had done for the English
system. He wished to get behind formal professions, to escape from
legal definitions, and to explore the actual workings of institutions.
"My purpose," he repeated in letter after letter and wherever appropriate elsewhere, is "to show . . . our constitutional system as it
looks in operation." Critics who have discovered Wilson's dependence on Bagehot and his reliance upon well-established information
have discovered no more than Wilson himself well knew.[63]

Congressional Government was acclaimed at once. Wilson dedicated his work to his father, whose identification with his son almost
burst proper Presbyterian bonds. "Your book," confessed Woodrow
Wilson's adoring parent, "has been received and gloated over." [64]
The young author had additional evidence of the influence of his
thought. Chapters had been read to the Adams seminar and had
received the approbation of master and apprentice alike. He had
been understandably apprehensive. "I read at the Seminary last

night," he wrote to his future wife, "and my audience looked as tired as I was when I got through. They applauded (to wake themselves up) and Dr. Adams praised. . . . Seriously, I think I made a very favourable impression." But the Seminary records attest that "Mr. Wilson's work is better than anything in that line that has been done heretofore in the Seminary." [65] Within a few weeks the first printing had been sold out, and Gamaliel Bradford, immersed in similar studies, reviewed the book for *The Nation*. After paying the author and his work the largest of compliments, Bradford said, "His book is evidently modelled on Mr. Bagehot's *English Constitution,* and it will, though the praise is so high as to be almost extravagent, bear comparison with that inestimable work," [66] than which little could have been added to please Wilson more.

Wilson's triumph was incomplete,[67] for *Congressional Government* failed to bring about the desired practical results. If congressmen and party managers ever read Wilson's words, they paid their meanings little heed.[68] Wilson hoped *Congressional Government* "would stand as a permanent piece of constitutional criticism by reason of some depth of historical and political insight." But it was not as an exercise in constitutional criticism that he was prompted to write. *Congressional Government* was meant "to *stir* thought and to carry irresistible practical suggestion. . . . I carefully kept all advocacy of particular reforms out of it, because I wanted it to be . . . a permanent piece of work . . . but I hoped at the same time that it might catch hold of its readers' convictions and set reform a-going in a very definite direction." [69] Not until those who made politics their business felt the need of knowing the man who was their president did they turn to his books. A new edition of *Congressional Government* was issued in 1913, and Americans had learned since 1885 that an analysis of government functions was not without some point.

Congressional Government was a study of classic proportions. Others had surveyed parts of the same field,[70] few with such learning and incisiveness, none with such felicity and clarity of expression. Wilson had in truth accomplished something like the feat of Bagehot. He gave life to the study of government; in the pages of *Congressional Government* institutions came alive. Government functioned in dynamic human relationships with palpable consequences in the lives and actions of men. If for no other reason *Congressional Government* is a great book.

Wilson's career as a scholar began with *Congressional Government.* Princeton, Virginia, and Hopkins were preparatory for the triple office of student, teacher, and writer. Woodrow Wilson's stature as the first citizen of the Republic has obscured his activity as a leading citizen of the republic of letters.[71] He was after all a college professor from 1885 to 1902, a university president from 1902 to 1910. Only in the decade following was he able to realize his ambition in public office. Successively governor of New Jersey, president of the United States, and for a brief span the first statesman of the world, he imprinted his personality and his cause on the record of humanity. His last years were spent dying.

Woodrow Wilson was a student and teacher before he became a statesman. Despite his devotion to the ideal of service as a politician, reformer, and statesman—words which should mean the same thing but do not—it was with books, ideas, and professors that he spent most of his time and energy. While still a Princeton undergraduate, he entered into a "solemn covenant" [72] with a friend to do everything in his power to help his fellow man. Service to mankind became the guiding purpose and passion of his life, and never did he release himself from this youthful vow. This purpose gives meaning and unity to his whole existence as teacher, writer, and politician. He was not simply a teacher of history or politics; he was a teacher of ideas forged for living. Woodrow Wilson was no scholar's scholar. He wrote essays on political theory and public affairs as well as volumes of history to teach himself and teach his country. Nor was he a politician simply to satisfy an urge for prestige and power; he was a politician in the service of mankind, a democratic leader who, having learned about national and world problems, tried to teach his growing constituency.

When Wilson became professor of jurisprudence at Princeton in 1890, he was already a seasoned teacher. He had taught at Bryn Mawr and at Wesleyan University and had given special lectures annually at Hopkins. He was singularly successful. If he had failings, they were the failings of virtue. Brilliant as a lecturer, as his students testified then and thereafter, he always made his classes a source of pleasure and inspiration. Wilson, recalled one Bryn Mawr student, was "the most interesting and inspiring teacher I ever heard." He was not disdainful of detail, but he regarded it as part of his function to weld detail into a meaningful synthesis. For undergraduates, accustomed to the formal presentation of facts, this was something of a novelty. As one of them later remembered, "He was a little impatient of detail, not that he did not recognize the importance of detail, but that the fundamental underlying laws and causes, whether of economic, political, or social problems, fascinated him and absorbed his best energies." [73] To attain mastery of the latter, nothing was too hard, and he reported on a subsequent occasion that he never worked harder than in preparing his college lectures. He believed that "some of the subtlest and most lasting effects of genuine oratory have gone forth from secluded lecture desks into the hearts of quiet groups of students" [74] and he was bound to emulate those who had mastered the art of cogent speech. The portals of the Senate chamber might forever remain closed, but the classroom lectern was not without its appeal. He strove for a "mastery over the class," for he would have his hearers "get exactly what I have to give them." [75]

Even when he had satisfied his own hypercritical standards, he realized that teaching was not his real objective. After he had captured Bryn Mawr and knew how good he was and how much better he could be, he stated his ultimate purpose. To his old Princeton classmate he wrote: "For in the thinking and writing I am trying to do, I constantly feel the disadvantages of the *closet:*

> I want to keep close to the *practical* and the *practicable* in politics; my ambition is to add something to the *statesmanship* of the country, if that something be only thought, and not the old achievement of which I used to dream when I hoped that I might enter practical politics. I seek, therefore, in the acquaintances I make, not other "professors," not other *book*-politicians, but men who have direct touch of the world; in order that I may study affairs rather than doctrine. But the "practical men" I meet have not broad horizons; *they* are *not* students of affairs: they learn what they know rather by friction than by rational observation; they are at the opposite extreme from the man of books, who are all horizon,— and the one extreme is as fatal to balanced thought as the other.[76]

Nothing could stay his interest in politics. If he could not be the senator from Virginia or an assistant secretary of state, he would be a "literary politician," [77] a statesman of ideas. He was so meticulous an artist of the spoken word that form and substance of expression were always of first importance. Words were the vessels for his thought, his lectures the instruments of his ideas. This is scarcely deserving of criticism, although Wilson has often been criticized for attending to form at the expense of content.[78] The stricture is largely without foundation, unless it be argued that undergraduates were unable to profit by brilliant synthesis. If it is just to censure him for an insensitivity to economics as related to politics,[79] it is probably fairer to point out that such correlations developed later in American intellectual history. Wilson was aware of economic forces; he had not yet learned to put economics and politics hypothetically together. It was enough that he saw the politics of democracy in a new and vital relation: after he had left the university, he learned a new economics in the school of democratic politics.[80]

Wilson was as dedicated to the written word as to the spoken word. Soon after his establishment at Bryn Mawr, he outlined a vast project embracing no less than the entire history and philosophy of politics. The opus was never written, but the purposes then taking shape in his mind illumine his character and his mental development. "I want to come at the true conception of the nature of the modern democratic state by way of an accurate definition of the exposition of the history of democratic development." [81] The projected political philosophy was to deepen and expand *Congressional Government* and provide the requisite background for contemporary institutions. "As we can know persons only from what they say and do, and the manner of their acting and speaking," he explained to Horace Scudder, one of the editors of the *Atlantic,* "so we can know governments only from what *they* say and do and the manner of their speech and action." Wilson had already come close to a politician's theory of politics in *Congressional Government;* he had now reached it. "But in governments and persons alike we can look beneath the surface, if we have discernment enough, and so discover more of *character* than any amount of *a priori* speculation." He would dig as deeply as possible beneath the surface "of our democratic government in particular" in order to find "its *essential character* by way of a thorough knowledge of all its outward manifestations of character." [82]

The philosophy of politics, affectionately referred to in the Wilson family as P.O.P.,[83] was the book of Wilson's dreams. Wilson slaved to prepare himself for the writing of it and while he never succeeded, the effort was far from barren. His own learning was the most important by-product. Properly to undertake the P.O.P., he felt he should study the governments of the world, and to study comparative government he had to study German. He tussled with stubborn German treatises on *Staatsrecht* and *Stasstswissenschaft* and contemplated a trip to Germany to further his language and his writing, unharassed by the young ladies of Bryn Mawr.[84] The plan never materialized, but *The State,* "a dull fact book," [85] was a part of his program of self-education. As always the final end was the same. "All the country needs is a new and sincere body of thought in politics, coherently, distinctly, and boldly uttered by men who are sure of their ground." [86]

In between the inception and publication of *The State,* Wilson moved from Bryn Mawr to Wesleyan, where he remained for two years. The Wesleyan years were happy and fruitful, virtually unruffled by failure or antagonism. His intellectual powers, now highly developed, gave him a sense of worth and mastery that compensated for his unremitting effort.[87] During the Princeton period his productive creativity reached its peak. Almost immediately after *The State,* an invitation came from Albert Bushnell Hart to contribute the final volume to the *Epochs of American History* series. Wilson eagerly accepted, for the decades of the sectional clash leading up to the Civil War, and the eventful decades from Reconstruction to his own times, fascinated him. *Division and Reunion 1829–1889,*[88] the Wilson history least criticized by specialists,[89] was finished in 1893. The book was remarkable for its style and its balance. It was one of a small company of volumes dealing with American division and reunion, dating from this period, unmarred by hatred and bias, the more remarkable because its author was a Southerner who loved the South. Wilson expounded the thesis that the South was right in law but wrong in history; the North wrong in law but right in history. He also advanced the interpretation, later generally espoused, that the Civil War was the war of American nationality. Wilson suggested that America was a "confederation of sections" before the great internal conflict, not a nation of united states. The reciprocal influence of Turner and Wilson was suggested by Wilson's broader vision of sectionalism and his appreciation of the rise of the new West. The clash was a multiple conflict of three sections in evolution, not simply a conflict between North and South; not slavery and antislavery merely, but expansion and conflict.[90]

Woodrow Wilson's longest historical work, though by no means his masterpiece, was a five-volume *History of the American People.* The Princeton professor had a reputation as a scholar with a style. Literary editors persistently urged him to write for their journals and since his need for cash was as constant as his ambition, he found it uncommonly hard to refuse.[91] The *History* first ran serially in magazines and was published in multivolume form in 1902.[92] Successful both as articles and books, they fully accomplished Wilson's purpose: to educate himself and the American people. There was adequate evidence of the former in the extent of his comprehension, of the latter in the reception and sale of the work.[93]

The first volume of the *History* covered the seventeenth century, with emphasis on the English settlements. The second, the eighteenth-century volume, dealt with the preliminaries of the Revolution, the Revolution itself, and the war of American independence.[94]

The Confederation, the founding of the Republic, and the critical changes from Jefferson to Jackson comprised the subjects of the third. The exposition in this section of Jeffersonian and Jacksonian democracy was one of Wilson's finest achievements.[95] From Jackson to the Civil War was the span of the fourth, and the fifth covered from Reconstruction to the beginning of the twentieth century. As the *History* was written for general consumption instead of for the specialist's delectation, there were no footnotes.[96] Almost all chapters, however, were equipped with extended bibliographies, and three of the five volumes were buttressed by appendixes. The work was superbly illustrated, some illustrations having been especially executed for the purpose. But it was so profusely illustrated as to distract and confuse the reader rather than to aid him.[97]

The History of the American People has been generously condemned by diverse specialists. Not great history either then or now, it would yet be unwarranted to dismiss it. Wilson's *History* was a protest against existing historiographical trends. It was an objection to the soliloquy of the monograph and a reaffirmation of his faith in knowledge for individual use and social profit.[98] *The History of the American People* was unique; the first general history of such chronological sweep written by an historian of Southern lineage. Wilson incorporated the substance of *Division and Reunion* in the *History* and with the substance came the balance, the perspective, and the relative freedom from partisanship. He had already said his same words concerning division, Reconstruction, and reunion, but in the *History* he said them to a different and much wider audience. Also repeated was the theory that the war was the catalyst of American nationality, a theory which, regardless of its validity, was balm to the wounds of unreconstructed Confederates and unrelenting Unionists alike.[99] Frederick Jackson Turner, reviewing the *History*, aimed lethal thrusts at its weaknesses but concluded: "It is impossible to find in similar compass or by any other single author so sustained and vital a view of the whole first cycle of American history." [100]

The *History* was all Turner said of it. While it could be pointed out—as Bliss Perry did—that the style was more suited to the ear than to the eye, it was fast-moving, interesting, and sustained.[101] The writing betrayed all Wilson's characteristic weaknesses and peculiarities, but it was the best-written narrative of American history in print.[102] It was a vast improvement on Bancroft, for it was compact as well as dramatic. It bore no comparison to Hildreth, for it was never dull. None could say of Wilson's history that it was a compendium of unrelated facts. Neither John Bach McMaster, Hermann von Holst, James Ford Rhodes, nor James Schouler displayed anything like Wilson's literary charm, and he attempted so much more, even if, as in some instances, he managed only by "grace of overheroic compression." [103] Henry Adams and Francis Parkman are Wilson's peers, and it may well be doubted whether anyone since has equaled them. Wilson came close to accomplishing for the history of America what John Richard Green accomplished for the history of England.

Wilson is pathetically vulnerable, nevertheless, and Turner's critical scalpel laid the *History* bare. He was best as a "critic of politics, more at home in characterizing political leaders and trends of events than in dealing with the deeper undercurrents of economic and social change." [104] This was eminently true. Wilson was a dramatic historian; he rarely explored hypothetical meanings in his general historical writings. On the other hand, to have been able to do so for the whole course of American development from Columbus to McKinley was more than anyone could fairly ask. He was infinitely better in dealing with the years 1829 to 1876 in *Division and Reunion* than almost anywhere in the *History*. He was at his best in *Congressional Government* because he plumbed beneath the surface, even if he did not plumb everywhere. But this was not because he was a better political scientist than he was an historian. It was because he took infinite pains to examine the concepts with which he was working and to spin out their manifold relations, to test and retest them against the living realities of contemporary ideas and institutions. Turner's criticism of his treatment of the Revolution was devastating for exactly this reason. Wilson, said Turner, failed to understand "the important facts of economic and political significance that were so powerful in shaping the sections during that period, in preparing the way for American political parties and institutions." While this criticism was justified, Turner was one of the few historians who understood the economic and political implications of sectionalism in the period from 1763 to 1776.[105]

Wilson's analysis of American political parties and institutions, regardless of its limitations, was unparalleled. Shortly after the *History* Wilson delivered a series of lectures at Columbia, later published as *Constitutional Government in the United States*.[106] These essays represent the culmination of his thought; they continue and extend the thesis of *Congressional Government*. Wilson remained the critic of American political institutions and the opponent of a separation of powers that resulted in institutional isolation. As in 1885, he found the House and Senate sufficient to themselves, the executive hampered, and the Supreme Court virtually independent. The government of the United States was static. Modeled on the principles of Newtonian physics, it required rethinking in terms of Darwinian dynamics. While in 1885 he found the presidency ineffective, in 1907 he found the executive office the key to responsibility. "That part of the government, therefore, which has the most direct access to opinion has the best chance of leadership and mastery; and at present that part is the President." The president alone represented all the people and if once he won "the admiration and confidence of the country . . . no other single force. . . ." [107] could possibly compete with him. Democracy and leadership were now joined. Not cabinet government, but party organization and executive leadership became the Wilsonian solutions of the democratic dilemma. Bosses and corruption existed, to be sure, but Americans had to learn to entrust leaders with power adequate to the tasks of government. Party leadership and responsibility were the critical problems of representative democratic government. Wilson was still a conservative, hostile to labor, opposed to federal intervention, friendly to state action.[108] He was often clearer in enunciating principles than in exemplifying them.[109] But he was to learn something of Darwinian dynamics on the road to the White House.[110]

Wilson's essays and addresses contain some of his best historical and political writings.[111] Among these "The Truth of the Matter" [112] is an exposition of his philosophy of history. He paid deference to fact and to fact finders; he applauded the virtues of scientific historiography.[113] Historical truth was not obtained, however, by the simple acquisition of data, for history "consists of things which are invisible as well as things which are visible." Mere chronology, which Wilson himself so largely followed in the *History*, "may or may not be the arrangement which most surely brings the truth of the narrative to light; and the best arrangement is always that which displays, not the facts themselves, but the subtle and else invisible forces that lurk in the events and in the minds of men—forces for which events serve only as lasting and dramatic words of utterance." The historian was enjoined to go beyond the facts and their compilation. "Of what service is it that the historian should have insight if we are not to know how the matter stands in his view?" [114] With a clarity of his own he defined the historian's practice:

> Unquestionably every sentence of true history must hold a judgment in solution. All cannot be told. If it were possible to tell all, it would take as long to write history as to enact it, and we should have to postpone the reading of it to the leisure of the next world. A few facts must be

selected for the narrative, the great majority left unnoted. But the selection—for what purpose is it to be made? For the purpose of conveying *an impression* of the truth. Where shall you find a more radical process of judgment? The "essential" facts taken, the "unessential" left out! . . . It is in this that the writing of history differs, and differs very radically, from the statement of the results of original research. The writing of history must be based upon original research and authentic record, but it can no more be directly reconstructed by the piecing together of bits of original research than by the mere reprinting together of state documents.[115]

Woodrow Wilson's place in American historiography needs reappraisal. As historian, Wilson cannot be dismissed simply because he became a major political figure during the later years of his life. To say that he was potentially great yet never fulfilled his promise because he was primarily a political scientist and secondarily an aspirant for political office, violates logic at both points. Had he devoted his full talent and energy to division and reunion or to the issues of constitutional government, he almost certainly would have been a greater scholar. Such a judgment is not only too literal, but it concedes the conclusion of greatness in the premise of criticism.[116] He frequently wrote at the request of editors, but the imputation that his thought was aimless on that account is groundless.[117] A consistent intellectual objective permeates his life as well as his work. To disagree with Wilson's evaluation of intellectual priorities is anyone's privilege; to cavil at his intellectual honesty is no one's right. Whether he was a success or failure as president is still debated. His greatness in the presidency, however, has little to do with the merits of the point of view presented in *The Federalist* as compared with the interpretation presented in *Constitutional Government*. He was, of course, inconsistent. He was certainly more theoretical than concrete. But who can develop intellectually and escape inconsistency? Who before Wilson so penetratingly appraised the functions of democracy in political action? As long as men continue to be identified with the democratic experiment, Woodrow Wilson—historian, political scientist, politician—will command respect and attention.

Wilson owed a great intellectual debt to Frederick Jackson Turner. From Turner Wilson caught the vision of the significance of the frontier and of sectionalism. From Turner and from H. B. Adams came Wilson's interpretation of the Civil War as a conflict embracing all sections. Although Wilson was older and one of his teachers, Turner and Wilson became intimate friends.[118] Turner talked about the significance of the frontier with Wilson in the house where both of them lived, and they were frequently locked in discussion of such historical topics as the substance of American nationality or the misinterpretation of the South and the West.[119] When president of Princeton, Wilson sought without success to lure Turner to New Jersey. Turner, more successful in promoting academic migration, was instrumental in calling Richard T. Ely and Charles Homer Haskins, both ornaments at Hopkins, to Wisconsin.[120]

Herbert Baxter Adams, however, taught them both. Adams gave Wilson leave to follow his intellectual bent; Adams presided over the early stages of Turner's graduate work. The Adams seminar and the Hopkins influence permeated the academic institutions of the South. George Petrie at the Polytechnic Institute in Alabama acquired an Adams doctorate in 1892 and began to teach "by the laboratory method." [121] A new group of scholars who were to regenerate Southern history came out of his historical "laboratory," among them William L. Fleming, Albert B. Moore, Frank L. Owsley, Herman C. Nixon, and William O. Scroggs. Hopkins began the modern study of southern history before Columbia under John W. Burgess and William A. Dunning extended and improved it.[122]

Hopkins, said Charles W. Eliot of Harvard at the twenty-fifth anniversary of its founding, was not only "a strong and potent school" of graduate studies; it "has lifted every other university in the country." [123] What was true of learning in general was true of history in particular. At Hopkins the "scientific" study of history first properly began. Southern history was revived, and the investigation of institutions assumed new importance. Colonial development in English America, educational ideas and practices, the evolution of legal forms were given a new impetus. Examinations of party government and comparative democratic institutions came out of the Baltimore seminaries. The history of the West and the concepts of the frontier and the section finally acquired academic sponsorship and prestige. John Spencer Bassett went to Smith, William Peterfield Trent to Columbia, James Albert Woodburn to Indiana.[124] Frederick Jackson Turner went to Wisconsin, Charles McLean Andrews to Yale, Woodrow Wilson to Princeton. Eliot had not overstated the case.

The scientific historians of the nineteenth century enriched American thought less by philosophy than by scholarship. Although their writings when not superseded have for the most part been revised, they stenciled their lives in the American tradition of learning. Historians attain greatness by forcing others to think; they attain immortality by forcing some to think differently. Every historian worthy of a footnote has either made a convert or sired a critic. The scientific historians taught their students, their colleagues, and the public, and they taught more than fragments of American history. They instructed a generation in the virtues of intellectual constancy and the values of intellectual discovery. They made research a continuing excitement, and fidelity and integrity a practicing creed; accuracy was only another name for honesty and critical analysis, not only of documents, as priceless an attribute as any in the whole array of scientific methods. By their faith in the power of human intelligence and their persistent use of it, they bolstered the faith of their successors in the capacity of man to know and to understand.

But the scientific historians also changed the image of the historians' ideal. The broad philosophical sweep represented by Edward Gibbon and Thomas Babington Macaulay was exchanged for empirical virtues. Gibbon mastered a series of epochs, and Macaulay mastered a culture; modern scholars mastered the particular topic and the particular time span. The monograph became the vehicle of the scientific historians, and precision stood high in their code. Literary yearnings were suppressed; strivings for effect were abandoned for the drama latent in the sequence of events. Like the microscope, the monograph enlarged detail for which the grand periods of Gibbon were unsuited. While historians continued to admire the Macaulay rhythm, they developed different standards of craftsmanship.

History was severed from philosophy as decisively as it was separated from literature. Literature was no more hostile to history than philosophy was hostile to science. But the scientific historians, sensitive to the history of history, chose to be "right" rather than philosophical or artistic. They preferred the facts, if only they could acquire them, to hypotheses conceived as guides to meaning. And if data were lacking in whole or in part, they were unwilling to mask their ignorance with speculation. History and literature were separated less because historians demeaned resplendent prose than because history had always been considered a branch of literature. Science valued "the truth," not the way in which explorers reported it. Emancipation demanded devotion to validity; if historians were fated to use words as tools they were not fated to be entrapped by them. If the scientific historians equated literature with undisciplined imagination, it must be admitted that many an earlier historian seemed less interested in fact than in fancy.[125]

Antipathy toward philosophy was the reflection of an antipathy toward abstraction, an aversion for speculation rather than speculative thought. The scientific historian learned from the laboratory scientist to distrust untestable deductions from *a priori* premises. Both were suspicious of theories unsupported by proof, of concepts not grounded in demonstrable logic. Rigorous thinking was acclaimed by all, but for the scientific historians such thinking had to be unconditioned. Philosophy belonged to the philosophers, and the members of the scientific school professed to have none of it. The philosophy of history, once honored by philosophers and historians alike, became a tyrannous phrase. Experience came to be the antithesis of speculation, fact the antithesis of idea. The vocabulary of historical learning bristled with critical adjectives applied to history tinged with philosophy. It was vain and idle, biased and partial, speculative and theoretical. Above all, it was unscientific. Critics in historical journals castigated their fellows suspected of philosophy. To be discovered with an avowed philosophy was an indiscretion sufficient to place the historian in jeopardy. Science had purportedly emancipated itself from philosophy and scientific historians could hardly lay claim to scientific status if they espoused what scientists had already rejected. "If one must choose between a school of history whose main characteristic is *espirit,*" wrote a champion of scientific history, "and one which rests upon a faithful and honest effort to base its whole narration upon the greatest attainable number of recorded facts, we cannot longer hesitate." [126]

These distinctions, however, were often more neatly categorized in the minds of later analysts than in the minds of the scientific historians themselves.[127] Yet, worship of fact frequently tended to demean the role of reason. Data sometimes became more significant than concepts, and emphasis upon method contributed to a neglect of meanings. Precision was the word for science, and the pressures of writing scientific history limited the canvas, if not the vision, of the practicing historian. The more rigorous the monograph, the less it seemed to answer the questions which, if historians no longer asked themselves, others were asking the historian. In fact, many of the questions others were asking seemed not to be asked by the historian at all. Deepening specialization overtook the historian as well as the rest of organized learning.

Specialization fostered restive intellectual dissatisfaction and ultimately produced a quest for synthesis. Data yielded by the pursuit of the particular defied quantitative comparison with anything that had gone before. But what did data piled upon data signify? What did the innumerable monographs, monographs that ordinary libraries could no longer house, signify? Actually, each new interpretation and each new emphasis indicated a yearning for more inclusive meanings. And the search began with the standard bearers of science themselves. Those whose formal works were sparked with criticisms of speculation were themselves engaged in it. Those who deplored a philosophical approach were themselves in search of it.

John William Burgess was a philosopher of history. Herbert Baxter Adams elevated the comparative method into a principle of organization. And Adams was able to make the comparative method a key to meaning because it was the correlation of a theory of social growth. Frederick Jackson Turner's early nationalism was a revolt against eastern and European influences explicit in the cultural formula of Herbert Baxter Adams. "The Significance of the Frontier" was designed as a synthesis of American experience. After Turner's early nationalism had been modulated by constant reflection, the frontier theory remained an interpretive hypothesis; the idea of the section, a concept. Herbert Levi Osgood and George Louis Beer —and later Charles McLean Andrews—found in the mutation of institutions an organic factor which helped to explain change and stability. Economic interpretations were not beholden to Karl Marx alone or to the seeming pervasiveness of the material; they were efforts toward intellectual integration. Social and intellectual history were courageous attempts to probe beneath the surface in the hope of discovering a larger significance. The urban approach was likewise the historiographical aspect of a search for unifying principles, a theoretical comparison between urbanism as a way of life and its rural opposite. A quest for larger meanings, for synthesis, began to emerge even before it became a fully developed movement in the early decades of the twentieth century.

XXII

History at Columbia:
The Postwar South and
the American Colonies

Johns Hopkins was rivaled by other graduate schools[1] whose historical seminars performed similar scholarly functions. At Columbia, other scholars in response to identical urgings[2] were anxious to revamp their own college and to build their own university. Attempts to provide graduate instruction at Columbia between 1852 and 1864 never emerged beyond the planning stage. In the latter year, the Columbia School of Mines, conceived as the first step in a larger project, was established, and Columbia's first doctorates were granted under its auspices.[3] When Burgess came to Columbia as professor in 1876, he found the character of advanced work scarcely better than at Amherst. The faculty as a whole was unreceptive, and Burgess regarded his idea of a graduate faculty in history and political science as "so progressive" that he dared not "broach it for a long time." [4] With the help of the trustees, the Burgess program was adopted, and the graduate school began to operate in the academic year 1880–81. In addition to Burgess the faculty consisted of three others. Richmond Mayo-Smith, a former Burgess student at Amherst who had done further study at Berlin, offered courses in English history and economics. Another Burgess man with the same academic affiliations, Edmund Munroe Smith, presided over Roman institutions and comparative jurisprudence. The third, Clifford R. Bateman, of Amherst and Heidelberg, surveyed the field of administrative law in America and Europe. Bateman died early in the career of the graduate school and was succeeded by Frank J. Goodnow in 1883. Also from Amherst, Goodnow completed his training at the École libre des sciences politiques, model for Columbia's formative activities, and remained at Columbia until he became president of Johns Hopkins in 1914.[5] Burgess taught the political history of the United States and of continental Europe, comparative law, and the history of diplomacy, in addition to a course in international law. While the first decade of Columbia's graduate life was one of struggle, by 1900 its future was no longer insecure.[6]

The excitement of launching a new university was the same for the men of Columbia as for the men of Hopkins.[7] Burgess, like Herbert Baxter Adams, was a great administrator, but the initial years at Hopkins were far more glamorous. Daniel Coit Gilman was an academic statesman with a vision neither F. A. P. Barnard nor Seth Low, could match.[8] And among Columbia's first scholars there was no Royce, Dewey, or Veblen; in history, no Frederick Jackson Turner or Woodrow Wilson. But Burgess captured the abilities of a number of promising students in a stellar Amherst class and at Columbia's graduate beginnings he helped to guide three who became famous in American life and letters. Daniel De Leon became a leader of American socialism. Nicholas Murray Butler, a philosopher of education, followed Low as president of Columbia, and Theodore Roosevelt followed McKinley as president of the United States.[9]

The second generation of the Columbia social science faculty far outdistanced the academic founders. Except for Burgess himself, the students trained by the first quadrumvirate had more direct and lasting influence on intellectual development than their teachers. Edwin R. A. Seligman and John Bates Clark in economics, F. H. Giddings in sociology, and John Bassett Moore in international law were powerful personalities and powerful intellects who did much to give permanent shape to their specialties. Columbia's own doctors of philosophy began another great historiographical tradition. William A. Dunning made the university famous as a northern center of southern study. Herbert Levi Osgood gave Columbia an international reputation for research in American institutions. Stressing their transplantation and transformation in colonial America, he offered suggestive departures for explorations in the history of law and government, economics, and administration. Dunning's seminar resulted in rewriting the history of the post-Civil War South. Osgood's seminar contributed to a revision of the interpretation of British imperial policy and the American Revolution. William R. Shepherd, Latin

American expert, helped to place the process of colonization and settlement in the larger context of European cultural diffusion. William M. Sloane was in charge of the history of Europe, particularly France, and James T. Shotwell after 1900 added his wide learning and breadth of view. By that time James Harvey Robinson had been asked to join the Columbia ranks, and Columbia had become one of the foremost centers of historical study in America.[10]

Many devoted and brilliant teachers collaborated in making the history department at Columbia, and William A. Dunning was one of them. The son of a New Jersey carriage maker with artistic tastes, Dunning was born in Plainfield in 1857. He took his graduate and undergraduate degrees at Columbia and spent an invigorating year at Berlin under Heinrich von Treitschke. Historian and political scientist like Burgess, he divided his intellectual energy between both, and received double honors. He became the leading historian of reconstruction and the leading American historian of western political thought. The American Historical Association and the American Political Science Association each elected him to its presidency, and while he shared the making of political scientists with others, he acquired something like a monopoly of Reconstruction historians. Dunning's seminar in southern history was a center of reinterpretation. Together with his students, Dunning recast the historiography of the Reconstruction period.[11] Columbia University historians were among the great revisionists of modern times. Herbert Levi Osgood, James Harvey Robinson, and Charles A. Beard wrote the books that changed our minds about the meaning of the past and the meaning of history. Dunning wrote a new sequel to Appomattox and changed the mind of a generation.

It was Dunning the teacher as well as Dunning the scholar who made such an achievement possible. He was a rare teacher who imparted enthusiasm together with knowledge. He made raw students into ripe scholars, and he also made them his friends. From him they learned the worth of intellectual effort and the vitality of history. Never pedantic, his learning was as mellow as his thought was penetrating. Students looked forward to his classes not only because his words were full of wisdom, but because they were full of wit. He made the life of learning a life of enjoyment, and his followers could never do him the honor they thought he deserved. "To those . . . whose work as graduate students was directed by him, he is forever the beloved 'Old Chief,' whose shining personality, keen intellect, warm personal interest, and painstaking guidance placed them under obligation too great ever to be fully discharged and bound them to him by ties of warm affection." [12] Teachers who evoke such loyalties deserve no less.

The famed Reconstruction series, emanating from Dunning's seminar, vindicated his reputation as a teacher of teachers. Better evidence would be hard to find, for the Reconstruction monographs, collaborative assault on southern history from Johnson to Hayes, long remained unequaled. Beyond the capacities of a single scholar, few projects have so completely altered historical opinion. In terms of general comparison, the Dunning series is more thorough than the Hopkins studies. The Columbia series is based on a wider and more diverse range of materials, is more fully documented from original sources, and more closely integrated in overall objective.[13] Whatever their weaknesses, and they are many, Dunning's students diligently re-examined assumptions and presented what they regarded as a fairer judgment of the postbellum South.

James W. Garner's *Reconstruction in Mississippi* (1901)[14] was the first of the series. A native of Mississippi, Garner believed that a frank and dispassionate account of Reconstruction was long overdue. Writing as an unbiased scholar rather than as a southerner, he nevertheless felt that only a southerner could write the sort of history he had in mind. Only a southerner could comprehend the nature of the southern problem and the impact of Reconstruction plans on southern society—a conviction frequently professed and just as frequently denied. Garner's book was a good one, but it was heavily weighted on the political and constitutional side. While sections were reserved for the discussion of education, the Freedmen's Bureau, and similar matters, the tone, like Dunning's own, was political. With two notable exceptions this was more or less true of the entire series.[15] Also true of the whole was the assumption that Radical plans were ill-conceived and often only incidentally concerned with their avowed purposes. Reconstruction was detrimental to the South, disregarded the lessons of the southern past, and marred the southern future. This theme was accompanied by the suggestion that Radical planners and Radical agents had economic axes of their own to grind, and that they ground them fast with exceedingly large results. [16]

The Reconstruction series bears the Dunning stamp.[17] Dunning's students spun out their facts on the thread of politics. Passions of war had distorted truth, and the vanquished had been accorded the usual treatment at the hands of the victors. Dunning scholars demonstrated that war had interfered with temperate appraisal. Writers of the postwar generation adopted a view of Reconstruction premised on their view of rebellion. Save for those who loyally resisted Confederate pretensions, the whites of the South were traitors. Peace simply transformed fighting rebels into defeated rebels. Wars need only be declared but peace has to be made, and declarations of peace did not change treason into loyalty. The South had to be reconstructed; southerners had to be reformed. And if reformation of sentiment was too much to be expected, southerners had to be controlled by the force of legislation and the force of arms. Defeated rebels were no different from seceding rebels in mind and heart, for both aimed at the perversion of the Union. Having failed to capture the government by political connivance before 1861 and having failed to disrupt it on the field of battle, their purposes remained the same. Hardly less suspect than unreconstructed rebels were Northern Democrats, as susceptible to southern blandishments after the war as before it. If the North, having won the war, was to win the peace, the old political alliances were not to be renewed. Traitors were not to be restored to power. This became the politics of the "bloody shirt" in national debate. It became the historiography of sectional guilt in national history. The Radical Reconstruction program was the measure of patriotism in politics; it was the test of cogency in historical judgment. Federal arms had saved the nation; Radical Reconstruction was to restore the Union. Southern resistance was treason all over again, the mark of an unregenerate South.[18]

William A. Dunning and his research corps filed a factual demurrer. If they complicated the problem by insistence upon careful discrimination, they restored a note of moderation. All Southerners were not rebels, all Democrats were not disloyal. Nor were all Republicans missionaries of the general welfare or all Negroes angelic innocents. There was apparently more to Radical Republican Reconstruction plans than had met myopic patriotic eyes. Moreover, as Dunning himself made plain, Reconstruction was not exclusively sectional. There was more than the simple challenge of northern plans and the equally simple southern response. Reconstruction was a national problem. Nor was it quite as singularly political as some who have appraised Dunning have supposed:

> Many things contributed to keep conditions in the South in the forefront of contemporaneous interest; and the historian cannot but feel the influence of this fact. Moreover, few episodes of recorded history more urgently invite thorough analysis and extended reflection than the struggle through which the Southern whites, subjugated by adversaries of their own race, thwarted the scheme which threatened permanent subjugation to another race. From the point of view of social and political science in general, the South bulks largest in the history of reconstruction. But

our point of view in the present volume is different. We must regard the period as a step in the progress of the American nation. In this aspect the North claims our principal attention. The social, economic, and political forces that wrought positively for progress are to be found in the record, not of the vanquished, but of the victorious section. In this record there is less that is spectacular, less that is pathetic, and more that seems inexcusably sordid than in the record of the South; but moral and dramatic values must not have greater weight in the writing than they have had in the making of history.[19]

While Dunning's followers did not abandon his controlling assumptions, some of them deviated from the Garner pattern of presentation. Walter L. Fleming, one of the most prolific of southern historians, envisaged Reconstruction much more inclusively. In its apportionment, *The Civil War and Reconstruction in Alabama* (1905) differs appreciably from Garner's *Mississippi*. Fleming took industry, education, and religion into historical account along with legislative acts and political purposes. A half century ago such factors as clothes, drugs, and the manner of living were causes and effects customarily omitted from consideration.[20] Fleming was cast in the Dunning mold. He stemmed from comfortable southern stock, the son of a Georgia planter who was a Confederate cavalryman. As a student at Alabama Polytechnic Institute, he came under the tutelage of George Petrie, a Dixie product of the Hopkins seminar. At the Institute, he earned his bachelor's and master's degrees in 1896 and 1897 respectively and, while a graduate student, taught English and history at his alma mater. Mustered out of the army after the Spanish-American War, he went to Columbia University and Dunning's seminar in 1900.

Once he acquired his doctorate in 1904, Fleming made the South of the Reconstruction era inseparable from the rest of his life. At the University of West Virginia he initiated the university *Documents on Reconstruction,* a monthly compilation of source materials. The following year his doctoral study of the war and reconstruction in Alabama appeared, succeeded by his collection of the Ku Klux Klan and his exhaustive *Documentary History of Reconstruction.* He moved from West Virginia to Louisiana State University and finally to Vanderbilt, but his productive energies never lessened. Woodrow Wilson offered him a post at Princeton, and the twelve Southerners who in the twentieth century took their defiant stand with Dixie's past, dedicated their minority report to him.[21] On the other hand, William E. B. Du Bois, looking at the history of Reconstruction from another angle, took him severely to task for misrepresenting the Negro and perverting the whole southern story. "Fleming's 'Documentary History of Reconstruction' is done by a man who has a thesis to support, and his selection of documents supports the thesis. His study of Alabama is pure propaganda." Du Bois supplied an important corrective to Reconstruction history, not without a generous bias of his own.[22]

Contemporary with Fleming and in every sense his peer was Ulrich Bonnell Phillips. Also a Georgian, he was educated in the university of his native state and proceeded to Columbia for his doctorate. Fleming represents the Dunning strain in pure form; Phillips represents a fruitful blend. Political and constitutional history of the Dunning variety interested him but mildly. It was not until he heard Frederick Jackson Turner lecture on sectionalism that he discovered a conceptual tool for the understanding of southern history.[23] He eschewed Reconstruction for the prewar years, and his thesis *Georgia and State Rights*[24] owed as much to the historian of the frontier West as to the historian of the Reconstruction South.

Though a highly effective teacher, Phillips was not in the Turner-Dunning class. Dunning and Turner produced scholars as well as scholarship, but Phillips is memorable for his own production record. Within thirty-two years, according to one of his bibliographers, he wrote five volumes, edited four books of documents, contributed fifty-five articles to the journals in addition to about as many reviews.[25] Phillips' writings, largely confined to the antebellum South, are divided among three specialties: politics, transportation, and labor. *Georgia and State Rights,* his maiden monographic effort, was in certain ways his best. As an example of "scientific" history, it bears comparison with almost any other. Little was left undone: the sources in public archives and private hands were resolutely tracked down with the result that Georgia's political history from the Revolution to secession is fully, not to say minutely, surveyed. It is not only adequately but economically surveyed, for Phillips compressed these crowded years into three chapters. It was an exemplary digest, useful but undistinguished except for its industry. Yet when Phillips, with the aid of Turner's concept of sectionalism, came to interpret Georgia's politics he made an enduring contribution to understanding. The hypothesis of sectionalism, the independent variable in the Georgia equation, made it possible to organize the bewildering multiplicity of political, economic, and social factors. Economic differences followed the lines of sectional differences, and the latter was correlated with soil. Such a conceptual integration gave meaning to political change and political stability, which in the impeccable Turner manner Phillips charted on illustrative maps.[26]

In the field of transportation, Phillips turned out polished and highly competent expositions, none more nearly complete than the *History of Transportation in the Eastern Cotton Belt to 1860.*[27] Yet, the plantation and slavery were closest to his mind, and it was here that he made his lasting scholarly mark. John R. Commons' stolid *Documentary History of American Industrial Society* opens with two volumes of sources compiled and edited by Phillips. Evidence of his unflagging search for materials, *Plantation and Frontier Documents*[28] also displayed how these twin concepts were coupled in his thought. They supply, as one appraiser concluded, a key to his productivity and to his method. The house that Phillips built was carefully planned. He drew up the blueprints himself and once drawn he permitted no extravagant alterations.[29] *American Negro Slavery,* and *Life and Labor in the Old South,*[30] no less than *Georgia and State Rights,* are variations on a single theme, the Negro and the slavery system. For Phillips the Negro was "the central theme of Southern history." [31]

While Phillips was a worthy exemplar of scientific history in the southern field, Dunning remained the unchallengeable *magister.* A commemorative volume, *Essays in Southern History and Politics,*[32] presented to him in 1914, recognized the power of his personality as well as the power of his mind. In a communication addressed "To the Authors, all and singular of Studies in Southern History and Politics," Dunning placed his own contributions and those of his students in a sensitively proportioned estimate.

> I had a subconscious impression that I was pretty familiar with the field in a general way; but I do not think there is one of your essays from which I have not derived chastisement and correction as to facts and valuable suggestion as to points of view and interpretation. If the reading public will profit as much as I have from the Studies, your need of approbation from your fellow-citizens will be rich indeed. Very likely, however, there will not be an adequate recognition of your work at the present time. But a definitive interpretation of the Old South and its extinction, as they appeared to your generation, will be sought by thousands of students in the future; and you have the satisfaction of knowing that your volume will stand through the ages as such an interpretation—as the dominate judgment of American historical scholarship in the first quarter of the twentieth century.[33]

The history of the Old South and its demise changed by Dunning's students had first been changed by Dunning. *Essays on Civil War and Reconstruction* and *Reconstruction, Political and Economic, 1865–1877,*[34] summarize the views of specialist scholars in the post-Civil War era. They illustrate, and illustrate effectively, the first revisionist phase in the cycle of reconstruction history.

The cycle of Reconstruction history passed through three stages. Among the spoils of war, conventionally assigned to the victor, are the spoils of history. The history made by the Radical Reconstructionists became all but official before the restoration of southern rule in the seventies.[35] But literary expressions of southern attitudes were never wanting. *Why the Solid South?*,[36] for example, written by Southern members of Congress, was published in 1890. It was the year of the Lodge Force Bill,[37] and many had grown weary of Republican excesses. More histrionic than historical, *Why the Solid South?* suggested a revulsion of feeling by no means confined to southern congressmen. The next year, James Ford Rhodes, in the initial volume of his *History of the United States from the Compromise of 1850,*[38] exposed a series of Republican prejudices; year after year Dunning and his Columbia scholars added conceptual and factual data which further dissolved them. Rhodes and Dunning were refreshingly novel. They wrote without rancor. They deplored polemics in the guise of history and they tried to formulate judgments of what they believed had actually happened. Frequently one set of stereotypes was substituted for another. Republican historiography stressed the threat of the South to the nation; the revisionists stressed the threat of the Radical Republicans to the South. The revisionists denuded Republican propaganda of its shallow pretensions and stripped Scalawags and Carpetbaggers of even the simpler virtues. They exchanged heroes, for the southern white—misunderstood, wronged, harried by vengeance—became the revisionists' hero. And the Negro, always the central theme of Southern history, was conceived as ready for freedom only under the tutelage of his erstwhile masters.

The third stage of Reconstruction historiography matured as sectional identification waned. Between the two world wars a different culture fashioned different objectives. When the Old South had in fact become the New South, America had become a new nation. Economic revolutions and economic depression gave new weight to economic interpretations, and caste, class, and social conflict took precedence over sectional animosities. But the most recent schools of historians, Negro historians among them, have not yet eradicated Dunning's classic conceptions. They still remain. Also remaining is the less complicated traditional view of the Old South with which southern men of letters, historians included, continue to take their trenchant stand.[39]

Leadership, unquestionably Dunning's while he lived, gradually passed into other hands. As chief mentor of Columbia doctoral students in southern studies, he continued to train the men who wrote the monographs. But Dunning was immersed in explorations of his own. The *Political Science Quarterly,* which he managed from 1894 to 1903, received his careful editorial attention until his death in 1922. His *History of Political Theories, Ancient and Medieval,*[40] devoured his time and his substance.[41] The final volume, *From Rousseau to Spencer,* did not appear until 1920, thirteen years after his summary of Reconstruction in the *American Nation* series. With Frederic Bancroft he edited the *Reminiscences of Carl Schurz,* and in 1914 came his thought-provoking *British Empire and the United States.*[42]

Phillips, finishing at Columbia in 1902, went to Wisconsin, where, added to the advantage of association with Turner, he had a clear mandate to cultivate the history of the South. After a relatively brief sojourn at Wisconsin and Tulane, he settled at Michigan from 1911 to 1929 before going to Yale with his seminar on the South.

Slightly prior to Phillips' appointment at Michigan, William Edward Dodd accepted a position at the University of Chicago, a post he held for twenty-five years. A Southerner by birth and training, Dodd differed from Phillips in many important respects. Phillips was at his best in the seminar, Dodd on the lecture platform. Dodd was an expert of synthesis, while Phillips was less receptive to large-scale generalization. Both received their preliminary education and early teaching experience in the South; both reached a fullness of mind and service in the North. Phillips leaned to the conservative side. Dodd made the sources of the democratic faith, in the South and in the nation, in thought and in deed, the work of his life.[43] But together Dodd, Phillips, and Dunning opened the modern period of Southern historiography.[44]

A Columbia school of institutional history complemented the Columbia school of Southern history. Herbert Levi Osgood, a Burgess student, grounded the institutional approach in meticulous research and outlined a revised framework for the investigation of colonial America. After him the study of the colonial period and the revolutionary struggle moved in a different intellectual orbit. Born on a Maine farm in 1855, Osgood was graduated from Amherst, fifth in a class of seventy-seven, twenty-two years later. The philosopher-president, Julius Seeyle, and Anson D. Morse,[45] the historian, each helped to stretch his mind. But it was Burgess, the maker of historians, who shaped Osgood's intellectual life and gave direction to his career.[46] Thus equipped, Osgood taught Worcester Academy boys for two years before taking up formal learning once more. Amherst provided him with an A.M. degree in 1880 and a year at Yale enabled him to work with William Graham Sumner, professor of political and social science, whose trenchant essays made him a national figure. Burgess then proposed Germany, and Osgood was disposed to heed his advice. After additional preparation during which he laid siege to the language, he took up residence at the University of Berlin in 1882. Amherst was a far academic cry from Berlin, and Osgood reveled in his opportunities. He heard Adolf Wagner lecture on socialism, Gustav Schmoller on economic history, and Rudolf von Gneist on English and Prussian constitutionalism. Treitschke's incomparable eloquence stirred him even when he rejected Treitschke's ideas, and he was impressed by Heinrich von Sybel's plea for the preservation of historical sources. Occasionally, and from a distance, he saw the eighty-six-year-old Ranke, still an active scholar, who gave him a feeling of kinship with the immortals. The short year ultimately ended, and, returning to the United States, he taught briefly at Amherst and Smith until he joined the staff of the Brooklyn High School where he remained until 1889.[47]

The secondary schools, as Dixon Ryan Fox observed,[48] neither demand nor deserve men of secondary worth, and Osgood's service to Brooklyn was outstanding. Residence in Brooklyn, moreover, made further study at Columbia a relatively easy matter. At Columbia as at Amherst Burgess was the prime mover, and it was under his guidance that Osgood prepared a paper on "Rodbertus and Scientific Socialism" which appeared in the *Political Science Quarterly*. Adolf Wagner's influence was also apparent in Osgood's study of Proudhon and in his dissertation, *Socialism and Anarchism,* which brought him a Columbia doctorate in 1889.[49] The respective domains of Wagner and Burgess were secondary to his main research, for even before *Socialism and Anarchism* was completed, he published an essay in 1887 on England and the colonies.[50] But the study of England and her colonies as Osgood conceived it was not foreign to the teachings of Wagner, Schmoller, or Burgess. Osgood's volumes on the America of the seventeenth and eighteenth centuries were legal and institutional in orientation. They were as much concerned with economics and economic theory as with government and administration. Osgood had simply delimited a geographical area and defined a topic. He believed it could be managed within the time allotted him. To begin it, English history and the English sources of American institutions were prerequisite, and he deserted Brooklyn and Brooklyn High for London and the Public Record Office. After fifteen months Burgess called him back to Columbia. Columbia became his permanent academic home in 1890; the colonies had already become his permanent research interest. English constitutional development and European history were among his course offerings until William M. Sloane and James Harvey Robinson joined the history faculty. But he concentrated from the very beginning. His course on the "Political History of the Colonies and the American Revolution" dated from 1891. The first two volumes on the seventeenth century were published in 1902, the third in 1907. He made two further research trips to England in preparation for writing on the eighteenth century, and the four eighteenth-century volumes appeared six years after his death.[51]

Osgood led the scholar's life. He prepared his materials with studious care, and even his presentations at Brooklyn High School are marked with the investigator's touch. His class notes, still preserved, were interlined and annotated as new thought and new research enlarged his understanding.[52] The "Political History of the Colonies and the American Revolution," properly labeled an "investigation course," at first surveyed the entire field. As his knowledge expanded, his course boundaries contracted. In 1898, the year 1689 served as the dividing point; after 1914 the American Revolution was separately studied.[53] In his first article on the subject in 1887, he attacked the simple thesis, then a respected commonplace, that British imperialism intended subversion, which the colonials were manfully determined to thwart. British colonial policy may have been imperialistic; it was neither illegal nor wicked. Rather, it was inconsistent and ill-conceived. Colonials had no greater affinity for freedom and virtue than other Englishmen across the water. The Americans were actually "more concerned with community independence than with individual liberty or social progress."[54]

The problem that worried Osgood was a real one. He stated it with an unvarnished directness (in 1891) while reviewing a celebrated book on the Revolution. "How . . . is it possible for an historian to do justice to the American Revolution—a revolt which destroyed the unity of the empire and involved great constitutional changes,—without making the reader understand what was the character of the political structure thus assailed? . . . The colonial revolt, like every other similar movement, involved questions both of right and of fact. The former are quite as important to the historian as the latter; for it is only through the adequate treatment of these that justice can be done to the institutions attacked." Was the principle of no taxation without representation a valid and reasonable proposition? To this question Osgood replied that for the English aristocracy it was "a thoroughly revolutionary doctrine." Historians of the colonial period and the American Revolution had been prejudiced and partial. As a result, there was no adequate treatment of either. "The truth is until American historians cease to attempt to defend a dogma, and begin in earnest the effort to understand the aristocratic society which existed in England and the democracy which was maturing here, and the causes of the conflict between the two, we shall not have a satisfactory history either of the colonial period or of the revolution. The Englishman too who carries his party prejudices into the work will reach no better results." [55] Osgood made the effort and reached the best results attained up to that point. If the history of the colonial period and the Revolution became more complicated, it also became more reasonable. The history of the colonies for those with whom Osgood shared his knowledge became a part of the history of Europe and of the British Empire. Colonial history was more than "the background of American history," and the Revolution was more than the beginning of the United States. No longer an immaculate event devoutly to be described, it became a secular process seriously to be studied.[56]

Enthusiasm for Osgood is almost exclusively limited to scholars. General readers of history have never taken his seven volumes to their hearts and even among the learned they are less frequently read than praised. For specialists, close familiarity with Osgood is the minimum price of competence, a price not always exhilaratingly paid. Readers of Osgood with a zest for knowledge provide their own excitement; he rarely offers it. He seldom allowed himself to veer from his objective, but his spare prose is clear, and he perfected it as deliberately as he imposed limitations on his subject matter.

> The political and social sciences have now reached such development that it is impossible to present in a single view all known aspects of any period of history. A choice must be made between those which are distinctly political and those that are social, and upon one or the other the emphasis must be laid. This should be done not in a narrow or exclusive spirit, but with a due regard to the fact that political events and forms of government are very largely the product of social causes, while institutions in their turn are the avenues through which social forces act. In this work attention will be specially directed to forms of government and to the forces and events from which their development has sprung.

Material of a social or economic nature will be utilized not directly for its own sake, but for a light which it may throw on political growth. In other words, an attempt will be made to interpret early American history in the terms of public law. The treatment of material will be subordinated to that end.[57]

A specialist's specialist, Osgood wrote a monograph on the American colonies, although it was a monograph seven volumes long.

The seven volumes produced a crop of new ideas and a batch of new scholars.[58] The seventeenth century acquired a novel and sharper outline; the eighteenth century acquired documented substance.[59] After Osgood's cultivation, the American colonies were seen to have grown out of English roots transplanted in new-world soil. Osgood was indisputably right in insisting that there were two sides to the growth of America, and that the American side could not be severed from the English. In fact, they had to be seen together, for both altered markedly in response to the other. Osgood furnished historians with an imperial view of colonial development and an institutional view of social change.

American colonial history, especially when studied from the institutional standpoint, is not limited or narrow in its bearings. Its outlook is broad, and the issues with which it is connected affect deeply the history of the world at large. Viewed in one connection, it is the record of the beginnings of English-American institutions. Looked at from another point of view, it fills an important place in the history of British colonization. It leads outward in two directions, toward the history of the greatest of federal republics, and toward the later and freer development of the greatest of commercial empires. If the colonial and the imperial forces which were operating can be fully traced and clearly revealed, the significance of the period in its twofold connection will be made apparent.[60]

Robert Livingston Schuyler, commemorating Osgood, wrote that his students learned "the worth of historical research and . . . the high responsibility of the historian's calling," a tribute Osgood would have appreciated as much as the judgment that he was the "first historian to undertake a scientific study of the origins of the American Republic." [61] The Osgood students, far from failing the master, did him the greatest honor. They adopted his controlling ideas.

First among Osgood's disciples was George Louis Beer. Beer was born in New York in 1872, the son of an immigrant family whose fortune in the tobacco trade America helped to enhance. Columbia awarded him an A.B. in 1892, and he continued his studies in the graduate school, which throve in part because it attracted students like him.[62] Burgess and Seligman were helpful guides, but Osgood was his most resourceful tutor. Burgess proposed the institutional history of the American colonies to Osgood.[63] Osgood proposed a study of the British commercial system to Beer.[64] Both acted upon the advice and neither had reason to regret it. *The Commercial Policy of England toward the American Colonies,*[65] Beer's M.A. essay, written before he had attained his majority, amplified in detail what Osgood had already suggested in outline. Beer's volume widened the secular gap in the dyke of American patriotism and it was widened with the intellectual tools forged in Osgood's seminar. The English side, as Osgood called it, was forcefully presented by Beer and he avowedly tried to correct the impression that "England consciously pursued an egotistic and tyrannical policy." [66] His fundamental purpose was to trace the history of mercantilism in the details of commercial policy and to illustrate the motive behind British economic administration.

The tobacco trade in the days of the Stuarts, chastely described in Beer's pages, was profitably described in the pages of Beer's own ledgers.[67] So capably did he handle his business affairs that he was able after 1903 to devote all his time to scholarship. Having taught briefly at Columbia, he married Seligman's niece and retired, following Osgood to the Public Record Office to permit the documents to tell him the story he wished to write.[68] Beer was an economic historian but he was just as well aware as Osgood that the institutions of economic life do not operate alone. It is "frequently far more important to know what people at the time thought were the results, rather than what these actually were," for Beer was convinced that history was largely "based on social psychology." [69] But the specialist, regardless of the breadth of his vision, is forced to limit his scope.

Beer's scope was as broad as his subject was panoramic. The economic organization of the British empire from 1578 to 1765 was his substantive and chronological aim, but he was not prepared to slight motivation outside conventional economic categories. He first published a volume on the years 1754 to 1765, which, presenting materials never before treated and covering a subject then highly obscure, met with warm scholarly approbation.[70] He demonstrated conclusively, irrespective of specific deductions, that printed sources in the United States were insufficient for proper understanding and that previous historical inferences were inaccurate and unsound. His specific deductions were arresting. The "ideal of a self-sufficient commercial Empire" exacted as high a price of the mother country as of the colonies and the entire ideal was directed less toward selfish profit than toward defense, which "was the rock upon which the old

Empire shattered itself." [71] From the period of the Seven Years' War, Beer went back to the origins of British commercial policy in 1578 and finally to the "old colonial system," the period 1660 to 1688. The gap in the series, 1688 to 1754, was to be filled in by four projected volumes that were never written. [72] Beer's accomplishment was a major one and his professional colleagues were not tardy in noting it. His results brilliantly complemented Osgood's pioneering work. Both were superb examples of scientific history in method, style, and faith. Beer and Osgood prized thought more than piety and were willing to follow wherever it might lead. There was no substitute for research and both were eager to look for newer explanations, whether they collided with established convictions or not. Beer presented new documentary evidence for historical consideration and he presented it in an unconventional theoretical structure. And the theoretical structure, hammered out by Osgood and elaborated by Beer, began the intellectual movement by which our ideas of colonial history have been revised.

Yet Beer was but one of Osgood's products. The number of Osgood students is impressively large. And more impressive than the quantity of Osgood's followers is the quality of their achievements. Each British colony in America recruited at least one historian from the Osgood seminar. [73] Two of Osgood's students embarked on revisions of their own. Charles A. Beard typified the cross currents of American historiography as it came to full maturity. He established canons and criteria of his own, and in volume after volume he flung a series of challenges at traditional historical sanctities. The Constitution, the motives of the Founding Fathers, the role of economics in historical causation, and the philosophy of scientific history itself were subjected to his corrosive speculation and his encyclopedic data. Arthur M. Schlesinger, Sr., surveyed the activities of the colonial merchants in the American Revolution in the Osgood-Beer spirit and tightened the links of evidence into a new viewpoint of American history. After Schlesinger had expanded the Osgood thesis with fresh documentary detail, he went on to formulate new viewpoints of his own. [74]

Osgood's followers later went their several ways. But it was Herbert Levi Osgood, pupil of John William Burgess, and Charles McLean Andrews, pupil of Herbert Baxter Adams, who exemplify the science of history in the second generation. And they exemplified it through the comparative institutional approach to American colonial history. [75] While Adams and Burgess upheld the Teutonic hypothesis, Osgood and Andrews, rejecting it, evolved a different formula for the comparative method.[76] Although they criticized the assumptions of Teutonic origins, they were evolutionists none the less. They explicitly avowed a continuity of English and American institutions. They marshaled the data of English institutional origins, charted the course of change during the evolutionary process of transplantation and interaction, and compared them in various stages of alteration. The assumptions of continuity often resulted in giving the "English side" undue stress. While an important corrective, the doctrine of change and continuity obscured factors of discontinuous change, the emergence of novel institutions in both England and America.

Younger than Osgood by eight years,[77] Charles McLean Andrews hailed from Wethersfield, Connecticut, and was graduated from Trinity College in Hartford. Osgood and Andrews received their doctorates simultaneously in 1889; the first at Columbia, the second at Hopkins. Andrews left Baltimore at once and began an association with Bryn Mawr that lasted eighteen years. From 1907 to 1910 he taught at Hopkins before moving to Yale, where he remained until his retirement in 1931. As one of the leading scholars in early American history, he made the New Haven university a center of colonial studies.

Andrews and Osgood held substantially similar views. Both were convinced that studies in colonial history were unbalanced. Too much weight had customarily been given to American affairs, too little to correlative English conditions.[78] Andrews frequently accorded the English side as much consideration as the American. Andrews moreover normally conceived the colonies as including the empire in the western hemisphere. Canada and the British West Indies formed a unit in his mind, for he consistently maintained an imperial, if not a global, perspective:

> My . . . purpose has been to deal with the colonies in large measure from the vantage ground of their origin. To write as one standing among them and viewing them at close range is to crowd the picture and to destroy the perspective. We must study the colonies from some point outside of themselves, and to the scholar there is only one point of observation, that of the mother country from which they came and to whom they were legally subject.
>
> Furthermore, I have included . . . not only the original thirteen colonies but those of Canada and the West Indies also. No distinction existed between them in colonial times and none should be made now by the writer of colonial history. Only by viewing the colonies as a whole and comparatively can a treatment be avoided which is merely provincial on one side or topical on the other.[79]

American history was English history before it became Anglo-American. Both stages had to develop and alter before American history could properly begin. Even the Revolution itself, Andrews felt, was a colonial rather than an American issue.[80] Ordinarily Andrews' histories are made up of three separable parts: England, England's colonies, and their interrelationships.

English history was a precondition to any serious study of America. The works of Osgood and Andrews show a detailed knowledge of the English background. Andrews persistently searched for manuscripts and other documents. The "facts" were objects of veneration for Osgood as for Andrews, but it was the English "facts," previously slighted, which had now to be restored. Discovery of abundant manuscript materials, long unused, went far to convince modern colonial historians that understanding of America had yet to begin. An unrivalled command of English manuscript materials bearing on America led Andrews to conclude that "no systematic attempt has ever been made by British or American historians to discover the extent and value of the material contained in British archives relating to American history." [81] He agreed with Osgood that the period 1690 to 1750 had been "unduly neglected." Although events were more exciting before 1689 and more dramatic after 1754, the neglected period was one of significant institutional change, without a comprehension of which neither England nor America could be understood.[82]

Between Andrews and Osgood there was intellectual harmony. There was also disagreement. Osgood had dissented from Burgess, Andrews from Herbert Baxter Adams. Andrews took serious exception to Osgood's interpretation, and others have taken exception no less serious to Andrews. Andrews found Osgood too legal and institutional.[83] As a result, Osgood had confounded the forms of social organization with economic realities. Economic factors had been neglected, and to neglect economics was "to miss some of the deeper currents of colonial life." Insufficient consideration had been given to such factors as "rising prices, debt, the cost of living, the growth of regional and radical feeling, and the bearing of commerce and the increase of wealth on legislation." [84] Andrews also argued that Osgood had given inadequate emphasis to English conditions to such a degree that it appeared "difficult for him to understand just what was the British outlook before 1763." [85] Osgood leveled exactly the same charge at others and in almost identical words.[86] Of Andrews it was later said that his great work was too legal in tone, that he had overestimated the importance of the ruling classes, that he disparaged the lower orders and gave undue attention to the English side. Critics alleged that he had written a conservative colonial history, that he in turn had minimized the "growth of regional and radical feeling" and had failed to probe "into the workings of economic forces." [87]

Historiography in America had come of critical age. Scientific historians themselves had begun to question the premise of objectivity and to raise doubts concerning the philosophy of the science of history. Said Andrews, when the twentieth century had reached its first quarter: "Objective history is merely nonpartisan history. To write objectively is merely to write with the detachment of the onlooker rather than with the prejudice of the advocate and to draw conclusions from the evidence itself and not from prepossessions already existing in the writer's mind. History viewed through Whig or Tory spectacles . . . and used to defend a doctrine, a theory, or a philosophy—all such history is a bad guide for the public because it does not tell the truth." [88] Curtis Nettels, colonial historian at Cornell, averred that Tory spectacles were just what Andrews wore.

Men thought and wrote from different points of vantage. They advanced different sets of facts differently conceived. And different speculative or cultural attitudes gave a different coloration to the evidence. Scholars could afford to differ. Indeed, they could not afford permanently to agree.

XXIII

Harvard and Cambridge

Graduate study began as tentatively at Harvard as at Columbia. In 1825, George Ticknor, professor of French and Spanish literature, was instrumental in securing permission for "resident graduates" of other institutions to continue their studies at Harvard. However, no graduate school developed from this offer of academic hospitality. The University Lecture System, inaugurated in 1863 by President Thomas Hill, and thereafter regarded by Charles W. Eliot as the genesis of the graduate division, turned out to be mainly scientific. Hill's innovation no more served as a graduate school than Eliot's "University Courses of Instruction" of 1870, which were soon allowed to lapse.[1]

Advanced offerings in history at Harvard commenced with Henry Adams.[2] Harvard and the Adams family were well accustomed to each other. Henry Adams, never able to elude his noble ancestors, was preceded by them at Harvard as everywhere else. Before Eliot became president of the university in 1869, Charles Francis Adams, Henry's father, had been offered the post, and John Quincy Adams had been Boylston professor of rhetoric from 1806 to 1809. In fact, there was scarcely a period without an Adams in the Harvard service.[3]

Eliot had no reason to suppose that Henry Adams was available for a Harvard appointment. Adams had already decided to make politics his career and was preparing to moor himself in Washington

444

for the purpose. He had been offered the editorship of *The North American Review*, which he promptly refused.[4] When Eliot's invitation to become an assistant professor of history reached him, Adams was in Europe. He refused the invitation though somewhat less peremptorily than the *North American* editorship.[5] Eliot was unwilling to take "no" for an Adams answer. He was too heavily committed to plans for change at Harvard to lose the kind of opportunity he believed Adams presented. As for Adams, "he could see no relation whatever between himself and a professorship. He sought education; he did not sell it. He knew no history; he knew only a few historians; his ignorance was mischievous because it was literary, accidental, indifferent." [6] When he met Eliot, he frankly told him so. Eliot, as Adams reported the interview, replied: "If you will point out to me anyone who knows more, Mr. Adams, I will appoint him." Adams accepted the appointment at once. He was to serve for five years, and so that Ephraim W. Gurney, a Harvard historian, might be free for the duties of the deanship, Adams also agreed to head the *North American*.[7]

It was unquestionably true that Adams was technically unprepared to teach medieval history. But if Adams was honestly disturbed by his lack of preparation, his sponsors were not. What they wanted Adams possessed in more than full measure. He had demonstrated his literary skill in the pages of the *North American*. As a staunch advocate of reform in politics, he had earned the right to wear the badge of liberalism. He was widely read and as widely traveled. Since Eliot and Gurney wanted men of charm and cultivation as aides in the battle against entrenched Harvard conservatism, they could not have done better than to secure Henry Adams. Nor could his Harvard sponsors have been disappointed. While the *North American* did not at once become the social catalytic for which they hoped, it was not because Adams had failed to try. Had doubts of Adams' devotion to reform ever existed, his editorial conduct would have been enough to dispel them. *The North American Review* had a part in the education of Henry Adams. It served to develop his mind and to improve his style. He exercised his editorial authority vigorously, not to say arbitrarily, and many contributions were written to his order. English history, English law, and English historians were the subjects he chose to review, and these helped immeasurably to build a body of knowledge in the field of his teaching and to provide a background in the field in which he was later to write.

Adams set about teaching with energy, and his course Medieval Institutions was a departure from conventional Harvard practice.

Eliot and Gurney had wished for a nonconformist, and they had one. Whatever Adams later wrote in the *Education,* he was an immediate and unqualified success. Students admired him even when they failed to understand him. He dazzled the brilliant with his powers and shocked the humdrum by his irreverence. The discerning were soon aware that much of his iconoclasm was pose. It was just as quickly apparent that he respected first-class minds and that he tried to provoke thinking by disagreement. The perceptive discovered that meanings and interrelationships were more important than the "facts" that illustrated them. Medieval Institutions turned into an undergraduate seminar. Half a dozen students would meet at his house, where Adams cross-examined them and the texts, and they cross-examined the sources and each other. Henry Osborn Taylor, who as an Adams student already gave indication that the Middle Ages were to capture his mind, preferred Adams to any of his teachers. "He is so clearheaded and analyzes history so well; also he despises as I do the barren accumulation of knowledge." [8]

Adams himself wrote the best description of his course and of his students, although he ends on a characteristic note of pessimism:

> Adams found himself obliged to force his material into some shape to which a method could be applied. He could think only of law as subject; the Law School as end; and he took, as victims of his experiment, half-a-dozen highly intelligent young men who seemed willing to work. The course began with the beginning, as far as the books showed a beginning, in primitive man, and came down through the Salic Franks to the Norman English. Since no textbooks existed, the professor refused to profess, knowing no more than his students, and the students read what they pleased and compared their results. As pedagogy, nothing could be more triumphant. The boys worked like rabbits, and dug holes all over the field of archaic society; no difficulty stopped them; unknown languages yielded before their attack, and customary law became familiar as the police court; undoubtedly they learned, after a fashion, to chase an idea, like a hare, through as dense a thicket of obscure facts as they were likely to meet at the bar; but their teacher knew from his own experience that his wonderful method led nowhere and they would have to exert themselves to get rid of it in the Law School even more than they exerted themselves to acquire it in the college. Their science had no system, and could have none, since its subject was merely antiquarian. Try as hard as he might, the professor could not make it actual.[9]

Nevertheless, Adams studied hard. He read widely, thought deeply, and during a European trip sought out the master historians whose ideas kept churning in his mind.[10] Soon he was given the Medieval Institutions for honors' candidates alone. As his interest mounted, he informed Eliot and the Harvard fellows that he was willing to give instruction to a group of doctoral candidates. Eliot and the fellows promptly accepted this generous proposal, and graduate work in history at Harvard was begun.[11] From these beginnings came the contributions of Henry Adams to American historiography: the Adams seminar, the *Essays in Anglo-Saxon Law,* and the first Adams students.[12]

Study of English law and institutions was the Adams prologue to America. English legal history, the development of English liberties, were the background to the transplantation of English institutions overseas. Adams had already begun to plan for a course in American colonial history, a course that became Harvard's celebrated "History V." [13] Meanwhile, his contract having run out, he accepted another five-year appointment in 1875. Colonial history was assigned to his student, Henry Cabot Lodge, and Adams turned to his "History VI," the history of the United States from 1789 to 1840. The United States from 1789 to 1840 belonged particularly to Henry Adams; it was that part of the history of the United States which included the administrations of John Adams and John Quincy Adams.[14]

Henry Adams took various views of his historical writings and he invariably accounted his teaching a failure. Yet when he chose to retire in 1877 he had already created a school of history and established a tradition of historical scholarship. He restored history to the undergraduate curriculum and brought the nineteenth-century version of scientific history to Harvard. Through his students, products of his classes and his seminar, he generated an intellectual evolution. Ernest Young followed him into Medieval Institutions and became a full professor in 1888. When he died shortly thereafter, his place was filled by Charles Gross, an outstanding medievalist trained at Göttingen. Gross taught the Constitutional History of England, a course begun by Adams and continued by Charles H. McIlwain, and taught in turn by Gross. J. Laurence Laughlin, who collaborated with Adams on the study of Anglo-Saxon Law, moved into economics finally at the University of Chicago, and Henry Osborn Taylor became the historian of the medieval mind. Ephraim Emerton and Albert Bushnell Hart returned to Cambridge and Harvard after earning German doctorates; the first to teach the Middle Ages and ecclesiastical institutions, the second, American history and government. Edward Channing made Harvard noteworthy for the study of the history of the United States and himself for the writing of it. Henry Cabot Lodge studied with Adams, worked in collaboration with him, and remained his life-long friend. He not only shared Adams' devotion to the history their respective ancestors had made, but he shared his passion for politics. In 1881 he entered the Massachusetts House of Representatives and began a political career which effectively stifled his earlier interest in scholarship.[15]

Henry Cabot Lodge owes his position in American historiography to Henry Adams. Not that Lodge lacked native ability, for he was in fact superior to many a scholar whose achievements have received more generous tribute. Nor did he lack the advantages of an excellent training. He had the advantage of Harvard, of Harvard Law School, and of Henry Adams. It was Adams who brought out the best in Lodge, and once the search for education separated Adams from Lodge and the yearnings of ambition separated Lodge from scholarship, Lodge lost touch with a mind and personality of the Adams stamp.[16] Lodge, said Adams, "was a creature of teaching" and he did not mean his own. He meant the Cabot lineage, the background connections of the Boston Lodges, for he was "Boston incarnate—the child of his local parentage." The difference between Lodge and Adams was that while both tried to outgrow their local parentage, Lodge failed more completely in Henry Adams' terms than Adams himself. Perhaps, as Adams conjectured, it was because "his ambition led him to be more," [17] but in public life as distinguished from the life of thought, the limitations of local parentage are likely to prove more disastrous. With Lodge, Adams always had the last word: "he never could feel perfectly at ease whatever leg he stood on, but shifted, sometimes with painful strain of temper, from one sensitive muscle to another, uncertain whether to pose as an uncompromising Yankee, or as pure American." [18]

Lodge performed brilliantly in the Adams seminar. At the suggestion of his teacher, he undertook a search of Germanic law to discover the links between its concepts and those of English common law. Anglo-Saxon law, the doctrine of continuity, and the Teutonic hypothesis were the major ideas of the seminar, and Lodge acquitted himself in the prescribed German manner. He was so thorough and so promising that Adams felt no hesitancy in suggesting him for the American colonial history course. Had Eliot any reservations, he failed to act on them, and Lodge appeared as an instructor in history in the year 1876–77. Adams had earlier displayed his confidence in Lodge when he offered him, though only twenty-four years of age, an assistant editorship of *The North American Review*. Flattered, Lodge hardly needed to consider. And a rare chance it was, for Adams taught him not only history but style. He made him responsible for seeing the journal through to publication, a function

Lodge performed with growing skill and judgment. The assistant editor also wrote for the *Review*.[19] One of his early pieces was an essay on Hamilton, the hero of his youth and of his maturity. Adams did not share his student's adulation for the adversary of Thomas Jefferson. "I dislike Hamilton," he told Lodge, and he had a good Adams reason for his aversion. Hamilton, he felt, was an "adventurer." "The very cause of your admiration is the cause of my distrust; he was equally ready to support a system he disbelieved in as one that he liked." [20]

Lodge and Adams did not see American history eye to eye. Student gossip in the Yard had it that Adams interpreted the American past from the radical and democratic point of view, Lodge from a conservative and aristocratic one. Adams remained undisturbed. Lodge's Federalism, he said, had "as good a right to expression in the college" as his own Republicanism.[21] Differences such as these did not prevent Lodge and Adams from joining together in sympathetic collaboration. It was as a result of this partnership that Lodge performed his best work. Also involved in this venture were their honorable ancestors and their New England honor.

Adams and Lodge merged their minds in a long review of Hermann von Holst's *Constitutional and Political History of the United States*. Holst, a leading Continental interpreter of the American past, surveyed the vicissitudes of sovereignty in American theory and practice. In the course of his appraisal he came upon separatist episodes unrelated to slavery and the South. The doctrine of nullification and threats of secession, he reported, were heard in New England during the sectional controversies of Jefferson's and Madison's administrations. John Quincy Adams, breaking Federalist party lines, had thrown his support to Jefferson's Embargo Act. The Embargo Act, mooring the merchantmen of Federalist shippers to New England wharfs, angered Massachusetts merchants, who excoriated their wayward representative in the precise language of special interests. Twenty years later, in the presidential campaign of 1828, Jacksonians revived the incident to prove President Adams disloyal to party. Adams, anxious to remain in office, retorted sharply. The Massachusetts Federalists of 1808 had lost whatever claim on his loyalty they had once possessed and, he insisted, he had told them so in unmistakable written words. As members of the Essex Junto—a group of prosperous merchants representing the ports of the North Shore together with their Boston allies—they had conspired against the United States and had threatened, none too vaguely, to withdraw from the Union. When Holst was writing, John Quincy Adams' reply to the Federalists could not be found. Since the evidence was lacking, the probity of President Adams was in doubt.[22]

The reputation of President John Quincy Adams was but one of those weighed in Holst's historical balance. A chief member of the Essex Junto was George Cabot, a direct progenitor of Henry Cabot Lodge. Cabot had been the president of the Hartford Convention, which issued the challenge to national sovereignty. Lodge, always given to ancestor worship, was already engaged in a life of George Cabot. Henry Adams found his grandfather's long-lost reply among the family papers. Adams published *Documents Relating to New England Federalism, 1800–1815,* the first clear manifestation of his revived interest in American history.[23] In the introduction Adams was able to prove that if his grandfather had deserted his party, he had not deserted his country. Lodge published *The Life and Letters of George Cabot,*[24] in which he was able to show that his well-known kinsman, though a member of a secessionist group, did not belong to its most violent wing. Each reviewed the work of the other. Adams found Lodge too eager to exonerate Cabot, and Lodge found Adams too gentle to his presidential grandfather.

George Cabot, Lodge's maiden effort aside from his part in *Anglo-Saxon Law,* was a worthy effort and a good biography. The *Cabot* was followed in 1881 by a *Short History of the English Colonies in America,* which showed how well he had digested the materials of his Harvard course and how much he had profited from contact with Henry Adams. A life of Alexander Hamilton in 1882 and a study of Daniel Webster in 1883, both in the *American Statesmen* series, were his last unhampered scholarly ventures. After his election to Congress in 1887, politics easily won the uneven battle with learning. From 1887 to 1892 he was re-elected to the House, and in 1893 he was elevated to the United States Senate, a seat he occupied until his death in 1924. As a teacher, his tenure was altogether too short to mellow his mind or to deepen his maturity. Yet he taught long enough to influence Edward Channing, who, annoyed by Lodge's dogmatism, vowed he would become a better historian.[25]

Edward Channing was actually more the student of Henry Adams than of Henry Cabot Lodge.[26] Adams was a positive force in his development, and he later referred to him as "the greatest teacher" he had "ever encountered."[27] From Adams Channing learned the technique of scholarship coupled with standards of literary craftsmanship. The *History of the United States During the Administration of Thomas Jefferson,* at which its author sometimes scoffed,

Channing acclaimed a masterpiece. So highly, in fact, did he regard it that he relinquished a notion to write on Jefferson's first presidency, since Adams had done it definitively. When Channing came to prepare his own *Jeffersonian System* in the *American Nation* series, he relied on the Adams volumes and on some of the materials he had helped his teacher to collect.[28]

Channing was as purely a New England product as Lodge or Adams. Margaret Fuller was his aunt, and William Ellery Channing was his father, both transcendentalist critics whose hallowed origins strengthened their uncompromising protests. He was born in Dorchester, Massachusetts, in 1856, and barely strayed from Boston and Cambridge. Five years after he received his Harvard diploma in 1873, he became an instructor in history, and he continued to teach at Harvard until 1929. After earning his Ph.D. in 1880, he took himself off to Europe for a year of travel. When he returned he had fully made up his mind that American history and the teaching of it were to consume his life.[29]

Channing would very much have liked to get into the Harvard teaching swing at once, but his undiluted New England lineage proved to be a temporary barrier. Eliot, whose first duty was to Harvard, was apprehensive about inbreeding in New England's first families, and Channing represented too many of them. There was sufficient living evidence to justify Eliot's fears, but Channing had resolved to stand or fall on what he himself could do. When the first vacancy occurred in Harvard's historical ranks, Albert Bushnell Hart rather than Channing was called to fill it. For these purposes, at least, to have been born in Clarksville, Pennsylvania, was an advantage, and it was not until Channing had shown his mettle in various ways about the Yard, together with an increase in the American history enrollment, that Channing acquired the colonial history course. As a teacher Channing emulated the iconoclasm of his master. He liked nothing better than to demolish historical sanctities, especially when they concerned the historical great and particularly members of his own illustrious tribe. Myths existed only for Channing to explode, and though he chided undergraduates unmercifully, they continued to clamor for his courses because everyone knew it paid to take them. Membership in his graduate seminars was particularly prized. A carefully selected few were admitted, and they learned to respect Edward Channing no less than the stuff out of which his history was made.[30]

Notwithstanding Channing's gifts as a teacher, his claim to greatness rests upon his published work. *Town and County Government in the English Colonies* was awarded a prize in 1883. Herbert Baxter Adams, one of the judges in the contest, arranged for its publication in the *Johns Hopkins Studies,* although it was critical of the Teutonic theory of American institutional origins. Channing had already read parts of the monograph before its publication at the first meeting of the American Historical Association.[31] At the invitation of the editor, he wrote two chapters for Justin Winsor's *Narrative and Critical History:* "The Companions of Columbus" and "The War in the Southern Department." [32] *The Narragansett Planters, A Study in Causes,* also in the *Johns Hopkins Studies,* appeared in 1886.[33] Channing tried his now practiced hand at historical composition with a broader sweep. With Thomas Wentworth Higginson[34] he issued an *English History for American Readers* in 1893, and for the English reading public he wrote *The United States of America, 1765–1865,* three years later. *A Students' History of the United States* (1898), a successful text, had a considerable sale, in part because of its pacific and balanced tone.[35]

Channing laid the plan for a full-scale history of the United States while still in college, and most of his research was undertaken with that plan in mind.[36] This was called "The Great Work" by his friends and co-workers, and little was permitted to interfere with its preparation. *The Planting of a Nation in a New World, 1000–1600,* the first of six volumes, was ready in 1905. The remaining five were printed within the next twenty years. Edward Channing's *History* was a singular triumph. Bancroft's seemingly endless parade of volumes ended where the history of a nation began. Hildreth bettered Bancroft's chronological record by reaching the year 1821. But Channing began with the Norsemen and aimed to plow his solitary way to the end of the nineteenth century. He was the last American historian to make the attempt: the only twentieth-century American historian to have conceived it possible. Edward Channing reached his goal by fierce determination and an almost single-minded perseverance to realize his scholar's dream. When he left his Widener Library office on January 6, 1931, he had a large portion of the seventh volume, projected to reach 1900, under control. The next day he was dead, and the seventh volume remained unpublished.

Channing's chronological coverage has made his *History* significant. The *History,* however, is not great. The personality of the author is stamped on nearly every page of the work, but the *History* suffers by comparison with Francis Parkman or with Henry Adams. The six volumes are linked together by the power of Channing's mind and they possess a unity which no co-operative undertaking could have achieved. Evidence of sharp insights and growing comprehension are by no means lacking. There are scores of perceptive passages and discerning judgments. Facts there are in abundance, and many of them appeared in the *History* for the first time. But there is no synthesis, no overarching analysis of American life and American experience. Channing was a narrative historian, but his narrative is without the sustained Parkman brilliance or the penetrating Adams depth. Like his "scientific" historical peers, Channing strove for detachment, but his prejudices remain implicit in his assumptions, though they rarely are overt in his judgments. Monographs, printed documents, original sources crowd his footnotes. He thought little of the value of newspapers as historical sources.[37] Printed documents appear more frequently among his references than manuscripts, and he made admirable use of the vast specialized bibliography of his day. Reliance upon monographs was so marked a feature of Channing's method that Charles A. Beard—a scholar noted as much for his caustic wit as for his learning—reviewing the sixth volume, pronounced it the best guide for those interested in discovering what doctors of philosophy had said about the Civil War.[38]

There is much unanimity about the merits of Channing's work. Disagreements relative to the extent of his bias have divided the authorities, but the "reader soon surmises," to use the language of one of his most reasonable critics, "that the author lived on the Atlantic seaboard."[39] Channing's Atlantic-seaboard background accounted not only for his predilection for oceans, ships, and commerce; it likewise accounted for the interpretation of the British colonial system and the American Revolution. Official astigmatism and "commercialism" seemed in Channing's thinking to have been fundamental in bringing the imperial rupture about. He failed, and failed completely, to comprehend the significance of the frontier and the meanings of sectionalism. This failure warped his presentation of the Revolution, of the so-called "Critical Period," of the movement for the Constitution, and the social struggle between the sections from 1789 to 1865. His social and geographical origins, possibly without conscious intent, led him into a mild form of racialism. The threat of a French empire in colonial America was for him a "Gallic peril," and its final outcome was ordained by English superiority, if not indeed by English destiny. "Foreigners" was a term employed with slurring undertones, and virtue was apparently more abundantly distributed among English or Anglo-Saxon strains in the population than among others. There is no real understanding of immigration anywhere either at the beginnings of American history or at any of its later stages. Slighting of the West and of sectionalism crippled his understanding; slighting of nonpolitical forces marred his interpretation.[40] Channing's *History* is a political and a constitutional history. Belatedly he came into intellectual contact with economic, social, and intellectual factors, but it was never more than a surface contact. Ideas, religion, and economics were never truly a part of his causal sequences. If he had a philosophy of history, it does not obtrude in his narrative. His grand thesis of human progress, of the ultimate dominance of nationalism over particularism, never blatantly asserted, remains uncritical and unconvincing. But the *History* "will always represent certain qualities of coherence and uniformity." [41] With this seasoned judgment few can properly differ.

Channing's contemporary and occasional collaborator, Albert Bushnell Hart, also shared in the wisdom of Henry Adams during his undergraduate days. He then went to Germany to study with Hermann von Holst, at that time an outstanding European authority on American history, and acquired a Freiburg doctorate. Eliot appointed him to the history faculty in 1883, and Hart taught American history and American government to Harvard students until his retirement in 1926. As professor emeritus, he was a familiar figure in Boston and Cambridge and at the meetings of the American Historical Association up to his death just before his eighty-ninth birthday.[42] Someone once referred to him as "The Last Leaf on the Tree," [43] and so he was. He was one of the last survivors of the young pioneers, one of the remaining members of the original group who formed the American Historical Association in 1884. As such he witnessed the astounding series of changes in the teaching and writing of American history that he, as teacher, editor, and superlative organizer, did so much to assure.

An excellent teacher, Hart at once became a tradition and has since become a legend. He awakened among his students an active sense of participation in American history. He was a captivating lecturer, dramatic, intense, appealing. Adams was a provocative teacher because he operated on the principle that the "only privilege a student had that was worth his claiming, was that of talking to the professor, and the professor was bound to encourage it. His only difficulty . . . was to get them to talk at all. He had to divine schemes to find out what they were thinking about, and induce them to risk criticism from their fellows." [44] Adams made students ask questions, and Channing shocked students out of their complacency so that they queried their contemporaries and sometimes even themselves. Hart also "wanted to teach . . . something not wholly useless." Faced with large classes, which Adams always felt "stifles the student," [45] he used every device to enlist and retain their interest. Above all, he tried to implicate them and their lives in the materials he was engaged in presenting. For many, at least, he succeeded in communicating the importance of the American past. Adams, Channing, and Hart set Harvard's standards for teaching American history.[46]

Hart had a passion for orderly sequence and a genius for developing it. He advised teachers of American history "to lay down certain fundamental principles" in a clear and unmistakable manner so as "to leave them sharply defined in the minds of the students." Hart's principles had an additional purpose: they were to be "so framed as to correct a few of the more dangerous popular errors about the real relations of the United States to other countries." For the guidance of his colleagues, he published a list of eight points. The first two stated the continuity of history, its evolutionary growth, and genetic relationships. "No nation has a *history disconnected* from the rest of the world: The United States is closely related, in point of time, with previous ages; in point of space, with other civilized countries." Social institutions, in the second place, "are a growth, and not a creation." The Constitution was such an institution and was itself "constantly changing with changes in public opinion." The third injunction acknowledged the source of American institutions as Teutonic derived through England, thus justifying a colonial emphasis in American historical treatment. It likewise justified, as in the teaching of Henry Adams, an emphasis on English medieval law and institutions as the background of the American heritage. His last five points, dealing specifically with national history, illustrated Hart's method and emphasis. They likewise illustrated some of the reasons for his success as teacher and writer:

4. The growth of our institutions has been *from local to central:* the general government can, therefore, be understood only in the light of the early history of the country.

5. The *principle of union* is of slow growth in America: the Constitution was formed from necessity, and not from preference.

6. Under a *federal form of government* there must inevitably be a perpetual contest of authority between the States and the general government: hence the two opposing doctrines of States-rights and of nationality.

7. *National political parties* naturally appeal to the federal principle when in power, and to the local principle when out of power.

8. When parties become distinctly sectional, a *trial of strength* between a part of the States and the general government must come sooner or later.[47]

Lecturing and teaching were only two of Hart's many competencies. He was an organizer and promoter, an editor and an author. Almost a hundred volumes of American history and biography bear his name as editor, compiler, joint author, or author. There is a biography of Salmon P. Chase, studies of the formation of the union, of slavery and abolition, the Monroe Doctrine, the new South, and of American ideals. He edited documents, sources, collections. Historiographically significant series appeared under his editorship: *Epochs of America, The American Citizens Series, American Patriots and Statesmen, The Commonwealth History of Massachusetts,* and *The American Nation.* The American Historical Association borrowed his talents for its committee of seven to investigate the problems of teaching history. Study of George Washington and Theodore Roosevelt was furthered by his promotional zeal, and he served as historian of the United States Commission for the Celebration of the Two Hundredth Anniversary of the Birth of George Washington. With Edward Channing, he edited *American History Leaflets,* and the *Cyclopedia of American Government* with others. In 1896, Channing, Hart, and Frederick Jackson Turner produced the first important *Guide to the Study and Reading of American History,* a reference of inestimable value to teachers and students. At the very least, Albert Bushnell Hart was the "most useful historical worker of his generation." [48]

Hart's work as an editor was more than simply useful. *The American Nation* series was a brilliant editorial accomplishment. Hart had a capacity, essential for editors, of making contributors perform, and he had the further capacity, rarer in editors, of making them perform at their best. The matter was first proposed in the council of the American Historical Association in 1898, and in 1899 a committee, with Hart as chairman, was appointed. The committee originally consisted of Charles Francis Adams, Herbert Baxter Adams, William Archibald Dunning, John Bach McMaster, Frederick Jackson Turner, and Moses Coit Tyler. Hart's genius as an organizer and promoter had much to do with the success of the series. The plan became an operating program in 1900, the first volume appeared in 1904, and the twenty-five additional volumes and a separate index were published four years later.[49]

The American Nation series was the professional answer to the ubiquity of the monograph. Its sponsors were convinced that "a new history of the United States" was required, since a "comprehensive work by a competent writer" simply did not exist. Hart reviewed the dilemma of American historical scholarship as it appeared to the professors at the turn of the century. "Individual writers have treated only limited chronological fields. Meantime there is a rapid increase of published sources and of serviceable monographs. . . . On the one side there is a necessity for an intelligent summarizing of the present knowledge of American history by trained specialists; on the other hand there is need for a complete work, written in un-technical style." [50] *The American Nation* was not "to be simply a political and constitutional history." It was, wrote Hart, to include "the social life of the people, their religion, their literature, and their schools. It must include their economic life, occupations, labor systems, and organizations of capital. It must include their wars and their diplomacy, the relations of community with community, and of the nation with other nations." [51] While the results fell considerably short of the mark, the whole was an admirable synopsis of specialist thought. Actually, it possesses a double value: it is a survey of the substance of American history as then conceived and an expression by professionals of the nature and scope of history.

The plan of the series provided for twenty-seven separate but co-operatively planned studies divided into five groups. Fifteen volumes, evenly distributed among the first three groups, were classified under the general categories: "Foundations of the Nation," "Transformation into a Nation," and "Development of the Nation." The total emphasis, irrespective of individual deviations, was nationalistic, the rise and development of distinctively American institutions and attitudes in America. Of the last two divisions, "Trial of Nationality" and "National Expansion," six volumes were allocated to the first and seven to the second. More than half of the series was thus focused on the period before the division of the Union, five to the background of the division itself, and seven to the years of reunion. Such weighting of the Civil War, considered appropriate to the theme of developing nationhood, was nevertheless disproportionate. Recognition was granted, as in the Winsor series, to the European background and to the non-English cultural factors operative in the founding of America. Once the European background was covered up to 1660, European influences were introduced only when "appropriate." An entire volume was dedicated to the discussion of American foreign affairs during the modern era. Serious attention was accorded the rise of the West and the westward extension of the

American frontier. Geography, ethnology, and anthropology find place in a study of "the bases of American history," suggesting an awareness of the new humanistic approaches to social science.[52]

Albert Bushnell Hart and his editorial associates did not exaggerate the need for a "comprehensive" work of American history by an author of unmistakable "competence." Channing's first volume followed the birth of *The American Nation,* and Winsor's *Narrative and Critical History* stopped for all practical purposes at the War of 1812. George Bancroft and Richard Hildreth, whatever their merits, fell far short of Hart's chronological demands. There was one individual whose competence was beyond reasonable doubt and who had already come fairly close to realizing Hart's objective. "Mr. John Fiske," wrote Hart, who fully surveyed the prospects and limitations of the project during a preliminary canvass, "is the only man whose writings include considerable parts of the whole area." [53] But John Fiske had more than done his historical share and was already numbered among the dead before the series was fairly launched.

Yet, if any single individual could have written *The American Nation* series, it was John Fiske. As a matter of fact, he almost did write a comparable series on his own. There are eleven Fiske volumes dealing with the years before 1789, another on the Mississippi Valley in the Civil War, and still another on the evolution of American political ideas. A three-volume survey of America shows him to have been the principal author, and he wrote two texts, one on American history and the other on American government. Several other volumes and scores of articles in the American field comprise only a segment of his stupendous bibliography. As one of the outstanding popularizers of science in America and as a leading exponent of evolutionary theory, his writings on Darwinism, philosophy, and religion almost matched his prolific record in recounting his country's past. He was one of the most successful popular lecturers, perhaps the most successful popular speaker, on American historical topics. Between 1888 and 1893 he delivered more than five hundred lectures on American themes. But John Fiske, philosopher, historian and popularizer extraordinary, was a phenomenon from the beginning.

Born Edmund Fiske Green in 1842 at Hartford, Connecticut, he early suggested genius. At the age of seven, ancient history and Caesar's prose constituted his usual intellectual fare. At eight he attacked the English literary classics, including all of Shakespeare, and emerged unscathed. Greek diverted him at nine, and when he was eleven he was ready for the historians, Froissart, Gibbon, Robertson, and Parkman. Apparently he succeeded in capturing history instead of being captured by it, for at this stage of his precocity he sat down and wrote out a chronology for his guidance. Without recourse to books or other reference, he jotted down a list of sequential dates from A.D. 1000 to 1820. At the end of another two years he had covered most of the principal Latin authors, including the historians, Tacitus, Sallust, Suetonius, and Livy. By the time of his fifteenth birthday he could read such Greek writers as Herodotus and Plato with ease. Having mastered Greek and Latin, he had no trouble with other languages. He took up German without help, kept a journal in Spanish, and acquired reading facility in French, Italian, and Portuguese. For Sanskrit and Hebrew, he required the assistance of a teacher.[54] "O my dear!" he wrote in 1864 to the girl who was to become his wife, "there is nothing in this world like SCIENCE, nothing so divine as the life of a scholar!" [55]

Docility was unlikely in one of such brilliance. Fiske questioned his elders, particularly his theological superiors, and quickly found himself banned from the orthodox Congregational fold. He was labeled an unbeliever in his teens, an agnostic while at college, and an infidel throughout most of his later life. The inflexibly devout could neither understand nor forgive his espousal of Darwinism and his advocacy of a philosophy of science. Although Fiske was profoundly religious, his contributions to a restatement of theism and his service in assessing the conflicting claims of science and religion have seldom been appreciatively understood.[56]

Fiske chose Harvard over Yale because he felt Harvard was more difficult as well as more liberal. He entered the sophomore class in 1860, was graduated in 1863, and received an LL.B. from the law school in 1865.[57] Eliot, braving criticism but bent on reform, appointed Fiske a special lecturer in philosophy to give a course on the Positive Philosophy.[58] Since Fiske as an undergraduate had come close to dismissal after having been apprehended with a volume of Auguste Comte at chapel, his appointment to lecture on Positivism was something of a justification.[59] For another brief period immediately following, Fiske taught as an instructor in history. The overseers resisted Eliot's choice and accepted Fiske grudgingly. The appointment ended June 1870, but in 1872 he became assistant librarian of Harvard College, an office he held until 1879.[60]

Fiske's preoccupation with American history dates from his tenure as a Harvard librarian. He began his lecturing career in 1879 and by the nineties he had an impressive list of publications to his credit. For one not specially trained as a historian, he was admirably prepared. His native capacities were unusual, his reading was broad, and his knowledge of philosophy and science exceptional. His linguistic equipment was infinitely better than that of most European-trained historical scholars. He possessed stores of energy, wrote with ease and charm, and spoke gracefully and effectively. Spirit and style made John Fiske a popular historian. A philosophy of history assured him of a place in historiography.[61]

John Fiske was the Bancroft of his generation. His writing and lecturing gave the history of America a new general appeal and a new public status. He captivated the educated public as none but Bancroft had been able to captivate it. Meaning was infused into the American past by the broad sweep he imparted to history. Fiske's prose invited his readers to share his sense of the dramatic. He was adept at conveying thought and feeling by the use of words, and when he himself was moved his readers were moved with him.[62] A Boston newspaper, reporting his Old South Church lectures of 1884 on the American Revolution, commented that it "was not easy to explain the secret of the orator's charm." The writer, however, revealed the secret without difficulty:

> Mr. Fiske makes no gestures, and indulges in no high-flown rhetoric; but his manner is extremely easy and graceful and his . . . method of presentation brings us face to face with persons and events as if we had seen and known them. The character of George Washington has never before been so impressively depicted in so few words. Part of the effect, no doubt, is due to the surpassing beauty of his language.[63]

Nothing escaped him. On his first trip to the Pacific Northwest he was stirred as seldom before and, after a precise description of the scenery, he wrote ecstatically to his wife:

> Where is this going to help my History, do you ask? Why, when I describe the great exploring expedition of Lewis and Clark, who in Jefferson's time *discovered* this country and won it for the United States. Won't I put some poetry into my account of it when I get to it? I will make it one of the features of my History. Nobody has begun to do justice to that wonderful expedition, and most people know nothing about it. The brave men who did this *on foot* deserve to be immortalized. I'll give them their due. I *feel* it all now; and that alone would be worth the trip.[64]

And it was. His letters like his life were crammed with impressions, with the robust reactions of a brimming spirit.

Fiske wrote approximately a volume a year. Once he completed an entire manuscript in forty-three days of uninterrupted work.[65] He was forever writing, traveling, speaking, and planning to write, to travel, or to speak. But he reveled in every minute of it. The image of Fiske as a drone, burrowing in libraries, pouring over old manuscripts, and pontificating about the results of his research is a caricature. He did burrow in libraries and pour over old manuscripts and sometimes he pontificated in the most irritating manner. But every book was a spiritual experience, every manuscript a lusty exhilaration. Boxes of books were constantly arriving at his Cambridge home, the results of ransacking the bookstores wherever he went. They were all bargains, but when he acquired an eighteenth-century edition of the complete works of Voltaire he shipped his early nineteenth-century set off to Bartlett's book shop in Boston for sale.[66] His book finds, his lectures, his audiences, his triumphs are recounted in letters to his mother, his wife, and his children. And he was never without the time to write them. He did his reading on trains, his research in libraries away from home while on lecture tours or in his own book-crammed study on Berkeley Street in Cambridge. There was also time for responses to people and to ideas. There was always time for music, for the admiration of lovely women, for food, and for wine. Fiske sang and played the piano adequately and he loved to hear the music made by others. Often he lectured on music and literary topics. Food and drink were not inconsequential, and there are long instructions to his wife about the menus of dinners to be given with epicurean éclat or accounts of dinners that had been eaten with pleasure and recalled with relish. There was a gusto in Fiske that explains why he did so much and why he did much of it well. Considered one of the learned men of his time, he garnered rewards of every kind; degrees, invitations, and praise. His greatest reward was the fullness of his crowded life. He made his own everlasting pleasure and, good evolutionist that he was, left his reputation to the keeping of the future.[67]

Fiske's long adventure in American studies began with *American Political Ideas*. Published in 1885, it grew out of his initial lecture series at Boston's Old South Church in 1879.[68] American political ideas began, appropriately enough for John Fiske, with the discovery and colonization of America. Thomas H. Huxley, whose friendship dated from early Darwinian days, invited him to repeat the Old South series at University College, London. The response to Fiske and to American history was so great that Huxley asked him to "treat of some of the philosophical aspects" the following year before the Royal Institution.[69] The three lectures making up this small book were the result. They present Fiske's philosophy of history and his view of the place of America in the development of the world. A cosmic philosopher, as he was frequently called, Fiske found a place for history in his evolutionary scheme of things. While he altered the emphasis of certain phases, the broader outlines of his cosmic philosophy remained unchanged from the time he wrote his own two-volume work with that imposing title.[70]

American political ideas were discussed "from the standpoint of universal history." It was impossible, Fiske explained, "thoroughly to grasp the meaning of any group of facts, in any department of study, until we have duly compared them with allied groups of facts; and the political history of the American people can be rightly understood only when it is studied in connection with that general process of political evolution which has been going on from the earliest times, and of which it is itself one of the most important and remarkable phases." [71] The incisiveness with which he set forth the hypothesis of institutional continuity and the comparative method is as clear as in Edward A. Freeman, in John William Burgess, or in Herbert Baxter Adams. "The government of the United States is not the result of special creation, but of evolution," he wrote in the conceptual language of Charles Darwin and Herbert Spencer which had molded his thought.[72] "As the town-meetings of New England are lineally descended from the village assemblies of the early Aryans; as our huge federal union was long ago foreshadowed in the little leagues of Greek cities and Swiss cantons; so the great political problem which we are . . . solving is the very same problem upon which all civilized peoples have been working ever since civilization began." And what was the universal problem of civilized man? It was: "How to insure peaceful concerted action throughout the Whole, without infringing upon local and individual freedom in the Parts." [73] John Adams would have had no difficulty in agreeing with this statement of the problem or with Fiske's interpretation of the American Revolution already presaged in the principle.

American history was a part of the process of evolution. American history did "not begin with the Declaration of Independence, or even with the settlements of Jamestown or Plymouth; but it descends in unbroken continuity from the days when stout Arminius in the forests of northern Germany successfully defied the might of imperial Rome. In a more restricted sense, the statesmanship of Washington and Lincoln appears in the noblest light when regarded as the fruition of the various works of De Montfort and Cromwell and Chatham." [74] The American Revolution, as a contemporary historian expressed it, was a revolution of gentlemen, by gentlemen, and for gentlemen, the continuation of the struggle for English liberties on American soil. It was a decorous affair, unsullied in its proper aspects by violence. Instances such as the attack on Governor Hutchinson's home were acts of mob violence. This specific instance was "an event in the history of crime, and belongs to such incidents as fill the Newgate Calendar." The Boston Tea Party, on the other hand, was "majestic and sublime," though no less technically criminal. To Fiske the American Revolution belonged to a realm Jennings B. Sanders has called political metaphysics.[75]

If much of Fiske's philosophy is contained in *American Political Ideas,* the book also contains many of his basic prejudices. Aryans were of the master race, the great carriers of civilization in the Burgess and Freeman sense. "The indomitable spirit of English liberty," wrote Fiske, "is alike indomitable in every land where men of English race have set their feet as masters." This was one of the great lessons of world history on the political level: the victory of the forces of civilization over barbarian peoples. Hence "the greatest work which the Romans performed in the world was to assume the aggressive against.menacing barbarism, to subdue it, to tame it, and to enlist its brute force on the side of law and order." [76] The work of Caesar in conquering the Gauls and bringing them within the bastion of civilization "was as thoroughly done as anything that was ever done in human history, and we ought to be thankful to Caesar for it every day that we live." Wars were therefore sometimes just or at least historically justifiable. It was the manifest destiny of the master race to extract the red fangs of the barbarians, even if their own claws were bloodied in the process.

Fiske had established what for him was an historical premise. The logic of Fiske's premise made the defeat of France in 1763 a dramatic turning point in history. "I am fully prepared to show that the conquest of the North American continent by men of the English race was unquestionably the most prodigious event in the political annals of mankind." [77] Even Fiske regarded this statement as somewhat bold, and he proceeded to explain it more fully. Throughout history Aryan culture had first to resist and then to civilize the barbaric peoples. Part of this struggle involved Catholicism and "the great Protestant outbreak against the despotic pretensions of the Church." The Catholic Church "in its antagonism to the rival temporal power" had once been on the side of popular liberty, but thereafter it "sought to enthrall" the people "with a tyranny far worse than that of irresponsible king or emperor." [78] The issue was fought out on the battlefields of Europe with Holland and England on one side and Spain and the pope on the other. With the discovery of America, the course of history altered. "The race which here should gain the victory was clearly destined hereafter to take the lead in the world." England and the English transplanted the tradition to America. "When the neighbouring civilization of an inferior type—I allude to the French in Canada—began to be seriously troublesome, it was struck down at a blow." [79]

Triumphant Aryanism and a mild anti-Catholicism were only two of Fiske's prejudices. Tariffs and other forms of government "paternalism" raised the temperature of his blood and of his prose. Protection, "our shameful tariff," was finally to meet its "doom." [80] A form of Spencerian social statics dominated Fiske's thought. When he came to discuss what he regarded as unwise monetary legislation, anger captured his words. Wherever "unsound" currency legislation reared its debased head, Fiske smote it down with shrill verbal blows. Whether in Virginia in 1607, in Massachusetts in 1690, or during the Confederation era from 1783 to 1787, the post-Civil War years, or the Bryan crusade, inflation was an unsound, wicked, and unwarranted governmental interference with the reign of natural law.[81] While these views recur throughout his writings, they were especially sharp and especially important as presented in *The Critical Period.*[82] This volume stamped its interpretation of the movement for the Constitution on the American historical mind. Still widely prevalent as a causal analysis, the most careful subsequent research has been unable completely to dislodge it. Fiske gave the years 1783 to 1789 a name and a character. He made them so critical that a strong central government seemed the only logical solution to chaos. Among the factors making for chaos was inflation which had created "a true Bryanite paradise." Eastern merchants held sound ideas about the currency; the Western farmers were misled in part by "a rather feeble creature named Daniel Shays." [83]

Prejudice mars but does not destroy Fiske's value. *The Critical Period* contains some of his most persuasive writing, which probably accounts for the persistence of his ideas. It also contains penetrating sketches of the members of the Convention of 1787 and one of the best descriptions of the first presidential inauguration. *The Beginnings of New England,*[84] also notable for its literary quality, presents the thesis of *American Political Ideas* at much greater length and with luxuriant historical detail. Fiske espoused interpretations now less commonly held, but he had read and absorbed a great deal of history. Other data is needed to explain why power in the western world moved from the Mediterranean to the Atlantic, but the problem is still a pertinent part of American history. And Fiske was doubtless correct in insisting that the history of the United States more properly begins at that period of crucial transition than at Plymouth or at Watling's Island. The discovery of America fascinated Fiske as much as it fascinated others, and allowed him further to develop this theme. In *Discovery of America,* often pronounced his most gifted book, he covered all the topics implied by the title. Aboriginal America formed an appropriate part of his interest, as did the history of Spanish exploration, conquest, and settlement. Fiske did not spare detail and his notes, frequently disquisitions in themselves, indicated that he put his linguistic skills to constant use. The conceptual emphasis still merits historical consideration. And Fiske's contention that the history of the United States represents less of a special creation than an evolution remains a standpoint more often endorsed than applied.[85]

Fiske's prejudices are as invalid now as when he held them. His faith in a law of progress has been voted old-fashioned, and his understanding of evolution would now be considered naïve. But his history was never provincial, just as it was never dull. If John Fiske did not write great history, he did history great service. Men still read Fiske, and much of what he wrote still deserves to be read.[86]

Visitors to Cambridge in the waning years of the nineteenth century asked to have John Fiske's house identified together with Washington's elm and Harvard's colonial halls. If this was fame, it was a satisfaction few professional historians enjoyed. Despite his early wish, Fiske did not become a university professor nor were his numerous doctorates formally acquired. Yet he was far better known to the educated public than most academic scholars, and he taught more students on the lecture circuit than the graduate professor in the seminar.[87] The scholar's scholar whose revisions initiated critical trends earned other satisfactions largely confined to the universities and the life of the profession.

XXIV

History in the Old West
and the New

Andrew Dickson White, an outstanding scholar and teacher, became first president of Cornell University and one of America's great educational statesmen.[1] As a Yale student, history had been his preferred subject. The textbook recitations and uninspired lectures repelled him. In contrast, he found the French and German universities exciting as a result of lively and imaginative instruction. His European experience awakened in him "a new current of ideas," ideas, however, not confined to the subject of history alone, but related to and interwoven with ideas about teaching and ways in which it should be improved. When he returned to Yale as a resident postgraduate student in 1856, he was eager to aid in the renovation of university education. But his zeal was not matched by a plan of action until, dropping in on a talk being given by President Francis Wayland of Brown University, he was stirred by the comment that the West was to be the focus of the American future.[2] "The best field of work for graduates is now in the *West,*" said Wayland, "our country is shortly to arrive at a switching-off place for good or evil; our Western States are to hold the balance of power in the Union, and to determine whether the country shall become a blessing or a curse in human history." [3] Wayland had political rather than educational considerations in mind, but the remark gave White's undirected motives the quality of purpose. He immediately determined to seek a history appointment in some western college. A sally of letters to friends brought him an offer from the University of Michigan, and October 1857 found him in Ann Arbor.

Many of White's impressions about the teaching of history had already appeared in various publications. He had evaluated American teaching against the background of his knowledge of German universities in an article entitled "German Instruction in General History." [4] From a close study of the life of Thomas Arnold, headmaster of Rugby after 1828, he had drawn two inferences that continued to guide his own thinking in later life, whether as professor, writer, or educational administrator.[5] One was that the historian fulfilled his calling to the extent that he succeeded "in bringing young men into fruitful trains of thought regarding present politics." He also learned "how real an influence an earnest teacher might . . . exercise upon his country." [6] History of the White variety was taught for social purposes, for immediate practical usages. He was no less objective on that account, but history for history's sake alone did not really enlist his ardor. His concern for students, for their immediate needs and for the course of their future made him a sensational teacher. The Michigan students from 1857 to 1864 learned both to respect his mind and to admire his character. But triumph over student lethargy did not come without determined struggle. Only White's total commitment to the vitality of history, demonstrated in class after class, was able to dispel the dismal reputation the subject had acquired among undergraduates. White worked earnestly and used every teaching device he had learned from his tutors or that his own creativity could fashion.[7] He trained himself to lecture without notes so as not to interrupt the flow of his thought. He read from the original materials whenever appropriate because "no declamation upon the boldness of Luther," for example, "could impress thinking young men as did citation from his 'Erfurt Sermon.' " [8]

White's dynamism achieved striking results. Charles Kendall Adams[9] responded to White's teaching and strove to emulate him. The son of a Vermont farmer who migrated with his family to Iowa in 1856, Adams rose from farm boy to university president through a sequence which became increasingly common as learning changed from a vocation to a profession. His academic beginnings were as inauspicious as the circumstances of his birth. He was admitted to the University of Michigan without adequate preparation and pressured by poverty to work his own way. It was by sheer ability, perseverance, and White's patronage that he was able to complete the course. White was his constant guide and benefactor. When White left Ann Arbor in 1864 to serve as state senator in Albany, New York, Adams was made an assistant professor of history and advanced to a professorship in 1867. His sponsor's judgment was not misplaced, for Adams was a well-liked teacher from the start. Once he received his professorship, he went abroad for further study and when he returned from Germany in 1869, he brought the "seminar method" [10] with him. Admittedly somewhat elementary, when Adams introduced it, he carefully developed the seminar method to meet the requirements of undergraduates and graduates alike. White also suggested the preparation of the *Manual of Historical Literature*[11] to Adams, a compilation rare in its day and invaluable to workers during the youth of the profession. The *Manual* was planned as a collaboration, but as Adams explained, White "was called to the making of history at a foreign court, while I was left to talk and write about it at home." [12] They did, however, collaborate in many other ways. Intellectually, they concurred in their attitudes concerning the purpose and meaning of history. History was valued by both as a "preparation for the affairs of politics and statesmanship." [13] Such conceptions of history did not quite approximate the professed intentions of the scientific historians. Although both highly esteemed strict logical procedures and the methods of science, as historians their main object in the words of Adams was to fit "men to conduct properly the large interests of communities and states." Method, or an essential part of it, Adams defined as "the ability to grasp what may be called the strategic parts of a situation by instinctive or intuitive methods." Historical conclusions were not reached "by any clearly defined or definable process, but rather by the method of conjecturing the value and importance of contingent elements," a device particularly necessary "when the conditions of a strictly logical process are wanting." [14]

Adams and White left their imprint on historiography as statesmen of education. They piloted adolescent universities to greatness and achieved in their own lives the goals they set for others. While their teaching was significant and their writings memorable, they also participated in the creation of "communities and states." They fitted men for larger interests like their own.[15]

Moses Coit Tyler flourished in the universities grounded by White and Adams. The Tylers were as ancient as Plymouth. One Tyler line brought forth John Tyler, tenth president of the United States; another, Moses Coit Tyler, pioneer historian of American letters and first professor of American history in the nation.[16] As a Yale undergraduate in the fifties, and even before, Tyler could never quite determine whether teaching, preaching, or writing was to be his career. When he decided upon theology at Yale in 1857 and went to Andover, he was less sure than his action implied. He never took a theological degree, functioned as a minister from 1859 to 1862, and later wrote: "I was not built for a parson." [17] But he had a deeply religious bent, which always colored his outlook and motivated his conduct. Actually, he became a parson again in 1883 and was ordained a clergyman of the Episcopal Church.[18]

Tyler's brief encounter with the ministry did not fill the needs of his life, and he withdrew to find a new calling. A family had to be supported, but he wrote when he could; at one point he entered the journalistic controversy in behalf of Vassar and female education.[19] He went to Boston where transcendentalists, former abolitionists, and the literary giants accorded him a vicarious membership among the elect. Also in Boston he met Dr. Dio Lewis, exponent of novel health methods, and enrolled in his Normal Institute of Physical Education. Musical gymnastics bolstered Tyler's indifferent constitution, and as he gained strength and vigor the Lewis regimen gained a convert. In 1863 Tyler went to England as a Lewis propagandist. He remained until 1866, first lecturing on the virtues of musical gymnastics, then expanding his repertoire to include American topics.[20] Tyler developed into a first-class orator, and his writings on England for American journals gave restraint and balance to his style. When he returned home he had two new arrows to shoot from his sagging theological bow. He planned to make his living as a journalist and by lecturing. In 1867 he was offered an appointment as professor of rhetoric and English literature at the University of Michigan. Barring the interludes, when institutional religion reclaimed him and journalism in an official capacity deflected him, he remained at Michigan until Andrew Dickson White brought him to Cornell in 1881.

Diverse experience and limitless zeal combined to make Tyler an outstanding teacher. Impatient of the ways in which literature was taught, he rejected linguistic autopsy for literary analysis. He insisted that students look for ideas and for beauty both in literary analysis and literary creation. Students found so fresh an approach hard to resist and they heartily responded to the professor's appeal and integrity.[21] Meanwhile, Tyler read literature and history, trying to define his ultimate objective as a scholar. More and more he inclined toward American history, politics, and ideas.[22] The "golden Buckle" [23] enlarged his imagination and punctuated his thought. Could he do for America what Buckle had done for England? Could he do anything in the serious study of American ideas with obligations to students and classes and without the resources of a research library? In 1873 he resigned from Michigan and accepted an offer to become literary editor of *The Christian Union*. Journalism and religion were in his New England bones, but for Tyler at least the combination was not unfortunate.[24]

Life in New York City was an unceasing contest between duties in the editorial rooms of *The Christian Union* and the study of American history. Whenever possible he made American history serve his remunerative work. He lectured, he wrote reviews, and in September 1874 he went back to the University of Michigan. Tyler's restlessness was for the time being over, and work on his history of American literature, an unformed design since his European years, could now properly begin. In November 1878, *A History of American Literature, 1607 to 1765,* appeared in two impressive volumes.[25] Moses Coit Tyler had become "the first great historian of the national mind expressed in literature." [26]

What Tyler had done had never been done before. Here were two large volumes that ended before most compilations of American writings began. And most of the books dealing with American letters were compilations and little more. To begin in 1607 and to stop in 1765 was an innovation in itself. Customarily, American literature was believed to have commenced with the Revolution; everything preceding 1776 was English. Tyler, of course, had studied all the general works in the fields of his specialty and he learned whatever he could. But no treatment of ideas during the colonial period existed; in fact, there was little to be found in the province of ideas for any period. Materials were available—scattered, obscure, and sometimes unknown—and someone had to find, organize, and assimilate them. This was the contribution made by Tyler.[27] He marshaled the materials and wove them into an intellectual history, a synthesis of ideas. The whole scheme was original. Tyler's approach to intellectual history was as modern as the moderns. "There is but one thing more interesting than the intellectual history of a man," wrote Tyler, "and that is the intellectual history of a nation."

> The American people, starting into life in the early part of the seventeenth century, have been busy ever since in recording their intellectual history in laws, manners, institutions, in battles with man and beast and nature, in highways, excavations, edifices, in pictures, in statues, in written words. It is in written words that this people, from the very beginning, have made the most confidential and explicit record of their minds. It is in these written words, therefore, that we shall now search for that record.[28]

Tyler had only just begun his writing career. *The Literary History of the American Revolution* was the planned sequel to *A History of American Literature, 1607 to 1765,* and he agreed in 1881 to write a volume on Patrick Henry for the *American Statesmen* series.[29] Fame was pleasant but it was also distracting. White had offered him the professorship at Cornell, and Tyler had his usual difficulties reaching a decision. Finally, as sure as he could be that going to Ithaca was the "will of God," he accepted the Cornell post. From time to time the old questionings would seize him, and he would wonder whether he was really doing God's work until in 1884, settled once more, he was able to pour contentment into his diary:

> The most satisfying privileges in life have come to me here. I can imagine how I might be happier even than I now am; but never before have I been so happy—so deeply, soundly, solidly happy. The great fermentations of existence are done. I have found my niche, my sphere, my vocation, my horizon, even my burial place.[30]

With such tranquillity the latent drive returned, and he set about his work with gusto. The *Patrick Henry* was finished in March 1887. *Patrick Henry* was not only a good book, but also a fine example of scientific history. It was as accurate as Tyler could make it, and because of his accuracy and judgment Patrick Henry lost something of his heroic schoolbook character and regained stature as a thinking and acting man.[31]

During his sabbatical year, 1888–89, Tyler went to Europe again. It was typical that, having decided on Germany, he studied the language. German was far from easy even for Tyler, but he did not allow the intricacies of its grammar to master him. At the age of fifty-three, he went back to school, to the University of Leipzig, to hear the professors White and Adams held in such high esteem.[32] The *History* was not forgotten. In England again, he spent long hours of research in the British Museum, and when he returned to Ithaca, resumed writing in earnest. Tyler was always having ideas about work in progress and works he wanted to do. He decided to end his *History* in 1783 instead of 1815 as initially planned, thus hastening its completion.[33] He also decided to get out a little book on three of his favorite characters—Timothy Dwight, Joel Barlow, and George Berkeley—taken from chapters in *A History . . . 1607 to 1765. Three Men of Letters,* published in 1895, turned out exceedingly well. The Barlow essay, the least satisfactory historically, suffers from Tyler's failure to understand Barlow's intellectual debt to the French Revolution. The Dwight section is competent, graceful in the smooth Tyler style. But Berkeley is splendidly done, and in the opinion of Tyler's biographers, ranks with the finest in Sainte-Beuve.[34] *The Literary History of the American Revolution,* coming two years later, established Tyler's command of the historian's method and the writer's craft.[35]

The degree of difference between *A History of American Literature* and *The Literary History* is the degree of Tyler's growth during twenty years. Tyler's history of the colonial mind is phenomenal book covering more than a century and a half of literary expression. Tyler's history of the revolutionary mind covers only eighteen years (1765–83), but they were years of sharp and bitter controversies. "The plan of the author," Tyler explained, as the true exponent of the newer ways in history,

> has been to let both parties in the controversy—the Whigs and the Tories, the Revolutionists and the Loyalists—tell their own story freely in their own way, and without either of them being liable, at our hands, to posthumous outrage in the shape of partisan imputations on their sincerity, their magnanimity, their patriotism, or their courage.[36]

This alone could insure Tyler's intention

> to set forth the inward history of our Revolution—the history of its ideas, its spiritual moods, its motives, its passions, even of its sportive caprices and its whims, as these uttered themselves at the time, whether consciously or not, in the various writings of the two great parties of Americans who promoted or resisted that great movement.[37]

Tyler had reached heights of understanding, and as a result the Loyalists were accorded full literary justice. Such impartiality was unusual enough, but Tyler accomplished other novelties. He was a social historian before the rise of social history and he hewed against the political and constitutional grain of his professional university colleagues, for the whole plan and tone of *The Literary History of the American Revolution* implied a changing emphasis. Tyler was also explicit:

> One result of this method . . . is an entirely new distribution of the tokens of historic prominence. . . . Instead of fixing our eyes almost exclusively, as is commonly done, upon statesmen and generals, upon party leaders, upon armies and navies, upon Congress, upon parliament . . . and instead of viewing all these people as the sole or the principal movers and doers of the things that made the American Revolution, we here for the most part turn our eyes away toward certain persons hitherto much neglected, in many cases wholly forgotten—toward persons who, as mere writers, whether otherwise prominent or not, nourished the springs of great historic events by creating and shaping and directing public opinion during all that robust time . . . who . . . illustrate . . . the majestic operation of ideas, the creative, a decisive play of spiritual

forces, in the development of history, in the rise and fall of nations, in the aggregation and the division of races.[38]

Moses Coit Tyler "nourished the springs of great . . . events" and directed opinion during a new "robust time." He too illustrates "the majestic operation of ideas . . . in the development of history. . . ." Tyler died in 1900 and after the passage of more than half a century, no one, including Vernon Louis Parrington, his most noted successor, has fundamentally challenged his great work.

When Tyler arrived at the University of Michigan in 1867, William Francis Allen, a young classical historian, left Harvard to teach at Wisconsin.[39] When Tyler exchanged Michigan for Cornell in 1881, graduate instruction in history had already been firmly established. Michigan was granting the doctorate, and a new school of social studies, headed by Charles Kendall Adams, had been founded. Between 1885 and 1895, eight universities, in addition to Hopkins, Columbia, Harvard, Yale, and Michigan, were offering graduate work leading to advanced degrees.[40] Among them was the University of Wisconsin, where Allen began what Frederick Jackson Turner was to continue.

Allen was bountifully equipped. Technically a classicist, he did not limit himself to ancient language and literature or to the history of the classical world. Wisconsin selected him to preside over language and history, but soon his duties were restricted to Latin and history. Finally, in 1886, he was responsible for history alone.[41] His conception of history was as broad as his knowledge. Bancroft's old Göttingen mentor, Arnold H. L. Heeren, impressed him, as he had Bancroft, with the need for integrating concepts. Detailed learning was valuable only if it was meaningful; it acquired meaning by the exploration of relationships with other concepts and other bodies of learning. In 1796, Heeren wrote *Historical Researches into the Politics, Intercourse, and Trade of the Principal Nations of Antiquity,*[42] as a history of Mediterranean culture. Three of the six volumes traced the development of Asian nations, two were devoted to African society, and the final volume was devoted to Greece. Greek and Latin for Allen were instruments for the communication of ideas; ideas were embedded in cultures. The ancient world did not end with the Romans, and Allen's historical interests did not stop with the empire. Europe was the legacy of classical civilization; America was the offspring of Europe. Heeren's *History of the Political System of Europe and its Colonies from the Discovery of America to the Independence of the Autumn Continent* (1809), which Bancroft translated in 1828,[43] was a study of reciprocal culture contacts Bancroft,

Allen, and Turner owed much to its provocative suggestions. Heeren and Allen were specialists of the type who constantly searched for continuities, relations, and meanings. They taught Frederick Jackson Turner to seek for the significance of historical change. *Significance* was not only a key word in the Turner vocabulary; it was a part of the Turner methodology.

When Allen returned from his period of European study, he associated himself with the work of the Freedmen's Aid Society and the United States Sanitary Commission, then engaged in reconstructing the South. Out of this experience came Allen's edition of *Slave Songs of the United States,* a collection of Negro melodies taken down on the spot. The collection, one of the first of its kind, is suggestive of Allen's catholicity of interest. Music was for him an historical source of understanding, a body of living data which offered insights into human needs and behavior. The same cultural approach marks his section of *Ancient History for Colleges and High Schools* and his *Short History of the Roman People.*[44] The latter study, finished the night before he died in 1889, was seen through the press by Turner. In a brief introduction, Turner wrote:

> To him Roman society presented itself as an entirety, so that the political, economic, literary, and the religious elements in the life of the Roman people could not be understood in isolation, but only in relation to each other. While thus he considered society as a whole, he found in Roman history two fundamentally important series of events, each of which influenced the other: first, the policy and process by which the Roman Dominion was secured and organized during the Republic, its reorganization under the Empire, and final disruption at the time of the German migrations; and secondly, the social and economic causes of the failure of self-government among the Romans, and the working of the same forces under the Empire. In connection with these fundamental considerations, the land question is treated, and the history of literature and religion is carefully traced.[45]

Allen, like Turner, exerted a profound influence as an innovator in the method of teaching history. He rebelled against the prevailing techniques and set himself to devising new ones. Recitations based on memorizing events and dates culled from textbooks were abhorrent to him. When these had been learned, he asked, "What, after all, do we possess? Only a skeleton, to be clothed with the flesh and blood of history." Facts and dates had their place, they supplied the elemental framework for historical thought, but "no historical fact is of any value except so far as it helps us to understand human nature or the working of historic forces." [46] He offered his students a device called the "topical method." After he had prepared a list of topics, students were invited to make a choice and were then expected to read as widely as possible on every aspect of the subject. Allen explained:

> The topical method is successful in proportion to the abundance and accessibility of books of reference. In American history it works best, and here I employ no other. . . . I combine with it constant map-drawing. . . . It is, of course, impossible to design topics which cover the whole ground. It is possible, however, to select for this purpose all the names and events of first importance, and it is one of the advantages of the topical method that it thus affords an opportunity to emphasize those facts of history which most need emphasis. It is the special function of the teacher to supplement the topics, to point out their relative importance and their connection with one another, and to help the student in acquiring a complete and accurate general view.[47]

Students were put on their mettle and given a large scope of independence. The investigation culminated in an oral report before which the student was required to put a synoptic outline on the board. For undergraduates and graduates alike this was excellent training. It was excellent training for Turner, who attributed his whole competence to Allen's teaching. Allen, he is reported once to have said, "taught me all the history I know." [48]

Turner's tribute, while warm and gracious, was far too generous. Yet Allen contributed markedly to Turner's early growth. He gave him friendship, understanding, and support that every maturing student desperately requires but so few ever receive. He also gave Turner his conception of the meaning of history, a vision of its social purpose, and a grasp of the mastery of practice. From Allen, Turner derived a breadth of view, a feeling for correlation and a respect for commanding ideas. It was not enough for Turner later to outline the history of the fur trade in Wisconsin. He was concerned with its character and influence. The fur trade had to be explored, and exploration was an adventure in meanings. Turner had to discover its significance, which implied that it had to be studied in relation to economics, geography, immigration, and the growth of the West, itself a part of the growth of America. Allen made geography basic to westward expansion. Turner became the great historian of the westward movement of peoples in America, but Allen had earlier perceived a relationship between population movements in Roman and American history. He had also perceived connections between ideas and institutions; connections between government, geography, capital formation, and immigration. And within these multiple relationships he detected the "historic forces" making for stability and change.

Turner began his teaching with Allen's *Historical Topics*. The plotting of economic, social, and political changes on maps became a notable feature of his seminars. Turner and his students became famous because they looked for relations where few had sought them earlier. It appeared "certain" to one of the most sensitive students of Turner's intellectual origins "that without a knowledge of Roman history, understood in a philosophical spirit," he "would not have come upon his discovery." [49] Turner's knowledge of Roman history and his introduction to the philosophical spirit was William Francis Allen's gift to American history and to American historiography.

Frederick Jackson Turner was born in Portage, Wisconsin, November 14, 1861. [50] His parents were migrants from New England, and Wisconsin was young enough when Turner was a boy to provide a rich background of the early West. His father, Andrew Jackson Turner, was named for the seventh president of the United States, and Turner's middle name was a token of pride in his paternity and the democratic faith of the Turner generations. His was a rare brilliance compounded of insight and a capacity for making subtle distinctions. Nor was his intellectual development sporadic; it was, on the contrary, a progressive, finely modulated growth. The most important educational factor of Turner's youth was his determination to study at the University of Wisconsin, and the most important coincidence of his life was Allen's presence on the faculty. By his junior year in 1883, Turner was enrolled in Allen's class and sharpening his wits on Allen's topics. Still under twenty-five in 1885, Turner returned to the University of Wisconsin as a graduate student after a journalistic fling on a Madison paper. Three elements combined to produce the basic tools of his effectiveness. [51] As an undergraduate Turner acquired a classical education. Also as an undergraduate he had distinguished himself in oratory, and as a first-year graduate student he was a tutor of oratory and rhetoric. As a pupil of promise and charm he won the friendship of Allen. The first two elements helped to make him an effective public speaker and classroom lecturer. They gave a distinctive character to his prose, which was always clear, muscular, and proportioned. He needed only a knowledge of history, and he had Allen to teach him.

Turner's courses had the leavening Allen touch, and their content clarifies Turner's intellectual position as an historian. He became an assistant professor immediately after his Hopkins year in 1889, a full professor at the age of twenty-nine in 1890. In addition to American history, he offered a survey of society from primitive times to the emergence of the modern period. Later he lectured on ancient history and on Europe in the nineteenth century. In 1891, Charles Homer Haskins, Turner's old Hopkins friend and already a promising medievalist, joined the Wisconsin ranks. Together they constituted the department and shared the seminar instruction. Haskins, whose early work had been in the American field, had much in common with Turner, who was more than casually familiar with ancient and European history. During this Wisconsin period, moreover, history was a part of the school of economics, political science, and history inaugurated in 1892.[52] Turner was a social scientist by training and temperament. The history of the American West was his specialty, but Turner was a historian of the world. "Local history," he said, "must be read as part of world history." [53]

President T. C. Chamberlain initiated the extension department at Wisconsin in 1891. Turner, already a prominent member of the faculty, was invited to participate in its opening. He prepared an address designed to place the field of history in proper Extension perspective. "The Significance of History," published that year, states Turner's convictions with the eloquence of clarity. "The focal point of modern interest is the fourth estate, the great mass of the people," wrote Turner, suggesting the emphasis that exponents of the "new history" were later to stress.

> History has been a romance and a tragedy. In it we read the brilliant annals of the few. The intrigues of courts, knightly valor, palaces and pyramids, the loves of ladies, the songs of minstrels, and the chants from cathedrals pass like a pageant, or linger like a strain of music as we turn the pages. But history has its tragedy as well, which tells of the degraded tillers of the soil, toiling that others might dream, the slavery that rendered possible the "glory that was Greece," the serfdom into which decayed the "grandeur that was Rome"—these as well demanded their annals.[54]

The social historians were never to say it more adequately, and Turner himself wrote the annals of tillers of the American earth who tilled to fulfill a dream. Turner also anticipated the insistence of subsequent economic historians that: "Far oftener than has yet been shown have . . . underlying economic facts affecting the breadwinners of the nation been the secret of the nation's rise or fall, by the side of which much that has passed as history is the merest frippery." [55]

History was the past, but the past was not to be honored for itself alone. Nor could the past be understood in isolation. "Today," he argued as a philosopher of history, "we understand Roman history better than did Livy or Tacitus." The explanation lay in factors of growth, evolution, genetic continuity. Contemporaries understand the past better "not only because we know how to use the sources better but also because the significance of events develops with time, because today is so much a product of yesterday that yesterday can only be understood as it is explained by today." Turner was unwilling to amputate the past by depriving it of a present. "The present is simply the developing past, the past the undeveloped present." [56] In Turner's interpretation this was to be no antiquarian worship, no love of yesterdays without thought of tomorrows. "The goal of the antiquarian is the dead past; the goal of the historian is the living present." [57]

History conceived as politics was valid only in the Aristotelian sense as the total life of mankind. Turner was an evolutionist. He believed in the genetic principle and the comparative method, even if his hypotheses and conclusions differed from the Hopkins historical school.

> By unconscious inheritance, and by conscious striving after the past as part of the present, history has acquired continuity. Freeman's statement that into Rome flowed all the ancient world and out of Rome came the modern world is as true as it is impressive.[58]

Rome lived in the immediate present.

> When the inaugural procession passes toward the Senate chamber, and the president's address outlines the policy he proposes to pursue, there is Rome! You may find her in the code of Louisiana, in the French and Spanish portions of our history, in the idea of checks and balances in our constitution.[59]

History could not be split up into segments of time and place. There were no rigid breaks, no truly separable departments of human life and thought. History was a unity as well as a continuity.

The sublimity of history, however, did not deprive it of its uses. Turner quoted the noted German historian, Johann Gustav Droysen, with approval: "History is the 'Know Thyself' of humanity—the self-consciousness of mankind." Turner was not intimidated, he did not shrink from speaking of "the utility of historical studies." [60] And among the utilities of history was the power that knowledge of history gave to man. "To enable us to realize the richness of our inheritance, the possibility of our lives, the grandeur of the present—these are some of the priceless services of history." [61] The function of history was also the training for citizenship. This was the purpose of the public school, of the university, and of university extension. The American educational system contrasted unfavorably with the European. "Count the roll in Senate and House, cabinet and diplomatic service—to say nothing of the state governments—" he challenged, "and where are the names famous in history and politics?" [62] America had no Niebuhr, historian and state councilor, no historians like Macaulay, Morley, and Bryce, who were also active and honored members of Parliament. Questions of public policy could be answered by knowledge alone, but men of knowledge in America all too rarely united scholarship and government service.

Training for citizenship as understood by Frederick Jackson Turner—and by Andrew Dickson White, Charles Kendall Adams, and Moses Coit Tyler—demanded knowledge of one's own history. American meanings could not be fully grasped without an awareness of their European connections. Turner called for a recognition of cultural interdependence. "Consider," he wrote in a remarkable passage,

> how our vast Western domain has been settled. Louis XIV devastates the Palatinate, and soon hundreds of inhabitants are hewing down the forests of Pennsylvania. The bishop of Salzburg persecutes his Protestant subjects, and the woods of Georgia sound to the crack of Teutonic rifles. Presbyterians are oppressed in Ireland, and soon in Tennessee and Kentucky the fires of pioneers gleam. These were but the advance guards of the mighty army that has poured into our midst ever since." [63]

If overzealous disciples later made a fetish out of Turner's dictum that the frontier was the most American part of America, they did so at the risk of severing the unity of history and Turner's conception of it. The men and women on the frontier

> have come to us historical products, they have brought to us not merely so much bone and sinew, not merely so much money, not merely so much manual skill, they have brought with them deeply inrooted customs and ideas. They are important factors in the political and economic life of the nation.
> Our destiny is interwoven with theirs; how shall we understand American history without understanding European history? The story of the peopling of America has not yet been written. We do not understand ourselves. [64]

Turner's own statements are more reliable than the assumptions others have made about him. The essay on the significance of history is a preview of his intellectual future. He escaped from provincialism, and he escaped it not only because he was versed in the history of Rome and the ancient world. He learned to observe cultural sequences from the very start, to make comparisons between past and present, and to evaluate differences between Europe and America. When he expressed resentment that American history had too long been written by the wise men of the East, he was far from demanding that America ignore its European affinities. Our history, said Turner in a hundred different ways, "is only to be understood as a growth from European history under the new conditions of the New World." [65] He insisted that the influence of the West be included in any synthesis of the forces that had made and were then making America. If he remained unimpressed by historical efforts to establish precise connections between American ideas, institutions, and other cultural forms in the German forests, he did not reject the concept of cultural linkages. He was to supply a different emphasis and a new series of hypotheses. The wilderness might indeed master the colonist, but it did not destroy him. It simply forced him to change himself and some of his ways. Turner was studying the history of the world in America and describing the alterations in the modes of behavior and the modes of thought created by the impact of an America that was itself changing. The problem of government, for example, was the same in Rome as in Virginia. Turner's task was to discover how American differences altered the fabric of society and transformed ideas and institutions. For Turner as for Allen the captivating problem was the same as for Heeren: the interactive impact of Europe and America. The ultimate purpose of raising the issue in the first place was to find out how man changed in the process of mastering the environment, and the effects of such changes on the continuing struggle for human fulfillment.

Meanwhile, Turner continued to give himself to the university, the social instrument of his creative intent. He was as committed to further social science and graduate work as President Chamberlain. As part of their plan, they induced Richard T. Ely, a stellar younger economist and Turner's Hopkins teacher, to come to Madison to lead the newly created school of economics, political science, and history.[66] Turner offered Ely arguments convincing to them both. Wisconsin was to become the pioneer graduate university of the West, and it was to be graduate work rooted in the duties of citizenship. With Ely in economics, Haskins and Turner in history, the three Hopkins men were ready to re-enact the dramatic Hopkins role. Chamberlain left Wisconsin in 1891 to accept a geology professorship at the recently opened University of Chicago. But Charles Kendall Adams, having just exchanged the presidency of Cornell for the presidency of Wisconsin, carried on the enthusiasm for graduate instruction in the social studies and the humanities.

A Turner school existed in a triple sense. In 1893 Turner delivered his great address on the significance of the frontier in American history before the American Historical Association meeting in Chicago.[67] This address, suggestively called an "historiographical Declaration of Independence," [68] was probably the most influential single essay ever written by an American historian. Not only did it elicit critical comment and appreciative support, it also produced an enormous amount of research and speculation that still continues. The essay elevated Turner to the front rank of American historical scholars; the ideas inspired a rethinking of the national record. When the council of the American Historical Association selected Turner together with Francis Parkman as the two leading American historians of the half century,[69] they recognized officially what every scholar knew. No one had surpassed Parkman in historical sweep and brilliance of execution. No one had matched Turner in conceptual impact and pervasiveness of influence. In 1900 a school of history was created by the University of Wisconsin with Turner as its director.[70] Wisconsin had become a prairie Johns Hopkins, Turner a Wisconsin Herbert Baxter Adams. Even before the century closed, a Univeristy of California historian concluded that Wisconsin was "at the head in History." [71]

If Wisconsin was truly "at the head" in history, others were not far behind. At the University of Pennsylvania, where there had been no teaching in American history for nearly thirty years, there was a historical renaissance during the period of Wisconsin's fame. In 1850 William Bradford Reed had been appointed to the faculty and together with his brother, Henry Reed, offered work in international law and American history. When the former, a Whig and later Democratic politician, became minister to China in 1857, American history disappeared from the curriculum until John Bach McMaster came to the Wharton School of the University in 1883.[72] There he remained for thirty years, adding volumes to his *History of the People of the United States,* and distinction to the department. His associate in medieval civilization, Dana Carleton Munroe, was captured by Wisconsin when Turner had to yield up Charles Homer Haskins to Harvard in 1902. But Edward Potts Cheyney, himself a McMaster student, remained at Pennsylvania, where he made the history of England, general European history, and the "background of American beginnings" clearer to generations of college and university students. And in 1891 James Harvey Robinson, fresh from Freiburg by way of Harvard and Indiana, was added to the academic company. Until 1895, when he left for Columbia, he shared the thoughts of these scholars on the problems of history and invited them to share in his own. McMaster was already the historian of the people; Cheyney and Robinson were to give Americans a new history.[73]

Wisconsin had another potent rival in the West. The University of Chicago, with William Rainey Harper, a Yale theologian, as president, was scouring the field for the best available academic talent. Although Harper had the financial resources to offer salaries considerably higher than the professorial average, the university was as yet no more than a blueprint backed by Rockefeller money and Harper's determination. Meeting with one rebuff after another, Harper, capitalizing on internal dissension at Clark University, swooped down on President G. Stanley Hall's faculty and, in what has since become known as "Harper's Raid," induced many of the foremost Clark scientists to abandon Worcester for Chicago. Wisconsin was also vulnerable. Its president, T. C. Chamberlain, accepted a call to fill a chair in geology, and both Turner and Haskins received attractive offers. Turner and Haskins refused, bartering a willingness to remain for the assurance that graduate instruction at Madison would be strengthened.[74] Harper succeeded in luring one professorial celebrity after another, and in 1892 he induced Hermann von Holst to leave Freiburg and become head professor of history.[75]

Holst possessed a reputation few native scholars could rival. He was the leading specialist in American history in Europe. By 1891 his *Verfassung und Demokratie der Vereinigten Staaten von America* was completed and appeared in eight stately volumes of translation between 1876 and 1892. *John C. Calhoun,* a biography in the *American Statesmen* series in 1882, was followed by an essay on John Brown in 1889.[76] As professor at the University of Freiburg, he had stature, as a German and a foreigner so proficient in the history of the national past, his academic attractiveness dazzled Harper and accomplished a major feat, since Hopkins, Cornell, and Clark were eager to avail themselves of his services.

Holst had a personal history almost as dramatic as the history about which he wrote. His birth in the Russian province of Livonia in 1841 was one of the few conventional facts in his life. His parents were German, his father was a minister of the Lutheran faith in orthodox Russia, and he was one of ten children. His family roots in Baltic Russia were five centuries deep. Education was a struggle, and he battled to win it against the obstacles of his father's death and the poverty of a large family. The battle seemed to be won at Heidelberg in 1865, when Holst received his doctorate in history, but it turned out to be simply another phase of his struggle. Holst became ill and so remained for the rest of his existence; he had pawned his health in exchange for his education.

French history was Holst's first specialty. He wrote his doctoral dissertation on Louis XVI and absolutism, and was able to supplement his knowledge by personal experience with an absolutism of a different historical type. An attempted assassination of Czar Alexander II took place in 1866, while Holst was teaching at the University of St. Petersburg. The attempt failed, but the totalitarian reaction was swift and devastating. Academic freedom in Czarist Russia was as lacking as political freedom was nonexistent, and Holst had to wait until he was out of the country to say what he thought. He said it in a pamphlet published at Leipzig in 1867, and he said it fervently. The pamphlet cost Holst his job and his country and ended his specialist research in French history. Soon he was a steerage passenger on his way to America, where, like countless other Europeans, he hoped to find freedom. Like other Europeans, too, he had nothing but his faith and his knowledge.[77]

If the czar deprived Holst of a career, America provided him with another. How he was rescued from poverty, became a special student of America, and rose to eminence in the United States and in Europe is one of the epics of American historiography. Beginning as a laborer, he worked as hard as his weakened physical condition permitted. German contacts and his learning secured him odd jobs until the aid of the Prussian historian Heinrich von Sybel, and changes in German politics, provided him with a mission. The advance of liberalism in Germany, signalized by the North German Confederation of 1867, invited comparison with the political evolution of the United States. Germany required popular political education, and those who recognized the need decided that a study of American electoral processes would be helpful. Sybel's counsel was enlisted, and Sybel suggested Holst. Holst began his work with enthusiasm but soon concluded that in order to explain the politics of America, he had to write a history of the United States. From this point onward, he was marked for fame.

Further European changes assisted the rapid rise of his fortunes. The Franco-Prussian War provided Bismarck with the excuse to absorb Alsace-Lorraine within the new German Empire, and when the University of Strassburg was reopened, Holst was offered the position of assistant professor of American history and constitutional law. He assented with pleasure, married a Vassar girl, and left for Strassburg where he taught with joyous contentment. He also worked on his history, and the first volume appeared in German in

1873 at the close of his first happy year in Alsace. The first volume of *Verfassung und Demokratie* supplied Holst with academic prestige glittering enough to produce a call to Freiburg as professor of modern history. Seven years after his steerage trip to America, in 1874, he occupied a distinguished university chair, had embarked upon a new research career, and had a recognized standing in the European community of scholars. Freiburg was to be his home for eighteen years, and he returned there to die in 1904.[78]

The second volume of the *History* (1878) amplified Holst's renown, and he received a Prussian fellowship to spend a year in America. He lectured at Hopkins and Cornell, met many American scholars, and toured those sections of the country he had not visited before. When next he came to the United States in 1883, it was as a member of a company of guests invited by the Northern Pacific Railroad to grace the occasion of the opening of its line. He observed the proceedings, lectured at Harvard, and was accorded the adulation Americans reserve for distinguished European visitors. When he came to America as a Chicago professor, Americans thought well of him, and he had every reason to think well of them.[79]

Estimates of Holst's position in American historiography rest upon *The Constitutional and Political History of the United States,* his major historical work. Everything else he wrote, in the American field at least, were elaborations, summaries, or extensions of the dominating thesis presented in this large study. The seven volumes cover the years from 1750 to 1861; the first three survey the century beginning in 1750 and ending in 1850; the last four volumes treat the eleven years from the Compromise of 1850 to the inauguration of Lincoln in 1861.[80] Such a distribution of emphasis seems disproportionate, but Holst did not think so. He was writing a history of American democracy and politics in terms of slavery, and slavery was a moral problem. With other historians, not only German ones, he believed in the immutability of principles, "the eternal principles or right and morals, against which no law can prevail," and "the entire struggle against the slavocracy was based on the moral reprehensibleness of slavery." [81]

Although Holst shared prepossessions concerning morals and slavery with others, they account for most of his lapses in logic. National sovereignty, he contended, preceded the legal existence of the several states. The national union, in law as well as in fact, antedated the transition from individual colonial status to individual statehood. National sovereignty existed prior to state sovereignty and therefore to federalism. The first volume of his *History* opened with the observation:

> The opinion is not uncommon in Europe, that American politics, up to the outbreak of the civil war, were exceedingly complicated and difficult to understand. Such, however, is not the case. If we do not allow ourselves to be confused by matters of secondary consideration, and once get hold of the right thread, it soon becomes evident that the history of the United States, even as far back as the colonial period, is unusually simple, and the course of their development consistent in a remarkable degree.

The "right thread" was not easy to disentangle from the matted design of historical development. It was not immediately apparent in the Articles of Confederation nor in the Constitution, and he was under obligation to explain. Holst did not find explanation difficult.

> Beginning with the Continental Congress of 1774, the people, by recognizing its authority, placed themselves on a revolutionary footing, and did so not as belonging to the several colonies, but as a moral person; for to the extent that congress assumed power to itself and made bold to adopt measures national in their nature, to that extent the colonists declared themselves prepared henceforth to constitute one people, inasmuch as the measures taken by congress could be translated from words into deeds only with the consent of the people.

Until the Articles of Confederation were adopted in March, 1781, this continued to be the legal situation. Congress continued a revolutionary body,

> which was recognized by all the colonies as *de jure* and *de facto* the national government . . . the binding force of which on the whole people had never been called in question. The individual colonies, on the other hand, considered themselves, up to the time of the Declaration of Independence, as legally dependent upon England and did not take a single step which could have placed them before the mother country or the world in the light of *de facto* sovereign states. They remained colonies until the "representatives of the United States" in the name of the good people of these colonies solemnly declared "these united colonies" to be "free and independent states." The transformation of the colonies into "states" was, therefore, not the result of the independent action of the individual colonies.[82]

The Articles of Confederation recognized the existence of the states and hence introduced the principle of federalism. Americans, said Holst, "ventured to out-do the mystery of the Trinity by endeavoring to make thirteen one while leaving one thirteen." [83] Washington, together with other exponents of national power and patriotic sentiment, was cited with pointed approbation. "The world," wrote George Washington, "must feel and see that the Union or the states individually are sovereign as best suits their purposes; in a word, that we are one nation today and thirteen tomorrow. Who will treat with us on such terms?" [84] Great though the confusion within the family of nations, domestic confusion was the more disastrous and the more permanent. Divided internal authority was the historical consequence. Establishment of state sovereignty, regardless of federal powers, was the prelude to states' rights, states' rights the preface to compromise enshrined in the Constitution of 1789. This was the "right thread" of American history. Slavery was the great disruptive force, the great compromise of the constitutional convention. The unwillingness of the Founding Fathers squarely to face the implications of slavery explained "all the internal conflicts of the Union up to the year 1865."

> Calhoun and his disciples were not the authors of the doctrine of nullification and secession. The question is as old as the constitution itself, and has always been a living one, even when it has not been one of life and death. Its roots lay in the actual circumstances of the time, and the constitution was the living expression of these actual circumstances.[85]

Compromise guaranteed peril, for it prevented a clear declaration of national sovereignty. And the absence of an unambiguous national power entangled the future in disaster. Sectional and economic groups were presented with a constitutional argument for special and local purposes and created the conflict between the "opposing tendencies" dominating American life before the war. The conflict did not truly begin at any single point after 1789, it was latent in the federal-state system. Each party to the dispute claimed to defend the Constitution as the inexorable controversy was intermittently resumed. But the North was on the side of right, not as Woodrow Wilson said, because the North was right in history but wrong in law. The North was right because it was right in law and in history. For Holst the distinction was meaningless.[86]

Holst's unitary interpretation justified his allocation of space and emphasis. And it was conviction, not arrogance, which induced him to say in his comment cited earlier "that the history of the United States . . . is unusually simple." Simple though it was for Holst, it had the simplicity of a classic epic. It demanded a climax of dramatic intensity, a finality that the war between the sections ultimately provided. But the war was more than a drama; the issues were parts of a continuing process which neither began nor ended at Appomattox.

Slavery for Holst was the standard of judgment of forces, of events, and of men. The moral principles violated by slavery were transcendental principles. He accordingly could not appreciate the difference between the need for preserving the Union at all costs, regardless of the existence of slavery, and the issue of slavery itself. While Lincoln was one of his great heroes, and Holst was aware of what Lincoln said and did, he misconceived his purpose. Henry Clay, as the "great compromiser," did not appear as a stalwart figure, and Daniel Webster was but slightly more acceptable. Stephen Douglas was no "little giant" for Holst, he was a little Lucifer who always acted from motives of the sheerest self-interest.

> Douglas, whose exterior and manners revealed to a marked and sometimes almost a disgusting extent the coarseness and half-culture of the growing west, who had an adroit tongue, a sharp, natural understanding, great presence of mind, a large measure of shrewdness that borders on cunning, who was always alert and at the right place, and who always presented himself with the entire coarse *aplomb* of the bold, influential, half-educated contestant who is filled with immeasurable confidence in himself.[87]

He found excuses for Calhoun, praised John Brown, and completely misunderstood Thomas Jefferson.

> It was not a difficult matter for Jefferson to act in opposition to his theories; and it was still easier for him to reconcile himself to a contradiction between his words and his deeds. Ambition was the sovereign trait in his character. He was always willing to sacrifice much of favorite theories to his feverish thirst for power and distinction, the more especially as his eminently practical instinct caused him often to doubt the tenableness of his ideal systems. Moreover, as he, partly from interest and partly because misled by his idealistic reveries, concealed his ambition under the mask of the greatest simplicity, stoical indifference, and even of disinclination to accept any political honor or dignity, so, too, his conscience was not precisely what would be called tender in weighing and measuring of words, whether his own or those of others. Such a character could scarcely always resist the temptation to make ink and paper say what in his opinion they ought to say. His mode of thought, which was a mixture of about equal parts of dialectical acuteness and of the fanaticism of superficiality, as shortsighted as it was daring, made this matter of no difficulty. Hence it is that not the slightest weight should be attached *a priori* to his interpretation of the constitution.[88]

Holst's preoccupation led him to misinterpret events as well as men. Obviously he found Southern culture typified by the institution of slavery; the North was culturally identifiable by its absence. States'-rights doctrine and special interest inevitably merged. He was almost as rigidly a cultural determinist as certain modern students whose premises lead them to create two separate nationalisms: one in the North, the other in the South. The concept of an "aggressive slavocracy" devoted to sectional expansion was accepted without reservation, and the westward movement became an appendage of sectional power politics. Texas and earlier territorial acquisitions were conspiracies, the Mexican war a Southern imperialistic venture. Conservative Southern Whigs were fearful of what territorial acquisition might do to the South and to the Union, but it was a fear based on concern with slavery. The Kansas-Nebraska Act, a typical Douglas stratagem, was the consequence of slavery, and the Dred Scott case involved the Supreme Court in guilt.

> The Dred Scott decision would . . . remain the greatest political atrocity of which a court has ever been guilty, even if the reasoning of Chief Justice Taney, who delivered the opinion of the majority, were as unassailable and convincing historically and constitutionally, as it was, in fact, wrong, sophistical and illogical. [89]

Holst's powers of organization and capacity for synthesis were nevertheless remarkable. His search for materials was truly prodigious, and he treated a number of segments of the subject without the guidance of precursors. With John Bach McMaster he shares pioneering honors in the use of newspapers, except that he used them primarily to test public attitudes on political questions, whereas McMaster used them as sources for social life. Holst consulted obscure items whenever he had knowledge of their existence; he also relied extensively on printed documents, particularly the *Congressional Globe.* No serious scholar since his time has ventured into the domain of government and administration without consulting official records. Political history rather than constitutional history properly understood makes up the bulk of the Holst volumes, but there are interesting sidelights on economic factors. History in America was viewed as part of the history of civilization, for Holst was far from provincial in his general outlook, but his catholicity bears a closer kinship to Hegel than to the standpoint of comparative anthropology. While he says much of individuals and the attributes of their personalities, the events of history seem to respond to the power of forces rather than to the will of men.[90]

The origins of Holst's biases are reasonably apparent. He was first of all a mid-nineteenth-century German. Reasons for his uncompromising rejection of slavery are probably lodged in his religious training and the circumstances of his intellectual growth. Nurtured in the *Freiheit* of the German university, he and his teachers had the nineteenth-century liberal philosophy in common. Holst had enough intimate experiences with despotism to recognize some of its manifestations. And in the politics of the years before the Civil War there were indications of despotic tendencies. Holst erred only in finding them all on one side. Part of his certainty emanated from a belief in progress, one of the persistent strands of European liberalism as of the American faith in the golden day of industrial miracles. He lived exclusively in the North and knew the South only as a tourist; otherwise he might have been less dogmatic and insistent. But the North was his American home, and his friends and associates, largely Northerners, indoctrinated his attitudes and confirmed the outlines of his bias. The North German Confederation, the Franco-Prussian War, and the creation of the German Empire were exhilarating experiences of his own life. As historians like Holst understood it, German history from 1867 to 1871 was a glowing record of progress, a progress welded together by national sentiment and centralized organization. German federation failed; German nationalism and centralized power established German unity.[91]

To account for Holst's swift eclipse is easier than to account for his temporary renown. Often classed with the scientific historians, he was not actually one of them. His handling of materials did not always follow the rules laid down by the orthodox canon. When he first began to publish, general historians of superior capacity were scarce. The publication of his first volume in English coincided with the opening of Johns Hopkins (1876), and the panoramic survey, for the time being, was eclipsed by the guildman's monograph. Holst enjoyed a brief monopoly. Just when he was bringing his series to a close, James Schouler, John Bach McMaster, and the incomparable Henry Adams began to challenge public attention. The year after Holst presented his last volume in English (1892), James Ford Rhodes presented his first. But the year 1893 is memorable in American historiography less because of the advent of Rhodes than because of the advent of Turner. Turner and the frontier hypothesis altered the meanings historians subsequently identified with the political and constitutional history of the United States.

XXV

Historians Without Portfolio

Once the doctorate became the certificate of historical competence, every graduate student became an author by requirement. But the publications of the scientific historians seldom provided the pleasures Woodrow Wilson derived from John Richard Green or the joy the "golden Buckle" gave to Moses Coit Tyler.[1] The historians who continued to captivate the historians remained the immortals. Herodotus and Thucydides were still the classics.[2] Gibbon and Macaulay had more admirers among historians in America than native craftsmen with the exception of Prescott, Motley, and Parkman. Parkman was the favorite writer of the scientific historians and his name almost acquired the halo of a substantive. Specialist monographs, in editions limited by the public and the publishers alike, went out of print with depressing regularity. Parkman, on the other hand, was constantly available and constantly reprinted.[3]

University administrators like Nicholas Murray Butler or Charles Kendall Adams took justifiable pride in their achievement. Herbert Baxter Adams alone among department executives kept a map on which to register the conquests of Hopkins doctors.[4] But graduate teachers everywhere were identified with the progress of learning. Each new scholar and each new volume enriched the sum of knowledge. Henry Adams was far less sanguine, and Henry Adams did not stand alone. Multiplication of published research did not by itself equal knowledge or guarantee wisdom. Henry Adams stated bluntly

490

that much of what passed for scholarship was simply pedantry.[5] Others, though less pessimistic, did not wholeheartedly believe that meaning spontaneously erupted from the pages of carefully circumscribed dissertations. Special studies were not necessarily significant because they were special. *The American Nation* project was unconsciously a confession. It was designed to integrate the mounting special knowledge about the history of the United States. *The American Nation* series had another purpose suggestive of inner professional disquiet: to provide an interesting and reliable account of national development for general educated consumption.

Professional historians frequently lamented that they were engaging in soliloquy rather than dialogue.[6] Progress did not always appear as striking outside the universities as it appeared within the guild. As research pressures made scholarship more specialized and technical, others were prompted to seek their own meanings in the historical record. Particular motives obviously induced individuals to attempt historical reconstruction, but there were also general motivations. The historian without portfolio expressed an intellectual restiveness; the wish to emulate the historical great implied a subtle disapproval of conventional academic performance. History was too important to be confined to experts. None disparaged the expert's function in the economy of learning, but other experts and the educated public were entitled to share in the wisdom distilled from expert knowledge. Historians without portfolio received careful attention from the professionals and prolonged attention from the interested public. They represented a deeply felt need of professionals and nonprofessionals alike, the need for clarification and understanding.

During the first stage of specialization after the Civil War, five noteworthy historians were recruited from without the professional fold. One was a research scientist who set himself against the specialist trend even before it had fairly begun. His conception of history and the assumptions upon which it was based still provoke controversy. Another was a lawyer who, distressed by the gaps in the national record, was the first to write a consecutive narrative of American history from the first to the so-called second American Revolution following the peace between the states. The third, a successful businessman, retired from a lucrative occupation to write an historical series upon which he spent the remainder of his life. The fourth was a naval officer, whose writings, frequently compared with those of Richard Hakluyt, had a measurable influence on history's course. The fifth was a politician whom the experts elected to the

presidency of the American Historical Association and the majority
of the people elected to the presidency of the United States.[7]

John William Draper still lives in the immortality of historical
results.[8] Although historians habitually use the language of social
process, they almost always think in terms of particular events.
Louis Daguerre, for example, has been transformed into a word that
suggests the beginnings of photography. The name of Samuel F. B.
Morse, enshrined in a code, has virtually become a synonym for the
telegraph. But the creative work of Draper entered into both—and is
linked with the subsequent developments of Edison, Eastman, and
Marconi. Innovations in the teaching of science and advances in
medical education are more readily associated with Benjamin Rush
and Abraham Flexner than with Draper, who had a full part in developing them. Recognition for stimulating scientific thought in
America goes to Benjamin Franklin, to Benjamin Silliman, and to
Willard Gibbs; there is rarely praise for Draper. In an age when the
writing of history was dominated by Sparks, Bancroft, and Hildreth
and distinguished by the heroic trinity of New England—Prescott,
Motley, and Parkman—few are likely to think of the author of *The
Civil War* and *The Intellectual Development of Europe*. Even the
phrase "the conflict of religion and science" usually suggests Andrew
Dickson White, who wrote a famous book with a similar title, rather
than John William Draper, who borrowed it for a volume of his own.
Draper was a historian of ideas and an interpreter of science as well
as an experimentalist. Just before the Civil War, when only forty-
five, he published *Human Physiology* which marked the end of his
career as a research scientist. Thereafter he devoted himself to synthesis: *The Intellectual Development of Europe, Thoughts on the
Future Civil Policy of America, The Civil War,* and *The Conflict
Between Religion and Science*.[9]

Draper's life, interesting on its own account, bears intimately on
the molding of his thought. He was born into a family of devout
Methodists in Lancashire, England, in 1811, and went to the University of London in 1829 to study under the auspices of the dissenters, Benthamites, and utilitarians who founded it. There he studied
chemistry and *materia medica,* besides jurisprudence with John
Austin. Though he learned his subjects of study well, he learned
more than what was presented in class. He learned about living and
working in a great urban center, an excellent laboratory for Benthamite doctrines of institutional utility. When he was twenty-one in
1832, he migrated to Virginia, where his mother's kin resided. His
sisters had opened "The Misses Draper Seminary for Girls" in

Mecklenberg County, where Draper was able to set up a laboratory and pursue his research. After completing his studies for a medical degree at the University of Pennsylvania in 1836, he returned to Virginia and taught chemistry and natural philosophy at Hampden-Sydney College. Soon he removed to New York to teach college chemistry and botany at New York University. Draper had already begun his experiments with light at Hampden-Sydney. Daguerre's method of capturing camera images was announced in 1839, and, although Draper was certainly not the first to do so, he and Samuel F. B. Morse co-operated to perfect the process of camera portraiture. In 1841 he combined with others in establishing the New York University Medical School, with which he worked energetically. He continued to experiment in photography—actually in the wider field of the chemical reactions of light—until 1850, when physiology was added to his teaching load. Six years later Draper left the laboratory and the microscopic study of the universe for historical reconstruction and the study of society.[10]

Draper was caught in the web of history. He felt himself hemmed in by the tight boundaries of specialisms. While he continued to teach students the creed and the data of science, he rebelled against the incapacity stemming from partial training. Compelled to seek for larger meanings, he straddled two worlds and two traditions. As an experimental scientist, Draper belonged by training, if not by temperament, to the professionals. By temperament, and in a lesser degree by training, he belonged to the western tradition of intellectual synthesis. As a laboratory scientist, he hewed close to the experimental line, professing to accept nothing until empirically proved. As a builder of intellectual systems, he deduced conclusions from *a priori* assumptions. Draper himself would not have admitted that he had left the laboratory, and he was not conscious that he had done so. He believed he was continuing his investigations and bringing the postulates of experimental science to their logical social conclusions. History was for him an extension of natural science, a series of sociological implications deducible from the science of physiology.

The universe and therefore society was in Draper's conception a rational order. Man was capable of fathoming meanings of growth, and once meanings were established, intelligence decreed that they be applied. Within the limits of cosmic possibilities and human knowledge, change could be effected by human minds and human wills. Faith in human intelligence, organized knowledge, and directed social change were not exclusively the legacy of science. Draper's faith came as well from the influences of his Methodist youth and his early utilitarian contacts. The positivism of Auguste Comte, first directly and later more intimately, entered into the making of his belief. Like Comte, he trusted only the primacy of "concrete" scientific results and deplored the "futility" of metaphysics.[11]

Methodism, Benthamism, and Comtism were woven into Draper's science of society. If the combination made him a whole man, it split his scientific personality. Intimations were already contained in his writings: Methodism and utilitarianism conceived man as free if not equal in a universe governed by inferential laws; positivism confirmed freedom and progress and made science the key to the cosmos; God, the Great Artificer of eighteenth-century deism, remained safely remote in the rationalist's heaven.

Draper's first appearance on the world stage of scientific debate occurred at the Oxford meeting of the British Association for the Advancement of Science in 1860. A better occasion and a better platform could hardly have been chosen, for the meeting was not an ordinary one. Ordinary business was transacted, and ordinary communications were read. But in Section D, "Zoology and Botany, including Physiology," members of the association were scheduled to discuss a new theory on the origin of species by means of natural selection, or the preservation of favored races in the struggle for life. *The Origin of Species* was the title of Charles Darwin's epoch-making book published the year before. Listed on the program of this section was John William Draper, whose paper was entitled: "On the Intellectual Development of Europe, Considered with Reference to the Views of Mr. Darwin and Others that the Progression of Organisms is Determined by Law."

Drama was in the Oxford air, for the adversaries of Mr. Darwin and their clerical allies were determined to make the most of this auspicious occasion to "smash Darwin." The hall was so crowded· with frocked churchmen, Oxford undergraduates, and ladies and gentlemen that another and larger meeting place had to be secured. They had come to witness the fray and to join in the chorus of approbation or dissent, according to their views of science, theology, or public decorum. The meeting has become so celebrated an incident and so variously reported that no one is exactly certain of what actually occurred. Samuel Wilberforce, bishop of Oxford (nicknamed "Soapy Sam"), a master rhetorician, attended as the champion of the anti-Darwinian forces at the meeting. The bishop displayed his brilliance as an orator and revealed his ignorance of the issues. While his unfamiliarity with biology was excusable, his conduct was not. At one point he turned and asked Thomas H. Huxley whether it was on his grandfather's or his grandmother's side that he claimed descent from an ape. Huxley, who until that moment had not made up his mind how to handle either the situation or the bishop, whispered to his neighbor: "The Lord hath delivered him into mine hands." Wilberforce carried the day with the audience, but Huxley made the scholar's point: he would rather take his descent from wherever it came than to misuse his talent to obscure an intellectual issue in behalf of a treasured preconception.[12]

The emotions of the Oxford meeting have blurred Draper's part in it. Bishop Wilberforce's histrionic encounter with Professor Huxley has been taken as a kind of shorthand to define the meaning of the debate and to recapture its tone. Everybody knows that Draper was there, since his address was the main one, but what he said merits recollection. It was a high point in Draper's life. The paper preceded the Wilberforce-Huxley clash, and the audience was so eager for the blood of the Darwinian battle that they could scarcely listen. They disliked the "Yankee accents" of the Lancashire scientist from America, but the former Englishman was in his element. This was Europe, England, and the British Association, and Draper had the scientific' recognition he craved. It did not matter that Huxley thought Draper "droned" or that unpleasant comments from the audience interrupted his remarks: he was reading an important paper at the British Association.[13]

The paper was unquestionably important. Draper endorsed Darwin and incorporated his version of Darwinian evolution into the interpretation of the intellectual development of Europe. He thereby provided Wilberforce and the anti-Darwinian forces at the meeting with confirmation of a significant point; once grant the initial assumption, the hypothesis of evolution applied everywhere. More importantly, Draper summed up his social views as a scientist and outlined the science of society he was subsequently to elaborate. Law governed in the organic as in the inorganic world, and, once understood, "we have gained a philosophical guide for the interpretation of the past acts of nations, and a prophetic monitor of their future, so far as prophecy is possible in human affairs." [14] An inseparable link in Draper's thought united the physical world of science and the human world of man. "All organisms, and even men," he is reported to have said at the Oxford meeting,

> are dependent for their physical characteristics, continuance, and life, on the physical conditions under which they live; that the existing apparent invariability presented by the world of organization is the direct consequence of the physical equilibrium; but that, if that should suffer modifi-

cation, in an instant the fanciful doctrine of the immutability of species would be brought to its proper value. The organic world appears to be in repose because natural influences have reached an equilibrium.[15]

Draper was unequivocal about the rise and fall of civilizations.

He showed that the advances of men are due to external and not to interior influences, and that in this respect a nation is like a seed, which can only develope [sic] when conditions are favourable, and then only in a definite way; that the time for psychical change corresponds with that for physical, and that a nation cannot advance except its material condition be touched.[16]

He would on no account limit the sway of the natural. He would not sacrifice a jot of reason. But having held to the scientific faith in natural law and rationality, how was man to find room for will? It was an ancient problem, and Draper, for all his older science and its newer Darwinian additions, did not greatly improve on the historic response.

Although probably formulated before the Oxford meeting address, *The Intellectual Development of Europe* contained a part of Draper's answer.[17] His purpose was sharp, his statement clear. "Social advancement is completely under the control of natural law as is bodily growth. The life of an individual is a miniature of the life of a nation." [18] "I have," he said,

asserted that the control of natural law in the shaping of human affairs—a control not inconsistent with free-will any more than the unavoidable passage of an individual as he advances to maturity and declines in old age is inconsistent with his voluntary actions; that higher law limits our movements to a certain direction, and guides them in a certain way.[19]

The Intellectual Development of Europe was greater as a tribute to Edward Gibbon than to Charles Darwin. Whether Draper fully understood Darwin was questionable; that he failed completely to follow him was certain. Like *The History of the Decline and Fall of the Roman Empire, The Intellectual Development* presented culture as an evolutionary process, save that universal progress rather than the interminable fusion of growth and decay was Draper's theme. Draper's most probing analyst described his philosophy as a mixture of "Shakespeare's seven ages of man and Comte's three stages of thought." [20] Draper advanced a cyclical theory of history, and for Draper cyclical development was a predetermined cosmic law.[21]

Groups of men, or nations are disturbed by the same accidents, or complete the same cycle as the individual. Some scarcely pass beyond infancy, some are destroyed on a sudden, some die of mere old age. In this confusion of events, it might seem altogether hopeless to disentangle the law which is guiding them all, and demonstrate it clearly.[22]

Draper's *Intellectual Development* possessed more significance as a record of his own mental and spiritual growth than of the development of European ideas. As a source book charting the mind of an era, the work has inestimable value. While Draper would make no compromise with anthropocentrism, he believed that science enabled man to know the universe and therefore know himself. Knowledge permitted man and societies to exchange illusion for reality. If knowledge lessened man's importance in the universe, it increased man's stature in the world. The laws of science were from God; knowledge of the laws was fashioned by human reason. It followed that truth alone could make man free. And truth, eternally in conflict with error, resulted from the conflict. *The Intellectual Development* is the history of the struggle between false opinion and its gradual conquest. Organized religion was among the interests resisting the development of truth, but Draper would not place religious opinion under an interdict of science. He stressed especially the sins of the Catholic Church in opposition to science, but he never suggested interference with the Church except to protect the holy right of man to question and the divine right of man to change. The Reformation was a landmark in intellectual history, the "predestined issue of sectarian differences and dissensions is individual liberty of thought." [23]

The dissensions produced by the Reformation continued in the American Revolution, which for Draper was the second stage in the conflict of creeds. "State and the Church were solemnly and openly dissevered from one another." The American Revolution was an epoch in intellectual freedom as well as political freedom.

> A grand and imposing religious unity implies tyranny to the individual; the increasing emergence of sects gives him increasing latitude of thought —with their utmost multiplication, he gains his utmost liberty. In this respect, unity and liberty are in opposition; as the one diminishes, the other increases.[24]

Draper's brave new world rested on the twin pillars of freedom and progress.

The Intellectual Development was the façade of the edifice Draper had yet to build. In 1865, he gave four lectures on "The Historical Influences of Natural Causes" to the New-York Historical Society. With additions, these lectures became *Thoughts on the Future Civil Policy of America,* followed by *A History of the Civil War.* The *Civil Policy* was a continuation and an amplification of

The Intellectual Development.[25] "The aim of all science is prevision," he proclaimed with confidence from the preface, and "the Historian, who relies on the immutability of Nature," has it within his power to "predict the inevitable course through which a nation must pass." [26] How could a knowledge of nature be applied to man and society? He propounded a Draper axiom: the physical environment was basic to social understanding, social control, and social progress. The masses of men are not initially moved by argument; they are controlled by the physical environment that they can themselves control only by knowledge and manipulation. Man must be attuned to his environment and place himself in correspondence with it.[27]

Draper gave prominence to the geographic factor in history. American development was conditioned by land. Abundance of land made Americans mobile and endowed them with a spirit of independence. Movement of the American people, he advised, should be encouraged by the government in every way, for a free movement of the population was as beneficent as a free movement of ideas. The movement of peoples was "the true method for . . . preventing communities from falling into Asiatic torpor, and contracting senseless antipathies against each other." [28] He read Americans a lesson out of their recent history to drive home the influence of climate on cultural development and the role of social mobility in mitigating its effects. "Had the Southern States for the last ten years been pervaded by an unceasing stream of Northern travel in every direction, the civil war would not have occurred." [29] The westward movement of the American people created a social atmosphere favorable to individualism. Pioneer types deluded themselves in thinking they were sufficient unto themselves. The actual experience of pioneering for most men, excepting the lone frontiersman on the edge of civilization, demonstrated that to do things alone there were prior things that men had to do together.

The significance of the frontier was the clue to the significance of America. European democracies differed essentially from American democracies: "the former are destructive, the latter constructive." [30] American society, as Turner remarked, constantly began over again on the frontier, as Americans, untrammeled by institutions unsuited to frontier needs, were able to fashion novel ones. Europeans contemplating change were invariably confronted by old institutions; reform always involved a ripping away and a tearing apart. The development of democracy in America had the appearance of a natural evolution. Similar European developments seemed more like a violent uprooting.

Westward expansion left plundered provinces behind it. Exploitation of the land impoverished a continent but opened the way for social learning. Penalties were exacted for the butchery of resources. Here the plainest injunctions of science were violated, and the results could be predicted with certainty.[31] How could these fatal errors be avoided? Government must be clothed with power sufficient to meet such needs, and the needs could be met by using the knowledge of experts, the wisdom of the competently trained. But the problem of the expert in a free society was not easy to solve. To say with Draper that an elite is democratically safe because its members shared in the general culture simply removed the problem to a different level of complexity.

Draper's three-volume *History of the Civil War* followed the *Civil Policy* almost at once. He wrote it under adverse conditions, but it was not without interest. The Secretary of War, Edward M. Stanton, came to the aid of the historian with documents. General William T. Sherman dispatched letters and papers for his use.[32] Without exact references, it is difficult to determine how Draper profited from this largesse, although it is clear that his descriptions of campaigns and battles were enlivened by such data. Discussions of the causes of the Civil War give the work its import. Sectional differences, he asserted, were in the first instance the work of climate. He presented a picture of sectional divergencies now common to historians of the war, who base sectionalism on geography and culture on sectionalism. Slavery, though intrinsically evil, was less the cause than the result of sectional antagonisms. Slavery intensified sectional feeling and contributed to a tighter integration of southern society. Yet, the South offered an engaging illustration of Draper's inclusive thesis. Climate, having made the southern man, made him rural, agricultural, and devoted to the single crop. Hence, southern culture as contrasted with northern, tended to be less mobile, more conservative, less diverse, and more resistant to change. Ideas were static; there was less clash of conflicting attitudes and principles. When it is understood "how much the actions of men are controlled by the deeds of their predecessors, and are determined by climate and their natural circumstances, our animosities lose much of their asperity, and the return of kind feelings is hastened." [33] This was a cool tone for a member of the war generation, and even if the environmental interpretation made Draper abjure moral impeachment, it was a rare mood.

The *History of the Conflict Between Religion and Science* was Draper's best-known book. A volume of the *International Scientific*

Series, it was published by Appleton in 1874. It was a smaller version of *The Intellectual Development* with new material added to meet the immediate situation.[34] To Draper and a number of his contemporaries there seemed to be a new crisis in the relations of church and state. The most dramatic aspect of the crisis turned on organized ecclesiastical efforts to stifle Darwin, a revival for Draper of the ancient attacks on scientific innovation. There was also evidence of a revival of clerical aggression marked by an interference, particularly by the Roman Catholic Church, in the internal affairs of sovereign states. The Syllabus of Errors, promulgated by the Vatican in 1864, the Vatican Council of 1869–70, and Bismarck's *Kulturkampf* of 1871 appeared to point to a new stage of the controversy Draper had already traced.[35] Again he defined the boundaries. It was a conflict "of two contending powers, the expansive force of human intellect on one side, and the compression arising from traditionary faith and human interests on the other." [36] Whoever the enemy, it was the old crusade. Freedom of inquiry could not be arbitrarily limited, the right to differ could not be institutionally suppressed. Draper, himself a profoundly religious man, had no conscious anti-Catholic bias. He could not, however, condone interference with the progress of science on the part of Catholicism, which for him symbolized the current threat.

Draper grossly overstated the case, for science and its intemperate protagonists had become the votaries of a new revelation. He wrote:

> Roman Christianity and Science, nevertheless, are recognized by their respective adherents as being absolutely incompatible; they cannot exist together; one must yield to the other; mankind must make its choice— it cannot have both.[37]

Draper demanded that religion accept the world of his understanding, which meant that churchmen were to embrace scientific concepts as the revelation of divine purpose and scientists as alone competent to interpret it. From this point of view there was no real conflict, but for those regarded by Draper as the enemy, this was just where the conflict began.

Whether Draper's belief in individual freedom derived from the intoxication of discovery or from the faith of his Wesleyan fathers, he hoped for a trained capacity which would remake the malleable parts of the world. Yet, control over cosmic forces was the reward of knowledge, not of faith—unless it was the faith of knowledge. And it was climate (used in the broadest sense) and the environment, not divine sparks kindled in individual souls, which were the sources of control and change. As a sober citizen, he looked to the expert to lead the common man—a delegation of power which without responsible controls has always been a threat to democracy. He was unwilling to yield anything of the sacred right to differ, although in logical consequence it was a freedom to agree with the consensus of the competent rather than to differ from it.

Science revealed a new universe; history transmitted an old world of values. Draper accepted the universe but he accepted it on his own terms. The paradoxes with which he dealt were latent in the issues, his confusions were the confusions of his time. If they still remain exciting, it is not because we lust for dilemmas. It is because the dilemmas still are ours.[38]

The history of ideas owes much to John William Draper. *The Intellectual Development of Europe* marked the initiation of many a young scholar, for Draper made creative thought the catalytic of his own historical thinking. He was one of the most successful popular exponents of the role of science in civilization. Scholars were urged to study historical processes as clues to the meanings of the life of mankind. As one of the formulators of a science of society, he argued persuasively for the unity of knowledge as a method of social analysis and as a measure of the integrity of scholarship.

Draper longed to revise the social universe. James Schouler's ambition, more modest, was also less formidable. He simply wished to rewrite the record of the American past and to make American history whole.[39] Schouler was disturbed because there was a lack of comprehensive or unified treatment he considered necessary. Bancroft had covered the beginnings of the American experiment and managed successfully to establish the Federal Republic in his uniquely glowing account. Yet the Revolution had only begun with the winning of independence, and the history of the United States of America merely commenced with the creation of the Union. Schouler, like Draper, was anxious that history might count in the battles men were constantly forced to wage. He too believed that "the grand lessons of human life" were latent in historical experience, which it was the business of the historian to "deduce" and his duty to "inculcate." [40]

Schouler, born in 1839, was a talented youth. Afflicted by precocity, he is said at an early age to have devoured Dickens, Shakespeare, Macaulay, and Scott. A hearing difficulty first apparent in his Harvard student days later resulted in deafness. This infirmity had a bearing in altering his professional plans. He showed promise in music, played the piano, the organ, and sang with the Harvard Glee Club. After graduation, he taught at St. Paul's School in Concord,

New Hampshire, but when the teaching position of his choice did not materialize he decided to study law. Two years of apprenticeship in a law office sufficed to prepare him for the bar, but his hearing deteriorated as a result of illness contracted during army service. The law, practiced in Boston and dealing with veterans' claims against the government, was financially rewarding and required another office at the national capital. Schouler's effectiveness as an advocate was impaired by his growing deafness, and he gradually turned more of his energy to the writing of legal texts. The first of these appeared in 1870, and three or four years later he again took up residence in Boston to practice in the probate court and to write his law books.[41]

Schouler's literary strivings and his interest in America were whetted by his sojourn in the Washington of the Reconstruction era. He had already made tentative efforts at historical authorship and probably formed the intention of writing the *History of the United States of America Under the Constitution* early in his adult life. The first volume was published in 1880, four more in the next eleven years, the sixth in 1899, and the seventh in 1913. Other studies and other activities crowded these years. The seven volumes of the *History* were matched by seven more scholarly productions between 1893 and 1908.[42] The law school of Boston University appointed him to its faculty in 1883, and in 1890 he began to lecture on American constitutional history at Johns Hopkins. The Hopkins connection, lasting seventeen years, brought him into close association with Herbert Baxter Adams, an advantage for any man and the good fortune of any historical student.[43]

James Schouler wrote his history to fill what he conceived to be an imperative need. "There is no narrative in existence from which one may safely gather the later record of our country's career." [44] There were, of course, respectable historical offerings to which one could repair, but there was "no narrative . . . of ample historical scope prepared from a critical and minute study of the copious materials of the past." The venerable Mr. Bancroft's masterly achievements then stopped "short of the constitutional era," [45] and the work of Mr. Hildreth, though entitled to praise, was thirty years old and thus marked "with the horizon line of his generation." [46] New sources piled high in government archives, some yet unprinted, accented the necessity for revision. Schouler attested to the accuracy of Hildreth. Accuracy of detail was one thing, interpretation another. "I am constrained to differ with him in many particulars," Schouler announced at the very outset, "most widely as to the estimate of our political leaders and their motives; the plan, too, the expression, the historic unities of his work by no means coincides with those herein favored." [47]

The *History* grew beyond its initial plan. Originally conceived as a five-volume work ending with the election of Lincoln, Schouler added one on the Civil War and one on Reconstruction. "I seem to have been borne onwards by some invisible current, where I had repeatedly thought myself in port," [48] he felt under obligation to explain to his readers, but the chief and undeniable merit of the seven volumes is the chronological range. The *History* is dominated by politics and organized on a strict temporal plan. After introductory sections on the Confederation, the constitutional convention and "A More Perfect Union," Schouler surrendered to the presidential synthesis, which he followed with but two exceptions throughout the first five volumes. Every presidential administration provided the title for a chapter, which was then subdivided into sections for each Congress. [49] Schouler's scheme of presentation explains Dunning's student impression that Americans had devoted "all their waking hours outside of mealtime . . . to politics, with a view to save the Constitution of the United States from the Slavocrats." [50] Draper had already attacked the narrow emphasis on politics in American historiography, and others were soon to attack it again, but it was political and constitutional history that Schouler wrote.

Yet, there are intimations of departure in Schouler. Within the tight confines of the presidential synthesis and the tighter ones of chronology, he inserted a considerable amount of social and cultural material. They are literally inserted, rarely assessed. [51] The well-known seventh chapter in the second volume is a noteworthy exception to the general Schouler rule. "The United States of America in 1809" [52] is hardly up to the Henry Adams standard, but that Schouler was capable of first-class performance is more than proved by his *Americans of 1776*. [53] There is much to be recorded on the credit side of the Schouler ledger. He made full use of the sources whenever possible and he was among the first to use the manuscript collections of five American presidents—Monroe, Jackson, Van Buren, Polk, and Johnson. [54] The Reconstruction chapters are particularly valuable, as Schouler's was an early effort to rehabilitate the reputation of Andrew Johnson. He "felt deeply that this much maligned President needed a vindication . . . and . . . that the vindicator ought to be myself." [55] Schouler was able to reappraise Johnson on the basis of his examination of the Johnson papers in the Library of Congress and the publication of part of the Gideon Wells diary in

The Atlantic Monthly of 1910–11.[56] A considerable section of the Reconstruction story and the Grant regime is personal recollection. The Library of Congress, the Boston Public Library, and the Boston Atheneum were systematically exploited, but his documentation unfortunately represents a narrow selection.[57]

Schouler was a political historian because "public events" represented his conception of the essence of history.[58] An event should be evaluated "by its own light, by its own contemporaneous record." [59] He recognized the need for a judicious weighing of the evidence. He was after all an excellent lawyer, and he had the scholar's goal of disinterested assessment.[60] But there were limits. "Let us have earnestness . . . ," he enjoined the historians, "for the writer . . . most distrusted is he . . . who gains no earnestness at all from his subject, but who remains wholly neutral, negative, and external." [61] And Schouler never failed to "inculcate the lesson" whenever he could. He castigated Southerners and held them accountable for the Mexican War. They were also held accountable for the Civil War. Jefferson and Lincoln were idols; Calhoun and Jefferson Davis were admitted to Schouler's court only to be sentenced.[62]

The *History* received the approbation to which it was entitled. Its merits were recognized, its service in bridging the sequential breaks in American historical writing applauded. Schouler's other works were respectfully considered, and his *Americans of 1776* still retains its initial worth. He received professional honors, among them election to the presidency of the American Historical Association. But the way of the historian without portfolio was sometimes hard. At least Schouler thought so. Even after his *History* had earned him stature, and honors of the most flattering kind had been bestowed upon him, he felt deprived. He tried hard to secure an honorary degree through the influence of President Daniel C. Gilman of Hopkins and his friend Herbert Baxter Adams. To Adams he wrote in 1899:

> Let it all pass, now. I shall never appear again as an *applicant* for earthly honors as long as I live. Very likely, after my final volume of history is issued, next October, I shall take up a post-graduate study at Harvard, with the view of *earning* a Ph.D. in course there. In that way I may get into the green pastures.[63]

The chief secondary authority upon whom Schouler relied was James Ford Rhodes, author of *History of the United States from the Compromise of 1850*.[64] The nine volumes of Rhodes, presenting a portrait of America from Abraham Lincoln to Theodore Roosevelt, gave the writer an assured rank. Rhodes was an unusual person and his professional success was remarkable. His educational training was highly informal, and when he launched himself upon a historical career at the age of thirty-seven, he placed his preparation in his own capable hands. Praised by his contemporaries as a great historian, he lectured at Harvard and Oxford, was elected to membership in the Massachusetts Historical Society, and was made president of the American Historical Association.[65] He earned no academic degree, but Harvard, Yale, Wisconsin, and Oxford, among others, awarded him honorary ones. Noted public figures, scholars of international repute, presidents of the United States, and senators were his friends and associates, whose approbation sweetened his life. Unlike James Schouler, he was given invaluable source material by his friends, and he had to fend off encroachments threatening the completion of his work. The redoubtable Lord Acton himself asked Rhodes to prepare the American section of the *Cambridge Modern History;* Rhodes reluctantly had to refuse.[66]

Rhodes was born in Cleveland, Ohio, in 1848.[67] His father was a cousin of Stephen A. Douglas and one of the founders of the coal industry in Ohio. Both facts were of ruling importance in the evolution of Rhodes the historian. From the first came an accentuation of interest in national politics for father and son; from the second, a fortune that smoothed the path to eminence. James Ford Rhodes wrote an autobiographical fragment in which he tells of his early public-school education in Cleveland. It was unconventional and good. His teachers tried to relate what was going on in the world to their teaching, and with Rhodes they succeeded. When he was twelve in 1860, just entering high school, Lincoln had been elected to the presidency, and Rhodes and his father were Democrats. "I cannot praise too highly the encouragement the boys received from the master . . . to devote their attention to an accurate comprehension of public affairs. While he was an ardent Republican and most of the boys were with him, there was always the disposition to give the handful of Democratic boys a fair opportunity for the free expression of their opinions." [68] The Civil War also received consideration from master and students, and when Rhodes graduated in 1865, aged seventeen, he had a "thirst for history and literature." [69]

Rhodes finished high school without Latin or mathematics, lack of preparation considered so fundamental that college on a regular basis was out of the question. The College of the City of New York admitted him as a special student in 1865, where Benjamin N. Martin, a now-forgotten history teacher of force and competence,[70] kept his youthful enthusiasms alive. At Martin's suggestion he read Macaulay's *Essays,* "whose charm was great to a boy of seventeen." [71] Draper's *Intellectual Development of Europe* marked "an epoch" in his mental life; for the first time he perceived the range of speculation. But Buckle transported him. "I was mastered. In my mind I became a disciple." There was, he recorded, "no purer pleasure than to be able to produce such a book." He attended lectures on geology given by Draper, who fascinated him with his "great reputation," his "scientific spirit," and "his great desire to get at the truth." [72] The following year, 1867, he went to the old Chicago University and studied J. S. Mill, William Hamilton, R. W. Emerson, and Herbert Spencer. That summer his parents took him to Europe, and he spent the three succeeding years in study and travel on the Continent and in Britain. While in Paris he listened to Édouard Laboulaye at the Collège de France lecture on Montesquieu's *Spirit of the Laws* and then moved on to Berlin to study metallurgy at the school of mines. This was the real parental purpose and finally in 1870, Rhodes was immersed in coal, iron ore, and pig iron in Cleveland. Coal and iron remained his activity until 1885, when, ready to retire, he closed up his desk and gave himself up to the profession of letters.[73]

James Ford Rhodes formulated his plans early and he was the sort of man who, having made a resolve, was likely to see it through to completion. He set himself a three-year course of reading and study. Soon he submitted himself to historical baptism in the *Magazine of Western History,* which began to publish in Cleveland in 1884. His first piece was on the Cleveland coal and iron industry. His second was a review of the second volume of John Bach McMaster's ground-breaking social history, just then beginning to appear. Rhodes was by now in midstream and he had made up his mind about certain phases of the historian's craft. He approved of McMaster's content and he approved particularly that none had to conjecture about the historian's opinions, which were clearly and unmistakably set forth. This, he pronounced, "is the proper way to write history." [74]

And this was the way Rhodes wrote his own. At first he had merely a history of the Republican party from 1850 to 1858 in contemplation, but holding the boundary lines fixed was an unequal struggle. The Republican party grew into the *History* and by the time he reached the sixth volume he had extended the terminal date to 1877, a chronological extension which was to occur twice until, in the final complete edition, he closed his account in 1908 with the end of Theodore Roosevelt's administration. In 1909 he offered his collected *Historical Essays* to the public, and in 1913 his Oxford series, *Lectures on the American Civil War, 1861–1865,* delivered the year before, was published.[75]

Rhodes' preparation for his later career was certainly unorthodox but by no means inadequate. His reading was extensive, generally self-selected and covered a thought-compelling range. Study of the printed word was generously amplified by successive European travels, which for Rhodes were largely planned tours of field study. When he began his American history, he knew far less about his own country than he knew about England and the ancient world. This should not necessarily count as a disadvantage; any real understanding of the American background demanded such knowledge.[76] But he had a number of decided opportunities not ordinarily open to the usual college professor. For one whose historical province encompassed the revolutions in economics, fifteen years of successful business operation was easily the equivalent of a graduate seminar. For one whose main theme was politics, a close connection with an astute political manager was worth any number of academic courses in government. Rhodes' sister married Mark Hanna, the most notorious "political boss" of the age, who knew a great deal more about politics than many a university professor. Hanna and his brother-in-law shared business offices in Cleveland for years, and their later contacts were always intimate and frequent. Moreover, his own life was coincident with the history he endeavored to depict. He had vivid impressions of the Civil War. Stephen A. Douglas was his kinsman, who had visited at his father's house, and almost all the leading figures of the postwar years were his friends, among them Carl Schurz, Henry Cabot Lodge, Theodore Roosevelt, William Howard Taft, and Elihu Root. Curiously enough, these invaluable advantages were not reflected in his scholarship. His *History* does not demonstrate a mastery of economic analysis, and his understanding of politics was even less acute.

Rhodes suffered from lack of a broadly based training. He believed, as did Schouler, that honesty, integrity, and a good intelligence were by themselves sufficient for an adequate understanding of intricate social processes. A growing number of trained scholars were beginning to realize that there was more to historical craftsmanship than the collection of sources and the calm presentation of their contents in ordered sequences. Much before the time that Rhodes consented to stop, Frederick Jackson Turner and James Harvey Robinson told their colleagues that the "new" sciences of man were the prerequisites for historical explanation. The fundamental historical errors of James Ford Rhodes owe their origin to these deficiencies.[77]

The final volumes of the *History* are inferior to the first ones. Specifically, the eighth and ninth volumes, which came thirteen years after the seventh, are not comparable with the earlier standard. His knowledge of the leading participants in the decades from the end of Reconstruction to the end of Roosevelt's presidency apparently hindered rather than helped him. Instead of critically evaluating their outlook on the questions of public life, he accepted it uncritically. Their outlook was almost certainly his own, but there is little indication that he ever seriously pondered the indictment of American dissent. The social and political meanings of finance, businessman though he was, eluded him and appeared in his pages simply as factors of unrest. Up to the Civil War slavery supplied a unifying thread; after the war there was no discernible theme.[78]

All nine volumes are marred by difficulties that they manifest in common. Whether before or after the Civil War, Rhodes showed scant appreciation of the West as a force in American development. As his underlying assumptions were political, it is difficult to see how he could have missed the elemental implications of western bills in Congress and the sectional votes of western representatives. Barring the concept of sectionalism, western attitudes on land, improvements, and money questions required explanation. Nor is it easy to understand, given slavery as the schematic link of Rhodes' prewar discussion, how the deeper connections between territorial expansion and slavery failed to confront him. When he first began to write, historical materials and the concepts based upon them were not yet all in print, but Turner had delivered his great address on the significance of the frontier before Rhodes completed his third volume. The third volume dealt with the years 1860 to 1862, the latter the date of the Homestead Act. The revisions were made after Turner's ideas and Turner's students had revolutionized historical conceptions. One can only agree with a careful student of James Ford Rhodes that the revisions, seriously intended, indicate that he purposely excluded the West from consideration.

Stranger still was Rhodes' failure comprehensively to treat the upsurge of economic alterations in American civilization. The contention that the dominance of slavery muffled economics might, if valid, cover the first seven volumes, although it will not suffice for the remainder. He had earlier written on coal and iron, and he deplored a disregard of economics in the work of others. If, like the omission of the West, it resulted from conscious choice, it was a choice that was indefensible.[79]

Personalities were Rhodes' forte, and it was in the assessment of men that he did his best historical writing. Thucydides and Tacitus served him as models, and he wished to write an epic of elemental clashes, but he wrote episodic history instead. Not a philosophical thinker, he was persevering, courageous, and intelligent. Historians ever since have had recourse to his work mainly, it is true, to refute him. But, like Schouler, he staked out the historian's claim to a period then uncultivated. Rhodes himself regarded the classical historians as unexcelled, yet he admired the modern historians for their superiority in the "connection" they made of materials, "in criticism and detailed analysis in the study of cause and effect, in applying the principle of growth, of evolution." [80] These were virtues indeed, but they were precisely those which Rhodes himself conspicuously lacked.

If renown is the measure of greatness, Alfred Thayer Mahan, rather than James Ford Rhodes, achieved it. Undoubtedly one of the better-known historians, Mahan's reputation rests as much on his propagandistic writings as upon his historical research. From his studies he drew plausible lessons for national guidance and he urged them upon his countrymen with unrelenting pressure and the full weight of a specialist's authority. Although the course of world history toward nationalism, expansion, and armaments would have occurred without Mahan, his influence was considerable. And the direction of global events from Theodore Roosevelt to Woodrow Wilson suggested to many that his pronouncements were not without historical foundation.

Little in Mahan's early life suggested what he was later to become.[81] He was born at West Point in 1840, where his father was a professor of engineering. At sixteen he secured an appointment to Annapolis through the sponsorship of Jefferson Davis, who had once served with the elder Mahan and who was then secretary of war. A conscientious student at the Naval Academy, he stood high in his class, but the records do not indicate that he was marked by the navy for any special grooming. Being graduated in 1859, he received his commission and saw service, mostly in blockading squadrons, during the Civil War. The next two decades were the normal peacetime years in the life of a navy officer. One breach in the routine of a normal naval career occurred: Mahan wrote a book. *The Gulf and*

Inland Waters,[82] one of a series on naval warfare in the Civil War, was published in 1883. Though quite a satisfactory performance, the book was not much better than scores of others in its class.

Mahan's literary venture produced a deviation in predictable naval routine.[83] He was invited to lecture on naval history and tactics at the newly instituted Naval War College at Newport, Rhode Island. When the invitation arrived, Mahan was with his ship in South American waters, and he accepted with alacrity. He had to wait nearly two years before he could start his assignment, but he began to prepare immediately. The ship's store of books and the English Club at Lima, Peru, served as his library. He reported to Newport in August 1886, ready to lecture. Now a naval captain of forty-six, he was about to become a historian. *The Influence of Sea Power on History, 1660–1783,* came out in 1890, and Mahan, still a navy captain, was also a celebrated man of letters.[84]

Within fifteen short years following the *Influence of Sea Power,* he produced one book after another and became an outstanding authority on the sea and its history. He filled the presidential office at the Naval War College and, after spending half a lifetime in the service, voluntarily retired in 1896. During the Spanish-American War he was a member of the Naval War Board and in 1899 he represented the United States as delegate to the Hague Peace Conference. Oxford and Cambridge crowned him with distinctions in 1894; in 1895, 1897, and 1900 respectively Harvard, Yale, and Columbia granted him an honorary LL.D. The American Historical Association elected him its president in 1902, and the navy made him a rear admiral in 1906. Sea power and history made Alfred Thayer Mahan a personage.[85]

Once Mahan agreed to lecture at the Naval War College, he was constrained to find a central topic. He read Theodor Mommsen's *History of Rome* in Lima. "It suddenly struck me . . ." he wrote, "how different things might have been could Hannibal have invaded Italy by sea, as the Romans often had Africa, instead of by the long land route; or could he, after arrival, have been in free communication with Carthage by water." Mahan had his "clew."

> I would investigate coincidentally the general history and naval history of the past two centuries, with a view to demonstrating the influence of events of one upon the other. Original research was not within my scope, nor was it necessary to the scheme.[86]

He disclaimed credit for developing any principles of naval warfare.

> I learned the few, very few, leading considerations in military combination; and in these I found the key by which, using the record of sailing

navies and the actions of naval leaders, I could elicit, from the naval history upon which I had looked despondingly, instruction still pertinent.[87]

For the correlative historical materials he "relied upon the usual accredited histories." To Bacon and Raleigh he acknowledged full indebtedness, as they "had epitomized in a few words the theme on which I was to write volumes." [88] Mahan took hold of their suggestions, investigated them fully, and presented them with elaborate illustration to the modern world. *The Influence of Sea Power Upon History* received prompt attention and unrestrained admiration in the reviews. Mahan also accomplished what many another scholar yearned to effect. He converted men to his views, the men, as it happened, whose position in public life made it possible for them to translate Mahan's principles into action. Theodore Roosevelt, who in slightly more than a decade was to be president of the United States, was ecstatic, and Henry Cabot Lodge, already a member of Congress and soon to ascend to the Senate, was impressed. Mahan was not responsible for the expansion of the American navy, but he helped to construct the attitudes of many of its foremost advocates.[89] Mahan; at work on *The Influence of Sea Power upon the French Revolution and Empire,* applied for permission to remain ashore while completing it. The permission, eventually granted, was at first refused. "It is not the business of a naval officer to write books," wrote the chief of the Bureau of Navigation. Every book Mahan wrote enhanced the prestige of the navy and strengthened his own reputation. *Sea Power in its Relation to the War of 1812,* published in 1905, ended his researches. The rest of his work was propaganda, artful and earnest, and calculated to influence national policy and public opinion.[90]

The mainsprings of Mahan's thought are not difficult to discover. The practice of history did not involve "merely . . . giving every fact and omitting none," he told the historians who assembled in 1902 to listen to his presidential address. To do so, Mahan almost said, consigned the scholar to futility. The function of the historian was

> not merely to accumulate facts, at once in entirety and in accuracy, but to present them in such wise that the wayfaring man . . . shall not err therein. Failing here, by less or more, the historian, however exhaustive his knowledge, by so far shares the fault of him who dies with his treasures of knowledge locked in his own brain. He has not perfectly communicated his gifts and acquirements to his brethren.

Facts must be subordinated to an "essential unity," if the historian was to capture meaning for himself as well as for the wayfarer. He roundly approved Dr. Johnson's distinction that some things might well be "worth seeing, but not worth going to see." Admiral Mahan was reminded of the seaman who calculated the position of his ship to the hundredth part of a mile. This, he confessed,

> was perhaps a harmless amusement, only wasteful of time, but when he proceeded to speak of navigation as an exact science, he betrayed to my mind a fallacy of appreciation, symptomatic of mental defect.[91]

Some facts were assuredly less significant in certain relations than in others, but how, some must have thought, can one tell what an unknown fact will reveal about another fact before its relations are discovered?

Mahan's concern was less speculative than practical, although his practical emphasis was speculatively tinged. Research alone was not necessarily difficult nor necessarily reserved for first-class minds. The creativity requisite for the discovery of meaning was of the highest order of historical genius. Mahan offered a military analogy. "Not every good general of a division can handle a hundred thousand men, so in history it is more easy duly to range a hundred facts than a thousand." Mildly the admiral taunted the historians:

> That informing spirit which is indispensable to the highest success is the inestimable privilege of nature's favored few. But to study the facts analytically, to detect the broad leading features, to assign to them their respective importance, to recognize their mutual relations, and upon these data to frame a scheme of logical presentation—all this is within the scope of many whom we should hesitate to call artists, and yet who are certainly capable of being more than chroniclers, or even than narrators.

Between Froissart and Ranke there was a difference. Without significance there could be no history; there could only be chronicle. For Mahan there was "a plan of Providence, which in its fulfillment we call history." For Mahan there was a plan:

> Each particular incident, and group of incidents, becomes as it were a fully wrought and fashioned piece, prepared for adjustment in its place in the great mosaic, which the history of the race is gradually fashioning under the Divine overruling.[92]

Mahan's intent as historian was to demonstrate the rise of British sea power from 1660 to 1815. England became the dominant force in European politics and France lost the imperial race. Sea power was the reason for British success and for French failure. Three times France went down to defeat because she had no navy sufficient to counter British maritime strength. Commerce was basic to sea power; sea power was basic to commerce. Mahan was opposed to protective tariffs and a proponent of reciprocity, which, he explained, was not free trade but a policy mitigating the protective principle. Without expanding trade, national prosperity was imperiled and individual well-being jeopardized. Trade must be carried in ships, and a navy must protect them. As long as Britain ruled the waves, she ruled the world. And when British admirals in war or in peace had directed affairs from the bridge of their ships, the ultimate ends of mankind were secure.[93]

When Mahan came to the War of 1812, his vision remained fixed on the ocean. The causes of the war were maritime causes; he had no knowledge of the territorial expansionists of 1812 or of the agricultural depression in the Mississippi Valley. Great Britain had wronged the United States and violated her rights.[94] Locked in struggle with Napoleon, the British did only what they had to do, and Americans could protect themselves and their honor by recourse to war alone. Was Britain justified in employing methods that made American recourse to war inevitable? If Britain was carrying the torch of liberty that Napoleon threatened to extinguish, was the United States justified in going to war against Britain? Mahan never fled from these dilemmas.

There was always a higher law. There was always a higher principle to which particular events were subordinated. Naval strength guaranteed national prosperity and national power. But all nations could not control the oceans. Who was "entitled" to command? The answer was to be found in the "Divine overruling." Nations, like men, were "instruments" of God's purposes. Mahan could take God's part in taking sides with Britain against France, with America against Spain, with England against Germany, with Europe and America against the East. And the divine intent, Mahan was sure, converged with the interests of the Occident, of Christianity, and with those destined to uphold them. Expansion of trade required a merchant marine, a merchant marine a navy, and a navy required naval bases. The universe Mahan surveyed was a closed universe, a world bounded by the seven seas.[95]

"Captain Mahan has met the requirements necessary for an historian of the first class," [96] wrote Theodore Roosevelt of the master protagonist of sea power. Roosevelt paid a greater tribute to Mahan's genius, for as assistant secretary of the navy and as president, he indicated to what extent he subscribed to Mahan's teachings. While the naval captain was doing his routine duty in the New York navy yard, Roosevelt, then a Harvard student, was reading *The Naval History of Great Britain*.[97] The account of the War of 1812 offended his patriotism and outraged his sense of fairness. He decided to investigate the matter for himself. With characteristic impetuosity, he delved into the sources, read whatever came his way, and wrote a book of his own. *The Naval War of 1812* was published in 1882, when Roosevelt, two years out of Harvard, was twenty-four. The author later dismissed it as dull, but it soon became standard in England and America.

Roosevelt had found the career he had been seeking during his last days in Cambridge. He had been elected to the New York State Assembly in 1882 and he never really forsook public life thereafter. He never forsook history either, for Roosevelt was too volatile a personality, too filled with energy, to find complete satisfaction in a single calling. The most remarkable fact about Theodore Roosevelt is that he did so many things and so many of them well. Judgment of his history must take account of his many-sided character and his total immersion in every aspect of the life that he lived. By any ordinary standards, it is miraculous that Roosevelt wrote at all. But ordinary standards do not apply to Theodore Roosevelt.[98]

Roosevelt was one of the principal American authorities on the strenuous life. Election to the New York legislature coincided with *The Naval War of 1812*. He wrote his life of Thomas Hart Benton at a furious clip while ranching in Dakota, and under these conditions he also composed a biography of Gouverneur Morris. While United States civil-service commissioner from 1889 to 1895, he produced a volume on New York and, in collaboration with Henry Cabot Lodge, *Hero Tales from American History. The Winning of the West,* Roosevelt's stellar historical contribution, was begun while he held the former office and was finished when he was president of the police commission of New York City. In fact, some of the later parts of *The Winning of the West* were written at police headquarters. *Oliver Cromwell* appeared when he was governor of New York. After Roosevelt went to Washington as vice president and president, his strenuous political life interfered with his rate of production, although not with his literary activity. He delivered carefully prepared lectures at Oxford, the University of Berlin, and at the American Historical Association. His output of state papers, letters, articles, and reviews on subjects outside of history and politics was constant. But all this was not impossible for a man who, awaiting his political fate at the Republican National Convention of 1900, read Thucydides.[99]

Reading Thucydides did not make Roosevelt calm. He was forever doing something and preparing to do something else. After three years in the State Assembly, he required a change of pace and scene. A cowboy's activity in Dakota was apparently a relief after the turmoil of Albany. The saddle and the range sufficed for his body, and nature always charged his mind. But when John T. Morse asked him to write for the *American Statesmen* series, he promptly agreed to furnish two biographies, studies of Thomas Hart Benton and Gouverneur Morris. The Benton was completed in approximately four months. Four months is an incredibly short time, but not inconceivable if one was full of the subject, had everything at hand, and worked incessantly. Roosevelt was not a Benton student, had almost nothing at hand, and was "pretty sleepy, all the time." His exhaustion did not come from slaving over Benton. He was exhausted because he was cowpunching, and when on the roundup he was on horseback "fourteen to sixteen hours a day." [100] Toward the end of his Benton labors, he asked Henry Cabot Lodge to send him some materials or have somebody look up the data. Roosevelt was desperate. When he reached the years after 1850 in Benton's life, he wrote to Lodge:

> I have nothing whatever to go by; and, being by nature both a timid and, on occasions, by choice a truthful man, I would prefer to have some foundations of fact, no matter how slender, on which to build. . . . He was elected once to Congress; who beat him when he ran the second time? What was the issue? Who beat him, and why, when he ran for Governor of Missouri? And the date of his death? I hate to trouble you . . . but the Bad Lands have much fewer books than Boston has.[101]

Normally, such circumstances would have produced a monstrosity. Such was far from the case, although there were of course unmistakable signs of rapid writing and equally quick thought. Roosevelt's was not a contemplative mind, and he rarely allowed himself time for protracted thinking. The West was congenial to his spirit, he responded to its primitive challenges. First, he felt it intuitively and later he came to know it. Benton, the frontiersman, the spokesman for the new region, had a psychology he could understand and appreciate. He admired Benton, and the volume contains much warm, sympathetic writing.[102] The opposite is true of the Morris book. Roosevelt did more work, although he worked almost as fast, but he did not enter into Morris' purposes as fully as he did into Benton's. He found Morris to be an "entertaining scamp," but he laced into him "savagely for his conduct in 1812–15." [103] Roosevelt, having celebrated Morris' services in somewhat extravagant language, wrote:

> Throughout the War of 1812 he appeared as the open champion of treason to the nation, of dishonesty to the nation's creditors, and of cringing subserviency to a foreign power. It is as impossible to reconcile

his course with his previous career and teachings as it is to try to make it square with the rules of statesmanship and morality. His own conduct affords a conclusive condemnation of his theories as to the great inferiority of a government conducted by the multitude, to a government conducted by the few who should have riches and education.[104]

There was good writing but no research in *Hero Tales from American History,* which is memorable chiefly as reflective of Roosevelt's love of country. He and Lodge joined their pens to pay homage to American patriots and to inspire others to do so. The *New York,* a volume in *Historic Towns,* edited by E. A. Freeman, had appeared four years earlier and was frankly based upon existing authorities that Roosevelt had learned to use with critical dexterity.[105] *Oliver Cromwell,* the least worthy of his compositions, was more a portrait of Roosevelt himself than of the Puritan leader. It was, as a discerning Englishman remarked, "a fine imaginative study of Cromwell's qualifications for the governorship of New York." Roosevelt, again in the full tide of action, had just literally sheathed his sword after leading the Rough Riders in Cuba, "and his account of the 'Sixty-seventh Troops,' of which Cromwell was originally captain, might almost be a description of 'Troop K' of the Rough Riders." [106]

Roosevelt was more than a Cromwellian leader of the Rough Riders, although Roosevelt's image of himself has helped historians to assess his character. Theodore Roosevelt's character does not reflect any single psychological mood. He also had an image of himself as a scholar, and if he identified with his heroes in *The Winning of the West,* the identification does not lessen its value. Roosevelt loved the West and had come to know it well. Like Parkman, whom he greatly admired and to whom he dedicated his volumes about the West, he had an intimate knowledge of the country. Roosevelt was the man of action that Parkman respected, the kind of man, whole as Parkman was not, with the makings of a virile thinker. Roosevelt did not quite meet Parkman's ideal, but there are spirit and scholarship in *The Winning of the West,* and Roosevelt's claim to serious historical consideration depends upon it.[107]

The Winning of the West is Roosevelt's best historical work. It was, he said emphatically, a labor of love to write "the great deeds of the border people," [108] but plenty of hard and consistent labor went into it. His preface, reminiscent of Parkman's, catalogued his sources. The catalogue was impressive and included the printed government documents and manuscript materials not then as common as Turner's influence was later to make them. Turner, reviewing the volumes, gave them the kind of praise only a thorough expert could give. Roosevelt had the credentials for describing how the West was won. Turner meant that Roosevelt was prepared to write it not alone because he had studied the materials appreciatively but because he had, in Roosevelt's words

> guarded . . . herds of branded cattle, and shaggy horses, hunted bear, elk, and deer, established civil government, and put down evil-doers, white and red, on the banks of the Little Missouri and among the wooded, precipitous foothills of the Bighorn, exactly as did the pioneers who a hundred years ago previously built their logcabins beside the Kentucky or in the valleys of the Great Smokies. The men who have shared in the fast-vanishing frontier life of the present feel a peculiar sympathy with the already long-vanished frontier life of the past.[109]

Roosevelt's western chronicle begins with the expulsion of the French from the valley of the Ohio and concludes with the acquisition of the territory of Louisiana from Napoleon. The introductory chapter, "The Spread of the English-Speaking Peoples," [110] demonstrated Roosevelt's breadth and Roosevelt's insight. Regardless of its faults, mostly the result of an irrepressible nationalism, the essential points were firmly laid down.

> The Americans began their work of western conquest as a separate and individual people, at the moment when they sprang into national life. It has been their great work ever since. All other questions save those of the preservation of the Union itself and the emancipation of the blacks have been of subordinate importance when compared with the great questions of how . . . they were to subjugate that part of their continent lying between the eastern mountains and the Pacific. Yet the statesmen of the Atlantic seaboard were often unable to perceive this, and indeed frequently showed the same narrow jealousy of the communities beyond the Alleghenies that England felt for all America.[111]

With unconcealed pride he set metes and bounds, but he set them with a Turneresque sweep:

> The story of how this was done forms a compact and continuous whole. The fathers followed Boone or fought at King's Mountain; the sons marched south with Jackson to overcome the Creeks and beat back the British; the grandsons died at the Alamo or charged to victory at San Jacinto. They were doing their share of a work that began with the conquest of Britain, that entered on its second and wider period after the defeat of the Spanish Armada, that culminated in the marvelous growth of the United States. The winning of the West and Southwest is a stage in the conquest of a continent.[112]

And he ends on the same level of understanding:

> The territories which had been won by war from the Indians and by treaty from Spain, France, and England, and which had been partially explored, were not yet entirely our own. Much had been accomplished

by the deeds of the Indian-fighters, treaty-makers, and wilderness-wanderers; far more had been accomplished by the steady push of the settler folk themselves, as they thrust ever westward, and carved states out of the forest and the prairie; but much yet remained to be done before the West would reach its natural limits, would free itself forever from the pressure of outside foes, and would fill from frontier to frontier with populous commonwealths of its own citizens.[113]

Publisher and author had first agreed on a larger plan. When Roosevelt in 1896 was furiously writing the final chapters, the affairs of state had once again enmeshed him. His publisher, Putnam, and Theodore Roosevelt for that matter, could not successfully compete with the United States navy, the war with Spain, and the vice-presidential office.

Although crammed with dramatic episodes of which Roosevelt always made the most, *The Winning of the West* was the history of a movement.[114] Roosevelt was caustic in his criticism of the historians, whose writings left their readers groping for significance. His comments on scholars who chose to regard compilations of fact untinged by relevance as history were unmistakably blunt. "Unfortunately with us," he wrote to Sir George Otto Trevelyan, a historian he, together with others, considered great,

> it is these small men who do most of the historic teaching in the colleges. They have done much real harm in preventing the development of students who might have a large grasp of what history should really be. They represent . . . the excellent revolt against superficiality . . . but they have grown into the opposite . . . belief that research is all in all . . . and that the ideal history of the future will consist not even of the work of one huge pedant but of a multitude of articles by a multitude of small pedants.[115]

The function of history, as interpreted by Roosevelt, was a philosophical one requiring the establishment of relevancies and criteria of importance. American historians failed to perform the historical function adequately. "We have a preposterous little historical association which, when I was just out of Harvard and very ignorant, I joined." Eight years later, as its president, he addressed "the conscientious, industrious, painstaking little pedants." [116]

At Oxford, as Romanes lecturer in 1910, Roosevelt gave forceful expression to his precepts. With great care he prepared a paper on "Biological Analogies in History," on which he had consulted with Henry Fairfield Osborn of the Natural History Museum. The new science of man was[117] his message, and Darwin was his text. Historians "who would fully treat of man must know at least something of biology . . . and especially of that science of evolution which is inseparably connected with the great name of Darwin." Charles Darwin had given Roosevelt an invigorating clue, for "Darwin and Huxley succeeded in effecting a complete revolution in the thought of the age, a revolution as great as that caused by the discovery of the truth about the solar system." [118] Since Darwinian ideas bore so suggestively on the life of man and society, historians could hardly avoid them. He did not permit himself to lay down the conceptual laws implicit for history; indeed, he cautioned against the dangers of rigid analogies.

Of one conclusion he was entirely certain. Historians who did not write well were unlikely to be remembered. They would not only be forgotten, their ideas would be forgotten with them. Darwin and Huxley had a revolutionary effect because they had acquired a mastery of English prose. Great history, like great science, he informed the American historians in 1912, was also great literature. He had not changed his mind about historians, but he had slaved over his American Historical Association address. "I am to deliver a beastly lecture—'History as Literature'"—he wrote Lodge, and he didn't believe much good would come of it. Historians of the American Historical Association did not "believe that history is literature." Lodge did, however. "The only history the world will ever read," he replied to Roosevelt, "is the history that is literature, and the excellent gentlemen who heap up vast masses of facts render valuable service to history and the historian, but they are not read." [119] Roosevelt told the historians:

> The great historian must be able to paint for us the life of the plain people, the ordinary men and women, of the time of which he writes. He can do this only if he possesses the highest kind of imagination.
> He must tell us of the toil of the ordinary man in ordinary times, and of the play by which that ordinary toil was broken. He must never forget that no event stands out entirely isolated. He must trace from its obscure and humble beginnings each of the movements that in its hour of triumph has shaken the world. [120]

Roosevelt was on the side of the historiographical future. Although many of his auditors were not yet ready to grant his assumptions, they were soon to debate them. The "New History" was still new. Theodore Roosevelt was but one of its heralds.

XXVI

Henry Adams

Theodore Roosevelt wore the robes of learning as easily as he wore the apparel of a cowboy or the uniform of the Rough Riders. To write on the American West and merit Turner's approval was to receive the nod from Clio herself. Among those who listened to his presidential address at the American Historical Association in 1912, few could equal his record as historian. Hardly anyone could match his total achievement. Roosevelt had earned the right to chide the historians. He accused them of neglect of science, of desertion of philosophy, and of indifference to literature. He urged them to shift their focus to higher and broader vistas. Historical scholarship, he insisted, must be meaningful.

Theodore Roosevelt affronted the historians; Henry Adams accused them. When Adams left Harvard in 1877 further to pursue his education, he was dissatisfied with the way history was taught and written.[1] "A teacher," he wrote

> must either treat history as a catalogue, a record, a romance, or an evolution; and whether he affirms or denies evolution, he falls into all the burning faggots of the pit. He makes of his scholars either priests or atheists, plutocrats or socialists, judges or anarchists, almost in spite of himself. In essence incoherent and immoral, history had either to be taught as such—or falsified.[2]

Adams, he said, was unwilling to do either.

He had no theory of evolution to teach, and could not make the facts fit one. He had no fancy for telling agreeable tales to amuse sluggishminded boys, in order to publish them afterwards as lectures. He could still less compel his students to learn the Anglo-Saxon Chronicle and the Venerable Bede by heart. He saw no relation whatever between his students and the Middle Ages unless it were the Church, and there the ground was particularly dangerous. He knew better than though he were a professional historian that the man who should solve the riddle of the Middle Ages and bring them into the line of evolution from past to present, would be a greater man than Lamarck or Linnæus; but history had nowhere broken down so pitiably, or avowed itself so hopelessly bankrupt, as there. Since Gibbon, the spectacle was almost a scandal. History had lost even the sense of shame. It was a hundred years behind the experimental sciences. For all serious purpose, it was less instructive than Walter Scott and Alexandre Dumas.[3]

His gesture was the most eloquent anyone could make. He gave up teaching.

Henry Adams is a study in paradox. One of the most accomplished of American historians said of the *History* that "for clarity . . . and sheer intelligence . . . ," Henry Adams, "had not then, and has not since, been equaled." Carl Becker neither erred nor exaggerated. The *History* stands unrivaled, the best single piece of literary craftsmanship in American historiography.[4] Of the *Education,* unique in American literature and among the finest examples of autobiographical writing in the English language, William A. Dunning predicted that it would "never fail to command the homage due to genius." [5] Yet Henry Adams accounted his teaching futile, his writings dull, and his life a failure.

The acclaim later accorded Henry Adams would greatly have amused him. After his Harvard tenure, he represented historical traits most academic historians disparaged. Scholars continued to praise the *Essays in Anglo-Saxon Law,*[6] but he disowned the institutional history on which his students had nourished him. His *Albert Gallatin,* an admirable instance of multiple skills and a preview of his concepts of democratic leadership, was barely noticed.[7] Even Adams, for all his Jovian aloofness, was sufficiently annoyed to write E. L. Godkin, editor of *The Nation,* in mild protest. It was bad enough that the reviews, parading a learning palpably derived from Adams himself, were unappreciative. It was worse that *The Nation,* listing the significant books in American history for 1879, ignored the *Gallatin* and cited only a volume of Holst which had been translated during the year.[8]

While the important study of Albert Gallatin was neglected, the

Adams history finally received copious praise.[9] But the praise was not only belated, it was conferred on a variety of writing already out of fashion. The initial response to Adams was meager indeed. For Adams there were few of the honors that came to Bancroft, little of the immediate recognition that came to Parkman, nothing like the flattering Parkman sale.[10] When as a youngster Adams reviewed the tenth edition of Sir Charles Lyell's *Principles of Geology,* he had written a long, considered, and graceful essay in keeping with the magnitude of Lyell's effort and the significance of Lyell's accomplishment.[11] There were no such reviews for Henry Adams. Adams stood in the great literary tradition. With the heroic historians of New England, history for Adams was a work of art. But Adams also stood in the tradition of scientific history. No less than Burgess, he was master of the seminar. No less than Herbert Baxter Adams, he gave law and institutions a dominating priority. He made politics the loom of national life, although he did so for reasons the scientific historians did not share. Adams, however, represents a reversal of the normal transition. Historians in general deserted literary and philosophical history for the scientific mode. Adams deserted conventional scientific history for the history of civilization.

An understanding of the *History* requires an understanding of Adams' intent. The *History* was part of a cosmic inquiry. Adams sought to discover the meaning of America, which led him to seek for the meaning of mankind. Chronology was incidental, for Adams' questions encompassed the universe. Nothing less than total unity would suffice. He demanded answers to key questions: why had civilization deluded man with its promise? Why had the American experiment failed? Why had there been a degradation of democracy? If it was an age of optimism for most Americans, it was for him an age of disillusionment. It was the age of paradoxes, but few had the courage and the wit to analyze them. Henry Adams had both.

Adams wished to discover the connections between the ways of man and the ways of the universe. *Mont-Saint-Michel and Chartres*[12] and *The Education of Henry Adams* continued the investigation begun with the history of the United States from 1800 to 1817. "Any schoolboy," he wrote,

> could see that man as a force must be measured by motion, from a fixed point. Psychology helped here by suggesting a unit—the point of history when man held the highest idea of himself as a unit in a unified universe. Eight or ten years of study had led Adams to think he might use the century 1150–1250 . . . as a unit from which he might measure motion down to his own time, without assuming anything as true or untrue, except relation. The movement might be studied at once in philosophy

and mechanics. Setting himself to the task, he began a volume which he mentally knew as "Mont-Saint-Michel and Chartres: a Study of Thirteenth-Century Unity." From that point he proposed to fix a position for himself, which he could label: "The Education of Henry Adams: a Study of Twentieth-Century Multiplicity." With the help of these two points of relation, he hoped to project his lines forward and backward indefinitely.[13]

Adams constantly projected lines in both directions. The *History* looked backward to discover the meaning of America against the background of Europe and it looked forward to discover its destiny. From Jefferson's first inaugural in 1801 to the end of the second war with England were years of special pertinence.

> In 1815 for the first time Americans ceased to doubt the path they were to follow. Not only was the unity of their nation established, but its probable divergence from older societies was also well defined. Already in 1817 the difference between Europe and America was decided. In politics the distinction was more evident than in social, religious or scientific directions; and the result was singular.[14]

The singular historical consequence was the creation of the American character; the unity of the American character exposed its divergence from the European. "Opinions might differ," Adams concluded, "whether the political movement was progressive or retrograde, but in any case the American, in his political character, was a new variety of man." [15]

The lines of power implicit in American development had matured.

> That Europe, within certain limits, might tend toward American ideas was possible, but that America should under any circumstances follow the experiences of European development might thenceforward be reckoned as improbable. American character was formed, if not fixed.[16]

The history of the United States had fashioned a cultural mold, a mold in which men thought, felt, and acted. All men, according to the Adams formula, responded to "the lines of force that attract their world." [17] Like other societies, the United States had produced its own lines of force.

If Henry Adams was a nationalist, he was a nationalist on speculative grounds. Even before the appearance of the *History,* he unmistakably made the point in a *North American Review* essay.

> If the historian will only consent to shut his eyes for a moment to the microscopic analysis of personal motives and idiosyncrasies, he cannot but become conscious of a silent pulsation that commands his respect, a steady movement that resembles in its mode of operation the mechanical action of Nature herself.[18]

Specific American events documented the steady movement and distinguished the new world from the old. "The force of the national movement" was apparent in social and individual action. Adams granted his readers a fleeting vision of the American democratic future.

> If they were right in thinking that the next necessity of human progress was to lift the average man upon an intellectual and social level with the most favored, they stood at least three generations nearer than Europe to their common goal. The destinies of the United States were certainly staked, without reserve or escape, on the soundness of this doubtful and even improbable principle, ignoring or overthrowing the institutions of church, aristocracy, family, army, and political intervention, which long experience had shown to be needed for the safety of society. Europe might be right in thinking that without such safeguards society must come to an end; but even Europeans must concede that there was a chance, if no greater than one in a thousand, that America might, at least for a time, succeed. If this stake of temporal and eternal welfare stood on the winning card; if man actually should become more virtuous and more enlightened, by mere process of growth, without church or paternal authority; if the average human being could accustom himself to reason with the logical processes of Descartes and Newton—what then?[19]

Were this in fact to occur, Adams went on, titillating himself and tantalizing his readers, "no one could deny that the United States would win a stake such as defied mathematics." [20] Still unwilling to predict the democratic millennium with unflinching certainty, he was equally unwilling to leave the possibility unexpressed.

> Stripped for the hardest work, every muscle firm and elastic, every ounce of brain ready for use, and not a trace of superfluous flesh on his nervous and supple body, the American stood in the world a new order of man. From Maine to Florida, society was in this respect the same, and was so organized as to use its human forces with more economy than could be approached by any society of the world elsewhere. Not only were artificial barriers carefully removed, but every influence that could appeal to ordinary ambition was applied. No brain or appetite active enough to be conscious of stimulants could fail to answer to the intense incentive. Few human beings, however sluggish, could long resist the temptation to acquire power; and the elements of power were to be had in America almost for the asking. Reversing the old-world system, the American stimulant increased in energy as it reached the lowest and most ignorant class, dragging and whirling them upward as in the blast of a furnace.[21]

Adams was an exponent of comparative analysis. To his former student, Henry Cabot Lodge, he explained that absence of inclusive concepts made for bias. "Unless you can find some basis of faith in general principles," he cautioned Lodge, whose undiluted New England Federalism irritated him, some theory of the progress of civilization which is outside and above all temporary questions of policy, you must infallibly think and act under the control of the man or men whose thought, in the times you deal with, coincide most nearly with your prejudices.[22]

Adams placed his faith in the idea of civilization, a creative principle that gave the *History* its absorbing interest. The "progress of civilization" itself, if it did not always suggest improvement, at least supplied points of convergence for the lines of force which propelled change and explained it. Although nationalist sentiment throbs through the nine volumes, nationalism was subsidiary, a line of social movement documenting the curve of mutation. The idea of civilization, not nationalism, offers insight into Adams' thought. The *History* charted the difference between Europe and America. The *Education* recorded the evolution of Henry Adams, *Mont-Saint-Michel* the contrast between the twelfth and the twentieth centuries. If the history of the United States created democracy, *Mont-Saint-Michel* contrasted modern diversity with medieval unity. Modern diversity alienated man; medieval unity gave man spiritual peace.

The *History* therefore was as much a history of Europe as of America. America furnished the plot of the narrative, a plot that could only be unraveled in European perspective. Europe was mired in a state of "decrepitude." Constant wars "withdrew many hundred thousand men from production, and changed them into agents of waste," thus compounding degeneration with decay. Europeans might perhaps have survived so ceaseless a drain upon human and natural resources, "but behind this stood aristocracies sucking their nourishment from industry, producing nothing themselves . . . ," which pressed "on the energies and ambition of society with the weight of an incubus." The resulting political and social contrast would have been predictable was it not already discernible. In Europe "common men could not struggle; the weight of society stifled their thought. In America the balance between conservative and liberal forces was close, but in Europe conservatism held the physical power of government." [23]

American conditions made for a distinctive nationalism; American nationalism bred a particular type of man. War was outside the constellation of American drives.[24] Americans, wisely or not, resorted to almost any device to avoid armed conflict. Jefferson's policy of avoidance in the Napoleonic years proceeded from the loftiest idealism. And Jefferson's moral sense and social purpose were simply expressions of the moral sense and social purpose characteristic of average Americans. When Napoleon's ambition drew the

United States into a conflict neither Jefferson nor Madison could prevent, American energy and resourcefulness proved Adams' point. He drew up a list of unbelievable American wonders.

> No European nation could have conducted a war, as the people of America conducted the War of 1812. The possibility of doing so without destruction explained the existence of the national trait, and assured its continuance.[25]

The old commonwealths, Virginia and Massachusetts, demonstrated less resourcefulness than such newer commonwealths as Ohio and Tennessee, but

> the better test of American character was not political but social, and was to be found not in the government but in the people.[26]

The record was the more unbelievable because so utterly unexpected. European nations, adept at war, had trained navies to do their destructive bidding. No nation had less experience and fewer modern craft at hand than the United States. But the Americans perfected the clipper ship, which gave them a naval ascendency European nations had striven for ten centuries to attain. American ships were better constructed, swifter, more easily manned, and cheaper than those of their competitors.

> The Americans resorted to expedients that had never been tried before, and excited a mixture of irritation and respect in the English service, until Yankee smartness became a national misdemeanor.[27]

American naval craft outmaneuvered the English and outclassed the French. The French had failed to interfere seriously with English commerce, but as soon as the American cruiser made its belligerent appearance in ocean lanes, the British Admiralty was beseiged with demands for countermeasures.

There was hardly an end to the list of daring Yankee inventiveness. Americans were as resplendently successful on land as on sea. The English found American gunnery more expert, and hence more fatal, than the hitherto unexcelled British. The British explained their discomfiture, arguing that there had been few improvements since none were needed earlier. American weapons and marksmanship shocked the British into respect for American capacity.[28] Partly as the result of training at West Point,[29] the strides made in military engineering were startling. "None of the works," Adams reported, himself astounded at the record of a pacific people, "constructed by a graduate of West Point was captured by the enemy; and had an engineer been employed at Washington . . . the city would have easily been saved." [30] General science produced Fulton's steamboat, but Fulton's torpedo was a subtle and complicated invention of the first class. "The chief function of the American Union," he concluded, finally clinching his case,

> was to raise the average standard of popular intelligence and wellbeing, and at the close of the War of 1812 the superior average intelligence of Americans was . . . admitted.[31]

Confidence in the "progress of civilization" resulted from a confidence in science.[32] A general scientific outlook rather than any direct experience with science itself swayed Henry Adams at this stage of his career. Interest in science began as a Harvard undergraduate. The lectures of Louis Agassiz, the brilliant Swiss naturalist whose enthusiasm for science captivated everyone, captivated Adams as well. "The only teaching that appealed to his-imagination," he later wrote,

> was a course of lectures by Louis Agassiz on the Glacial Period and Palæontology, which had more influence on his curiosity than the rest of the college instruction altogether.[33]

What particularly appealed to Adams was Agassiz's idealistic interpretation of science, brimful of purpose and final cause. Adams ignored Agassiz's belligerent certainty and his thunderous denunciation of evolutionary theories, and carried away impressions of Agassiz's power to integrate scientific details and to build a unified philosophical pattern. While Adams was a member of the American legation in London during the sixties, an invigorating group of English intellectuals became his friends. Among them was Sir Charles Lyell.[34] Lyell's friendship produced the famous review of the *Principles* which demonstrated that Adams still resembled Agassiz more closely than Lyell. The methods of the new science as practiced by Darwin at this time eluded him.[35] Auguste Comte had a more direct bearing upon the ideas of the *History*.[36] "I pass my intervals from official work," he wrote in 1863, "in studying De Tocqueville and John Stuart Mill, the two high priests of our faith." To the French author of *Democracy in America* he paid particular tribute. "I have learned to think De Tocqueville my model, and I study his life works as the Gospel of my private religion." [37] Adams, as he told posterity in *The Education,* restrained by his New England background from becoming a Marxist, "became a Comteist within the limits of evolution." [38] When Adams, forsaking Harvard and Cambridge, settled down to write the *History* in Washington, it was the author of the *Positive Philosophy* who helped to guide his pen.

Adams adopted Comte's basic classification of cultural development. The well-known Comtean stages—the theological, the metaphysical, and the scientific[39]—are traceable in the *History*. Questing from the vantage point of the scientific era, Adams employed the idea of civilization as a unifying principle. Democracy, the essence of American nationalism, was the fruition of the scientific stage. Adams shared the positivist's faith that scientific methods and conclusions could be applied to society with predictable results. He reveled in stages. The seventeenth of August, 1807, the date the *Clermont* ploughed through the Hudson upstream, was the beginning of a new era in America,

> a date which separated the colonial from the independent stage of growth; for on that day, at one o'clock in the afternoon, the steamboat, "Clermont" . . . started on her first voyage.[40]

Social processes came to a full, measurable stop, although few were immediately conscious of it. The *Clermont* was so epochal a turning point that by comparison "the medieval barbarisms of Napoleon . . . signified little more" to America "than the doings of Achilles and Agamemnon." [41]

Search for laws implied a search for controls; social controls implied social determinants. When cultural determinants were discovered, wisdom helped man to attune to them. Understanding of "the lines of force" was statesmanship; to live in response to their meaning was sagacity. Individuals counted for less than forces. Half jocularly, he later expressed regret that he had even tried to explain Jefferson and Madison. To Samuel J. Tilden, a patrician Democratic reformer who came within an ace of the presidency in 1876, he wrote:

> They appear like mere grasshoppers kicking and gesticulating on the middle of the Mississippi River. . . . They were carried along on a stream which floated them, after a fashion, without much regard to themselves.

Henry Adams was a determinist. "My own conclusion," he continued in the Tilden letter of 1883,

> is that history is simply social development along the lines of weakest resistance, and that in most cases the line of weakest resistance is found as unconsciously by society as by water.[42]

Man's fate was determined by the uncontrollable forces of the physical universe. The *History* explored the possibilities of human control within such limits. The famous series of questions, still pertinent, with which the *History* closed underscored his assumptions.[43]

A new episode in American history began in 1815. New subjects demanded new treatment, no longer dramatic but steadily tending to become scientific. The traits of American character were fixed; the rate of physical and economical growth was established, and history, certain that at a given distance of time the Union would contain so many millions of people, with wealth valued at so many millions of dollars, became thenceforward chiefly concerned to know what kind of people these millions were to be. They were intelligent, but what paths would their intelligence select? They were quick, but what solution of insoluble problems would quickness hurry? They were scientific, and what control would their science exercise over their destiny? They were mild, but what corruptions would their relaxations bring? They were peaceful, but by what machinery were their corruptions to be purged? What interests were to vivify a society so vast and uniform? What ideals were to ennoble it? What object, besides physical content, must a democratic continent aspire to attain? For the treatment of such questions, history required another century of experience.[44]

Adams was a clinician of integrity. While in one of its dimensions the *History* is a study of the limitations imposed upon man, in another it is a study of how man made the most of these limitations. The *History* explored the character of others; in *The Education* Adams explored his own, for Adams was a censor of public morality.[45] History was the constant interplay of dynamic forces, a struggle between the inner resources of men and the resistless pressures of the cosmos. If man was to survive, an adjustment had somehow to be made, but the conflict was the drama of living.

"The scientific interest of American history," said Adams, "centered in human character." European history was dominated by individual personalities; American "individuals" were important, chiefly as types.[46] There was no room for great men in Adams' theory of history. "With hero-worship like Carlyle's, I have little patience," he wrote to the philosopher William James in what amounted to a lecture on free will. "In history heroes have neutralized each other, and the result is no more than would have been reached without them." Heroes in Carlyle's sense may not exist, yet one man was not the same as another. Adams was too firmly committed to the Comtean notion of a "speculative class" to discount the role of leadership. "Nevertheless," he added, "you could doubtless at any time stop the entire progress of human thought by killing a few score of men." If it were true that a "few hundred men represent the entire intellectual activity of the whole thirteen hundred million," did they have opportunity for free, untrammeled choice? Adams had his answer. "They drag us up the cork-screw stair of thought, but they can no more get their brains to run out of their especial convolutions than a railway train (with a free will of half an inch on three thousand miles) can run free up Mount Shasta." [47]

Adams studied American personalities because in America individuals typified the evolution of the race. "The interest in such a subject exceeded that of any other branch of science," for, as he ominously remarked, "it brought mankind within sight of its own end." [48] Biographical ventures preceded the *History*.[49] He assessed Federalist leaders in the *Documents Relating to New England Federalism,* he struggled with the erratic Virginian, John Randolph, and he drew the portrait of Albert Gallatin with sympathetic understanding. Randolph was wanting by Adams' standards. Brilliance and courage availed but little against the forces that shattered him.

> More than any other southern man he felt the intense self-confidence of the Virginian, as contrasted with his northern rivals, a moral superiority which became disastrous in the end from its very strength; for the resistless force of northern democracy lay not in its leaders or its political organization, but in its social and industrial momentum, and this was the force against which mere individuality strove in vain.[50]

Albert Gallatin, not Jefferson or Madison, was the hero of the *History*.

> After long study of the prominent figures of our history, I am more than ever convinced that for combination of ability, integrity, knowledge, unselfishness, and social fitness, Mr. Gallatin has no equal.

This was high commendation, and Adams, stern in his judgments, was rarely effusive.

> He was the most fully and most perfectly equipped statesman we can show. Other men, as I take hold of them, are soft in some spots and rough in others. Gallatin never gave way in my hand or seemed unfinished. That he made mistakes I can see, but even in his blunders he was respectable.[51]

Adams was merely following the evidence faithfully, and it is curious that Gallatin, never fully appreciated, is still accorded only second-class eminence. He was a man of practical wisdom in the Adams sense and provided ballast for the theoretical flights of his more idealistic associates.[52] As secretary of the treasury, the most imaginative after Hamilton, he worried less about counting assets than ways of using them. And he made valiant efforts to bring a greater measure of reality to Jefferson's dream. He counseled Jefferson on every critical occasion, and for the most part wisely. He advocated defensive preparations after the *Chesapeake* incident. He took issue with his chief on the efficacy of gunboats then already antiquated. A lover of peace, though not at all costs, he tried to help Jefferson avert the War of 1812, but when the war was over it was Gallatin who went to Ghent to help write the peace. For such public service the presidency was the only decent reward. But Gallatin selflessly made way for Monroe and in true republican style retired to Pennsylvania to cultivate the science of ethnology. This was a test of greatness, and Adams honored him for it. "To my mind," Adam wrote to Henry Cabot Lodge, who by Adams' criteria was not a statesman cast in the Gallatin mold,

> the moral of his life lies a little deeper than party politics and I have tried here and there rather to suggest than to assert it.

Adams preferred suggestion to assertion. But he unmistakably asserted his opinion on the meaning of Gallatin's career.

> The inevitable isolation and disillusionment of a really strong mind— one that combines force with elevation—is to me the romance and tragedy of statesmanship. The politician who goes to his grave without suspecting his own limitations, is not a picturesque figure; he is only an animal.[53]

While Jefferson more than suspected his own limitations, he does not always appear to good advantage in the *History*. Jefferson's virtues were always balanced by his faults. He was "awkward in the intellectual restraints of his own political principles," [54] a characteristic awkward indeed for a political leader in the Adams universe, where restraints were imposed by the realities of existence. Jefferson's interests led him to widen rather than to narrow the bounds

> of every intellectual exercise; and if vested with political authority, he could no more resist the temptation to stretch his powers than he could abstain from using his mind on any subject merely because he might be drawn upon ground supposed to be dangerous.[55]

The Virginia and Kentucky Resolutions, in other words, adequate as a political stratagem, could scarcely serve as a philosophy of government. Jefferson as president was destined to become a broad constructionist and an exponent of government power by the qualities of his mind as well as by the force of circumstances.

> Prone to innovation, he sometimes generalized without careful analysis. He was a theorist, prepared to risk the fate of mankind on the chance of reasoning, far from certain of some of its details. His temperament was sunny and sanguine, and the . . . philosophy of New England was intolerable to him. He was curiously vulnerable, for he seldom wrote a page without exposing himself to attack. He was superficial in his knowledge, and a martyr to the disease of omniscience.[56]

Adams' view of Jefferson was a nineteenth-century view. But whatever the final judgment of Henry Adams, he recognized those other facets of Jefferson's thought which made shortcomings a measure of greatness.

> Jefferson aspired beyond the ambition of a nationality, and embraced in his view the whole future of man. That the United States should become a nation like France, England, or Russia, should conquer the world like Rome, or develop a typical race like the Chinese, was no part of his scheme. He wished to begin a new era. Hoping for a time when the world's ruling interests should cease to be local and should become universal . . . Few men have dared to legislate as though eternal peace were at hand . . . but this was what Jefferson aspired to do.[57]

It was, thought Adams, a visionary dream, impractical in the world of forces symbolized by Napoleon. But it was a noble vision. Yet Jefferson for Adams was a welter of conflict and contradictions.

> Excepting his rival Alexander Hamilton, no American has been the object of such estimates so widely differing and so difficult to reconcile. Almost every other American statesman might be described in a parenthesis. A few strokes of the brush would paint the portraits of all the early Presidents with this exception, and a few more strokes would answer for any member of their many cabinets; but Jefferson could be painted only touch by touch, with a fine pencil, and the perfection of the likeness depended upon the shifting and uncertain flicker of its semi-transparent shadows.[58]

The analysis of character "touch by touch" revealed Adams as a consummate artist and made the *History* a masterpiece.

Contrasting personality types provided dramatic antithesis, but there was another variety of drama in the Adams method. Adams used documents to attain both dramatic intensity and logical precision.[59] Adams allowed the documents to speak. Jefferson's own words, adroitly selected, enter into the narrative to convict him of an almost neurotic compulsion to avoid the obligations of his office. In this given instance, Madison, heir apparent of the Virginia dynasty, had already been named by the Republicans as Jefferson's successor. Adams cited Jefferson against himself to illustrate his irresolution, his longing to fly to the safety of Monticello, his unwillingness to take a stand or to formulate a policy. Adams contrived to let Jefferson indict himself. Lest any doubt be permitted to linger, he called in Jefferson's friends to bear witness, and Mr. Gallatin's words were entered into the record. "Both Mr. Madison and myself," Gallatin testified,

> concur . . . that considering the temper of the Legislature it would be eligible to point out to them some precise and distinct course. . . . But I

think we must, or rather you must, decide the question absolutely, so that we may point out a decisive course either way to our friends.[60]

The cumulative effect was overwhelming. Adams, not yet satisfied, summoned Jefferson's opponents to the witness box, certain that violent comments would now seem mild.

> So freely did he express his longing for escape that his enemies exulted in it as a fresh proof of their triumph. Josiah Quincy, his fear of the President vanishing into contempt,—a dish of skim-milk curdling at the head of our nation—writing to the man whom eight years before Jefferson had driven from the White House, gave an account of the situation differing only in temper from Jefferson's description of himself.[61]

With seeming impartiality, Adams offered a letter written by Josiah Quincy to his immortal great-grandfather:

> Fear of responsibility and love of popularity are now master-passions, and regulate all movements. The policy is to keep things as they are, and wait for European events. It is hoped the chapter of accidents may present something favorable within the remaining three months; and if it does not, no great convulsion can happen during that period. The Presidential term will have expired, and then—away to Monticello, and let the Devil take the hindmost. I do believe that not a whit deeper project than this fills the august mind of your successor.[62]

To permit the documents to speak for themselves was scientific historical method, for the documents presumably told what actually occurred. But it was Adams who told the story, and his connective links told it the way he wished it told. The historian, he had once written in criticism of the great English constitutional scholar, Bishop Stubbs, "must be an artist. He must know how to keep the thread of narration always in hand, how to subordinate details, and how to accentuate principles." [63] Adams could not control the total situation as could a novelist, but as historian he could control the documents. The result, as William Jordy concluded, created "a mathematical sense of precision; an almost mechanistic sense of cause and effect." [64]

Adams finished the *History* in 1890.[65] According to his own account, he was through with such matters. American history, he averred, was dull. He insisted that he and his friend, John Hay, who had edited Lincoln's papers, had written all the American history worth writing. If Adams was through with American history, he was far from through with history. Actually, he was not through with American history either. Custom has already established distinctions between one segment of Adams' life and another: Adams the historian and Adams the theorist, Adams the probing scholar and Adams the frustrated man. Such conventional distinctions are too neat to be natural, too contrived to transform Henry Adams into a split personality.[66] Adams could not investigate civilization without investigating his own. He could not venture to explain mankind without assessments of individual men. He had to attempt to explain himself, if he were to attempt to explain others. He could not, in other words, assess the idea of civilization without asking whether civilization had retrograded or advanced. If, as he believed, civilization had failed, he could not avoid an analysis of the American character, which, having produced democracy, was fated to disappear. Accordingly, *The Education,* designed to explain Henry Adams to himself, involved a larger question. If the "standard formulas" had failed for Henry Adams, they had failed for everyone else. The prime dramatic purpose of *Mont-Saint-Michel and Chartres* was to compare modern chaos with medieval order, but it was also a response to the tensions of his spirit which gave inner meanings to his quest for unity.

Marian Hooper Adams, his wife, committed suicide on December 6, 1885.[67] What happened to Adams following this catastrophe can scarcely be conjectured. He went on a trip to Japan with the artist, John La Farge, almost immediately. The rest of his life reads like a travelogue. He returned to finish the *History,* but in August 1891, he and La Farge went off on an eighteen-month trip to the South Seas, to Tahiti, Fiji, Samoa, Australia, and back to the United States by way of Europe. Thereafter his existence was an epic of restlessness. His peregrinations, global in extent, took him to Cuba, Mexico, and Egypt. Europe was virtually an annual affair. He went to the Rockies, to California, to Chicago, and to Canada. He was always on the move and always ready to go somewhere else.[68] Always he returned to his Washington home on Lafayette Square that Henry Hobson Richardson, a leading architect of these years, had built for him and his wife adjacent to another he had designed for John Hay, secretary of state.[69] Always he returned to his friends, his books, his curios, and his coins. Often he was to be found, alone with his thoughts, in Washington's Rock Creek Cemetery, where, according to his own specifications, Augustus Saint-Gaudens had executed a monument to the memory of his wife, a monument called "Silence," which was ultimately to be his own.[70]

The decade from 1890 to 1900, seemingly as desultory as his travels, was a time of profound reflection. Intrigued by Tahiti and by its fullness of life, he wrote a history of the royal house, based in part upon the oral testimony of its queen.[71] In 1894, he told John Hay: "I really enjoy writing that link of history. It shows me, too, why I loathe American history." Sharp, pessimistic distinctions were forming in his mind. "Tahiti is all literary. America has not a literary conception. One is all artistic. The other is all commercial." There already were ominous conclusions. "Both are about equally bankrupt. That is their only marked resemblance." [72] The note of catastrophe was clear, but Adams was learning. He was learning that everything could not be subjected to reason, that his sophistication sometimes hindered rather than helped him to understand the Tahitians. Yet, when he came to write the royal history, he could not let the queen's uninhibited words tell the story. He had to direct the flow of narrative in his own finely chiseled prose. But he had begun to see the world in what for him was unaccustomed light. As the pupil of La Farge, he studied painting and for the first time color and form appeared to him in ways he had never really known existed.

Adams seeped up learning everywhere. His friends, a small coterie of rare spirits, were every whit as immersed in living as Adams. They were rare because they so uniquely offered strength and stature to each other and so finely balanced his needs with their own.[73] La Farge was a kindred seeker; John Hay was another companion in spirit. Clarence King, an erudite and stimulating geologist, tutored Adams in science as La Farge tutored him in art.[74] King was for Adams "the best companion in the world";[75] the three, Adams, King, and Hay[76] were as inseparable as their separate activities permitted. When apart, their correspondence tightened the thread of contact, and the letters Adams wrote them are among the best guides to his mind and heart. Increasingly, his associations were with women. His "nieces in wishes" crowded his Washington house and gave the aging man pleasure and repose. Adams, he wrote in *The Education,* truthfully but not without exaggeration, "owed more to the American woman than to all the American men he had ever heard of." [77] They were, he said, in the nineteenth century at least, "much better company than the American man." And as symbolized by the Virgin, they had "once been supreme." [78] Why women, still a potent force of energy in the scheme of the universe, were no longer recognized as occupying a commanding position, was a speculative issue that meant much to him.

Young men were also numbered among his friends. One of them, George Cabot Lodge, son of the senator, a youthful poet of considerable promise, died prematurely in 1909. At the request of the Lodge family, Adams wrote a memoir of him. Adams felt the loss of "Bay" Lodge keenly and he was as poignantly moved by the futility of his brief life. Lodge, he believed, had failed because there was little response to poetry in Boston or, for the most part, in the world. The bonds tying Adams and "Bay" Lodge together were many, among them the personal bond of living in a society that failed to appreciate their talents.

> Of Bay Lodge I cannot speak with the smallest calm, because the loss is so personal. The superb exuberance of youth which can find no outlet except in self-assertion, and no appeasement except in defiance of commonplace, was the very last of my social foundations. Nothing remains. I look around over the whole field of human activity, and can see no one else to offer a ray of light.[79]

The early optimism had already been seared out of Henry Adams. In 1893 he had been elected president of the American Historical Association. The obligation of his office required an address, and Adams contrived to be in Mexico when he was scheduled to give it. Instead, he sent a letter from Guadalajara to Herbert Baxter Adams, which was read at the annual meeting in December 1894.[80] "The Tendency of History" publicly marked his departure from professional orthodoxy and his rejection of confidence in accepted historical formulas. Darwinian evolution, he informed the historians, had at first intimated a "cheerful optimism" no longer warranted. The only alternative to futility was a science of history. Adams had begun another stage of his education, which was to lead to the formulation of his dynamic theory of history. But the Adams message did not lead the historians anywhere.

The last eighteen years of Adams' life, from 1900 to 1918, were years of furious activity. He wrote the *Mont-Saint-Michel and Chartres* and *The Education,* as well as *A Letter to American Teachers of History* and *The Rule of Phase Applied to History,* during the first decade of the new century. The *Mont-Saint-Michel and Chartres,* first privately printed, was issued for the public in 1913 by the American Institute of Architects. *The Education,* also printed privately, was posthumously published in 1918. *A Letter* appeared together with *The Rule of Phase* in 1919. Brooks Adams republished the two later items and the "Tendency of History" as *The Degradation of the Democratic Dogma,* a title as deceptive as it was provocative. *The Tendency of History,* issued in 1928, contained *A Letter* and *The Rule of Phase* but did not include the complete essay from which the title of the book was taken.[81]

Adams' oscillations of mood and activity were not so sharp as they sometimes seem. When Harvard beckoned him, he gave up journalism. When he left Harvard for Washington in 1877, he gave up teaching. When he returned from his South Sea trip with La

Farge, he announced that he had done with American history. Specifically, all this was true. Adams abandoned journalism as a profession; he never abandoned the purpose that persuaded him to consider it in the first place. As a responsible member of the "speculative class," he was committed to exert power over social change. The *History* was not journalism, but one of its objectives was to aid Americans—and Europeans—to see themselves as a historian of civilization saw them. The *History* attempted to place America and democracy in evolutionary perspective so that mankind might see its end.[82]

After Harvard, Adams never taught again. He refused an offer from Johns Hopkins, and it seems clear that he had no desire to join a university faculty as a teacher of history. But the remainder of his life was one long teaching experience. *The Education* is the journal of a man learning.[83] Adams was teaching himself and being taught, and like other Americans he was chiefly important as a type. He addressed "The Tendency of History" and *A Letter to American Teachers of History* to instruct his historical colleagues. He wrote the *Chartres* to instruct himself, but he also wrote it together with *The Education* and *The Rule of Phase Applied to History* to instruct others. He hoped to exert power on university education. In a preface to the *The Rule of Phase,* recently unearthed by Harold Dean Cater, he expressed the earnest wish that his suggestions might serve

> as a universal formula for reconstructing and rearranging the whole scheme of University instruction so that it shall occupy a field of definite limits, distinct from the technical. In that case, he will conceive of the University as a system of education grouped about History; a main current of thought branching out, like a tree, into endless forms of activity, in regular development, according to the laws of physics; and to be studied as a single stream, not as now by a multiversal, but a universal law; not as a scientific but as a historical unity; not as a practice of technical handling, but as a process of mental evolution in history, controlled, like the evolution of any series of chemical or electrical equilibria, by one general formula. University education, organized on this scheme, would begin by ceasing to compete with technical education, and would found all its instruction on historical method.[84]

Adams contributed an article to the first issue of the *American Historical Review* in 1895. The essay, on Count Edward de Crillon, an intriguing Frenchman who served as an intermediary between the United States and an English agent in 1812,[85] presented fresh materials from the French Foreign Office, correcting and amplifying what he had already written in the *History*.[86] The occasion permitted him to stress the inescapable margin of error in historical method.

According to mathematicians, every man carries with him a personal error in his observation of facts, for which a certain allowance must be made before attaining perfect accuracy. In a subject like history, the personal error must be serious, since it tends to distort the whole subject, and to disturb the relations of every detail. Further, the same allowance must be made for every authority cited by the historian. Each has his personal error, varying in value, and often unknown to the writer quoting him. Finally, the facts themselves carry with them an error of their own; they may be correctly stated, and still lead to wrong conclusions. Of the reader's personal error nothing need be said. The sum of such inevitable errors must be considerable.[87]

How could there be synthesis based on accumulated error? How is conceptual unity to be found in a multiplicity of doubtful facts? What were the standards by which a fact became "a fixed and documented starting point?" [88] He was certain, as he later expressed it— and historians would have found it intellectually suicidal to disagree —that "History has no use for multiplicity; it needed unity; it could study only motion, direction, attraction, relation." [89] The alternative was chaos. Adams strove to avoid "the futile folly of the infinite," [90] and to find a unity in the welter of multiplicity.

The scope and direction of Adams' thought altered, but the ultimate purposes remained. The *Chartres,* as Adams avowed, was "involved in the same doubt" as *The Education.*[91] "The three last chapters of the *Education,*" he explained to Whitelaw Reid, editor of the New York *Tribune,* were the "Q.E.D. of the three last chapters of *Chartres.*" [92] And *The Rule of Phase,* as he told the historian J. Franklin Jameson, was only a "supplementary chapter" of *The Education.* Moreover, he added, "The form of presenting all this, from the 12th Century till today (in the *Chartres,* the *Education,* and the supplementary chapter), was intended in order to make it literary and not technical. I trust you will not let yourself be beguiled by the form." [93] In reality, Adams had undertaken a work of art. History, sociology, mathematics, and physics were the materials of an artistic purpose. The dynamic theory of history was not intended for scientists and historians alone; it was intended for all mankind.

The Adams writings represented a single expression. *The Education* without the *Chartres* or the *Chartres* with *The Education* are basically incomprehensible. Together they constitute one of the finest examples of symbolic interpretation in American letters. Science for Adams was an artistic instrument; physics a symbolic device. *The Rule of Phase,* he confided to his brother, Brooks Adams, "was . . . put together in order to see whether the pieces could be made to fit. . . . The fools begin at once to discuss whether the theory was true." [94] The dynamic theory of history was simply a part of the "speculative inquiry." He undertook it, "not to prove its truth, but to prove its convenience." [95] Adams was a Socrates in two senses: he would spur the process of dialectical exploration and he would serve as a gadfly of dull-witted complacency.

The *Chartres* therefore was an esthetic experience. For a single imaginative moment, he strove to capture the spirit of a past age and to fix it precisely as a starting point in the thought and feeling of his readers. The *History,* as distinguished from the *Chartres,* displayed a conscious awareness of the role of the imagination, of the artistry of literary purpose, and the extent to which the documentary historian could make use of them. When he wrote the *History,* his emotional life was still impoverished. It had not yet been enriched by La Farge, by Saint-Gaudens, and by Clarence King. He had yet to make his travels and experience the full impact of Marian Adams' death, the simplicity of Tahiti, and the changes wrought by the power of coal and electricity in his own western world. In his remembrances of things past, Adams tried, as Proust did later, to ignore the imperative of time. But Adams could not ignore time completely, for the comparison between the serenity of the Middle Ages and the descriptions of the modern age to some extent depended upon a temporal equation.

The *Chartres* was addressed to women, to his nieces real and fancied. Baiting the modern male, Adams asked whether, controlled as he was by the "central power houses" of his time, man could have any feeling for art or literature. Also baiting the historians, Adams ignored historical questions relating to the exactitude of times and places.[96] Scholars' queries gave him no pause. He was creating a drama, the drama of cultural unity symbolized in the Gothic architecture of the cathedrals of France and incarnated in the worship of the Virgin.

> *Brave though we be, we dread to face the Sphinx,*
> *Or answer the old riddle she still asks.*
> *Strong as we are, our reckless courage shrinks*
> *To look beyond the piece-work of our tasks.*[97]

Adams asked his nieces and hence his readers to leave their sophistication behind them as they embarked on their pilgrimage to Mont-Saint-Michel and Chartres.[98] He asked his fellow scholars to leave their theories locked in their monographs, for one had first to feel before one could understand. He was asking the modern world not to conform to their culture, at least while they tried to grasp the meaning of another. Adams could fume at conformity in finely measured words. He had been doing it throughout his intellectual life in his novels, biographies, and histories. But Adams was limited by some of his own conformist drives. He admonished his nieces to leave every scrap of knowledge safely stored away, but he himself rushed back and forth from guidebooks to art historians—and occasional visits to libraries. He was stretched on the rack of his own personality. The urge of his artistic impulse brought only partial surrender. His artistic sense was too tardily awakened, and his inhibitions were too deeply imbedded in his New England subconscious. The idea that art and thought were separable, if not exclusive, was virtually an Adams axiom. Sophistication and the overtrained mind thwarted the emotions. With conviction he wrote of the need for combining them, but he could not fully succeed in combining them himself. If once he felt the full power of line and form from buttress to pinnacle, he still felt compelled to check the data. He could not let Chartres envelop him completely; he already knew Saint Thomas Aquinas. Saint Francis stirred him, but he had already seen himself in the mirror of logic. For Adams it was too late. Chartres was a heavenly glimpse, not a divine vision. The Virgin was an esthetic experience, not a spiritual conversion.

The Education of Henry Adams preceded *The Rule of Phase Applied to History,* which was probably written before *A Letter to American Teachers of History.* While all were interrelated parts of a creative whole, *The Education* is inseparably the companion of the *Chartres.* Together they represent Adams at his greatest, Adams the artist, Adams the philosopher, Adams the historian. Any work so provocatively ambivalent was certain to be variously appraised. The volumes were at once too subtle and too forthright, too metaphysical and too ironical to allow for unruffled agreement. Adams would have been pleased with the number and diversity of commentators. The critical elaboration of the obvious would have irritated him. Adams struggled as all men must who seek to communicate novel thought or personal feeling. He struggled against what Alfred North Whitehead called the obtuseness of language, with words at once too fragile to bear the intimacy of private thought and too opaque to reflect the nuances of meaning. But Adams compounded the struggle. He refined a subtle literary device, an artistic goal with a philosophic purpose. He employed irony with premeditated sharpness so that what he actually said evoked what was deliberately left unsaid.

While *The Education* is almost all the things that have been said about it, *The Education* is all of them at once. It is imaginative and scientific, serious and ironical, certain and tentative, mystical and realistic, erroneous and true. Not designedly autobiographical, it is yet intimately personal. Regardless of what may be said of *The Education,* it is impossible to study Adams without it. It is just as essential for an understanding of America during the years from 1838 to 1905. An earlier century speaks to America through the pages of *The Education,* and it speaks with the voice of an Adams.

The Education is the history of the complexity of modern life. Multiplicity had succeeded unity, and complexity was constantly increasing at an accelerated rate. The result was chaos. As historian, Adams had undertaken the arrangement of sequences.

> He had even published a dozen volumes of American history for no other purpose than to satisfy himself whether, by the severest process of stating, with the least possible comment, such facts as seemed sure, in such order as seemed rigorously consequent, he could fix for a familiar moment a necessary sequence of human movement.[99]

But he was unable to fix any facts which seemed sure for a familiar moment. "Where he saw sequence, other men saw something quite different, and no one saw the same unit of measure." Adams had to find a unit of measure, no matter where it might lead. The objective of the historian "is to triangulate from the widest possible base to the farthest point he thinks he can see, which is always far beyond the curvature of the horizon." Adams triangulated far beyond the curve of the horizon. "Satisfied that the sequence of men led to nothing and that the sequences of their society could lead no further, while the mere sequence of time was artificial, and the sequence of thought was chaos, he turned at last to the sequence of force." [100]

Two scientific theories dominated the thought of the nineteenth century. One, biological evolution, seemingly premised universal progress; the other, the dissipation of cosmic energy, seemingly premised universal decay. Adams found evolutionary dynamics unacceptable; he found universal degradation the law of life. Historians for the most part accepted evolutionary doctrines uncritically. They assumed progress and garnered hope from the record of civilization. Yet, man was the latest in the evolutionary series and the twentieth century the culmination of the remotest past. As the most recent cosmic phenomenon, humanity represented dissolution rather than progress. Its very development implied a diminution of energy in the limited cosmic supply.

The dynamo was the symbol of the twentieth century, as the Virgin was the symbol of the thirteenth. Adams "found himself lying in the Gallery of Machines at the Great Exposition of 1900, his histori-

cal neck broken by the sudden irruption of forces totally new." [101]
The dynamo was a miracle of force and power. While it demonstrated man's dominance over nature, it also demonstrated nature's dominance over man. Paradoxically, it was the symbol of man's conquest of himself. The very purpose for which man had devised it, the harnessing of power, would ultimately destroy mankind in the very act of using it. And the dynamo was simply the epitome of an entire historical process. The simple lever dissipated energy no less than the complicated motors invented by Samuel P. Langley. Thought itself was a force, and the cumulative expenditure of precious power, of Galileo, Newton, and Edison, had also to be computed in the total loss. Adams had seen the rise of coal, he had witnessed the technological revolution. Coal, electricity, motors, and dynamos used up the energy of the universe with improvident waste and incredible speed, and nothing was certain but doom. Adams' own expenditure of energy was formidable. He had made a truly fabulous effort. But, as he himself intended, the dynamic theory of history was more of a suggestion than a conclusion.

The insinuations of *The Education* were parts of its design. For Adams "the details of science meant nothing; he wanted to know its mass," [102] a technical concept he seldom used with scientific precision. Symbolic contrasts mattered more than scientific accuracy. Judgment must rest upon his creative intent, not on the gross materials out of which his dramatic contrasts were shaped. "The charm of the effort," wrote Adams to Barrett Wendall, the literary historian who had once listened to his Harvard lectures, "is not in winning the game but in playing it." [103]

If Henry Adams was a prophet of doom, it was in keeping with his character that he should enjoy it. Even his pessimism was paradoxical. His was a pessimism with a relish, and he could contemplate the death of the sun while living life to the brim. His friends knew him well. Augustus Saint-Gaudens told Hay that should in fact "the world blow up . . . nobody would care except Henry Adams who would shriek and yell with delight and derision as he sailed into the air." [104] It was in keeping with his character too that when he followed his own compelling intellectual drives, he should banter and chide and cajole. He was deadly serious about the rule of phase applied to history and the letter he wrote to his historical colleagues in America. He could not help overstating his case that progressive evolution was folly in the light of the universality of entropy. But his was the unpopular side and the minority view.[105]

Yet how could he deny that social energy was a true form of energy when he had no reason for existence, as professor, except to describe and discuss its acts.[106]

Adams hammered home the point—in fact, he labored it—that unless historians were content to collect facts as geologists collected fossils, history had to become a science.[107] Indeed, there was no way of preventing it:

> If life was to disappear, the forms of Vital Energy known as Social Energy, must also, presumably, go to increase the Entropy of the Universe, thus proving—at least to the degree necessary and sufficient to produce conviction in historians—that History was a Science.[108]

Anyone but Henry Adams would have accounted himself a success. Adams accounted himself a failure. But if Adams was truly a failure, the society, not Adams, had failed. Henry Adams ignored his own precept. Education, he taught, should teach men to act "by choice, on the lines of force that attract their world." He eschewed the major lines of force of his own society perhaps because he was an Adams, or perhaps, being an Adams, he was incapable of coming to terms with the kind of world it was. He abjured power by means of wealth. Adams had sufficient financial resources to do what he wanted, but he was no nabob. The nabobs of the gilded age repelled him, and Adams rarely lost the chance to scoff at money and the men who made it—although he was free from financial cares because of those who made it for him and those who administered it afterwards. He likewise abjured power by means of the Adams standing and the Adams name. While he detested the new society and its materialistic standards, he resented the indifference of the new society to the Adams values and the Adams heritage. None could deliberately ignore an Adams, but the lords of steel and the barons of coal were impervious to his existence. The difference between the House of Adams and the House of Morgan was the difference between two centuries of American history. President Grant, as far as Henry Adams was concerned, may have been enough to upset Darwin, but it was U. S. Grant, not Charles Francis Adams—nor indeed Henry Brooks Adams—who sat in the White House.

Adams' pride in the Adams name was more than the simple worship of his republican ancestors. He thought less of the coincidence of his birth than of his patrimony. He was· a beneficiary of intelligence and a trustee of morality. The "want of a moral sense," wrote Adams in the *History,* "was one more proof that the moral instinct had little to do with social distinctions." [109] Aaron Burr conspired against his country not because he lacked gentility and breeding. Timothy Pickering demonstrated that he loved New England more than he loved the Union, but it was his lack of integrity, not breeding, that proved his undoing. The House of Adams was memorable because its members were endowed with the moral sense. The Adams integrity was the legacy of Henry Adams, and he never forgave his society for being unable to make use of it.

John Adams, second president of the United States and great-grandfather of Henry Adams, had displayed his integrity on numerous occasions before a United States existed to honor him. One had only to recall honest John Adams defending British soldiers charged with murder in a hostile Boston court. One had only to recall ex-president John Quincy Adams, Henry's grandfather, dying on the floor of the Congress. Henry Adams himself recalled his grandfather in whose Quincy study he heard talk of the "slave power" as he listened to the formulation of plans to oppose it. They were the plans of an unpopular minority. Organization of a minority was integrity in political action, and Henry's father, Charles Francis Adams, became the Free Soil party's candidate for vice-president. Adams remembered his father as minister in London during the Civil War and his own role as legation secretary when the Union cause was as unpopular in official circles as the United States had been when his great-grandfather was United States minister in England. He recalled his father's activity and his own in behalf of liberal reform in the seventies. If the members of the fourth generation of the House of Adams were without the moral sense, it would have been hard to find it elsewhere. But no one in official Washington sought to harness the power of the Adams legacy in behalf of the common weal. For an Adams, a political career was as normal as Quincy, and Quincy was as outmoded in the new America as Adams himself. It was hardly amazing that Henry Adams felt he had to account for it.

Henry Adams had to account for himself; later historians have had to account for Henry Adams. There is no finer history than the Adams history, no more courageous attempt to decipher the meanings of human experience. Adams flung his challenge in the teeth of the universe. Failure was inescapable. Had he succeeded—an idea impossible to contemplate—he would have created a new world and a new religion.[110] Adams fulfilled the demands of his reason; he could not fulfill the demands of the cosmos.

Adams, however, did fill an urgent need in the world of historical scholarship. He challenged the professional historians as he challenged the universe. He called for revisions and re-examinations of historical intent that professionals had ultimately to heed. "Nothing in education is so astonishing as the amount of ignorance it accumulates in the form of inert facts." [111] Without hypotheses, facts were meaningless, no matter how many of them historians were able to accumulate. Concepts were intellectual unities, and such unities, fragile though they were, alone enabled scholars to grope for understanding. A science of history as Adams envisaged it, may not have been possible, but Adams' achievement was to put science and history together. Human energy and social acts, regardless of the conceptual framework, he rightly maintained, are inseparably parts of the natural universe. Thereafter no serious historian could afford to separate them. If historians were to make any sense of man, they had to make sense of the world.

Scholars, Adams warned, were too dependent on reason. Again and again he demonstrated by his thought and by his example that there was more to human experience than the mind alone could unravel. La Farge had twitted him that he reasoned too much and he twitted modern scholars in turn. "The mind resorts to reason for want of training," [112] training in seeing and feeling, as well as thinking. Reality is stubborn enough not to yield to so-called reality alone. Adams "did his damndest" with ideas, but they were not only the ideas of reason, they were imaginative ideas and the ideas of insight. Adams learned that only the total personality could approximate the totality of experience. "Unity is vision; it must have been part of the process of learning to see." [113]

With Adams, though not because of him, the world shifted its course. Adams' life represents a cross-section of the American mind in transition. America had passed from the agricultural-rural stage to the urban-industrial stage, from relative simplicity to increasing complexity. Unity made for optimism, doubt was the companion of multiplicity. The dynamo had come to stay. Scholarship was obligated to face the questions that it was the duty of Henry Adams to ask.

Notes

Abbreviations of Works Cited

CHAL: W. P. Trent, John Erskine, Stuart P. Sherman, and Carl Van Doren (eds.), *The Cambridge History of American Literature* (3 vols., New York, 1917, 1918, 1921; one-volume edition [complete], 1933).

DAB: Allen Johnson (ed.), *Dictionary of American Biography* (20 vols., New York, 1928–37).

Jernegan Essays: William T. Hutchinson (ed.), *The Marcus W. Jernegan Essays in American Historiography* (Chicago, 1937).

Kraus: Michael Kraus, *A History of American History* (New York, 1937).

LHUS: Robert Spiller, Willard Thorp, Thomas H. Johnson, and Henry Seidel Canby (eds.), *Literary History of the United States* (3 vols., New York, 1949).

NCHA: Justin Winsor (ed.), *Narrative and Critical History of America* (8 vols., Boston, 1884–89).

INTRODUCTION

[1] Karl R. Popper, *The Logic of Scientific Discovery* (New York, 1961), 16; italics in original.

[2] *Ibid.,* 16–17.

[3] George Santayana, *Skepticism and Animal Faith* (New York, 1955), 8.

[4] Alfred North Whitehead, *Science and the Modern World* (New York, 1948), 49.

[5] George Santayana, *The Life of Reason* (New York, 1955), 9, 10.

[6] Henri Bergson, *Creative Evolution* (New York, 1944), 27.

[7] *Boswell's Life of Johnson,* edited by George Birkbeck Hill; revised

and enlarged edition by L. F. Powell (6 vols., Oxford, 1934–50), I, 424–25.

CHAPTER I

1 Frederick J. E. Woodbridge, *The Purpose of History* (New York, 1916), 17. Bert James Loewenberg, "American History in College Education," *Essays in Teaching,* Harold Taylor (ed.), (New York, 1950), 117.
2 Morris R. Cohen, *The Meaning of Human History* (La Salle, Ill., 1947), 84–85.
3 Gaetano Salvemini, *Historian and Scientist* (Cambridge, Mass., 1939), 27. Bert James Loewenberg, "Some Problems Raised by Historical Relativism," *Journal of Modern History,* XXI (Mar. 1949), 17–20. Charles Gray Shaw, *Trends of Civilization and Culture* (New York, 1932), 624–25.
4 William R. Shepherd, "The Expansion of Europe," *Political Science Quarterly,* XXXIV (Mar. 1919), 43–60; (June 1919), 210–25; (Sept. 1919), 392–412. Loewenberg, "American History in College Education," 117.
5 Ralph Turner, *The Great Cultural Traditions* (2 vols., New York and London, 1941), I, vii.
6 Salvemini, *Historian and Scientist,* 60. Loewenberg, "American History in College Education," 119.
7 Woodbridge, *Purpose of History,* 40, 89.
8 *Ibid.*
9 Cohen, *Meaning of Human History,* 7, 6.
10 Woodbridge, *Purpose of History,* 49.
11 *Ibid.,* 46.
12 *Ibid.,* 49.
13 *Ibid.,* 46.
14 *Ibid.,* 45.

15 *Ibid.*
16 Cohen, *Meaning of Human History,* 84.
17 Woodbridge, *Purpose of History,* 17. Current practice of periodization is analyzed in Thomas C. Cochran, "The Presidential Synthesis in American History," *American Historical Review* (July 1948), LIII, 748–59.
18 Matthias Thórdarson, *The Vinland Voyages* (New York, 1930), is a modern survey of the evidence, valuable particularly for the analysis of geographical factors; Arthur M. Reeves, *Finding of Wineland the Good* (London, 1890), translates the documents and is equipped with an excellent critical introduction. The most accessible volume containing the sagas and bibliographical analysis is J. E. Olson (ed.), "The Voyages of the Northmen," *The Northmen, Columbus and Cabot* (New York, 1906), one in the series entitled *Original Narratives of Early American History,* of which J. Franklin Jameson is the general editor. John Fiske, *The Discovery of America* (Boston, 1892), I, ch. 2, is still worth reading, and the account in Edward Channing, *A History of the United States* (New York, 1928), I, 2–6, is one of the most judicious.
19 The reference to Adam of Bremen is cited in Reeves, *Wineland,* 92. It is not particularly informative. But cf. C. R. Beazley, *The Dawn of Modern Geography,* 300–1420 (3 vols., Oxford, 1897–1906), II, 9.
20 Thórdarson, *Vinland Voyages,* 1–5; Olson, 4–5. Reeves does not regard the Flat Island book as reliable; Fiske does.
21 Shepherd, "Expansion of Europe."
22 William H. George, *The Scientist*

in *Action: A Scientific Study of his Methods* (London, 1936), 128.

23 See, for example, Silvio Zavala, *New Viewpoints on the Spanish Colonization of America.* (Philadelphia, 1943), 3, 4.

24 William Van Loon [Hendrik Willem Van Loon], *America* (New York, 1927), 34. Cf. Fiske, *Discovery of America,* I, 256, 257.

CHAPTER II

1 This document is cited and translated by Samuel Eliot Morison, *Admiral of the Ocean Sea. A Life of Christopher Columbus* (Boston, 1946), 105. The omissions are Morison's. Salvador de Madariaga's *Christopher Columbus* (New York, 1940) presents a different view at many points. The older studies are still valuable because they depict the evolution of critical alteration in interpretation and reveal the growth of the Columbus legend. Washington Irving's *History of the Life and Voyages of Christopher Columbus* (3 vols., New York, 1828), discussed below, is a classic and still remains one of the best introductions to the subject. Justin Winsor, *Christopher Columbus, and How He Received and Imparted the Spirit of Discovery* (Boston, 1891), is indispensable. John Fiske, *Discovery of America,* I, 335–516, vies with Irving for charm of style. The critical works of Henry Harrisse and Henry Vignaud are cited hereafter in specific instances. Clements R. Markham, *Life of Christopher Columbus* (London, 1892), is a distinguished historical study. Edward G. Bourne, *Spain in America, 1450–1580* (New York and London, 1904),

throws light on every aspect of the problems discussed in this chapter. Bourne's bibliographical comments on the Columbus literature are particularly informative, 323–25. See also Justin Winsor (ed.), *Narrative and Critical History of America* (8 vols., Boston and New York, 1884–89), I, chs. 1 and 2, by William H. Tillinghast and Winsor respectively. This work is hereafter cited as *NCHA.*

2 The original of the *Santángel Letter* has been lost.

3 The *Santángel Letter* is reprinted in Bourne, "Letter from Columbus to Luis de Santángel," *Northmen, Columbus and Cabot,* 263–71. There are two printed copies of this letter in existence, one of which is in the New York Public Library. Morison, *Admiral of the Ocean Sea,* 322–23.

4 According to some accounts, see Bourne, *Northmen, Columbus and Cabot,* 261. For Morison's version, *Admiral of the Ocean Sea,* 322–23.

5 A. P. Newton, in *Great Age of Discovery* (London, 1932), 97, also for bibliographical details; Bourne, *Northmen, Columbus and Cabot,* 262.

6 Bourne, *Northmen, Columbus and Cabot,* 270–71.

7 Charles E. Nowell, "The Columbus Question," *American Historical Review,* XLIV (July 1939), 802–22, is an admirable summary. See Edward Channing's comments, *A History of the United States,* II, 28–30. Morison's are the most recent and seem to the present writer the most judicious, *Admiral of the Ocean Sea,* 54–55. Newton's brief analysis is suggestive at every point, *Great Age of Discovery,* 73–102. Charles M. Andrews, *The Colonial Period in American*

History (4 vols., New Haven, 1934–38), is an outstanding work by an outstanding scholar, who, I, 11, n. 1, critically evaluates some of the controversial Columbus literature. His assessment of the maps and the Toscanelli letter are especially important. William H. Tillinghast, "The Geographical Knowledge of the Ancients Considered in Relation to the Discovery of America," in *NCHA,* I, 33–58.
8 Nowell, in "The Columbus Question," 802–22. For example, Henry Vignaud, "Proof that Columbus Was Born in 1451: A New Document," *American Historical Review,* XII (Jan. 1907), 270–79; Vignaud, "Columbus a Spaniard and a Jew," *American Historical Review,* XVIII (Apr. 1913), 505–12.
9 The evidence on these points is summarized by A. P. Newton, "Columbus and His First Voyage," *Great Age of Discovery,* 76–77; Henry Harrisse, *Christophe Colomb: son origine, sa vie, ses voyages, sa famille. . . .* (2 vols., Paris, 1884–85). Henry Vignaud, *Critical Study of the Various Dates Assigned to the Birth of Christopher Columbus: the Real Date, 1451* (London, 1903).
10 On the Toscanelli letter, Andrews, *Colonial Period,* I, 11, n. 1, is illuminating; Morison, *Admiral of the Ocean Sea,* 78; Vignaud, *Toscanelli and Columbus* (London, 1902²).
11 João de Barros, the Portuguese historian, for example, Morison, *Admiral of the Ocean Sea,* 54–55.
12 A. P. Newton, "Asia or Mundus Novis?" *Great Age of Discovery,* 104–26. Morison, *Admiral of the Ocean Sea,* 54, 55–57. George E. Nunn, *The Geographical Conceptions of Columbus* (New York, 1924), 54–90, but Morison thus disposes of the argument: "Around 1900 men began to write about Columbus who were so bright as to 'discover' what had been hidden for centuries; even though they had but a small fraction of the documentary evidence, and none of the oral and visual evidence available to Columbus' contemporaries. Vignaud, in two stout volumes and numerous pamphlets, built up the hypothesis that Columbus was not looking for 'The Indies,' had no idea of sailing to China; he was simply searching for new Atlantic islands of whose existence he had secret information, in order to found a valuable estate for himself and his family. Having passed the position where he expected to find these lands, and made land much further west, he concluded that he had reached Asia. Then, with his son Ferdinand and Las Casas as fellow conspirators, Columbus falsified the *Journals*—forged the Toscanelli letter, even annotated the margins of his books, to prove that he had been looking for Asia all along!" 55.
13 Irving B. Richman, *The Spanish Conquerors* (New Haven, 1921), 35, n. 1. Vignaud, *Histoire critique de la grande entreprise de Christophe Colomb* (Paris, 1911).
14 Morison, *Admiral of the Ocean Sea,* 54–55.
15 Ferdinand Columbus' biography of his father exists in an Italian translation by Alfonso de Ulloa, published in Venice in 1571. The title is excessively long and is usually referred to simply as the *Historie.* See, in general, E. G. Bourne, "Introduction," *The Northmen, Columbus and Cabot,* 87 ff. The abstract of Las Casas

is in the *Historia de las Indias* (5 vols., Madrid, 1875). The history of the third voyage is in vol. II, pp. 220–317, reprinted in Bourne, 319–66. It was this history which first appeared in Antonio de Herrera, *Historia general . . . de las Indias Occidentales. . . .* (Madrid, 1601–15). Bourne's bibliographical remarks in *Spain in America*, 323–24, are also helpful. For Las Casas, Joseph Sabin, *A List of Printed Editions of the Works of Fray Bartolomé de Las Casas, Bishop of Chiapa* (New York, 1870).

16 Antonio Montesinos actually anticipated Las Casas. On the general topic, see Lewis Hanke, *Struggle for Justice in the Spanish Conquest of America* (Philadelphia, 1949), the leading modern authority on Las Casas. Also worthy of remembrance in this crusade are the Franciscans of Guatemala in general and Juan de Zumárraga and Vasco de Quiroga; see Silvio Zavala, *New Viewpoints . . . ,* 56. The general philosophy of the Spanish in this period is discussed by Zavala in this volume, in an essay, "Spanish Colonization and Social Experiments," 104 ff., and Hanke has contributed an important study, *The First Social Experiments in America* (Cambridge, Mass., 1935). A. W. Lauber, *Indian Slavery in Colonial Times Within the Present Limits of the United States* (New York, 1913), should also be consulted. Fundamental to the whole problem is Ricardo Levene, *Introducción a la historia del derecho indiano* (Buenos Aires, 1924). Lewis Hanke, "Bartolomé de Las Casas, An Essay in Hagiography and Historiography," *The Hispanic American Historical Review*, XXXIII (Feb. 1953),

136–51, summarizes some of the fundamental issues of the Las Casas controversy.

17 F. A. MacNutt, *Bartholomew de Las Casas* (New York, 1909), contains the best account. The *Brevissima* was published in Seville in 1552. For Morison's opinion, *Admiral of the Ocean Sea*, 51, 155; Fiske, *Discovery of America*, I, 335.

18 N. Andrew N. Cleven, (ed.), *Readings in Hispanic American History* (Boston and New York, 1927), is a convenient collection of important documents, many of which are not to be found elsewhere. For the decree creating Las Casas "Protector of the Indians," 221–22.

19 On this and other related problems the works of Lewis Hanke previously cited are explicit.

20 Cleven, *Readings in Hispanic American History*, 226–33.

21 *Ibid.,* and references to Hanke already cited.

22 William H. Prescott, *History of the Conquest of Mexico* (3 vols. London and New York, 1901), II, 235, and comments, 12 n.

23 Morison, *Admiral of the Ocean Sea*, 51.

24 A. P. Newton, "Christopher Columbus and His First Voyage," *The Great Age of Discovery*, 89, is an excellent short account.

25 Hanke, "Bartolomé de Las Casas," *The Hispanic American Historical Review*, XXXIII (Feb. 1953), 149, and references there cited.

26 Fiske, *Discovery of America*, II, on Peter Martyr. Peter Martyr's work has been translated by F. A. MacNutt, *De orbe novo: The Eight Decades of Peter Martyr d'Anghiera.* (New York, 1912). Peter Martyr was made official historian by the Spanish court in 1520; the first part—

"decade"—of his work had already appeared. Of these decades there are eight, half of which were published before he died in 1526, the whole in 1530. Newton, "Christopher Columbus and His First Voyage," *Great Age of Discovery*, 98–102. Prescott's comments, II, 96–98, should on no account be missed. They are amplified in his *History of the Reign of Ferdinand and Isabella, the Catholic* (3 vols., London, 1902), II, 74.

27 A. P. Newton, "Christopher Columbus and His First Voyage," *Great Age of Discovery*, 99.

28 Cited *Ibid.*, 100. Vespucci's letters unquestionably first chronologically belong to a category different from Martyr's *Decades*.

29 Cited *Ibid.*, 102.

30 Fiske, *Discovery of America*, II, 36.

31 George Ticknor, *History of Spanish Literature* (3 vols., Boston and New York, 1871), II, 38, 21 n. The title of Gonzalo Fernández de Oviedo's work is *Historia general y natural de las Indias Occidentales*, published by the Spanish Academy of History (4 vols., Madrid, 1851–55).

32 Ticknor, *Spanish Literature*, II, 39, 23 n.

33 *Ibid.*, II, 40, 24 n. Herrera was made "Historiographer of the Indies" by Philip II. Prescott, *History of the Conquest of Mexico*, II, 91–94, contains an excellent account of Herrera, in which Prescott makes some pertinent remarks concerning Herrera's "slavish adherence to chronology," 92. "It is, indeed," Prescott concludes, "a noble monument of sagacity and erudition; and the student of history, and still more the historical compiler, will find himself unable to advance a single step among the early colo-

nial settlements of the New World without reference to the pages of Herrera." 93.

34 Antonio Pastor, a noted student of Spanish literature, regards Fernández de Oviedo's work as "the most entertaining collection of early 'Americana' that exists." Newton, cited in "Spanish Civilization in the Great Age of Discovery," *Great Age of Discovery*, 18; for Morison's opinion, *Admiral of the Ocean Sea*, 53.

35 Antonio de Herrera y Tordesillas, *Historia general de los hechos de los castellanos en las islas y tierra firme del mar Océano* (5 vols., Madrid, 1601–15); Ticknor, *Spanish Literature*, III, 217–18.

36 Edward P. Cheyney, *Dawn of a New Era* (New York and London, 1936), 1.

37 Germán Arciniegas, *Caribbean: Sea of the New World* (New York, 1946), 13.

38 Excellent critical discussions of the literature as well as the evidence are in Fiske, *Discovery of America*, I, 447 ff; Bourne, *Spain in America*, 67–68, 88, and for bibliography, 330 ff; Justin Winsor, *Columbus*, 538–55. The Hakluyt Society has printed the Vespucci letters; Clements R. Markham, *Letters of Amerigo Vespucci* (London, 1894); briefer extracts have been issued by the Old South Association, *Old South Leaflets*, No. 90.

39 Arciniegas, *Caribbean*, 14–15, 17–21, 45–46.

40 Channing, *History of the United States*, I, 45, 46; Fiske, *Discovery of America*, II, 34–37, 39, 44–46.

41 Channing, *History*, I, 43; Fiske, *Discovery of America*, II, 157, 159, 163.

42 Edward G. Bourne, "The Naming of America," *American His-*

torical *Review*, X (Oct. 1904), 41.

⁴³ On Waldseemüller *NCHA*, II, 147–48.

⁴⁴ Cleven, *Readings in Hispanic American History*, 98.

⁴⁵ *Ibid.*, 100.

⁴⁶ *Ibid.*, 102, 103.

⁴⁷ See Washington Irving, *Voyages of the Companions of Columbus* (London, 1831); *The Decades* of Peter Martyr contains a famous sketch of Balboa.

⁴⁸ Arciniegas, *Caribbean*, 82 ff.

⁴⁹ Bernal Díaz del Castillo, *The True History of the Conquest of Mexico* (New York, 1927), with an introduction by Arthur D. Howden Smith, was first published in London in 1800; it is as important for Cortés as for Díaz. See also Salvador de Madariaga, *Hernán Cortés Conqueror of México* (New York, 1941); Francis A. MacNutt, *Fernando Cortés and the Conquest of Mexico, 1485–1547* (New York, 1909); Prescott's *History of the Conquest of Mexico* remains, of course, incomparable. J. Bayard Morris, *Hernando Cortés Five Letters 1519–1526* (New York, 1929). See also A. P. Maudsley (ed. and tr.) Bernal Díaz del Castillo, *The True History of the Conquest of New Spain* (5 vols., London: The Hakluyt Society, 1909–16).

⁵⁰ They were so impressed that they often imaginatively projected what in fact was not there. See Fiske, *Discovery of America*, I, 125, citing Lewis Morgan, *Ancient Society* (New York, 1877), 186 n.: "The histories of Spanish America may be trusted in whatever relates to the acts of the Spaniards, and to the acts and personal characteristics of the Indians; in whatever relates to their weapons, implements and utensils, fabrics, food and raiment, and things of a similar character. But in whatever relates to Indian society and government, their social relations and plan of life, they are nearly worthless, because they learned nothing and knew nothing of either. We are at full liberty to reject them in these respects and commence anew; using any facts they may contain which harmonize with what is known of Indian society." Fiske summarizes both the material and the bibliography, I, 100–02. Among those who, before Morgan, expressed a like skepticism were William Robertson, the Scotch historian of Amercia, and Albert Gallatin, who was a philologist as well as a statesman. William Robertson, *History of America*, 9th ed. (London, 1800), III, 274, 281, J. A. Stevens, *Albert Gallatin* (Boston, 1884), 386–96.

⁵¹ Morris, *Hernando Cortés Five Letters* . . . xli–xlviii.

⁵² *Ibid.*, xli.

⁵³ *Ibid.*, xli–xliii.

⁵⁴ *Ibid.*, xli–xliii; Prescott, *Conquest*, II, 425.

⁵⁵ Morris, *Cortés* . . . *Letters*, 86–89. "For I am desirous that your Majesty should know of matters concerning this land, which is so great and marvellous that . . . your majesty may well call himself Emperor of it with no less reason than he now does of Germany." Morris, 31; see also 84–85. Prescott, II, 426.

⁵⁶ Prescott, I; II, 425 ff. Madariaga, *Cortés*, chs. xvi, xvii.

⁵⁷ Díaz, *True History of the Conquest, passim*.

⁵⁸ James A. Robertson has translated the narrative of Antonio Pigafetta, *Magellan's Voyage Round the World* (2 vols., Cleveland, 1906); Fiske, *Discovery of*

America, II, 195–211. Bourne, *Spain in America*, 120–21.

[59] Bourne, *Spain in America*, 132.

[60] Robertson, *Magellan's Voyage.*

[61] Ticknor, *Spanish Literature*, II, 36–37; Morris, *Cortés Letters*, xxix.

[62] Díaz, *History of the Conquest of Mexico;* on his general trustworthiness, Prescott, I, 473 n., who has reservations about it.

[63] Smith, introduction to Díaz, *The True History*, vi–xv.

[64] The best survey of this whole subject from the pen of one of the acknowledged masters is Herbert E. Bolton, *The Spanish Borderlands* (New Haven, 1921), to which an admirable critical bibliography is attached, 297 ff.

[65] Frederick W. Hodge (ed.), "The Narrative of Alvar Núñez Cabeza de Vaca," *Spanish Explorers in the United States, 1528–1543, Original Narratives of Early American History* (New York, 1907), 3. Cabeza's *Relación* was first printed in 1542 at Zamora, 126. See also A. F. A. and Fanny Bandelier (eds.), *The Journey of Alvar Núñez Cabeza de Vaca* (New York, 1905). The first printed reference to bison is in Hodge, 68 ff. Woodbury Lowery, *Spanish Settlements Within the Present Limits of the United States: Florida, 1562–1574* (New York, 1905). Edward W. Lawson, *The Discovery of Florida and its Discoverer Juan Ponce de León* (St. Augustine, 1946).

[66] Bolton's account is superlative, *Spanish Borderlands*, ch. 2.

[67] Theodore H. Lewis (ed.), "The Narrative of the Expedition of Hernando de Soto by the Gentleman of Elvás," *Spanish Explorers in the Southern United States*, 136; Hodge, ". . . Cabeza de Vaca," 136. First published in Portugal in 1557, *The Narrative of the Gentleman of Elvás* appeared in French in 1685. An English translation appeared in 1686, made from the French edition of 1685 (Hakluyt had already made an English rendering in 1609).

[68] T. Maynard, *De Soto and the Conquistadores* (New York, 1934).

[69] Ray A. Billington, *Westward Expansion* (New York, 1949), 22.

[70] Lewis, ". . . Gentleman of Elvás," 129–272.

[71] *Ibid.*, 233; Bolton, *Spanish Borderlands*, 78.

[72] Frederick W. Hodge (ed.), "The Narrative of the Expedition of Coronado, by Pedro Castañeda," *Spanish Explorers in the Southern United States*, 281–387.

[73] *Ibid.*, 284.

[74] Herbert E. Bolton, "The Mission as a Frontier Institution in the Spanish-American Colonies," *American Historical Review*, XXIII (Oct. 1917), Herbert E. Bolton and Mary Ross, *The Debatable Land* (Berkeley, Calif., 1925); John T. Lanning, *The Spanish Missions of Georgia* (Chapel Hill, N.C., 1935); Verne E. Chatelain, *The Defenses of Spanish Florida, 1565–1763* (Washington, D.C., 1941).

[75] The achievement of Spain in colonizing the new world is nothing short of startling, and the failure of historians of the United States really to take serious note of it is scarcely less so. As late as 1933, Herbert E. Bolton, pioneer student of American continental history, eloquently stressed the imperative need for a fuller comprehension of the epic of greater America. Yet the conventional phrases denoting the problem are more frequently used than creatively applied. Wrote Arthur M. Schlesinger and

Dixon Ryan Fox: "In the broad view of the New World the history of the United States, despite our fond appropriation of the term 'American,' is only local history." Herbert I. Priestley, *The Coming of the White Man, 1498–1848,* vol. I of A. M. Schlesinger, Sr., and D. R. Fox (eds.), *A History of American Life* (13 vols., New York, 1927–1948), xvii. Edward P. Cheyney, *European Background of American History, 1300–1600,* vol. 1 of Albert B. Hart (ed.), *The American Nation: A History* (New York, 1904), xxvii, 79.

CHAPTER III

1 The "rise and fall of New France," wrote R. G. Thwaites, "is the most dramatic chapter in American history." For Thwaites this was more than simply a dramatic episode, for "no history of the American nation can be considered complete that does not . . . outline the remarkable career of Canada under the French. . . ." R. G. Thwaites, *France in America, 1497–1763* (New York, 1905), xix; William B. Munro, *Crusaders of New France* (New Haven, 1918); George M. Wrong, *The Rise and Fall of New France* (2 vols., New York, 1928).
2 Francis Parkman, *Pioneers of France in the New World.* (Boston, 1927), xix.
3 *Ibid.,* 189, 191. H. P. Biggar, *Precursors of Jacques Cartier* (Ottawa, 1911).
4 Parkman, *Pioneers of France,* 231–32, where Parkman evaluates the controversial literature on this aspect of the subject. For

his own conclusion, 197. The letter in question has been reprinted in *Old South Leaflets,* No. 17. Wrong's opinion is stated in *Rise and Fall of New France,* I, 47–48.
5 Channing, *History of the United States,* I, 91. *NCHA* III, 184–98; Benjamin F. DeCosta, *Magazine of American History,* VI (Jan. 1881), 68–70.
6 Parkman, *Pioneers of France,* 203. The picture itself is reproduced in the Centenary Edition of Parkman's *Works.*
7 Parkman, *Pioneers of France,* 207.
8 Champlain, who followed Cartier, was inclined to belittle Cartier's contribution: W. L. Grant (ed.), *Voyages of Samuel de Champlain, 1604–1618, Original Narratives of Early American History* (New York, 1907), 22. Since Cartier's explorations took him inland almost nine hundred miles from the Atlantic and his achievement includes the discovery of the St. Lawrence, it is impossible to do so. H. P. Biggar, "The First Explorers of the North American Coast," *Age of Discovery,* 144. See also, Henry S. Burrage (ed.), *Early English and French Voyages, 1534–1608, Original Narratives of Early American History* (New York, 1906); H. P. Biggar (ed.), *The Voyages of Jacques Cartier* (Ottawa, 1924). Biggar has also edited *A Collection of Documents Relating to Jacques Cartier and the Sieur de Roberval* (Ottawa, 1930). Stephen Leacock has written an interesting biography of Cartier, *Mariner of St. Malo* (Toronto, 1930). The pertinent Cartier writings are reprinted in Henry S. Burrage (ed.), *Early English and French Voyages, Original Narratives of*

Early American History (New York, 1930).

9 Parkman, *Pioneers of France,* 185–86, 263 ff. Grant (ed.), *Voyages of Champlain,* reprints important materials, all the more so because the best source on Champlain is Champlain himself. See also E. G. and A. N. Bourne, *The Voyages and Explorations of Samuel de Champlain 1604–1616 Narrated by Himself* (2 vols., New York, 1906); H. P. Biggar, *The Early Trading Companies of New France* (Toronto, 1901), besides its significance as a monograph, contains a most valuable bibliography. *NCHA,* IV, 103–22.

10 For bibliographical details of this and other Champlain writings, Grant (ed.), *Voyages of Champlain,* "Introduction." On Champlain's experience in the Spanish colonial world, Wrong, *Rise and Fall of New France,* I, 137–39. When Parkman recounted these events he relied upon the original of Champlain then in possession of Aymar de Clermont, Seigneur de Chastes, patron of Champlain, *Pioneers of France,* 243, n. 1. Parkman described the journal as having been written "in clear, decisive, and somewhat formal handwriting of the sixteenth century, garnished with sixty-one colored pictures, in a style of art which a child of ten might emulate," 242. Burrage, *Early English and French Voyages,* 35, gives additional bibliographical information.

11 Grant (ed.), *Voyages of Champlain,* 5, 6.

12 John M. Brown, *Collections of the Maine Historical Society* (1876), 1st ser., VII, cited by Grant (ed.), *Voyages of Champlain,* 10.

13 Grant (ed.), *Voyages of Champlain,* 10.

14 *Ibid.*

15 Parkman, *Pioneers of France,* ch. 2; Wrong, *Rise and Fall of New France,* 78 ff. P. Gaffarel, *Histoire du Brésil français* (Paris, 1878).

16 Parkman, *Pioneers of France,* 24–27; Wrong, *Rise and Fall of New France,* I, 78–82. A. Heulhard, *Villegagnon, roi d'Amérique* (Paris, 1897).

17 Parkman, *Pioneers of France,* 1–4, chs. 3–7.

18 *Ibid.,* 4–5.

19 The quotation of Ribault is from Richard Hakluyt cited by Parkman, *Pioneers of France,* 37. P. Gaffarel, *Histoire de la Floride française* (Paris, 1875). Louise P. Kellogg, a principal authority on these matters, has written the biography of Ribault for the *DAB,* XV, 533. Marc Lescarbot, *Histoire de la Nouvelle France* (Paris, 1609), is one of the most significant primary sources.

20 The translation is in Hakluyt's *Divers Voyages* (London, 1582). See Parkman, *Pioneers of France,* 38 n.; Channing, *History,* I, 94–98. Jean Ribaut [Ribault], *The Whole and True Discovery of Terra Florida* (De Land, Florida, 1927), a volume published by the Florida State Historical Society with notes by H. P. Biggar and a biography by Jeannette T. Connor. John G. Shea, "Ancient Florida," in *NCHA,* II, 231–98. Daniel Garrison Brinton, *Notes on the Floridian Peninsula; Its Literary History, Indian Tribes and Antiquities* (Philadelphia, 1859), is the study of a pioneer anthropologist.

21 Parkman, *Pioneers of France,* 48–67. See Richard Hakluyt, *Principal Navigations, Voyages, Traffiques, and Discoveries of*

the English Nation, Everyman Library ed. (8 vols., New York, 1907), VI, 227; cf. George B. Parks, Richard Hakluyt and the English Voyages, American Geographical Society, Special Publication No. 10 (New York, 1928), 263.

22 The translation from Laudonnière is cited in Parkman, Pioneers of France, 53. See the biography of Laudonnière by Louise P. Kellogg, DAB, XI, 30.

23 Stefan Lorant, The New World, The First Pictures of America (New York, 1946), is the most readily accessible reference for Jacques Le Moyne. See particularly Lorant's note on Le Moyne and the Brevis Narratio, 280–81, 30–31.

24 Fiske, Discovery of America, II, 511–22; NCHA, II, 260–83.

CHAPTER IV

1 C. M. Andrews, The Colonial Period of American History (4 vols., New Haven, 1934–38), I, 25. On this chapter and those following C. M. Andrews and F. G. Davenport, Guide to the Manuscript Material for the History of the United States to 1783, in the British Museum, in minor London Archives, and in Libraries of Oxford and Cambridge (Washington, 1908), is indispensable.

2 Franklin T. McCann, English Discovery of America to 1585 (New York, 1952), who writes, "We can hardly understand the English discovery of America before 1585 unless we first consider English knowledge of the earth." The fundamental volumes dealing with English geographical concepts in this period are by E. G. R. Taylor, Tudor Geogra-

phy, 1485–1583 (London, 1930), and Late Tudor and Early Stuart Geography, 1583–1650 (London, 1934). James A. Williamson has made these issues his special province; see his Maritime Enterprise, 1485–1588 (Oxford, 1913). "Yet for sixty years after 1492 not a single geographical work of any importance was published in England to record an English interest in the new age or in the science that was expanding to account for it." G. B. Parks, R. Hakluyt, 5. C. N. Robinson and John Leyland, "The Literature of the Sea," in The Cambridge History of English Literature, A. W. Ward and A. R. Waller (eds.) (14 vols., Cambridge and New York, 1907–17), IV, 77–79. Parks has compiled a highly serviceable bibliography, "List of English Books on Geography and Travel to 1600," Parks, Hakluyt, 269–77.

3 H. P. Biggar, "The First Explorers of the North American Coast," A. P. Newton (ed.), Great Age of Discovery, 132–33. James A. Williamson, The Voyages of the Cabots and the English Discovery of North America under Henry VII and Henry VIII (London, 1929). For Andrews' evaluation, Colonial Period, I, 19, n. 1.

4 Biggar, "The First Explorers of the North American Coast," 141. Henry S. Burrage, (ed.), Early English and French Voyages, Original Narratives of Early American History (New York, 1930). These narratives are "chiefly from Hakluyt."

5 William Wood, Elizabethan Sea-Dogs (New Haven, 1921), 14–15.

6 McCann, English Discovery of America, 69–97; Robinson and Leyland, Cambridge History of

English Literature, IV, 80–85, 87–88.

[7] McCann, *English Discovery of America,* 70.

[8] The quotation from Lee is cited in James E. Gillespie, *The Influence of Overseas Expansion on England to 1700* (New York, 1920), 251. E. J. Payne, "The New World," *The Cambridge Modern History,* A. W. Ward, G. W. Prothero, and Stanley Leathes (eds.) (14 vols., New York and London, 1902–24), I, 56–58. G. Dudok, *Sir Thomas More and His Utopia* (Amsterdam, 1924); Parks, *Hakluyt,* 6–7.

[9] Parks, *Hakluyt,* 6–7.

[10] *Ibid.* See also, McCann, *English Discovery of America,* 49, 84–85.

[11] Parks, *Hakluyt,* 8; McCann, *English Discovery of America,* 187–88.

[12] McCann, *English Discovery of America,* 187–88.

[13] *Ibid.*

[14] Parks, *Hakluyt,* 7.

[15] Andrews, *Colonial Period,* I, 53.

[16] "The need of knowledge of America cannot be too strongly emphasized." Parks, *Hakluyt,* 99. For an account of the steady growth of knowledge concerning America in Europe, consult Justin Winsor, *Cartier to Frontenac* (Boston and New York, 1894). Beazley, *The Dawn of Modern Geography,* II, 17–111.

[17] Parks, *Hakluyt,* 14, 39–45. A. J. Gerson, *The Organization and Early History of the Muscovy Company* (New York, 1912). On the significance of Russia and the connections of the Merchant Adventurers and the Russian (and Muscovy) Company, Boise Penrose, *Travel and Discovery in the Renaissance, 1420–1620* (New York, 1962), 213–17, 239–43.

[18] Gillespie, *The Influence of Over-seas Expansion,* 234; Parks, *Hakluyt,* 21. "The fact that the world had materially changed was at length made plain." 22. McCann, *English Discovery of America,* believes Eden to have been more important in promoting colonization and discovery than Hakluyt, xiii, 121–37.

[19] Eden's "death in 1576 transferred to the younger Hakluyt the duties of historian; but to Eden remains the credit for breaking out a path from English insularity, for publishing the first important works on geography since Caxton." Parks, *Hakluyt,* 23. Edward Arber (ed.), *The First Three English Books on America* (London, 1885). Robinson and Leyland, *Cambridge History of English Literature,* IV, 80–81; Gillespie, *The Influence of Overseas Expansion,* 234.

[20] Giambattista Ramusio (1485–1577) was Hakluyt's predecessor and in some respects his model. Educated at Venice and Padua, he went into the service of the Venetian Republic in 1505. He served as secretary of the Senate in 1515 and became in 1533 the secretary of the Council of Ten. *Navigationi e viaggi* appeared in three volumes. Vol. I was published in 1550, III in 1556. The second volume appeared posthumously (1579).

[21] Burrage, *Early English and French Voyages,* 113; Gillespie, *Overseas Expansion,* 235. Hawkins' own account is *A True Declaration of the Troublesome Voyage of Mr. John Hawkins to the parts of Guinea and the West Indies in the years of our Lord 1567 and 1568.* J. A. Williamson, *Sir John Hawkins* (Oxford, 1927).

22 Burrage, *Early English and French Voyages*, 113.
23 Parkman, *Pioneers of France*, 89-95.
24 *Ibid.*, 91.
25 Channing, *History of the United States*, I, 120. For the original account, *The World Encompassed by Sir Francis Drake, carefully Collected out of the notes of Master Francis Fletcher.* . . . (London, 1628). Burrage, *Early English and French Voyages*, 152-73.
26 Vilhjalmur Stefansson (ed.), *The Three Voyages of Martin Frobisher* (2 vols., London, 1938). David B. Quinn (ed.), *The Voyages and Colonizing Enterprises of Sir Humphrey Gilbert* (London, 1940). The Gilbert voyages are in Burrage, *Early English and French Voyages*, 179-222; Gillespie, *Overseas Expansion*, 235.
27 Burrage, *Early English and French Voyages*, 177, 178, from which the quotation is taken. Burrage gives sufficient bibliographical data on the writings of the Gilbert ventures. Parks, *Hakluyt*, 78.
28 Parks, *Hakluyt*, 70-71; Gillespie, *Overseas Expansion*, 235.
29 Parks, *Hakluyt*, 70.
30 *Ibid.*, 78-79.
31 "Whatever was known of the Newfoundland region, the country south of it was virtually unknown in England. . . . Few Englishmen had been known to sail any distance from the fishing banks. Foreigners had been more active; but their records were not available in England. In making the turn south Gilbert had sailed into a void." Parks, *Hakluyt*, 99.
32 Among the many studies of Raleigh, Milton Waldman, *Raleigh* (London, 1928), is one of the best. Louise Creighton, "Sir Walter Raleigh," *Cambridge History of English Literature*, IV, 59-65. Burrage, *Early English and French Voyages*, 303 ff.
33 Burrage, *Early English and French Voyages*, 233-41.
34 Parks, *Hakluyt*, 112. Channing, *History*, I, 128. A number of the accounts of early voyages to Virginia are reprinted in Burrage, *Early English and French Voyages*, 247-321 (among which John White's writings are included). For Hariot, see *Narrative of the First English Plantation of Virginia* (London, 1588). Bibliographies may be found in *NCHA*, III, 121-26. Stefan Lorant, *The New World*, reproduces White's watercolors, 185-224. Special mention should be made of the following: Henry Stevens, *Thomas Hariot, the Mathematician, the Philosopher and the Scholar* (London, 1900); Randolph G. Adams, "An Effort to Identify John White," *American Historical Review*, XLI (Oct. 1935), 87-91; Wesley F. Craven has written the biography of White in *DAB*, XX, 110-11.
35 Data on this particular point are summarized by Parks, *Hakluyt*, 178 ff.
36 James A. Williamson contributed an introduction to Parks' *Hakluyt*. The quotation is at xiv; for Parks' own statement, 2. See also comments, 3. Hakluyt was much influenced by his uncle, a scholarly lawyer of the same name. Parks discusses this somewhat obscure figure and assesses his influence, 25-28. Parks ultimately concludes: "It is hardly too much to say that Hakluyt's is the most important historical work of the century," 183. On the Cartier translation, 64; on Ribault, 71-72, 114.
37 Full bibliographical details on

The Particular Discourse on the Western Planting . . . (1584) are given by Parks, *Hakluyt,* 261, 87–88. Burrage, *Early English and French Voyages,* xix, is less full. Four manuscript copies apparently were made. Hakluyt never printed the *Discourse,* and until the mid-nineteenth century the four copies were believed lost. The president of Bowdoin College, seeking data on the history of Maine, discovered a copy in 1867. It was published by the Maine Historical Society in 1877. See Parks' comments, 90, 91. Other interpretations mentioned above are supported by Parks, 110.

38 Parks, *Hakluyt,* 63–64. The bibliography of Hakluyt's writings is adequate on every score—even for the specialist: Appendix III, "Hakluyt's Writings," 260–68. Henry Stevens, *Bibliotheca Americana* (London, 1861).

39 The quotation from Hakluyt is in Parks, 123.

40 Parks' analysis of the *Discourse* is cogent and convincing, 72, 211–12.

41 Lorant, *New World,* 274 ff; 283–84; Parks, *Hakluyt,* 161–63.

42 Parks, *Hakluyt,* 130, 175–76.

43 Parks appraises Hakluyt's work in whole and in part in *Hakluyt,* 130. He believes the *Principal Navigations* takes its place "with the chronicles of Holinshed and Stow, with Camden's *Britannia,* with the historical plays of the new theater and with Spenser's *Faërie Queene,*" 131–32, and further, 178 ff., all of which, however, contain mythical elements. "Beginnings" such as "from the time of King Arthur" should not be taken literally. Criticism has been directed at Hakluyt's accuracy in editing. He made some changes in Cabot's

record of the first expedition to Newfoundland and took certain liberties with his materials generally. Despite the eminence of the critics, it must be remembered that Hakluyt was a sixteenth-century scholar and, as Parks insists, "he was not better than his time." 182 ff.

CHAPTER V

1 Jarvis M. Morse, "John Smith and his Critics; A Chapter in Colonial Historiography," *Journal of Southern History,* I (May 1935), 123–37; Wilberforce Eames, *A Bibliography of Captain John Smith* (New York, 1927). Lyon Gardiner Tyler (ed.), *Narratives of Early Virginia 1606–1625, Original Narratives of Early American History* (New York, 1930), 27–29, which also contains enough of Smith for ordinary purposes. An excellent edition, however, was made by Edward Arber, *Travels and Works of Captain John Smith . . .* (2 vols., Birmingham, England, 1884).

2 *A true relation of such occurrences and accidents of noate as hath hapned in Virginia since the first planting of that Collony* (London, 1608). Another edition of Smith's works is by Charles Deane (Boston, 1866). For an interpretation which does not agree with that given above, see John Spencer Bassett, "The Historians," *CHAL,* I, 16.

3 Moses Coit Tyler, *A History of American Literature During the Colonial Period 1607–1765* (2 vols. in one, New York and London, 1898), I, 21.

4 Morse, "John Smith and his Critics," 123–27; *LHUS,* I, 32–33; J. G. Fletcher, *John Smith—*

Also Pocahontas (New York, 1928).

5 Kraus, *History of American History* (New York, 1937), 24–25.

6 Tyler, *American Literature*, I, ch. 2. James Truslow Adams has written the biography in the *DAB*. J. Franklin Jameson, *The History of Historical Writing in America* (Boston and New York, 1891), is skeptical of Smith, especially 11. Also critical of the present viewpoint is E. K. Chatterton, *Captain John Smith* (New York and London, 1927). *LHUS*, III, 725–27.

7 *Generall Historie of Virginia, New-England and the Summer Isles* (London, 1624). Details of editions and reprints are given in Tyler (ed.), *Narratives of Early Virginia*, 291–93.

8 Jameson, *Historical Writing*, 11 ff.; Chatterton, *Smith*, 141 ff. Fletcher, *John Smith*. Of great historiographical interest is an early historical effort of Henry Adams, "Captain John Smith," *North American Review*, CIV (Jan. 1867), 1–30.

9 Tyler (ed.), *Narratives of Early Virginia*, 116–17.

10 Perry Miller and Thomas H. Johnson, *The Puritans: A Sourcebook of Their Writings* (New York, 1938), 398.

11 *Ibid.*, 400.

12 Franklin B. Dexter in *NCHA*, III, 264–69, also 283–88. Worthington C. Ford (ed.), *History of Plymouth Plantation*, Massachusetts Historical Society (2 vols., Boston, 1921). Samuel Eliot Morison contributed the biographical sketch in the *DAB* and has prepared a new edition of the *History* (New York, 1953). It is to be observed that the Bible with which Bradford was so familiar was the Geneva Bible rather than the King James

version. On his style, E. F. Bradford, "Conscious Art in Bradford's History of Plymouth Plantation," *New England Quarterly*, I (Apr. 1928), 133.

13 There is neither an adequate biography nor a full bibliography of Bradford. Morison's writings are best for both. *LHUS*, III, 412–14.

14 Miller and Johnson, *Puritans*, 98.

15 *Ibid.*, 101.

16 *Ibid.*, 102.

17 *Ibid.*, 87–89, sums up the views of modern criticism.

18 *NCHA*, III, 286; Jameson, *Historical Writing*, 14–15; Tyler, *American Literature*, I, 117.

19 Nathaniel Morton, *New-England's Memoriall* (Cambridge, Mass., 1669). Miller and Johnson, *Puritans*, 81–82.

20 Samuel Eliot Morison, *The Puritan Pronaos: Studies in the Intellectual Life of New England in the Seventeenth Century* (New York, 1936), 174–75, 118.

21 Quoted in Perry Miller, *Orthodoxy in Massachusetts* (Cambridge, Mass., 1933), 28. The author of the second comment was Giles Widdowes; he is cited by Miller, 41.

22 S. E. Morison, *Builders of the Bay Colony* (Boston, 1930), 51–104, is one of the most penetrating volumes written on the leaders of this period, including Winthrop. Robert C. Winthrop, *Life and Letters of John Winthrop* (2 vols., Boston, 1864–67). James K. Hosmer (ed.), *Winthrop's Journal, Original Narratives of Early American History* (2 vols., New York, 1908). There is a bibliographical guide to reprints and editions in *LHUS*, III, 782. Of particular moment are Stanley Gray, "The Political Thought of John Winthrop," *New England Quarterly*, III (Oct.

1930), 681–705, and Vernon Louis Parrington, *Main Currents in American Thought* (3 vols., New York, 1927–30), I, 38–50. Perry Miller, *The New England Mind* (New York, 1939), 422–28.

23 Hosmer, *Winthrop's Journal*, I, 240.

24 *Ibid.*, I, 116–17.

25 The best and most incisive brief analysis of Puritanism is Miller's and Johnson's, "Introduction," *Puritans*, 1–79, and Miller's *New England Mind* is one of the ripest studies in the entire field of ideas in America. See, particularly, chs. 1, 3, 4–9. One of Miller's great contributions is the clarification of the role of Ramus in the intellectual history of Puritanism; see Appendix A, "The Literature of Ramus' Logic in Europe," 493–501.

26 Morison, *Puritan Pronaos*, chs. 2, 7.

27 Brooks Adams, *The Emancipation of Massachusetts: The Dream and the Reality* (Boston and New York, 1919); Parrington, *Main Currents of American Thought*, I, 38–75, 118–47; S. H. Brockunier, *The Irrepressible Democrat Roger Williams* (New York, 1940), 282–89. George E. Ellis, *The Puritan Age and Rule in the Colony of Massachusetts Bay, 1629–1685* (New York, 1927), 143–44.

28 Miller and Johnson, *Puritans*, 181, 184, 188. Miller, *New England Mind*, 416–19, 429–30.

29 Miller and Johnson, *Puritans*, 22.

30 Theodore Hornberger, "Puritanism and Science: The Relationship Revealed in the Writings of John Cotton," *New England Quarterly*, X (Sept. 1937), 503–15; Hornberger, "The Date, the Source, and the Significance of Cotton Mather's Interest in Science," *American Literature*, VI (Jan. 1935), 413–20, S. E. Morison, "The Harvard School of Astronomy in the Seventeenth Century," *New England Quarterly*, VII (Mar. 1934), 3–24. Miller and Johnson are superlative on this aspect of Puritan thought, *Puritans*, 729–38. Miller, *New England Mind*, 221. Morison, *Pronaos*, 234–69.

31 Miller, *New England Mind*, 111–53, 271–73; but cf. John Dewey, *Logic the Theory of Inquiry* (New York, 1938), 81–98; John Dewey, *Reconstruction in Philosophy* (New York, 1920), 103–31.

32 Miller and Johnson, *Puritans*, 82–90. See also Morison, *Pronaos*, ch. 8.

33 "Theirs was a social structure with its corner-stone resting on a book." Tyler, *American Literature*, I, 89.

34 London, 1648.

35 Parrington, *Main Currents in American Thought*, I, 53–62; but see Miller and Johnson, *Puritans*, 291.

36 George L. Walker, *Thomas Hooker, Preacher, Founder, Democrat* (New York, 1891), makes Hooker a democrat. This and other studies with a similar orientation should be checked against Perry Miller's "Thomas Hooker and the Democracy of Early Connecticut," *New England Quarterly*, IV (Oct. 1931), 663–712, and Andrews, *Colonial Period*, II, 67–99. James Truslow Adams has written the sketch in the *DAB*. See Tyler's comments, *American Literature*, I, 193–203. There is a full bibliography in *LHUS*, III, 568–69.

37 Tyler, *American Literature*, I, 142.

38 Morison, *Builders of the Bay Colony*, 128–29. On his "atro-

cious" English and the reasons for it, 127. *LHUS*, III, 718–19.

39 Miller and Johnson, *Puritans*, 121.

40 Tyler, *American Literature*, I, 212.

41 *Ibid.*, I, 213.

42 Henry Bamford Parkes, "John Cotton and Roger Williams Debate Toleration, 1644–1652," *New England Quarterly*, IV (Oct. 1931), 735–56; Andrews, *Colonial Period*, I, 462–95. J. H. Tuttle, "Writings of Rev. John Cotton," *Bibliographical Essays: A Tribute to Wilberforce Eames* (Cambridge, 1924), 363–80. James T. Adams is the author of the essay in the *DAB*. See *LHUS*, III, 456–57.

43 Brockunier, *Roger Williams*, chs. 4, 7–8; 125.

44 J. Franklin Jameson (ed.), *Johnson's Wonder-Working Providence 1628–1651, Original Narratives of Early American History* (New York, 1910).

45 *Ibid.*, 21.

46 Cited in Morison, *Builders*, 53.

47 *LHUS*, III, 252.

48 Miller, *New England Mind*, 229–31.

49 *Ibid.*, 229; Miller and Johnson, *Puritans*, 98; Hosmer, *Winthrop's Journal*, II, 18.

50 Miller, *New England Mind*, 228.

51 *Ibid.*

52 Thomas Letchford, *Plain Dealing; Or, News from New England* (London, 1642) in *Collections of the Massachusetts Historical Society*, third series, III (1833), 25–128. E. E. Hale (ed.), "Note-Book Kept by Thomas Letchford, Esq., Lawyer, in Boston, Massachusetts Bay, from June 27, 1638, to July 29, 1641," *Transactions and Collections of the American Antiquarian Society*, VII (1885).

53 Miller, *New England Mind*, 454.

54 Miller and Johnson, *Puritans*, 108.

55 Andrews, *Colonial Period*, II, 363, n. 1. Morton's activity inspired John Lothrop Motley's novels *Morton's Hope: Or the Memoirs of a Provincial* (2 vols., New York, 1839) and *Merry-Mount: A Romance of the Massachusetts Colony* (2 vols., New York and Cambridge, Mass., 1849) and Nathaniel Hawthorne's story "The Maypole of Merry Mount."

56 Cf., however, Nathaniel Ward's *Simple Cobbler of Agawam* (1647). Morison, *Builders of the Bay Colony*, 217–43, is the best sketch.

57 Cited in Kraus, 60.

58 The quotation is from Mather's *Magnalia Christi Americana* (London, 1702) and is cited in Miller and Johnson, *Puritans*, 503.

59 Tyler, *American Literature*, II, 133. William Hubbard, *A Narrative of the Troubles with the Indians in New-England*, Samuel G. Drake (ed.) (2 vols., Roxbury, Mass., 1865).

60 The work was produced in 1677 and later appeared in England with the title *The Present State of New England*. William Hubbard, *A Generall History of New-England, from the Discovery to MDCLXXX*. Hubbard was called "the careless Hubbard" by Alexander Young; Tyler, *American Literature*, II, 134.

61 Tyler, *Ibid.*, II, 136.

62 *Ibid.*, II, 135.

63 *Collections of the Massachusetts Historical Society*, second series, Vols. V-VI (1815).

64 Morison, *Pronaos*, 176–81, says most of what needs to be known with charm and wit. Kenneth B. Murdock, "William Hubbard's 'Narrative.' " *Proceedings of the*

564 / NOTES

American Antiquarian Society, LII (1943), 15–37.

[65] Samuel G. Drake (ed.), *The Old Indian Chronicle: Being a Collection of Exceeding Rare Tracts Written and Published in the Time of King Philip's War. . . .* (Boston, 1836). Charles H. Lincoln (ed.), *Narratives of the Indian Wars, 1675–1699, Original Narratives of Early American History* (New York, 1913), contains Cotton Mather's and Mary Rowlandson's narratives. Morison, *Pronaos,* discusses Captain Church, Mrs. Rowlandson, and Cotton Mather in relation to their activities as historians of the Indian wars, ch. 8. Tyler, *American Literature,* I, 146–57.

[66] George H. Haynes, *Representation and Suffrage in Massachusetts, 1620–1691* (Baltimore, 1894); Brooks Adams, *Emancipation of Massachusetts;* T. J. Wertenbaker, *The First Americans* (New York, 1929), chs. 5–6, 10, 13; James T. Adams, *Provincial Society* (New York, 1927), chs. 2, 5, 9; Perry Miller, "The Half-way Covenant," *New England Quarterly,* VI (Dec. 1933).

[67] John Norton, *The Heart of N-England rent* (1659), cited in Miller and Johnson, *Puritans,* 379. Miller, *New England Mind,* 230–31.

[68] Miller and Johnson, *Puritans,* 379.

[69] *Ibid.,* 185.

[70] These events are recounted in *Ibid.,* 185–86. There was also a threat of the Anglican Church becoming the established church in the colonies.

[71] Tyler, *American Literature,* II, 73.

[72] *Ibid.,* II, 64–67. Consult *LHUS,* III, 640–44, for full bibliography of Cotton Mather; for Increase Mather, 644–46. Thomas J.

Holmes has compiled *Increase Mather: A Bibliography of His Works* (2 vols., Cleveland, 1913). The best full-length biography is Kenneth B. Murdock, *Increase Mather: The Foremost American Puritan* (Cambridge, 1925), and he also contributed the sketch for the *DAB.* For revealing selections, Miller and Johnson, *Puritans, 335–40, 340–48, 348–50,* and *passim.*

[73] Tyler, *American Literature,* II, 74. Adams, *Emancipation of Massachusetts,* 66.

[74] Tyler, *American Literature,* II, 74.

[75] In Kraus, 66.

[76] Charles Francis Adams, *Massachusetts, Its Historians and Its History* (Boston, 1893), 67.

[77] Tyler, however, felt that "as an historian, he was unequal to his high opportunity." *American Literature,* II, 83.

[78] Barrett Wendell's study, *Cotton Mather: The Puritan Priest* (New York, 1891, reissued, 1926), remains standard. Kenneth Murdock's essay in the *DAB* carries the authority of the specialist. Parrington has interesting points to make about all the Mathers, "The Mather Dynasty," *Main Currents in American Thought,* I, 98-117.

[79] Nor was Puritan faith, as already pointed out, based exclusively upon reason. The Bible was, of course, the main authority. But since the Bible did not and could not tell all, reason was required to interpret it. Miller, in a brilliant passage, makes the necessary qualification: "That Protestantism appealed to the authority of the Bible is a platitude of history. That the Calvinists were vehement asserters of its finality is also common knowledge. What is frequently for-

gotten is that without a Bible, this piety would have confronted chaos. It could not have found guidance in reason, because divine reason is above and beyond the human; not in the church, because God is not committed to preserving the orthodoxy or purity of any institution; not in immediate inspiration, because inward promptings are as apt to come from the Devil as from God; not from experimental science, because providence is arbitrary and unpredictable; not from philosophy, because philosophy arises from the senses, which are deceptive, or from innate ideas, which are corrupted, or from definitions of the attributes, which are mental creations. Unless the formless transcendence consents, at some moment in time, to assume the form of man and to speak 'after a humane manner,' men will have nothing to go upon. In the Bible God has so spoken. He has not therein uttered the naked truth about Himself, He has not revealed His essence; His secret will remain secret still, as we witness daily in the capricious orderings of providence. The Bible contains His revealed will, tells men what is expected, but does not explain why, for if it were explained men could never understand their relation to the whole drama of creation." *New England Mind,* 19, 20.

[80] Morison, *Builders,* 125–26.

[81] Thomas J. Wertenbaker, *The Puritan Oligarchy* (New York, 1947), ix, chs. 5–6, 9–10. Brockunier, *Roger Williams,* chs. 20–21. Morison, *Builders,* 56–57; James Truslow Adams, *Founding of New England* (Boston, 1921), 144, 419, 154, 365; Miller, *New England Mind,* chs. 3–4. Adams,

Emancipation of Massachusetts, 2.

[82] Brooks Adams, *Emancipation of Massachusetts;* Ralph Barton Perry, *Puritanism and Democracy* (New York, 1944), 3–61. Parrington, *Main Currents in American Thought,* I, 16–75. Adams, *Emancipation of Massachusetts,* 9–10.

[83] Wertenbaker, *Puritan Oligarchy,* 343–44: "the nation was founded neither upon the ideals and institutions of the Pilgrims nor of the Puritans who followed them."

[84] Adams, *Emancipation of Massachusetts,* 34, 41 n. 1. Andrews, *Colonial Period,* I, 269 n. 2; 291 n. 1. Adams, *Founding of New England,* 456, 278.

[85] Herbert L. Osgood, "Political Ideas of the Puritans," *Political Science Quarterly,* VI (June, Sept., Dec. 1896), 3, with which the interpretation given in this chapter does not agree. Liberalism and tolerance were alien to the framework of Puritan thought: Miller, *Orthodoxy in Massachusetts,* 61–62. Adams, *Emancipation of Massachusetts,* 6, 42–44. Miller, *New England Mind,* 91–92; C. K. Shipton, "A Plea for Puritanism," *American Historical Review,* XL (Apr. 1935), 460–67. Also the same author's "The New England Clergy of the Glacial Age," *Publications of the Colonial Society of Massachusetts,* XXXII (1937), 25–54; "The New England Frontier," *New England Quarterly,* X (Mar. 1937), 25–36. Kenneth B. Murdock, "The Puritan Tradition in American Literature," *The Reinterpretation of American Literature,* Norman Foerster (ed.) (Cambridge, 1949).

[86] Miller, *Orthodoxy in Massachusetts,* 162.

[87] Then, continued Richard Mather,

"We see not how another can be lawfull; and therefore if a company of people shall come hither, and here set up and practise another we pray you thinke not much, if we cannot promise to approve of them." Cited in Miller, *Orthodoxy in Massachusetts,* 162; also 163. "It appears to me that if ever a case could be made out for religious persecution it was in early Massachusetts Bay. The Colony had not been founded with a view to establishing religious liberty. The phrase 'liberty of conscience' which the puritans frequently used, did not mean to them what it means to-day. Their consciences had been hampered in England by the necessity to subscribe to religious tests and oaths, by conformity, by the difficulty of living the good life in a corrupt atmosphere; they sought a refuge where they would have liberty to live according to their own consciences. For the consciences of Anglicans and sectaries they were not concerned. Toleration had never been offered or promised to the immigrants. 'The design of our first Planters,' wrote John Cotton, 'was not Toleration; but were professed Enemies of it . . . their business was to settle, and (as much as in them lay) secure Religion to Posterity, according to that way which they believed was of God.' An invitation to all sects to take refuge in New England might attract 'so many as would sinke our small vessel; whereas in that greater ship of England, there is no such danger of those multitudes to founder the same.' " Cited in Morison, *Builders,* 115–16.

88 Hosmer, *Winthrop's Journal,* II, 238, 239.

89 Miller and Johnson, *Puritans,* 209–10.

90 Miller, *Orthodoxy in Massachusetts,* 173.

91 "Older writers, particularly in New England and Virginia, found in the words 'liberties, franchises, and immunities' something akin to universal rights. No such interpretation is possible. The words are to be taken literally, as meaning just what they were understood to mean in England at that time. They have nothing to do with civil liberty, self-government, or democracy; they were strictly legal, tenurial, and financial in their application." Andrews, *Colonial Period,* I. 86 n. 1. See also Morison, *Builders,* 83. J. T. Adams, *Founding of New England,* 143–44. See, however, Morison, *Builders,* 85, 86; Miller, *Orthodoxy in Massachusetts,* 37.

92 Morison, *Builders,* 126. "When the discipline was carried to America, it was put immediately to uses exactly opposite to those it had served in England. Instead of being the shield of an attacking party, it suddenly became the platform of a ruling oligarchy; instead of being invoked to delimit the sway of kings and prelates, it was now employed to rule a populace. Whereas the supporters of the polity had formerly stifled its democratic tendencies to preserve their respectability, they now were compelled to chain them to maintain their power. Consequently, though they carried over the idea of limitation of church officers by the fundamental law of God and by the corporate will of the society, they now had to make sure that such limitation would not prevent the ministers from holding the throttle." Miller, *Orthodoxy in*

Massachusetts, 176; see also 53. Morison, *Puritan Pronaos,* 7.

93 Ernest Sutherland Bates, *American Faith* (New York, 1940), 9. J. T. Adams, *Founding of New England,* 143–44. Sanford H. Cobb, *The Rise of Religious Liberty in America* (New York, 1902).

94 The controversy, of course, is much wider in scope than Puritanism and New England. It begins in the twentieth century with the work of Max Weber (1904–05). Weber's thesis is presented in *The Protestant Ethic and the Spirit of Capitalism* (London, 1934). Although Weber's analysis has certain connections with Marx, the viewpoint is actually opposed to economic determinism. Indeed, it has been argued that Weber's thesis is primarily a psychological interpretation of economic causation. See H. M. Robertson, *Aspects of the Rise of Economic Individualism.* (Cambridge, England, 1935), which remains the most distinguished critique of Weber and his followers. R. H. Tawney, *Religion and the Rise of Capitalism* (New York, 1926), the work of a leading British historian, is the classic in this field. The works of S. E. Morison and James T. Adams, already cited, represent the most important American versions of the general controversy. Harold J. Laski has brilliantly presented the leading cultural and intellectual facets in *The Rise of European Liberalism* (London, 1936). Note, however, Miller's comments, *New England Mind,* 43, and Herbert W. Schnieder, "The Puritan Tradition," *Wellsprings of the American Spirit,* F. E. Johnson (ed.) (New York, 1948), 1–13. These concepts are of continuing importance; they are more fully explored as they later impinge on altering developments.

95 Miller, *New England Mind,* 398 ff.; Miller and Johnson, *Puritans,* 383–85, 396–400.

96 This point is admirably instanced by John Cotton in a letter to Lord Saye and Sele: "Nor neede your Lordship feare (which yet I speake with submission to your Lordships better judgment) that this corse will lay such a foundation, as nothing but a mere democracy can be built upon it. Bodine [Bodin] confesseth, that though it be *status popularis,* where a people choose their own governors; yet the government is not a democracy, if it be administred, not by the people, but by the governors, whether one (for them it is a monarchy, though elective) or by many, for then (as you know) it is aristocracy. In which respect it is, that church government is justly denied (even by Mr. Robinson) to be democratical, though the people choose their own officers and rulers." Miller and Johnson, *Puritans,* 211.

97 Miller, *Orthodoxy in Massachusetts,* 176; Morison, *Builders of the Bay Colony,* 85–86; Wertenbaker, *Puritan Oligarchy,* 339–40.

98 See above, 107.

99 Miller, *Orthodoxy in Massachusetts,* 13, 21, 47–48. "The Congregational polity resulted from an elaborate preparation; it was based upon a complex body of Biblical exegesis that could not be mastered on a single voyage." xii–xiv.

100 Miller, *New England Mind,* ch. 14.

101 Morison, *Builders of the Bay Colony,* 85, 86. But it is difficult to agree with his comment that "In a sense . . . this sort of

franchise was democratic, for it made no account of social standing or estate." Regardless, however, of this point, if one were not a member of the "community of saints," one was really out of the community. See Andrews, *Colonial Period*, I, 438.
102 *Journal*, II, 238.

CHAPTER VI

1 Swethland refers to Sweden. A basic source for a number of Virginia writers discussed in this chapter is Alexander Brown, *The Genesis of the United States* (2 vols., New York, 1890). Among other things Brown is noted for his extreme anti-Smith point of view. Jarvis M. Morse, *American Beginnings* (Washington, D.C., 1952), summarizes many of these early writers, 35–41.
2 L. G. Tyler (ed.), *Narratives of Early Virginia*, 97–98.
3 *Ibid.*, 331–32. Whitaker was the author of *Good News from Virginia* (London, 1613), reprinted in facsimile in 1936, which details in fresh, straightforward prose the nature of both the country and its inhabitants. Moses Coit Tyler, *American Literature*, I, 46 ff., *LHUS*, III, 258.
4 *Observations gathered out of a Discourse of the Plantation of the Southerne Colonie in Virginia by the English, 1606. Written by that Honorable Gentleman, Master George Percy* is reprinted in L. G. Tyler (ed.), *Narratives of Early Virginia*, 5. Percy was in Virginia twice, first from Sept. 1609 to the coming of Sir Thomas Gates in May 1610 and again from Mar. to May 1611. Moses Coit Tyler, *American Literature*, I, 40–41.

5 L. G. Tyler, *Early Narratives of Virginia*, 3–4.
6 London, 1615. See *LHUS*, III, 258.
7 Tyler, *American Literature*, I, 41–45, has copious extracts. *LHUS*, III, 258.
8 The quotation is from the title itself and is cited in Tyler, *American Literature*, I, 42.
9 The Pocahontas incident is referred to above. See also Andrews, *Colonial Period*, I, 142, n. 1. *NCHA*, III, 160, 211–12.
10 For Pory, and also for Strachey and Smith, the best study is by Howard Mumford Jones, "The Literature of Virginia in the Seventeenth Century," *Memoirs of the American Academy of Arts and Sciences* (Boston, 1946), 16–28. Tyler, *American Literature*, I, 48–51.
11 Michael Drayton, the English poet, wrote to Sandys:
   And, worthy George, by industry and use,
   Let's see what lines Virginia will produce.
   Go on with Ovid, as you have begun
   With the first five books. . . .
   Tyler, *Ibid.*, I, 53, 55–58.
12 Father White's Latin work is titled *Relatio Itineris in Marylandiam* and was not rediscovered until 1832, when it was found in Rome. *Ibid.*, 60 n. 1. Tyler's discussion of White is informative. The English version, known as Father Andrew White's Narrative, is reprinted in Clayton C. Hall (ed.), *Narratives of Early Maryland, 1633–1684, Original Narratives of Early American History* (New York, 1910), 29–45. The introduction gives full bibliographical data, 27. L. B. Wright, *The Cultural Life of the American Colonies* (New York, 1957), 166.

[13] London, 1656. See Tyler, *American Literature*, I, 61. Hall, *Narratives of Early Maryland* contains a reprint, *Leah and Rachel, or, The Two Fruitfull Sisters, Virginia and Mary-Land*, 277–308.

[14] Clayton C. Hall has written a brief sketch of Alsop, which precedes the reprint of *A Character of the Province of Maryland, Narratives of Early Maryland*, 340–87. Tyler, *American Literature*, I, 65–69. Alsop's account had the added importance of having been written by an indentured servant. By far the best biographical source is the work itself.

[15] A reprint of Beverley's *History* was prepared by Charles Campbell (Richmond, Va., 1855); see Louis B. Wright's study "Beverley's *History of The Present State of Virginia*. . . . (1705): A Neglected Classic," *William and Mary Quarterly*, third series, I (July, 1944), 49–64, is first rate; Tyler, *American Literature*, II, 264–67. Beverley's life is best handled in his own prefaces. Wright, *Cultural Life of American Colonies*, 167.

[16] Tyler, *American Literature*, II, 264. Another exponent of the imperial point of view was William Douglass, author of a two-volume work, *A Summary, Historical and Political . . . of the British Settlement in North-America* (London, 1755). A Scotchman, he was a trained doctor who settled down to practice in Boston in 1718. Some have acclaimed him the best historian of the colonial period. Max Savelle, *Seeds of Liberty* (New York, 1948), 427, 382–83, a view not shared by Jarvis M. Morse, *American Beginnings*, 196. At any rate he was among the first to regard the colonies as a unit. Morse contributes a good sketch of him, 196–200.

[17] Kraus, 73.

[18] Tyler, *American Literature*, II, 260. There is no suitable biography of Blair.

[19] London, 1727.

[20] Louis B. Wright, *The First Gentlemen of Virginia, Intellectual Qualities of the Early Colonial Ruling Class* (San Marino, Calif., 1940) is the best full account in this area. The quotation is at 312. John Spencer Bassett has published *The Writings of Colonel William Byrd* (New York, 1901), equipped with a splendid introduction. Thomas J. Wertenbaker is the author of the sketch in the *DAB*, and Richmond Croom Beatty has written *William Byrd of Westover* (Boston and New York, 1932).

[21] Louis B. Wright, one of the acknowledged experts, reports that more has been written about the Byrds than any other colonial Virginia family. *First Gentlemen of Virginia*, 312 n. 1. A representative bibliography is cited above, note 20.

[22] *Ibid.*, 329.

[23] Quotation from Kraus, 76.

[24] Wright, *First Gentlemen of Virginia*, 336–37.

[25] William Stith, *The History of the First Discovery and Settlement of Virginia. . . .* (Williamsburg, Va., 1747). Kraus, 93; Tyler, *American Literature*, II, 279–82. It was William Byrd who helped Stith get at the records of the Virginia Company. Mention must also be made of *The Present State of Virginia* (London, 1724), by Hugh Jones, a mathematician as well as an historian, who gives one of the finest accounts of the state of colonial society.

26 Both quotations from Stith are cited by Kraus, 93.

27 John Spencer Bassett, "The Historians, 1607–1783," *CHAL*, I, 26–27, 30. Parrington, *Colonial Mind*, 194 ff.

28 There is a reprint of Lawson's *History*, edited by Francis L. Harris (Richmond, Va., 1937). Pertinent bibliographical facts may be found in *LHUS*, III, 259. Tyler, *American Literature*, II, 283–89. Lawson called his work *A New Voyage to Carolina containing the Exact Description and Natural History of that Country. . . .* (London, 1709).

29 Kraus, 122–24. For other figures see Tyler, *American Literature*, II, 289–98; Morse, *American Beginnings*, 69–90.

30 *LHUS*, III, 255.

31 Tyler, *American Literature*, II, 207.

32 *LHUS*, III, 255.

33 Quoted in Tyler, *American Literature*, II, 208. Denton continues specifically: "Here any one may furnish himself with land, and live rent-free; yet, with such a quantity of land that he may weary himself with walking over his fields of corn and all sorts of grain."

34 The best source of information on these two genial Dutchmen is Bartlett B. James and J. Franklin Jameson (eds.), *Journal of Jasper Danckaerts, 1679–1680, Original Narratives of Early American History* (New York, 1913). The introduction presents all the necessary data, xv–xxv. See 43–89 on New York culture, personages, and incidents, 166–251.

35 Miller and Johnson, *Puritans*, 407.

36 *Ibid.*, 410.

37 *Ibid.*, 408–09.

38 *The History of the Five Indian Nations Depending on the Province of New York in America* (New York, 1727) is distinguished as the first truly scholarly study of its subject. The biography of Colden by Alice M. Keys, *Cadwallader Colden: A Representative Eighteenth Century Official* (New York, 1906), is more concerned with politics than with history and literature. Morse, *American Beginnings*, 121–24; Lawrence C. Wroth, *An American Bookshelf, 1755* (Philadelphia, 1934), appendix X.

39 In 1728.

40 Tyler, *American Literature*, II, 223–25. Smiths abound both in American history and in American historiography. William Smith wrote of New York, Samuel Smith of New Jersey. A native American of Quaker stock, he was born in 1720, and his *History of the Colony or Nova-Caesarea . . .* appeared in 1765. It covers the New Jersey scene up to 1721. But there are more documents than data about Smith in the volume. Morse, *American Beginnings*, 226–27.

41 Mary K. Spence, *William Penn: A Bibliography* (Harrisburg, Pa., 1932), William J. Beeck, *William Penn in America* (Philadelphia, 1888), and S. M. Janney, *Life of William Penn* (Philadelphia, 1852), are among the standard older biographies. William Hull, *William Penn: A Topical Biography* (New York, 1937), is one of the most satisfactory modern studies. An important account of Penn's background is Mabel R. Brailsford, *The Making of William Penn* (New York, 1930). Edward C. O. Beatty, *William Penn as a Social Philosopher* (New York, 1939). A list of the publications and editions of Penn's own writ-

ings is given in *LHUS*, III, 687–88. See also Albert Cook Meyers (ed.), *Narratives of Early Pennsylvania, West New Jersey and Delaware, 1630–1707, Original Narratives of Early American History* (New York, 1912), 199–201.

42 *Some Account of the Province of Pennsilvania* is reprinted in Cook, *Early Pennsylvania;* the quotation is at 200.

43 *LHUS*, III, 687–88; Tyler, *American Literature*, II, 228, 231, 235; Morse, *American Beginnings*, 77–78.

44 William Warren Sweet, *Religion in Colonial America* (New York, 1942), 210–36. J. T. Hamilton, *A History of the Church Known as the Moravian Church* (Bethlehem, Pa., 1900); S. M. Janney, *History of the Religious Society of Friends from its Rise to the Year 1828* (4 vols., Philadelphia, 1859–67); Rufus M. Jones, *The Quakers in the American Colonies* (London, 1911); Walter A. Knittle, *Early Eighteenth Century Palatine Emigration* (Philadelphia, 1937); John M. Mecklin, *The Story of American Dissent* (New York, 1934); Jacob J. Sessler, *Communal Pietism among Early American Moravians* (New York, 1933).

45 John Horsch, *Catalogue of the Mennonite Historical Library in Scottdale, Pennsylvania* (Scottdale, Pa., 1929). W. W. Sweet, *Religion in Colonial America,* 210–11, 274–323.

46 Cook, *Early Pennsylvania,* 355–59. The account of Daniel Pastorius, *Circumstantial Geographical Description of the Lately Discovered Province of Pennsylvania,* which first appeared in Leipzig and Frankfort in 1700, is reprinted in Cook, 360–448.

47 Cook, *Early Pennsylvania,* 438.

The Life of Francis Daniel Pastorious, the Founder of Germantown, by Marion D. Learned (Philadelphia, 1908), is the best and fullest account.

48 Carl and Jessica Bridenbaugh, *Rebels and Gentlemen, Philadelphia in the Age of Franklin* (New York, 1942), 89–90, 310. Austin K. Gray, *The First American Library* (Philadelphia, 1936).

49 *LHUS*, III, 507–16. Franklin's role in the making of American historiography is treated below, 179.

50 There is no study in American historiography comparable to Ernst Troeltsch, *The Social Teachings of the Christian Churches* (2 vols., New York, 1931). One does not have to endorse the point of view to recognize its breadth of scholarship and depth of scope.

51 Miller, *New England Mind,* Miller and Johnson, *Puritans,* and Morison, *Puritan Pronaos,* have already been referred to in various connections.

52 Henry K. Rowe, *The History of Religion in the United States* (New York, 1928); Sweet, *Religion in Colonial America;* also his *Religion in the Development of American Culture, 1765–1840* (New York, 1952); Willard L. Sperry, *Religion in America* (New York, 1946); Sweet, *The Story of Religions in America* (New York and London, 1930); Ernest Sutherland Bates, *American Faith* (New York, 1940).

53 "It is strange," writes Hall, "that in all that has been written about the United States in recent years little has been said about our religious history." T. C. Hall, *The Religious Background of American Culture* (Boston, 1930), vi.

54 See above, 108 and n. 94.

55 One may legitimately quarrel with many of the specifics in Bates' treatment of the American faith; but few would quarrel with his viewpoint. "The democratic faith demands whole men, not half-men. The compartmentalized philosophy which separates economics from life, which degrades scholars into specialists . . . is fundamentally inconsistent with the democratic spirit. And the whole man is the moral man, concerned everywhere with values, a field too often preempted by religion." Bates, *American Faith*, 13. For intimations of synthesis, see Ralph Henry Gabriel, *The Course of American Democratic Thought* (New York, 1940), 3–66. The extensive bibliography compiled by Herbert W. Schneider, *A History of American Philosophy* (New York, 1946), 250–57, suggests the validity of the point. Recent strivings to adjust these deficiencies are treated in later divisions of this work.

56 See *LHUS* III, 178–80, 74–75, 90.

57 J. T. Adams and R. V. Coleman (eds.), *Dictionary of American History* (5 vols., New York, 1940).

58 Although religion is treated in every volume, the plan of the *History of American Life* is topical and chronological (13 vols., New York, 1927–48); it was edited by Arthur M. Schlesinger, Sr., and Dixon Ryan Fox.

59 Frank H. Foster, *A Genetic History of New England Theology* (Chicago, 1907).

60 A. V. G. Allen, *Jonathan Edwards* (Boston, 1890); Arnold Lunn, *John Wesley* (New York, 1929); W. W. Walker, *Ten New-England Leaders* (Chicago, 1901), are typical biographical studies.

61 Brockunier's volume has already been cited. Ola E. Winslow, *Jonathan Edwards, 1703–1758* (New York, 1940); Perry Miller, *Jonathan Edwards* (New York, 1949).

62 Schneider, *History of American Philosophy;* G. H. Townsend, *Philosophical Ideas in the United States* (New York, 1934); W. H. Werkmeister, *A History of Philosophical Ideas in America* (New York, 1949).

63 Reinhold Niebuhr, *The Irony of American History* (New York, 1952); Merle E. Curti, *The Growth of American Thought* (New York and London, 1943), 50–78; Henry Steele Commager, *The American Mind* (New Haven, 1950), 162–95. Richard Niebuhr's earlier study, *The Social Sources of Denominationalism* (New York, 1929), is fundamental as illustrative of the present writer's view.

64 Sweet, *Religion in Colonial America*, vii.

65 P. G. Mode, *Sourcebook and Bibliographical Guide for American Church History* (Menasha, Wis., 1920). From this point of view, the bibliographical discussion in Anson Phelps Stokes, *Church and State in the United States* (3 vols., New York, 1950), I, li–lxvii, is enlightening. On Catholicism, Wilfred Parsons, *Early Catholic Americana: A list of Books and Other Works by Catholic Authors in the United States, 1729–1820* (New York, 1939); John G. Shea, *History of the Catholic Church in the United States* (4 vols., New York, 1886–92); Theodore Maynard, *The Story of American Catholicism* (New York, 1942). On Jews, Peter Wiernik, *History of the*

Jews in America from the Period of the Discovery of the New World to the Present Time (New York, 1931); Lee M. Friedman, *Early American Jews* (Cambridge, 1934), is a compilation illustrating antiquarian emphasis in this segment of the field; Lee J. Levinger, *A History of the Jews in the United States* (Cincinnati, 1930); Oscar I. Janowsky (ed.), *The American Jew: A Composite Picture* (New York, 1942). Particularly important is A. S. W. Rosenbach, *An American Jewish Bibliography. . . .* (Baltimore, 1926), which carries the listings up to 1850.

66 Literary strivings of the Spanish, French, Swedish, and Dutch writings, 1607–1763, find virtually no place in discussions of the building of America during these years. See, for example, R. U. Pane, *English Translations from the Spanish, 1484–1943: A Bibliography* (New Brunswick, N.J., 1944); Henry R. Wagner, *The Spanish Southwest, 1542–1794: An Annotated Bibliography* (2 vols., Albuquerque, New Mexico, 1937). For French literature, *LHUS,* III, 294–96; Swedish, 299–300; Dutch and Pennsylvania German, 286–89.

67 Much the same is true of the Indians, whose history has been written largely by their conquerors. Scholarly studies come considerably after the period of the beginnings, *LHUS,* III, 212. The story of the Negro and other ethnic groups follows a similar sequence.

CHAPTER VII

1 Hans Kohn, *The Idea of Nationalism* (New York, 1944), 263–325; Carlton J. H. Hayes, *The Historical Evolution of Modern Nationalism* (New York, 1931), 13–17; *Nationalism,* a group study by members of the Royal Institute of International Affairs (London, New York, and Toronto, 1939), 115–43; Michael Kraus, *The Atlantic Civilization: Eighteenth Century Origins* (Ithaca, N.Y., 1949), 123–58.

2 Bert James Loewenberg, "Power and American Ideals," *The Standard,* XXXVII (Dec., 1950), 106–20, from which some of these sentences are taken.

3 *Ibid.,* 110.

4 See below, where these ideas are exemplified by contemporaries.

5 Harold J. Laski, "Introductory: The Age of Reason," in *The Social and Political Ideas of Some Great French Thinkers of the Age of Reason* (ed.), F. J. C. Hearnshaw (London, 1930), 21, 22. "With the American Nation, for the first time, a nation was born, not in the dim past of history, but before the eyes of the whole world." Kohn, *Nationalism,* 271.

6 Sydney G. Fisher, "The Legendary and Myth-Making Process in Histories of the American Revolution," *Proceedings of the American Philosophical Society* (1912), LI, 72; Kohn, *Nationalism,* 278–80. See also Michel-Guillaume Jean de Crèvecoeur, *Letters from an American Farmer* (London, 1782).

7 Loewenberg, "Power and American Ideals," 111.

8 Alfred North Whitehead, "Aspects of Freedom," *Freedom Its Meaning* (ed.), Ruth Wanda Anshen (New York, 1940), 65.

9 Carl L. Becker, *The Heavenly City of the Eighteenth Century Philosophers* (New Haven, 1932), 29–30. "The American national consciousness is based

upon the conviction of being different from other nations—different not in representing a peculiar and unique development of human history but in realizing, as the first people, with the greatest possible approximation to perfection, the general trend of human development toward a better rational order, greater individual liberty, and basic equality." Kohn, *Nationalism*, 291.

10 Kraus, *Atlantic Civilization*, 230. Becker, *Heavenly City*, 110–11, notes that, three times revised, it went through 54 editions before the end of the eighteenth century. Raynal has been regarded as so influential that he is sometimes ranked with Rousseau, and his writings are compared with the *Social Contract*. Kraus, *Atlantic Civilization*, 230. F. J. C. Hearnshaw, "Rousseau," in *Great Thinkers of the Age of Reason*, 168–93. Jacob S. Schapiro, *Condorcet and the Rise of Liberalism* (New York, 1934), ch. xxii. The superb study of R. R. Palmer, *The Age of the Democratic Revolution* (2 vols., Princeton, N.J., 1959), is fundamental.

11 Voltaire's early interest in America is set forth in the *Lettres sur les Angles* (1734), in which he wrote of the Quakers with lyric intensity; also *Traité sur la Tolérance* (1763). In *Essai sur les Moeurs*, William Penn and the "Holy Experiment" provide excellent foils for his comments concerning Catholicism. Bernard Faÿ, *The Revolutionary Spirit in France and America* (New York, 1927), 13. J. B. Black, "Voltaire," *Great French Thinkers of the Age of Reason*, 136–69.

12 Faÿ, *Revolutionary Spirit*, 9.

13 *Ibid.*, 129.

14 *Ibid.*, 91, 90, 81; Kraus, *Atlantic Civilization*, 230.

15 Indeed, the English press in the earlier stages referred to the conflict as a civil war. Fred J. Hinkhouse, *The Preliminaries of the American Revolution as Seen in the English Press, 1763–1775* (New York, 1926), 198-99. Cecil Headlam, "The American Revolution and British Politics 1776–1783," *The Cambridge History of the British Empire* (eds.), J. H. Rose, A. P. Newton, and E. A. Benians (Cambridge, England, and New York, 1929), I, 763.

16 Curtis P. Nettles, *George Washington and American Independence* (Boston, 1951), 103.

17 D. M. Clarke, *British Opinion and the American Revolution* (Cambridge, 1930), 152–53.

18 Adams was elected to membership in an English organization known as "Supporters of the Bill of Rights," *Ibid.*, 155, 152, 153.

19 London, 1776.

20 Citation from Kraus, *Atlantic Civilization*, 224–25.

21 Hinkhouse, *Preliminaries of the American Revolution*, 194.

22 Clarke, *British Opinion*, 159, 289.

23 Francis Wharton, *The Revolutionary and Diplomatic Correspondence of the United States* (Washington, D.C., 1889), II, 474, cited in Clarke, *British Opinion*, 170.

24 Kraus, *Atlantic Civilization*, 221–22.

25 *Ibid.*, 221–22, William B. Cairns, *British Criticism of American Writings, 1783–1815* (Madison, Wis., 1918). Robert E. Spiller, *The American in England During the First Half Century of Independence* (New York, 1926). Reginald Coupland, *The American Revolution and the British Empire* (London, 1930). Robert B. Heilman, *America in English Fiction, 1760–1800* (Baton Rouge, La., 1937). See also,

Palmer, *Democratic Revolution,* David P. Crook, *American Democracy in English Politics* (Oxford, 1963), L. B. Namier, *The Structure of Politics at the Accession of George III* (New York, 1957), Herbert Butterfield, *George III and the Historians* (London, 1957).

26 This argument, of course, worked both ways. It could also be argued that if the empire was severed in one place, it could be severed in another. Hinkhouse, *Preliminaries of the American Revolution,* 199.

27 Michael Kraus, "American and the Irish Revolutionary Movement in the Eighteenth Century," *The Era of the American Revolution,* Richard B. Morris (ed.) (New York, 1939), 338.

28 Becker, *Heavenly City,* 33–34; Kraus, *Atlantic Civilization,* 232. What has been said of Goethe, Schiller, and Lessing was also true of Klopstock, Herder, and Wieland. Kraus, 232, reports that "the German magazines printed many contributions that spoke of America as an escape for the disheartened and the disinherited."

29 Schmohl's volume was published in 1782. Kraus, *Atlantic Civilization,* 232, 233 n. 1.

30 T. K. Gorman, *America and Belgium* (London, 1925); Kraus, *Atlantic Civilization,* 235–36.

31 *LHUS,* III, 97: Kraus, *Atlantic Civilization,* 234, n. 43. R. Garlick, *Philip Mazzei, Friend of Jefferson* (Baltimore, 1933).

32 The quotations from Pownall and Priestley are from Kraus, *Atlantic Civilization,* 239, 253. John C. Miller, *Origins of the American Revolution* (Boston, 1943), 165–231, 168–97.

33 Loewenberg, "Power and American Ideals," 106–20, 110.

CHAPTER VIII

1 Woodrow Wilson, *The New Freedom* (New York, 1913), 79–80.

2 Woodrow Wilson, *Co.:gressional Government* (Boston and New York, 1913), 205–06, 187, 328.

3 Fisher, "Mythmaking," 55, 56.

4 See ch. VII above and chs. IX-X below.

5 Loewenberg, "Power and American Ideals," 115.

6 Howard Fast (ed.), *The Selected Work of Tom Paine* (New York, 1945), *Common Sense,* 31.

7 This phrase is from Merrill Jensen, *The New Nation* (New York, 1950), 4.

8 Philip Guedalla, *Fathers of the Revolution* (New York and London, 1926), chs. 1–3.

9 Guedalla, *Fathers of the Revolution,* 112.

10 Curtis P. Nettles, *George Washington and American Independence* (Boston, 1951), 12.

11 Claude Halstead Van Tyne, *The Loyalists in the American Revolution* (New York, 1929), 190 ff.

12 *LHUS,* II, 131.

13 *Ibid.*

14 Charles F. Mullett (ed.), *Some Political Writings of James Otis* (Columbia, Mo., 1929), reprints the *Vindication* and *The Rights of the British Colonies Asserted and Proved* as well as other Otis writings. Mullett also contributes an excellent introduction. William Tudor, *The Life of James Otis of Massachusetts* (Boston, 1823), is still a work of major importance. While frequently inaccurate, it comes from the pen of John Adams' law student who knew his teacher's friend.

15 Tyler, *Literary History of the American Revolution* (2 vols., New York, 1941), I, 31.

16 *Ibid.*

17 *Ibid.,* I, 32, n. 2.

18 *Ibid.*, I, 33–34. See Tudor, *Otis,* 63 ff.

19 Randolph G. Adams, *Political Ideas of the American Revolution* (New York, 1939), 34. Tyler, *Literary History of the American Revolution,* I, 31. Tudor, *Otis,* 485–86.

20 *Vindication of the Conduct of the House of Representatives of Massachusetts Bay* (Boston, 1762).

21 John Adams claimed too much for the *Vindication.* "Look over the declaration of rights and wrongs issued by Congress in 1774. Look into the Declaration of Independence in 1776. Look into the writings of Doctor Price and Doctor Priestley. Look into all the French constitutions of government; and, to cap the climax, look into Mister Thomas Paine's 'Common Sense,' 'Crisis,' and 'Rights of Man.' What can you find that is not to be found, in solid substance, in this 'Vindication of the House of Representatives'?" Quoted by Tyler, *Literary History of the American Revolution,* I, 44.

22 Here, says Tyler, Otis "reveals the habit of his mind, wherein gravity and frolic, logic and sarcasm, all rush together for expression. And the entire pamphlet is but an amplification of the ideas and feelings which color these words,—an avowal of loyalty to the king so hyperbolical as to suggest its dangerous nearness to irony, a robust assertion of colonial rights under the British constitution, all blended with mirthful and contemptuous allusions to any man who should deny or qualify these rights." *Ibid.,* 43.

23 *Vindication* in Mullett, *Writings of James Otis,* 23.

24 *The Rights of the Colonies Asserted and Proved* (Boston, 1764). See Tyler, *Literary History of the American Revolution,* I, 51, 77.

25 Quoted in *LHUS,* I, 133–34.

26 *Ibid.,* Wrote Otis, in *Considerations on Behalf of the Colonists* (1765), the powers of government are "originally and ultimately in the people; . . . and they never did in fact freely, nor can they rightfully, make an absolute, unlimited renunciation of this divine right. It is ever in the nature of things given in trust, and on a condition the performance of which no mortal can dispense with, namely, that the person or persons on whom the sovereignty is conferred by the people, shall incessantly consult their good. Tyranny of all kinds is to be abhorred, whether it be in the hands of one, or of the few, or of the many." Tyler, *Literary History of the American Revolution,* I, 48.

27 The purpose of this pamphlet, says Tyler, "was not to bring about a revolution, but to avert one." *Ibid.,* 51.

28 Paul L. Ford (ed.), *The Writings of John Dickinson: Vol. I, Political Writings, 1764–1774* (Philadelphia, 1895), of which nothing beyond the first volume was published. R. T. H. Halsey (ed.), *Letters from a Farmer in Pennsylvania* (New York, 1903), of which the original edition appeared in Philadelphia (1767). For pertinent comment, see Charles Francis Adams (ed.), *Familiar Letters of John Adams and His Wife, Abigail Adams, During the Revolution* (Boston, 1875), 11, 45, 59, 84, 133, 256. R. G. Adams, *Political Ideas of the American Revolution,* 77–84. Charles J. Stillé, *The Life and Times of John Dickinson, 1732–1808* (Philadelphia, 1891), re-

mains incomparably the best biographical study. There are thought-provoking observations in Parrington, *Main Currents,* I, 219–32. Bibliographies are available in W. F. Taylor, *A History of American Letters* (New York, 1936), 486–87 and *LHUS,* III, 470–72.

29 Tyler, *Literary History of the American Revolution,* II, 33.

30 Nettles, *George Washington,* 102–03.

31 For a list of Dickinson's offices, see Tyler, *Literary History of the American Revolution,* II, 22.

32 Additional state papers from Dickinson's pen are listed. *Ibid.,* 23, 25, and notes.

33 Tyler puts this nicely. He urged Americans "to save their rights as men, without losing their happiness as British subjects," *Ibid.,* I, 234.

34 1767–68.

35 Tyler, I, 234.

36 Actually twenty-one of twenty-five papers.

37 These bibliographical facts have been gathered from *LHUS,* I, 135–36, and Tyler, *Literary History of the American Revolution,* I, 237.

38 Quoted in Tyler, *Ibid.,* 236.

39 R. G. Adams, *Political Ideas of the American Revolution,* 76–77.

40 James Wilson, *Considerations on the Nature and Extent of the Legislative Authority of the British Parliament* (Philadelphia, 1774). R. G. Adams, "The Legal Theories of James Wilson," *Political Ideas of the American Revolution,* 134.

41 S. E. Morison (ed.), *Sources and Documents illustrating the American Revolution 1764–1788* (Oxford, 1929), 108.

42 Merrill Jensen, *The New Nation* (New York, 1950), 19.

43 Zoltán Haraszti, *John Adams and*

the *Prophets of Progress* (Cambridge, Mass., 1952), is a highly suggestive discussion, 1–13, 26–48.

44 Quoted *Ibid.,* 1.

45 *Ibid.,* 3.

46 *Ibid.,* 13.

47 Charles Francis Adams (ed.), *The Works of John Adams* (10 vols., Boston, 1850–56).

48 On Sparks and Washington, see below, 217–18.

49 For a discussion of Jefferson, see below, 180–81.

50 Haraszti, *Adams,* 10.

51 *Ibid.,* 10, 11.

52 Theodore Parker, *Historic Americans* (Boston, 1870), a volume of four studies devoted to Franklin, Washington, Adams, and Jefferson. Although not published until 1870, they were written in 1858. Haraszti, *Adams,* 305, n. 1.

53 For the interchange between John Adams and Mercy Otis Warren, see below, 190. C. F. Adams (ed.), *Familiar Letters of John Adams and His Wife,* 25.

54 Haraszti, *Adams,* 10, 11.

55 Studies of John Adams are not so numerous as one might wish. In vol. I of the *Collected Works* is a biographical memoir by Charles Francis Adams. It was begun by John Quincy Adams and finished by Charles Francis Adams. James Truslow Adams, *The Adams Family* (Boston, 1930), makes a number of significant observations; see also Gilbert Chinard, *Honest John Adams* (Boston, 1933). C. M. Walsh, *Political Science of John Adams* (New York, 1915), devotes but seven pages to the years 1765–87. An important corrective to the Walsh treatment, and in itself a fundamental essay, is R. G. Adams, "John Adams as a Britannic Statesman," *Political Ideas of the Am-*

erican Revolution, 86–108. Zoltán Haraszti has made a number of studies of Adams, some of which are reprinted in his *Adams,* already cited. Two other studies, interesting from different points of view, are John T. Morse, Jr., *John Adams* (Boston, 1884), and Clifford Smyth, *John Adams, the Man Who was Called "Father of American Independence"* (New York, 1931). Recent studies of John Adams belong to a different phase of scholarship and are appraised in a later portion of the present work.

56 Catherine Drinker Bowen, *John Adams and the American Revolution* (Boston, 1950), is in a class by itself.

57 Paul Wilstach (ed.), *Correspondence of John Adams and Thomas Jefferson, 1812 . . . 1826* (Indianapolis, 1925), 117–18. *The Adams Papers* are now in process of publication by the Harvard University Press.

58 E. E. Schattschneider, *Party Government* (New York, 1942), 5–16; Wilson, *Congressional Government,* 311, 307–10, 7. J. Allen Smith, *The Spirit of American Government* (New York, 1907), 3–10, 28–35, 135–85.

59 B. F. Wright, Jr., *American Interpretations of Natural Law* (Cambridge, Mass., 1931), 120–21, with which Haraszti, *Adams,* 310, n. 5 disagrees. The best source for a study of Adams' ideas of man, society, and government is the *Works.* A convenient source is Adrienne Koch and William Peden (eds.), *The Selected Writings of John and John Quincy Adams* (New York, 1946). By all odds the best source is Adams' own, *A Defence of the Constitutions of the Government of the United States of America* (1794).

60 Adams, *Defence of the Constitutions,* preface. An adequate bibliography will be found in *LHUS,* III, 377–79.

61 On Montesquieu see Paul M. Spurlin, *Montesquieu in America, 1760–1801* (Baton Rouge, La., 1940). The quotation from Adams is cited in Haraszti, *Adams,* 28; from Madison, Saul K. Padover (ed.), *The Complete Madison* (New York, 1953), 162. After paying his respects to Montesquieu as an "oracle who is always consulted and cited on this subject," Madison continues, "On the slightest view of the British Constitution, we must perceive that the legislative, executive, and judiciary departments are by no means totally separate . . . he [Montesquieu] did not mean that these departments ought to have no *partial agency* in, or no *control* over, the acts of each other." 162–63.

62 Walter Bagehot, *The English Constitution* (New York, 1930), 78–79, 295.

CHAPTER IX

1 Quoted in John C. Miller, *Sam Adams Pioneer in Propaganda* (Boston, 1936), 398. Zoltán Haraszti, "Adams' Political Philosophy," *John Adams,* 26–48.

2 This point is elaborated with learning and insight by Charles M. Bakewell, "The Philosophical Roots of Western Culture," in F. S. C. Northrop (ed.), *Ideological Differences and World Order* (New Haven, Conn., 1949), 69–89.

3 Miller, *Sam Adams,* 7, 8, 354–400.

4 Tyler, *Literary History of the American Revolution,* II, 4.

5 Miller, *Sam Adams,* 360–61, 370,

380, indicates the effects of changing conditions on Adams' views. But note 390–91.
[6] Quoted, *Ibid.*, 391.
[7] Tyler, *Literary History of the American Revolution*, II, 2.
[8] Both references, *Ibid.*, 3.
[9] Committees of correspondence had earlier been used by merchant organizations in the first stages of the controversy.
[10] *Ibid.*, 8.
[11] Burton J. Hendrick, *The Lees of Virginia* (Boston, 1935), 189.
[12] Harry A. Cushing (ed.), *The Writings of Samuel Adams* (4 vols., New York, 1904–08), are indispensable for any study of Adams. The biographies of Miller and Harlow, already cited, are valuable and informative. Tyler, *Literary History of the American Revolution*, II, 3–16, is a spirited account.
[13] The sketch of Paine by Crane Brinton, *DAB*, XIV, 159–66, is the best brief statement. Moncure D. Conway, *The Life of Thomas Paine* (2 vols., Boston, 1892), remains the most comprehensive study, despite the author's identification with his hero. Harry Hayden Clark has edited selections from Paine's works, *Thomas Paine: Representative Selections* (New York, 1944), which contains an exciting introductory essay and a carefully annotated bibliography. A more recent bibliographical listing may be found in *LHUS*, III, 674–78. Tyler's comments, *Literary History of the American Revolution*, I, 452–74, are still illuminating.
[14] "The cause of America is, in great measure, the cause of all mankind." Paine, *Common Sense*, introduction, 3. All references to Paine's works are from Clark's edition of *Selections*.
[15] Paine, *Common Sense*, 4.

[16] *Ibid.*, 18.
[17] *Ibid.*, 19.
[18] *Ibid.*, 20.
[19] *Ibid.*
[20] *Ibid.*, 21.
[21] *Ibid.*, 22.
[22] *Ibid.*
[23] *Ibid.*
[24] *Ibid.*
[25] The italics are Paine's. *Ibid.*, 23. For a digest of contemporary opinion, Richard Frothingham, *The Rise of the Republic of the United States* (Boston, 1873), 476.
[26] Number I of the *Crisis* papers was published Dec. 18, 1776. *The Crisis*, 45. The italics are in the original.
[27] *The Crisis*, 45.
[28] The second *Crisis* paper was a retort (Jan. 13, 1777) to Lord Howe, who had issued a series of proclamations designed to bring about peace. Paine's purpose was to prevent whatever success Howe might have achieved. In this paper, Paine attacked the Loyalist elements in the population as well as his Quaker coreligionists who refused to take up arms. The third *Crisis* paper, appearing two years after the battle of Lexington, was a summary of events up to that date. It was a message calculated to enlist support for the Revolution on all fronts and from all elements of the population. Here Paine attacks the Tories, who could no longer be tolerated. The fourth *Crisis* paper was stimulated by the battle of the Brandywine, Sept. 11, 1777, in which Washington and the Continental Army were again defeated and in which Paine tried to lift the morale of soldiers and civilians alike. The fifth *Crisis* paper, Mar. 21, 1778, was devoted to General Washington, whom his enemies, after Washington's defeat at German-

town, the loss of Philadelphia, and the victory of Gates over Burgoyne at Saratoga in Oct., sought to supplant. Paine had spent the winter with Washington at Valley Forge and was much impressed with his greatness. The sixth *Crisis* paper, Oct. 20, 1778, is aimed at the British Commission which came over with General Clinton, successor to Howe, that tried to split off the Americans from their French allies. On Nov. 21, the Commission having failed, Paine addressed the seventh *Crisis* to "The People of England," calling attention to the fallacies of British propaganda with special reference to trade and taxes. Approximately eighteen months elapsed before the eighth *Crisis* paper appeared. Again he addressed the English people (Mar. 1780), pointing out that conquest of America by the British was extremely unlikely. June 9, 1780, is the date of the ninth issue of the *Crisis,* in which Paine asserts the threat to America was over. But Paine was far from correct. In Aug. 1780 Gates was defeated at Camden. French aid arrived in the form of Rochambeau's fleet in July, but the French did not attack. The battle of King's Mountain was won, but in September Benedict Arnold's defection made the American cause look bleak. Paine's *Crisis Extraordinary,* Oct. 6, 1780, dealt with taxation. He pled for public support on grounds of sheer self-interest. Contrasting American and English taxation and other financial measures, he argued that American measures were better and cheaper. By Mar. 5, 1782, the date of the tenth *Crisis* paper, the war was virtually over. Cornwallis had surrendered in Oct.

1781, but George III was for carrying on the conflict. Paine answered the king, and pointed out to Americans that the war had to be completely won before they could allow themselves to relax. After the North ministry fell in May 1782, the new government attempted to split the Franco-American alliance and make a separate peace. The eleventh *Crisis* paper, May 22, 1782, is devoted to exposing this move and to presenting the case against it. The twelfth *Crisis* paper, Oct. 29, 1782, addressed to the new ministry of Lord Shelburne, insists that no peace with Britain was possible unless based upon full independence. The final *Crisis* paper, number thirteen, Apr. 19, 1783, begins "The times that tried men's souls, are over and the greatest and completest revolution the world ever knew, gloriously and happily accomplished." Here he entered a plea for union, for a real united states.

29 Paine published materials relating to the Deane affair which were classified as confidential. Although he violated his trust by doing so, he was apparently motivated by patriotic zeal. Jensen, *New Nation,* 368, 370.

30 *Public Good,* 354–66. This essay was published in Philadelphia, Dec. 30, 1780. The subtitle reads, *Being an Examination into the claim of Virginia to the Vacant Western Territory, and of the Right of the United States to the Same: to Which is Added Proposals for Laying off a New State, to be Applied as a Fund for Carrying on the War, or Redeeming the National Debt.*

31 *Public Good,* 365. Jensen, *New Nation,* 230.

32 The first part of *The Rights of Man* was ready in Feb. 1791, and

a few copies were issued; it was finally published in an adequate edition, Mar. 13, 1791. Clarke, *Paine,* 421.

33 *Rights of Man,* 162.

34 *Ibid.,* Pt. II, 173. Italics are in the original.

35 *Ibid.*

36 *Ibid.*

37 *Ibid.*

38 "If there is a country in the world, where concord, according to common calculation, would be least expected, it is America. Made up, as it is, of people from different nations, accustomed to different forms and habits of government . . . it would appear that the union of such a people was impracticable; but by the simple operation of constructing government on the principles of society and the rights of man, every difficulty retires. . . ." *Ibid.,* 179–80.

39 *Ibid.,* 185.

40 *Ibid.,* 198–99.

41 *Ibid.,* 200.

42 *Ibid.,* 204.

43 "What is called a *republic* is not any *particular form* of government. It is wholly characteristical of the purport, matter, or object for which government ought to be instituted, and on which it is to be employed, *res-public,* the public affairs, or the public good; or, literally translated, the *public thing.* Every government that does not act on the principle of a republic, or, in other words, that does not make the *res-publica* its whole and sole object, is not a good government. Republican government is no other than government established and conducted for the interest of the public, as well individually as collectively." The italics are Paine's. *Rights of Man, Ibid.,* 191.

44 *Ibid.,* 193.

45 Dec. 1792.

46 Clark, *Paine,* 434–35.

47 *Letter to George Washington,* 393, and Clark's notes, *Paine,* 436.

48 In Dec. 1793.

49 The first section of *The Age of Reason* appeared in 1794, the second in 1796.

50 Clark, *Paine,* 427. The italics are Paine's. An extended list of the replies to *The Age of Reason* is in A. E. Morse, *The Federalist Party in Massachusetts to the Year 1800* (Princeton, N.J., 1909), 217–19.

51 Leonard W. Labaree, *Conservatism in Early American History* (New York and London, 1948), 146.

52 Chatham's remarks are to the point. Commenting on the addresses and memorials presented to the British government, he said, "for solidity of reasoning, force of sagacity, and wisdom of conclusion, under such a complication of difficult circumstances, no nation or body of men can stand in preference to the General Congress at Philadelphia. I trust it is obvious to your lordships, that all attempts to impose servitude upon such men, to establish despotism over such a mighty continental nation, must be vain, must be fatal." Quotation in Tyler, *Literary History of the American Revolution,* I, 330.

53 Technically, Galloway was a conservative rather than a Tory. He finally became a Loyalist. He followed the British army to New York after the evacuation of Philadelphia in 1778 and shortly thereafter removed to England, where he died in 1803. Pertinent on the Loyalists is Lorenzo Sabine, *Biographical*

Sketches of Loyalists of the American Revolution (2 vols., Boston, 1864), rev. ed., Van Tyne, *Loyalists in the American Revolution.* Jonathan Boucher, *Reminiscences of an American Loyalist, 1738–1789*, Jonathan Boucher (ed.) (Boston, 1925). Stimulating comment is to be found in Tyler, *Literary History of the American Revolution,* I, 293–315; on Boucher, I, 316–28; II, 79–129. Philip Davidson, *Propaganda and the American Revolution 1763–1783* (Chapel Hill, N.C., 1941), 249–337.

54 Clarence H. Vance (ed.), *Letters of a Westchester Farmer 1774–1775* (White Plains, N.Y., 1930). Walter Chambers, *Samuel Seabury: A Challenge* (New York, 1932), is the most modern biographical account. E. E. Beardsley, *Life and Correspondence of the Right Reverend Samuel Seabury* (Boston, 1881). Van Tyne, *Loyalists in the American Revolution,* 136.

55 Quoted in Tyler, *Literary History of the American Revolution,* I, 335.

56 *Ibid.*

57 *Ibid.,* 336–37.

58 *Ibid.,* 340.

59 *Ibid.,* 343.

60 Davidson, *Propaganda and the American Revolution,* 252; Tyler, *Literary History of the American Revolution,* I, 392–95.

61 Quotation. *Ibid.,* 394.

62 *Ibid.,* 394–95.

63 Galloway's plan is reprinted in Morison, *The American Revolution,* 117. His own account constitutes a vital historiographical record, *Historical and Political Reflections on the Rise and Progress of the American Revolution* (London, 1780). Ernest H. Baldwin, *Joseph Galloway, the Loyal-*

ist Politician: A Biography (Philadelphia, 1902).

64 For historiography of Washington and Franklin, see below, 214–18.

65 Guedalla, *Fathers of the Revolution,* 288.

66 For an opposite view see Thomas Carlyle, *On Heroes, Hero-Worship, and the Heroes in History* (London, n.d.), 1, 2.

67 For Adams, see above, 160–64.

68 Haraszti, *John Adams,* 46, a comment made to Haraszti by Harold Laski.

69 And, of course, Thomas Jefferson and Benjamin Franklin.

70 See below, ch. X.

71 Guedalla, *Fathers of the Revolution,* 299–300.

72 "That period was preeminently the turning-point in the development of political society in the western hemisphere," wrote John Fiske, whose volume, *The Critical Period in American History 1783–1789* (Boston and New York, 1888), set a fashion in historiography. The quotation is at vi. See Jensen, *New Nation,* xi–xii, and the same writer's *The Articles of Confederation* (Madison, Wis., 1940).

73 Jensen, *New Nation,* 19, 426–27.

CHAPTER X

1 J. Franklin Jameson, *The American Revolution Considered as a Social Movement* (Princeton, N.J., 1940). For a discussion of Hildreth, see below, ch. XIV.

2 M. C. Tyler's narrative is adequate for the essential details. *Literary History of the American Revolution,* II, 423–28. A more modern version which does not differ substantially may be found in Merrill Jensen, *New Nation,* 96–99.

3 *The History of the Rise, Progress, and Establishment of the Independence of the United States of America* was published in London in 1788. The following year a three-volume American edition appeared, and a second American edition in 1794 published in New York.

4 Letter to General Gates, Oct. 16, 1782, cited in Tyler, *Literary History of the American Revolution*, II, 424.

5 Letter to Gates, *Ibid.*, 425.

6 Adams was critical. He was "somewhat vain, and not accurate or judicious; very zealous in the cause, and a well-meaning man, but incautious." Adams, *Works*, II, 424, in *DAB*, VII, 426. But see Jensen's opinion, *New Nation*, 96–99. The fear of giving offense to living participants was a real one. Charles Thomson, secretary of the Continental Congress during the Revolution, is said to have burned the manuscript he had written rather than to take the risk of giving offense. Fisher, "The Legendary and Myth-Making Process in Histories of the American Revolution," *Proceeding of the American Philosophical Society*, II (1912), 57.

7 *Ibid.*, 58.

8 Orin G. Libby, "A Critical Examination of William Gordon's History of the American Revolution," American Historical Association, *Annual Report* (1899), I, 367–88.

9 E. B. Greene, *Revolutionary Generation, 1763–1790* (New York, 1943), 395; Fisher, "Myth-Making," 58; John Spencer Bassett, "The Historians," *CHAL*, II, 104.

10 Fisher, "Myth-Making," 63. Actually many of Gordon's statements have been corroborated by documents since published, particularly for the year 1775.

11 Greene, *Revolutionary Generation*, 395.

12 Jensen, *New Nation*, 93–95. Kraus, 127–29.

13 David Ramsay, *The History of the American Revolution* (2 vols., Philadelphia, 1789; 2 vols. in one, London, 1793). David Ramsay, *The History of the Revolution of South-Carolina, from a British Province to an Independent State* (2 vols., Trenton, N.J., 1785). Page Smith, "David Ramsay and the Causes of the American Revolution," *William and Mary Quarterly*, 3rd. ser., xvii (Jan. 1960), 51–77.

14 Orin G. Libby, "Ramsay as a Plagiarist," *American Historical Review* VII (July 1904), 697–703. But Fisher hailed him as standing alone in understanding "that the dispute . . . was irreconcilable and could never have been settled by conciliation." "Myth-Making," 63–64.

15 *Ibid.*, 64. But John Spencer Bassett concludes that his volumes were "well read by an uncritical generation." "The Historians," *CHAL*, II, 105.

16 Mercy Warren wrote in a fine Addisonian style. Bassett, however, thought her work "loosely written." He admitted that "for a long time" her volumes "furnished the average New Englander his knowledge of the Revolution." *Ibid.*, 105.

17 On feminist grounds for example, *LHUS*, III, 122.

18 She has been styled "the poet laureate and, later, historical apologist for the patriot cause." *DAB*, XIX, 484. Mercy Warren's literary reputation rests upon *The Adulateur. A Tragedy as it is now Acted in Upper Servia* (Boston, 1773), *The Group,*

As Lately Acted and to be Re-Acted to the Wonder of all Superior Intelligences, nigh Headquarters at Amboyne (Boston, 1775), and *Poems Dramatic and Miscellaneous* (Boston, 1790).

[19] Alice Brown, *Mercy Warren* (New York, 1896).

[20] *History of the Rise, Progress and Termination of the American Revolution* (3 vols., Boston, 1805).

[21] Brown, *Warren*, 207.

[22] Tyler, *Literary History of the American Revolution*, II, 421.

[23] In 1781 the Warrens purchased Hutchinson's house in Milton, where they lived for ten years. *DAB*, XIX, 484–85.

[24] Quoted in Brown, *Warren*, 207.

[25] Cited in Kraus, 145.

[26] Quoted in Brown, *Warren*, 161–162.

[27] *Ibid.*, 224, 225.

[28] *DAB*, I, 60–61; *LHUS*, III, 88.

[29] *DAB*, I, 60–61.

[30] Kraus, 143.

[31] *DAB*, III, 279–80, is a brief but substantial account. For further detail, see Kraus, 146–47.

[32] Philadelphia, 1799. Burk's study of Irish songs appeared in the *Richmond Enquirer*, May 27, 1808. There is no study of Burk, but his journals are in the possession of the New York Historical Society.

[33] Kraus (146–47) cites the bibliographical details of the *History of Virginia*, Vol. IV, which was brought to a conclusion by others.

[34] Herbert B. Adams, *The Life and Writings of Jared Sparks* (2 vols., Boston, 1893), I, 420–21. Another contemporary history of the Revolution by John Andrews appeared in 1786. It was based on material provided by *The Annual Register*. Nevertheless, some attention was given to the anti-Whig point of view. Fisher,

"Myth-Making," 62, rightly stigmatizes Andrews as "a mere dull chronicler and summarizer."

[35] Carlo Botta's history was translated by George Alexander Otis with the title *History of War of Independence of the United States of America* (3 vols., Philadelphia, 1820–21). The fourth edition (1834) contains an interesting "Biography of the Author," facing vi.

[36] Fisher, "Myth-Making," 67.

[37] Adams, *Jared Sparks*, II, 93.

[38] "A modern reader has difficulty in getting through a single chapter. The popularity of such a tedious compilation is hard to understand, unless it was that our people were pleased because it was a French and Italian defense of our American institutions." Fisher, "Myth-Making," 67.

[39] Jefferson's comments are quoted in the "Translator's Notice to the Second Edition."

[40] But Belknap himself was an impeccable patriot, although no democrat. Jensen, *New Nation*, 93.

[41] Charles W. Cole, "Jeremy Belknap: Pioneer Nationalist," *New England Quarterly*, X (Dec. 1937), 743–51. Jane M. Belknap, *Life of Jeremy Belknap with Selections from His Writings* (New York, 1847). Jameson, *Historical Writing*, 86.

[42] Jeremy Belknap, *The History of New Hampshire* (2 vols., Boston, 1791).

[43] Kraus, 75.

[44] J. Franklin Jameson, *The History of Historical Writing in America* (Boston, 1891), 86.

[45] For Daniel Leonard and other Tory writers, see above, 175–79.

[46] On general historical grounds it is easy to agree with Tyler that Hutchinson shared with Joseph Galloway the "supreme place

among American statesmen opposed to the Revolution." *Literary History of the American Revolution,* I, 370.

[47] Thomas Hutchinson, *The History of the Colony (and Province) of Massachusetts Bay* (3 vols., Boston and London, 1795–1828). Lawrence S. Mayo has edited the *History* based on a collection of Hutchinson's copy of the first two volumes and the MS. of the third (3 vols., Cambridge, Mass., 1936), which contain a biographical sketch and the editor's notes. Hutchinson also compiled *A Collection of Original Papers Relative to the History of the Colony of Massachusetts-Bay* (Boston, 1769), which was reprinted in 2 vols. (Albany, N.Y., 1865). Peter O. Hutchinson (ed.), *The Diary and Letters of Thomas Hutchinson* (2 vols., Boston, 1884, 1886). James K. Hosmer, *Life of Thomas Hutchinson* (Boston, 1896).

[48] Mercy Otis Warren as cited by Tyler, *Literary History of the American Revolution,* II, 422–23. See above, 189.

[49] *Ibid.,* 394; for the opinions of others, 395.

[50] J. T. Adams, *Revolutionary New England, 1691–1776* (Boston, 1923), 370. "He [Hutchinson] displays a rare impartiality considering that he was himself one of the chief actors."

[51] V. L. Parrington, *Main Currents,* I, 196.

[52] Despite, continues Parrington, a "praiseworthy care for accuracy and impartiality." *Ibid.,* 196.

[53] Tyler, *Literary History of the American Revolution,* II, 395. Bassett, "The Historians," says, "It was long before there appeared among them one who could be ranked with Hutchinson, though some of them wrote

well and displayed great industry. The stream was wider than formerly, but it was not so deep." "The Historians," *CHAL,* II, 104.

[54] On Prince and Stith, see above, 119.

[55] On Bradford and Winthrop, see above, 86–87.

[56] Parrington, *Main Currents,* I, 196; James K. Hosmer, *Samuel Adams* (Boston, 1885), 259; Carl L. Becker, *The Declaration of Independence* (New York, 1922), 72.

[57] Parrington, *Main Currents,* I, 195. Greene, *Revolutionary Generation,* 216–19. Virginia D. Harrington, *The New York Merchant on the Eve of the Revolution* (New York, 1935). Arthur M. Schlesinger, Sr., *The Colonial Merchants and the American Revolution* (New York, 1918), is the definitive study.

[58] For a discussion of these loyalist writers, see above, 151–53.

[59] Merle Curti, "The American Scholar in Three Wars," *Journal of the History of Ideas,* III (June 1942), 241–48.

[60] Fisher, "Myth-Making," 60, 61, 62. These views are elaborated in the same writer's *True History of the American Revolution* (Philadelphia and London, 1902), 169–81. For data on other contemporary histories of the Revolution, Kraus, 108. Of particular interest and importance is the work of Jedidiah Morse, for an account of which see below, 206–7. A notable work was written by John Drayton, *Memoirs of the American Revolution, From its Commencement to the Year 1776 inclusive. . . .* (2 vols., Charleston, S.C., 1821). These were begun by the author's father, William Henry Drayton, who represented South Carolina in the Continental Congress.

Much of his manuscript was destroyed at his death because it was felt to contain too much confidential data. Materials for two volumes escaped destruction, and these were used by his son. Tyler, *Literary History of the American Revolution*, II, 419.
61 Jensen, *New Nation*, 426–27. Tyler, *Literary History of the American Revolution*, I, 499–503.
62 Arthur M. Schlesinger, Sr., *New Viewpoints in American History* (New York, 1928), 181. They should, he continues, "explain why the Revolution has had to be re-discovered and re-constructed from the source materials by the present generation of historians."

CHAPTER XI

1 Jedidiah Morse, who quotes Thomas Hutchins, the first geographer of the United States, cited in Jensen, *New Nation*, 111.
2 Jensen, *New Nation*, 178.
3 *Ibid.* John Fiske, *Critical Period*, 174–81.
4 Thomas C. Cochran, "The Presidential Synthesis in American History," *American Historical Review*, LIII (July 1948), 751. Guy Stanton Ford, "Some Suggestions to American Historians," *American Historical Review*, XLIII (Jan. 1938), 267–68. See also Oscar and Mary F. Handlin, *Commonwealth: Massachusetts, 1774–1861* (New York, 1947). Louis Hartz, *Economic Thought and Democratic Thought: Pennsylvania 1776–1860* (Cambridge, Mass., 1948).
5 Hans Kohn, *The Idea of Nationalism* (New York, 1944), 291, 294.

6 Dumas Malone, *Jefferson the Virginian* (Boston, 1948), 201.
7 For discussion of Noah Webster, see below, 208–10. William B. Cairns, in *British Criticisms of American Writings, 1783–1815* (Madison Wis., 1918), discusses English reactions to American speech. "However detestable personal pride may be," wrote Noah Webster, "yet there is a national pride and a provincial, that are the noblest passions of a republican patriot. . . . For my own part, I frankly acknowledge, I have too much pride not to wish to see America assume a national character. I have too much pride to stand indebted to Great Britain for books to learn [sic] our children the letters of the alphabet." Cited in Harry L. Warfel, *Noah Webster Schoolmaster to America* (New York, 1936), 53. Allen O. Hansen, *Liberalism and American Education in the Eighteenth Century* (New York, 1926), 45, 56, 80–81, 235, 240–42, 247.
8 Erasmus Root, *An Introduction to Arithmetic for the Use of the Common Schools* (Norwich, Conn., 1796), preface, cited in Merle E. Curti, *The Growth of American Thought* (New York and London, 1943), 138–39.
9 Warfel, *Webster*, 90–92. Webster endorsed the motto of Mirabeau and placed it on some of his title pages: "Begin with the infant in the cradle; let the first word he lisps be Washington."
10 Frederick L. Pattee (ed.), *The Poems of Philip Freneau* (3 vols., Princeton, N.J., 1902), II, 304.
11 Noah Webster, *A Grammatical Institute of the English language. . . .* (Hartford, Conn., 1784), 14, cited in Warfel, *Webster*, 59–60. "It is the business of *Americans* [Webster's italics] to select the wisdom of all nations . . . to add

superior dignity to this infant Empire and to human nature."

12 *Memoirs of the American Academy of Arts and Sciences* (Boston, 1785), I, 3–4. The American Philosophical Society advocated similar views, Hansen, *Liberalism in American Education,* 109–10.

13 Curti, *American Thought,* 153.

14 Hansen, *Liberalism and American Education,* 87, 88, 120–21. For the views of Noah Webster on this subject, Warfel, *Webster,* 47–48. Edward F. Humphrey, *Nationalism and Religion in America, 1774–1789* (Boston, 1924), is the outstanding reference on this topic.

15 Curti, *American Thought,* 146.

16 *Ibid.,* 146. Isaiah Thomas founded the American Antiquarian Society (1812) in Worcester, Massachusetts.

17 Hansen, *Liberalism and American Education,* 40, 41, 56. Nathan G. Goodman, *Benjamin Rush, Physician and Citizen: 1746–1813* (Philadelphia, 1934).

18 *DAB,* XIII, 245–47. Morse was as impassioned a Federalist as he was a patriot, a "Pillar Adamant in the temple of Federalism." William B. Sprague, *The Life of Jedidiah Morse* (New York, 1874), contains considerable material of value.

19 *Geography Made Easy* appeared in 1784 and went through twenty-five editions during Morse's life. *The American Geography; or a View of the Present Situation of the United States of America* (Elizabeth Town, N.J., 1789).

20 Cited in Kraus, 153.

21 Sprague, *Morse,* 196, 205.

22 J. S. Bassett, "The Historians," *CHAL,* II, 115. Morse also wrote (together with another) an essay on New England which became part of the supplement to the 1801 American edition of the *Encyclopaedia Britannica.* Eventually this essay, expanded and rewritten, became a history of New England, *A Compendious History of New England. . . .* 3rd ed. (1820), which began with the Reformation rather than with Columbus or Adam. It was this volume which brought about a bitter quarrel between Morse and Hannah Adams, who accused him of borrowing her data. On the issues involved and the pamphlets produced as a result, see the sketch in the *DAB,* XIII, 245–47. Morse's *Annals* resemble the history of Abiel Holmes, father of Oliver Wendell Holmes, *American Annals; or a Chronological History of America from the Discovery. . . .* (2 vols., Boston, 1805), which is discussed in Catherine Drinker Bowen, *Yankee from Olympus* (Boston, 1944), 18–19.

23 F. L. Mott, *A History of American Magazines: 1741–1850* (New York, 1930), 23.

24 *LHUS,* III, 36.

25 Cited in Kohn, *Nationalism,* 276.

26 Jefferson to Adams, August 1, 1861. Paul Wilstach (ed.), *Correspondence of John Adams and Thomas Jefferson* (Indianapolis, 1925), 136.

27 The italics are Webster's, and the quotation is cited in Warfel, *Webster,* 59.

28 *LHUS,* III, 92, 218. See also, 36, 187, 119. For its eighteenth-century successes, Warfel, *Webster,* 71. Webster taught patriotic nationalism with grammar and through his selection of readings: "In the choice of pieces, I have not been inattentive to the political interests of America. Several of those masterly addresses of Congress, written at the commencement of the late revolution, contain such noble, just and

independent sentiments of liberty and patriotism, that I cannot help wishing to transfuse them into the breasts of the rising generation." Cited in Warfel, *Webster*, 86.

29 *Ibid.*, 53, 3, see also, 78.

30 *Ibid.*, 1.

31 *Ibid.*, 56–57.

32 *LHUS*, III, 189–90. There is an excellent brief survey of dictionaries in Warfel, *Webster*, 287–90; for Webster's dictionary, 364–66. Webster's views were not universally acclaimed. Joseph E. Worcester (1784–1865) acrimoniously disagreed. His *Comprehensive Pronouncing and Explanatory Dictionary of the English Language* (1830) hewed to the British grammatical line. A "dictionary war" ensued, involving charges of plagiarism and countercharges of fraud, which is suggestively recounted by Warfel, 366–68. A minor engagement of the "war" was fought by Jeffersonians who objected to Webster's definition of "Federal" and "Federalist." "A friend to the Constitution of the U. States," Warfel, 315. See Mott, *American Magazines: 1741–1850*, 235.

33 The quotation is from the preface and is cited by Warfel, *Webster*, 362. The original title page of the *Dictionary* is reproduced on 363.

34 In Feb. 1785 Webster wrote a pamphlet of 48 pages, entitled *Sketches of American Policy*, facsimile edition (New York, 1937). The material is divided into four categories: Theory of Government; Governments on the Eastern Continent; American States; or the principles of the American Constitutions contrasted with those of European States; and Plan of Policy for improving the Advantages and perpetuating the Union of the American States. The quotation appears in Warfel, *Webster*, 112, 113. The pamphlet referred to is Richard Price's *Observations on the Importance of the American Revolution* published in 1784. The Rousseau reference is to the *Social Contract.*

35 Warfel, *Webster*, 114–45, 214, 329.

36 Warfel quotes from Webster's works on the subject, *Ibid.*, 115. See also 119–49, 150–70.

37 *Ibid.*, 436.

38 *Ibid.*, 116.

39 Vernon L. Parrington has edited selections from the leading Hartford writers, *The Connecticut Wits* (New York, 1926), which has a critical introductory essay and a bibliography. Leon Howard has written the principal study, *The Connecticut Wits* (Chicago, 1943).

40 M. C. Tyler, *Three Men of Letters* (New York and London, 1895), 146–47, 166–69.

41 The quotation is from *The Columbiad*, Book VIII, 79–80. Barlow had a prevision of a federation of nations based on American experience:

There stands the model, thence he long shall draw
His forms of policy, his traits of law;
Each land shall imitate, each nation join
The well based brotherhood, the league divine
Extend its empire with the circling sun,
And band the peopled globe within its federal zone.

42 In 1774.

43 Ray A. Billington, *Westward Expansion* (New York, 1967), 212–13, 219–20.

44 Charles B. Todd, *Life and Letters of Joel Barlow, LL.D.* (New York and London, 1886), has not been outmoded by Theodore A. Zunder, *The Early Days of Joel Barlow, a Connecticut Wit: His Life and Works from 1754 to 1787* (New Haven, 1934), which is excellent for the period covered. Howard, *Connecticut Wits,* 135–65, 271–341, covers the later period of Barlow's life. Suggestive for the entire span of Barlow's life is John Dos Passos, "Citizen Barlow of the Republic of the World," *The Ground We Stand On* (New York, 1941), 256–380. Recent periodical literature is listed in *LHUS,* III, 397.

45 Mott, *American Magazines: 1741–1850,* 176, 186, 232, 257. Warfel calls *The Columbiad* a "tin-plated epic," *Webster,* 116.

46 Dos Passos, *The Ground We Stand On,* 262–64, 269, 300–305, 315.

47 Dumas Malone, *Jefferson and the Rights of Man* (Boston, 1951), 218–19, 223–24, 230–31.

48 *Advice to the Privileged Orders in the Several States of Europe, Resulting from the Necessity and Propriety of a General Revolution in the Principle of Government* (London, 1792, 1795).

49 *The Political Writings of Joel Barlow* (New York, 1796), 142–144.

50 *A Letter to the National Convention of France, on the Defects of the Constitution of 1791, and the Extent of the Amendments which ought to be Applied* (London, 1792). For the circumstances of the genesis of this letter, see Dos Passos, *The Ground We Stand On,* 311–12.

51 *Ibid.,* 326–41.

52 After his return to America, Barlow prepared in 1806 a *Prospectus for a National Institution to be Established in the United States* (Washington, 1806), published anonymously, which was a plan for a national university. At the suggestion of Jefferson he translated Volney's *Ruins of Empire* and Brissot de Warville's *Travels to the United States.* Dos Passos, *The Ground We Stand On,* 367, on his projected history of the American Revolution, 366.

53 *Ibid.,* 274–75.

54 Mott, *American Magazines: 1741–1850,* 183, 48, 52. Edward H. O'Neill, *A History of American Biography: 1800–1935* (Philadelphia, 1935), 155–58. *LHUS,* I, 198–200, summarizes Washington's reputation in Europe.

55 This is from the *Massachusetts Magazine* for 1793, quoted in Mott, *American Magazines: 1741–1850,* 53.

56 In Lord Byron's tribute:

The first—the last—the best—
The Cincinnatus of the West,
Whom envy dared not hate,
Bequeathed the name of Washington,
To make men blush there was but one.

Washington's surrender of power was celebrated as unique.

57 The standard study is L. C. Wroth, *Parson Weems* (Baltimore, 1911). Weems was born in 1759, studied medicine in Europe, and became an Anglican minister in 1784. He relinquished his professional calling in 1792 and became a seller and author of books instead. He represented Mathew Carey, the Philadelphia publisher, in the South. An excellent summary is presented by Dixon Wecter, "President Washington and Parson Weems," *The Hero in America* (New York, 1941), 99–147, in which certain discordant and

dissenting views are appropriately noted.

[58] "Prescott, Motley and Parkman are mere children when compared with him." Fisher, "Myth-Making," 64. In 1912, when Fisher wrote, *The Life of Washington* was reported as still selling, 65. See also O'Neill, *American Biography*, 157. For a favorable impression of Weems from Robert Lewis, nephew of Washington, see H. B. Adams, *Sparks*, II, 39, and Edward Channing, *History of the United States*, IV, 57; V, 278–79.

[59] *A History of the Life and Death, Virtues and Exploits of General George Washington* was the title of the first edition (Philadelphia, 1800). The fifth edition, *The Life of George Washington, with Curious Anecdotes Equally Honorable to Himself and Exemplary to His Young Countrymen . . . by a former rector of Mt. Vernon Parrish* (Philadelphia, 1806). The first edition was reprinted in New York (1927). The fifth edition contains the cherry tree and other legends.

[60] These figures are cited by Kraus, 161. Wecter, *Hero in America*, gives different figures: fifty-nine editions before 1850, seventy-nine up to 1921, 133.

[61] These references to Weems are cited in Wecter, *Hero in America*, 135. Weems was also the author of a life of General Francis Marion and of Benjamin Franklin as well as of a book on temperance. The following verses appeared in recent years, when debunking of Washington was in flower:

Let others echo Rupert Hughes
And mix up motes and beams—
The anecdotes that I peruse
Were told by Parson Weems.

Above iconoclastic views
That little hatchet gleams!
"I cannot tell a lie," I choose
The Washington of Weems.

[62] John Marshall, *The Life of George Washington* (5 vols., Philadelphia, 1804–07).

[63] O'Neill, *American Biography*, 158. Jameson, *Historical Writing*, 84. Despite some high praise, few now regard Marshall's *Life* as significant scholarship.

[64] On the whole subject of Marshall's venture as historian, consult Albert J. Beveridge, *The Life of John Marshall* (4 vols., Boston and New York, 1916–1919), III, 223–66. The quotation from Jefferson is at 267. For other comments, mostly negative, 269–71.

[65] The first volume contains but two brief references to Washington. Vol. II begins with Washington's birth, and there is brief mention of the significance of Washington's assumption of command. The two succeeding volumes are much superior both as to general quality and coverage of the subject. The third ends with the year 1779, and the fourth ends with the war. The last volume is in every way the best and is devoted to the final sixteen years of Washington's life.

[66] Francis Glass, *Washington ii Vita* (New York, 1835).

[67] Aaron Bancroft, *The Life of George Washington, Commander-in-Chief. . . .* (2 vols., Boston, 1826).

[68] David Ramsay, *The Life of George Washington* (New York, 1807).

[69] Sparks is treated in the next chapter. For a listing of Washington biographies, Edward H. O'Neill, *Biography by Americans* (Philadelphia, 1939), 381–86.

[70] Washington Irving, *Life of George Washington* (5 vols., New York, 1856–59). William A. Bryan, *George Washington in American Literature, 1775–1865* (New York, 1952).

[71] O'Neill, *American Biography*, 166.

[72] Woodrow Wilson, *George Washington* (New York, 1896). Henry Cabot Lodge, *George Washington* (2 vols., Boston, 1889), of which a revised edition was published in 1898. Worthington C. Ford (ed.), *The Writings of George Washington* (14 vols., New York, 1889–93).

[73] Wecter, "Poor Richard: The Boy Who Made Good," *Hero in America*, 52–53.

[74] The *Autobiography* was first published completely by John Bigelow in 1868. See *LHUS*, III, 511.

[75] The title of the first edition is *The Life of Benjamin Franklin; With Many Choice Anecdotes and Admirable Sayings of the Great Man. . . .* (Philadelphia, 1817). The leaders of the era are, of course, incorporated in the revisions of recent times and are treated subsequently in appropriate places.

[76] Wecter, *Hero in America*, 74.

CHAPTER XII

[1] Pride in America, heightened by the War of 1812 and the westward expansion of population, stimulated serious interest in the records of the nation's past. Avid collectors and editors made available to later scholars documents that broadened the scope of understanding and opened the portals of criticism. Private literary treasures and local self-consciousness were supplemented by the activity of famous editors whose names have long sparkled in monographic footnotes. Hezekiah Niles, who earned a somewhat doubtful immortality by giving his name to two midwestern towns, edited the *Baltimore Evening Post* during the major portion of the European crisis of the Napoleonic period, founded *Niles' Weekly Register,* and was responsible for the appearance of *Principles and Acts of the Revolution in America* (Baltimore, 1822). Jonathan Elliot prepared an edition of the debates on the federal constitution, familiarly known to students as Elliot's *Debates. Debates in the several State Conventions on the Adoption of the Federal Constitution. . . .* (4 vols., Washington, 1836). A fifth volume, usually referred to as Vol. V of the *Debates,* is *Debates on the Adoption of the Federal Constitution in the Convention held at Philadelphia* (Washington, 1845) and contains Madison's notes. No less well known are the *American Archives,* edited by Peter Force, with the financial assistance of the government and the collaboration of the clerk of the House of Representatives. These were published in nine volumes in Washington between 1837 and 1853 and cover the years from 1774 to 1776. Also noteworthy is Peter Force, *Tracts and Other Papers Relating Principally to the . . . Colonies in North America* (4 vols., Washington, 1836–46); one of the earliest and most important is Ebenezer Hazard, *Historical Collections* (2 vols., Philadelphia, 1792–94). For other activities contemporary with Hazard and earlier, see above, ch. VIII. John Spencer Bassett, *The Middle Group of American Historians*

(New York, 1917), ch. V, contains a full discussion of most of these individuals. Mott, *American Magazines: 1741–1850*, 268–70.

2 H. B. Adams, *The Life and Writings of Jared Sparks* (2 vols., Boston, 1893), I, 373.

3 On the influence of mechanical and other techniques in the development of organized scholarship, see below, ch. XVII.

4 On the editorial controversy, O'Neill, *American Biography: 1800–1935*, 40. There were always two sides to the controversy. Edward Everett wrote in 1838 that it would be "impossible to point to a sentence in his volumes, penned for the gratification of a prejudice personal or national." Adams, *Sparks*, II, 288. Judge Story warned against making any changes because it would "perhaps be deemed a liberty not required, and very unfair." Joseph Story to Sparks, Oct. 19, 1833. *Ibid.*, II, 283–84.

5 Adams, *Sparks*, I, 6.

6 The facts of Sparks' early life are set forth in *Ibid.*, 4–18. Thomas Powell, *The Living Authors of America* (New York, 1850). James Parton, "Jared Sparks: From the Carpenter's Bench to the Presidency of Harvard College," *Triumphs of Enterprise, Ingenuity, and Public Spirit* (Hartford, Conn., 1871), 131–37.

7 Mostly by teaching.

8 Adams, *Sparks*, I, 30–31. In his argument for educational opportunity for women, he made the point that hard intellectual work was not detrimental to health.

9 *Ibid.*, 51.

10 *Ibid.*, 65.

11 *Ibid.*, 112, for his theological studies, 87–88. On the Newton essay, 83.

12 *Ibid.*, 169.

13 *Ibid.*, 263. Sparks' southern activities also gave him a brief contact with Thomas Jefferson, upon whom he called in 1820 and to whom he presented his first book on theological issues, 173. About his feelings concerning slavery he wrote: "I really have a great deal of fellow-feeling for these poor Africans, . . . while I actually keep out of the desert, and suffer my zeal to evaporate in reviews," 109, n. 1. *An Inquiry into the Comparative Moral Tendency of Trinitarian and Unitarian Doctrine. . . .* (Boston, 1823), was Sparks' first book and the one he presented to Jefferson.

14 As his chief biographer avers, *Ibid.*, I, 165.

15 *Ibid.*, I, 199. Also, I, 178.

16 A quarterly begun Jan. 1, 1823, and continued until Mar. 1826. It contained selections from Locke, Newton, and Penn and was designed to show the basic argument of such figures on the elements of religion. *Ibid.*, I, 204, also 202. Mott, *American Magazines: 1741–1850*, 204.

17 *Ibid.*, I, 189 n. 1, 190.

18 *Ibid.*, 179.

19 Mott, *American Magazines: 1741–1850*, 130.

20 The general subject of historical coverage in periodicals is treated in A. H. Shearer, "American Historical Magazines," *Mississippi Valley Historical Review*, IV (Mar. 1918), 484 ff. Sparks had objected that *The North American Review* was too local even before he became editor, Mott, *American Magazines: 1741–1850*, 200; Adams, *Sparks*, I, 242, 367, 422. An exceedingly able article covering aspects of this topic is Robert E. Streeter, "Association Psychology and Literary Nationalism in the *North American*

Review," *American Literature,* XVII (Mar. 1945), 243–54, and references in note 25.

21 *North American Review* (1821), new series, I, 433–35.

22 Sparks to Lucas Alamán, Mexican secretary of state, Sept. 27, 1825. Adams, *Sparks,* I, 297.

23 Alexander H. Everett to Sparks, Nov. 18, 1826. "I doubt whether the President of the United States has a higher trust to be accountable for than the editor of the 'North American.' " *Ibid.,* I, 286.

24 *Ibid.,* I, 292, 297.

25 He regarded the Holy Alliance as "a confederation of despotism." *Ibid.,* I, 319–20. Arthur P. Whitaker, *The United States and the Independence of Latin America, 1800–1830* (Baltimore, 1941), 565–70, is a comprehensive summary of this relatively unknown phase of Sparks' career. See also, Adams, *Sparks,* II, 299–320, for a discussion and summary of Sparks' articles in the *North American* and of those he encouraged others to write.

26 *Ibid.,* I, 389.

27 *Ibid.,* I, 390.

28 *Ibid.,* on Apr. 2, 1824.

29 Sparks to Alexander Everett, Sept. 12, 1826. "The materials have never been collected; they are still in the archives of the States, and in the hands of individuals." *Ibid.,* I, 509.

30 *Ibid.,* II, 215.

31 "I shall be obliged to examine these papers with great care, and if I can prepare them for publication at the same time I shall be effecting a double purpose." Adams, *Sparks,* II, 215.

32 Herbert Baxter Adams describes this month, probably correctly, as "Certainly the most important month of study in his whole life." He describes the collection, probably incorrectly, as "the richest

historical inheritance which ever came into the hands of an American scholar." *Ibid.,* II, 11.

33 Sparks met Mill, "the author of a work on political economy and another on India." Among the subjects of conversation with Mill and others were American institutions: "I was surprised to find . . . these gentlemen extremely ill-informed on all these topics." *Ibid.,* II, 60.

34 *Ibid.,* 79–80, 71.

35 *Ibid.,* 85.

36 *Ibid.,* 89, 96, 99.

37 *Ibid.,* 143, 319, 329–30. The details are recorded at 319.

38 *Life of John Ledyard the American Traveler; Comprising Selections from his journals and Correspondence* (Cambridge, Mass., 1828). Adams, *Sparks,* I, 372–75, 386. Jefferson, who knew Ledyard in Paris, gave Sparks some aid in its preparation, as did Lafayette, 274, n. 1.

39 William H. Prescott to Sparks, Apr. 13, 1828. Adams, *Sparks,* II, 51 n. 1.

40 *Diplomatic Correspondence of the American Revolution* (12 vols., Boston, 1829–30); *Writings of George Washington Being his Correspondence, Addresses, Messages, and other Papers, Official and Private* (12 vols., Boston, 1834–37); *Life of Gouverneur Morris, with Selections from His Correspondence and Miscellaneous Papers* (3 vols., Boston, 1832).

41 "A pioneer in this enterprise . . . ," Adams, *Sparks,* II, 186. The *National Almanac* began in 1863; see 183–86.

42 *Ibid.,* II, 187.

43 *Ibid.,* 189–90.

44 Sparks nearly succeeded in getting John Quincy Adams to contribute. He wrote Sparks he would have agreed "were I in a

condition to write the life of any other person while that of my father is upon my hands." John Quincy Adams to Sparks, Dec. 1, 1832. *Ibid.*, II, 193. *LHUS*, III, 116.

45 Adams, *Sparks*, II, 334. On Feb. 22, 1834, Sparks noted in his journal that he had made a publisher's agreement for the Franklin work, 340.

46 George Bancroft to Sparks, Nov. 28, 1832. *Ibid.*, II, 191–92.

47 Timothy Pitkin, *A Political and Civil History of the United States of America. . . .* (2 vols., New Haven, 1828).

48 *A Collection of the Familiar Letters and Miscellaneous Papers of Benjamin Franklin* (Boston, 1833).

49 See above, note 46.

50 Sparks' view was in general more humanistic. While he was certainly eloquent in praise of Franklin and his accomplishments, he made him more of a man, less of a saint. See above, note 5.

51 George Bancroft to Sparks, Feb. 18, 1830. O'Neill, *American Biography*, 39.

52 *Works of Benjamin Franklin; with Notes and a Life of the Author* (10 vols., Boston, 1836–40).

53 Adams, *Sparks*, II, 348–49.

54 Sparks to John Quincy Adams, Mar. 5, 1838. *Ibid.*, 345.

55 The editors of the *LHUS*, III, 116, remark: "Its notes are still useful, and it has been unjustly abused with little reason for its 'corrections' of Franklin's text." *NCHA*, VIII, 422; Paul Leicester Ford, *Franklin Bibliography* (Brooklyn, N.Y., 1889), 273; Adams, *Sparks*, II, 358–59.

56 Robert Rantoul and the Reverend George Putnam were also mem-

bers. Adams, *Sparks*, II, 366–67.

57 In 1838.

58 In 1834. Adams, *Sparks*, II, 369, 372.

59 The lectures were organized as follows: the Causes of the Revolution, the First Continental Congress, the Declaration of Independence, the Confederation of States, Money and Finances of the Revolution, the Continental Army, Military operations of the Revolution, Treaty of alliance between France and the United States, naval operations, Franco-American co-operation during the Revolution, peace attempts during the war, Treaty of peace, and the close of the war. *Ibid.*, 419.

60 *Ibid.*, 369.

61 June 1840.

62 Adams, *Sparks*, II, 378.

63 *Ibid.*, 384. "There is a suspicion that I shall find something on the Boundary Question." 385. For the role Sparks actually did play in what Daniel Webster called the "battle of the maps" during the negotiations leading up to the Webster-Ashburton Treaty (1842), see L. Martin and S. F. Bemis, "Franklin's Red-Line Map," *New England Quarterly*, X (Mar. 1937), 105–11. Sparks, however, found his map, not in London, but in Paris.

64 Adams, *Sparks*, II, 384.

65 *Ibid.*, 385.

66 By the State Paper Office. *Ibid.*, 385. These papers covered the years 1763–74.

67 *Ibid.*, 386–87.

68 Adams, *Sparks*, II, 386–87. The *Bibliotheca Americana; or A Chronological Catalogue of the Most Curious and Interesting Books, Pamphlets. . . . Upon the Subject of North and South America, from the Earliest Period to the Present. . . .* (Lon-

don, 1789), is ascribed to Arthur Homer in collaboration with others.

69 Adams, *Sparks*, II, 388–89.

70 *Ibid.*, 389.

71 *Ibid.*, 388.

72 The second series contained fifteen duodecimo volumes. Among the more distinctive were A. H. Everett on Patrick Henry, Francis Bowen on James Otis, John Gorham Palfrey on William Palfrey, George W. Greene on Nathaniel Greene, and Sparks on La Salle, Pulaski, Jean Ribault, and Charles Lee. The series also contained a reprint of the Ledyard. For discussion, see O'Neill, *American Biography*, 39; Adams, *Sparks*, II, 204–07; Mott, *American Magazines: 1741–1850*, 421.

73 Sparks had been proposed twenty years earlier, in 1828, as a compromise candidate. Adams, *Sparks*, II, 464, n. 1.

74 *Ibid.*, II, 479.

75 On March 23, 1851, he was injured in an accident while crossing the bridge between Boston and Cambridge. He had already been suffering from a neuralgic pain which was aggravated by the accident. *Ibid.*, II, 464, n. 1.

76 *Ibid.*, II, 479.

77 *Ibid.*, II, 468–69, 435.

78 On Sparks' career as Harvard's president, *Ibid.*, II, 435–78. Samuel E. Morison, *Three Centuries of Harvard, 1636–1936* (Cambridge, Mass., 1942), 280–82, 289.

79 Adams, *Sparks*, II, 547.

80 1853 to 1866.

81 1857 to 1858. Sparks was in Paris at the time of the attempted assassination of Napoleon III.

82 Adams, *Sparks*, II, 554, n. 1.

83 "The subject of his projected history became a sacred one among all who were familiar with him, and even in his family it was passed over in silence," said Brantz Meyer of Baltimore, one of his close friends. *Ibid.*, 554.

84 *Ibid.*, 556.

85 For the extent of Sparks' aid to Gilpin and Randall. *Ibid.*, 556–557. Among others, John C. Hamilton for his volume on Alexander Hamilton, Benson Lossing for his field book on the American Revolution, and Frederick Kapp for his biographies of De Kalb and of Steuben.

86 George Bancroft to Sparks, May 13, 1853, *Ibid.*, 310.

87 Sparks wrote to Trescot: "The fairness with which you have spoken of the motives and characters of the principals and actors is worthy of much praise." *Ibid.*, 558–59. William Henry Trescot, *Diplomatic History of the Administration of Washington and Adams* (Boston, 1857).

88 Adams, *Sparks*, I, xxii. See Sydney G. Fisher, "Myth-Making," 56.

89 Sparks' comments are in Adams, *Sparks*, I, 571–72.

90 Bernhard Knollenberg, *Washington and the Revolution* (New York, 1940), 151–55. O'Neill, *American Biography*, 39–40.

91 Adams, *Sparks*, II, 199. A different and public statement, which appeared as an advertisement for the first edition of the first series of the *Library of American Biography*, is cited by O'Neill, *American Biography*, 41.

92 Carlo Botta's history was translated as *History of the War of the Independence of the United States of America* (3 vols., Philadelphia, 1820–21) by George Alexander Otis. Sparks used Botta as a text in his Harvard course. Adams, *Sparks*, II, 93. James Grahame, *The History of*

the United States of North America from the Plantation of the British Colonies till their Assumption of National Independence (4 vols., 1827–36), with which Sparks was not greatly taken. Adams, *Sparks,* I, 554; II, 217. Christoph Daniel Ebeling was the author of *Erd-beschreibung und Geschichte von Amerika* (5 vols., Hamburg and Bonn, 1787–1816), a substantial work, but not accessible to most Americans because of the language barrier.

CHAPTER XIII

1 In 1814.
2 John Dewey, "James Marsh and American Philosophy," *Journal of the History of Ideas,* II (Apr. 1941), 131; Oliver Wendell Holmes, *Ralph Waldo Emerson. John Lothrop Motley: Two Memoirs* (Boston and New York, 1892), 114. Orie William Long, *Literary Pioneers* (Cambridge, Mass., 1935), 108–58. Henry D. Gray, *Emerson: A Statement of New England Transcendentalism as Expressed in the Philosophy of its Chief Exponent* (Stanford University, Calif., 1917). Frederic I. Carpenter (ed.), *Ralph Waldo Emerson: Representative Selections. . . .* (New York, 1934), xi–xlviii.
3 Van Wyck Brooks, *The Flowering of New England* (Boston, 1937), chs. 1–6.
4 Mott, *American Magazines: 1741–1850,* 302–05, contains a first-class sketch. See also, George Park Fisher, *Life of Benjamin Silliman* (2 vols., New York, 1866), and Edward S. Dana and others, *A Century of Science in America, with Special Reference to the American Journal of Sci-*

ence, 1818–1918 (New Haven, 1918), 13–59.
5 1831.
6 Emerson's *Nature* appeared in 1836. Kenneth W. Cameron has edited the most recent edition in the *Scholars' Facsimiles and Reprints* (New York, 1940), with index and bibliography.
7 Mott, *American Magazines: 1741–1850,* 410–11. Holmes, *Emerson,* 142, 307. Brooks, *Flowering,* 111–15, 121–22. For the purposes of the present volume, George W. Cooke, *Ralph Waldo Emerson: His Life, Writings, and Philosophy* (Boston, 1881), is most revealing, as it was published during the last year of Emerson's life. Bliss Perry, *Emerson Today* (Princeton, 1931), and Van Wyck Brooks, *The Life of Emerson* (New York, 1932), are also helpful. One of the most important critical studies is F. O. Mathiessen, *American Renaissance Art and Expression in the Age of Emerson and Whitman* (New York, 1941), 3–175. See also Matthew Arnold, "Emerson," *Discoveries in America* (Boston, 1885), and Paul E. More, "Emerson," *CHAL,* I, 349–62. On Longfellow, the earliest biography, despite its inaccuracies, best serves this chapter: Samuel Longfellow, *The Life of Henry W. Longfellow* (2 vols., Boston, 1886). Of particular usefulness is Lawrence Thompson, *Young Longfellow, 1807–1843* (New York, 1938). Long, *Literary Pioneers,* 159–98, is basic.
8 Mark A. DeWolfe Howe, *The Life and Letters of George Bancroft* (2 vols., New York), is a fundamental source, particularly for Bancroft's published correspondence. Howe's comments are usually suggestive, I, 9, 13.

The most recent and the best study ever made of Bancroft is by Russel B. Nye, *George Bancroft, Brahmin Rebel* (New York, 1944), in which Bancroft's student years are discussed, 33–59. Long, *Literary Pioneers,* 108–158.

9 Edward Everett wrote in *The North American Review* that Irving was the best writer of English prose. Mott, *American Magazines: 1741–1850,* 408, 174, 408–09, 392. Van Wyck Brooks, *The World of Washington Irving* (New York, 1944), 195–213, 214–61. 399–425. The most recent study is by Stanley T. Williams, *The Life of Washington Irving* (2 vols., New York, 1935). Of special pertinence for the present purpose is George S. Hellman, *Washington Irving, Esquire: Ambassador at Large from the New World to the Old* (New York, 1925), as is Henry A. Pochmann's introduction to *Washington Irving: Representative Selections. . . .* (New York, 1934), xi–xcii. On Cooper, Thomas R. Lounsbury, *James Fenimore Cooper* (Boston, 1882), is still the best study. Robert E. Spiller, *Fenimore Cooper: Critic of His Times* (New York, 1931), is exceedingly clear on Cooper's travels in Europe and his social ideas. For Bryant's estimate of Cooper, William Cullen Bryant, *Orations and Addresses* (New York, 1873), 45–91. Parrington, *Main Currents,* II, 222–237; Preston A. Barba, *Cooper in Germany* (Bloomington, Ind., 1914); Robert E. Spiller, *The American in England. . . .* (New York, 1926), 300–45. On Bryant, Cairns, *British Criticism of American Writings* (Madison, Wis., 1918), 158–64; Parrington, *Main Currents,* II, 238–46.

10 In 1837.

11 In 1839.

12 Hawthorne's *Twice-Told Tales* appeared in 1837. See, in general, George E. Woodberry, *Nathaniel Hawthorne* (Boston, 1902). Important is Leslie Stephen. "Nathaniel Hawthorne," *Hours in a Library* (New York, 1875), I, 204–37; Brooks, *Flowering,* 210–227.

13 Brooks, *World of Washington Irving,* 443–56. For some contemporary evaluation of Poe, Mott, *American Magazines: 1741–1850,* 498; of Lowell, 412; of Melville, 416. Edmund C. Stedman, "James Russell Lowell," *Poets of America* (Boston, 1885), 304–48. William C. Brownell, *American Prose Masters* (New York, 1909), 271–335. Parrington, *Main Currents,* II, 460–72. Brooks, *Flowering,* 505–25. On Poe, Arthur H. Quinn, *Edgar Allan Poe: A Critical Biography* (New York, 1941), is excellent, but George E. Woodberry's *The Life of Edgar Allan Poe, Personal and Literary, with His Chief Correspondence with Men of Letters* (2 vols., Boston, 1909, rev. ed.), well repays examination. Stedman, *Poets of America,* 225–72. C. P. Cambiaire, *The Influence of Edgar Allan Poe on France* (New York, 1927). John E. Englekirk, *Edgar Allan Poe in Hispanic Literature* (New York, 1934).

14 Biographical details of Bancroft's early life are in Nye, *Bancroft,* 4–16, and Howe, *Bancroft,* I, 9, 13. William Milligan Sloane, "George Bancroft—In Society, In Politics, In Letters," *Century Magazine,* XI (Jan. 1887), 473–487. Sloane was at one time Bancroft's secretary.

15 At Exeter the Reverend Hosea Hildreth, professor of natural

philosophy and mathematics and father of the historian Richard Hildreth, was one of his teachers.

16 Howe, *Bancroft*, I, 1.

17 In May 1818, he was taken to see old John Adams by Andrews Norton to consult with him on the advisability of going abroad to study theology. Adams did not think much of it, but Bancroft went anyway. Although he pursued his theological studies with typical diligence, he soon abandoned its study. Nye, *Bancroft*, 39, 63, 64.

18 See below, 248–50 for references to Bancroft's explication of his own philosophy.

19 H. C. Strippel, "A Bibliography of Books and Pamphlets by George Bancroft." Howe, *Bancroft*, II, 331–41, which does not include periodical writings unless separately reprinted. More recent is the bibliography compiled by Nye, *Bancroft*, 227–30. John Spencer Bassett (ed.), *Correspondence of George Bancroft and Jared Sparks, 1823–1832, Smith College Studies in History* (Northampton, Mass., 1915), II, 2, 70, note.

20 J. Franklin Jameson, "Early Days of the American Historical Association," *American Historical Review*, XL (October, 1943), 5.

21 He not only broke down academic provincialisms, but he helped to break down conventional stereotypes. This was particularly true of the image Massachusetts literary men had of Goethe as a vile, immoral man. Bancroft shared this view, but when he actually met Goethe he found his impression was really unaffected by Goethe's soiled shirt. Goethe's conversation interested young Bancroft in German literature, and Bancroft's interests were almost always followed by study. See his "Schiller's Minor Poems," *North American Review*, XVI (Oct. 1823), 268–80, "Goethe's Werke," *North American Review*, XIX (Oct. 1824), 303–25; "German Literature," *The American Quarterly Review*, II (Sept. 1827), 171–86, III (Mar. 1828), 150–73, IV (Sept. 1828), 157–90; "German Poetry," *The American Quarterly Review*, X (Sept. 1831), 194–210. For Bancroft and Goethe, see an article with that title by O. W. Long, *Studies in Philology*, XXXVIII (Oct. 1931), 820–29. Nye, *Bancroft*, 76 ff., 80–81.

22 Harvard appointed him tutor in Greek for the year 1822–23. Among other pieces the following are of interest: "Heeren's *Politics of Ancient Greece*," *North American Review*, XVIII (Apr. 1824), 390–406, "Herder's Writings," XX (Jan. 1825), XXXII (Apr. 1831), 344–67.

23 His general manner and German methods irritated almost everyone. The students in particular disliked him intensely, but they learned more Greek than ever before. Howe, *Bancroft*, I, ch. II; Nye, *Bancroft*, 60–84. See particularly, "On Harvard University," *North American Review*, XXXII (July 1831), 216–66. Long, "Joseph Green Cogswell," *Literary Pioneers*, 93.

24 Adams, *Jared Sparks*, I, 338. John Spencer Bassett, "The Round Hill School," *Educational Review*, I (Apr. 1891), 341–44. Long, "Joseph Green Cogswell," *Literary Pioneers*, 93–101.

25 Nye, *Bancroft*, 60–61.

26 Cited in Kraus, 217. See Nye, *Bancroft*, 48. Bancroft to Sparks, Sept. 20, 1824. Adams, *Sparks*, I, 335.

27 *Ibid.*, 338.

28 Nye, *Bancroft,* 78–79.
29 Bancroft to Sparks, Sept. 20, 1824, Adams, *Sparks,* I, 335.
30 Howe, *Bancroft,* II, 102.
31 "In New England," writes Nye, "there were but two ways to attain eminence—to make history or to write it. Accordingly, he set out to do both." Nye, *Bancroft,* 84.
32 Walt Stewart, "George Bancroft," *Jernegan Essays,* 4. For general background clarifying Bancroft's political role: A. B. Darling, *Political Changes in Massachusetts, 1824–1828* (New Haven, 1925); Frederick J. Turner, *The United States* (New York, 1935); Arthur Schlesinger, Jr., *The Age of Jackson* (Boston, 1945), especially, chs. 7–10, especially 255–57, 419; John Spencer Bassett, *Middle Group of American Historians* (New York, 1917).
33 Cited in Nye, *Bancroft,* 87.
34 Cited in Kraus, 220.
35 Nye, *Bancroft,* 88–89. The Reverend Aaron Bancroft had been a faithful Federalist, and Bancroft's first marriage brought him into the circle of the Dwights, as conservative a group of Whigs as one could find in Boston.
36 "The Bank of the United States," *North American Review,* XXXII (Jan. 1831), 21–64.
37 Nye, *Bancroft,* 90–91; Stewart, "Bancroft," *Jernegan Essays,* 5–6. Schlesinger, *Jackson,* chs. 7–10, but see also Bray Hammond, "Jackson, Biddle, and the Bank of the United States," *Journal of Economic History,* VII (May 1947), 1–23, and the same writer's review of Schlesinger, VI (May 1946), 79–84, in the same journal.
38 *Boston Courier,* Oct. 23, 1834.
39 Nye believes Bancroft "planned his career in politics cleverly and carefully" and that "for political skill and astuteness he had few equals in Massachusetts or, for that matter, in all New England." *Ibid.,* 90, 108. Brooks, *Flowering,* 130–31.
40 Bancroft's political activity began with his Fourth of July speech in 1826, which was followed by his part in the Bank controversy. In 1834 he received the nomination of the Anti-Masons for the Massachusetts legislature. He refused nomination by the Workingmen's Party, but stood for the Anti-Masons and was defeated. Bancroft's plan was to get Democratic leaders to see that only by combining forces with the Workingmen's Party and the anti-Masonic groups could the Democrats successfully challenge Whig control.
41 Schlesinger, *Age of Jackson,* 254–257.
42 Nye, *Bancroft,* 102.
43 *Ibid.,* 102, but see Adams, *Sparks,* II, 292–93.
44 Nye, *Bancroft,* 102.
45 *Ibid.,* 104.
46 *Ibid.,* 106.
47 Alfred Goldberg, "School Histories of the Middle Period," *Historiography and Urbanization,* Eric F. Goldman (ed.) (Baltimore, 1941), 174–76.
48 A brief statement of the various editions is in Stewart, "Bancroft," *Jernegan Essays,* 11. See also Nye, *Bancroft,* 286–87, 296–97. References to the publication of volumes in the text are to the first edition, *The History of the United States from the Discovery of the Continent* (10 vols., Boston, 1834–74); references to content, chapters, quotations, and analysis are to the Centenary Edition, *History of the United States of America, from the Discovery of the Continent* (6 vols., Boston,

1876–79). This edition is also the "Thoroughly Revised Edition." The quotation from the preface is from the first volume of the first edition.

49 "Introduction," I, 1, 2.

50 "The Office of the People in Art, Government, and Religion," *Literary and Historical Miscellanies* (New York, 1855), 408–09. "'From his early German training and continued study of metaphysics, Mr. Bancroft was probably the most philosophical of all American historians." Adams, *Sparks,* II, 198. Bancroft's comment on Hegel is interesting in this connection. He wrote to Edward Everett from Germany: "I took a philosophical course with Hegel. But I thought it lost time to listen to his display of unintelligible words." Long, *Literary Pioneers,* 248, n. 53.

51 When Bancroft delivered the address "The Office of the People" in 1835, Ralph Waldo Emerson's *Nature* was not to appear for a year. The philosophy presented in this address had been Bancroft's for a least a dozen years before the development of the transcendentalist movement. "If reason is a universal faculty, the universal decision is the nearest criterion of truth." "Office of the People," 415. Mind, wrote Bancroft, "eludes the power of appropriation; it exists only in its own individuality; it is a property which cannot be confiscated and cannot be torn away; it laughs at chains; it bursts from imprisonment; it defies monopoly. A government of equal rights must, therefore, rest upon mind; not wealth, not brute force, the sum of the moral intelligence of the community should rule the State." 421–22. Nye, *Bancroft,* 101.

52 "Office of the People," 408–09. Howe, *Bancroft,* II, 119–20.

53 "Office of the People," 410, 415, 421. "The public happiness is the true object of legislation, and can be secured only by the masses of mankind themselves awakening to the knowledge and care of their own interests." 422. "The duty of America is to secure the culture and happiness of the masses by their reliance on themselves." 423. "Thus the opinion we respect is . . . not the opinion of one or of a few, but the sagacity of the many." 425. "The measure of the progress of civilization is the progress of the people." 427.

54 See below, 254–55.

55 See Kraus, 224.

56 Bancroft, *History,* II, ch. XXXII, "Progress of France in North America," ch. XXXIII, "France and the Valley of the Mississippi," ch. XXXIV, "France Contends for the Fisheries and the Great West." On Indians and Indian culture, ch. XXXVI, "The Aborigines East of the Mississippi. Their Languages," ch. XXXVII, "Their Manners, Polity, and Religion," ch. XXXVIII, "Their Nature and Origin."

57 *Ibid.,* ch. XLI.

58 Carl L. Becker made the most of an irrefutable example in "Labelling the Historians," *Everyman His Own Historian* (New York, 1935), 134–42, Nye, *Bancroft,* 104, Stewart, "Bancroft," *Jernegan Essays,* 22–23.

59 For the reference to Cabot, vol. I, 67; to Virginia, 87.

60 Becker, "Labelling the Historians," 139.

61 Vol. III, 4. Fisher, "Myth-Making," 68–69, praised the earlier volumes, but wrote "in the Revolution he became merely a scholarly Weems. . . ."

⁶² Vol. III, 4. "The authors of the American Revolution avowed for their object the welfare of mankind, and believed that they were in the service of their own and all future generations. Their faith was just; for the world of mankind does not exist in fragments, nor can a country have an isolated existence. All men are brothers; and all are bondsmen for one another," 5.

⁶³ Bancroft to Buchanan, March 24, 1848: "I can only say for myself that my residence in Europe has but quickened and confirmed my love for the rule of the people, and I do not believe that any arrangement of political power short of universal suffrage, can give to freedom the security which it needs in planning legislation suited to the advancement of the race." Howe, *Bancroft,* II, 33. Bancroft's wife has helped us to understand this phase of their joint career. Elizabeth Davis Bancroft, *Letters from England, 1846–1849* (New York, 1904).

⁶⁴ See, ch. XV of present study.

⁶⁵ See above, ch. XIII of present study.

⁶⁶ John Gorham Palfrey (1796–1881) was theologian as well as historian. Graduated from Harvard in 1815, he became pastor of Boston's Brattle Street Unitarian Church and professor of sacred literature at his alma mater. Palfrey was also active in politics. He was a member of the Massachusetts legislature (1842–43), was secretary of state (1844–1847), represented Massachusetts as Whig congressman (1847–1849) and was postmaster of Boston (1861–67). He edited *The North American Review* (1835–43), but his historical reputation rests exclusively upon his four-volume history of New England. *A Compendious History of New England from the Discovery by Europeans to the First General Congress of the Anglo-American Colonies* (3 vols., Boston, 1858–64); the fourth was published in 1875. See Charles Francis Adams, "The Sifted Grain and the Grain Sifters," *American Historical Review,* VI (Jan. 1901), 221.

⁶⁷ Nye, *Bancroft,* 187.

⁶⁸ For a discussion of Hildreth, see below, ch. XIV.

⁶⁹ Kraus, 257–60.

⁷⁰ Nye, *Bancroft,* 188.

⁷¹ Bancroft stated his view tersely: "The principle on which the separation was demanded, rested on a fallacy which would leave us no country, no state, no social band: it was the doctrine of individualism, pushed to its extremest limit." Cited *Ibid.,* 212.

⁷² *Ibid.,* 209. He had regarded Lincoln as "brainless and incompetent." Five years later he had changed his mind, and he told a mourning crowd in Union Square, New York, that Lincoln who had been "scoffed at by the proud as unfit for his station . . . , pursued a course of wisdom and kindness, harboring not one vengeful feeling or purpose of cruelty." *Ibid.,* 225.

⁷³ *Ibid.,* 215, 218.

⁷⁴ *Ibid.,* 219–20.

⁷⁵ *Ibid.,* 220.

⁷⁶ *Ibid.,* 228–29.

⁷⁷ William A. Dunning, "More Light on Andrew Johnson," *Truth in History* (New York, 1937), 83–88, 90–92. Nye, *Bancroft,* 230–31.

⁷⁸ Dunning, "More Light on Andrew Johnson," 89. Nye, *Bancroft,* 232–33.

⁷⁹ *Ibid.,* 234.

⁸⁰ Bancroft dealt with military his-

tory in this volume, and many a revolutionary hero lost his halo. Bancroft indeed was as lethal as Hildreth in altering reputations, though he said less about it in advance. But the descendants took a dim view of the historian's forthrightness and came to the defense of their ancestors. What is known as the "war of the grandsons" followed the battles, some of which were fought with angry pamphlets. See Bancroft's account of Joseph Reed, Vol. V, 457, 341, 461–62, especially note, 388–90. Of General Philip Schuyler he wrote: "The courage of the commander being gone, his officers and his army became spiritless; and, as his only resource, he solicited aid from Washington with unreasoning importunity." Vol. V, 581. Other revelations concerning Generals Sullivan and Greene produced the "pamphlet war," for which see Nye, *Bancroft*, 237–38.

81 Vol. VI, 77–95.

82 *Ibid.*, 78.

83 *Ibid.*, ch. XXVIII, "The United States and George III," ch. XXIX, "The United States and France, 1778," ch. XXXVII, "The King of Spain Baffled by the Backwoodsmen of Virginia, 1778–1779."

84 *Ibid.*, ch. XXI, "Germany and the United States, 1778," ch. XXXII, "The Relations of the Two New Powers, 1778."

85 Nye, *Bancroft*, 238.

86 Dunning, "More Light on Andrew Johnson," 83 ff. Dunning's discovery did not occur until 1905.

87 Nye, *Bancroft*, 249–50.

88 *Ibid.*, 255–58, especially 257.

89 *Ibid.*, 273, 275.

90 *Ibid.*, 255.

91 When Bancroft's final volume appeared, the writing of history had entered a new era. See below, ch. XVII. Bancroft had not been outmoded, but the impact of new ideas had passed him by. The essence of the change is indicated by a reviewer who asked testily: "Will Mr. Bancroft inform us what are the intuitions of reason, a faculty hitherto concerned with deduction?" Cited *Ibid.*, 286. He wrote in the "Prefatory Note" of the Centenary Edition: "Every noteworthy criticism that has come under observation has been carefully weighed, accepted for what it was worth, and never rejected, except after examination. The main object has been the attainment of exact accuracy; so that, if possible, not even a partial error may escape correction. Very few statements disappear before the severer application of the rules of historical criticism . . . and simplicity and clearness has been the constant aim. Vol. I, Chaps. v–vi. Bancroft had learned a part of the language of the new scholarship, but he was never to learn the new concepts.

92 The final volume of the *History* marked the end of forty years of work on this monumental project. They were forty crowded years, constantly interrupted by other duties and the pressure of great events in which Bancroft took part.

93 Bancroft wrote occasional pieces for periodicals in addition to his major research activity, among them one on Washington, on Clay, and on Lowell, Nye, *Bancroft*, 295.

94 The first volume of the Centenary Edition and the remaining five were not only carefully revised, but demonstrated Bancroft's response to general criticism. The belligerent patriotism,

to which there had been so much objection, was tempered. But the philosophy remained unimpaired.

95 *Ibid.*, 296.

96 He still maintained something of his old pace, rising early and putting in a day of work, which was the envy of far younger men.

97 George Ticknor Curtis, *History of the Origin, Formation, and Adoption of the Constitution of the United States* (2 vols., New York, 1854–58).

98 Bancroft's history of the formation of the Constitution is significant for its scholarship. He left no manuscript possibility unturned. The Peter Force Collection was made available to him by the Library of Congress, he used the archives of the states whenever possible and he tapped the literary resources of the contemporaries of the period. Through his European and diplomatic connections, he obtained the reports of French representatives to the United States (1782–1790), and materials from Dutch, Spanish, and Austrian depositories. Nye, *Bancroft*, 288.

99 *History of the Formation of the Constitution of the United States of America* (2 vols., New York, 1882).

100 Bancroft felt he could readily bring the *History* to 1840, a period he believed he knew quite well. Nye, *Bancroft*, 296.

101 *History of the Formation of the Constitution*, preface.

102 "The Last Revision" (1886) developed the changes of the Centenary Edition still further. Stewart, "George Bancroft," *Jernegan Essays*, 11.

103 *Martin Van Buren to the End of his Public Career* (New York, 1889), a task that the reviewers pretty generally agreed might well have been left unfinished.

Begun as a campaign biography, it had most of the attributes of a campaign biography when completed.

104 Howe, *Bancroft*, II, 107.

105 *Ibid.*, 107.

106 *Ibid.*, 106. Henry Adams, a devastating critic, wrote Francis Parkman, Dec. 21, 1884, and delivered himself of a meaningful rebuke. See below, 305–6.

107 Howe, *Life and Letters*, I, 205–206.

108 Kraus, 230.

109 Adams, *Sparks*, II, 353, n. 1.

110 Nye, *Bancroft*, 99. In an address before the New York Historical Society in 1854, Bancroft turned again to these themes. "No science has been reached, no thought generated, no truth discovered, which has not from all time existed potentially in every human mind. The belief in the progress of the race does not, therefore, spring from the supposed possibility of his acquiring new faculties, or coming into the possession of a new nature," 483–84. "The necessity of the progress of the race follows, therefore, from the fact, that the great Author of all life has left truth in its immutability to be observed, and has endowed man with the power of observation and generalization," 488, "Oration Delivered before the New York Historical Society, The Progress of Mankind," *Literary and Historical Miscellanies*, 481–517.

111 Stewart, "George Bancroft," *Jernegan Essays*, 21–23. Emerson, "Hildreth, Draper and Scientific History," *Historiography and Urbanization*, 146. Bancroft himself wrote "There is no faculty I would more desire to possess in an eminent degree than

cool, practical judgment." Sparks, *Adams,* I, 335.

[112] See note 91 above. Bancroft's address before the American Historical Association in 1886, "Self-Government," revealed how far removed Bancroft was from the younger generation of historians. When Bancroft used the words "law," "development," "critical spirit," he was not thinking in terms of the modern scientific quest; he was still thinking in terms of the idealistic philosophy. See Nye, *Bancroft,* 296.

CHAPTER XIV

[1] Van Wyck Brooks, *Flowering of New England,* 4–9. Prescott, Motley, and Parkman are treated in ch. XV.

[2] 1805–65.

[3] Ray A. Billington, Bert James Loewenberg, and Merle Colby, *Massachusetts: A Guide to its Places and People* (Boston, 1937), 223–24.

[4] Donald E. Emerson, *Richard Hildreth* (Baltimore, 1946), is a well-rounded biographical treatment upon which the present writer has relied heavily. Emerson has promised a full-length historiographical analysis, part of which appears in his essay "Hildreth, Draper, and 'Scientific History,'" *Historiography and Urbanization,* 139–53. Kelly, "Richard Hildreth," *Jernegan Essays,* 25–42, contains helpful suggestions and information. Kenneth B. Murdock is the author of the account in the *DAB,* IX, 19–20. Kraus, 243–54. Martha M. Pingel, *An American Utilitarian: Richard Hildreth as a Philosopher* (New York, 1958), is a more recent study.

[5] Emerson, *Hildreth,* 31, 43, 69,

80. Efforts to unravel the problem of Richard Hildreth must certainly take his failure to achieve success and recognition into account.

[6] Nye, *Bancroft,* 287. Emerson, *Hildreth,* 143.

[7] A post was available at Harvard when Sparks resigned to assume the presidency in 1849. Whether Hildreth expected seriously to be considered, there was some talk about it. In any event, it was Francis Bowen of *The North American Review* who received the appointment. Bowen was deprived of his position in 1851, and this time Hildreth applied for it. Had his application met with favor, his financial burdens would have been considerably lessened. His rejection embittered him. Emerson, *Hildreth,* 136–39.

[8] Mrs. Hildreth to John A. Andrew, governor of Massachusetts, Feb. 4, 1861. "I therefore intend to go on to Washington to see Mr. Lincoln this week, tho 'I tread thro' blood . . .' I do not find this an age of *delicacy* [italics hers] and I have fallen into the common weakness— [of] which my sensitive and true-hearted husband would be forever exempt." Cited *Ibid.,* 159.

[9] William Dean Howells, *Literary Friends and Acquaintances* (New York, 1900), 97–98.

[10] Notably Edward Channing, Samuel E. Morison, "Edward Channing: A Memoir," *Proceedings of the Massachusetts Historical Society,* LXIV (1930–32), 260. Among others were James Ford Rhodes and James Schouler. M. A. DeWolfe Howe, *James Ford Rhodes, American Historian* (New York, 1929), 26; James Schouler, *History of the United States under the Consti-*

tution (5 vols., Washington, D.C., 1886–91), I, iii, iv. These historians, however, seem not to have read Hildreth's other works. See Emerson, *Historiography and Urbanization,* 142; G. P. Gooch, *History and Historians in the Nineteenth Century* (London, 1913), 407–08; J. S. Bassett, "Later Historians," *CHAL,* II, 108–09.

11 Emerson, *Historiography and Urbanization,* 142.

12 Emerson has made the richest contribution on this point in both his writings on the subject already cited. Kelly has also made pertinent observations on the "problem." See also Arthur M. Schlesinger, Jr., "The Problem of Richard Hildreth," *New England Quarterly,* XIII (June 1940), 223–45.

13 Specific citations to Hildreth's works appear below.

14 John Stuart Mill, *Dissertations and Discussions* (3 vols., New York, 1874), I, 379–80.

15 Hildreth to Caroline Weston, Nov. 26, 1841, Emerson, *Hildreth,* 110.

16 Emerson, *Historiography and Urbanization,* 143.

17 See references cited above, 275–277. Hildreth, *History of the United States of America* (6 vols., New York, 1849–52), first edition. Subsequent editions appeared in 1856, 1863, and 1880. References are to the latter.

18 "Advertisement," *History,* I, vii, ix. "A Note: Hildreth on Bancroft's *History,*" Appendix I, Emerson, *Hildreth,* 163–68. Theodore Parker put his finger on one of the significant aspects of difference. In a letter to Francis Parkman, Sept. 22, 1851, he wrote: "The historian cannot tell all; he must choose such as, to him, clearly set forth the Idea

of the nation—or man—he describes. Bancroft chooses one set of facts, Hildreth another—and how different the N.E. of Bancroft from H.'s N.E." Mason Wade, *Francis Parkman,* 312. Although Hildreth was doubtless chagrined that Bancroft had an influence denied to him, he was not unappreciative of Bancroft's work. In his revision of 1880 he referred to a New York historian and to "Bancroft's new volumes —fruits, at least in part, of laborious and protracted researches on the part of their accomplished author among European colonial records." Hildreth, *History,* I, ix. A copy of Hildreth's *History,* belonging to Bancroft and now in the New York Public Library, contains Bancroft's marginal notes, Emerson, *Hildreth,* 165, n. 6.

19 *Ibid.,* 164.

20 Oliver Wendell Holmes, father of the late justice, once remarked that the sons of ministers were exceptionally fortunate. The lack did not affect his own son, but Emerson, Parker, Lowell, Bancroft, and Hildreth had whatever advantages such paternity brought.

21 Brooks, *Flowering,* 21–45. Hildreth was eighth in a class of fifty-three. Bancroft was certainly more precocious and earned greater distinction at his Harvard commencement. Nye, *Bancroft,* 18–27.

22 *Ibid.,* 81–82, 139. On Hildreth, see below, 272–73.

23 Hildreth soon became less enthusiastic about law as a career and the utility of the legal profession. Emerson, *Hildreth,* 42–43, suggests that a part of this disillusionment may have come from Bentham.

24 *The Slave, or Memoirs of Archy*

Moore (2 vols., Boston, 1836), has the distinction of being the first antislavery novel.

25 *Despotism in America or, an Inquiry into the Nature and Results of the Slave-Holding System in the United States* (Boston, 1840), possesses a number of points of historical interest. Among other things it contains Hildreth's analysis of the development of democracy in America, in the course of which Thomas Jefferson fares somewhat better than he was later to fare in the *History.*

26 In 1840. He edited the Guiana *Chronicle* and the *Royal Gazette.*

27 In addition to *The Theory of Morals* and *The Theory of Politics,* he planned more translations of the works of Bentham, a life of Jesus, a universal history, a history of the Christian religion, a history of the United States, and various other items, Emerson, *Hildreth,* 97–98.

28 Letter to Caroline Weston, Jan. 8, 1841, *Ibid.,* 99.

29 The reviews, including that of Orestes A. Brownson, are digested and appraised, *Ibid.,* 106–108.

30 Some critics, like Brownson, identified Hildreth with transcendentalism. But his reliance on Hume, Bentham, and Locke could hardly have pleased transcendentalist ears, which were always attuned to the infinite.

31 See above, n. 12.

32 From *A Letter to Andrews Norton on Miracles as the Foundation of Religious Faith* (Boston, 1840), cited in Emerson, *Hildreth,* 90. Hildreth commented that he detested "all forms of cant, especially the so fashionable twin cants of a spasmodic, wordy rhetoric and a transcen-

dental philosophy. . . ." "Advertisement," *History,* I, xi.

33 Emerson, *Hildreth,* 99.

34 *Ibid.,* "Advertisement," *The Theory of Morals: An Inquiry Concerning the Law of Moral Distinctions and Variations and Contradictions of Ethical Codes* (Boston, 1844). Emerson, *Hildreth,* 101.

35 *Ibid.,* 102.

36 *Ibid.,* 103.

37 *Ibid.,* 104.

38 Hildreth's formulation of moral theory is subject to the inherent weaknesses of the utilitarian formula. At this point it is pertinent only to mention one or two basic confusions. Bentham and Hildreth assume that the search for pleasure and the escape from pain are alone among the objects of desire. Their analysis is based on a psychological compulsion, for in the utilitarian argument there is no place for what should be sought; to achieve pleasure and to avoid pain *is* the human objective. This assumption gives mankind a native and inherent character, namely, selfishness. Man acts in terms of his own individual ends, and they are selfish ends. The theory further is vulnerable, because it fails to take different *qualities* into consideration. Objects provide pleasures, and different objects yield different qualities of pleasure. Pleasure cannot be conceived apart from the objects that produce them.

39 Emerson, *Hildreth,* 110. Hildreth to Caroline Weston, Nov. 26, 1841. *Ibid.,* 110, who points out that Hildreth was reading Bacon at this juncture.

40 Emerson, *Hildreth,* 106–07.

41 Orestes A. Brownson, an acute observer, was quick to perceive the source of Hildreth's intel-

lectual inspiration. He "is substantially, a Benthamite—for his slight modification of Benthamism amounts, practically, to nothing at all. . . . He has studied Bentham till his head is more confused, if possible, than was ever Bentham's own head, and till even his heart appears to have lost all of its native appreciation of right and wrong." Cited in Emerson, "Hildreth, Draper, and 'Scientific History,' " *Historiography and Urbanization*, 150.

42 Emerson, *Hildreth*, 107.

43 *The Theory of Politics: An Inquiry into the Foundations of Governments and the Causes and Progress of Political Revolutions* (New York, 1853). It is Emerson's view that the poor reception accorded *The Theory of Morals* induced Hildreth to defer publication. When it finally appeared, it was probably altered to incorporate the events of the revolutions of 1848. In any case, it was written during the South American period and therefore before the *History*. Emerson, *Hildreth*, 114, 115. Hildreth called attention to this volume for the benefit of those critics who had dismissed the *History* as of no philosophical account, 145. He probably did not, as Kelly avers, publish the *Treatise* "in answer" to such objections. Kelly, "Richard Hildreth," *Jernegan Essays*, 39.

44 *Theory of Politics*, 267, as cited in Emerson, *Hildreth*, 147. See also, 145–46.

45 *Ibid.*, 148. Marx was not yet at school when Bentham died in 1832. Later, Marx described him as "the insipid, pedantic, leather-tongued oracle of the commonplace intelligence of the nineteenth century," Karl Marx, *Capital* (Everyman edition, London and New York, 1951), II, 671.

46 *Theory of Politics*, 271, as cited in Emerson, *Hildreth*, 149.

47 Caroline Negus not only made the *History* possible in all these vital ways; she also made it possible in a material way. As a painter, she suppressed her larger ambitions and devoted herself to portraits and miniatures. Hildreth was for a time free of financial worries. In addition, their home attracted many artists and musicians, and these contacts added to Hildreth's understanding and enjoyment. Mrs. Hildreth regarded her husband as "a living Encyclopedia and History."

48 Hildreth, *History*, IV, vii–viii. The major reviews are admirably summarized in Emerson, *Hildreth*, 131–32.

49 Emerson, *Hildreth*, 133–34. Kelly, "Richard Hildreth," *Jernegan Essays*, 32.

50 Hildreth, *History*, I, ix.

51 *Ibid.*, Vol. I, 339.

52 *North American Review*, LXXIII (1851), 413–27, 431–37.

53 *History*, I, 329, 402.

54 *Ibid.*, I, 402.

55 Élie Halévy, A *History of the English People in the Nineteenth Century*, E. I. Watkin and D. A. Barker, translators (5 vols., New York, 1924–34), I, 86.

56 In 1853 he wrote in the "Advertisement" to the *History*, "Indeed, I am encouraged to entertain the idea of bringing down my narrative of American affairs, in a Third Series of two additional volumes, to the end of the presidential term which has just closed. . . ." *History*, I, xi. The quotation in the text is cited in Emerson, *Hildreth*, 142.

57 Kelly, "Richard Hildreth," *Jernegan Essays*, 29. *LHUS*, III, 115.

58 Kelly, "Richard Hildreth," *Jernegan Essays*, 26.

59 Roy F. Nichols, *The Disruption of American Democracy* (New York, 1948), 9–10. Nor were the Jacksonians any less confused in the decade of the thirties, Arthur M. Schlesinger, Jr., *Age of Jackson*, 424–25. Hildreth, once a candidate for the lower house in Massachusetts on the Whig ticket, was referred to as "this *Snapping Turtle Abolitionist.*" The broadside began: "CAN ANY TRUE WHIG VOTE FOR *RICHARD HILDRETH*—that notorious Hildreth, so justly styled the 'unprincipled'?" Emerson, *Hildreth*, 65.

60 *Ibid.*, 128.

61 *The History of Banks: to which is added, a Demonstration of the Advantages and Necessity of Free Competition in the Business of Banking* (Boston, 1837). *Banks, Banking, and Paper Currency* (Boston, 1840). Emerson has compiled a full bibliography of the known published writings of Hildreth, "Bibliography of the Published Writings of Richard Hildreth," Emerson, *Hildreth*, Appendix II, 169–72. The references to the banking publications are at 170–71.

62 Schlesinger, *Age of Jackson*, 144–148, 164–65, 225. Emerson, *Hildreth*, 85–88.

63 *The People's Presidential Candidate, or The Life of William Henry Harrison of Ohio* (Boston, 1839).

64 Schlesinger, *Age of Jackson*, 267–82.

65 Emerson, *Hildreth*, 123. "I only wish," he wrote, "to secure for all of us the liberty to worship according to our own ideas."

66 *Ibid.*, 71.

67 See above, n. 30.

68 *A Joint Letter to Orestes A. Brownson and the Editor of the North American Review: In which the Editor of the North American Review is proved to be no Christian, and little better than an Atheist.* Emerson, *Hildreth*, 171, 122.

69 Mill, *Utilitarianism, Liberty, and Representative Government* (Everyman Library, New York, 1950), 125–26.

70 *"Our First Men:" A Calendar of Wealth, Fashion and Gentility, containing a list of those persons taxed in the City of Boston, credibly reported to be worth ONE HUNDRED THOUSAND DOLLARS; with biographical notices of the principal persons* (Boston, 1846). Emerson, *Hildreth*, 126, 171.

71 *Native-Americanism Detected and Exposed. By a Native American* (Boston, 1845), Emerson, *Hildreth*, 125.

72 *Ibid.*, 63–68.

73 *Ibid.*, 152.

74 Hildreth, *History*, I, ix, xii.

75 *Ibid.*, II, 150.

76 *Ibid.*, 149.

77 *Ibid.*, 151.

78 *Ibid.*, IV, 293.

79 *Ibid.*, 297–98.

80 *Ibid.*, 352.

81 *Ibid.*, 292–93.

82 *Ibid.*, 455.

83 *Ibid.*, 293.

84 *Ibid.*, 296.

85 *Ibid.*, 296–97. Italics mine.

86 *Ibid.*, III, 473.

87 *Ibid.*, 472.

88 *Ibid.*, 484.

89 *Ibid.*, 401, 547–48.

90 *Ibid.*, IV, 343–45.

91 Jeremy Bentham, *Theory of Legislation* (2 vols., Boston, 1840). Emerson, *Hildreth*, 90–93.

92 The literature on utilitarianism and utilitarian thinkers is extensive. Leslie Stephen, *The English Utilitarians* (3 vols., London,

1912), is a good introduction. Vol. I is devoted to Bentham. More incisive and critical is Élie Halévy, *The Growth of Philosophic Radicalism*, Mary Morris, trans. (London, 1949), with a preface by A. D. Lindsay, which is critical and informative. Part I of this work covers Bentham. Ernest Albee, *A History of English Utilitarianism* (London, 1902), ch. IX, points out the connections between William Paley and Bentham, 165–90. F. R. Leavis (ed.), *Mill on Bentham and Coleridge* (London, 1950), is prefaced by a discursive but interesting introduction. Mill, *Utilitarianism, Liberty and Representative Government* (Modern Library edition, New York, 1950), 1–80, contains Mill's own analysis of the movement of which he was the most important exponent. A. D. Lindsay wrote the "Introduction," vii–xxix. The most revealing evaluations of Bentham's influence are to be found in Mill, *Utilitarianism*, and Halévy, *Philosophic Radicalism*, 479–514, 296–310.

93 Emerson, *Hildreth*, 67.

94 *Ibid.*, 94.

95 See above, n. 49.

96 Emerson, *Hildreth*, 99.

97 Halévy, *Philosophic Radicalism*, 433–55, especially 451. Stephen, *English Utilitarians*, 241–42.

98 "It can indeed be said that the idea of a philosophy of history is totally foreign to Bentham's thought. It is . . . fundamental to James Mill.". Halévy, *Philosophic Radicalism*, 273. What was true of the father was even more true of the son. John Stuart Mill differed from Bentham in many ways, none more basically than with regard to history. As a radical reformer, he quickly realized that to mold the present,

its roots in the past had to be understood.

99 Emerson, *Historiography and Urbanization*, 170. Kelly, "Richard Hildreth," *Jernegan Essays*, 30–31, remarks that Hildreth failed "to present any general interpretation," which resulted perhaps from "the absence of any adequate philosophy to guide the historian in the selection of his facts." But Kelly neglects to explain how a philosophy "to guide the historian" was to conform to the canons of science as then understood, particularly by Hildreth himself.

CHAPTER XV

1 Van Wyck Brooks, *Flowering of New England*, 339. G. P. Gooch, *History and Historians in the Nineteenth Century* (London, 1913), 417.

2 Harry Thurston Peck, *William Hickling Prescott* (New York and London, 1926), 54. Brooks, *Flowering*, 138.

3 Ruth Putnam, "Prescott and Motley," *CHAL*, II, 133.

4 Wilbur Schramm, *Francis Parkman: Representative Selections* (New York, 1938), an excellent and helpful volume, contains selections from Parkman's "Autobiography," 4, 13, 14. ". . . For here . . . the forest drama was more stirring and the forest stage more thronged with appropriate actors than in any other passage of our history." 14.

5 *Ibid.*, 14.

6 *Ibid.*

7 The facts of Prescott's life are sympathetically set forth in Peck, *Prescott*, 13–38. Putnam, "Prescott and Motley," *CHAL*, II, 123–24. William Charvat and Michael Kraus, *William Hickling*

Prescott: Representative Selections (New York, 1943), contains interesting material, xi–cxxviii. Brooks, *Flowering*, 136–43, is excellent. Roger B. Merriman's article in the *DAB*, X, 196–200, is an appreciative but judicious summary, particularly suggestive because Merriman was a leading American expert on the history of Spain. George Ticknor's biography, *Life of William Hickling Prescott* (Boston, 1864), is the work of a close friend and is valuable on that account. Prescott's reviews are listed in Charvat and Kraus, cxxxi–cxxxv. H. B. Adams, *Jared Sparks*, I, 235.

8 Peck, *Prescott*, 48. Putnam, "Prescott and Motley," *CHAL*, II, 125. Interest in Spanish literature and history in Prescott's time is briefly set forth in Charvat and Kraus, *Prescott*, xxx–xxxvi. On Prescott's contact with Ticknor, Peck, *Prescott*, 47, Brooks, *Flowering*, 141–42, and Brooks, *World of Washington Irving*, 317–24.

9 Charvat and Kraus, *Prescott*, xlix–lx. Peck, *Prescott*, 63–64.

10 John Fiske, *A Century of Science and Other Essays* (Boston and New York, 1900), 201–02.

11 Putnam, "Prescott and Motley," *CHAL*, II, 127. Peck, *Prescott*, 31–32, 34–35. The various editions of Prescott's works are listed in *LHUS*, III, 700–01, and in Charvat and Kraus, *Prescott*, cxxxi. The major works referred to in the text of this chapter are *A History of the Reign of Ferdinand and Isabella, the Catholic* (3 vols., Boston and London, 1837); *A History of the Conquest of Mexico, with a Preliminary View of the Ancient Mexican Civilization and the Life of Hernando Cortés* (3 vols., New York and London, 1843); *A*

History of the Conquest of Peru, with a Preliminary View of the Civilization of the Incas (2 vols., New York and London, 1847); *A History of the Reign of Philip the Second* (3 vols., Boston and London, 1855–58).

12 Putnam, "Prescott and Motley," *CHAL*, II, 127. Peck, *Prescott*, 45–47, 56–61. Prescott himself wrote on Scott, "Sir Walter Scott," *North American Review*, XLVI (Apr. 1838), 431–74. See also Charvat and Kraus, *Prescott*, xxxviii–xl.

13 Peck, *Prescott*, 129, considers *Ferdinand and Isabella* "a solid piece of work," notwithstanding the legitimate criticisms which may be brought against it, 130. Charvat and Kraus, *Prescott*, lxix–lxx.

14 Putnam, "Prescott and Motley," *CHAL*, II, 128. A Tory reviewer wrote in the *British Quarterly Review:* "His style is too often sesquipedalian and ornate; the stilty, wordy, false taste of Dr. Channing without his depth of thought; the sugar and sack of Washington Irving without the half-pennyworth of bread—without his grace and polish of pure, grammatical, careful Anglicanism." Peck, *Prescott*, 124. Contemporary reviews are listed in Charvat and Kraus, *Prescott*, cxxxii–cxxxiii.

15 Putnam, "Prescott and Motley," *CHAL*, II, 128.

16 Peck, *Prescott*, 134.

17 *Ibid.*, 135, 161, whose eloquent praise is also a synopsis of Prescott's method: "Every event is made to bear directly upon the development of this leading motive. The art of Prescott in this book is the art of a great dramatist who keeps his eye and brain intent upon the true catastrophe, in the light of which alone the

other episodes possess significance." 135. Charvat and Kraus,
Prescott, lxxi–lxxiv, analyze the
content of the study. Channing,
History of the United States, I,
19 n.

18 Peck, *Prescott,* 160–62, but "nowhere has Prescott written with
greater skill."

19 *Ibid.,* 161.

20 *Ibid.,* 107.

21 Putnam, "Prescott and Motley,"
CHAL, II, 129–30.

22 Charvat and Kraus, *Prescott,*
lxxvii. Peck, *Prescott,* 171. Putnam, "Prescott and Motley,"
CHAL, II, 129. Contemporary
reviews are listed in Charvat and
Kraus, *Prescott,* cxxxiv.

23 Peck, *Prescott,* 172.

24 Brooks, *Flowering,* 323–42. Oli-
ver Wendell Holmes, *John Lothrop Motley: A Memoir* (Boston,
1879). George W. Curtis (ed.),
*The Correspondence of John
Lothrop Motley* (2 vols., New
York, 1889). Excellent recent
and critical bibliographies are
available: *LHUS,* III, 664–66,
and Chester P. Higby and Bradford T. Schantz, *John Lothrop
Motley: Representative Selections*
(New York, 1939), cxxxv–clxi.
The article on Motley in the
DAB, XIII, 282–87, by Edward
P. Cheyney, a distinguished
American student of English
and European history, is the best
brief account. Putnam, "Prescott
and Motley," *CHAL,* II, 131–47,
is suggestive.

25 "And so shall be accused, very
justly perhaps, of the qualities
for which Byron commended
Mitford, 'wrath & partiality.'"
Peck, *Prescott,* 166. He later,
however, developed a passion for
reform, see below, note 29.

26 Putnam, "Prescott and Motley,"
CHAL, II, 132.

27 Long, *Literary Pioneers,* 199–
224.

28 Putnam, "Prescott and Motley,"
CHAL, II, 134; Long, *Literary
Pioneers,* 212–13, 259 n. 22.
Higby and Schantz, *Motley,* xvi–
xviii. *Morton's Hope: or The
Memoirs of a Provincial,* (2
vols., New York, 1839). *Merry-
Mount: A Romance of the Massachusetts Colony* (2 vols., Boston and Cambridge, Mass.,
1849).

29 Putnam, "Prescott and Motley,"
CHAL, II, 135–36. Motley's interest in politics was a progressive growth. As he matured as
a scholar and as an observer of
the events of his times, he became increasingly identified with
social and political issues and
their relation to American ideals
and with what he believed to be
America's destiny. He became, in
short, and in spite of his temperament and background, more of
a democrat, less of a theoretical
republican liberal. See the discussion "Political and Social
Ideals," Higby and Schantz,
Motley, xxv–lxx, the best survey
thus far of its subject.

30 Putnam, "Prescott and Motley,"
CHAL, II, 135.

31 The most notable in this con-
nection is the article "Peter the
Great," *North American Review,*
LXI (Oct. 1845), 269–319.
Higby and Schantz, *Motley,*
xviii.

32 Putnam, "Prescott and Motley,"
CHAL, II, 136.

33 Higby and Schantz, *Motley,*
lxxxii.

34 Charvat and Kraus, *Prescott,*
xxxiv.

35 Editions of Motley's works are
listed in *LHUS,* III, 664–66, and
Higby and Schantz, *Motley,*
cxxxv–cxxxviii.

[36] Putnam, "Prescott and Motley," *CHAL,* II, 137.

[37] Bakhuysen van der Brink was chief archivist of the Netherlands. His review and Fronde's are quoted in Putnam, "Prescott and Motley," *CHAL,* II, 137–139.

[38] Peck compares Motley and *Prescott,* 176–79, and holds Motley "unsurpassed" as a narrator, the most "literary" of the "literary historians." But he adds: "Unlike Prescott, he understands the philosophy of history and delves beneath the surface to search out and reveal the hidden causes of events. Yet first and last and all the time, he is a partisan." 177. Higby and Schantz, *Motley,* lxxxiii–cxii, present and historical and critical evaluation. Bassett, *Middle Group of American Historians,* 223–32. John Fiske, "Spain and the Netherlands," *The Unseen World, and Other Essays* (Boston, 1876), wrote: "If here Motley exhibits any serious fault, it is perhaps the natural tendency to *take sides.*" 234. Gooch, *History and Historians,* approves of Prescott and Motley and is critical of Parkman, 385–94.

[39] Mason Wade, *Francis Parkman, Heroic Historian* (New York, 1942), is the most recent and most satisfactory treatment. Charles Haight Farnham, *A Life of Francis Parkman* (Boston, 1901), is still valuable. Schramm's introductory material is extraordinarily helpful, *Parkman,* xiii–cxvi; the listing of biographical and critical studies cxxx–cxli, is carefully annotated. Wade, author of the leading Parkman study, has also edited *The Journals of Francis Parkman* (2 vols., New York, 1947). For additional studies and sources, consult, *LHUS,* III, 680–82.

[40] "Autobiography," Schramm, *Parkman,* 4–5, Farnham, *Parkman,* 187.

[41] Schramm, *Parkman,* xxv; "Autobiography," 5. Farnham, *Parkman,* 52, 130.

[42] Don C. Seitz, *Letters from Francis Parkman to E. G. Squier* (Cedar Rapids, Iowa, 1911), 28.

[43] Farnham, *Parkman,* 136, 138, 169. "Autobiography," Schramm, *Parkman,* 5–6, xxiv–xxxi, and Wade, *Parkman,* 292–97, 324–28, fully cover this problem.

[44] Seitz, *Letters from Parkman to Squier,* 23–24.

[45] Fiske, *Century of Science,* 204.

[46] John Spencer Bassett (ed.), *Letters of Francis Parkman to Pierre Margry, Smith College Studies in History* (Northampton, Mass., 1923), VIII, Nos. 2 and 3, covers this point as completely as it needs to be. See also Farnham, *Parkman,* 155–57, and Wade, *Parkman,* 389–91.

[47] Schramm, *Parkman,* xlv, n. 88. Farnham, *Parkman,* 157–59.

[48] "I have visited and examined every spot where events of any importance in connection with the contest took place, and I have observed with attention such scenes and persons as might help to illustrate those I meant to describe. In short, the subject has been studied as much from life and in the open air as at the library table." *Montcalm and Wolfe* (2 vols., Boston, 1885), I, ix; II, 436–42. Since Parkman's volumes were reprinted in various editions with different combinations and different titles, the bibliographical history is somewhat confusing. S. E. Morison renders the confusions clear in *The Parkman Reader* (Boston, 1955), 519–21.

⁴⁹ Farnham, *Parkman*, 181–82. For Parkman's review of Cooper, *North American Review*, LXXIV (Jan. 1852), 147–61. For others, with annotations, Schramm, *Parkman*, cxxv–cxxiv; see also lii–liii. And when Parkman dispensed censure, it was sometimes savage. Reviewing Schoolcraft's Indian opus, he wrote: "It is a singularly crude and illiterate production stuffed with blunders and self-contradictions giving evidence on every page of a striking unfitness either for history or philosophical inquiry, and taxing to the utmost the patience of those who would extract what is valuable in it from its oceans of pedantic verbiage." Wade, *Parkman*, 398.

⁵⁰ Farnham, *Parkman*, 199. Schramm, *Parkman*, lvi.

⁵¹ *Montcalm and Wolfe*, II, 287.

⁵² "My business was observation and I was willing to pay dearly for the opportunity of exercising it." Wade, *Parkman*, 260.

⁵³ California was added to the title, "a sly publisher's trick," simply to capitalize on current public interest. Wade, *Parkman*, 318. The eighth revised edition (Boston, 1895), carried the note: "The 'Oregon Trail' is the title under which this book first appeared. It was afterwards changed by the publisher, and is now restored to the form in which it originally stood in the Knickerbocker Magazine."

⁵⁴ *The Oregon Trail: Sketches of Prairie and Rocky-Mountain Life* (Boston, 1895), 60–61.

⁵⁵ Wade, *Parkman*, 222–25.

⁵⁶ *The Conspiracy of Pontiac and the Indian War after the Conquest of Canada* (2 vols., Boston, 1874), sixth edition, I, ix–x.

⁵⁷ *Ibid.*, I, x.

⁵⁸ *Ibid.*, II, 313.

⁵⁹ The scholars to whom Parkman was indebted had made singularly important additions to the knowledge of his field. Edmund Bailey O'Callaghan had issued a two-volume history of New Netherlands and became famous among students for his documentary compilation, *Documentary History of the State of New York* (4 vols., Albany, 1949–1951). John Gilmary Shea, the most prominent early Catholic historian in America, was a specialist in Parkman's own area of study. His *History of the Catholic Church in the United States* (4 vols., New York, 1886–92) and *History of the Catholic Missions among the Indian Tribes of the United States, 1529–1854* (New York, 1854), were of great help to Parkman, despite a different point of view. For Shea, Draper, and O'Callaghan, see below, ch. XVII. Wade, *Parkman*, 298, briefly mentions others; O'Callaghan and Shea at greater length, 342–45. Schramm has worked out a chronological table of Parkman's trips in the field during the years between 1841 and 1887, including trips to Canada and Europe, *Parkman*, xlvi–xlviii, 90 n.

⁶⁰ He had even met and talked with a man who had known Pontiac himself. *Ibid.*, 305.

⁶¹ *Conspiracy of Pontiac*, I, chs. 1–3.

⁶² *Ibid.*, I, 46–47.

⁶³ A bibliography of Parkman's horticultural articles, pieces on social issues and reviews, some of which are cited below, have been compiled by Wade, *Parkman*, 454–56.

⁶⁴ Farnham, *Parkman*, 29–30, Wade, *Parkman*, 350–51.

⁶⁵ "The art of horticulture is no leveler. Its triumphs are achieved

by rigid systems of selection and rejection, founded always on the broad basis of intrinsic worth. The good cultivator propagates no plants but the best"—Parkman wrote in *The Book of Roses* (Boston, 1866), as cited by Wade, *Parkman,* 353, in which, Wade remarks, "his social ideas are mirrored in his horticultural ones."

66 Farnham, *Parkman,* 31.

67 *Vassall Morton: A Novel* (Boston, 1856), is largely autobiographical in character and illumines Parkman's psychological development, his basic attitudes, and his aspirations. This suggestion is presented and brilliantly sustained by Wade, *Parkman,* 328, 330. It "is close self-analysis, cloaked in fictional terms." 332, 333–40. Farnham, *Parkman,* describes *Vassall Morton* as simply "a failure" as a novel, 189, but recognizes its "autobiographic touch," 237. See also 305–06, 314, 336. Schramm, *Parkman,* lxi, lxx–lxxvi, xcii–xciii.

68 *The Jesuits in North America in the Seventeenth Century* (Boston, 1940), 552.

69 Editions of Parkman's major works are listed in *LHUS,* III, 680. A fuller and annotated bibliography is to be found in Schramm, *Parkman,* cxxi–cxliv, which contains, in addition, references to the contemporary reviews of the separate studies. Wade's "Bibliographical Note," *Parkman,* 453–56, is probably the most complete listing of Parkman's published writings. But see n. 48 above.

70 Joe Patterson Smith, "Francis Parkman," *Jernegan Essays,* 56–57, summarizes these appraisals. See also Edward Channing, *History of the United States,* V, 305. Fiske wrote, referring to the whole work, "it clearly belongs . . . among the world's few masterpieces of the highest rank, along with the works of Herodotus, Thucydides, and Gibbon." *Century of Science,* 264.

71 Wade, *Parkman,* 428–29.

72 Smith, "Parkman," *Jernegan Essays,* 57–59; Schramm, *Parkman,* c; Channing, *History of the United States,* V, 305. Edward G. Bourne, *Essays in Historical Criticism* (New Haven, 1913), expressed an opinion, which has since become general, that Parkman "chose to picture the past rather than reason about it." 285. Clarification of the heroic historians as "literary" and "romantic" is virtually universal. Bassett, "Later Historians," *CHAL,* III, 188.

73 Farnham, *Parkman,* 147–49. Wade, *Parkman,* 440, 373, 387, for a significant letter to Parkman from the Abbé Henri S. Casgrain; Schramm's view will be found in *Parkman,* xcviii–xcix.

74 Clarence W. Alvord, "Francis Parkman," *Nation,* CXVII (Oct. 10, 1923), 394–96. Parkman's love of nature is perhaps best expressed in *Conspiracy of Pontiac,* at the point he seeks to explain why certain whites, captured by Indians, are unenthusiastic about the prospect of release. "To him who has once tasted the reckless independence, the haughty self-reliance, the sense of irresponsible freedom, which the forest life engenders, civilization thenceforth seems flat and stale." II, 237; see also 238–39. For discussions of Turner, Roosevelt, and Draper, see chs. XXIV, XXV.

75 Schramm, *Parkman,* c, cvi–cvii.

76 *The Old Regime in Canada* (Bos-

ton, 1874), 394, 229, 207–14, 215–30.

77 "Puritanism was not an unmixed blessing," he wrote in *Montcalm and Wolfe.* "Its view of human nature was dark, and its attitude toward it one of repression. It strove to crush out not only what is evil, but much that is innocent and salutary. Human nature so treated will take its revenge, and for every vice that it loses find another instead." I, 26.

78 "A New England village of the olden time—that is to say of some forty years ago—would have been safely and well governed by the votes of every man in it; but, now that the village has grown into a populous city, with its factories and workshops, its acres of tenement-houses, and thousands and ten thousands of restless workmen, foreigners for the most part, to whom liberty means license and politics means plunder . . . the public good is nothing and their own most trivial interests everything." "The Failure of Universal Suffrage," Schramm, *Parkman,* 165–66.

79 Parkman's antagonism to democracy may be traced in the following articles, in *The North American Review:* "The Failure of Universal Suffrage," CXXVII (July-Aug. 1878), 1–20; "The Woman Question," CXXIX (Oct. 1879), 303–21; "The Woman Question Again," CXXX (Jan. 1880), 16–30. In the first essay, reprinted in Schramm, *Parkman,* 159–80, the matter is stated succinctly, ". . . the present danger is not above but beneath, and where the real tyrant is organized ignorance, led by unscrupulous craft, and marching, amid the applause of fools, under the flag of equal rights." 159–60.

80 "England succeeded and France failed. The cause lies chiefly in the vast advantage drawn by England from the historical training of her people in habits of reflection, forecast, industry, and self-reliance." And again, "The Germanic race, and especially the Anglo-Saxon branch of it, is peculiarly masculine, and, therefore, peculiarly fitted for self-government. It submits its action habitually to the guidance of reason, and has the judicial faculty of seeing both sides of a question." *Old Régime,* 396, 397–98. *Conspiracy of Pontiac,* 47–48.

81 Joseph Schafer, "Francis Parkman, 1823–1893," *Mississippi Valley Historical Review,* X (Mar. 1924), 351–64.

82 Wade, *Parkman,* 311–14, in which Parker was saying in effect that the conception of the *Pontiac* was a dramatic, not a logical, scheme.

83 *Ibid.,* 448.

CHAPTER XVI

1 William E. Dodd, *Expansion and Conflict* (Boston, 1915), v. Edwin C. Rozwenc (ed.), *Slavery as a Cause of the Civil War* (Boston, 1961), v.

2 Harry J. Carman, *Social and Economic History of the United States* (2 vols., Boston, 1934), II, iii.

3 The phrase is Frederick Jackson Turner's.

4 W. A. Dunning, "A Generation of American Historiography," *Truth in History and Other Essays* (New York, 1937), 155.

5 Henry P. Beers, *Bibliographies in American History* (New York, 1938), 163–64, Oscar Handlin, Arthur M. Schlesinger, Samuel E. Morison, Frederick Merk, Arthur M. Schlesinger, Jr., and Paul H.

Buck (eds.), *Harvard Guide to American History* (Cambridge, 1954), 361–66, 371–98—hereinafter cited as *Harvard Guide*.
[6] Hal Bridges, *Civil War and Reconstruction* (Washington, D.C., 1957), 1.
[7] The following suggest the variety of special topics: Clement Eaton, "Censorship of the Southern Mails," *American Historical Review* XLVIII (Jan. 1943), 266–80. A. H. Abel, *The American Indian as Slaveholder and Secessionist* (2 vols., Cleveland, 1915–19). M. L. Bonham, *The British Consuls in the Confederacy* (New York, 1911). Gray Wood, *The Hidden Civil War: The Story of the Copperheads* (New York, 1942). A. B. Moore, *Conscription and Conflict in the Confederacy* (New York, 1924). Ella Lonn, *Foreigners in the Confederacy* (Chapel Hill, N.C., 1940). Bell I. Wiley, *The Life of Johnny Reb, the Common Soldier of the Confederacy* (Indianapolis, 1943). Fred A. Shannon, *The Organization and Administration of the Union Army, 1861–1865* (2 vols., Cleveland, 1928). George W. Adams, *Doctors in Blue: The Medical History of the Union Army in the Civil War* (New York, 1952). Robert C. Black, III, *The Railroads of the Confederacy* (Chapel Hill, N.C., 1952). Thomas Weber, *The Northern Railroads in the Civil War, 1861–1865* (New York, 1952). James P. Baxter, III, *The Introduction of the Ironclad Warship* (Cambridge, 1933). J. D. Bulloch, *The Secret Service of the Confederate States in Europe* (2 vols., London, 1883). F. B. Simpkins and J. W. Patton, *The Women of the Confederacy* (Richmond, Virginia, 1936). W. M. Robinson, Jr., "Prohibi-tion in the Confederacy," *American Historical Review*, XXVII (Oct. 1931), 50–58. Bell I. Wiley, *The Plain People of the Confederacy* (Baton Rouge, 1943). Bell I. Wiley, *Southern Negroes, 1861–1865* (New Haven, 1938). Ella Lonn, *Salt as a Factor in the Confederacy* (Baltimore, 1933). Ella Lonn, *Desertion During the Civil War* (New York, 1928).
[8] The following is a representative selection: Ben Ames Williams (ed.), Mary B. Chestnut, *A Diary from Dixie* (Boston, 1949). Howard Swiggett (ed.), *A Rebel War Clerk's Diary at the Confederate State Capitol* (2 vols., New York, 1935). H. S. Commager (ed.), *The Blue and the Gray: The Story of the Civil War as Told by Participants* (2 vols., Indianapolis, 1950). George M. Dallas, *A Series of Letters from London Written During the Years 1856–60* (Philadelphia, 1869). Milo M. Quaife (ed.), *The Diary of James K. Polk* (Chicago, 1910). Tyler Dennett (ed.), *Lincoln and the Civil War in the Diaries and Letters of John Hay* (New York, 1939). M. A. DeWolfe Howe (ed.), *Home Letters of General Sherman* (New York, 1909). William H. Russell, *My Diary, North and South* (Boston, 1863). Joseph Schafer (ed.), *Intimate Letters of Carl Schurz, 1841–1869* (Madison, Wis., 1928). Dwight L. Dumond (ed.), *Letters of James Gillespie Birney, 1831–1857* (2 vols., New York, 1938). Gilbert H. Barnes and Dwight L. Dumond (eds.), *Letters of Theodore Dwight Weld, Angelina Grimké Weld, and Sarah Grimké, 1822–1844* (2 vols., New York, 1934). John A. Cawthon (ed.), "Letters of a North Louisiana Private to His

Wife, 1862–1865," *Mississippi Valley Historical Review*, XXX (Mar. 1944), 533–50.

9 Among the many recollections, the following are most important: J. H. Browne, *Four Years in Secessia* (Hartford, Conn., 1865). Dunbar Rowland (ed.), *Jefferson Davis, Constitutionalist: His Letters, Papers and Speeches* (10 vols., Jackson, Miss., 1923). Fannie A. Beers, *Memories: A Record of Personal Experience and Adventure During Four Years of War* (Philadelphia, 1891). Frank B. Moore (ed.), *The Rebellion Record: A Diary of American Events, with Documents, Narratives, Illustrative Incidents, Poetry, etc.* (12 vols., New York, 1864–68), is an important contemporary collection. Myrta L. Avary, *Recollections of Alexander H. Stephens. . . .* (New York, 1910). An excellent bibliography of materials of this character has been compiled by Bruce Caton in *A Stillness at Appomattox* (New York, 1954), 386–91.

10 A fuller discussion of historians as biographers will be found in a later part of this study. Among the indispensable studies J. G. Randall, *Lincoln the President* (2 vols., New York, 1945), is one of the best of recent studies, but Lincoln biography is a subject in itself. See David M. Potter, *The Lincoln Theme and American National Historiography* (Oxford, 1948). Zachary T. Johnson, *The Political Policies of Howell Cobb* (Nashville, Tenn., 1929). Allen Johnson, *Stephen A. Douglas* (New York, 1908). Douglas S. Freeman, *R. E. Lee: A Biography* (4 vols., New York, 1934–35), supersedes all other accounts and has become a classic. Laura A. White,

Robert Barnwell Rhett: Father of Secession (New York, 1931). Rudolph von Abele, *Alexander H. Stephens* (New York, 1946). Carl B. Swisher, *Roger B. Taney* (New York, 1935). U. B. Phillips, *The Life of Robert Toombs* (New York, 1913). J. H. Parks, *John Bell of Tennessee* (Baton Rouge, La., 1930). Pierce Butler, *Judah P. Benjamin* (Philadelphia, 1907). Oswald Garrison Villard, *John Brown* (New York, 1943). Albert B. Hart, *Salmon P. Chase* (Boston, 1899). Carl Schurz, *The Life of Henry Clay* (2 vols., Boston, 1887). G. G. Van Deusen, *The Life of Henry Clay* (Boston, 1937). G. I. Milton, *The Eve of Conflict: Stephen A. Douglas and the Needless War* (Boston, 1934). F. J. and W. P. Garrison, *William Lloyd Garrison, 1805–1879* (4 vols., New York, 1885–89). C. B. Going, *David Wilmot, Free-Soiler* (New York, 1924).

11 Douglas S. Freeman, *The South to Posterity: An Introduction to the Writing of Confederate History* (New York, 1939), is basic to an understanding of the subject. Materials on Fort Sumter, on which the bibliography is extensive, generally concern politics and theories of the causes of the war rather than military history. Burton J. Hendrick, *Lincoln's War Cabinet* (Boston, 1946), is important for the development of overall policy making. A. C. Inman (ed.), *Soldier of the South: General Pickett's War Letters to His Wife* (Boston, 1928). T. Harry Williams, *Lincoln and His Generals* (New York, 1952). Douglas S. Freeman, *Lee's Lieutenants: A Study in Command* (3 vols., New York, 1942–44). Gamaliel Bradford, *Lee the American* (Boston,

1912). G. F. R. Henderson, *Stonewall Jackson and the American Civil War* (2 vols., New York, 1936). Allen Tate, *Stonewall Jackson, the Good Soldier* (New York, 1928). Don C. Seitz, *Braxton Bragg, General of the Confederacy* (New York, 1924). E. B. Long (ed.), U. S. Grant, *Personal Memoirs* (Cleveland, 1952). Lamont Buchanan (ed.), *A Pictorial History of the Confederacy* (New York, 1951). D. H. Donald, H. D. Milhollen, and H. Kaplan (eds.), *Divided We Fought: A Pictorial History of the War, 1861–1865* (New York, 1952). A. M. Stickles, *Simon Bolivar Buckner, Borderland Knight* (Chapel Hill, N.C., 1940). H. J. Eckenrode and B. Conrad, *George B. McClellan: The Man Who Saved the Union* (Chapel Hill, N.C., 1941). Naval history has also been covered extensively. See, for example, William H. Parker, *Recollections of a Naval Officer, 1841–1865* (New York, 1883). John Bigelow, *France and the Confederate Navy, 1862–1868* (New York, 1888). J. T. Scharf, *History of the Confederate States Navy* (New York, 1887).

12 This point is exemplified by studies of Jefferson Davis. William E. Dodd, *Jefferson Davis* (Philadelphia, 1907); H. J. Eckenrode, *Jefferson Davis, President of the South* (New York, 1923); Allen Tate, *Jefferson Davis: His Rise and Fall* (New York, 1929); Varina H. Davis, *Jefferson Davis: Ex-President of the Confederate States of America* (New York, 1890). Another excellent example is Alexander H. Stephens, *The Reviewers Reviewed. A Supplement to the "War Between the States," etc., with an Appendix in Review of "Reconstruction,"* So-Called (New York, 1872). The most comprehensive study of Civil War historiography is by Howard K. Beale, "What Historians Have Said About the Causes of the Civil War," *Theory and Practice in Historical Study: A Report of the Committee on Historiography* (New York, 1946), 55–102. William K. Boyd, "Political Writing Since 1850," *CHAL,* III, 337–53. John Spencer Bassett, "Later Historians," *CHAL,* 180–82. Thomas J. Pressly, *Americans Interpret Their Civil War* (Princeton, N.J., 1954) is the most recent study. "Literature and Conflict," *LHUS,* I, 563–68, surveys the outstanding literary writings during the crisis years. A full discussion of modern Civil War historiography is reserved for a later volume of this study.

13 Beale, *Theory and Practice in Historical Study,* 58–60. Edward Pollard, *Southern History of the Great Civil War in the United States* (New York, 1866).

14 Henry Wilson, *History of the Rise and Fall of the Slave Power in America* (3 vols., Boston, 1872–77).

15 Russel B. Nye, "The Slave Power Conspiracy," *Science and Society* (Summer 1946), 10, 262–74 is reprinted in Rozwenc, *Slavery as Cause of Civil War,* in which the quotations are at 29.

16 Frank I. Owsley, "The Fundamental Cause of the Civil War: Egocentric Sectionalism," *Journal of Southern History,* VII (Feb. 1941), 3–18.

17 Russel B. Nye, *Fettered Freedom* (East Lansing, Mich., 1949,) 223–31, 248–49.

18 Jesse T. Carpenter, *The South As a Conscious Minority, 1789–1861* (New York, 1931), 127–

70. Kenneth M. Stampp, *And the War Came* (New Orleans, 1950), 31–45. Important in this connection is Sidney D. Brummer, *The Judicial Interpretation of the Confederate Constitution* (New York, 1914). Arthur C. Cole, "The South and the Right of Secession in the Early Fifties," *Mississippi Valley Historical Review,* I (Dec. 1914), 376–99. Sidney George Fisher, *The Trial of the Constitution* (Philadelphia, 1862).

19 Jefferson Davis, *The Rise and Fall of the Confederate Government* (2 vols., New York, 1881), and *A Short History of the Confederate States of America* (New York, 1890). Alexander H. Stephens, *A Constitutional View of the Late War Between the States, Its Causes, Character, Conduct and Results.* . . . (2 vols., Philadelphia, 1867). "Minority Report: The Tradition of the Old South," *LHUS,* I, 607–16, carries the report down to the present with suggestive observations.

20 Stephens, *Constitutional View,* I, 9–12.

21 Henry Cleveland, *Alexander H. Stephens, in Public and Private: With Letters and Speeches* (Philadelphia, 1866), 721.

22 John W. Burgess, *The Civil War and the Constitution* (2 vols., New York, 1901), I, 75–76.

23 Charles E. Merriam, *The Political Philosophy of John C. Calhoun* (New York, 1914). Edward A. Pollard, *The Lost Cause* (New York, 1866). Nathaniel W. Stephenson, "A Theory of Jefferson Davis," *American Historical Review,* XXV (July 1926), 701–07. W. W. Willoughby, *The American Constitutional System* (New York, 1904), 70–80. John W. Draper and James Schouler, noted historians without academic portfolio, popularized the Burgess thesis. John W. Draper, *History of the American Civil War* (3 vols., New York, 1867–1870). James Schouler, *History of the United States under the Constitution* (7 vols., Washington, D.C., 1882–94), IV–VI. Hermann E. von Holst, German student of American life, first at Johns Hopkins and later at the University of Chicago, added currency to the competing hypotheses of constitutional law in his *The Constitutional and Political History of the United States* (8 vols., Chicago, 1877–1892).

24 Arthur M. Schlesinger, Sr., "The States Rights Fetish," *New Viewpoints in American History* (New York, 1928), 243, 220–42, strips the argument of historical validity. Herman V. Ames (ed.), *State Documents on Federal Relations* (Philadelphia, 1906), is a fundamental source collection. Frank L. Owsley, *States Rights in the Confederacy* (Chicago, 1925). Henry M. Wagstaff, *State Rights and Political Parties in North Carolina, 1776–1861* (Baltimore, 1906).

25 Roy F. Nichols, "Federalism versus Democracy," Roscoe Pound, Charles H. McIlwain, and Roy F. Nichols (eds.), *Federalism as a Democratic Process* (New Brunswick, N.J., 1942), 49. But see Leonard D. White, *The States and the Nation* (Baton Rouge, La., 1953).

26 Charles A. and Mary R. Beard, *The Rise of American Civilization* (2 vols., New York, 1927), ch. VI, 51.

27 Nichols, "Federalism versus Democracy," 50.

28 Arthur Bestor, *State Sovereignty and Slavery* (Springfield, Ill., 1961), 3.

29 Burgess, *Civil War and the Constitution*, I, 16.

30 William B. Munro, *The Makers of the Unwritten Constitution* (New York, 1930), 2. Smith, *The Spirit of American Government*, 331–60.

31 Beale, in *Theory and Practice in Historical Study*, 65.

32 Stampp (ed.), *The Causes of the Civil War*, 69.

33 *Social Forces in American History* (New York, 1911), vii, 263, 284; also 218: ". . . reasons [for the Civil War] are not found either in the wickedness of chattel slavery, nor the growing moral consciousness of the North." And 218: "The attitude of the various sections of the country toward chattel slavery has always been determined directly by the dominant economic interests of the section in question." Beale, in *Theory and Practice of Historical Study*, 69–70. A. M. Schlesinger, Sr., has called attention to Turner's influence in the formulation of economic interpretations. Schlesinger, *New Viewpoints*, 69. Turner's influence on Civil War historiography combined in underscoring economic and sectional considerations.

34 C. A. and Mary Beard, *Rise of American Civilization*, 51.

35 Louis M. Hacker, "Revolutionary America: An Interpretation of Our History," *Harper's Magazine*, CLXX (March 1935), 411, 438–40. Beale, in *Theory and Practice in Historical Study*, 72–73. A good statement of the Marxian view will be found in Richard Emmall, "Interpretations of the American Civil War," *Science and Society*, I (Winter, 1937), 127–36. The best statement, however, is Karl Marx and Friedrich Engels, *The Civil War in the United States* (New York, 1937).

36 J. T. Carpenter, *South As a Sectional Minority*, 17–21, 29–33. Randall, *Civil War and Reconstruction*, 111–13. Craven, *Coming of the Civil War*, 5–10. Allan Nevins, *The Emergence of Lincoln* (2 vols., New York and London, 1950), I, 6, 7, 18, 283–84.

37 Kohn, *The Idea of Nationalism*, 10–20.

38 Channing, *United States*, VI, 6–12.

39 Rollin G. Osterweis, *Romanticism and Nationalism in the Old South* (New Haven, 1949). Southern nationalism may be viewed as the suppressed premise of cultural integration. But what was truly and unmistakably Southern? What were the ingredients of Southern nationalism? To fashion an emblem of stars and bars, to select a "national" anthem was a simple matter, but this cannot be said to denominate a culture. Cultures are the results of historical processes; they cannot be fashioned out of a series of unique events. Milan, Tuscany, and Piedmont became Italy. Yet the course by which Alabama, Virginia, and South Carolina became parts of the Confederacy was a course of a different order. Romans and Milanese were not Italians in the sense that Georgians, Texans, and Carolinians were Americans before and after Richmond became the seat of the Confederate States of America. If there was a Southern nationalism, it represents conventional historical processes in reverse. Dynastic rulers—Hapsburgs, Bourbons, Romanovs—kept national minorities in subjection. National miorities sought independence from

the domination of foreign oppressors on the basis of the right of national self-determination. Southern nationalistic tendencies were tendencies within a cultural unity. Secession separated Americans from other Americans. Instead of creating a unity, a unity was severed. A suggestive discussion of some of these issues, though not relating to the Civil War, is Boyd C. Shafer, "Men Are More Alike," *American Historical Review,* LVII (Apr. 1952), 593–612. See Avery O. Craven, *The Repressible Conflict, 1830–1861* (Baton Rouge, La., 1939), 4–7. F. E. Chadwick, *Causes of Civil War* (New York and London, 1936), 4–14.

40 Henry Seidel Canby, "Introduction," Stephen Vincent Benet, *John Brown's Body* (New York, 1941), viii.

CHAPTER XVII

1 See, for example, Theodore D. Woolsey and others, *The First Century of the Republic: A Review of American Progress* (New York, 1876).

2 *LHUS,* III, 3, 5, 7–13; II, 805; *Harvard Guide,* 59. Arthur E. Bostwick, *The American Public Library* (New York and London, 1929), 5–19. S. H. Ditzion, *Arsenals of a Democratic Culture; a Social History of the American Public Library Movement in New England and the Middle States, 1850–1900* (Chicago, 1917), is one of the best volumes on this subject. S. S. Green, *Public Library Movement in the United States, 1853–1893* (Boston, 1913). The Library of Congress, founded in 1800, did not begin to exert a dominant influence until almost a hundred years later. It was not until 1870

that it began to receive copies of books copyrighted in America, and its modern existence really commences in 1899 with the appointment of Herbert Putnam as librarian. David C. Mearns, *The Story Up To Now: The Library of Congress, 1800–1946* (Washington, 1947).

3 J. S. Bassett, "Later Historians," in *CHAL,* III, 171.

4 See above, 306.

5 "The greatness of the eighteenth century lies in the fact that it was prepared to fuse with other universes of knowledge, to seek and apply the clues which science, philosophy, and practical experience, were in a position to place in its hands." J. B. Black, *The Art of History* (New York, 1926), 18.

6 Ibid., 5. And a president of the American Historical Association was later to say: "Human conduct, whether individual or group, is so complex and varied that history, when it attempts to describe it, cannot afford to overlook any of its manifestations, whether recorded in statistics, economics, political science, sociology, ethnology, anthropology, or psychology." Guy Stanton Ford, "Some Suggestions to American Historians," *American Historical Review,* XLIII (Jan. 1938), 268.

7 A list of historical societies together with the dates of their foundation will be found in Bassett, "Later Historians," *CHAL,* III, 172–73. *Harvard Guide,* 82–87. J. Franklin Jameson, *History of Historical Societies* (Savannah, Georgia, 1914). H. L. Carson, *History of the Historical Society of Pennsylvania* (Philadelphia, 1940). Constance M. Green, "The Value of Local History," Caroline F. Ware (ed.), *The Cultural Ap-*

proach to History (New York, 1940).

8 J. Franklin Jameson, "The Present State of Historical Writing in America," *Proceedings of the American Antiquarian Society,* n.s., XX (1911), 413–14. This subject is discussed in Bassett, "Later Historians," *CHAL,* III, 172 ff. and by H. Hale Bellot, *American History and American Historians* (London, 1952), 25–26.

9 *Harvard Guide,* 163–68, lists historical journals and historical society publications.

10 Wisconsin, 1846; Minnesota, 1849. The Mississippi Valley Historical Association, founded in 1907, was until recently largely regional in its objectives and interests.

11 Joseph Schafer is the author of the sketch in the *DAB,* V, 441–442. A more recent account is in Bellot, *American Historians,* 29. Lyman Copeland Draper, *Kings Mountain and Its Heroes* (Cincinnati, Ohio, 1881). Draper items are listed in *CHAL,* III, 173.

12 In 1840.

13 Bellot, *American Historians,* 29.

14 Schafer, in *DAB,* V, 441–42.

15 The first volume of the *Collections* appeared in 1855.

16 Reuben G. Thwaites, *The State Historical Society of Wisconsin* (Madison, Wis., 1898). F. J. Turner, *Reuben Gold Thwaites: A Memorial Address* (Madison, Wis., 1914). Clarence W. Alvord, "A Critical Analysis of the Work of Reuben Gold Thwaites," Mississippi Valley Historical Association, *Proceedings,* VII (1913–1914), 321–23. Kraus, 493–95. Bellot, *American Historians,* 30.

17 Turner, *Thwaites,* 27–28.

18 Carl L. Becker, "Frederick Jack-

son Turner," *Everyman His Own Historian,* 200–11.

19 *Original Journals of the Lewis and Clark Expedition* (8 vols., New York, 1904–05).

20 *Jesuit Relations and Allied Documents, 1610–1791* (73 vols., Cleveland, 1896), containing the French originals with translations.

21 See below, 306.

22 *Early Western Travels, 1748–1846* (32 vols., Cleveland, 1904–1907).

23 Turner, *Thwaites,* 27, 28.

24 C. Crittenden and Doris Godard, *Historical Societies in the United States and Canada: A Handbook* (Washington, D.C., 1944). Bellot, *American Historians,* 27–37.

25 J. S. Bassett's treatment of the "Great Subject" is brief but adequate. "Later Historians," *CHAL,* III, 183–88. Kraus, 293–97.

26 Kraus, 294.

27 Bassett, "Later Historians," *CHAL,* III, 185–86.

28 For Winsor's writings, Bassett, "Later Historians," *CHAL,* III, 186, from which the quotation from Winsor is taken.

29 The scope of Harrise's contribution may be gleaned from the listing of his works in *CHAL,* IV, 735; also Bassett, "Later Historians," *CHAL,* III, 184–85.

30 Kraus, 296–97.

31 Bassett, "Later Historians," *CHAL,* III, 185.

32 Edward G. Bourne as quoted in Bassett, "Later Historians," *CHAL,* III, 185.

33 Joseph Sabin (ed.), *Bibliotheca Americana; A Dictionary of Books Relating to America from its Discovery to the Present Time* (29 vols., New York, 1868–1936). For dates of publication of the volumes published under the editorship of Sabin, Wilberforce Eames, and Robert W. G.

Vail, see H. P. Beers, *Bibliographies in American History* (New York, 1942 [revised ed.]), 34.

34 *LHUS*, III, 21.

35 See below, chs. XVIII–XXVI.

36 Orville A. Roorbach (ed.), *Bibliotheca Americana; Catalogue of American Publications . . . from 1820 to 1860 . . . Together with a list of Periodicals Published in the United States* (4 vols., New York, 1852–61; reprinted 4 vols., New York, 1939). James Kelly (ed.), *American Catalogue of Books Published in the United States from Jan. 1861 to Jan. 1871* (2 vols., New York, 1871; reprinted 2 vols., New York, 1938).

37 British Museum, *Catalogue of Printed Books* (95 vols., London, 1881–1900. Supplement, 1900–1905, 13 vols. There is a photographic reprint in 58 vols., Ann Arbor, Mich., 1946–50).

38 *American Catalogue of Books, 1876–1910* (New York, 1876–1910). *United States Catalog: Books in Print*, 1899 (Minneapolis, 1900) which continues to 1928 and is thereafter followed by the *Cumulative Book Index*, which began publication in 1898. See Constance M. Winchell, *Guide to Reference Books* (Chicago, 1967), 32.

39 *Poole's Index to Periodical Literature, 1802–1881* (rev. ed., Boston, 1891). Five supplements carry it through 1906. See Winchell, *Guide*, 145. Poole's is succeeded by *Readers' Guide to Periodical Literature* (New York, 1900–). *Ibid.*

40 Guides to federal documents are listed in *Harvard Guide*, 113–15; to state documents, 115–17.

41 Laurence F. Schmeckebier, *Government Publications and Their Use* (Washington, 1939), 5–6. Ben Perley Poore, (ed.), *De-*

scriptive Catalogue of the Government Publications of the United States, September 5, 1774–March 4, 1881 (Washington, D.C., 1885).

42 *Harvard Guide*, 73, 113.

43 John G. Ames (ed.), *Comprehensive Index to the Publications of the United States Government, 1881–1893* (2 vols., Washington, D.C. 1905). Schmeckebier, *Government Publications*, 11, 13, 25–29.

44 Bassett, "Later Historians," *CHAL*, III, 176.

45 *The General Laws and Liberties of Connecticut Colonies* (Hartford, 1865).

46 *Harvard Guide*, 131–39.

47 Bassett, "Later Historians," *CHAL*, III, 173.

48 J. Q. Adams, *Memoirs*. U. S. Grant, *Personal Memoirs* (2 vols., New York, 1885–86). Horace Greeley, *Recollections of a Busy Life* (New York, 1868). Thomas W. Higginson, *Cheerful Yesterdays* (Boston, 1898). Julia Ward Howe, *Reminiscences* (Boston, 1899). G. B. McClellan, *McClellan's Own Story* (New York, 1887). Hugh McCulloch, *Men and Measures of Half a Century* (New York, 1888). S. J. May, *Recollections of Our Anti-Slavery Conflict* (Boston, 1869). Josiah Quincy, *Figures of the Past, from the Leaves of the Old Journals* (Boston, 1883).

49 For example, James G. Blaine, *Twenty Years of Congress: From Lincoln to Garfield* (2 vols., Norwich, Conn., 1884–86). Benjamin F. Butler, *Autobiography and Personal Reminiscences* (Boston, 1892). Allan Pinkerton, *Thirty Years a Detective* (New York, 1894). W. D. Armes (ed.), Joseph Le Conte, *Autobiography* (New York, 1903). Simon New-

comb, *Reminiscences of an Astronomer* (Boston, 1903).

50 Bassett, "Later Historians," *CHAL,* III, 173.

CHAPTER XVIII

1 William R. Shepherd, "John William Burgess," Howard W. Odum (ed.), *American Masters of Social Science* (New York, 1927), 3.

2 *Ibid.,* 23–57; Bernard E. Brown, *American Conservatives: The Political Thought of Francis Lieber and John W. Burgess* (New York, 1951), 103–78; Dixon Ryan Fox, *Herbert Levi Osgood* (New York, 1924), 22–23, 30. Herbert L. Osgood, *The American Colonies in the Seventeenth Century* (3 vols., New York, 1904–07), I, iv. John W. Burgess, *Reminiscences of an American Scholar* (New York, 1934), 4–190, provides a revealing autobiographical sketch that is paralleled at a number of interesting points by Nicholas Murray Butler, *Across the Busy Years* (2 vols., New York, 1939), especially I, 68, 96–97, 134, 173–75.

3 John W. Burgess, "On Methods of Historical Study and Research in Columbia University," in G. Stanley Hall (ed.), *Methods of Teaching and Studying History* (Boston, 1886), 220. See also Burgess, *Reminiscences,* 213–14; Butler, *Across the Busy Years,* I, 69, 366; Charles A. Beard, *Public Policy and the General Welfare* (New York, 1941), 141, 143; David Easton, *The Political System* (New York, 1953), 156.

4 John W. Burgess, *The Foundations of Political Science* (New York, 1933), vi, 75–76, 80; Morris R. Cohen, *American Thought* (Glencoe, Ill., 1954), 130.

5 Stow Persons (ed.), *Evolutionary Thought in America* (New Haven, 1950), 44–83; Bert James Loewenberg, "Darwinism Comes to America, 1859–1900," *Mississippi Valley Historical Review,* XXVIII (Dec. 1941), 339–68; Richard Hofstadter, *Social Darwinism in American Thought, 1860–1915* (Philadelphia, 1944), 1–36; Eric F. Goldman, *Rendezvous with Destiny* (New York, 1952), 92–94.

6 John Herman Randall, Jr., and George Haines, IV, "Controlling Assumptions in the Practice of American Historians," *Theory and Practice in Historical Study* (New York, 1946), 23–24, 35–37.

7 "Teutonic political genius stamps nations as the political nations *par excellence,* and authorizes them, in the economy of the world, to assume the leadership in the establishment and administration of states." Burgess, *The Foundations of Political Science,* 40.

8 W. Stull Holt (ed.), *Historical Scholarship in the United States, 1876–1901, as Revealed in the Correspondence of Herbert Baxter Adams* (Baltimore, 1938), 7–18.

9 Bert James Loewenberg, "Some Problems Raised by Historical Relativism," *Journal of Modern History,* XXI (Mar. 1949), 17–23.

10 See, for example, Allen Johnson, *The Historian and Historical Evidence* (New York, 1926), 157–176.

11 W. A. Dunning, "A Generation of American Historiography," *Truth in History,* 157.

12 Burgess, *Reminiscences,* 343. See also Charles A. and Mary R. Beard, *The American Spirit,* (New York, 1942), 3–18, and

Nicholas Murray Butler's "Foreword," in Burgess, *Foundations of Political Science*, v.

[13] In 1844.

[14] W. R. Shepherd in Odum (ed.), *Masters of Social Science*, 24–29. Burgess, *Reminiscences*, 4–190, an autobiographical sketch. On Seelye and Amherst, see Thomas Le Duc, *Piety and Intellect at Amherst College, 1865–1912* (New York, 1946), 40–61.

[15] Burgess, *Reminiscences*, 190–244, 322–41.

[16] Burgess, *The Middle Period, 1817–1858* (New York, 1897).

[17] Burgess, *The Civil War and the Constitution, 1859–1865* (2 vols., New York, 1904, 1906).

[18] Burgess, *Reconstruction and the Constitution, 1866–1876*, (New York, 1902).

[19] Burgess, *The Administration of President Hayes* (New York, 1916).

[20] "On Methods of Historical Study," in Hall (ed.), *Methods of Teaching and Studying History*, 219.

[21] *Ibid.*, 218. Italics in original.

[22] *Ibid.*, 220.

[23] Francis Darwin (ed.), *More Letters of Charles Darwin* (2 vols., London, 1903), I, 195.

[24] Thomas H. Huxley, *Methods and Results* (New York, 1896), 62. This essay first appeared in 1887.

[25] Georg W. F. Hegel, *Lectures on the Philosophy of History*, translated by J. Sibree (London, 1890), 9, 11. But "it is indispensable that Reason should not sleep that reflection should be in full play. To him who looks upon the world rationally, the world in its turn, presents a rational aspect. The relation is mutual."

For an excellent introduction to Hegel, see Jacob Loewenberg's "Introduction," in his *Hegel: Selections* (New York, 1929). See also A. D. Lindsay, "Hegel, the German Idealist," in F. J. C. Hearnshaw (ed.), *Social and Political Ideas of the Age of Reconstruction* (London, 1932), 52 ff.

[26] Hegel, *Philosophy of History*, 8–9. The italics are Hegel's. "The only Thought which Philosophy brings with it to the contemplation of History, is the simple conception of *Reason;* that Reason is the Sovereign of the World; that the history of the world, therefore, presents us with a rational process. This conviction and intuition is a hypothesis in the domain of history as such. In that of Philosophy it is no hypothesis. It is there proved by speculative cognition."

[27] Herbert Marcuse, *Reason and Revolution* (New York, 1941), 23.

[28] The German word *Geist* is translated both as spirit and as mind. Hegel used the two meanings interchangeably.

[29] John W. Burgess, "Political Science and History," *American Historical Review*, II (Apr. 1897), 403.

[30] Hegel, *Philosophy of History*, 18.

[31] Burgess, *The Civil War and the Constitution*, I, 44.

[32] *Ibid.*, 134–35.

[33] *Ibid.*, 44.

[34] *Ibid.*

[35] John M'T. E. M'Taggart, *Studies in the Hegelian Dialectic* (Cambridge, England, 1922), 205.

[36] Burgess, "Political Science and History," *American Historical Review* II (Apr. 1897), 407–08.

[37] Burgess, *Foundations of Political Science*, 89. Cf. Hegel, *Philosophy of History*, 25: "A State is then well constituted and internally powerful, when the private interest of its citizens is one with

the common interest of the State."
38 Burgess, *Foundations of Political Science*, 89.
39 *Ibid.*, 90.
40 *Ibid.*, 90–92.
41 *Ibid.*, 53. "There is one thing, however," Burgess added, "which modifies this divergence between the idea and the concept of the state, and that is the dependence, after all, of the speculative philosopher upon objective realities to awaken his consciousness of the idea. This brings the two nearer together. It makes the idea the pioneer of the concept."
42 Cited in William M. McGovern, *From Luther to Hitler* (Boston, 1941), 282.
43 Jacob Loewenberg (ed.), *Hegel*, 79. Italics in original.
44 *Ibid.*, 113. Cf. Burgess' comment that only "the Roman and the Teuton have realized the state in its approximately pure and perfect character. From them the realized propaganda must go out, until the whole human race shall come to the consciousness of itself, shall realize its universal spiritual substance, and subject itself to the universal laws of its rationality." Burgess, *Foundations of Political Science*, 71.
45 The quoted phrases are in Burgess, *Foundations of Political Science*, 55–56. See also Burgess, *Political Science and Comparative Constitutional Law* (2 vols., Boston, 1890–09), I, 67.
46 Loewenberg (ed.), *Hegel*, 444.
47 Burgess, *Foundations of Political Science*, 56. "With us the government is not the sovereign organization of the state. Back of the government lies the constitution; and back of the constitution the original sovereign state, which ordains the constitution." *Ibid.*, 61. Cf. Hegel in *The Philosophy*

of Law: "It is absolutely essential that the constitution, though having a temporal origin, should not be regarded as made. It (the principle of constitution) is rather to be conceived as absolutely perpetual and rational, and therefore as divine, substantial, and above and beyond the sphere of what is made." Loewenberg (ed.), *Hegel*, 448. The interpolated phrase is Hegel's.
48 Burgess, *The Reconciliation of Government with Liberty* (New York, 1915), 98.
49 Burgess, *Foundations of Political Science*, 100.
50 John Dewey, *The Public and Its Problems* (New York, 1927), 8–9.
51 Burgess, *Reminiscences*, 401.
52 Burgess, *Foundations of Political Science*, 129.
53 *Ibid.*, 93, 89.
54 Bert James Loewenberg, "The Process of Democracy and Political Parties," *Labor and Nation*, VII (Fall 1951), 10–16.
55 Jacob Loewenberg (ed.), *Hegel*, 456.
56 *Ibid.*, 458.
57 Burgess, *Foundations of Political Science*, 130.
58 *Ibid.*, 136.
59 Burgess, *Reminiscences*, 397. Edwin Mims, Jr., *American History and Immigration* (Bronxville, N.Y., 1950), 18.
60 Burgess, *Foundations of Political Science*, 7.
61 Burgess, *Reminiscences*, 248. "If I were to be called upon to state in a few sentences the inferences to be drawn from my treatment of the great subject, I would say that the book [*Political Science and Comparative Constitutional Law*] represents the Teutonic nations . . . as the great modern state builders, that it presents the national state, that is, the self-

conscious democracy as the *Ultima Thule* of political history; that it justifies the temporary imposition of Teutonic order on unorganized, disorganized, or savage people for the sake of their own civilization and thus in the world society." *Ibid.*, 254.

62 Mims, *American History and Immigration*, 18. Brown, *American Conservatives*, 132, gives a lucid discussion of this point.

63 Burgess, *Foundations of Political Science*, 47, 139–40; Brown, *American Conservatives*, 133–135.

64 Shepherd, "John William Burgess," in Odum (ed.), *American Masters of Social Science*, 53.

CHAPTER XIX

1 John Martin Vincent, "Herbert Baxter Adams," Odum (ed.), *Masters of Social Science*, 127. Holt (ed.), *Historical Scholarship in the United States, 1876–1901: As Revealed in the Correspondence of Herbert B. Adams* (Baltimore, 1938), 7–10.

2 Quoted in Vincent, "Herbert Baxter Adams," 102. John Spencer Bassett, "Herbert Baxter Adams," *DAB*, I, 67–69. Holt (ed.), *Historical Scholarship*, 27–28.

3 Vincent, "Herbert Baxter Adams," 104. Daniel C. Gilman, *Bluntschli, Lieber, and Laboulaye* (Baltimore, 1884), 13–22. Herbert B. Adams, *Bluntschli's Life Work* (Baltimore, 1884). Holt (ed.), *Historical Scholarship*, 29–30. Brown, *American Conservatives*, 119–20.

4 Burton J. Hendrick, *The Life and Letters of Walter H. Page* (3 vols., New York, 1922–25), I, 23–30; III, 21–91. James E. Creighton (ed.), *Papers in Honor of Josiah Royce on His Sixtieth Birthday* (New York, 1916). Ralph Barton Perry, *The Thought and Character of William James* (2 vols., Boston, 1935). Morison, *Three Centuries of Harvard, 1636–1936* (Cambridge, 1942), 377–453.

5 Cited in Kraus, 312.

6 Louis N. Wilson (ed.), *Granville Stanley Hall* (Worcester, Mass., 1925). G. Stanley Hall, *Life and Confessions of a Psychologist* (2 vols., New York, 1923).

7 Paul T. Homan, "Thorstein Veblen," Odum (ed.), *Masters of Social Science*, 231–70. Joseph Dorfman, *Thorstein Veblen and His America* (New York, 1935). R. L. Duffus, *The Innocent at Cedro: A Memoir of Thorstein Veblen and Some Others* (New York, 1944), is valuable for its reminiscences. Paul A. Schilpp (ed.), *The Philosophy of John Dewey* (Evanston and Chicago, 1939).

8 Turner is discussed below, 423–427, 472–74. The quotation is cited in Kraus, 313.

9 Fulmer Mood (ed.), *The Early Writings of Frederick Jackson Turner* (Madison, Wis., 1938), 22.

10 Bellot, *American Historians*, 16. Actually, the first seminar on the German model was introduced into America by Charles Kendall Adams in 1869 at the University of Michigan. Charles Kendall Adams to Herbert B. Adams, Feb. 9, 1886. Holt (ed.), *Historical Scholarship*, 79, but, as Charles K. Adams says himself, "For a considerable number of years the work was still rather elementary." *Ibid.*

11 Herbert B. Adams, "Special Methods of Historical Study," in Hall (ed.), *Methods of Teaching History;* the diagram is reproduced at 147. Adams often had

the diagram published; see Holt (ed.), *Historical Scholarship,* 69.

12 Herbert B. Adams, *The Study of History in American Colleges and Universities* (Washington, D.C., 1887), 175.

13 Holt (ed.), *Historical Scholarship,* 94 n.1.

14 John Spencer Bassett to Adams, Apr. 3, 1899, *Ibid.,* 270. George W. Knight to Adams, Apr. 18, 1899, 271.

15 *Ibid.,* 181.

16 Bassett to Adams, Nov. 15, 1898. *Ibid.,* 259–66.

17 William P. Trent to Adams, Nov. 13, 1890. *Ibid.,* 142–43. Italics in original.

18 David Kinley to Adams, Feb. 16, 1901, *Ibid.,* 298–99. Italics in original.

19 John M. Vincent to Adams, Feb. 15, 1892, *Ibid.,* 180. Italics in original.

20 For a discussion of this point, see ch. XIII, 239, and esp. ch. XX.

21 Holt (ed.), *Historical Scholarship,* 71; also 108: James K. Hosmer felt that the Association "may be regarded as your creation." Vincent, "Herbert B. Adams," *Masters of Social Science,* 113.

22 Holt (ed.), *Historical Scholarship,* 111, 108, 121.

23 George W. Kirchwey to Adams, Mar. 7, 1888, *Ibid.,* 111.

24 Adams to Andrew D. White, Feb. 4, 1890, *Ibid.,* 127.

25 The first volume of the first series was published in 1883.

26 Edward A. Freeman, "An Introduction to American Institutional History," *The Johns Hopkins University Studies in Historical and Political Science,* first series, I (Baltimore, 1883).

27 Adams to Daniel C. Gilman, July 3, 1882, Holt (ed.), *Historical Scholarship,* 55–56. Italics in original.

28 Adams, "Special Methods of Historical Study," Hall (ed.), *Methods of Teaching History,* 136–39.

29 Adams to Gilman, Dec. 22, 1890, Holt (ed.), *Historical Scholarship,* 145–46.

30 Committee on Historiography, *Theory and Practice in Historical Study,* 37–39. Edward N. Saveth, *American Historians and European Immigrants, 1875–1925* (New York, 1948), 13–64.

31 Arthur O. Lovejoy, *The Great Chain of Being* (Cambridge, Mass., 1936). Lovejoy in this now classic volume traces the complicated origins and history of the ideas making up the unit concept of the "great chain of being." Plato who contributed significantly to its substance could never have anticipated its later importance to pre-Darwinian biologists nor the uses post-Darwinian biologists derived from it. Literature on this topic is abundant. For a general comment see, George Boas, "A. O. Lovejoy as Historian of Philosophy," *Journal of the History of Ideas,* IX (Oct. 1948), 404–11. See note 35.

32 See above, 245, 271ff.

33 See chapter following.

34 Cited in Committee on Historiography, *Theory and Practice in Historical Study,* 37.

35 Hannis Taylor to Adams, May 26, 1888, quotes an earlier letter in which Adams expressed his notion of the whole theory of Germanic origins tersely. His project had "the possibility of tracing the great stream of American democracy to its earliest English source. Hegel somewhere says that the passing over of the world-spirit from one nation to another is the chief

content of the world's history. In this transitional process, from the spirit of Anglican to American liberty, lies your grand opportunity. An American interpretation of English history in its relation to the rise of this great federal republic, the lineal descendant of those early Germanic tribal federations. . . ." This reference is to Hegel the philosopher. Holt (ed.), *Historical Scholarship*, 113. John G. Palfrey, *A Compendious History of New England* (4 vols., Boston, 1858–75), 113. Adams' own writings on this subject are more instructive than anything written about it. "The Germanic Origins of New England Towns," *The Johns Hopkins Studies in Historical and Political Science*, first series, II (Baltimore, 1883). The following are also in the same series: "Saxon Tithingman in America," IV (1883); "Norman Constables in America," VIII (1883); "Village Communities of Cape Ann and Salem," IX–X (1883). Committee on Historiography, *Theory and Practice in Historical Study*, 37–38. For a critique of "classical evolutionism," Alexander Goldenweiser, "Leading Contributions of Anthropology to Social Theory," Harry E. Barnes and Howard Becker (eds.), *Contemporary Social Theory* (New York and London, 1940), 433–53. See also E. W. Bemis, "Local Government in Michigan and the North West," *The Johns Hopkins University Studies in Historical and Political Science*, first series, V (Baltimore, 1883). Also in the *Johns Hopkins Studies . . .* are Allen Johnson, "The Genesis of a New England State," first series, XI (1883); Jesse Macy, "Institutional Beginnings in a

Western State," second series, VII (1884); Edward Channing, "Town and Country Government in the Colonies," second series, X (1884); J. Elting, "Dutch Village Communities on the Hudson River," fourth series, I (1886). Adams, *Study of History in American Colleges;* William Stubbs, *Lectures on Early English History*, A. Hassal (ed.) (London and New York, 1906), lectures 10, 13, 18, 19; Robert H. Lowie, *The History of Ethnographical Theory* (New York, 1937), chs. v, vi, vii.

36 Albion W. Small, *Origins of Sociology* (Chicago, 1924), 328 n.

37 Adams to Frederic Bancroft, April 6, 1887, Holt (ed.), *Historical Scholarship*, 99.

38 *Ibid.*, 11.

39 For discussion of Osgood, Andrews, and colonial history, see ch. XXII. The epigram has also been ascribed to others. During the latter half of the nineteenth century, it was practically in the public domain.

40 Charles M. Andrews, "Some Recent Aspects of Institutional Study," *Yale Review*, I (Feb. 1893), 384.

41 See n. 34, above. Adams continues: "In Wisconsin, Professor Allen, the original pioneer, has joined in the work, supported by his Seminary of advanced students." See also, *Early Writings of . . . Turner*, 18.

42 Frederick Jackson Turner, "The Significance of the Frontier in American History," *The Frontier in American History* (New York, 1921), 2.

43 *Ibid.*

44 "Our early history is the study of European germs developing in an American environment. Too exclusive attention has been paid by institutional students to

the Germanic origins, too little to the American factors." *Ibid.,* 3.

45 Edwin Mims, Jr., *American History and Immigration,* 16–18. Marcus Lee Hansen, *The Atlantic Migration, 1607–1860* (Cambridge, Mass., 1940), xiii–xvii, 3–78, Marcus Lee Hansen, *The Immigrant in American History* (Cambridge, Mass., 1940), 191–217. Arthur M. Schlesinger, Sr., edited the two volumes after Hansen's death.

46 See above, 362.

47 Burgess, *Reminiscences,* 397.

48 Hansen, *Immigration in American History,* Schlesinger (ed.), 28–29, Mims, *American History and Immigration,* 18–20.

49 Adams, "Germanic Origin of New England Towns," in *Johns Hopkins Studies,* II, first series (Baltimore, 1888), 8 and *passim.*

50 William Edward Hartpole Lecky, *Democracy and Liberty* (2 vols., New York, 1900), I, 135–36. J. Allen Smith, *The Spirit of American Government* (New York, 1907), 291–97. Bernard E. Brown, *American Conservatives,* 58–92.

51 For Burgess' attitude on this point, see above, 360–61.

52 Gooch, *History and Historians in the Nineteenth Century,* 352.

53 Writing of Bryce's treatment of political parties, Woodrow Wilson remarked, ". . . and certainly those who are farthest removed from the practical politician's point of view will gain from these chapters a new and vital conception of what it is to study constitutions in the. life." Wilson's review of Bryce from the *Political Science Quarterly,* IV (Mar. 1899), is reprinted in Robert C. Brooks (ed.), *Bryce's American Commonwealth Fiftieth Anniversary* (New York,

1939), 169–88. The quotation is at 176.

54 Woodrow Wilson, *Congressional Government* (Boston, 1913), 10.

55 But see H. B. Adams, "Jared Sparks and Alexis de Tocqueville," *The Johns Hopkins University Studies in Historical and Political Science,* sixteenth series, XII (Baltimore, 1898).

56 John W. Burgess, "The Methods of Historical Study and Research in Columbia College," Hall (ed.), *Methods of Teaching and Studying History,* 220.

57 "No less philosophic historian has ever lived." Gooch, *History and Historians,* 349, from which the quotation from J. R. Green's review is taken.

58 The development of social history will be discussed in a subsequent section of this study.

59 For example, Holt (ed.), *Historical Scholarship,* 244–45.

60 Frederick Jackson Turner referred to him "as the representative of the idea of University Extension, and the use of *libraries* in this end" (italics are Turner's). Turner to Adams, Sept. 27, 1890, Holt (ed.), *Historical Scholarship,* 137. Vincent, "Herbert B. Adams," Odum (ed.), *Masters of Social Science,* 117. The series in Baltimore was begun by Charles M. Andrews.

61 William R. Harper to Adams, Jan. 30, 1894, Holt (ed.), *Historical Scholarship,* 211–12.

62 Herbert B. Adams, "Seminary Libraries and University Extension," *The Johns Hopkins University Studies in Historical and Political Science,* fifth series, XI (Baltimore, 1887); "Notes on the Literature of Charities," fifth series, VIII (Baltimore, 1887), "Public Educational Work in Baltimore," seventeenth series (Baltimore, 1899).

63 Vincent, "Herbert B. Adams," Odum (ed.), *Masters of Social Science,* 119–21; Holt (ed.), *Historical Scholarship,* 210–11. *Thomas Jefferson and the University of Virginia,* U.S. Bureau of Education, Circulars of Information, No. 1 (Washington, D.C., 1888).

64 *The College of William and Mary: A Contribution to the History of Higher Education, with Suggestions for its National Promotion,* U.S. Bureau of Education, Circulars of Information, No. 1 (Washington, D.C., 1887). *The Study of History in American Colleges and Universities,* U.S. Bureau of Education, Circulars of Information, No. 2 (Washington, D.C., 1887).

65 Herbert B. Adams, "Special Methods of Historical Study," Hall (ed.), *Methods of Teaching and Studying History,* 113–47, 113 n. 1.

66 The contract is reprinted in Holt (ed.), *Historical Scholarship,* 81, n. 1.

67 Vincent, "Herbert B. Adams," Odum (ed.), *Masters of Social Science,* 114–16; Holt, (ed.), *Historical Scholarship,* 205–06.

CHAPTER XX

1 Bert James Loewenberg, "Darwinism Comes to America, 1859–1900," *Mississippi Valley Historical Review,* XXVIII (Dec. 1941), 339–68.

2 Emerton, "The Practical Method in Higher Historical Instruction," in Hall (ed.), *Methods of Teaching and Studying History,* 52.

3 *Ibid.,* 54.

4 *Ibid.,* 54–55.

5 George Burton Adams, "History and the Philosophy of History,"

American Historical Review, XIV (Jan. 1909), 235–36. John Martin Vincent, *Historical Research: An Outline of Theory and Practice* (New York, 1911), 251, makes clear that regardless of language, more than a conventional empiricism was required.

6 Allen Johnson, *The Historian and Historical Evidence* (New York, 1926), 2.

7 George Burton Adams, "History and the Philosophy of History," *American Historical Review,* XIV (Jan. 1909), 223.

8 Johnson, *The Historian and Historical Evidence,* 11–12, Charles V. Langlois and Charles Seignobos, *Introduction to the Study of History,* G. G. Berry, tr. (New York, 1912), 316.

9 "However primary the source, it is the testimony of a witness, and the perceptions, memories, and psychological idiosyncrasies of witnesses are notoriously unreliable. Moreover, the historian himself is a witness in the second degree so to speak, for he testifies to his readers what he perceived in the document. Historians themselves can be cross-examined at least by reference to the document itself. But the original chronicler can be attacked only by other documents, other data, and other concepts." *Ibid.*

10 "History is only the utilisation of documents." *Ibid.*

11 *Ibid.,* 317. Johnson, *The Historian and Historical Evidence,* "Preface," 45. Vincent, *Historical Research,* 122, 249.

12 Langlois and Seignobos, *Study of History,* 262–95.

13 John H. Randall, Jr., and George Haines, IV, in *Theory and Practice in Historical Study* (New York, 1946), 25. Morris R. Cohen, *The Meaning of Human*

History (La Salle, Ill., 1947), 77–78.

14 Johnson, *The Historian and Historical Evidence,* 160–62. See above, n. 10.

15 Johann Gottfried von Herder (1711–1803); Barthold Georg Niebuhr (1776–1831); Leopold von Ranke (1795–1886). Gooch, *History and Historians in the Nineteenth Century* (London, 1913), 14–24. Ernst Cassirer, *The Problem of Knowledge* (New Haven, 1950), 218–19.

16 Gooch, *History and Historians,* 9. Ernst Cassirer, *An Essay on Man* (New Haven, 1944), 172–73. Lord Acton, *A Lecture on the Study of History* (London, 1895), 49–50. Theodore H. von Laue, *Leopold von Ranke: The Formative Years* (Princeton, N.J., 1950).

17 Hajo Holborn, "The Science of History," Joseph R. Strayer (ed.), *The Interpretation of History* (Princeton, N.J., 1942), 71.

18 At its second annual meeting the American Historical Association elected Ranke "its sole honorary member." Jameson, "Early Days of the American Historical Association," *American Historical Review,* XL (Oct. 1934), 6. "No historian has approached his task with a more universal equipment of culture." Gooch, *History and Historians,* 77.

19 This much-quoted phrase has created great confusion. As Holborn points out, it simply means, "It only wants to show what actually occurred." But, more meaningfully, it should be rendered, "It wants merely to reconstruct the actual past." Holborn, "The Science of History," 73. Harry Elmer Barnes and Howard Becker (eds.), *Contemporary Social Theory* (New York and London, 1940), 20, n. 4.

20 Holborn, "Science of History," 63.

21 Barnes and Becker (eds.), *Contemporary Social Theory,* 19–21, 428.

22 Gooch, *History and Historians,* 77.

23 Antoine Guilland, *Modern Germany and Her Historians* (New York, 1915), 86.

24 Cassirer, *Problem of Knowledge,* 235.

25 Quoted in Guilland, *Modern Germany and Her Historians,* 91–93. See below, n. 47.

26 Cassirer, *Problem of Knowledge,* 224, 231–32.

27 Quoted in Guilland, *Modern Germany and Her Historians,* 99.

28 Cassirer, *Problem of Knowledge,* 234.

29 *Ibid.*

30 The phrase is Ranke's and is quoted, *Ibid.*

31 *Ibid.*

32 Quoted in Guilland, *Modern Germany and Her Historians,* 88, n. 1.

33 *Ibid.,* 112.

34 Holborn, "Science of History," 74. Cassirer, *Essay on Man,* 189. Cassirer, *Problem of Knowledge,* 232.

35 Guilland, *Modern Germany and Her Historians,* 93–96.

36 Cassirer, *Problem of Knowledge,* 239. "Of course the task of the historian was not to be mastered by intellect alone; it required, rather, a constant cooperation of the creative imagination, which alone was able to tie together into a genuine unity the isolated and widely dispersed facts. But the imagination of the historian is not striving to get beyond the actual events; it subordinates itself to experience and the investigation of what is real." See also 240–42, 235, 237.

37 See above, note 25.

[38] Acton, *Study of History*, 49–50.

[39] The ways that Henry Adams employed the hypotheses of Gibbs are discussed in Muriel Rukeyser, *Willard Gibbs* (New York, 1964), 408–15. Lankester is quoted in Johnson, *The Historian and Historical Evidence*, 158.

[40] Emerton, "The Practical Method in Higher Historical Instruction," Hall (ed.), *Methods of Teaching and Studying History*, 54.

[41] Cohen, *Meaning of Human History*, 77–78, 205–46. Morris R. Cohen and Ernest Nagel, *An Introduction to Logic and Scientific Method* (New York, 1934). E. W. Strong, "William Whewell and John Stuart Mill: Their Controversy About Scientific Knowledge," *Journal of the History of Ideas*, XVI (Apr. 1955), 209–31.

[42] Carl L. Becker, "What Are Historical Facts?" *The Western Political Quarterly*, VII (Sept. 1955), 327–40.

[43] Cohen, *Meaning of Human History*, 44.

[44] *Ibid.*

[45] "Physical science therefore rests on verified or uncontradicted hypothesis; and such being the case, it is not surprising that a great condition of its progress has been the invention of verifiable hypotheses." Thomas Henry Huxley, "The Progress of Science," *Methods and Results* (New York, 1896), 61–62. Johnson, *The Historian and Historical Evidence*, 157. Alfred North Whitehead, *Science and the Modern World* (New York, 1937), 63. Cohen, *Meaning of Human History*, 210.

[46] Burgess, "Methods of Historical Study and Research in Columbia College," Hall (ed.), *Methods of Teaching and Studying History*, 220; italics in original; see also 218.

[47] See above, 349, 351, 352.

[48] Andrew Dickson White, "Historical Instruction in the Course of History and Political Science at Cornell University," Hall (ed.), *Methods of Teaching and Studying History*, 76.

[49] Adams, "Special Methods of Historical Study," Hall (ed.), *Ibid.*, 126.

[50] Moses Coit Tyler as quoted in Adams, "Special Methods of Historical Study," *Ibid.*, 135, a specially prepared statement.

[51] Langlois and Seignobos, *Study of History*, 317.

[52] Acton, *Study of History*, 2.

[53] Viscount Morley, *Notes on Politics and History* (London, 1913), 51–52.

[54] *Ibid.*

[55] Marc Bloch, *The Historian's Craft* (New York, 1953), 47.

[56] H. B. Adams, "Special Methods of Historical Study," Hall (ed.), *Methods of Teaching and Studying History*, 127.

[57] Bloch, *Historian's Craft*, 41. "I would not be understood as disparaging ancient or old-world history, for, if rightly taught, this is the most interesting of all history; but I would be understood as emphasizing the importance of studying the antiquity which survives in the present and in this country." Adams, "Special Methods of Historical Study," Hall (ed.), *Methods of Teaching and Studying History*, 131.

[58] W. F. Allen, "Gradation and the Topical Method of Historical Study," in Hall (ed.), *Ibid.*, 235.

[59] Adams, "Special Methods of Historical Study," Hall (ed.), *Methods of Teaching and Studying History*, 137.

[60] H. B. Adams, "Germanic Origins of New England Towns," in *Johns Hopkins Studies*, first series, II (Baltimore, 1888), 8.

61 Charles M. Andrews, "Some Recent Aspects of Institutional Study," *Yale Review* I (February 1893), 384.

62 The "Teutonic hypothesis" is discussed above, 369, 370, 371. Roosevelt and Mahan, ch. XXV.

63 Cassirer, *Problem of Knowledge*, 170, who suggests that the gaps in the evidence for evolution can only be explained by this "deep-seated characteristic of general intellectual history in the nineteenth century."

64 *Ibid.*, 172. Italics in original.

65 Quoted in Cassirer, *Problem of Knowledge*, 171.

66 Cassirer, *Essay on Man*, 18.

67 Cassirer, *Problem of Knowledge*, 172. Johnson, *The Historian and Historical Evidence*, 155.

68 *Ibid.*, 224.

69 Bury, "Darwinism and History," *Evolution in Modern Thought* (New York, n.d.), 248.

70 Morris R. Cohen, "Einstein and His World," *The Faith of a Liberal* (New York, 1946), 47. Cohen, *Meaning of Human History*, 44.

CHAPTER XXI

1 See above, 233.

2 Jameson, *Historical Scholarship*, 4. Andrew Dickson White, *Autobiography* (2 vols., New York and London, 1922), I, 255. "John Franklin Jameson," *American Historical Review*, XLIII (Jan. 1938), 244. C. K. Adams, "On Methods of Teaching History," Hall (ed.), *Methods of Teaching and Studying History*, 208.

3 Kraus, 311–12. J. Franklin Jameson, "Early Days of the American Historical Association,"

American Historical Review, XL (Oct. 1934), 2.

4 It has been estimated that ten thousand Americans matriculated in German universities during the century from 1814 to 1914. Curti, *Growth of American Thought*, 582.

5 Holt (ed.), *Historical Scholarship*, 17. Theodore Clarke Smith, "The Writing of American History in America, from 1884 to 1934," *American Historical Review*, XL (Apr. 1935), 410–13.

6 See above, 337–38.

7 Holt (ed.), *Historical Scholarship*, 9.

8 Caroline F. Ware, "Introduction," Ware (ed.), *The Cultural Approach to History* (New York, 1940), 3.

9 Emerton, "The Practical Method in Higher Historical Instruction," Hall (ed.), *Methods of Teaching and Studying History*, 33, 51, 54. A. D. White, "Historical Instruction in the Course of History and Political Science at Cornell University," *Ibid.*, 75.

10 Emerton, "The Practical Method in Higher Historical Instruction," *Ibid.*, 33.

11 Hart, "Methods of Teaching American History," *Ibid.*, 5. White, "Historical Instruction in the Course of History and Political Science at Cornell University," *Ibid.*, 74.

12 H. B. Adams, "Special Methods of Historical Study," *Ibid.*, 120.

13 Emerton, "The Practical Method in Higher Historical Instruction," *Ibid.*, 32.

14 Burgess, "The Methods of Historical Study and Research in Columbia College," *Ibid.*, 216, 218. Italics in original.

15 Emerton, "The Practical Method

in Higher Historical Instruction," *Ibid.*, 38. Italics in original.

16 Adams, "Special Methods of Historical Study," *Ibid., passim.*

17 Emerton, "The Practical Method in Higher Historical Instruction," *Ibid.*, 59.

18 William E. Foster, "The Use of of a Public Library in the Study of History," *Ibid.*, 105–11. Henry E. Scott, "The Courses of Study in History, Roman Law, and Political Economy at Harvard University," *Ibid.*, 168–69. Adams, "Special Methods of Historical Study," *Ibid.*, 122–23.

19 Adams, "Special Methods of Historical Study," *Ibid.*, 147.

20 Emerton, "The Practical Method in Higher Historical Instruction," *Ibid.*, 58, 38. "One apparent obstacle to success in America lies in our almost universal system of grading students, by which all efforts, after a true scholarly standard, are hampered, and many of them wholly defeated," 58.

21 W. Carson Ryan, *Studies in Early Graduate Education,* Carnegie Foundation for the Advancement of Teaching, Bulletin Number Thirty (New York, 1939), 20–24, 26–29.

22 Adams, "Special Methods of Historical Study," in Hall (ed.), *Methods of Teaching and Studying History,* 122.

23 Holst is discussed in ch. XXV.

24 Ryan, *Studies in Early Graduate Education,* 40–43.

25 See above, 370–71.

26 Thomas H. Huxley, *American Addresses* (New York, 1877), 7–14; Holt (ed.), *Historical Scholarship,* 55, 85, 209, 269.

27 Holt (ed.), *Historical Scholarship,* 55.

28 See above, 369.

29 *American Historical Review,* XLIII (Jan. 1938), 243–352.

"He had no predecessor, and he will have no successor," 243. Jameson was graduated from Amherst in 1879, taught at Hopkins for six years after earning his doctorate in 1882, at Brown from 1888 to 1901; and in 1901 went to Chicago.

30 H. Hale Bellot, *American History and Historians* (London, 1952), 21. Under this program guides to American materials in Great Britain, Spain, Italy, Germany, Austria, Switzerland, Russia, Canada, Mexico, Cuba, and the West Indies were prepared and published. Manuscript materials were copied and made available in the Library of Congress. *American Historical Review,* XLIII (Jan. 1938), 245. Jameson remained as director of research until his retirement in 1928.

31 J. Franklin Jameson, "Studies in the History of the Federal Convention of 1787," American Historical Association, *Annual Report for the Year 1902,* I (Washington, D.C., 1903), 87–167. Allen Johnson, *The Historian and Historical Evidence,* 18–19. Jameson's *An Introduction to the Study of the Constitutional History of the States* (Baltimore, 1886) contains three essays published as one of the Hopkins *Studies,* of which it is a characteristic example. Also representative is *Essays in the Constitutional History of the United States in the Formative Period, 1775–1789* (Boston, 1889), which appeared under his editorship.

32 J. Franklin Jameson, "Early Days of the American Historical Association," *American Historical Review,* XL (Oct. 1934), 1–9.

33 *The American Revolution Considered as a Social Movement* (Princeton, N.J., 1926). See

Frederick B. Tolles, "The American Revolution Considered as a Social Movement: A Re-evaluation," *American Historical Review*, XL (Oct. 1954), 1–12. When seventy, Jameson became chief of the division of manuscripts of the Library of Congress and first occupant of the chair of American History. Instrumental in the creation of the Historical Manuscript Commission of the American Historical Association, he himself edited the letters of Phineas Bond, Stephen Higginson, and J. C. Calhoun. For his historiographical works and his volumes in the *Original Narratives Series*, of which he was editor, see his documentary publications, *American Historical Review*, XLIII (Jan. 1938), 245.

34 Bassett was preceded at Trinity by another Hopkins man, Stephen B. Weeks, who received his Ph.D. in 1891. Wendell H. Stephenson, "A Half Century of Southern Historical Scholarship," *The Journal of Southern History*, XI (Feb. 1945), 8–12.

35 Bassett to Adams, Jan. 16, 1896, Holt (ed.), *Historical Scholarship*, 242.

36 *Ibid.*, 266.

37 Bassett to Adams, Sept. 26, 1897, *Ibid.*, 246. Bassett also initiated the *Historical Papers of the Trinity College Historical Society* in 1897 and had an active hand in the establishment of the *South Atlantic Quarterly* in 1902. Stephenson, "Half Century of Southern Scholarship," 9.

38 Bassett to Adams, Nov. 15, 1898, 259. "I do not have the honor to agree with most of my fellow Anglo Saxons on the negro question." Holt (ed.), *Historical Scholarship*, 257.

39 *Constitutional Beginnings of North Carolina, The Johns Hopkins University Studies in Historical and Political Science*, twelfth series, III (Baltimore, 1894). "The Regulators of North Carolina, 1765–1771," American Historical Association *Annual Report for 1894* (Washington, D.C., 1895), 141–212. *Slavery and Servitude in the Colony of North Carolina, The Johns Hopkins University Studies*, fourteenth series, IV–V (Baltimore, 1896).

40 Stephenson, "Half Century of Southern Scholarship," 9.

41 *Anti-Slavery Leaders of North Carolina, The Johns Hopkins University Studies in Historical and Political Science*, sixteenth series, VI (Baltimore, 1898). *History of Slavery in North Carolina, The Johns Hopkins Studies*, seventeenth series, VII–VIII (Baltimore, 1899). *The Federalist System, 1789–1801* (New York and London, 1906).

42 John Spencer Bassett and J. Franklin Jameson (eds.), *Correspondence of Andrew Jackson* (7 vols., Washington, D.C., 1926–1935). Bassett also wrote the *Life of Andrew Jackson* (2 vols., New York, 1925).

43 Underwood: 1862–1929. Congressman (1895–96; 1897–1915), U.S. Senator (1915–1927).

44 Wendell H. Stephenson, "William P. Trent as a Historian of the South," *The Journal of Southern History*, XV (May 1949), 151–177, especially 151–53.

45 William P. Trent, *English Culture in Virginia, The Johns Hopkins Studies in Historical and Political Science*, seventh series, vols. V–VI (Baltimore, 1889). For his earlier studies on the University of Virginia and the role of H. B. Adams, see Stephenson, "Trent," 153–54.

46 Trent to Adams, Jan. 8, 1898,

Holt (ed.), *Historical Scholarship*, 249. "I must doubt whether five or ten years more of me in the South means much to either party." 250.

47 Trent to Adams, Jan. 8, 1898, *Ibid.*, 250. Italics in original.

48 William P. Trent, "The Case of Josiah Phillips," *American Historical Review*, I (Apr. 1896), 444–54.

49 William P. Trent, *William Gilmore Simms* (Boston, 1892); *Southern Statesmen of the Old Regime* (New York, 1897); *Robert E. Lee* (Boston, 1899). Trent was a guiding figure in the early history of the *Sewanee Review*, of which he was editor from its founding in 1892 to 1900. Associated with him in this enterprise was B. Lawton Wiggins, a Hopkins product of Basil L. Gildersleeve in classical studies. Stephenson, "Trent," 173.

50 Trent, *Simms*, 36–37, 147–48.

51 Stephenson, "Trent," 165. *Southern Statesmen* was dedicated to Roosevelt, *Lee* to Matthews.

52 Stephenson, "Trent," 167.

53 *Ibid.*

54 *Ibid.*, 170, who reports that by 1930 Trent had written 130 historical articles, 56 of them on Southern topics. His early study, "The Period of Constitution-Making in the American Churches," is in Jameson's *Constitutional History*, ch. IV.

55 For these purposes the most important sources for Wilson are Ray Stannard Baker, *Woodrow Wilson, Life and Letters* (8 vols., Garden City, New York, 1927–39). *Selected Literary and Political Papers* (3 vols., New York, 1925–27). William E. Dodd, *Woodrow Wilson and His Work*, (New York, 1927), is an excellent appraisal, as is Herbert C. Bell, *Woodrow Wilson and the People* (New York, 1945). A recent biography is by Arthur S. Link, *Wilson, the Road to the White House* (Princeton, New Jersey, 1947). William Diamond, *The Economic Thought of Woodrow Wilson* (Baltimore, 1943), is exceedingly helpful. Louis Martin Sears, "Woodrow Wilson," *Jernegan Essays*, 102–121. Kraus, 454–61. Marjorie L. Daniel, "Woodrow Wilson, Historian," *Mississippi Valley Historical Review* XXI (Dec. 1934), 361–74. Wilson was graduated from Princeton in 1879 and admitted to the Virginia bar in 1882.

56 "The profession I chose was politics," he wrote, "the profession I entered was the law. I entered the one because I thought it would lead to the other." Baker, *Wilson*, I, 109. Wilson entered Hopkins, Sept. 18, 1883. A graduate student (1883–85), he received his doctorate in 1886.

57 Baker, *Wilson*, I, 171.

58 *Ibid.*, I, 173.

59 *Ibid.*, I, 174, 178–79, 180. Wilson later changed his opinion of Adams and Hopkins. For Hopkins' opinion of Wilson, see Holt (ed.), *Historical Scholarship*, 91, notes.

60 This work was never published. Baker, *Wilson*, I, 213. Diamond, *Economic Thought*, 29.

61 "Cabinet Government in the United States," *International Review*, VI (Aug. 1879), 146–63, reprinted in *Selected Literary and Political Papers*, I, 1–29. *Congressional Government: A Study in American Politics* (Boston, 1885). Although criteria vary, judgments of the import of this book differ sharply. The opinion of Link, *Wilson*, 15, 17, does not coincide with the view presented here. See also Dodd,

Wilson, 21. Diamond, *Economic Thought,* 47–48. Baker, *Wilson,* I, 226. Charles Kendall Adams, *A Manual of Historical Literature* (New York, 1888), 670. L. M. Sears, "Wilson," *Jernegan Essays,* 107–08.

62 Baker, *Wilson,* I, 213–18.

63 *Ibid.,* "I have modelled my work chiefly on Mr. Bagehot's essays," 216.

64 *Ibid.,* I, 222.

65 *Ibid.,* I, 218–19. Bryce had read it with enthusiastic approval, 224.

66 Gamaliel Bradford, "The Progress of Civil Service Reform," *International Review,* XIII (Sept. 1882), 266–67.

67 Baker, *Wilson,* I, 224.

68 Dodd, *Wilson,* 22.

69 Baker, *Wilson,* II, 99.

70 Diamond, *Economic Thought,* 48, n. 31. Link, *Wilson,* 19.

71 Baker, *Wilson,* I, 246.

72 *Ibid.,* 103–04.

73 *Ibid.,* I, 261, 262. Alfred Pearce Dennis, "Princeton Schoolmaster," Houston Peterson (ed.), *Great Teachers* (New Brunswick, N.J., 1946), 134–35.

74 "An Old Master," *Selected Literary and Political Papers,* III, 4. "Are not our college classrooms . . . getting . . . a brief of *data* and bibliography?" 3.

75 Baker, *Wilson,* I, 301.

76 *Ibid.,* I, 280. Note Wilson's essay, "The Study of Politics," *Selected Literary and Political Papers,* III, 27–49.

77 Baker, *Wilson,* I, 226.

78 Frederic C. Howe, *The Confessions of a Reformer* (New York, 1925), 6–7.

79 Link, *Wilson,* 15; Diamond, *Economic Thought,* 26, 31, 37.

80 Diamond, *Economic Thought,* 37, 65, 69, 86–87, 123–24. Link, *Wilson,* 119, 123, 131–32.

81 Baker, *Wilson,* I, 272.

82 July 10, 1886. *Ibid.,* I, 273. Italics are Wilson's.

83 *Ibid.,* I, 274.

84 Wilson wrote to H. B. Adams that he wished to "see the constitutions of the continent *alive.* I *must* learn German as it cannot be learned from books, and I must see European politics and administration as no library can show them to me. As you know, what I go in for is the *life,* not the texts, of constitutions, the practice not the laws of administration." Wilson to H. B. Adams, Dec. 5, 1886, Holt (ed.), *Historical Scholarship,* 92. Italics in original. Baker, *Wilson,* I, 275–277.

85 *The State* (Boston, 1889). Diamond, *Economic Thought,* 39. Baker, *Wilson,* I, 275.

86 Baker, *Wilson,* I, 281.

87 *Ibid.,* I, 298–325.

88 *Ibid.,* I, 53, 306, II, 123–24. *Division and Reunion* (New York and London, 1893).

89 Dodd, *Wilson,* 28. Baker, *Wilson,* II, 123–24.

90 *Division and Reunion* (1909 ed.), 21 (distinctions between Jeffersonianism and Jacksonianism), 112–15 (reformation of parties, 1829–41), 211 (secession), 212 (sectionalization of the Union), 15–16, 24–26, 212 (influence of the West). In 1915 Wilson made a short speech in which this interpretation of the Civil War was stressed and expanded. "Meaning of the Civil War," *Selected Literary and Political Papers,* II, 123–25.

91 Baker, *Wilson,* II, 102–09. "The editors of the popular monthlies offer me such prices nowadays that I am corrupted." 119.

92 *A History of the American People* (5 vols., New York and London, 1902). Dodd, *Wilson,* 30.

93 Baker, *Wilson,* II, 113.

94 Thirty-three pages is devoted to "Before the English Came," I, 1–33; the remainder of the volume discusses "The Swarming of the English," 35–350. Vol. II is distinguished by the portrait of Sam Adams, 160, 174–78, 180, and the treatment of loyalism, for example, 264.

95 Wilson's criticism of the Confederation, III, 20–21, 53, is based less on the assumptions of "the critical period" than assumptions of his theory of government, a government with power to govern. On Loyalists, 24–28. The view of Daniel Shays is unfavorable, 58. For Wilson's political analysis of the years 1824–29, 266–91.

96 The discussion of political changes is continued in IV, "The Democratic Revolution," 1–38. On the Civil War, chs. iii, iv, v. Vol. V, 1–113, cover the Reconstruction era.

97 Helpful and well-chosen materials appear in the appendixes. Vols. II, III, IV.

98 Baker, Wilson, II, 126. Dodd, Wilson, 29–30. Link, Wilson, 30.

99 History, IV chs. iii–v. V, ch. i.

100 American Historical Review, VIII (July 1903), 763.

101 Daniel, "Wilson," Mississippi Valley Historical Review, 372. L. M. Sears, "Wilson," Jernegan Essays, 112–13.

102 A. P. Dennis, "Princeton Schoolmaster," H. Peterson (ed.), Great Teachers, 149–50. Link, Wilson, 30, n. 125.

103 F. J. Turner, American Historical Review, VIII (July, 1903), 763.

104 Ibid., 762.

105 Ibid., 763. Turner himself said: "But this is the period that has suffered at the hands of all our historians."

106 Constitutional Government in the

United States (New York, 1908). Diamond, Economic Thought, 48.

107 Constitutional Government, 68, 110, 80–81, 82–111.

108 For Wilson's views on labor, Diamond, Economic Thought, 70–72, 116–21. On role of government, 80, 87, 88. Link, Wilson, 111–12.

109 Suggestive in this connection is the fact that, although Wilson was living in or near Baltimore while writing Congressional Government, he never visited Congress. Baker, Wilson, I, 218. Dennis, "Princeton Schoolmaster," 143.

110 Link, Wilson, 189–95, 205 ff.

111 Sears, "Wilson," Jernegan Essays, 116.

112 "The Truth of the Matter," Selected Literary and Political Papers, III, 161–86.

113 Ibid., 161.

114 Ibid., 161, 165, 170.

115 Ibid., 170–71.

116 Wilson's status as historian is suggested by President Gilman's offer, after the death of Adams, to make him head of the Hopkins department. See Wilson's letter to Gilman, Mar. 18, 1901, Holt (ed.), Historical Scholarship, 91. Daniel, "Wilson," Mississippi Valley Historical Review, 375. Sears, "Wilson," Jernegan Essays, 113, 121.

117 Kraus, 455.

118 Dodd, Wilson, 27–28, 52. Baker, Wilson, II, 24, 124–25. Fulmer Mood (ed.), Early Writings of Frederick Jackson Turner, 20–21, 23, 27. Turner to H. B. Adams, Jan. 11, 1890, Holt (ed.), Historical Scholarship, 123, states his opinion of Wilson. The best evidence, of course, is Wilson's own thinking as it appeared in his work. An excellent illustration may be found in "The

Course of American History," *Selected Literary and Political Papers*, III, 213–47.

[119] See the comments in Baker, *Wilson*, II, 124, and excerpts from a letter written to Baker by Turner on the subject of Wilson. Dodd, *Wilson*, 27, 28, also writes on the basis of conversations with Wilson and a letter from Turner. "Turner," wrote Wilson, "and I were close friends. He talked with me a great deal about his idea. All I ever wrote on the subject came from him." Baker, *Wilson*, II, 125.

[120] Mood, *Early Writings of . . . Turner*, 21. Baker, *Wilson*, II, 43.

[121] Stephenson, "Half Century of Southern Scholarship," 15–16.

[122] The development of Southern historiography is treated in ch. XXII. Stephenson, "Half Century of Southern Scholarship," 16. For a Hopkins' man engaged in productive historical scholarship, Stephenson, "Trent," 155.

[123] Cited in W. Carson Ryan, *Studies in Early Graduate Education*, 3.

[124] Woodburn received his Ph.D. in 1890 and was professor of American History at Indiana (1890–1924). John Martin Vincent received his degree in the same year and ultimately became professor of European history at Hopkins and editor of the *Studies*. Other distinguished Hopkins doctors in history are John H. Latané, Bernard C. Steiner, J. C. Ballagh, George E. Howard, and John H. T. McPherson. A statistical account has been made by William B. Hesseltine and Louis Kaplan. "Doctors of Philosophy in History," *American Historical Review*, XLVII (July 1942), 727–800.

[125] Hesseltine and Kaplan, "Doctors

of Philosophy in History," 727. Johnson, *The Historian and Historical Evidence*, 101.

[126] "It is rather the evidence of a deeply-felt reaction from the false methods,—the dramatic form, the partisan purpose, the rhetorical elaboration, which mark the historical writing of the eighteenth century. The falseness of that method was so strongly felt that men avoided consciously any approach toward brilliant presentation." Emerton, "The Practical Method in Higher Historical Instruction," Hall (ed.), *Methods of Teaching and Studying History*, 41.

[127] Randall and Haines, *Theory and Practice in Historical Study*, 30–31. Edward N. Saveth (ed.), *Understanding the American Past* (Boston, 1954), 8–11.

CHAPTER XXII

[1] Ryan, *Studies in Early Graduate Education*, 7–14. Abraham Flexner, *Universities: American English German* (New York and London, 1930), 39–218. *A Quarter Century of Learning* (New York, 1931), lectures delivered at Columbia at the 175th anniversary of its founding.

[2] Burgess, *Reminiscences*, 161. Nicholas Murray Butler, *Across the Busy Years* (New York and London, 1939), 111–16, 134–75. Ryan, *Early Graduate Education*, 46–90. A. D. White, *Autobiography*, I, 257–65.

[3] The best running account is furnished by Burgess himself in *Reminiscences*, chs. vi, vii. Butler, *Across the Busy Years*, chs. iv, v. Dixon Ryan Fox, *Herbert Levi Osgood* (New York, 1924), 36–37. Ryan, *Early Graduate Education*, 10–13.

[4] Burgess, *Reminiscences*, 187.

[5] *Ibid.*, 183, 197–98. Richmond Mayo-Smith (1854–1901) later achieved a scholarly reputation in statistics with particular reference to social science. Mayo-Smith and his colleagues are appraised by Burgess, 217–18.

[6] *Ibid.*, 202. The Columbia *Studies in History, Economics and Public Law* appeared in 1891.

[7] Burgess' recollection of the launching of the graduate school is itself exciting and one of the best sections of his book *Reminiscences*, 194–97. See also White, *Autobiography*, I, 287–329, Ryan, *Early Graduate Education*, for a good account of William Rainey Harper and the beginnings of Chicago, 109–38.

[8] Frederick Augustus Porter Barnard (1809–89) became president in 1864. Seth Low (1850–1916) was president (1889–1901). Burgess' comments on both are naturally significant. *Reminiscences*, 173–78, gives a highly complimentary picture of Barnard. Low is discussed, 235–38. Butler's comments in *Across the Busy Years* are as interesting, 69–70, 95–96 on Barnard; 156–157 on Low for what is actually said as for what is left unsaid.

[9] Burgess, *Reminiscences*, 183, 211–16. Butler reciprocated, *Across the Busy Years*, 68.

[10] Carlton J. H. Hayes, "History," *Quarter Century of Learning*, 9–30. Burgess, *Reminiscences*, 244.

[11] Charles E. Merriam, "William Archibald Dunning," Odum (ed.), *American Masters of Social Science*, 131–45, especially 139. J. G. de Roulhac Hamilton, "Introduction," to Dunning, *Truth in History*, xi–xxviii, especially xvi.

[12] Hamilton, "Introduction," *Truth in History*, xi. Charles E. Merriam, "William Archibald Dunning," Charles E. Merriam and Harry Elmer Barnes, *A History of Political Theories: Recent Times* (New York, 1924), v–viii.

[13] Stephenson, "Half Century of Southern Historical Scholarship," 19–20.

[14] James W. Garner, *Reconstruction in Mississippi* (New York, 1901).

[15] C. Mildred Thompson, *Reconstruction in Georgia: Economic, Social, Political, 1865–1872* (New York, 1915), and Walter L. Fleming, *Civil War and Reconstruction in Alabama* (New York, 1905), are exceptions. Stephenson, "Half Century of Southern Historical Scholarship," 21, is excellent on this and all other related points.

[16] Howard K. Beale, "On Rewriting Reconstruction History," *American Historical Review*, XLV (Oct. 1939), 807–08. Stephenson "Half Century of Southern Historical Scholarship," 19–20.

[17] In addition to Garner, Thompson, and Fleming, the following volumes might also be mentioned: William W. Davis, *The Civil War and Reconstruction in Florida* (New York, 1913); J. G. de R. Hamilton, *Reconstruction in North Carolina* (New York, 1914); Benjamin B. Kendrick, *The Journal of the Joint Committee of Fifteen on Reconstruction* (New York, 1915); Charles W. Ramsdell, *Reconstruction in Texas* (New York, 1910); Edwin C. Wooley, *The Reconstruction of Georgia* (New York, 1901).

[18] C. Vann Woodward, *Origins of the New South* (Baton Rouge, 1951), 422. Howard K. Beale, *The Critical Year* (New York, 1930), 3.

[19] William Archibald Dunning, *Reconstruction, Political and Economic* (New York and London, 1907), xv–xvi.

[20] Fleming's Reconstruction volume has already been noted. Fletcher M. Green, "Walter Lynwood Fleming: Historian of Reconstruction," *The Journal of Southern History*, II (Nov. 1936), 497–521, presents a full discussion, and Stephenson's comments, "Half Century of Southern Historical Scholarship," are informative, 20 ff.

[21] Stephenson, "Half Century of Southern Historical Scholarship," 20–21. Green, "Fleming," 498–500. Fleming, *Documentary History of Reconstruction, Political, Military, Social, Religious, Educational, and Industrial, 1865 to the Present Time* (2 vols., Cleveland, 1906, 1907). W. L. Fleming (ed.), *Ku Klux Klan, Its Origins, Growth and Disbandment* by J. C. Lester and D. L. Wilson (New York and Washington, D.C., 1905), rare and out of print when Fleming republished it with a long introduction. Fleming, *The Sequel to Appomattox* (New Haven, 1919).

[22] W. E. Burghardt Du Bois, *Black Reconstruction* (New York, 1935), 720, but see 731–32.

[23] Wood Gray, "Ulrich Bonnell Phillips," *Jernegan Essays*, 357.

[24] U. B. Phillips, "Georgia and State Rights: A Study of the Political History of Georgia from the Revolution to the Civil War, with Particular Regard to Federal Relations," *American Historical Association, Report for 1901*, II (Washington, D.C., 1902).

[25] David M. Potter, "A Bibliography of the Printed Writings of Ulrich Bonnell Phillips," *Georgia Historical Quarterly*, XVIII (Sept. 1934), 270–82. Everett E. Edwards has also assembled a bibliography. "A Bibliography of the Writings of Professor Ulrich Bonnell Phillips," *Agricultural History*, VIII (Oct. 1934), 199–218.

[26] Gray, "Phillips," *Jernegan Essays*, 359, offers an extremely able presentation. Phillips continued his analysis in a more restricted form in "The South Carolina Federalists," *American Historical Review*, XIV (Apr. and July 1909), 529–43, 731–43.

[27] U. B. Phillips, *History of Transportation in the Eastern Cotton Belt to 1860* (New York, 1908).

[28] U. B. Phillips, *Plantation and Frontier Documents: 1649–1863, A Documentary History of American Industrial Society*, John R. Commons and others (eds.), Vols. I and II (Cleveland, 1909).

[29] Gray, "Phillips," *Jernegan Essays*, 361.

[30] U. B. Phillips, *American Negro Slavery: A Survey of the Supply, Employment and Control of Negro Labor as Determined by the Plantation Regime* (New York and London, 1918). *American Negro Slavery* (Boston, 1929).

[31] U. B. Phillips, "The Central Theme of Southern History," *American Historical Review*, XXXIV (Oct. 1928), 30–43.

[32] *Studies in Southern History and Politics, Inscribed to William A. Dunning* (New York, 1914).

[33] Dunning, *Truth in History*, xxi.

[34] W. A. Dunning, *Essays on the Civil War and Reconstruction and Related Topics* (New York, 1897), of which a revised edition appeared in 1931.

[35] Beale, "On Rewriting Reconstruction History," *American Historical Review*, XLV, 807.

[36] Hilary A. Herbert and others,

Why the Solid South? (Baltimore, 1890).

37 William B. Hesseltine, *The South in American History* (New York, 1943), 569.

38 James Ford Rhodes, *History of the United States from the Compromise of 1850*, I (New York, 1893).

39 Beale, "On Rewriting Reconstruction History," 808–09. Horace M. Bond, "Social and Economic Forces in Alabama Reconstruction," *Journal of Negro History*, IV (Feb. 1938), 14–15, and the same writer's *Negro Education in Alabama: A Study in Cotton and Steel* (Washington, D.C., 1939). Francis B. Simkins, "New Viewpoints of Southern Reconstruction," *The Journal of Southern History*, V (Feb. 1939), 49–61, is of fundamental importance. Roger W. Shugg, *Origins of Class Struggle in Louisiana: A Social History of White Farmers and Laborers During Slavery and After, 1840–1875* (Baton Rouge, 1939), suggestively illustrates the historiographical change of view.

40 Dunning's volumes on political theory are *History of Political Theories, Ancient and Medieval* (New York, 1905), and *From Rousseau to Spencer* (New York, 1920). In addition to Charles E. Merriam and Harry Elmer Barnes, the following were numbered among his political-science students: F. W. Coker, E. M. Borchard, Carleton J. H. Hayes, Alexander Goldenweiser, and Frank H. Hankins.

41 Dunning, *Truth in History*, xvii.

42 A full bibliography of Dunning's work may be found in *A Bibliography of the Faculty of Political Science, 1880–1930* (New York, 1931).

43 Stephenson, "Half Century of Southern Historical Scholarship," 26–30.

44 *Ibid.* Later developments dealing with the South and Reconstruction are assessed in a succeeding volume.

45 Fox, *Osgood*, 15 ff. E. C. O. Beatty, "Herbert Levi Osgood," *Jernegan Essays*, 271–93, 272. H. F. Coppock, "Herbert Levi Osgood," *Mississippi Valley Historical Review*, XIX (Dec. 1932), 394–413.

46 Burgess, *Reminiscences*, 159.

47 Fox, *Osgood*, chs. 1–3, cover his early life and preparation.

48 *Ibid.*, 28.

49 H. L. Osgood, "Scientific Socialism—Rodbertus," *Political Science Quarterly*, I (Dec. 1886), 560–94; "Scientific Anarchism," *Ibid.*, IV (Mar. 1889), 1–36. Fox, *Osgood*, 32–33; Beatty, *Jernegan Essays*, 273.

50 Osgood's articles and reviews are partially noted in Beatty, *Jernegan Essays*, 274, nos. 7 and 8. Fox, *Osgood*, 33, 47, 78, 79.

51 H. L. Osgood, *The American Colonies in the Seventeenth Century* (3 vols., New York, 1904, 1907); *The American Colonies in the Eighteenth Century* (4 vols., New York, 1924–25). Beatty, *Jernegan Essays*, 276–78 and notes.

52 Fox, *Osgood*, 38, 43–45.

53 *Ibid.*, 38, 39.

54 *Ibid.*, 46–48.

55 *Ibid.*, 49–50, 51.

56 *Ibid.*, 50–52, 59.

57 Osgood, *American Colonies in the Seventeenth Century*, I, xxv; *American Colonies in the Eighteenth Century*, I, ix.

58 Fox, *Osgood*, 150.

59 Beatty, *Jernegan Essays*, 290–91.

60 Osgood, *American Colonies in the Seventeenth Century*, I, xxxii.

61 Fox, *Osgood*, 157–58; 160–65, where tributes by Robert Living-

ston Schuyler and William R. Shepherd are reprinted.

62 Arthur P. Scott, "George Louis Beer," *Jernegan Essays*, 313–14.

63 Osgood, *American Colonies in the Seventeenth Century*, I, iv.

64 Scott, *Jernegan Essays*, 314.

65 George L. Beer, *The Commercial Policy of England Toward the American Colonies* (New York, 1893).

66 *Ibid.*, 7.

67 Scott, *Jernegan Essays*, 315–16.

68 In 1897, 1896, and 1903 respectively.

69 George L. Beer, *British Colonial Policy, 1754–1765* (New York, 1907), 201.

70 Scott, *Jernegan Essays*, 317.

71 Beer, *Colonial Policy, 1754–1765*, 201. Scott, *Jernegan Essays*, 317.

72 Scott, *Jernegan Essays*, 318.

73 Fox, *Osgood*, 150.

74 Beard and Schlesinger are reserved for treatment in later portions of this study.

75 *Theory and Practice in Historical Study*, 41.

76 *Ibid.*, 37–40.

77 Andrews was born in 1863.

78 Charles M. Andrews, "American Colonial History, 1690–1750," American Historical Association, *Annual Report 1898* (Washington, D.C., 1899), 49.

79 Charles M. Andrews, *The Colonial Period* (New York and London, 1912), vi–vii. Andrews' major work is *The Colonial Period of American History* (4 vols., New Haven, 1934–38).

80 C. M. Andrews, "The American Revolution: An Interpretation," *American Historical Review*, XXXI (Jan. 1926), 219–32.

81 Andrews, "American Colonial History, 1690–1750," 50. Andrews, "Materials in British Archives for American Colonial History," *American Historical Review*, X (Jan. 1, 1905), 325.

82 Andrews, "American Colonial History, 1690–1750," 49, 50–55.

83 Andrews in a review of Osgood, *American Historical Review*, XXXI (Apr. 1926), 532–37. H. L. Osgood, "The Study of American Colonial History," American Historical Association, *Annual Report 1898* (Washington, D.C., 1899), 63–73.

84 Andrews' review of Osgood, *American Historical Review*, XXXI (Apr. 1926), 536–37.

85 *Ibid.*

86 Above, n. 55. "Two political societies of quite different types were thus brought into conflict . . . the historian is bound to do justice to the character and aims of both." Fox, *Osgood*, 50–51.

87 Curtis Nettles, review of Andrews, *New England Quarterly*, X (Dec. 1937), 793–95.

88 C. M. Andrews, "These Forty Years," *American Historical Review*, XXX (Jan. 1925), 243–44. Abraham S. Eisenstadt, *Charles McLean Andrews* (New York, 1957).

CHAPTER XXIII

1 Morison, *Three Centuries of Harvard, 1636–1936*, 291–93, 345, 348–49. Ethel F. Fisk (ed.), *The Letters of John Fiske* (New York, 1940), 189–81, 194. Andrew D. White reported that immediately following the tenure of Jared Sparks as professor of history, there was no real teaching of history, and there were no trained teachers in the American field. *Autobiography*, I, 225. For Harvard before the era of Eliot, William G. Land, *Thomas Hill, Twentieth President of Harvard* (Cambridge, 1933), 193, 123–72.

[2] And with Eliot; see Morison, *Three Centuries*, 348–49.

[3] Ernest Samuels, *The Young Henry Adams* (Cambridge, Mass., 1948), 205, 214.

[4] Adams, *Education*, 308.

[5] Morison, *Three Centuries*, 348. For Adams' reply to Eliot, Harold D. Cater (ed.), *Henry Adams and His Friends* (Boston, 1947), 44–45.

[6] Adams, *Education*, 293.

[7] *Ibid.*, 294. To Charles Eliot Norton, Harvard College, Jan. 13, 1871. "As for my professorship, the less said of that, the better. A madder choice I can't conceive . . . but they said there was no one better." Cater, 54.

[8] Adams, *Education*, 299, 301–04. For the Taylor comment, probably fulsome, Samuels, *Young Henry Adams*, 217.

[9] Adams, *Education*, 302–03.

[10] Samuels, *Young Henry Adams*, 234, 238. Adams' reviews are among the best evidences of his own learning. See, "Freeman's Historical Essays," *North American Review*, CXIV (Jan. 1872), 193–96; "Freeman's History of the Norman Conquest," *Ibid.*, CXVIII (Jan. 1874), 176–81.

[11] Samuels, *Young Henry Adams*, 245–46.

[12] Henry Adams (ed.), *Essays in Anglo-Saxon Law* (Boston, 1876).

[13] Samuels, *Young Henry Adams*, 246–47; *Letters of John Fiske*, 378–79; Cater, 80–81.

[14] For Adams and his development as historian, ch. XXVI.

[15] Lodge, Young, and Laughlin contributed to the *Essays in Anglo-Saxon Law*, Stewart Mitchell, "Henry Adams and Some of His Students," *Proceedings of the Massachusetts Historical Society*, LXVI (1942), 294–312.

[16] Henry Cabot Lodge, *Early Mem-*
ories (New York, 1913), 186–87, 263, 181–86, 188–99.

[17] Adams, *Education*, 419.

[18] *Ibid.*, 420.

[19] Lodge, *Early Memories*, 240–41, 244–45; Samuels, *Young Henry Adams*, 247, 249, Kraus, 439.

[20] Samuels, *Young Henry Adams*, 25.

[21] *Ibid.*

[22] *Ibid.*, 272 ff. Holst is discussed, ch. XXIV; "Von Holst's History of the United States," *North American Review*, CXXIII (Oct. 1876), 328–61, is signed by Adams and Lodge.

[23] Henry Adams (ed.), *Documents Relating to New England Federalism, 1800–1815* (Boston, 1877).

[24] Henry Cabot Lodge, *Life and Letters of George Cabot* (Boston, 1877).

[25] Samuel E. Morison, "Edward Channing, a Memoir," *Proceedings of the Massachusetts Historical Society*, LXIV (Boston, 1932), 260, 279. For an example of Lodge's scholarship, see his life of George Cabot and *A Short History of the English Colonies in America* (New York, 1881), which was dedicated to Adams. *Alexander Hamilton* (Boston and New York, 1882).

[26] Kraus, 322.

[27] Morison, *Three Centuries*, 349.

[28] Kraus, 334.

[29] Morison, *Proceedings of the Massachusetts Historical Society*, LXIV, 260 ff.

[30] Morison, *Three Centuries*, 376. Ralph R. Fahrney, "Edward Channing," *Jernegan Essays*, 294–322.

[31] Edward Channing, *Town and County Government in the English Colonies of North America*, John Hopkins Studies, second series, X (Baltimore, 1883).

[32] For Winsor, see above, 337–38.

[33] Edward Channing, "The Nar-

ragansett Planters, A Study of Causes," *Johns Hopkins University Studies* . . . Fourth series, III (Baltimore, 1886).

34 Thomas W. Higginson and Edward Channing, *English History for American Readers* (New York, 1893).

35 Edward Channing, *A Student's History of the United States* (Boston, 1898).

36 Fahrney, *Jernegan Essays,* 295. Edward Channing, *History of the United States* (6 vols., New York, 1905–25). George W. Robinson (comp.), *Bibliography of Edward Channing* (Cambridge, 1932).

37 Fahrney, *Jernegan Essays,* 309.

38 *New Republic,* XLIV (Nov. 11, 1925), 310.

39 Fahrney, *Jernegan Essays,* 299.

40 *Ibid.,* 300.

41 *Ibid.,* 311.

42 Kraus, 395.

43 *American Historical Review,* XLIX (Oct. 1943), 193.

44 Adams, *Education,* 301–02.

45 *Ibid.*

46 Morison, *Three Centuries,* 349, 376, 387. Herman Ausubel, *Historians and Their Craft: A Study of the Presidential Addresses of the American Historical Association, 1884–1945* (New York, 1950), 160.

47 Hart, "Methods of Teaching American History," Hall (ed.), *Methods of Teaching History,* 3, 2, 1. Italics in original. Samuel E. Morison, "Albert Bushnell Hart, 1889–1939," Massachusetts Historical Society, *Proceedings,* LXVI (1936–41), 434–38.

48 *American Historical Review,* XLIX (Oct. 1943), 193.

49 Holt (ed.), *Historical Scholarship,* 276–77, 281–87.

50 See Hart's "Editor's Introduction to the Series," in Edward P. Cheyney, *European Background of American History* (New York

and London, 1904), *American Nation Series,* I, xv–xvii.

51 *Ibid.,* xvii. "Queries as to a Co-operative History of the United States under the Auspices of the American Historical Association," Holt (ed.), *Historical Scholarship,* 282–86, is the basic document recounting the evolution of the series. Hart edited the *Epochs of American History* (New York, 1891–93) with later editions and different authors. The first edition was composed of *The Colonies* by Reuben Gold Thwaites (1891), *Formation of the Union* by Hart (1892), and *Division and Reunion* by Woodrow Wilson (1893).

52 In this connection, special attention should be called to the volumes of Livingston Farrand, *Basis of American History,* and Hart's own *National Ideals Historically Traced.*

53 Holt (ed.), *Historical Scholarship,* 283–84.

54 Jennings B. Sanders, "John Fiske," *Jernegan Essays,* 144–70; T. S. Perry, *John Fiske* (Boston, 1906). John Spencer Clark, *The Life and Letters of John Fiske* (2 vols., Boston and New York, 1917). For an important autobiographical letter, Jan. 19, 1862, see Ethel Fisk, (ed.), *Letters of John Fiske,* 79–84. On his education and precocity, *Ibid.,* 3, 7, 15–34; languages, 40–43, 63, 72. In 1862, he wrote that "since I have been at Harvard, I have added Anglo-Saxon, Icelandic, Danish, Swedish, Dutch, Provençal and Roumanian, and have made a beginning in Chaldee and Sanskrit." 84.

55 *Ibid.,* 119.

56 Fiske as an infidel—and as deeply religious, Clark, *Life and Let-*

ters, I, 118; Fisk (ed.), *Letters of John Fiske,* 211–12, 379.

57 At Harvard and Harvard Law School, Fiske, *Letters,* 35, 37, 38–39; 55, 107, 118–19, 120–21, 130.

58 Clark, *Life and Letters,* I, 346–48, Fisk (ed.), *Letters,* 348, Morison, *Three Centuries,* 30, 89. Fiske's confirmation was approved by the narrow margin of 12–10, Morrison, 348. Fiske, *Letters,* 185, 333, 477.

59 See Fiske's own comments, Apr. 16, 1879, *Letters,* 378–79, also 183–85; Clark, I, 328, 373–74.

60 For Fiske as librarian, *Letters,* 213, 341. In 1879 he was appointed "to overhaul the history department," *Ibid.,* 417.

61 Fiske's activity as a popularizer of American history is most suggestively set forth by himself, *Ibid.,* 381, 417, 429.

62 For elaboration of this point, *Ibid.,* 401–02, 418–21, 430, 436, 473, 509, 417–18.

63 *Ibid.,* 503.

64 Portland, Oregon, June 3, 1887, *Ibid.,* 540–41.

65 *Ibid.,* 570.

66 *Ibid.,* 167; Clark, I, 135.

67 Rich insights into the many-sided activities of his life are provided in the following selections from his correspondence. *Letters,* 336, 392, 407, 412, 420, 422, 426, 460, 465, 467, 475, 482, 490, 494, 498, 500–21, 523, 577, 611, 630, 643.

68 John Fiske, *American Political Ideas Viewed from the Standpoint of Universal History* (New York, 1885).

69 In 1880. Fiske, *American Political Ideas,* 5. See also, *Letters,* 411–12, 430, 441.

70 *Ibid.,* 307. John Fiske, *Outlines of Cosmic Philosophy Based on the Doctrine of Evolution, with Criticisms on the Positive Philos-*

ophy (2 vols., Boston and New York, 1891). The first edition was published in 1874. See Fiske's letter to Charles Darwin, Apr. 20, 1880, *Letters,* 436. See also, *Ibid.,* 478, 523–24; *American Political Ideas,* 107, 123–25; Clark, I, 390. Fiske's own exposition is set forth in many places. For example, John Fiske, *The Beginnings of New England* (Boston and New York, 1889), 1–49.

71 *American Political Ideas,* 123–125.

72 *Ibid.,* 6.

73 *Ibid.*

74 *Ibid.,* 6–7.

75 Sanders, *Jernegan Essays,* 154.

76 *American Political Ideas,* 121, 110, 112.

77 *Ibid.,* 55.

78 *Ibid.,* 125–26.

79 *Ibid.,* 127–28.

80 *Ibid.,* 128.

81 *Ibid.,* 148–49.

82 Fiske, *The Critical Period of American History, 1783–1789,* 134–37. See the interesting letter written to Fiske by John Jay, the son and namesake of the famous statesman of the Revolutionary and "critical" periods, Nov. 30, 1888, *Letters,* 557.

83 Sanders, *Jernegan Essays,* 157, 156.

84 Fiske, *The Beginnings of New England,* 1–49.

85 *Discovery of America,* I, chs. 1–6.

86 For example, see comments of praise from E. A. Freeman, John Morley, and Charles Eliot Norton, *Letters,* 568, 570, 611.

87 *Ibid.,* 589, 600.

CHAPTER XXIV

1 Andrew D. White, *Autobiography,* I, 255. George L. Burr,

"Andrew Dickson White," in Lois O. Gibbons (ed.), *George Lincoln Burr: Selections from His Writings* (Ithaca, N.Y., 1943), especially 415–19. Walter P. Rogers, *Andrew D. White and the Modern University* (Ithaca, 1943). Carl L. Becker, *Cornell University: Founders and The Founding* (Ithaca, 1943).

2 White, *Autobiography*, I, 255.

3 *Ibid.*

4 On White as a teacher, Ruth Bordin, *Andrew Dickson White, Teacher of History, Michigan Historical Collections No. 8* (Ann Arbor, Mich., 1958), 3–17. Howard Mumford Jones and Thomas E. Casady, *The Life of Moses Coit Tyler* (Ann Arbor, Mich., 1933), 119.

5 White, *Autobiography*, I, 256.

6 *Ibid.*

7 Holt (ed.), *Historical Scholarship*, 79; Bordin, *White*, 11–15; Andrew Dickson White, *Outlines of a Course of Lectures in History* (Ann Arbor, Mich., 1860–61).

8 For the "Erfurt Sermon," together with other illustrations, White, *Autobiography*, I, 263.

9 *DAB*, I, 52–54; Charles Foster Smith, *Charles Kendall Adams: A Life-Sketch* (Madison, Wis., 1925).

10 Holt (ed.), *Historical Scholarship*, 79.

11 C. K. Adams, *Manual of Historical Literature*, vii-viii.

12 *Ibid.*, viii. White, *Autobiography*, II, 501–02.

13 Adams, *Manual*, 16.

14 *Ibid.*, 15–16.

15 *Ibid.*, 71, 400, 373; White, *Autobiography*, II, 575–82.

16 Jones and Casady, *Tyler*, 209. See also, Jessica Tyler Austen, *Moses Coit Tyler: Selections from His Letters and Diaries* (New York, 1911).

17 Jones and Casady, *Tyler*, 3, 209.

18 *Ibid.*, 63. See also, 75, 170.

19 *Ibid.*, 75–77.

20 *Ibid.*, 80, 95, 93.

21 See the assessment of President James B. Angell on Tyler's qualities as a teacher, *Ibid.*, 160–61.

22 *Ibid.*, 139–41.

23 *Ibid.*, 141.

24 *Ibid.*, 175.

25 Moses C. Tyler, *A History of American Literature, 1607–1765* (2 vols., New York, 1878).

26 Jones and Casady, *Tyler*, 175.

27 *Ibid.*, 189.

28 *A History of American Literature*, I, vii.

29 Moses C. Tyler, *Patrick Henry* (New York and Boston, 1887). *The Literary History of the American Revolution* (2 vols., New York and London, 1897).

30 Jones and Casady, *Tyler*, 220. See also 204.

31 *Ibid.*, 225–226, 233.

32 *Ibid.*, 26 ff.

33 *Ibid.*, 249.

34 Moses C. Tyler, *Three Men of Letters* (New York and London, 1895). Jones and Casady, *Tyler*, 254–55.

35 *Ibid.*, 257.

36 *Literary History*, I, v-vi.

37 *Ibid.*, vii-viii. Tyler had already written an article on the Loyalists, one of the early instances of an altering view. "The Party of the Loyalists in the American Revolution," *American Historical Review*, I (Oct. 1895), 24–45.

38 *Literary History*, I, vii-viii.

39 David B. Frankenburger and others, *William Francis Allen: Memorial Volume* (Boston, 1890), is a compilation of Allen's writings. See also *Proceedings of the Thirty-Seventh Annual Meeting of the State Historical Society of Wisconsin*,

1889 (Madison, 1890), 78–89.
[40] Charles F. Thwing, *The American and the German University* (New York, 1928). Ryan, *Studies in Early Graduate Education,* 13, 97.
[41] Merle Curti and Vernon Carstensen, *The University of Wisconsin, A History* (2 vols., Madison, Wis., 1949), I, 336. Holt (ed.) *Historical Scholarship,* 87–88.
[42] English translation (6 vols., Oxford, 1833). See Adams, *Manual,* 75–76.
[43] New York, (2 vols., New York, 1828), Adams, *Manual,* 205–06.
[44] Curti and Carstensen, I, 345–46.
[45] William F. Allen and P. V. N. Myers, *Ancient History for College and High Schools,* Part II. *A Short History of the Roman People* by William F. Allen, (Boston, 1890), v. Both were posthumously published.
[46] *History of the Roman People,* v-vi.
[47] Allen, "Gradation and the Topical Method of Historical Study," in Hall (ed.), *Methods of Teaching History,* 237.
[48] *The Early Writings of Frederick Jackson Turner,* with an introduction by Fulmer Mood (Madison, Wis., 1938), 9.
[49] Mood, *Turner,* 80.
[50] The authoritative bibliography compiled by Everett E. Edwards, *Ibid.,* 233–68 amended to 1938, together with listing of works about him, 269–72. A more recent listing and analysis is Ray Allen Billington, *The American Frontier,* (2nd ed., Washington, 1965), a leading student of Turner and his influence. Fulmer Mood, "The Origin, Evolution and Application of the Sectional Concept, 1750–1900," Merrill Jensen (ed.), *Regionalism in America* (Madison, Wis., 1951). Turner is accorded full analytical attention in the following volume.
[51] Merle E. Curti, *Frederick Jackson Turner* (Mexico, D. F., 1949), 9–38.
[52] Curti and Carstensen, I, 638; Mood, *Turner,* 35.
[53] "The Significance of History," Mood, *Turner,* 65.
[54] *Ibid.,* 48.
[55] *Ibid.*
[56] *Ibid.,* 52–53.
[57] *Ibid.,* 53.
[58] *Ibid.,* 56.
[59] *Ibid..* 57.
[60] *Ibid.,* 53, 58.
[61] *Ibid.*
[62] *Ibid.,* 61, 60.
[63] *Ibid.,* 63.
[64] *Ibid.,* 64.
[65] *Ibid.*
[66] Curti and Carstensen, I, 631.
[67] "The Significance of the Frontier in American History," initially delivered at a meeting of the American Historical Association at Chicago, July 12, 1893, is reprinted in Mood, *Turner,* 185–299. See n. 1 for pertinent information provided by Turner himself.
[68] Curti employs this phrase with reference to the "Significance of History" essay, but it properly describes all of Turner's essays, particularly this one. Mood, *Turner,* 18.
[69] Curti's essay on Turner, delivered at the Congress of Mexican and American historians and published by the Instituto Panamericano de Geografía e Historia, celebrates this judgment.
[70] Curti and Carstensen, I, 641.
[71] *Ibid.,* 643.
[72] Edward P. Cheyney, *History of the University of Pennsylvania 1740–1940* (Philadelphia, 1940), 231, 242–44, 290–91.
[73] *Ibid.,* 289; Herman Ausubel, *Historians and Their Craft,* 175–176; 347–50. William T. Hutch-

inson, "John Bach McMaster," *Jernegan Essays*, 122–43; Eric F. Goldman, *John Bach McMaster* (Philadelphia, 1943). These historians and the transitions they represent are reserved for later discussion.

74 Hall, *Life and Confessions of a Psychologist*, 296.

75 Charles R. Wilson, "Hermann Eduard von Holst," *Jernegan Essays*, 60–83. Ferdinand Schevill is the author of the sketch in *DAB*, IX, 177–79. See Eric F. Goldman, "Hermann Eduard von Holst," *Mississippi Valley Historical Review*, XXIII (Mar. 1937), 515, n. 12.

76 Hermann von Holst, *The Constitutional and Political History of the United States*, I (Chicago, 1876). The succeeding seven volumes are titled *The Constitutional History of the United States* (Chicago, 1876–92). Vol. VIII is the index volume. Details of the German editions and translations are given in Goldman, *Mississippi Valley Historical Review*, XXIII, 511, n. 1. Also by Holst are *John C. Calhoun* (Boston, 1883) and *John Brown*, edited by F. P. Stevens (Boston, 1888).

77 Wilson, *Jernegan Essays*, 61–64; Ferdinand Schevill, *DAB*, IX, 177–79.

78 *Constitutional History*, I, ix, Wilson, *Jernegan Essays*, 64–66.

79 *Ibid.* Also, Holt (ed.), *Historical Scholarship*, 35.

80 *Constitutional History*, I, x; Goldman, *Mississippi Valley Historical Review*, XXIII, 518.

81 *Constitutional History*, II, 109, 101–02; V, 459.

82 *Constitutional History*, I, 1, 5, 6; 223–24.

83 *Ibid.*, 16.

84 *Ibid.*, 17.

85 *Ibid.*, 19, n. 79.

86 *Ibid.*, 19.

87 *Ibid.*, III, 409–10; 11, 268.

88 *Ibid.*, I, 159–60.

89 *Ibid.*, VI, 25.

90 Goldman, *Mississippi Valley Historical Review*, XXIII, 529, 530–32.

91 Wilson, in *Jernegan Essays*, 64–65. Goldman, *Mississippi Valley Historical Review*, XXIII, 523.

CHAPTER XXV

1 See above, ch. XV, and various references in this chapter. For Henry Adams, "My favorite John Green was the flower of my generation." Cater, *Henry Adams and His Friends*, 133. See his "Green's Short History of the English People," *The North American Review*, CXXI (July 1875), 216–44.

2 See above, 331; ch. XXV *passim*.

3 The latest imprint from the Centenary Edition (12 vols., Boston, 1923) was in 1942. When this edition went out of print, Samuel Eliot Morison prepared the Parkman Reader (Boston, 1955); see 519–21 for a listing of editions and reprints. William R. Taylor (ed.), *The Discovery of the Great West: LaSalle* (Rinehart Editions, New York and Toronto, 1956). Cater, *Henry Adams*, 132–33.

4 See above, 367.

5 Henry Adams wrote his brother, Brooks, Mar. 19, 1909: "Of one hundred million people, not a single one truly cares what the Historical Association thinks." Cater, *Henry Adams*, 649. James B. Angell, *The Old and New Ideal of Scholars* (Ann Arbor, Mich., 1905).

6 See above, 331–32, 344–45.

7 Suggestively enough, all but one of these historians without portfolio were elected to the presi-

dency of the American Historical Association.

8 Donald Fleming, *John William Draper and the Religion of Science*, 1–56. Donald E. Emerson, "Hildreth, Draper, and Scientific History," in Goldman (ed.), *Historiography and Urbanization*, 139–70.

9 *Human Physiology. . . .* (New York, 1856); *A History of the Intellectual Development of Europe* (New York, 1863); *Thoughts on the Future Civil Policy of America* (New York, 1865); *History of the American Civil War* (3 vols., New York, 1867, 1868, 1870); *History of the Conflict Between Religion and Science* (New York, 1874).

10 Fleming, 1–64. Bert James Loewenberg, "The Sacred Right to Differ," *Saturday Review of Literature* (June 16, 1951), XXXIV, 38, is a review of Fleming, the substance of which is followed here.

11 Fleming, 58.

12 There are many accounts of this famous session, all different. Leonard Huxley (ed.), *Life and Letters of Thomas Henry Huxley* (2 vols., London, 1900), I, 180; Leonard Huxley (ed.), *Life and Letters of Sir Joseph Dalton Hooker* (2 vols., London, 1918), I, 525–27. Leslie Stephen (ed.), *Letters of John Richard Green*, (New York, 1901), 44.

13 Fleming, 165, 68–69.

14 *Intellectual Development of Europe*, II, 401.

15 Fleming, 69.

16 *Ibid.*, 75–76.

17 *Ibid.*, 74.

18 *Intellectual Development of Europe*, I, iii.

19 *Ibid.*, II, 400.

20 Fleming, 77.

21 *Intellectual Development of Europe*, I, 12.

22 Fleming, 86.

23 *Intellectual Development of Europe*, II, 226.

24 *Ibid.*, 237.

25 *Future Civil Policy in America*, iii.

26 *Ibid.*, iv.

27 *Ibid.*, 79, 159.

28 *Ibid.*, 86.

29 *Ibid.*

30 *Ibid.*, 265–67.

31 *Ibid.*, 168, 267–68.

32 Fleming, 113–14.

33 *American Civil War*, I, iii-iv.

34 *Conflict between Religion and Science*, viii, v-vii.

35 Fleming, 134.

36 *Conflict between Religion and Science*, 342.

37 *Ibid.*, 363.

38 Loewenberg, *Saturday Review*, XXXIV, 38.

39 Lewis E. Ellis, "James Schouler," *Jernegan Essays*, 88.

40 Ausubel, *Historians and Their Craft*, 34.

41 Ellis, *Jernegan Essays*, 84–101. The account in *DAB*, XVI, 459–460, is by John H. Latané.

42 Ellis, *Jernegan Essays*, 89. James Schouler, *The History of the United States of America, under the Constitution* (7 vols., Washington and New York, 1880–1913).

43 Holt, (ed.), *Historical Scholarship*, 248 n.

44 *History*, I, v.

45 *Ibid.*

46 *Ibid.*

47 *Ibid.*, vi.

48 *Ibid.*, vii, iii.

49 *History*, V, ch. xviii. An exception is Vol. II, ch. vii.

50 A letter from William A. Dunning quoted in Goldman, *John Bach McMaster*, 127–28. See *History*, VI, 311–12.

51 For insertions of nonpolitical materials, see *History*, I, 24, general delinquency; 238, emigrants,

redemptioners; 241, the pioneer life; 252, epidemics; 380, yellow fever.

[52] *Ibid.*, II, ch. vii.

[53] *Americans of 1776* (New York, 1906).

[54] *History,* VII, v.

[55] *Ibid.,* V, iii.

[56] Ellis, *Jernegan Essays,* 90.

[57] *History,* VII, iii. Ellis, *Jernegan Essays,* 90–91.

[58] *Historical Briefs* (New York, 1896), 23.

[59] *Ibid.,* 21.

[60] *Historical Briefs,* 24 n. "A New Federal Convention," American Historical Association, *Annual Report: 1897* (Washington, D.C., 1898), 21–34, is Schouler's presidential address.

[61] *Historical Briefs,* 62–65, 47; Ellis, *Jernegan Essays,* 92–93.

[62] *History,* VI, i; VII, 8; V, 211, 153, 504.

[63] Holt (ed.), *Historical Scholarship,* 275.

[64] Ellis, *Jernegan Essays,* 92, who has analyzed and tabulated Schouler's sources, reports that Rhodes is the most important authority for vol. VII. This represents a reversal of emphasis; earlier Schouler more frequently cited primary sources. James Ford Rhodes, *History of the United States from the Compromise of 1850 to the End of the Roosevelt Administration* (9 vols., New York, 1928), is the complete edition.

[65] Frederic Bancroft regarded Rhodes' volumes "the best work on American history" since Henry Adams and urged Herbert Baxter Adams to consider the appropriateness of an "office of honor" in the American Historical Association. Holt (ed.), *Historical Scholarship,* 237–38.

[66] In 1896, M. A. De Wolfe Howe, *James Ford Rhodes, American Historian* (New York, 1929), 93.

[67] Raymond C. Miller, "James Ford Rhodes," *Jernegan Essays,* 171–90, is a compact sketch. Dumas Malone contributed the piece in *DAB,* XV, 531–33. Howe, *Rhodes,* contains an autobiographical fragment, 17–29.

[68] Howe, 19.

[69] *Ibid.,* 20.

[70] *Ibid.,* 21.

[71] *Ibid.*

[72] *Ibid.,* 21, 22.

[73] *Ibid.,* 24, 25.

[74] *Ibid.,* 54–56.

[75] *Historical Essays* (New York, 1909); *Lectures on the American Civil War, 1861–1865* (New York, 1913).

[76] Howe, 143–44; Miller, *Jernegan Essays,* 176.

[77] Miller, *Jernegan Essays,* 180, 189.

[78] *Ibid.,* 175–76.

[79] *Ibid.,* 180–81.

[80] Rhodes' address as president of the American Historical Association is called "History," American Historical Association *Annual Report, 1899* (Washington, D.C., 1900), I, 45–63; Ausubel, *Historians and Their Craft,* 122–23, comments on these points and makes some of his own.

[81] Allen Wescott (ed.), *Mahan on Naval Warfare,* (Boston, 1941), xxxi. Wescott also contributed the biography in *DAB,* XII, 206–208; Julius W. Pratt, "Alfred Thayer Mahan," *Jernegan Essays,* 207–26. William E. Livezey, *Mahan on Sea Power* (Norman, Okla., 1947). Mahan's own autobiographical statement is in *From Sail to Steam, Recollections of Naval Life* (New York and London, 1907).

[82] *The Gulf and Inland Waters* (New York, 1883).

[83] Pratt, *Jernegan Essays,* 208.

84 *The Influence of Sea Power upon History, 1660–1783* (Boston, 1890).

85 Pratt, *Jernegan Essays*, 212–26.

86 Wescott (ed.), *Mahan*, xiii; Mahan, *From Sail to Steam*, 277.

87 *Ibid.*, Pratt, *Jernegan Essays*, 210.

88 *Ibid.*, 276. Mahan, "Subordination in Historical Treatment," *American Historical Association, Annual Report, 1902* (Washington, D.C., 1903) I, 49–63. Mahan's presidential address illustrates how he understood historical problems, 53–59.

89 Howard K. Beale, *Theodore Roosevelt and the Rise of America to World Power* (Baltimore, 1956), 22, 258–59. Roosevelt's review of Mahan: *Atlantic Monthly*, LXVI (Oct. 1892), 563–67; *Ibid.*, LXXI (Apr. 1893), 556–69; *Political Science Quarterly*, IX (Mar. 1894), 171; *New York Sun*, Dec. 26, 1897.

90 Wescott (ed.), *Mahan*, x, is the source for the comment of the Chief of the Bureau of Navigation. Mahan, *Influence of Sea Power upon the French Revolution and Empire, 1793–1812* (2 vols., Boston, 1892), Mahan, *Sea Power in its Relations to the War of 1812* (2 vols., Boston, 1905), Mahan collected some of his popular articles in *Retrospect and Prospect* (London, 1902). See listing in Wescott, 362.

91 Mahan, "Subordination in Historical Treatment," 52, 54, 57.

92 *Ibid.*, 57, 58, 61.

93 Pratt, *Jernegan Essays*, 215; Beale, *Theodore Roosevelt and the Rise of America to World Power*, 56, 85–86, 90; Wescott, 288, 299, 306.

94 Pratt, *Jernegan Essays*, 220–21. See J. W. Pratt, *Expansionists of 1898* (Baltimore, 1936).

95 Mahan, "Subordination in Historical Treatment," 63.

96 Albert Bushnell Hart and Herbert Ronald Ferleger (eds.), *Theodore Roosevelt Cyclopedia* (New York, 1941), 326, from a review of Mahan's *Life of Nelson*.

97 Harrison John Thornton, "Theodore Roosevelt," *Jernegan Essays*, 228. Roosevelt's comment on Mahan's book is in his own *The Naval War of 1812* (New York, 1926), xxiii.

98 Thornton, *Jernegan Essays*, 227–251; Theodore Roosevelt, *An Autobiography* (New York, 1926); R. C. Miller, "Theodore Roosevelt, Historian," J. L. Cate and E. N. Anderson (eds.), *Medieval and Historiographical Essays in Honor of James Westfall Thompson* (Chicago, 1938).

99 Jacob A. Riis, *Theodore Roosevelt the Citizen* (New York, 1904), 33.

100 Henry Cabot Lodge, *Selections from the Correspondence of Theodore Roosevelt and Henry Cabot Lodge* (2 vols., New York, 1925), I, 41–42.

101 *Ibid.*, 41.

102 *Ibid.*, 51, 59.

103 *Ibid.*, 57, 59; *Gouverneur Morris* (Boston, 1888), v–viii.

104 Lodge, *Correspondence of Roosevelt and Lodge*, I, 59; *Roosevelt Cyclopedia*, 356.

105 Henry Cabot Lodge and Theodore Roosevelt, *Hero Tales from American History* (New York, 1895).

106 *Oliver Cromwell* (New York, 1926). Comment quoted by Thornton, in *Jernegan Essays*, 235.

107 *The Winning of the West* (6 vols., New York, 1905).

108 *Ibid.*, I, 15.

109 *Ibid.*, 16.

110 *Ibid.*, 17–46.

[111] *Ibid.*, 40–41.

[112] *Ibid.*, 46.

[113] *Ibid.*, VI, 276–77.

[114] Thornton, *Jernegan Essays,* 237.

[115] Joseph Bucklin Bishop, *Theodore Roosevelt and His Times* (2 vols., New York, 1920), II, 139–40.

[116] *Ibid.*, 139–40. See Roosevelt's address as president of the American Historical Association, "History as Literature," *American Historical Review,* XVIII (Apr. 1913), 473–89.

[117] Lodge, *Correspondence of Roosevelt and Lodge,* II, 314. Roosevelt, "History as Literature," *Literary Essays,* 28–29.

[118] *Roosevelt Cyclopedia,* 554.

[119] Lodge, *Correspondence of Roosevelt and Lodge,* II, 427–28.

[120] Roosevelt, "History as Literature," *Literary Essays,* 19.

CHAPTER XXVI

[1] See above, ch. XXIII. The Adams bibliography is extensive. The most recent study, J. C. Levenson, *The Mind and Art of Henry Adams* (Boston, 1957), is among the best. William H. Jordy, *Henry Adams: Scientific Historian* (New Haven, 1952), is a masterly treatment of its subject. Jordy surveys the materials on Adams critically, 291–317. Robert A. Hume, *Runaway Star: An Appreciation of Henry Adams* (Ithaca, N.Y., 1951), is suggestive, see 245–65 for bibliography. Jordy, *Adams,* 35 n.

[2] *Education,* 300–01. In 1892 Adams wrote to his former Harvard student, Charles F. Thwing, then president of Western Reserve University, accepting the honorary degree he had offered. "I accepted the responsibility of education, and the result of several years experience was to satisfy me that all forms of education were necessarily wrong, and that my utmost hope must be that on the whole I had done no more harm than might probably have been done by the person who would have taught if I had not." Cater, *Henry Adams and His Friends,* 269.

[3] *Education,* 301. "I became overpoweringly conscious that any further pretense on my part of acting as instructor would be something worse than humbug, unless I could clear my mind in regard to what I wanted to teach. As History stands, it is a sort of Chinese play without end and without lesson." Roy F. Nichols, "The Dynamic Interpretation of History," *New England Quarterly,* VIII (June 1935), 163–64.

[4] Carl L. Becker, *Everyman His Own Historian,* 166. *History of the United States of America During the First Administration of Thomas Jefferson* (2 vols., New York, 1889); *History of the United States of America During the Second Administration of Thomas Jefferson* (2 vols., New York, 1890); *History of the United States of America During the First Administration of James Madison* (2 vols., New York, 1890); *History of the United States of America During the Second Administration of James Madison* (3 vols., New York, 1891).

[5] *Truth in History and Other Essays by William A. Dunning,* 214.

[6] See above, Cater, *Henry Adams,* 765.

[7] Henry Adams, *The Life of Albert Gallatin* (Philadelphia, 1879). Henry Adams (ed.), *The Writings of Albert Gallatin* (3 vols., Philadelphia, 1879). Cf., John A. Stevens, *Albert Gallatin,* (Bos-

ton, 1884). Raymond Walters, Jr., *Albert Gallatin* (New York, 1954). John Torrey Moore, Jr., "Albert Gallatin," *Atlantic Monthly*, XLIV (Oct. 1879), 513–21.

8 Cater, *Henry Adams*, 101–03. Another note to Godkin on the same subject, 103. Later Adams wrote to James Russell Lowell: "I am touched by your kindness to my poor ponderous Life of Gallatin. It is my one ewe lamb, or prize ox. No one has ever read it, or ever will, but perhaps, some centuries hence, antiquaries will use it. The documents may give it a use." *Ibid.*, 101.

9 Becker, *Everyman His Own Historian*, 149.

10 Jordy, *Henry Adams*, 298–302, assembles the critical responses to the *History*.

11 "Charles Lyell's Principles of Geology," *North American Review*, CVII (Oct. 1868), 465–501. Cater, *Henry Adams*, 42; Hume, *Runaway Star*, 61; Jordy, *Henry Adams*, 173 ff., 177–81, and bibliography, 309–11.

12 Henry Adams, *Mont-Saint-Michel and Chartres*, with an Introduction by Ralph Adams Cram (Boston, 1913). It was first printed in a limited edition of 150 copies (Washington, D.C., 1904).

13 Adams, *Education*, 434–35.

14 *History*, IX, 220. "As far as politics supplied a test, the national character had already diverged from any foreign type." *Ibid.*, 221.

15 *Ibid.*

16 *Ibid.*, IX, 220.

17 *Education*, 396 ff., 496 ff.

18 "Von Holst's History of the United States," *North American Review*, CXXIII (Oct. 1876), 328–61.

19 *History*, I, 158–59.

20 *Ibid.*, 159.

21 *Ibid.*, 159–60.

22 Jordy, *Henry Adams*, 73–74, n. 4.

23 *History*, I, 160–61.

24 *Ibid.*, IX, 226.

25 *Ibid.*

26 *Ibid.*, 227.

27 *Ibid.*, 228.

28 *Ibid.*, 231. See also, 234, 235.

29 Founded in 1802.

30 *History*, IX, 236.

31 *Ibid.*, 237.

32 Samuels, *Young Henry Adams*, 20–25. But cf. Jordy, *Henry Adams*, 91, 135–36.

33 *Education*, 60, 227; Samuels, *Young Henry Adams*, 17–22.

34 Samuels, *Young Henry Adams*, 123–24; *Education*, 123 ff.

35 Samuels, *Young Henry Adams*, 163–67.

36 Jordy, *Adams*, 113. Indeed Jordy believes that "Comte provides the master key to the History and to its meaning in Adams' life as well." *Ibid.*

37 Worthington C. Ford (ed.), *A Cycle of Adams Letters, 1861–1865* (2 vols., Boston, 1920), I, 281, 152.

38 *Education*, 225.

39 Jordy, *Henry Adams*, 98.

40 *History*, IV, 134–35; I, 75; V, 165; VI, 123; IX, 222, XI, 174–175, 195.

41 *History*, IV, 135.

42 Cater, *Adams*, 125–26. To Francis Parkman in the following year: "Democracy is the only subject for history. I am satisfied that the purely mechanical development of the human mind in society must appear in a great democracy so clearly, for want of disturbing elements, that in another generation psychology, physiology, and history will join in proving man to have a fixed and necessary development as that of a tree; and almost as unconscious." *Ibid.*, 134.

43 *Ibid.*, 480.

44 *History*, IX, 241–42.

45 Jordy regards the *History* as "the greatest moral history ever produced in America." *Adams*, 67. *Education*, 145–66.

46 *History*, IX, 222.

47 Cater, *Adams*, 122, 121, 125. *History*, IX, 222. For comment, Hume, *Runaway Star*, 75; Jordy, *Adams*, 46.

48 *History*, IX, 222.

49 Adams apparently prepared a MS on Aaron Burr which was not published. For a glimpse at the history of this episode, Jordy, *Henry Adams*, 49, n. 13; Levenson, *The Mind and Art of Henry Adams*, 134. Adams published studies of Napoleon, Toussaint L'Ouverture, and the Dominican revolt in the *Revue historique* in 1884; see Jordy, *Henry Adams*, 49, n. 14.

50 Henry Adams, *John Randolph* (Boston and New York, 1882), cf., William Cabell Bruce, *John Randolph of Roanoke, 1773–1833* (2 vols., New York, 1922). The introduction contains specific criticism of the Adams biography.

51 Cater, *Henry Adams*, 125.

52 Jordy, *Henry Adams*, 47.

53 *Ibid.*, 47–48.

54 *History*, I, 145.

55 *Ibid.*

56 *Ibid.*, I, 145–56. Jefferson's personality "belonged to the controlling influences of American history, more necessary to the story than three fourths of the official papers, which only hid the truth." *Ibid.*, 187.

57 *Ibid.*, 146–47.

58 *Ibid.*, 277.

59 Jordy, *Henry Adams*, 53 ff.

60 *History*, IV, 355.

61 *Ibid.*, 356–57.

62 *Ibid.*, 357.

63 "Stubbs' Constitutional History of England," *North American Review*, CXIX (July 1874), 233–244. See 235.

64 Jordy, *Henry Adams*, 56.

65 The last volumes were published in 1891.

66 Jordy, *Henry Adams*, 131, especially 27.

67 Richard P. Blackmur, "The Failure of Henry Adams," *Hound and Horn*, IV (Apr.-June, 1931), 442. Hume, *Runaway Star*, 20–23.

68 The chronology and pattern of Henry Adams' travels are essential to an understanding of his life and thought. The sequence may quickly be gleaned in Cater, *Henry Adams*, liii, 161–72, lviii-lix, 197–251, 161, 172–73, 196, 187–89, 248–52, 275, 305–15, 335–36, 285, 363–67, 429–30, 430–31, 431–32, 432–33, 517–18.

69 Hume, *Runaway Star*, 160–61; *Education*, 106.

70 Hume, *Runaway Star*, 329.

71 Henry Adams (tr. and ed.), *Memoirs of Marau Taaroa, Last Queen of Tahiti* (privately printed, 1893). Scholars' Facsimiles and Reprints republished the study (New York, 1947) with an introduction by Robert E. Spiller. Cater, *Henry Adams*, lviii.

72 *Ibid.*, 305.

73 David H. Dickason, "Henry Adams and Clarence King: The Record of Friendship," *New England Quarterly*, XVII (June 1944), 229–54. Cater's collection of letters fully documents the interdependence of these friendships. John La Farge, *An Artist's Letters from Japan* (New York, 1897); *Reminiscences of the South Seas* (New York, 1912); Royal Cortissoz, *John La Farge: A Memoir and a Study* (Boston, 1911).

74 Cater, *Henry Adams*, 195–96.

Robert E. Spiller, "Henry Adams," *LHUS*, II, 1094.

[75] Cater, *Henry Adams*, lxviii.

[76] *Education*, 422–23.

[77] *Ibid.*, 353. See a suggestive letter to George Cabot Lodge on this subject, Cater, *Henry Adams*, 543–44.

[78] *Education*, 384.

[79] Cater, *Henry Adams*, 663–64. "Bay was my last active tie to active sympathy with men. He was the best and finest product of my time and hope." *Ibid.*, 662. But see Levenson, *Henry Adams*, 379–83. Henry Adams, *The Life of George Cabot Lodge* (Boston and New York, 1911).

[80] Cater, *Henry Adams*, 278–79, 328–29. "The Tendency of History" was the subject of the letter and of his address.

[81] "The Tendency of History," American Historical Association, *Annual Report for 1894* (Washington, D.C., 1895), 17–23. Brooks Adams (ed.), *The Degradation of the Democratic Dogma* (New York, 1928). *The Tendency of History* (New York, 1928). *A Letter to American Teachers of History* (New York, 1910), which contains the first publication of "The Rule of Phase Applied to History." For critical bibliography, Jordy, *Henry Adams*, 302–303.

[82] *Education*, 315–16; *History*, IX, 222. Cater, *Henry Adams*, lxi.

[83] *Education*, ix–x. Holt (ed.), *Historical Scholarship*, 13.

[84] Cater, *Henry Adams*, 784; see especially "Editor's Note," 781.

[85] Henry Adams, "Count Edward de Crillion," *American Historical Review*, I (Oct. 1895), 51–69.

[86] *History*, IV, 176 ff.

[87] *Ibid.* Jordy, *Henry Adams*, 130.

[88] Cater, *Henry Adams*, 480.

[89] *Education*, 377–78.

[90] Concluding line of Adams' "Prayer to the Dynamo," reprinted in Hume, *Runaway Star*, 244.

[91] Cater, *Henry Adams*, 623.

[92] *Ibid.*

[93] *Ibid.*, 649–50.

[94] *Ibid.*, 638.

[95] Adams wrote to Henry Osborn Taylor, Jan. 17, 1905, "I have no object but a superficial one, as far as history is concerned. To me, accuracy is relative. I care very little whether my details are exact, if only my *ensemble* is in scale. You need to be thorough in your study. . . . Your middle-ages exist for their own sake, not for ours." (Italics in original), Cater, *Henry Adams*, 559; 782 for quotation in text.

[96] *Education*, 421–22. Hume, *Runaway Star*, 172.

[97] Stanza from Adams' "Prayer to the Virgin of Chartres," reprinted in Hume, *Runaway Star*, 241.

[98] *Mont-Saint-Michel*, xiii–xiv, 71, 91.

[99] *Education*, 382.

[100] *Ibid.*, 395, 382.

[101] *Ibid.*, 382.

[102] *Ibid.*, 377. The purpose of the *Education*, he wrote to Margaret Chanler in 1908, was "for revision, suggestion, corrections, and general condemnation." Cater, *Henry Adams*, 611.

[103] *Ibid.*, 645–46.

[104] *Ibid.*, lxxxiii–lxxxiv.

[105] "The pessimism or unpopularity of the law will not prevent its enforcement, if it develops superior force, even if it leads where no one wants to go." *Tendency of History*, 21. Also 22, 20.

[106] *Ibid.*, 9.

[107] *Ibid.*, 11.

[108] *Ibid.*, 13.

[109] *History*, III, 441.

110 George Santayana, *Reason in Science* (New York, 1906), 51–53.

111 *Education*, 379.

112 *Ibid.*, 370.

113 *Ibid.*, 392.

Select Bibliography

Abbreviations of Works Cited

CHAL: The Cambridge History of American Literature.
DAB: Dictionary of American Biography.
Jernegan Essays: The Marcus W. Jernegan Essays in American Historiography.
Kraus: Kraus, M., *A History of American History.*
LHUS: Literary History of the United States.
NCHA: Narrative and Critical History of America.

Abel, A. H., *The American Indian as Slaveholder and Secessionist* (2 vols., Cleveland, 1915–19).
Abele, Rudolph von, *Alexander H. Stephens* (New York, 1946).
Adams, Brooks, *The Degradation of the Democratic Dogma* (New York, 1928).
——, *The Emancipation of Massachusetts: The Dream and the Reality* (New York, 1919).
Adams, Charles Francis (ed.), *Familiar Letters of John Adams and His Wife, Abigail Adams, During the Revolution* (Boston, 1875).
——, *Massachusetts, Its Historians and Its History* (Boston, 1893).
——, "The Sifted Grain and the Grain Sifters," *American Historical Review*, VI (Jan. 1901).
—— (ed.), *The Works of John Adams* (10 vols., Boston, 1850–56).
Adams, Charles Kendall, *A Manual of Historical Literature* (New York, 1888).
——, "On Methods of Teaching History," in Hall, G. Stanley (ed.), *Methods of Teaching and Studying History* (Boston, 1886).

Adams, George Burton, "History and Philosophy of History," *American Historical Review*, XIV (Jan. 1909).

Adams, George W., *Doctors in Blue: The Medical History of the Union Army in the Civil War* (New York, 1952).

Adams, Henry, *A Letter to Teachers of History* (New York, 1910).

——, "Captain John Smith," *North American Review*, CIV (Jan. 1867).

——, "Charles Lyell's *Principles of Geology*," *North American Review*, CVII, (Oct. 1868).

——, "Count Edward de Crillion," *American Historical Review*, I (Oct. 1895).

—— (ed.), *Documents Relating to New England Federalism 1800–1815* (Boston, 1877).

——, "Freeman's *History of the Norman Conquest*," *North American Review*, CXVIII (Jan. 1874).

——, "Freeman's Historical Essays," *North American Review*, CXIV (Jan. 1872).

——, "Green's *Short History of the English People*," *North American Review*, CXXI (July 1875).

——, *History of the United States of America During the First Administration of Thomas Jefferson* (2 vols., New York, 1889).

——, *History of the United States of America During the Second Administration of Thomas Jefferson* (2 vols., New York, 1890).

——, *History of the United States of America During the First Administration of James Madison* (2 vols., New York, 1890).

——, *History of the United States of America During the Second Administration of James Madison* (3 vols., New York, 1891).

——, *John Randolph* (Boston, 1882).

——, *Memoirs of Marau Taaroe, Last Queen of Tahiti* (privately printed, 1893; available in Spiller, Robert E. (ed.), *Scholars' Facsimiles* (New York, 1947).

——, *Mont-Saint-Michel and Chartres* (Boston, 1913).

——, *The Education of Henry Adams* (Boston, 1918).

——, *The Life of Albert Gallatin* (Philadelphia, 1870).

——, "The Tendency of History," American Historical Association, *Annual Report for 1894* (Washington D.C., 1895).

—— (ed.), *The Writings of Albert Gallatin* (3 vols., Philadelphia, 1879).

——, "Von Holst's *History of the United States*," *North American Review*, CXXIII (Oct. 1876).

Adams, Herbert Baxter, *Bluntschli's Life and Work* (Baltimore, 1894).

——, "Jared Sparks and Alexis de Tocqueville," *The Johns Hopkins University Studies in Historical and Political Science*, sixteenth series, XII (Baltimore, 1898).

——, "Norman Constables in America," *The Johns Hopkins University Studies in Historical and Political Science*, VIII (Baltimore, 1883).

——, "Notes on the Literature of Charities," *The Johns Hopkins University Studies in Historical and Political Science*, fifth series, VIII (Baltimore, 1887).

——, "Public Educational Works in Baltimore," *The Johns Hopkins University Studies in Historical and Political Science*, seventeenth series, XII (Baltimore, 1899).

——, "Saxon Tithingmen in America," *The Johns Hopkins University*

Studies in Historical and Political Science, first series, IV (Baltimore, 1883).

———, "Seminary Libraries and University Extension," *The Johns Hopkins University Studies in Historical and Political Science,* fifth series, XI (Baltimore, 1887).

———, "Special Methods of Historical Study," in Hall, G. Stanley (ed.), *Methods of Teaching and Studying History* (Boston, 1886).

———, *The College of William and Mary: A Contribution to the History of Higher Education, with Suggestions for Its National Promotion,* United States Bureau of Education, Circulars of Information, No. I (Washington, D.C., 1887).

———, "The Germanic Origins of New England Towns," *The Johns Hopkins University Studies in Historical and Political Science,* first series, II (Baltimore, 1883).

———, *The Life and Writings of Jared Sparks* (2 vols., Boston, 1893).

———, *The Study of History in American Colleges and Universities,* United States Bureau of Education, Circulars of Information, No. II. (Washington, D.C., 1887).

———, *Thomas Jefferson and the University of Virginia,* United States Bureau of Education, Circulars of Information, No. I (Washington, D.C., 1888).

———, "Village Communities of Cape Ann and Salem," *The Johns Hopkins University Studies in Historical and Political Science,* first series IX–X (Baltimore, 1883).

Adams, James Truslow, *Provincial Society* (New York, 1927).

———, *Revolutionary New England, 1691–1776* (Boston, 1923).

———, *The Adams Family* (Boston, 1930).

———, *The Founding of New England* (Boston, 1921).

Adams, James Truslow, and Coleman, R. V. (eds.), *Dictionary of American History* (5 vols., New York, 1940).

Adams, Randolph G., "An Effort to Identify John White," *American Historical Review,* XLI (Oct. 1935).

———, *Political Ideas of the American Revolution* (New York, 1939).

Albee, Ernest, *A History of English Utilitarianism* (London, 1902).

Allen, A. V. G., *Jonathan Edwards* (Boston, 1890).

Allen, W. F., *A Short History of the Roman People* (Boston, 1890).

———, "Gradation and the Topical Method of Historical Study," in Hall, G. Stanley (ed.), *Methods of Teaching and Studying History* (Boston, 1886).

Allen, W. F., and Myers, P. V. N., *Ancient History for College and High Schools,* Part II (Boston, 1890).

Alvord, Clarence W., "A Critical Analysis of the Work of Reuben Gold Thwaites," *Mississippi Valley Historical Association Proceedings,* VII (1913–14).

———, "Francis Parkman," *Nation,* CXVII (Oct. 10, 1923).

Ames, Herman V. (ed.), *State Documents on Federal Relations* (Philadelphia, 1906).

Ames, John G. (ed.), *Comprehensive Index to the Publications of the United States Government 1881–1893* (2 vols., Washington, D.C., 1905).

Andrews, Charles M., "American Colonial History 1690–1750," American Historical Association, *Annual Report 1898* (Washington, D.C., 1899).

———, "Materials in British Archives for American Colonial History," *American Historical Review,* X (Jan. 1905).

——, "Some Recent Aspects of Institutional Study," *Yale Review*, I (1892–1893).

——, "The American Revolution: An Interpretation," *American Historical Review*, XXXI (Jan. 1926).

——, *The Colonial Period* (New York, 1912).

——, *The Colonial Period of American History* (4 vols., New Haven, 1934–38).

——, "These Forty Years," *American Historical Review*, XXX (Jan. 1925).

Andrews, Charles M., and Davenport, F. G., *Guide to the Manuscript Material for the History of the United States to 1783, in the British Museum, in minor London Archives, and in Libraries of Oxford and Cambridge* (Washington, D.C., 1908).

Angell, James B., *The Old and New Ideal of Scholars* (Ann Arbor, 1905).

Anshen, Ruth Nanda (ed.), *Freedom, Its Meaning* (New York, 1940).

Arber, Edward (ed.), *The First Three English Books on America* (London, 1885).

——, *Travels and Works of Captain John Smith. . . .* (2 vols., Birmingham, England, 1884).

Arciniegas, Germán, *Caribbean: Sea of the New World* (New York, 1946).

Armes, W. D. (ed.), Joseph Le Conte, *Autobiography* (New York, 1903).

Arnold, Matthew, "Emerson," *Discoveries in America* (Boston, 1885).

Austen, Jessica Tyler, *M. C. Tyler: Selections from His Letters and Diaries* (New York, 1911).

Ausubel, Herman, *Historians and Their Craft: A Study of the Presidential Addresses of the American Historical Association 1884–1945* (New York, 1950).

Avary, Myrta L., *Recollections of Alexander H. Stephens* (New York, 1916).

Bagehot, Walter, *The English Constitution* (New York, 1930).

Baker, Ray Stannard, *Woodrow Wilson Life and Letters* (8 vols., Garden City, 1927–39).

Baker, R. S., and Dodd, William E. (eds.), *The Public Papers of Woodrow Wilson* (6 vols., New York, 1925–27).

Bakewell, Charles M., "The Philosophical Roots of Western Culture," in Northrop, F. S. C. (ed.), *Ideological Differences and World Order* (New Haven, 1949).

Baldwin, Ernest H., *Joseph Galloway, The Loyalist Politician: A Biography* (Philadelphia, 1902).

Bancroft, Aaron, *The Life of George Washington, Commander-in-Chief. . . .* (2 vols., Boston, 1826).

Bancroft, Elizabeth Davis, *Letters from England, 1846–1849* (New York, 1904).

Bancroft, George, in *Boston Courier* (Oct. 23, 1834).

——, "German Literature," *The American Quarterly Review*, II (Sept. 1827).

——, "German Poetry," *The American Quarterly Review*, X (Sept. 1831).

——, "Goethe's *Werke*," *North American Review*, XIX (Oct. 1824).

——, "Heeren's *Politics of Ancient Greece*," *North American Review*, XVIII (Apr. 1824).

——, "Herder's Writings," *North American Review*, XX (Jan. 1825).

——, "Herder's Writings," *North American Review*, XXXII (Apr. 1831).

————, *History of the Formation of the Constitution of the United States of America* (2 vols., New York, 1882).

————, *Martin Van Buren to the End of his Public Career* (New York, 1889).

————, "On Harvard University," *North American Review,* XXXII (July 1831).

————, "Schiller's Minor Poems," *North American Review,* XVI (Oct. 1823).

————, "The Bank of the United States," *North American Review,* XXXII (Jan. 1831).

————, *History of the United States of America from the Discovery of the Continent* (6 vols., Boston, 1876). Last revision 1883–89.

————, *The History of the United States from the Discovery of the Continent to the Present Time* (10 vols., Boston, 1834–1835).

————, "The Office of the People in Art, Government, and Religion," *Literary and Historical Miscellanies* (New York, 1855).

Bandelier, Adolph F. A., and Fanny (eds.), *The Journey of Alvar Núñez Cabeza de Vaca* (New York, 1905).

Barba, Preston A., *Cooper in Germany* (Bloomington, Indiana, 1914).

Barlow, Joel, *Advice to the Privileged Orders in the Several States of Europe, Resulting from the Necessity and Propriety of a General Revolution in the Principle of Government* (London, 1792, 1795).

————, *A Letter to the National Convention of France, on the Defects of the Constitution of 1791, and the Extent of the Amendments which Ought to be Applied* (London, 1792).

————, *Prospectus of a National Institution to be Established in the United States* (Washington, D.C., 1806).

————, *The Political Writings of Joel Barlow* (New York, 1796).

Barnes, Harry E., and Becker, Howard (eds.), *Contemporary Social Theory* (New York and London, 1940).

Bassett, John Spencer (ed.), *Correspondence of George Bancroft and Jared Sparks, 1823–1832, Smith College Studies in History* (Northampton, Mass., 1915).

————, "Herbert Baxter Adams," *DAB,* I, 67–69.

———— (ed.), *Letters of Francis Parkman to Pierre Margry, Smith College Studies in History* (Northampton, Mass., 1923).

————, "The Historians," *CHAL* (as cited).

————, *Life of Andrew Jackson* (2 vols., New York, 1925).

————, *The Middle Group of American Historians* (New York, 1917).

————, "The Round Hill School," *Educational Review,* I (Apr. 1891).

————, *The Writings of Colonel William Byrd* (New York, 1901).

————, "The Regulators of North Carolina, 1765–1771," American Historical Association *Annual Report for 1894* (Washington, D.C., 1895).

————, *Slavery and Servitude in the Colony of North Carolina* (Baltimore, 1896).

Bassett, John Spencer, and Jameson, J. Franklin (eds.), *Correspondence of Andrew Jackson* (7 vols., Washington, D.C., 1926–35).

Bates, Ernest Sutherland, *American Faith: Its Religious, Political and Economic Foundations* (New York, 1940).

Baxter, James P., III, *The Introduction of the Ironclad Warship* (Cambridge, 1933).

Beale, Howard K., *The Critical Year* (New York, 1930).

——, *Theodore Roosevelt and the Rise of America to World Power* (Baltimore, 1956).

——, "What Historians Have Said About the Causes of the Civil War," *Theory and Practice in Historical Study: A Report of the Committee on Historiography* (New York, 1946).

——, "On Rewriting Reconstruction History," *American Historical Review,* XLV (Oct. 1939).

Beard, Charles A., *Public Policy and the General Welfare* (New York, 1941).

Beard, Charles A., and Mary R., *The American Spirit* (New York, 1942).

——, *The Rise of American Civilization* (2 vols., New York, 1927).

Beardsley, E. E., *Life and Correspondence of the Right Reverend Samuel Seabury* (Boston, 1881).

Beatty, Edward C. O., *William Penn as a Social Philosopher* (New York, 1939).

Beatty, Richmond Croom, *William Byrd of Westover* (Boston, 1932).

Beazley, C. R., *The Dawn of Modern Geography, 300–1420* (3 vols., Oxford, 1897–1906).

Becker, Carl L., *Cornell University: Founders and the Founding* (Ithaca, 1943).

——, "Labelling the Historians," in *Everyman His Own Historian* (New York, 1935).

——, *The Declaration of Independence* (New York, 1922).

——, *The Heavenly City of the Eighteenth Century Philosophers* (New Haven, 1932).

——, "What are Historical Facts?" *The Western Political Quarterly,* VII (Sept. 1955).

Beeck, William J., *William Penn in America* (Philadelphia, 1888).

Beer, George L., *British Colonial Policy 1754–1765* (New York, 1907).

——, *The Commercial Policy of England Toward the American Colonies* (New York, 1893).

Beers, Fannie A., *Memories: A Record of Personal Experience and Adventure During Four Years of War* (Philadelphia, 1891).

Beers, Henry P., *Bibliographies in American History* (New York, 1938).

Belknap, Jane M., *Life of Jeremy Belknap with Selections from His Writings* (New York, 1847).

Bell, Herbert, *Woodrow Wilson and the People* (New York, 1945).

Bellot, H. Hale, *American History and American Historians* (London, 1952).

Bemis, E. W., "Local Government in Michigan and the Northwest," *The Johns Hopkins University Studies in Historical and Political Science,* first series, V (Baltimore, 1883).

Bentham, Jeremy, *Theory of Legislation* (2 vols., Boston, 1840).

Bergson, Henri, *Creative Evolution* (New York, 1944).

Bestor, Arthur, *State Sovereignty and Slavery* (Springfield, Ill., 1961).

Beveridge, Albert J., *The Life of John Marshall* (4 vols., Boston, 1916–19).

Beverley, Robert, *History and Present State of Virginia,* Campbell, Charles (ed.) (Richmond, 1855).

Bigelow, John, *France and the Confederate Navy 1862–1868* (New York, 1888).

Biggar, H. P. (ed.), *A Collection of Documents Relating to Jacques Cartier and the Sieur de Roberval* (Ottawa, 1930).

————, *Precursors of Jacques Cartier* (Ottawa, 1911).

————, *The Early Trading Companies of New France* (Toronto, 1901).

————, *The Voyages of Jacques Cartier* (Ottawa, 1924).

Billington, Ray A., *America's Frontier Heritage* (New York, 1966).

————, *Westward Expansion* (New York, 1967).

Billington, Ray A., Loewenberg, Bert James, and Colby, Merle, *Massachusetts: A Guide to its Places and People* (Boston, 1937).

Bishop, Joseph Bucklin, *Theodore Roosevelt and His Times* (New York, 1920).

Black, J. B., *The Art of History* (New York, 1926).

Black, Robert C., III, *The Railroads of the Confederacy* (Chapel Hill, 1952).

Blackmur, Richard P., "The Failure of Henry Adams," *Hound and Horn,* IV (Apr.-June 1931).

Blaine, James G., *Twenty Years of Congress: From Lincoln to Garfield* (2 vols., Norwich, Conn., 1884–86).

Bloch, Marc, *The Historian's Craft* (New York, 1953).

Bolton, Herbert E., "The Mission as a Frontier Institution in the Spanish American Colonies," *American Historical Review,* XXIII (Oct. 1917).

————, *The Spanish Borderlands* (New Haven, 1921).

Bolton, Herbert E., and Ross, Mary, *The Debatable Land* (Berkeley, 1925).

Bond, Horace M., *Negro Education in Alabama: A Study in Cotton and Steel* (Washington, D.C., 1939).

————, "Social and Economic Forces in Alabama Reconstruction," *Journal of Negro History,* IV (Feb. 1938).

Bonham, M. L., *The British Consuls in the Confederacy* (New York, 1911).

Bordin, Ruth, "Andrew Dickson White, Teacher of History," *Michigan Historical Collections,* No. 8 (Ann Arbor, 1958).

Bostwick, Arthur E., *The American Public Library* (New York, 1929).

Botta, Carlo, *History of War of Independence of the United States of America,* George Alexander Otis (trans.) (3 vols., Philadelphia, 1820–21).

Boucher, Jonathan, *Reminiscences of an American Loyalist, 1738–1789* (Boston, 1925).

Bourne, Edward G., *Essays in Historical Criticism* (New Haven, 1913).

————, *Spain in America, 1450–1580* (New York, 1904).

————, "The Naming of America," *American Historical Review,* X (Oct. 1904).

Bourne, Edward G., and Bourne, A. N., *The Voyages and Explorations of Samuel de Champlain 1604–1616, narrated by Himself* (2 vols., New York, 1906).

Bowen, Catherine Drinker, *John Adams and the American Revolution* (Boston, 1950).

————, *Yankee from Olympus: Justice Holmes and His Family* (Boston, 1944).

Boyd, William K., "Political Writing Since 1850," *CHAL* (as cited), III (New York, 1921).

Bradford, E. F., "Conscious Art in Bradford's History of Plymouth Plantation," *New England Quarterly,* I (Apr. 1928).

Bradford, Gamaliel, *Lee the American* (Boston, 1912).

————, "The Progress of Civil Service Reform," *International Review,* XIII (Sept. 1882).

Bradford, William, *History of Plymouth Plantation* (ed.), Ford, Worthington C. (2 vols., Boston, 1921).

Brailsford, Mabel R., *The Making of William Penn* (New York, 1930).

Bridenbaugh, Carl, and Bridenbaugh, Jessica, *Rebels and Gentlemen, Philadelphia in the Age of Franklin* (New York, 1942).

Bridges, Hal, *Civil War and Reconstruction* (Washington, D.C., 1957).

Brinton, Daniel Garrison, *Notes on the Floridian Peninsula: Its Literary History, Indian Tribes and Antiquities* (Philadelphia, 1859).

British Museum Catalogue of Printed Books 1881–1900, The (58 vols., Ann Arbor, 1931–51).

Brockunier, Samuel H., *The Irrepressible Democrat Roger Williams* (New York, 1940).

Brooks, Robert C. (ed.), *Bryce's American Commonwealth Fiftieth Anniversary* (New York, 1939).

Brooks, Van Wyck, *The Flowering of New England* (Boston, 1937).

———, *The Life of Emerson* (New York, 1932).

———, *The World of Washington Irving* (New York, 1944).

Brown, Alexander, *The Genesis of the United States* (2 vols., New York, 1890).

Brown, Alice, *Mercy Warren* (New York, 1896).

Brown, Bernard E., *American Conservatives: The Political Thought of Francis Lieber and John W. Burgess* (New York, 1951).

Brown, John M., *Collections of the Maine Historical Society,* first series, VII (1876).

Browne, J. H., *Four Years in Secessia* (Hartford, Conn., 1865).

Brownell, William C., *American Prose Masters* (New York, 1909).

Bruce, William Cabell, *John Randolph of Roanoke* (2 vols., New York, 1922).

Brummer, Sidney D., *The Judicial Interpretation of the Confederate Constitution* (New York, 1914).

Bryan, William A., *George Washington in American Literature, 1775–1865* (New York, 1952).

Bryant, William Cullen, *Orations and Addresses* (New York, 1873).

Buchanan, Lamont (ed.), *A Pictorial History of the Confederacy* (New York, 1951).

Bulloch, J. D., *The Secret Service of the Confederate States in Europe* (2 vols., London, 1883).

Burgess, John W., *Political Science and Comparative Constitutional Law* (2 vols., Boston, 1890–91).

———, "Political Science and History," *American Historical Review,* II (Apr., 1897).

———, *Reconciliation of Government with Liberty* (New York, 1915).

———, *Reconstruction and the Constitution 1866–1876* (New York, 1902).

———, *Reminiscences of an American Scholar* (New York, 1934).

———, *The Administration of President Hayes* (New York, 1916).

———, *The Civil War and the Constitution, 1859–1865* (2 vols., New York, 1901).

———, *The Foundations of American Political Science* (New York, 1933).

———, "The Methods of Historical Study and Research in Columbia College," in Hall, G. Stanley (ed.), *Methods of Teaching and Studying History* (Boston, 1886).

———, *The Middle Period, 1817–1858* (New York, 1897).

Burr, George L., "Andrew Dickson White," in Gibbons, Lois O. (ed.), *George Lincoln Burr: Selections from His Writings* (Ithaca, 1943).

Burrage, Henry S. (ed.), *Early English and French Voyages, Original Narratives of Early American History* (New York, 1930).

———, *Early English and French Voyages, 1534–1608, Original Narratives of Early American History* (New York, 1906).

Bury, J. B., "Darwinism and History," *Evolution in Modern Thought* (New York, n.d.).

Butler, B. F., *Autobiography and Personal Reminiscences* (Boston, 1892).

Butler, Nicholas Murray, *Across the Busy Years* (New York, 1939).

Butler, Pierce, *Judah P. Benjamin* (Philadelphia, 1907).

Cairns, William B., *British Criticism of American Writings, 1783–1815* (Madison, 1918).

Cambiaire, C. P., *The Influence of Edgar Allan Poe on France* (New York, 1927).

Campbell, Charles, see Beverley, Robert.

Carlyle, Thomas, *On Heroes, Hero-Worship, and the Heroic in History* (London [1891]).

Carman, Harry J., *Social and Economic History of the United States* (2 vols., Boston, 1934).

Carpenter, Frederic I. (ed.), *Ralph Waldo Emerson: Representative Selections. . . .* (New York, 1934).

Carpenter, Jesse T., *The South As a Conscious Minority, 1789–1861* (New York, 1930).

Carson, H. L., *History of the Historical Society of Pennsylvania* (Philadelphia, 1940).

Cassirer, Ernst, *An Essay on Man* (New Haven, 1944).

———, *The Problem of Knowledge* (New Haven, 1950).

Cater, Harold (ed.), *Henry Adams and His Friends* (Boston, 1947).

Caton, Bruce, *A Stillness at Appomattox* (New York, 1954).

Cawthon, John A. (ed.), "Letters of a North Louisiana Private to His Wife, 1862–1865," *Mississippi Valley Historical Review*, XXX (Mar. 1944).

Chambers, Walter, *Samuel Seabury: A Challenge* (New York, 1932).

Channing, Edward, *A Student's History of the United States* (Boston, 1898).

———, *History of the United States* (6 vols., New York, 1905–25).

———, "The Narragansett Planters: A Study of Causes," *The Johns Hopkins University Studies in Historical and Political Science,* fourth series, III (Baltimore, 1886).

———, "Town and County in the Colonies," *The Johns Hopkins University Studies in Historical and Political Science,* second series, X (Baltimore, 1884).

Channing, Edward, and Higginson, Thomas W., *English History for American Readers* (New York, 1893).

Charvat, William, and Kraus, Michael, *William Hickling Prescott: Representative Selections* (New York, 1943).

Chatelain, Verne E., *The Defenses of Spanish Florida 1565–1763* (Washington, D.C., 1941).

Chatterton, E. K., *Captain John Smith* (New York, 1927).

Cheyney, Edward P., *Dawn of a New Era* (New York, 1936).

———, *European Background of American History, 1300–1600* (New York, 1904).

———, *History of the University of Pennsylvania 1740–1940* (Philadelphia, 1940).

Chinard, Gilbert, *Honest John Adams* (Boston, 1933).

Clark, Harry Hayden, *Thomas Paine: Representative Selections* (New York, 1944).

Clark, John Spencer, *The Life and Letters of John Fiske* (2 vols., Boston, 1917).

Clarke, D. M., *British Opinion and the American Revolution* (Cambridge, 1930).

Cleveland, Henry, *Alexander H. Stephens, in Public and Private: with Letters and Speeches* (Philadelphia, 1866).

Cleven, N. Andrew N. (ed.), *Readings in Hispanic American History* (Boston, 1927).

Cobb, Samuel H., *The Rise of Religious Liberty in America* (New York, 1902).

Cochran, Thomas C., "The Presidential Synthesis in American History," *American Historical Review,* LIII (July 1948).

Cohen, Morris R., "Einstein and His World," *Faith of a Liberal* (New York, 1946).

———, *The Meaning of Human History* (La Salle, Ill., 1947).

Cohen, Morris R., and Nagel, Ernest, *An Introduction to Logic and Scientific Method* (New York, 1934).

Colden, Cadwallader, *The History of the Five Indian Nations Depending on the Province of New York in America* (New York, 1727).

Cole, Arthur C., "The South and the Right of Secession in the Early Fifties," *Mississippi Valley Historical Review,* I (Dec. 1914).

Cole, Charles W., "Jeremy Belknap: Pioneer Nationalist," *New England Quarterly,* X (Dec. 1937).

Commager, Henry Steele, *The American Mind* (New Haven, 1950).

——— (ed.), *The Blue and the Gray: The Story of the Civil War as Told by Participants* (2 vols., Indianapolis, 1950).

Commons, John R., and others, *A Documentary History of American Industrial Society* (Vols. I and II, Cleveland, 1909).

Conway, Moncure D., *The Life of Thomas Paine* (Boston, 1892).

Coppock, H. F., "Herbert Levi Osgood," *Mississippi Valley Historical Review* XIX (Dec. 1932).

Cooke, George W., *Ralph Waldo Emerson: His Life Writings and Philosophy* (Boston, 1881).

Cortissoz, Royal, *John La Farge: A Memoir and a Study* (Boston, 1911).

Coupland, Reginald, *The American Revolution and the British Empire* (London, 1930).

Craven, Avery O., *The Repressible Conflict, 1830–1861* (Baton Rouge, 1939).

Creighton, James E. (ed.), *Papers in Honor of Josiah Royce on His Sixtieth Birthday* (New York, 1916).

Crittenden, C., and Godard, D., *Historical Societies in the United States and Canada: A Handbook* (Washington, D.C., 1944).

Curti, Merle, *Frederick Jackson Turner* (Mexico, D.F., 1949).

————, "The American Scholar in Three Wars," *Journal of the History of Ideas,* III (June, 1942).

————, *The Growth of American Thought* (New York, 1943).

Curti, Merle, and Carstensen, Vernon, *The University of Wisconsin, A History, 1848–1925* (2 vols., Madison, 1949).

Curtis, George Ticknor, *History of the Origin, Formation, and Adoption of the Constitution of the United States* (2 vols., New York, 1854–58).

Curtis, George W. (ed.), *The Correspondence of John Lothrop Motley* (2 vols., New York, 1889).

Cushing, Harry A. (ed.), *The Writings of Samuel Adams* (4 vols., New York, 1904–08).

Dallas, George M., *A Series of Letters From London Written During the Years 1856–1860* (Philadelphia, 1869).

Dana, Edward S., *et al., A Century of Science in America, with Special Reference to the American Journal of Science, 1818–1918* (New Haven, 1918).

Daniel, Marjorie L., "Woodrow Wilson," *Mississippi Valley Historical Review,* XXI (Dec. 1934).

Darling, A. B., *Political Changes in Massachusetts, 1824–1828* (New Haven, 1925).

Darwin, Francis (ed.), *More Letters of Charles Darwin* (2 vols., London, 1903).

Davidson, Philip, *Propaganda and the American Revolution, 1763–1783* (Chapel Hill, N.C., 1941).

Davis, Jefferson, *A Short History of the Confederate States of America* (New York, 1890).

————, *The Rise and Fall of the Confederate Government* (2 vols., New York, 1881).

Davis, Varina H., *Jefferson Davis: Ex-President of the Confederate States of America* (New York, 1890).

Davis, William W., *The Civil War and Reconstruction in Florida* (New York, 1913).

Dennett, Tyler (ed.), *Lincoln and the Civil War in the Diaries and Letters of John Hay* (New York, 1939).

Dennis, Alfred Pearce, "Princeton Schoolmaster," in Petersen, Houston (ed.), *Great Teachers* (New Brunswick, N.J., 1946).

Dewey, John, "James Marsh and American Philosophy," *Journal of the History of Ideas,* II (Apr. 1941).

————, *Logic: The Theory of Inquiry* (New York, 1938).

————, *Reconstruction in Philosophy* (New York, 1920).

Diamond, William, *The Economic Thought of Woodrow Wilson* (Baltimore, 1943).

Díaz del Castillo, Bernal, *The True History of the Conquest of Mexico* (New York, 1927).

Dickason, David H., "Henry Adams and Clarence King: The Record of a Friendship," *New England Quarterly,* XVII (June 1944).

Ditzion, S. H., *Arsenals of a Democratic Culture: A Social History of the American Public Library Movement in New England and the Middle States 1850–1900* (Chicago, 1917).

Dodd, William E., *Expansion and Conflict* (Boston, 1915).

————, *Jefferson Davis* (Philadelphia, 1907).

————, *Woodrow Wilson and his Work* (New York, 1927).

Donald, D. H., Milhollen, H. D., and Kaplan, H. (eds.), *Divided We Fought: A Pictorial History of the War 1861–1865* (New York, 1952).

Dorfman, Joseph, *Thorstein Veblen and His America* (New York, 1935).

Dos Passos, John, "Citizen Barlow of the Republic of the World," *The Ground We Stand On* (New York, 1941).

Douglass, William, *A Summary, Historical and Political . . . of the British Settlement in North-America* (London, 1755).

Drake, Samuel G. (ed.), *The Old Indian Chronicle: Being a Collection of Exceeding Rare Tracts Written and Published in the Time of King Philip's War. . . .* (Boston, 1836).

Draper, John William, *History of the Intellectual Development of Europe* (2 vols., New York, 1863).

————, *History of the American Civil War* (3 vols., New York, 1867–70).

————, *History of the Conflict Between Religion and Science* (New York, 1874).

————, *Human Physiology* (New York, 1856).

————, *Thoughts on the Future Civil Policy of America* (New York, 1865).

Draper, Lyman Copeland, *King's Mountain and Its Heroes* (Cincinnati, 1881).

Drayton, John, *Memoirs of the American Revolution, From its Commencement to the Year 1776, inclusive. . . .* (2 vols., Charleston, S.C., 1821).

DuBois, W. E. Burghardt, *Black Reconstruction* (New York, 1935).

Dudok, G., *Sir Thomas More and His Utopia* (Amsterdam, 1924).

Duffus, R. L., *The Innocent at Cedro: A Memoir of Thorstein Veblen and Some Others* (New York, 1944).

Dumond, Dwight L. (ed.), *Letters of James Gillespie Birney, 1831–1857* (2 vols., New York, 1938).

————, and Barnes, Gilbert H. (eds.), *Letters of Theodore Dwight Weld, Angelina Grimké Weld, and Sarah Grimké, 1822–1844* (2 vols., New York, 1934).

Dunbar, Rowland (ed.), *Jefferson Davis, Constitutionalist: His Letters, Papers and Speeches* (10 vols., Jackson, Miss., 1923).

Dunning, William A., *Essays on the Civil War and Reconstruction and Related Topics* (New York, 1897).

————, *From Rousseau to Spencer* (New York, 1920).

————, *History of Political Theories, Ancient and Medieval* (New York, 1905).

————, "More Light on Andrew Johnson," *Truth in History* (New York, 1937).

————, *Reconstruction Political and Economic* (New York, 1907).

————, *Truth in History and Other Essays by William Archibald Dunning* (New York, 1937).

Eames, Wilberforce, *A Bibliography of Captain John Smith* (New York, 1927).

Easton, David, *The Political System* (New York, 1953).

Eaton, Clement, "Censorship of the Southern Mails," *American Historical Review*, XLVIII (Jan. 1943).

Ebeling, Christoph Daniel, *Erdbeschreibung und Geschichte von Amerika* (5 vols., Hamburg, 1787–1816).

Eckenrode, H. J., *Jefferson Davis: President of the South* (New York, 1923).

Eckenrode, H. J., and Conrad, B., *George B. McClellan: The Man Who Saved the Union* (Chapel Hill, 1941).

Edwards, Everett E., "A Bibliography of the Writings of Professor Ulrich Bonnell Phillips," *Agricultural History,* VIII (Oct. 1934).

Elliot, Jonathan, *Debates in the several State Conventions on the Adoption of the Federal Constitution.* . . . (4 vols., Washington, D.C., 1836).

————, *Debates on the Adoption of the Federal Constitution in the Convention Held at Philadelphia* (Washington, D.C., 1845).

Ellis, George E., *The Puritan Age and Rule in the Colony of Massachusetts Bay 1629–1685* (New York, 1927).

Ellis, Lewis E., "James Schouler," *Jernegan Essays.*

Elting, J., "Dutch Village Communities on the Hudson River," *The Johns Hopkins University Studies in Historical and Political Science,* third series, I (Baltimore, 1886).

Emerson, Donald E., *Richard Hildreth* (Baltimore, 1946).

————, "Hildreth, Draper, and Science," in Goldman, Eric, (ed.), *Historiography and Urbanization* (Baltimore, 1941).

Emerton, E., "The Practical Method in Higher Historical Instruction," in Hall, G. Stanley (ed.), *Methods of Teaching and Studying History* (Boston, 1886).

Emmall, Richard, "Interpretations of the American Civil War," *Science and Society,* I (Winter 1937).

Englekirk, John E., *Edgar Allan Poe in Hispanic Literature* (New York, 1934).

Fahrney, Ralph R., "Edward Channing," *Jernegan Essays.*

Farnham, Charles Haight, *A Life of Francis Parkman* (Boston, 1901).

Farrand, Livingston, *Basis of American History* (New York, 1904).

Fast, Howard (ed.), *The Selected Work of Tom Paine* (New York, 1945).

Faÿ, Bernard, *The Revolutionary Spirit in France and America* (New York, 1927).

Fernández de Oviedo, Gonzalo, see Oviedo.

Fisher, George Park, *Life of Benjamin Silliman* (2 vols., New York, 1866).

Fisher, Sydney George, *The Trial of the Constitution* (Philadelphia, 1862).

————, *True History of the American Revolution* (Philadelphia, 1902).

————, "The Legendary and Myth-Making Process in Histories of the American Revolution," *Proceedings of the American Philosophical Society,* LI (1912).

Fisk, Ethel F. (ed.), *The Letters of John Fiske* (New York, 1940).

Fiske, John, *American Political Ideas Viewed from the Standpoint of Universal History* (New York, 1895).

————, *A Century of Science and Other Essays* (Boston, 1900).

————, *Outlines of Cosmic Philosophy Based on the Doctrine of Evolution with Criticism on the Positive Philosophy* (2 vols., Boston, 1874/1891).

————, "Spain and the Netherlands," *The Unseen World, and Other Essays* (Boston, 1876).

————, *The Beginnings of New England* (Boston, 1889).

————, *The Critical Period in American History, 1783–1789* (Boston, 1888).

————, *The Discovery of America* (2 vols., Boston, 1892).

Fleming, Donald, *John William Draper and the Religion of Science* (Philadelphia, 1950).

Fleming, Walter L., *Civil War and Reconstruction in Alabama* (New York, 1905).

———, *Documentary History of Reconstruction, Political, Military, Social, Religious, Educational and Industrial, 1865 to the Present Time* (2 vols., Cleveland, 1906–07).

———, *Ku Klux Klan, Its Origins, Growth and Disbandment by J. C. Lester and D. L. Wilson* (New York, 1905).

———, *The Sequel to Appomattox* (New Haven, 1919).

Fletcher, J. G. *John Smith—Also Pocahontas* (New York, 1928).

Flexner, Abraham, *Universities: American, English, German* (New York, 1930).

Force, Peter (ed.), *American Archives* (9 vols., Washington, D.C., 1837–53).

———, *Tracts and other Papers relating Principally to the . . . Colonies in North America* (4 vols., Washington, D.C., 1836–46).

Ford, Guy Stanton, "Some Suggestions to American Historians," *American Historical Review*, XLIII (Jan. 1938).

Ford, Paul Leicester, *Franklin Bibliography* (Brooklyn, 1889).

———, (ed.), *The Writings of John Dickinson: Vol. I, Political Writings, 1764–1774* (Philadelphia, 1895).

Ford, Worthington C. (ed.), *A Cycle of Adams Letters 1861–1865* (2 vols., Boston, 1920).

——— (ed.), *The Writings of George Washington* (14 vols., New York, 1889–93).

Foster, Frank H., *A Genetic History of New England Theology* (Chicago, 1907).

Foster, William E., "The Use of a Public Library in the Study of History," in Hall, G. Stanley (ed.), *Methods of Teaching and Studying History* (Boston, 1886).

Fox, Dixon Ryan, *Herbert Levi Osgood* (New York, 1924).

Frankenburger, David B., and others, *William Francis Allen: Memorial Volume* (Boston, 1890).

Freeman, Douglas S., *Lee's Lieutenants: A Study in Command* (3 vols., New York, 1942–44).

———, *Robert E. Lee: A Biography* (4 vols., New York, 1934–35).

———, *The South to Posterity: An Introduction to the Writing of Confederate History* (New York, 1939).

Freeman, Edward A., "An Introduction to American Institutional History," *The Johns Hopkins University Studies in Historical and Political Science*, first series, I (Baltimore, 1883).

Friedman, Lee M., *Early American Jews* (Cambridge, 1934).

Frothingham, Richard, *The Rise of the Republic of the United States* (Boston, 1873).

Gabriel, Ralph Henry, *The Course of American Democratic Thought* (New York, 1940).

Gaffarel, P., *Histoire de la Floride française* (Paris, 1875).

Galloway, Joseph, *Historical and Politcial Reflections on the Rise and Progress of the American Revolution* (London, 1780).

Garlick, R., *Philip Mazzei, Friend of Jefferson* (Baltimore, 1933).

Garner, James W., *Reconstruction in Mississippi* (New York, 1901).

Garrison, F. J., and Garrison, W. P., *William Lloyd Garrison, 1805–1879* (4 vols., New York, 1885–89).

George, William H., *The Scientist in Action: A Study of His Methods* (London, 1936).

Gerson, A. J., *The Organization and Early History of the Muscovy Company* (New York, 1912).

Gillespie, James E., *The Influence of Overseas Expansion on England to 1700* (New York, 1920).

Gilman, Daniel C., *Bluntschli, Lieber, and Laboulaye* (Baltimore, 1884).

Goldberg, Alfred, "School Histories of the Middle Period," in Goldman, Eric F. (ed.), *Historiography and Urbanization* (Baltimore, 1941).

Going, C. B., *David Wilmont, Free Soiler* (New York, 1924).

Goldenweiser, Alexander, "Leading Contributors of Anthropology to Social Theory," in Barnes, Harry E., and Becker, Howard (eds.), *Contemporary Social Theory* (New York, 1940).

Goldman, Eric F., "Herman Eduard von Holst," *Mississippi Valley Historical Review,* XXIII (Mar. 1937).

—————— (ed.), *Historiography and Urbanization* (Baltimore, 1941).

——————, *John Bach McMaster* (Philadelphia, 1943).

——————, *Rendezvous with Destiny* (New York, 1952).

Gooch, George P., *History and Historians in the Nineteenth Century* (London, 1913).

Goodman, Nathan G., *Benjamin Rush, Physician and Citizen: 1746–1813* (Philadelphia, 1934).

Gordon, William, *The History of the Rise, Progress, and Establishment of the Independence of the United States of America* (4 vols., London, 1788).

Gorman, T. K., *America and Belgium* (London, 1925).

Grahame, James, *The History of the United States of North America from the Plantation of the British Colonies till Assumption of National Independence* (4 vols., 1827–36).

Grant, U. S., *Personal Memoirs* (2 vols., New York, 1885–86).

Grant, W. L. (ed.), *Voyages of Samuel de Champlain, 1604–1618, Original Narratives of Early American History* (New York, 1907).

Gray, Austin K., *The First American Library* (Philadelphia, 1936).

Gray, Henry D., *Emerson: A Statement of New England Transcendentalism as Expressed in the Philosophy of its Chief Exponent* (Palo Alto, Calif., 1917).

Gray, Stanley, "The Political Thought of John Winthrop," *New England Quarterly,* III (Oct. 1930).

Gray, Wood, *The Hidden Civil War: The Story of the Copperheads* (New York, 1942).

——————, "Ulrich Bonnell Phillips," *Jernegan Essays.*

Greeley, Horace,.*Recollections of a Busy Life* (New York, 1868).

Green, Constance M., "The Value of Local History," in Ware, Caroline F. (ed.), *The Cultural Approach to History* (New York, 1940).

Green, Fletcher M., "Walter Lynwood Fleming, Historian of Reconstruction," *The Journal of Southern History,* II (Nov. 1936).

Green, S. S., *Public Library Movement in the United States, 1853–1893* (Boston, 1913).

Greene, E. B., *Revolutionary Generation, 1763–1790* (New York, 1943).

Guedalla, Philip, *Fathers of the Revolution* (New York, 1926).

Guilland, Antoine, *Modern Germany and Her Historians* (New York, 1915).

Hacker, Louis M., "Revolutionary America: An Interpretation of Our History," *Harper's Magazine*, CLXX (Mar. 1935).

Hakluyt, Richard, *Divers Voyages* (London, 1582).

———, *Principal Navigations, Voyages, Traffiques, and Discoveries of the English Nation* (Everyman edition, 8 vols., New York, 1907).

Hale, E. E. (ed.), "Note-Book Kept by Thomas Letchford, Esq., Lawyer, in Boston, Massachusetts Bay, from June 27, 1638, to July 29, 1641," *Transactions and Collections of the American Antiquarian Society*, VII (1885).

Halévy, Élie, *A History of the English People in the Nineteenth Century* (5 vols., E. I. Watkin and D. A. Barker, trs., London, 1924–34).

———, *The Growth of Philosophic Radicalism* (Mary Morris, tr., London, 1934).

Hall, Clayton C. (ed.), "Father Andrew White's Narrative," in *Narratives of Early Maryland, 1633–1684, Original Narratives of Early American History* (New York, 1910).

Hall, G. Stanley, *Life and Confessions of a Psychologist* (2 vols., New York, 1923).

——— (ed.), *Methods of Teaching and Studying History* (Boston, 1886).

Hall, T. C., *The Religious Background of American Culture* (Boston, 1930).

Halsey, R. T. H. (ed.), *Letters from a Farmer in Pennsylvania* (New York, 1903).

Hamilton, J. G. de R., *Reconstruction in North Carolina* (New York, 1914).

Hamilton, J. T., *A History of the Church Known as the Moravian Church* (Bethlehem, Pa., 1900).

Hammond, Bray, "Jackson, Biddle, and the Bank of the United States," *Journal of Economic History*, VII (May 1947).

Handlin, Oscar, and Handlin, Mary F., *Commonwealth: Massachusetts, 1774–1861* (New York, 1947).

Handlin, Oscar, Schlesinger, Arthur M., Morison, Samuel E., Merk, Frederick, Schlesinger, Arthur M., Jr., and Buck, Paul H. (eds.), *Harvard Guide to American History* (Cambridge, 1954).

Hanke, Lewis, "Bartolomé de Las Casas, An Essay in Hagiography and Historiography," *The Hispanic American Historical Review*, XXXIII (Feb. 1953).

———, *Struggle for Justice in the Spanish Conquest of America* (Philadelphia, 1949).

———, *The First Social Experiments in America* (Cambridge, 1935).

Hansen, Allen O., *Liberalism and American Education in the Eighteenth Century* (New York, 1926).

Hansen, Marcus Lee, *The Atlantic Migration, 1607–1860* (Cambridge, 1940).

———, *The Immigrant in American History* (Cambridge, 1940).

Haraszti, Zoltán, *John Adams and the Prophets of Progress* (Cambridge, 1952).

Harrington, Virginia D., *The New York Merchant on the Eve of the Revolution* (New York, 1935).

Harrisse, Henry, *Christophe Columb: son origine, sa vie, ses voyages, sa famille. . . .* (2 vols., Paris, 1884–85).

Hart, Albert Bushnell, "Editor's Introduction to the Series" (*The American Nation*), in Cheyney, E. P., *European Background of American History* (New York, 1904).

——— (ed.), *Epochs of American History* (New York, 1891–93).

————, "Methods of Teaching American History," in Hall, G. Stanley (ed.), *Methods of Teaching and Studying History* (Boston, 1886).

————, *National Ideals Historically Traced, 1607–1907* (New York, 1907).

————, *Salmon P. Chase* (Boston, 1899).

Hart, Albert Bushnell, and Ferleger, Herbert Ronald (eds.), *Theodore Roosevelt Cyclopedia* (New York, 1941).

Hartz, Louis, *Economic Policy and Democratic Thought: Pennsylvania 1776–1860* (Cambridge, 1948).

Hayes, Carlton J. H., "History," *A Quarter Century of Learning, 1904–1929* (New York, 1931).

————, *The Historical Evolution of Modern Nationalism* (New York, 1931).

Haynes, George H., *Representation and Suffrage in Massachusetts, 1620–1691* (Baltimore, 1894).

Hazard, Ebenezer, *Historical Collections* (2 vols., Philadelphia, 1792–94).

Headlam, Cecil, "The American Revolution and British Politics 1776–1783," in Rose, J. H., Newton, A. P., and Benians, E. A. (eds.), *The Cambridge History of the British Empire* (New York, 1929).

Hearnshaw, F. J. C. (ed.), *Social and Political Ideas of the Age of Reconstruction* (London, 1932).

Hegel, George W. F., *Lectures on the Philosophy of History,* translated by J. Sibree (London, 1890).

Heilman, Robert B., *America in English Fiction, 1790–1800* (Baton Rouge, 1937).

Hellman, George S., *Washington Irving, Esquire: Ambassador at Large from the New World to the Old* (New York, 1925).

Henderson, F. F. R., *Stonewall Jackson and the American Civil War* (2 vols., New York, 1936).

Herbert, Hillary, and others, *Why the Solid South?* (Baltimore, 1890).

Hendrick, Burton J., *Lincoln's War Cabinet* (Boston, 1946).

————, *The Lees of Virginia* (Boston, 1935).

————, *The Life and Letters of Walter Hines Page* (3 vols., New York, 1922–25).

Herrera y Tordesillas, Antonio de, *Historia general de las Indias Occidentales* (Madrid, 1601).

————, *Historia general de los hechos de los castellanos en las islas y terra firme del mar Océano* (5 vols., Madrid, 1601–15).

Hesseltine, William B., *The South in American History* (New York, 1943).

Hesseltine, W. B., and Kaplan, Louis, "Doctors of Philosophy in History," *American Historical Review,* XLVII (July 1942).

Heulhard, A., *Villegagnon, roi d' Amérique* (Paris, 1897).

Higby, Chester P., and Schantz, Bradford T., *John Lothrop Motley: Representative Selections* (New York, 1939).

Higginson, Thomas H., *Cheerful Yesterdays* (Boston, 1898).

Hildreth, Richard, *A Letter to Andrews Norton on Miracles as the Foundation of Religious Faith* (Boston, 1840).

————, *Banks, Banking, and Paper Currency* (Boston, 1840).

————, *Despotism in America, or an Inquiry into the Nature and Results of the Slave-Holding System in the United States* (Boston, 1840).

————, *Native-Americanism Detected and Exposed. By a Native American* (Boston, 1845).

——, *History of the United States of America.* . . . (6 vols., New York, 1849–52).

——, *"Our First Men": A Calendar of Wealth, Fashion and Gentility, containing a list of those persons taxed in the City of Boston, credibly reported to be worth ONE HUNDRED THOUSAND DOLLARS: with biographical notices of the principal persons* (Boston, 1846).

——, *The History of Banks: to which is added, a Demonstration of the Advantages and Necessity of Free Competition in the Business of Banking* (Boston, 1837).

——, *The People's Presidential Candidate, or the Life of William Henry Harrison of Ohio* (Boston, 1839).

——, *The Slave, or Memoirs of Archy Moore* (2 vols., Boston, 1836).

——, *The Theory of Morals: An Inquiry Concerning the Law of Moral Distinctions and Variations and Contradictions of Ethical Codes* (Boston, 1844).

——, *The Theory of Politics: An Inquiry into the Foundations of Governments and the Causes and Progress of Political Revolutions* (New York, 1853).

Hill, George Birkbeck (ed., revised and enlarged by Powell, L. F.), *Boswell's Life of Johnson* (6 vols., Oxford, 1934–50).

Hinkhouse, Fred J., *The Preliminaries of the American Revolution as seen in the English Press, 1763–1783* (New York, 1926).

Hodge, Frederick W. (ed.), "The Narrative of Alvar Núñez de Vaca," *Spanish Explorers in the United States 1528–1543, Original Narratives of Early American History* (New York, 1907).

Hofstadter, Richard, *Social Darwinism in American Thought* (Philadelphia, 1944).

Holborn, Hajo, "The Science of History," in Strayer, Joseph R. (ed.), *The Interpretation of History* (Princeton, 1942).

Holmes, Abiel, *American Annals: or a Chronological History of America from the Discovery* . . . (2 vols., Boston, 1805).

Holmes, Oliver Wendell, *John Lothrop Motley: A Memoir* (Boston, 1879).

——, *Ralph Waldo Emerson, John Lothrop Motley: Two Memoirs* (Boston, 1892).

Holmes, Thomas J., *Increase Mather: A Bibliography of His Works* (2 vols., Cleveland, 1913).

Holst, Hermann Eduard von, *John C. Calhoun* (Boston, 1883).

——, *The Constitutional and Political History of the United States* (8 vols., Chicago, 1876–92).

Holt, W. Stull (ed.), *Historical Scholarship in the United States 1876–1901: as Revealed in the Correspondence of Herbert Baxter Adams* (Baltimore, 1938).

Homan, Paul T., "Thorstein Veblen," in Odum, Howard W. (ed.), *American Masters of Social Science* (New York, 1927).

Hornberger, Theodore, "Puritanism and Science: The Relationship Revealed in the Writings of John Cotton," *New England Quarterly*, X (Sept. 1937).

——, "The Date, the Source, and the Significance of Cotton Mather's Interest in Science," *American Literature*, VI (Jan. 1935).

Horsch, John, *Catalogue of the Mennonite Historical Library in Scottdale, Pennsylvania* (Scottdale, Pa., 1929).

Hosmer, James K., *Life of Thomas Hutchinson* (Boston, 1896).

———, *Samuel Adams* (Boston, 1885).

——— (ed.), *Winthrop's Journal, Original Narratives of Early American History* (2 vols., New York, 1908).

Howard, Leon, *The Connecticut Wits* (Chicago, 1943).

Howe, Frederic C., *The Confession of a Reformer* (New York, 1925).

Howe, Julia Ward, *Reminiscences* (Boston, 1899).

Howe, Mark A. DeWolfe, *Home Letters of General Sherman* (New York, 1909).

———, *James Ford Rhodes, American Historian* (New York, 1929).

———, *The Life and Letters of George Bancroft* (2 vols., New York, n.d.).

Howells, William Dean, *Literary Friends and Acquaintances* (New York, 1900).

Hubbard, William, "A General History of New England from the Discovery to MDCLXXX," *Collections of the Massachusetts Historical Society,* second series, Vols. V–VI (1815).

———, *A Narrative of the troubles with the Indians in New-England,* Drake, Samuel G. (ed.) (2 vols., Roxbury, Mass., 1865).

Hull, William, *William Penn: A Topical Biography* (New York, 1937).

Hume, Robert A., *Runaway Star: An Appreciation of Henry Adams* (Ithaca, 1951).

Humphrey, Edward F., *Nationalism and Religion in America, 1774–1789* (Boston, 1924).

Hutchinson, Peter O. (ed.), *The Diary and Letters of Thomas Hutchinson* (2 vols., Boston, 1884–86).

Hutchinson, Thomas, *A Collection of Original Papers Relative to the History of the Colony of Massachusetts-Bay* (Boston, 1769).

———, *The History of the Colony (and Province) of Massachusetts Bay* (3 vols., Boston, 1795–1828).

Hutchinson, William T., "John Bach McMaster," in Hutchinson, William T. (ed.), *The Marcus W. Jernegan Essays in American Historiography* (Chicago, 1937); referred to as *Jernegan Essays.*

Huxley, Leonard (ed.), *Life and Letters of Sir Joseph Dalton Hooker* (2 vols., London, 1918).

——— (ed.), *Life and Letters of Thomas Henry Huxley* (2 vols., London, 1900).

Huxley, Thomas Henry, *American Addresses* (New York, 1877).

———, *Methods and Results* (New York, 1896).

Inman, A. C. (ed.), *Soldier of the South: General Pickett's War Letters to His Wife* (Boston, 1928).

Irving, Washington, *History of the Life and Voyages of Christopher Columbus* (3 vols., New York, 1828).

———, *Life of George Washington* (5 vols., New York, 1856–59).

———, *Voyages of the Companions of Columbus* (London, 1831).

James, Bartlett B., and Jameson, J. Franklin (eds.), *Journal of Jasper Danckaerts, 1679–1680: Original Narratives of Early American History* (New York, 1913).

Jameson, J. Franklin, *An Introduction to the Study of the Constitutional History of the States* (Baltimore, 1886).

———, "Early Days of the American Historical Association," *American Historical Review,* XL (Oct. 1934).

———— (ed.), *Essays in the Constitutional History of the United States in the Formative Period 1775–1789* (Boston, 1889).

———— (ed.), *Johnson's Wonder Working Providence 1628–1651, Original Narratives of Early American History* (New York, 1910).

————, "Studies in the History of the Federal Convention of 1787," American Historical Association, *Annual Report for the Year 1902*, I (Washington, D.C., 1903).

————, *The American Revolution Considered as a Social Movement* (Princeton, 1940).

————, *The History of Historical Societies* (Savannah, 1914).

————, *The History of Historical Writing in America* (Boston and New York), 1891).

————, "The Present State of Historical Writing in America," *Proceedings of the American Antiquarian Society*, New series, XX (1911).

Janney, S. M., *History of the Religious Society of Friends from its Rise to the Year 1828* (4 vols., Philadelphia, 1859–67).

————, *Life of William Penn* (Philadelphia, 1852).

Janowsky, Oscar I. (ed.), *The American Jew: A Composite Picture* (New York, 1942).

Jensen, Merrill (ed.), *Regionalism in America* (Madison, 1951).

————, *The Articles of Confederation* (Madison, 1940).

————, *The New Nation,* (New York, 1950).

Johnson, A., "The Genesis of a New England State," *The Johns Hopkins University Studies in Historical and Political Science,* first series, XI (Baltimore, 1883).

Johnson, Allen, *Stephen A. Douglas* (New York, 1908).

————, *The Historian and Historical Evidence* (New York, 1926).

Johnson, Zachary T., *The Political Policies of Howell Cobb* (Nashville, 1929).

Jones, Howard Mumford, "The Literature of Virginia in the Seventeenth Century," *Memoirs of the American Academy of Arts and Sciences* (Boston, 1946).

Jones, Howard Mumford, and Casady, Thomas Edgar, *The Life of Moses Coit Tyler* (Ann Arbor, 1933). (Based upon an unpublished dissertation from unpublished sources by Thomas Edgar Casady.)

Jones, Hugh, *The Present State of Virginia* (London, 1724).

Jones, Rufus M., *The Quakers in the American Colonies* (London, 1911).

Jordy, William H., *Henry Adams: Scientific Historian* (New Haven, 1952).

Kelly, James, *The American Catalogue of Books Published in the United States from January 1861 to January 1871* (2 vols., New York, 1871).

Kendrick, Benjamin B., *The Journal of the Joint Committee of Fifteen on Reconstruction* (New York, 1915).

Keys, Alice M., *Cadwallader Colden: A Representative Eighteenth Century Official* (New York, 1906).

Knittle, Walter A., *Early Eighteenth Century Palatine Emigration* (Philadelphia, 1937).

Knollenberg, Bernhard, *Washington and the Revolution* (New York, 1940).

Koch, Adrienne, and Peden, William (eds.), *The Selected Writings of John and John Quincy Adams* (New York, 1946).

Kohn, Hans, *The Idea of Nationalism* (New York, 1944).

Kraus, Michael, "American and the Irish Revolutionary Movement in the

Eighteenth Century," in Morris, Richard B. (ed.), *The Era of the American Revolution* (New York, 1939).

——, *History of American History* (New York, 1937); referred to as Kraus.

——, *The Atlantic Civilization: Eighteenth Century Origins* (Ithaca, 1949).

Labaree, Leonard W., *Conservatism in Early American History* (New York and London, 1948).

La Farge, John, *An Artist's Letters from Japan* (New York, 1897).

——, *Reminiscences of the South Seas* (New York, 1912).

Land, William G., *Thomas Hill: Twentieth President of Harvard* (Cambridge, 1933).

Langlois, Charles V., and Seignobos, Charles, *Introduction to the Study of History*, Berry, G. C. (tr.) (New York, n.d.).

Lanning, John T., *The Spanish Missions of Georgia* (Chapel Hill, 1935).

Las Casas, Bartolomé de, *Historia de las Indias* (5 vols., Madrid, 1875).

Laski, Harold J., "Introductory: The Age of Reason," in Hearnshaw, F. J. C. (ed.), *The Social and Political Ideas of Some Great French Thinkers of the Age of Reason* (London, 1930).

——, *The Rise of European Liberalism* (London, 1936).

Lauber, A. W., *Indian Slavery in Colonial times Within the Present Limits of the United States* (New York, 1913).

Laue, Theodore H. von, *Leopold Ranke: The Formative Years* (Princeton, 1950).

Lawson, Edward W., *The Discovery of Florida and its Discoverer Juan Ponce de Léon* (St. Augustine, 1946).

Lawson, John, *A New Voyage to Carolina containing the Exact Description and Natural History of that Country. . . .* (London, 1709).

Leacock, Stephen, *Mariner of St. Malo* (Toronto, 1930).

Learned, Marion D., *The Life of Francis Daniel Pastorius, The Founder of Germantown* (Philadelphia, 1908).

Leavis, F. R. (ed.), *Mill on Bentham and Coleridge* (London, 1950).

Lecky, William Edward Hartpole, *Democracy and Liberty* (2 vols., New York, 1900).

LeDuc, Thomas, *Piety and Intellect at Amherst College, 1865–1912* (New York, 1946).

Lescarbot, Marc, *Histoire de la Nouvelle France* (Paris, 1609).

Letchford, Thomas, *Plain Dealing: Or, News from New England* (London, 1642), in *Collections of the Massachusetts Historical Society*, third series, III (1833).

Levene, Ricardo, *Introducción a la historia del Derecho Indiano* (Buenos Aires, 1924).

Levenson, J. C., *The Mind and Art of Henry Adams* (Boston, 1957).

Levinger, Lee J., *A History of the Jews in the United States* (Cincinnati, 1930).

Lewis, Theodore H. (ed.), "The Narrative of the Expedition of Hernando de Soto by the Gentleman of Elvas," *Spanish Explorers in the Southern United States* (New York, 1907).

Libby, Orin G., "A Critical Examination of William Gordon's *History of the American Revolution*," American Historical Association, *Annual Report*, I (Washington, D.C., 1899).

——, "Ramsay as a Plagiarist," *American Historical Review*, VII (1901– July 1902).

Lincoln, Charles H. (ed.), *Narratives of the Indian Wars, 1675–1699, Original Narratives of Early American History* (New York, 1913).

Link, Arthur S., *Wilson: The Road to the White House* (Princeton, 1947).

Livezey, William E., *Mahan on Sea Power* (Norman, 1947).

Lodge, Henry Cabot, *A Short History of the English Colonies in America* (Boston, 1881).

———, *Early Memories* (New York, 1913).

———, *George Washington* (2 vols., Boston, 1889).

———, *Life and Letters of George Cabot* (Boston, 1877).

———, *Selections from the Correspondence of Theodore Roosevelt and Henry Cabot Lodge* (2 vols., New York, 1925).

Lodge, Henry Cabot, and Roosevelt, Theodore, *Hero Tales from American History* (New York, 1895).

Loewenberg, Bert James, "American History in College Education," in Taylor, Harold (ed.), *Essays in Teaching* (New York, 1950).

———, "Darwinism Comes to America 1859–1900," *Mississippi Valley Historical Review*, XXVII (Dec. 1941).

———, "Power and American Ideals," *The Standard*, XXXVII (Dec. 1950).

———, "Some Problems Raised by Historical Relativism," *Journal of Modern History*, XXI (Mar. 1949).

———, "The Sacred Right to Differ," *Saturday Review of Literature*, XXXIV (June 16, 1951).

———, "The Process of Democracy and Political Parties, *Labor and Nation*, VII (Fall 1951).

Loewenberg, Jacob (ed.), *Hegel: Selections* (New York, 1929).

Long, E. B. (ed.), *U. S. Grant, Personal Memoirs* (Cleveland, 1952).

Long, Orie W., "Bancroft and Goethe," *Studies in Philology*, XXXVIII (Oct. 1931).

———, *Literary Pioneers* (Cambridge, 1935).

Longfellow, Samuel, *The Life of Henry W. Longfellow* (2 vols., Boston, 1886).

Lonn, Ella, *Desertion During the Civil War* (New York, 1928).

———, *Foreigners in the Confederacy* (Chapel Hill, 1940).

———, *Salt as a Factor in the Confederacy* (Baltimore, 1933).

Lorant, Stefan, *The New World, The First Pictures of America* (New York, 1946).

Lounsbury, Thomas R., *James Fenimore Cooper* (Boston, 1882).

Lovejoy, Arthur O., *The Great Chain of Being* (Cambridge, 1936).

Lowery, Woodbury, *Spanish Settlements Within the Present Limits of the United States: Florida, 1562–1574* (New York, 1905).

Lowie, Robert H., *The History of Ethnographical Theory* (New York, 1937).

MacNutt, F. A., *Bartholomew de Las Casas* (New York, 1909).

———, *De Orbe Novo: The Eight Decades of Peter Martyr D'Anghiera* (New York, 1912).

———, *Fernando Cortés and the Conquest of Mexico, 1485–1547* (New York, 1909).

Macy, Jesse, "Institutional Beginnings in a Western State," *The Johns Hopkins Studies in Historical and Political Science*, second series, VII (Baltimore, 1884).

Madariaga, Salvador de, *Christopher Columbus* (New York, 1940).

———, *Hernan Cortés Conqueror of Mexico* (New York, 1941).

Mahan, Alfred T., *From Sail to Steam, Recollections of Naval Life* (New York [1907]).

——, "Subordination in Historical Treatment," American Historical Association, *Annual Report for 1902* (Washington, D.C., 1903).

——, *The Gulf and Inland Waters* (New York, 1883).

——, *The Influence of Sea Power on History, 1600–1783* (Boston, 1890).

Malone, Dumas, *Jefferson and the Rights of Man* (Boston, 1951).

——, *Jefferson the Virginian* (Boston, 1948).

Marcuse, Herbert, *Reason and Revolution* (New York, 1941).

Markham, C. R., *Letters of Amerigo Vespucci* (London, 1894).

——, *Life of Christopher Columbus* (London, 1892).

Marshall, John, *The Life of George Washington* (5 vols., Philadelphia, 1804–07).

Martin, L., and Bemis, S. F., "Franklin's Re-Line Map," *New England Quarterly*, X (Mar., 1937).

Marx, Karl, *Capital* (Everyman edition. 2 vols., London, 1951).

Marx, Karl, and Engels, Friedrich, *The Civil War in the United States* (New York, 1937). [Selected Published Writings.]

Mather, Cotton, *Magnalia Christi Americana* (London, 1702).

Mathiessen, F. O., *American Renaissance: Art and Expression in the Age of Emerson and Whitman* (New York, 1941).

Mattingly, Garrett, *The Armada* (Boston, 1959).

Maudsley, A. P. (ed. & tr.), Bernal Díaz del Castillo, *The True History of the Conquest of New Spain* (5 vols., London: The Hakluyt Society, 1908–1916).

May, S. J., *Recollections of our Anti-Slavery Conflict* (Boston, 1869).

Maynard, Theodore, *De Soto and the Conquistadores* (New York, 1930).

——, *The Story of American Catholicism* (New York, 1942).

McCann, Franklin T., *English Discovery of America to 1585* (New York, 1952).

McGovern, William M., *From Luther to Hitler* (Boston, 1941).

M'Taggert, John M'T. E., *Studies on the Hegelian Dialectic* (Cambridge, England, 1922).

Mearns, David C., *The Story Up To Now: The Library of Congress 1800–1946* (Washington, D.C., 1947).

Mecklin, John M., *The Story of American Dissent* (New York, 1934).

Merriam, Charles E., *The Political Philosophy of John C. Calhoun* (New York, 1914).

——, "William Archibald Dunning," in Odum, Howard W. (ed.), *American Masters of Social Science* (New York, 1927).

Merriam, Charles E., and Barnes, H. E., *A History of Political Theories: Recent Times* (New York, 1924).

Meyers, Albert Cook (ed.), *Narratives of Early Pennsylvania, West New Jersey, and Delaware, 1630–1707, Original Narratives of Early American History* (New York, 1912).

Mill, John Stuart, *Dissertations and Discussions* (3 vols., New York, 1874).

——, *Utilitarianism, Liberty, and Representative Government* (Modern Library edition, New York, 1950).

Miller, John C., *Origins of the American Revolution* (Boston, 1943).

——, *Sam Adams: Pioneer in Propaganda* (Boston, 1936).

Miller, Perry, *Jonathan Edwards* (New York, 1949).

———, *Orthodoxy in Massachusetts* (Cambridge, 1933).

———, "The Half-way Covenant," *New England Quarterly*, VI (Dec. 1933).

———, *The New England Mind: The Seventeenth Century* (New York, 1939).

———, "Thomas Hooker and the Democracy of Early Connecticut," *New England Quarterly*, IV (Oct. 1931).

Miller, Perry, and Johnson, Thomas H., *The Puritans, A Sourcebook of Their Writing* (New York, 1938).

Miller, R. C., "Theodore Roosevelt Historian," in Cate, J. L., and Anderson, E. N. (eds.), *Medieval and Historiographical Essays in Honor of James Westfall Thompson* (Chicago, 1938).

Milton, George F., *The Eve of Conflict: Stephen A. Douglas and the Needless War* (Boston, 1934).

Mims, Edwin, Jr., *American History and Immigration* (Bronxville, N.Y., 1950).

Mitchell, Stewart, "Henry Adams and Some of His Students," *Proceedings of the Massachusetts Historical Society*, LXVI (1942).

Mode, P. G., *Sourcebook and Bibliographical Guide for American Church History* (Menasha, Wis., 1920).

Mood, Fulmer (ed.), *The Early Writings of Frederick Jackson Turner* (Madison, 1938).

Moore, A. G., *Conscription and Conflict in the Confederacy* (Indianapolis, 1943).

Moore, Frank B. (ed.), *The Rebellion Record: A Diary of American Events* (12 vols., New York, 1868).

Moore, John Torrey, Jr., "Albert Gallatin," *Atlantic Monthly*, XLIV (Oct. 1879).

Morgan, Lewis, *Ancient Society* (Chicago [1877]).

Morison, Samuel Eliot, *Admiral of the Ocean Sea, A Life of Christopher Columbus* (Boston, 1946).

———, "Albert Bushnell Hart, 1889–1939," *Proceedings of the Massachusetts Historical Society*, LXVI (1936–44).

———, *Builders of the Bay Colony* (Boston, 1930).

———, "Edward Channing: A Memoir," *Proceedings of the Massachusetts Historical Society*, LXIV (1930–32).

———, "The Harvard School of Astronomy in the Seventeenth Century," *New England Quarterly*, VII (Mar. 1934).

——— (ed.), *The Parkman Reader* (Boston, 1955).

———, *The Puritan Pronaos: Studies in the Intellectual Life of New England in the Seventeenth Century* (New York, 1936).

———, *Three Centuries of Harvard, 1636–1936* (Cambridge, 1942).

——— (ed.), *Sources and Documents Illustrating the American Revolution, 1764–1788* (Oxford, 1929).

Morley, Viscount, *Notes on Politics and History* (London, 1913).

Morris, J. Bayard, *Hernando Cortés: Five Letters 1519–1526* (New York, 1929).

Morse, A. E., *The Federalist Party in Massachusetts to the year 1800* (Princeton, 1909).

Morse, Jarvis M., *American Beginnings* (Washington, D.C., 1952).

———, "John Smith and His Critics; A Chapter in Colonial Historiography," *Journal of Southern History*, I (May 1935).

Morse, Jedidiah, *The American Geography; or a View of the Present Situation of the United States of America* (Elizabeth Town, N.J., 1789).
Morse, John T., Jr., *John Adams* (Boston, 1884).
Morton, Nathaniel, *New England's Memorial* (Cambridge, 1669).
Motley, John Lothrop, *Merry-Mount: A Romance of the Massachusetts Colony* (2 vols., Boston and Cambridge, Mass., 1849).
————, *Morton's Hope: or the Memoirs of a Provincial* (2 vols., New York, 1839).
————, "Peter the Great," *North American Review*, LXI (Oct. 1845).
Mott, F. L., *American Magazines: 1741–1850* (New York, 1930).
Mullet, Charles F. (ed.), *Some Political Writings of James Otis* (Columbia, Mo., 1929).
Munro, William B., *Crusaders of New France* (New Haven, 1918).
————, *The Makers of the Unwritten Constitution* (New York, 1930).
Murdock, Kenneth B., *Increase Mather: The Foremost American Puritan* (Cambridge, 1925).
————, "The Puritan Tradition in American Literature," in Foerster, Norman (ed.), *The Reinterpretation of American Literature* (Cambridge, 1949).
————, "William Hubbard's 'Narrative,' " *Proceedings of the American Antiquarian Society*, LII (1943).
Nettles, Curtis P., *George Washington and American Independence* (Boston, 1951).
Newcomb, Simon, *Reminiscences of An Astronomer* (Boston, 1903).
Newton, A. P. (ed.), *Great Age of Discovery* (London, 1932).
Nichols, Roy F., "Federalism *versus* Democracy," in Pound, Roscoe, McIlwain, Charles H. and Nichols, Roy F. (eds.), *Federalism as a Democratic Process* (New Brunswick, N.J., 1942).
————, *The Disruption of American Democracy* (New York, 1948).
————, "The Dynamic Interpretation of History," *New England Quarterly*, VII (June 1935).
Niebuhr, Reinhold, *The Irony of American History* (New York, 1952).
Niebuhr, Richard, *The Social Sources of Denominationalism* (New York, 1929).
Niles, Hezekiah, *Principles and Acts of the Revolution in America* (Baltimore, 1822).
Nowell, Charles E., "The Columbus Question," *American Historical Review*, XLIV (July 1939).
Nunn, George E., *The Geographical Conceptions of Columbus* (New York, 1924).
Nye, Russel B., *Fettered Freedom* (East Lansing, Mich., 1949).
————, *George Bancroft: Brahmin Rebel* (New York, 1944).
Odum, Howard W. (ed.), *American Masters of Social Science* (New York, 1927).
Olson, J. E. (ed.), "The Voyages of the Northmen," *The Northmen, Columbus and Cabot* (New York, 1906).
O'Neill, Edward H., *A History of American Biography, 1800–1935* (Philadelphia, 1935).
————, *Biography by Americans, 1658–1936* (Philadelphia, 1939).
Osgood, Herbert Levi, "Political Ideas of the Puritans," *Political Science Quarterly*, VI (June, Sept., Dec. 1896).
————, "Scientific Anarchism," *Political Science Quarterly*, IV (Mar. 1889).

————, "Scientific Socialism—Rodbertus," *Political Science Quarterly,* I (Dec. 1886).

————, *The American Colonies in the Eighteenth Century* (4 vols., New York, 1924–25).

————, *The American Colonies in the Seventeenth Century* (3 vols., New York, 1904–07).

————, "The Study of American Colonial History," American Historical Association, *Annual Report for 1898* (Washington, D.C., 1899).

Osterweis, Rollin G., *Romanticism and Nationalism in the Old South* (New Haven, 1949).

Oswley, Frank L., *States Rights in the Confederacy* (Chicago, 1925).

————, "The Fundamental Cause of the Civil War: Egocentric Sectionalism," *Journal of Southern History,* VII (Feb. 1941).

Otis, James, *Vindication of the Conduct of the House of Representatives of Massachusetts Bay* (Boston, 1762).

————, *The Rights of the Colonies Asserted and Proved* (Boston, 1764).

Oviedo, Gonzalo Fernández de, *Historia general y natural de las Indias Occidentales* (4 vols., Madrid, 1851–55).

Padover, Saul K. (ed.), *The Complete Madison* (New York, 1953).

Palfrey, John Gorham, *A Compendious History of New England from the Discovery by Europeans to the First General Congress of the Anglo-American Colonies* (4 vols., Boston, 1858–64).

Palmer, R. R., *The Age of the Democratic Revolution* (2 vols., Princeton, New Jersey, 1959).

Pane, R. U., *English Translations from the Spanish, 1484–1943: A Bibliography* (New Brunswick, N.J., 1944).

Parker, Theodore, *Historic Americans* (Boston, 1870).

Parkes, Henry Bamford, "John Cotton and Roger Williams Debate Toleration, 1644–1652," *New England Quarterly,* IV (Oct. 1931).

Parkman, Francis, *La Salle and the Rediscovery of the Great West* (Boston, 1879).

————, *Montcalm and Wolfe* (2 vols., Boston, 1885).

————, *Pioneers of France in the New World* (Boston, 1885).

————, *The Book of Roses* (Boston, 1866).

————, *The Conspiracy of Pontiac and the Indian War after the Conquest of Canada* (6th ed., 2 vols., Boston, 1874).

————, "The Failure of Universal Suffrage," *North American Review,* CXXVII (July–Aug. 1878).

————, *The Jesuits in North America in the Seventeenth Century* (Boston, 1840).

————, *The Old Regime in Canada* (Boston, 1874).

————, *The Oregon Trail: Sketches of Prairie and Rocky-Mountain Life* (Boston, 1895).

————, "The Woman Question," *North American Review,* CXXIX (Oct. 1879).

————, "The Woman Question Again," *North American Review,* CXXX (Jan. 1880).

————, *Vassall Morton: A Novel* (Boston, 1856).

Parker, William H., *Recollections of A Naval Officer, 1841–1865* (New York, 1883).

Parks, George B., *Richard Hakluyt and the English Voyages,* American Geographical Society, *Special Publication,* No. 10 (New York, 1928).

Parks, J. H., *John Bell of Tennessee* (Baton Rouge, 1930).

Parrington, Vernon L., *Main Currents in American Thought* (3 vols., New York, 1927–30).

———— (ed.), *The Connecticut Wits* (New York, 1926).

Parsons, Wilfred, *Early Catholic Americana: A List of Books and Other Works by Catholic Authors in the United States, 1729–1820* (New York, 1939).

Parton, James, "Jared Sparks: from the Carpenter's Bench to the Presidency of Harvard College," *Triumphs of Enterprise, Ingenuity, and Public Spirit* (Hartford, Conn., 1871).

Pattee, Frederick L. (ed.), *The Poems of Philip Freneau* (3 vols., Princeton, 1902).

Payne, E. J., "The New World," in Ward, A. W., Prothero, G. W., and Leathes, Stanley (eds.), *Cambridge Modern History,* Vol. VIII (14 vols., Cambridge, England, 1902–24).

Peck, Harry Thurston, *William Hickling Prescott* (New York, 1926).

Penrose, Boies, *Travel and Discovery in the Renaissance, 1420–1620* (New York, 1962).

Persons, Stow (ed.), *Evolutionary Thought in America* (New Haven, 1950).

Perry, Bliss, *Emerson Today* (Princeton, 1931).

Perry, Ralph Barton, *Puritanism and Democracy* (New York, 1944).

————, *The Thought and Character of William James* (2 vols., Boston, 1935).

Perry, T. S., *John Fiske* (Boston, 1906).

Phillips, Ulrich Bonnell, *American Negro Slavery* (Boston, 1929).

————, *American Negro Slavery: A Survey of the Supply, Employment and Control of Negro Labor as Determined by the Plantation Regime* (New York, 1912).

————, "Georgia and State Rights: A Study of the Political History of Georgia from the Revolution to the Civil War with Particular Regard to Federal Relations," American Historical Association, *Annual Report for 1901,* II (Washington, D.C., 1902).

————, *History of Transportation in the Eastern Cotton Belt to 1860* (New York [1908]).

————, *Plantation and Frontier Documents: 1649–1863,* in Commons, J. R., and others (eds.), *A Documentary History of American Industrial Society* (10 vols., Cleveland, 1909–10, Vols. I and II, 1909).

————, "The Central Theme of Southern History," *American Historical Review,* XXXIV (Oct. 1928).

————, *The Life of Robert Toombs* (New York, 1913).

————, "The South Carolina Federalists," *American Historical Review,* XIV (Apr.–July 1909).

Pigafetta, Antonio, *Magellan's Voyage Round the World* (2 vols. [trans. James A. Robertson], Cleveland, 1906).

Pingel, Martha M., *An American Utilitarian: Richard Hildreth as a Philosopher* (New York, 1948).

Pinkerton, Allen, *Thirty Years a Detective* (New York, 1884).

Pitkin, Timothy, *A Political and Civil History of the United States of America. . . .* (2 vols., New Haven, 1828).

Pochmann, Henry A., *Washington Irving: Representative Selections. . . .* (New York, 1934).

Pollard, Edward A., *The Lost Cause* (New York, 1866).

Poore, Ben Perley (ed.), *A Descriptive Catalogue of the Government Publications of the United States . . . 1774–1881* (Washington, D.C., 1885).

Popper, Karl R., *The Logic of Scientific Discovery* (New York, 1961).

Potter, David M., "A Bibliography of the Printed Writings of Ulrich Bonnell Phillips," *Georgia Historical Quarterly,* XVIII (Sept. 1934).

———, *The Lincoln Theme and American National Historiography* (Oxford, 1948).

Powell, Thomas, *The Living Authors of America* (New York, 1850).

Pratt, Julius W., "Alfred Thayer Mahan," *Jernegan Essays.*

———, *Expansionists of 1898* (Baltimore, 1936).

Prescott, William H., *A History of the Conquest of Mexico, with a Preliminary View of the Ancient Mexican Civilization and the Life of Hernando Cortés* (3 vols., New York, 1843).

———, *A History of the Conquest of Peru, with a Preliminary View of the Civilization of the Incas* (2 vols., New York, 1847).

———, *A History of the Reign of Ferdinand and Isabella, the Catholic* (3 vols., Boston, 1837).

———, *A History of the Reign of Philip the Second* (3 vols., Boston, 1855–58).

———, "Sir Walter Scott," *North American Review,* XLVI (Apr. 1838).

Pressly, Thomas J., *Americans Interpret Their Civil War* (Princeton, 1954).

Priestley, Herbert I., *The Coming of the White Man* (New York, 1930).

Putnam, Ruth, "Prescott and Motley," *CHAL* (as cited), II (1918).

Quaife, Milo M. (ed.), *The Diary of James K. Polk* (Chicago, 1910).

Quincy, Josiah, *Figures of the Past from the Leaves of the Old Journal* (Boston, 1883).

Quinn, Arthur H., *Edgar Allan Poe: A Critical Biography* (New York, 1941).

Quinn, David B. (ed.), *The Voyages and Colonizing Enterprises of Sir Humphrey Gilbert* (London, 1940).

Ramsay, David, *The Life of George Washington* (New York, 1807).

———, *The History of the American Revolution* (2 vols., Philadelphia, 1789).

———, *The History of the Revolution of South-Carolina, from a British Province to an Independent State* (2 vols., Trenton, N.J., 1785).

Ramsdell, Charles W., *Reconstruction in Texas* (New York, 1910).

Randall, J. G., *Lincoln the President* (2 vols., New York, 1945).

Randall, John Herman Jr., and Haines, George, IV, "Controlling Assumptions in the Practice of American Historians," *Theory and Practice in Historical Study: A Report of the Committee on Historiography,* Social Science Research Council Bulletin 54 (New York, 1946).

Reeves, Arthur M., *Finding of Wineland the Good* (London, 1890).

Rhodes, James Ford, "History," American Historical Association, *Annual Report 1899,* I (Washington, D.C. 1900).

———, *History of the United States from the Compromise of 1850 to the End of Roosevelt's Administration* (9 vols., New York, 1928).

Ribault, Jean, see Ribaut, Jean.

Ribaut, Jean, *The Whole and True Discovery of Terra Florida* (De Land, Florida, 1927).

Richman, Irving B., *The Spanish Conquerors* (New Haven, 1921).

Riis, Jacob A., *Theodore Roosevelt the Citizen* (New York, 1904).

Robertson, H. M., *Aspects of the Rise of Economic Individualism* (Cambridge, England, 1935).

Robertson, William, *History of America* (2 vols., 9th English ed., London, 1800; 2nd American ed., Philadelphia, 1821–22).

Robinson, C. N., and Leyland, John, "The Literature of the Sea," in Ward, A. W., and Waller, A. R. (eds.), *The Cambridge History of English Literature*, Vol. IV (15 vols., Cambridge, England, 1907–1927).

Robinson, George W. (comp.), *Bibliography of Edward Channing* (Cambridge, 1932).

Robinson, W. M., Jr., "Prohibition in the Confederacy," *American Historical Review*, XXVII (Oct. 1931).

Rogers, Walter P., *Andrew D. White and the Modern University* (Ithaca, 1943).

Roorbach, Orville A. (ed.), *Bibliotheca Americana: Catalogue of American Publications . . . from 1820 to 1860 . . . together with a List of Periodicals Published in the United States* (4 vols., New York, 1852–60).

Roosevelt, Theodore, *Gouverneur Morris* (Boston, 1888).

———, "History as Literature," *American Historical Review*, XVIII, (Apr. 1913).

———, *Oliver Cromwell* (New York, 1926).

———, *The Naval War of 1812* (New York, 1926).

———, *The Winning of the West* (6 vols., New York, 1905).

Root, Erasmus, *An Introduction to Arithmetic for the Use of the Common Schools* (Norwich, Conn., 1796).

Rosenbach, A. S. W., *An American Jewish Bibliography. . . .* (Baltimore, 1926).

Rowe, Henry K., *The History of Religion in the United States* (New York, 1928).

Royal Institute of International Affairs, *Nationalism* (London, 1939).

Rukeyser, Muriel, *Willard Gibbs* (New York, 1964).

Russell, William H., *My Diary, North and South* (Boston, 1863).

Ryan, W. Carson, Studies in Early Graduate Education, Carnegie Foundation for the Advancement of Teaching, *Bulletin*, No. 30 (New York, 1939).

Sabin, Joseph, *A List of Printed Editions of the Works of Fray Bartolomé de las Casas, Bishop of Chiapa* (New York, 1870).

———, *Bibliotheca Americana: A Dictionary of Books Relating to America from its Discovery to the Present Time* (29 vols., New York, 1868–1936).

Sabine, Lorenzo, *Biographical Sketches of Loyalists of the American Revolution* (2 vols., Boston, 1864).

Salvemini, Gaetano, *Historian and Scientist* (Cambridge, 1939).

Samuels, Ernest, *Henry Adams—The Major Phase* (Cambridge, Mass., 1964).

———, *Henry Adams—The Middle Years* (Cambridge, Mass., 1958).

———, *The Young Henry Adams* (Cambridge, 1948).

Sanders, Jennings B., "John Fiske," *Jernegan Essays*.

Santayana, George, *Reason in Science* (New York, 1906).

———, *Scepticism and Animal Faith* (New York, 1955).

———, *The Life of Reason* (New York, 1935).

Savelle, Max, *Seeds of Liberty* (New York, 1948).

Saveth, Edward N., *American Historians and European Immigrants 1875–1925* (New York, 1948).

——— (ed.), *Understanding the American Past* (Boston, 1954).

Schafer, Joseph, "Francis Parkman, 1823–1893," *Mississippi Valley Historical Review,* X (Mar. 1924).

―――― (ed.), *Intimate Letters of Carl Schurz, 1841–1869* (Madison, 1928).

Schapiro, Jacob S., *Condorcet and the Rise of Liberalism* (New York, 1934).

Scharf, J. T., *History of the Confederate States Navy* (New York, 1897).

Schattschneider, E. E., *Party Government* (New York, 1942).

Schilpp, Paul A. (ed.), *The Philosophy of John Dewey* (Evanston, 1939).

Schlesinger, Arthur M., Sr., *New Viewpoints in American History* (New York, 1928).

――――, *The Colonial Merchants and the American Revolution* (New York, 1918).

―――― (ed.), Hansen, Marcus Lee, *The Atlantic Migration, 1607–1860* (Cambridge, 1940).

―――― (ed.), Hansen, Marcus Lee, *The Immigrant in American History* (Cambridge, 1940).

Schlesinger, Arthur M., Sr., and Fox, Dixon R. (eds.), *A History of American Life* (13 vols., New York, 1927–48).

Schlesinger, Arthur M., Jr., *The Age of Jackson* (Boston, 1945).

――――, "The Problem of Richard Hildreth," *New England Quarterly,* XIII (June 1940).

Schmeckebier, Laurence F., *Government Publications and Their Use* (Washington, D.C., 1939).

Schneider, Herbert W., *A History of American Philosophy* (New York, 1946).

――――, "The Puritan Tradition," in Johnson, F. E. (ed.), *Wellsprings of the American Spirit* (New York, 1948).

Schouler, James, "A New Federal Convention," American Historical Association, *Annual Report for 1897* (Washington, D.C., 1898).

――――, *History of the United States under the Constitution* (5 vols., Washington, D.C., 1886–91).

――――, *History of the United States under the Constitution* (7 vols., Washington, D.C., 1882–94).

Schramm, Wilbur, *Francis Parkman: Representative Selections* (New York, 1938).

Schurz, Carl, *The Life of Henry Clay* (2 vols., Boston, 1887).

Scott, Arthur D., "George Louis Beer," *Jernegan Essays.*

Scott, Henry E., "The Courses of Study in History, Roman Law, and Political Economy at Harvard University," in Hall, G. Stanley (ed.), *Methods of Teaching and Studying History* (Boston, 1886).

Sears, Louis Martin, "Woodrow Wilson," *Jernegan Essays.*

Seitz, Don C., *Braxton Bragg, General of the Confederacy* (New York, 1924).

――――, *Letters from Francis Parkman to E. G. Squier* (Cedar Rapids, Iowa, 1911).

Sessler, Jacob J., *Communal Pietism among Early American Moravians* (New York, 1933).

Shafer, Boyd C., "Men Are More Alike," *American Historical Review,* LVII (Apr. 1952).

Shannon, Fred A., *The Organization and Administration of the Union Army 1861–1865* (2 vols., Cleveland, 1928).

Shaw, Charles Gray, *Trends of Civilization and Culture* (New York, 1939).

Shea, John G., *History of the Catholic Church in the United States* (4 vols., New York, 1886–92).

Shearer, A. H., "American Historical Magazines," *Mississippi Valley Historical Review,* IV (Mar. 1918).

Shepherd, William R., "The Expansion of Europe," *Political Science Quarterly,* XXXIV (Mar., June, Sept. 1919).

Shipton, C. K., "A Plea for Puritanism," *American Historical Review,* XL (Apr. 1935).

———, "The New England Clergy of the Glacial Age," *Publications of the Colonial Society of Massachusetts,* XXXII (1933).

———, "The New England Frontier," *New England Quarterly,* X (Mar. 1937).

Shugg, Roger W., *Origins of Class Struggle in Louisiana: A Social History of White Farmers and Laborers during Slavery and After 1840–1875* (Baton Rouge, 1939).

Simpkins, F. B., "New Viewpoints of Southern Reconstruction," *The Journal of Southern History,* V (Feb. 1939).

Simpkins, F. B., and Patton, J. W., *The Women of the Confederacy* (Richmond, 1936).

Sloane, William Milligan, "George Bancroft—In Society, In Politics, In Letters," *Century Magazine,* XI (Jan. 1887).

Small, Albion W., *The Origins of Sociology* (Chicago, 1924).

Smith, Charles Foster, *Charles Kendall Adams: A Life-Sketch* (Madison, 1925).

Smith, J. Allen, *The Spirit of American Government* (New York, 1907).

Smith, John, *A true Relation of such occurrences and accidents of Noate as hath hapened in Virginia since the first planting of that collony* (London, 1608).

———, *The Generall Historie of Virginia, New-England and the Summer Isles* (London, 1624).

Smith, Theodore Clarke, "The Writing of American History in America from 1884–1934," *American Historical Review,* XL (Apr. 1935).

Smyth, Clifford, *John Adams, The Man Who Was Called "Father of American Independence"* (New York, 1931).

Sparks, Jared (ed.), *A Collection of the Familiar Letters and Miscellaneous Papers of Benjamin Franklin* (Boston, 1833).

———, *An Inquiry into the Comparative Moral Tendency of Trinitarian and Unitarian Doctrine. . . .* (Boston, 1833).

——— (ed.), *Diplomatic Correspondence of the American Revolution* (12 vols., Boston, 1829–30).

———, *Life of Gouverneur Morris, with Selections from his Correspondence and Miscellaneous Papers* (3 vols., Boston, 1832).

———, *Life of John Ledyard, the American Traveler: Comprising Selections from His Journals and Correspondence* (Cambridge, 1828).

——— (ed.), *Works of Benjamin Franklin; with Notes and a Life of the Author* (10 vols., Boston, 1836–40).

——— (ed.), *Writings of George Washington, Being his Correspondence, Addresses, Messages, and other Papers, Official and Private* (12 vols., Boston, 1834–1837).

Spence, Mary K., *William Penn: A Bibliography* (Harrisburg, Pa., 1932).

Sperry, Willard L., *Religion in America* (New York, 1946).

Spiller, Robert E., *Fenimore Cooper: Critic of His Times* (New York, 1931).

———, "Henry Adams," *LHUS,* II (New York, 1948).

————, *The American in England During the First Half Century of Independence* (New York, 1926).

Spiller, R. E., Thorp, Willard, Johnson, Thomas H., and Canby, Henry Seidel (eds.), *Literary History of the United States* (3 vols., New York, 1948); referred to as *LHUS*.

Sprague, William B., *The Life of Jedidiah Morse* (New York, 1874).

Spurlin, Paul M., *Montesquieu in America, 1760–1801* (Baton Rouge, 1940).

Stampp, Kenneth M., *And the War Came* (New Orleans, 1950).

———— (ed.), *The Causes of the Civil War* (Englewood Cliffs, N.J., 1959).

Stedman, Edmund C., "James Russell Lowell," *Poets of America* (Boston, 1885).

Stefansson, Vilhjalmur (ed.), *The Three Voyages of Martin Frobisher* (2 vols., London, 1938).

Stephen, Leslie (ed.), *John R. Green, Letters of John Richard Green* (New York, 1901).

————, "Nathaniel Hawthorne," *Hours in a Library* (New York, 1875).

————, *The English Utilitarians* (3 vols., London, 1912).

Stephens, Alexander H., *A Constitutional View of the Late War Between the States, Its Causes, Character, Conduct, and Results. . . .* (2 vols., Philadelphia, 1867).

————, *The Reviewers Reviewed: A Supplement to the "War Between the States," etc., with an Appendix in Review of "Reconstruction," So-Called* (New York, 1872).

Stephenson, Nathaniel W., "A Theory of Jefferson Davis," *American Historical Review*, XXI (Oct. 1915).

Stephenson, Wendell H., "A Half Century of Southern Scholarship," *Journal of Southern History*, XI (Feb. 1945).

————, "William P. Trent as a Historian of the South," *Journal of Southern History*, XV (May 1949).

Stevens, Henry, *Thomas Hariot, the Mathematician, the Philosopher and the Scholar* (London, 1900).

Stevens, John A., *Albert Gallatin* (Boston, 1884).

Stewart, Walt, "George Bancroft," *Jernegan Essays.*

Stickles, A. M., *Simon Bolivar Buckner, Borderland Knight* (Chapel Hill, 1940).

Stillé, Charles J., *The Life and Times of John Dickinson, 1732–1808* (Philadelphia, 1891).

Stith, William, *The History of the First Discovery and Settlement of Virginia* (Williamsburg, 1747).

Stokes, Anson Phelps, *Church and State in the United States* (3 vols., New York, 1950).

Streeter, Robert E., "Association Psychology and Literary Nationalism in *North American Review*," *American Literature*, XVII (Mar. 1945).

Stubbs, William, *Lectures on Early English History*, A. Hassal (ed.) (London and New York, 1906).

Sweet, William Warren, *Religion in Colonial America* (New York, 1942).

————, *Religion in the Development of American Culture, 1765–1840* (New York, 1952).

————, *The Story of Religions in America* (New York, 1930).

Swiggett, Howard (ed.), *A Rebel War Clerk's Diary at the Confederate State Capitol* (2 vols., New York, 1935).

Swisher, Carl B., *Roger B. Taney* (New York, 1935).

Tate, Allen, *Jefferson Davis: His Rise and Fall* (New York, 1929).

———, *Stonewall Jackson, The Good Soldier* (New York, 1928).

Tawney, R. H., *Religion and the Rise of Capitalism* (New York, 1926).

Taylor, E. G. R., *Late Tudor and Early Stuart Geography, 1583–1650* (London, 1934).

———, *Tudor Geography, 1485–1583* (London, 1930).

Taylor, W. F., *A History of American Letters* (New York, 1936).

Taylor, William R. (ed.), *The Discovery of the Great West: LaSalle* (New York [Rinehart edition], 1956).

Theory and Practice in Historical Study: A Report of the Committee on Historiography (Social Science Research Council, New York, 1946). Bulletin 54.

Thompson, C. Mildred, *Reconstruction in Georgia, Economic, Social, Political, 1865–1872* (New York, 1919).

Thompson, Lawrence, *Young Longfellow, 1807–1843* (New York, 1938).

Thordarson, Matthias, *The Vinland Voyages* (New York, 1930).

Thornton, Harrison John, "Theodore Roosevelt," *Jernegan Essays*.

Thwaites, R. G., *France in America 1497–1763* (New York, 1905).

———, *The State Historical Society of Wisconsin* (Madison, 1898).

Thwing, Charles F., *The American and the German University* (New York, 1928).

Ticknor, George, *History of Spanish Literature* (3 vols., Boston, 1871).

———, *Life of William Hickling Prescott* (Boston, 1864).

Todd, Charles B., *Life and Letters of Joel Barlow, LL.D.* (New York, 1886).

Tolles, Frederick B., "The American Revolution Considered as a Social Movement: A Re-evaluation," *American Historical Review*, XL (Oct. 1954).

Townsend, G. H., *Philosophical Ideas in the United States* (New York, 1934).

Trent, William P., "English Culture in Virginia," *The Johns Hopkins University Studies in Historical and Political Science*, seventh series, V–VI (Baltimore, 1889).

———, "The Case of Josiah Phillips," *American Historical Review*, I (Apr. 1896).

———, *William Gilmore Simms* (Boston, 1892).

———, *Robert E. Lee* (Boston, 1899).

———, *Southern Statesmen of the Old Regime* (New York, 1897).

Trescot, William Henry, *Diplomatic History of the Administration of Washington and Adams* (Boston, 1857).

Troeltsch, Ernst, *The Social Teachings of the Christian Churches* (2 vols., New York, 1931).

Tudor, William, *The Life of James Otis of Massachusetts* (Boston, 1823).

Turner, Frederick Jackson, *Reuben Gold Thwaites: A Memorial Address* (Madison, 1914).

———, *The Frontier in American History* (New York, 1921).

———, *The United States* (New York, 1935).

Turner, Ralph, *The Great Cultural Traditions* (2 vols., New York, 1941).

Tuttle, J. H., "Writings of Rev. John Cotton," *Bibliographical Essays: A Tribute to Wilberforce Eames* (Cambridge, 1924).

Tyler, Moses Coit, *A History of American Literature 1607–1765* (2 vols., New York, 1878).

————, *The Literary History of the American Revolution* (2 vols., New York and London, 1897).

————, "The Party of the Loyalists in the American Revolution," *American Historical Review*, I (October, 1895).

————, *Patrick Henry* (New York, 1887).

————, *Three Men of Letters* (New York, 1895).

Vance, Clarence H. (ed.), *Letters of a Westchester Farmer, 1774–1775* (White Plains, N.Y., 1930).

Van Deusen, G. C., *The Life of Henry Clay* (Boston, 1937).

Van Loon, William [Hendrik Willem], *America* (New York, 1927).

Van Tyne, Claude Halstead, *The Loyalists in the American Revolution* (New York, 1929).

Vignaud, Henry, "Columbus a Spaniard and a Jew," *American Historical Review*, XVIII (Apr. 1913).

————, *Critical Study of the Various dates assigned to the birth of Christopher Columbus: the real date, 1451* (London, 1903).

————, *Histoire critique de la grande entreprise de Christophe Colomb* (Paris, 1911).

————, "Proof that Columbus was Born in 1451: A New Document," *American Historical Review*, XII (Jan. 1907).

————, *Toscanelli and Columbus* (London, 1902).

Villard, Oswald G., *John Brown* (New York, 1943).

Vincent, John Martin, *Historical Research: An Outline of Theory and Practice* (New York, 1911).

Von Holst, Herman Eduard, see Holst, Hermann Eduard von.

Wade, Mason, *Francis Parkman: Heroic Historian* (New York, 1942).

———— (ed.), *The Journals of Francis Parkman* (2 vols., New York, 1947).

Wagner, Henry R., *The Spanish Southwest, 1542–1794: An Annotated Bibliography* (2 vols.), Albuquerque, N.M., 1937.

Wagstaff, Henry M., *State Rights and Political Parties in North Carolina 1776–1861* (Baltimore, 1906).

Waldman, Milton, *Raleigh* (London, 1928).

Walker, George L., *Thomas Hooker, Preacher, Founder, Democrat* (New York, 1891).

Walker, W. W., *Ten New-England Leaders* (Chicago, 1901).

Walsh, C. M., *Political Science of John Adams* (New York, 1915).

Walters, Raymond, Jr., *Albert Gallatin* (New York, 1954).

Warfel, Harry L., *Noah Webster; Schoolmaster to America* (New York, 1936).

Warren, Mercy, *Poems Dramatic and Miscellaneous* (Boston, 1790).

————, *History of the Rise, Progress, and Termination of the American Revolution* (3 vols., Boston, 1805).

————, *The Adulateur, A Tragedy as it is now Acted in Upper Servia* (Boston, 1773).

————, *The Group, As Lately Acted and to be Re-Acted to the Wonder of all Superior Intelligences, nigh Headquarters of Amboyne* (Boston, 1775).

Weber, Thomas, *The Northern Railroads in the Civil War 1861–1865* (New York, 1952).

Weber, Max, *The Protestant Ethic and the Spirit of Capitalism* (London, 1934).

Webster, Noah, *A Grammatical Institute of the English Language.* . . . (Hartford, Conn., 1784).

——, *Sketches of American Policy* (facsimile edition, New York, 1937).

Wecter, Dixon, "President Washington and Parson Weems," *The Hero in America* (New York, 1941).

Weems, Mason Locke, *The Life of Benjamin Franklin: With Many Choice Anecdotes and Admirable Sayings of the Great Man.* . . . (Philadelphia, 1917).

——, *The Life of George Washington, with Curious Anecdotes Equally Honorable to Himself and Exemplary to His Young Countrymen . . . by a Former Rector of Mt. Vernon Parrish* (Philadelphia, fifth edition, 1806).

Wendell, Barrett, *Cotton Mather: The Puritan Priest* (New York, 1891).

Werkmeister, W. H., *A History of Philosophical Ideas in America* (New York, 1949).

Wertenbaker, T. J., *The First Americans* (New York, 1929).

——, *The Puritan Oligarchy* (New York, 1947).

Wescott, Allen (ed.), *Mahan on Naval Warfare* (Boston, 1941).

Wharton, Francis, *The Revolutionary and Diplomatic Correspondence of the United States* (Washington, D.C., 1889).

Whitaker, Arthur P., *The United States and the Independence of Latin America, 1800–1830* (Baltimore, 1941).

Whitaker, Alexander, *Good newes from Virginia* (London, 1613).

White, Andrew Dickson, *Autobiography* (2 vols., New York and London, 1922).

——, "Historical Instruction in the Course of History and Political Science at Cornell University," in Hall, G. Stanley (ed.), *Methods of Teaching and Studying History* (Boston, 1886).

——, *Outlines of a Course of Lectures in History* (Ann Arbor, 1860–61).

White, Laura A., *Robert Barnwell Rhett: Father of Secession* (New York, 1931).

White, Leonard D., *The States and the Nation* (Baton Rouge, 1953).

Whitehead, Alfred North, "Aspects of Freedom," in Anshen, Ruth Wanda (ed.), *Freedom: Its Meaning* (New York, 1940).

——, *Science and the Modern World* (New York, 1948).

Wiernik, Peter, *History of the Jews in America from the Period of the Discovery to the Present Time* (New York, 1931).

Wiley, Bell I., *Southern Negroes, 1861–1865* (New Haven, 1938).

——, *The Life of Johnny Reb: The Common Soldier of the Confederacy* (Indianapolis, 1943).

——, *The Plain People of the Confederacy* (Baton Rouge, 1943).

Williams, Ben Ames (ed.), *Mary B. Chestnut, A Diary from Dixie* (Boston, 1949).

Williams, Harry T., *Lincoln and His Generals* (New York, 1952).

Williams, Stanley T., *The Life of Washington Irving* (2 vols., New York, 1935).

Williamson, James A., *Maritime Enterprise 1485–1588* (Oxford, 1913).

——, *Sir John Hawkins* (Oxford, 1927).

——, *The Voyages of the Cabots and the English Discovery of North America under Henry VII and Henry VIII* (London, 1929).

Willoughby, W. W., *The American Constitutional System* (New York, 1904)

Wilson, Charles R., "Hermann Eduard von Holst," *Jernegan Essays.*

Wilson, Henry, *History of the Rise and Fall of the Slave Power in America* (3 vols., Boston, 1872–77).

Wilson, Louis N. (ed.), *Graville Stanley Hall* (Worcester, Mass., 1925).

Wilson, James, *Considerations on the Nature and Extent of the Legislative Authority of the British Parliament* (Philadelphia, 1774).

Wilson, Woodrow, *A History of the American People* (5 vols., New York, 1902).

———, "Cabinet Government in the United States," *International Review*, VI (Aug. 1879).

———, *Congressional Government* (Boston, 1913).

———, *Constitutional Government in the United States* (New York, 1908).

———, *Division and Reunion* (New York, 1893).

———, *George Washington* (New York, 1896).

———, *Selected Literary and Political Pages* (3 vols., New York, 1925–27).

———, *The New Freedom* (New York, 1913).

———, *The State* (Boston, 1889).

Wilstach, Paul (ed.), *Correspondence of John Adams and Thomas Jefferson 1812–1826* (Indianapolis, 1925).

Winchell, Constance M., *Guide to Reference Books,* 8th ed. (Chicago, 1967).

Winsor, Justin, *Cartier to Frontenac* (Boston, 1894).

———, *Christopher Columbus, and how he Received and Imparted the Spirit of Discovery* (Boston, 1891).

——— (ed.), *Narrative and Critical History of America* (8 vols., Boston, 1884–89); referred to as *NCHA.*

Winslow, Ola E., *Jonathan Edwards, 1703–1758* (New York, 1940).

Winthrop, Robert C., *Life and Letters of John Winthrop* (2 vols., Boston, 1864–67).

Wood, William, *Elizabethan Sea-Dogs* (New Haven, 1921).

Woodberry, George E., *Nathaniel Hawthorne* (Boston, 1902).

Woodbridge, Frederick J. E., *The Purpose of History* (New York, 1916).

Woodbury, George E., *The Life of Edgar Allan Poe, Personal and Literary, with His Chief Correspondence with Men of Letters* (2 vols., Boston, 1909).

Woodward, C. Vann, *Origins of the New South* (Baton Rouge, 1951).

Wooley, Edwin C., *The Reconstruction of Georgia* (New York, 1901).

Woolsey, Theodore, and others, *The First Century of the Republic: A Review of American Progress* (New York, 1876).

Wright, B. F., Jr., *American Interpretations of Natural Law* (Cambridge, 1951).

Wright, Louis B., "Beverley's History and Present State of Virginia . . . 1705: A Neglected Classic," *William and Mary Quarterly,* third series, I (July 1944).

———, *The Cultural Life of the American Colonies, 1607–1763* (New York, 1957).

———, *The First Gentlemen of Virginia, Intellectual Qualities of the Early Colonial Ruling Class* (San Marino, Calif., 1940).

Wrong, George M., *The Rise and Fall of New France* (2 vols., New York, 1928).

Wroth, Lawrence C., *An American Bookshelf, 1755* (Philadelphia, 1934).

———, *Parson Weems* (Baltimore, 1911).

Zavala, Silvio, *New Viewpoints on the Spanish Colonization of America* (Philadelphia, 1943).

Zunder, Theodore A., *The Early Days of Joel Barlow, a Connecticut Wit: His Life and Works from 1754 to 1787* (New Haven, 1934).

Index

697

DATE DUE

6/1			
JUL 5 1973			
FEB 1 1976			
FEB 1 6 1976			
GAYLORD			PRINTED IN U.S.A.